Making the Best of Basics

Family Preparedness Handbook

The Family Preparedness Guide
for the
21ˢᵗ Century

James Talmage Stevens

Making the Best of Basics – *Family Preparedness Handbook*
12th EDITION – Print Version – 2010

Library of Congress Cataloging-in-publication Data: Library of Congress Catalog Card Number 75-953

LIBRARY FILE INFORMATION

641.4
Ste
    Stevens, James Talmage
    Making the Best of Basics: *Family Preparedness Handbook*;
    12th ed., Print Version 1.0
    Get Ready! Network, LLC ©2010.

    536 p. Illus. Soft Cover

    1. Family preparedness 2. Survival 4. Food – preservation

Disclaimer: The author and publisher disclaim all liability in connection with the use of *Making the Best of Basics—Family Preparedness Handbook.* It is intended only as an informative guide for those desiring to implement an in-home storage plan in an effort to be prepared for unknown future events over which one has little or no control. We have done our best to provide guidelines for implementing and utilizing in-home food storage. Our recommendations are based on experience and data from sources we believe reliable. Accordingly, the reader must take responsibility for decisions and the ultimate actions regarding his/her choice to effect any idea, suggestion, recommendation, instruction, or recipe in this *Handbook.*

The information offered herein is general and is made without guarantees by either the author or the publisher. The information is as accurate as humanly possible. However, given the amount and variety of choices in the marketplace, the differences in individual needs and tastes, and the fact that we have no control over quality, kinds, and types of possible substitutions and alternatives for virtually every item in our suggested items and quantities, we cannot be held responsible for the reader's ultimate choices or results.

You should get advice from local consultants, preparedness providers, and from government advisors in your area. Their local experience will be invaluable to your in your efforts in becoming prepared and **Making the Best of Basics.**

Making the Best of Basics

Family Preparedness Handbook

12th Edition
27th Printing
More than 765,000 copies sold!

The Family Preparedness Guide
for the
21st Century

Author of

Don't Get Caught with Your Pantry Down!
The Consumer's Reference Guide to the Preparedness Industry

Doctor Prepper

Get Ready! Network, LLC
9907 Cedar Crest Drive
Grey Forest TX 78023
www.DoctorPrepper.com

Making the Best of Basics

Family Preparedness Handbook

12th EDITION, 27th Printing – September 2010

Publication History

Date	Printing	Edition
02/74	First	First
03/74	Second	Second
08/74	Third	Second (*Special*)
08/74	Fourth	Third
03/75	Fifth	Third
07/75	Sixth	Fourth
06/76	Seventh	Fifth (*Special*)
08/76	Eighth	Fifth
10/76	Ninth	Fifth
11/76	Tenth	Fifth
02/77	Eleventh	Fifth
04/77	Twelfth	Sixth
03/80	Thirteenth	Sixth
11/80	Fourteenth	Seventh
02/82	Fifteenth	Eighth
02/96	Sixteenth	Ninth
06/97	Seventeenth	Tenth
11/97	Eighteenth	Tenth
6/98	Nineteenth	Tenth
9/98	Twentieth	Tenth
1/99	Twenty-first	Tenth
3/99	Twenty-second	Tenth
5/99	Twenty-third	Tenth
7/99	Twenty-fourth	Tenth
10/99	Twenty-fifth	Tenth
12/09	Twenty-sixth	Eleventh
0910	Twenty-seventh	Twelfth
10/10	Digital Edition	First

35   34   33   32   31   30   29   28

Making the Best of Basics has always been printed and produced proudly in the United States of America.

ACKNOWLEDGMENTS

I take this opportunity to express gratitude to the following persons—friends, family, and acquaintances over the years, including many professionals from the medical, educational, emergency preparedness, and food storage disciplines. They have shared their personal interests, their knowledge, and their innovative ideas for improvement in this 12th edition—our initial digital version.

Basics... is now a 36+ year veteran of the preparedness industry.

I'm truly grateful for the constant help and support from my wife, LeeDee, who not only believed it could be done, but gave me the means, the time, and the energy to undertake what I knew would be a continuing, extensive, long, and tedious journey.

Many thanks to the following people who also gave me often-needed encouragement: Randy Faulk, Sharon Iezzi, James Medina, Dennis Clements, and the digital expertise of Tab Hokamaier and Rich Fleetwood. I cannot begin to mention all my other friends and acquaintances who told me it was time... *to catch up with the future!*

Contributors to this new edition include some very specially qualified persons whose credentials you'll see in various chapters of this electronic book. They all accepted the opportunity to add their expertise to the previous work, making this edition the best of basics—and more. These include: Ruth Sebastian, J.D.; Dr. Rick Busch III and his wife Jennifer Busch; Meg Shehad, CEO of Gritman Essential Oils; Maryel Isham-Allen, CNC; Deanna DeLong; Barbara Salsbury; Pat Gorman; and many others who provided invaluable assistance in data collection, information utilization, and enthusiasm.

Many people—all friends—have provided specific information or given special help to prepare this most recent updated edition of **Making the Best of Basics**—*Family Preparedness Handbook.* It's no accident these people showed up in my life—just when they were needed. Some brought informational content, some gave needed guidance, and the others gave me the most important ingredient—motivation!

Thanks to Dr. Carlin Bartschi, M.D., and Dr. Zoltan Rona, M.D., for their medical advice. Zolly's health supplementation training was the wind beneath my wings these last few years when my get-up-and-go seemed to have dropped-down-and-died.

Also, Aaron Hopkins added the new cover, with a new look for the new generation. And then, just when needed, Rachel Mickelsen showed up to give a last look with the eye of an *artiste*.

What a joy to have met so many downright good people during the past months—actually, years! There have been many others along the path who have added to this book with their own stories, insights, suggestions, and information. Thanks to you each of you!

I am truly grateful for those who purchased the previous editions of **Basics**.... The basics of life haven't changed much over the 36 years I've been authoring, but I see tremendous changes in the attitude and appreciation of what our forefathers endured to give us so much—and sometimes we appreciate so little!

I'd so much like to help bring back the strength of those who built this nation with determination, faith, grit, and loyalty to provide the blessing of freedom we enjoy—without much thought of its cost to those past generations who gave their lives for the American dream. I hope this is partial repayment for the sacrifices they have made for all of us!

Truly, making the best of basics...

FOREWORD

This book has evolved as the conditions of my life changed—fortunately some things got better, and unfortunately some things didn't! As we've gone through health issues, financial issues, retirement issues, children and grandchildren issues––you name it—we've been shored up by our faith and our family preparedness plan. Now, as I go from senior citizen to geezer, I want to share some of my experiences, information, and knowledge with the new generation rising to take the reins of control in the newest economy.

The information, charts, tables, quotes, advisories, and opinions in this book reflect my intent to communicate what I feel is important in today's world of increasing uncertainty. I claim no special foresight into the future and possess no special skills for predicting future world events. I certainly am no clairvoyant, and make no presumption to be a foreteller of what is to come. However, neither am I deaf, dumb, nor blind to the escalation of discontent!

I believe the news is reporting ever-increasing violence in the world today. Could it be that we've become insensitive to ordinary suffering because of the increasing graphic nature of entertainment today?

It may be that we know more than we ever knew before due to some of these reasons:

- better communication technology;
- better use of visual tools;
- more/better reporters;
- more competition among increasing news organizations; and
- desire/need of the public for drama and trauma.

I do not want this book—or my efforts—to be characterized as having even a vestige of a *"gloomsday"* or *"doomsday"* mentality. I don't participate in *doomsday* or *gloomsday* thought, practice, or activities.

In reality, **Basics…** is a *gloomslayer* and *doomslayer* tool! Let it be so for you.

When asked what I perceive the value of **Basics…** to be for the reader, my answer is:

> **Basics**…*is the decoder ring to help those who want to protect their family from the effects of emergencies and disasters—whether natural, people-caused, or personal.*

We live in a great country. We can still choose what we want out of life. I have faith and hope it will always be so!

James Talmage Stevens
Author

DEDICATION

This 12th edition of **Making the Best of Basics** is dedicated to my wife, LeeDee, who accepted the trials this work required and encouraged me in the continuance of my walk on the preparedness path. She is a continuous, constant reminder of charity and peacefulness in our home and life.

Also dedicated to my parents, Ruth Virginia (Pace) and Ernest Dixon Stevens, whose mentoring and teaching about being ready for unforeseen events on the path of life made the twists and turns in my own life seem less tortuous. Their love was always patient and enduring. I appreciate them and love them for their great examples of acceptance and selflessness.

Perhaps in some small way, I can extend to others the same kind of support, caring, and motivation through this work—which is to *save lives*. My parents were exemplars of making the best of life's basics, and thankfully they left me a legacy of passion, industry, hard work, and thrift.

Making the Best of Basics

Family Preparedness Handbook

12th Edition – Print Version

TABLE OF CONTENTS

TABLE OF CONTENTS (continued)

TABLE OF CONTENTS (continued)

TABLE OF CONTENTS (continued)

TABLE OF CONTENTS (continued)

TABLE OF RECIPES AND DIRECTIONS

Fig. 122.—The Cook, drawn and engraved, in the Sixteenth Century, by J. Amman.

TABLE OF CHARTS, ILLUSTRATIONS, WORKSHEETS, QUICK-LISTS, QUICK-PLANS, AND QUICK-GUIDES

TABLE OF CHARTS, ILLUSTRATIONS, WORKSHEETS, QUICK-LISTS, QUICK-PLANS, AND QUICK-GUIDES (continued)

TABLE OF CHARTS, ILLUSTRATIONS, WORKSHEETS, QUICK-LISTS, QUICK-PLANS, AND QUICK-GUIDES (continued)

> *"In this work, when it shall be found that much is omitted, let it not be forgotten that much likewise is performed."*
>
> Dr. Samuel Johnson, 1775, upon completion of his dictionary

PARABLE OF GOMER

(from the Book of Gomer)

PART THE FIRST

Now these are the generations of Gomer, son of Homer, being the son of Omer.

2. And in the days of Gomer, Noah the Prophet went unto the people saying, "*Prepare ye for the flood which is to come; yea, build yourselves a boat, that ye may not perish.*"

3. Now, Gomer was of the Church, a faithful man indeed, verily a teacher in the Sunday School. And Gomer played with the ball team, yea, even pitched the ball, on the Church softball team.

4. And one day, Gomer's wife came and said unto him, "*Come, mine honorable husband, let us build unto ourselves a boat as the Prophet Noah commandeth, that we may not perish in the flood.*"

5. But behold, Gomer saith unto his wife, "*Worry not, dear wife, for if the flood should come, the government will provide boats for us.*"

6. And so, Gomer built not a boat for his family.

7. And Gomer's wife went unto Noah and she returned saying, "*Behold, my husband, the Prophet Noah saith unto us, 'Build a boat, that ye may preserve yourselves, for the government pays men not to grow trees, wherefore the government hath not the lumber to build for you a boat.'*"

8. And Gomer answered saying, "*Fear not, oh precious wife, for am I not the star pitcher on the Church's softball team? Wherefore, believest thou not that the Church will provide for us a boat that we perish not?*"

9. And Gomer's wife went again unto Noah. Then , she returned unto Gomer, saying, "*Behold, mine husband of great faith, the Prophet saith that the Church hath not enough lumber to build a boat for everyone, wherefore, mine husband, I pray thee to build for our family a boat that we might not perish in the promised flood.*"

10. And Gomer answered her saying, "*Behold, if we build a boat, when the flood cometh, will not our neighbors overcome us and take from us our boat? Wherefore, what doth it profit a man to build a boat under such adverse conditions?*"

11. And Gomer's wife went again unto Noah. She returned, again saying, "Behold, the Prophet Noah saith, 'Build unto yourselves a boat. Have faith, for if ye do the Lord's bidding, He will preserve your boat for your family.'"

12. But Gomer answered his wife, saying, "Behold, with these times of intense inflation and exceeding usury, the price of wood has become burdensome. If we but wait awhile, perhaps the price will become again more reasonable and we will have the means to buy without sacrifice. Then I will build for us a boat."

13. And Gomer's wife went again unto Noah, and she returned saying, "Thus saith the Prophet, build for yourselves a boat at this time, for the price of wood will not be less, but will continue to increase. Wherefore, oh my husband, build for ourselves a boat, that we perish not."

14. But Gomer answered his wife, saying, "Behold, my wife of many years and mother of my many children, hearken unto me. Yea, for more than 120 years Noah hath told us to build a boat to preserve ourselves from the flood, but hath the flood come? Nay, I say, nay! Wherefore, perhaps the flood will not come for another hundred and twenty years, and we would have perforce wasted our children's inheritance."

15. And Gomer's wife went again unto Noah and returned yet again saying, "The Prophet saith, he knows it has been 120 years, but nevertheless, the flood will come, wherefore, build now unto yourselves a boat."

16. And Gomer answered her saying, "Wherewith shall we get the shekels to build ourselves a boat, for are we not now indebted beyond our means with debt for our 4-room house, these new furnishings, the teeth of our precious children are in constant need of repair, and a new chariot driven by 8 horses with the top that comes off in fair weather? Wherefore, when our payments thereunto end, perhaps I shall then build our family a boat."

17. And Gomer's wife went again unto Noah and returned saying, "Behold, the Prophet saith that we should abate our conspicuous consumption, our weekend recreation, our dining at sumptuous buffets, and our annual vacations. He advises we commence to give to each other lumber for our vacations, family birthdays, and our anniversary, that we might thereby acquire enough lumber to commence to build unto ourselves a boat at this time."

18. But Gomer saith unto her, "What a burden to bear! Are we to cease enjoying our chosen lifestyle of comfort and ease, just because we are told by a prophet that we must build unto ourselves a boat at this time?"

19. Wherefore, Gomer having justified himself, built not himself a boat and continued in his conspicuous lifestyle, unconcerned about the prophecy of doom his wife had carried from the Prophet Noah.

20. And Gomer's wife was given to much anguish that he should not build a boat, but she had foresworn to honor and obey her husband and spake not again of the need for a boat.

1. And behold, it was some time later, in the early afternoon, a championship ball game was being played, wherein Gomer was at his highest level of performance of the season as he threw the ball to the opposing players.

2. Now Gomer, facing away from the bright sun, began to see great flashes of lightning in the far sky.

3. And though Gomer could not see over the distant horizon, he heard the sound of ominous, roaring thunder rolling over the land.

4. And Gomer, remembering the pleadings of his wife, suddenly began to fear and shake exceedingly.

5. And Gomer ran, yea, even from the field, unto the shop of the lumber merchant to buy himself a measure of lumber.

6. But behold, the lumber merchant's shop was crowded with great multitudes of eager buyers, all clamoring to buy their own measure of lumber, for they, too, had not wanted to prepare themselves a boat in time.

7. And as such, there was not enough lumber to be found in the entire village, for the multitudes were all demanding much lumber to build their boats.

8. And later in that same day, as the heavens were opened and the rains fell, were all the fountains of the deep opened, and the windows of heaven were broken up, and the floodwaters riseth throughout the whole land, Gomer began to have a deep fear.

9. And behold, Gomer had no boat for his woeful wife and his trusting family.

10. And the water rose above Gomer's waist. Now, Gomer's wife and his children clingeth unto him, hoping he had strength whereby he saveth them from the rising waters.

11. And his wife saith unto him, weeping and wailing, speaking through her gnashing teeth, as the waters rose unto her neck,

12. *"Behold, my slothful husband, did the Prophet Noah not tell thee so, when there was time to prepare a boat for thy family?"*

       ...There is no further record found of Gomer...or of his family...[1]

[1] **Parable of Gomer,** author unknown, courtesy of Christopher Parrett, editor @www.abysmal.com; published in LDS Preparedness Manual, Ver.6.01; Oct 1st, 2008, pp.6-7

From the Desk of Rich & Annie Fleetwood
Founders - SurvivalRing

SurvivalRing started in early 1997 as a single page focused on building up a network of like minded individual websites via the technology of Web rings. In 1999, SurvivalRing became a household name as Y2k chaos loomed on the horizon.

Over the next few years, hundreds of megabytes, and then gigabytes, were uploaded and shared via many different sections of SurvivalRing. Traffic to our site jumped to over 100,000 unique visitors a month, and hundreds of gigabytes (1000 megabytes per gigabyte) were downloaded each year.

Our new site design is the culmination of years of study, new software, intense discussion, and many sleepless nights. Database driven info, multimedia delivery, unlimited expansion and upgrade capability, and a uniform presentation of all SurvivalRing content gives you faster and better access to all the ebooks, software, media and more.

Since 1997, SurvivalRing has been focused on providing documents, downloads, and information to all visitors in all areas of family preparedness, survival, self-reliance, and self-sufficiency. As founders, Annie & I both returned to college to increase skills, add new experiences, and actually live some of the things we talk about… frugality, self reliance, self sufficiency, and survival skills. We currently live on 10 acres in rural Wyoming, and are always developing more content and media to share on the SurvivalRing and other SR network websites.

Never heard of us? Visit our **About Us** page for details on what we do and why. Visit our many **awareness pages** for history and details of past disasters and informational overviews. Drop by our **forums** and find lots of info on a myriad of topics, or over 1,200 new downloads in the forum downloads area. Our **chat room** is also available 24/7, and we have new content being uploaded every week. Questions? Comments? Use our **Contact page.** We also have **articles,** gigabytes of **downloads**, and I'll even personally respond to your emails if you're looking for specific info or are just getting started in preparedness.

Rich & Annie's lifestyle and experiences provided many key moments of having to learn self reliance and survival skills in a hurry. Weather disasters, home repairs, home schooling, car repairs, accidents, and more gave us reason to learn the hard way, and to avoid those situations in the future. Hurricanes & tornadoes wrecked some dreams and family, and were the real beginning of our quest for first learning, and then sharing solutions to regularly occuring threats.

All of the thousands of downloadable files, articles, web pages, and content offered on the SurvivalRing network are available to a global audience. The target audience is the family unit. Information, skills, resources, and how to's are offered that any family, individual, or group can use to focus on making themselves better prepared for LIFE. New to the idea of self reliance? We have a starter page for you.

Do you live in the USA? Have you ever suffered from severe weather? Earthquakes? Flooding? Crimes or warfare? Other Accidents or Mass disasters? Start by learning what natural threats occur where you live. We can help you with all these things that you really need to be concerned with.

We've got those downloads I keep mentioning above. Here are links to a LOT of them…

- Download Set One
- All Hazards – Downloads
- Bunker – Downloads
- Field Manuals – Downloads
- Civil Defense Classics
- Download Set Two
- Download Set Three
- NBC Preparedness – Downloads

Many more publications are on the way in the coming months and years. From where, you might ask? We have bookshelves full of original US and other nation civil defense and survival documents going back decades. DECADES.

Here's a sampling of just ONE stack of documents we have.

http://www.survivalring.org/about/the-project/

And, we have cleven PUBLISHED CD Rom and DVD Rom disks of multimedia, featuring documents, videos, audios, and more. More on the way soon. Intrigued? Read below.

Yes, we have data. We have ebooks. We have videos. We have community via our Forums, chat, and email lists.

How do we offer it all?

SurvivalCD.com is our publication company for our disks. We will be publishing videos, DVDs. podcasts, and even books in the coming future. All will be available online, as well as tangible, in your hand, products.

First, take a look below at our recent disk publications. Learn more about them at the SurvivalCD.com website.

Below you will find links to detailed info about our packages, as well as direct links to purchase our CD & DVD publications with **PayPal**. In association with James, and the digital launch of hs book, we offer the "Basics" sale of all our products, giving you 30% ALL of our products.

The "Basics" sales page is protected with the password *basics.* Enter *basics* in the password box at the page above, and you'll get access to the very special prices we're offering. Look for this…

PROTECTED: MAKING THE BEST OF BASICS SPECIAL

This post is password protected. To view it please enter your password below:

Password:

Submit

This post is password protected. Enter the password to view comments.

PACKAGE	Retail Price	Discount Price	You Save	Info	Buy Now
MassPak	$40.00	$28.00	$12	(info)	PayPal
DigiPak	$30.00	$21.00	$9	(info)	PayPal
HazardPak	$35.00	$24.50	$10.50	(info)	PayPal
Appropriate Tech	$55.00	$38.50	$16.50	(info)	PayPal
ATtackPak	$75.00	$52.50	$22.50	(info)	PayPal
LifePak	$100.00	$70.00	$30	(info)	PayPal
Pandemic	$10.00	$7.00	$3	(info)	PayPal
SRCC 1 year	$89.00	$62.30	$26.70	(info)	PayPal
CivDef Classics	$30.00	$21.00	$9	(info)	PayPal

We've been building our websites and creating new files for over 12 years now. We have no intentions of stopping in the future. SurvivalRing has become our life's passion. Come see what we've done…just for you.

Thanks for reading this page. We look forward to serving you. Questions or Comments? **Click Here.**

Rich and Annie Fleetwood
Summer 2010

Section I

A Preparedness Lifestyle

If you're going to do something, do it right. If something needs doing, do it now. If something's worth doing, do it right now!
Ernest D. Stevens (1909 – 2003)

Chapter 1

The Wake-Up Call

Like Gomer, in the introductory parable, you too have been forewarned—by federal, state, and local government leaders—and probably some spiritual leaders, too. They've all told you that you should be ever-vigilant and <u>prepared</u> for the unexpected, the unusual, and indeed, the realities of life. Maybe, unlike Gomer, you have always known that challenges are certain to lie in the undefined future and choose to be prepared. Or perhaps you're just now hearing the wake-up call.

Those of us who experienced the last decade of the 20th century and the first decade of this 21st century have witnessed unparalleled economic growth, social and political changes, progress in technological innovation, and achievements in our personal lives unforeseen and unrealized in the past. Sometimes such progress has been accompanied by the belief or hope that science, technology, and government can meet all the challenges of our times, tame the forces of nature, and fix everything that goes wrong.

Our unprecedented progress, however, has been accompanied by social change in which we've seen the eroding of our *traditional* values and the depletion of our earth's natural resources. Daily we are confronted with the evidence of our progress: air quality alert days; water use restrictions; *Don't Eat The Fish* signs along polluted rivers and lakes; men, women, and children standing on street corners with signs proclaiming *Will work for food* or just looking for a contribution to their personal cause; latchkey kids coming home to an empty house because both parents work to keep up their family lifestyle (or worse yet, only one parent, working to keep the rent paid); metal detectors in transportation hubs, public buildings, and even in our schools; increased security at airports; government services shutdowns; … the list seems endless.

And though we have had unparalleled growth we have also seen tremendous economic changes—rising unemployment, business closings, huge government deficits, Wall Street failures, just to mention a few.

And each week, it seems, we are challenged worldwide with natural occurrences and extreme weather somewhere: earthquakes, wildfires, flooding, snowstorms, droughts, hurricanes, tornados, fog, hailstorms, lightning strikes, excessive heat, etc.

And what about the ever-present threats to global health: the pandemics.

We do not have to be able to look too far into the future to see the challenges we are potentially facing.

The premise of **Making the Best of Basics** is that each family is subject to and vulnerable to some kind of risk, maybe even at a high risk, for a variety of disasters. The purpose of this book is to help you become prepared for them through <u>lifestyle</u> changes.

DISASTERS

What is a disaster? A disaster is by definition, a… *calamitous event beyond human control, usually occurring suddenly and causing great damage to property; or life-threatening and capable of causing death, injury or other emotional or financial hardship to individuals.*

There are, thankfully, only 3 types of disasters!

Let's take a moment to review these types of disasters:

1. **Natural disasters**—hurricane, typhoon, tornado, extreme cold of winter weather, extreme heat of summer weather, drought, flood, mudslide, woodland and grassland fire, wind, hail, rain, snow, ice, volcano, and tsunami—and various combinations of all these occur in Nature. Every day the unexpected occurs to some degree for each one of us—for some it may be the result of any one of these acts of Nature.

   Natural disasters can happen to any of us at any time. How many people have had their lives disrupted because of tornadoes, hurricanes, earthquakes, severe cold weather, drought, rain, or flooding?

   Just watch the Weather Channel to see the devastating effects that Nature is having on people around the world. Remember what happened to Dorothy and Toto in the fictional story of the Wizard of Oz after their house was hit by a Midwest tornado? Their story is a symbolic reminder of the tortuous path home after such events disrupt our lives.

   Even in our generally mild climate—though somewhat dry south central Texas area—we are currently experiencing (2009) a major drought and a regional disaster area has been declared.

   Just a little more than 10 years ago, we suffered two major floods—one was declared a regional disaster. It is interesting to note the drought and the flood of October 1998 were within a 4-month period—the first time ever in the Nation's history such opposite disaster types were declared in the same region in such a short period of time!

   The potential for damage to my own home was only a few feet away from our doorstep as a record 100-year flood surged across our front yard when a drainage ditch was inadequate for the unanticipated flow of water. That's why we sold our house and moved to a safer place!

2. People-caused disasters

You hear daily news reports about the types of man-caused events in our modern world and how they change the way each of us live:

- terrorism—nuclear, biological viruses, and chemical warfare
- local, state, & federal political decisions affecting taxes, healthcare, & education
- entire economies of foreign countries in gross inflation/deflation stagflation
- business closings
- banking failures
- technological advances replacing manpower
- job outsourcing to foreign countries
- fluctuating stock market prices in the US and abroad
- foreign stock markets plummeting
- business strikes
- corporate downsizing
- transportation-related accidents
- street crime—mugging, theft, and harassment, vandalism to personal and business property
- national and international conflicts
- business strikes
- civil disturbances, riots, and disorderly assembly
- etc., etc.

Often these disastrous events seem to be at a distance and not part of our own life, but eventually, they affect all of us at some level.

3. Personal disasters

Always the most life-changing events are those we experience directly and personally:

- illness or debility
- disability
- death of a spouse or someone in our family
- loss of income
- loss of home or possessions
- loss of any major asset
- divorce
- etc., etc.

The list goes on interminably—there are as many permutations as there are people! Certainly, these personal disasters may be the result of acts of Nature or other people-caused situations. No matter the cause, any of these occurrences could change your day-to-day life, as you know it.

You don't want to think that these types of things will happen to you, do you? Bad things happen only to other people. So you put off doing anything, sometimes until it is too late. Then when something does happen, you may find yourself dealing not only with the specific event but the associated problems that result from having not prepared for these situations.

My wife often shares with people how she was forced to deal with the emotional aspects of the unexpected death of her first husband and all the arrangements on short notice—with no anticipation of the event. She had major difficulties involving debts on a financial deal involving property and cattle her husband had initiated shortly before his death. She had chosen to be uninvolved in the project and subsequently was not prepared with information about the terms and conditions of the arrangements.

Your life will be easier before, during, and after a disastrous or emergency situation if you aren't pressured to sort out so many issues, on so many fronts, with so little information, in so little time, under the most stressful situations!

- <u>All</u> possibilities of disasters exist. Do you expect them all to happen to you? **No!**
- Should you spend your time <u>worrying</u> about disasters? **No!**—it's probably not the best use of your time.
- Can you be ready in case one should ever happen to you? **Yes, indeed!**

AT RISK

As our society becomes increasingly more complex and our space more crowded, greater numbers of people live and work in disaster-prone areas, and the potential for involvement in any of these disasters is enhanced. Today's lifestyle adds further pressure to the chances for *personal* disasters. The result is that greater numbers of communities and individuals are *at risk* of involvement in life-changing events.

When people become displaced, often they find themselves without adequate supplies for sustaining life, much less sustaining a near-normal lifestyle. So as the potential grows for more people to face *uncontrollable* life-changing events, economic self-reliance grows in importance as a significant focus of life management.

WHY WE DON'T PREPARE

It's certainly easy enough to understand why people don't prepare as past generations did. *Progress* and the resulting technological advancements of recent years seem to have lulled us into a false sense of security—believing we can have anything we want, anytime we want it, anywhere we want it—all without a penny in our pocket!

Control of our personal and family self-reliance—in reality our *real* security— has been replaced by the ease of obtaining credit, buy-now/pay-later plans, and ready availability in the stores of practically everything we want, delivered from over-stocked inventories for our consumption, regardless of our ability to meet the payments.

We take for granted the availability of public services such as water, sewer, electricity, natural gas, telephone service, and cable TV. Then there are the many privately-owned resources such as 24-hour supermarkets, convenience stores, full-service retailers, automated banking machines, debit and credit card merchandisers, tele-merchandising, drop-ship businesses, and the fastest-growing supermarket—online Internet merchandising—have addicted us to a high-technology, get-it-when-you-want-it, hand-to-mouth lifestyle.

Our nation's families are stretched thin financially, emotionally, and in terms of meaningful relationship time shared together in the home. As companies downsize their businesses, remaining employees are required to work more hours. Communication technology, with all of its advantages, also keeps people *on call* 24 hours a day.

We are a mobile society—families move across town and across country seeking better job opportunities. More and more women and men have the responsibility of parenting children alone, all the while maintaining a job—or two—to be able to provide money to reduce overwhelming financial obligations.

Unfortunately for today's family, there have never been so many distractions to interfere with the establishment of a family's preparedness or self-reliance program.

HOW PREPARED IS YOUR FAMILY?

Perhaps the questionnaire on the inside front cover will bring some light to the reality of your vulnerability. Take the test, grade yourself, then do what's required to be prepared.

If these questions—or rather, the answers to them—make you uncomfortable, now is the time for you to start to work on your family preparedness by using **Making the Best of Basics** as your *Family Preparedness Handbook*.

It's time to quit complaining about missed opportunities of the past, appreciating too little the opportunities of the present, and worrying too much about the opportunities of the future. Future time is tomorrow's time—whether it's tomorrow, next week, next month, or next year. The time to prepare is now!

Chapter 2

The Time to Prepare Is Now!

Certainly you've heard the story of the old man—now several generations back in time—who loved to listen to the striking of his grandfather clock? He enjoyed that clock so much, in fact, that he kept it in his bedroom against the far wall. After retiring each night, he would lie in his bed, half-awake, listening to the striking of that clock. Whenever the clock struck, he would sleepily count the chimes, knowing that all was well.

One night something must have gone wrong with the clock's mechanism. As it began to strike, the sleepy old man began to count. He counted to ten, eleven, twelve…then **thirteen!… fourteen!… fifteen!…** Suddenly he realized something had gone wrong and he was immediately wide-awake. He reached over, shook his wife, and said, *"Wake up, Ma! It's later than I ever knowed it to be!"*

Well, it's later than many of us realize, too!

The old man's *wake-up call—It's later than I ever knowed it to be*—serves to remind all of us during these challenging and chaotic times of the need for personal and family responsibility and individual creative genius. While it is important to recognize that each of us has a role to play in the ultimate survival and well-being of our world, we must first take responsibility for our own survival and well-being (and that of our family). To that end we apply our creativity so that eventually we can direct our time, talents, and resources to serving in a greater capacity.

We cannot expect science, technology, government, or anyone else to do our part. If **you** have heard the *wake up* call, the time for you and your family to prepare is **now**!

A MORE ACCEPTING ATTITUDE

To support your decision to prepare, you need to be aware there is currently a new, brighter, more accepting attitude towards family preparedness and family self-reliance. The news media are more tolerant in their reporting about survivalist, preparedness (individual and family), and self-reliance issues. The major national news organizations, news feeds, and local station *talking heads* are aware of and increasingly sympathetic—if not laudatory—of individual and community efforts being made to become prepared.

Now, serious tax dollars are being spent to promote preparedness in general by the broadcast media through the Homeland Security Department, FEMA, the American Red Cross, The Weather Channel, and other non-profit and for-profit organizations. If you access **www.ready.gov/america/npm08/intro.html,** you'll discover the federal government has provisions for a **National Preparedness Month** during September yearly!

YOU ARE NOT ALONE

Today, more people—individuals and families—are choosing respectfully, positively, and proactively to prepare for possible future chaos—whether from economic, political, or terrorist causation.

As part of the new movement in preparedness we find the rise of the *Preppers*. These are citizens who recognize their personal and family responsibilities and who **Plan Positively, Prepare Properly, and Perform Peaceably.**

A *Prepper* is one who essentially performs preparatory measures to diminish gradually the potential harmful effects of a disaster or emergency situation by carefully planning and deliberately acting before the event.

You, too, are a *Prepper* if you do any of the following:
- save money—in a sock or a bank account;
- buy new tires before the ones on your vehicle are bald;
- buy two pairs of shoes when they are on sale at ½ price;
- have a retirement account;
- advance your education;
- work hard to gain a raise or to be able to climb the corporate ladder; or
- eat healthily and exercise regularly.

There are probably hundreds of things people do to qualify them as *Preppers*. Recognize that in some or even many aspects of your life, you already have experience in being prepared. There is a growing contingent of urban and suburban *Preppers* organizations across the USA and Canada. There is a resource section at the end of the chapter with links and additional information for contacting them.

AVAILABLE RESOURCES

We're so fortunate in this great country to have the freedom to buy any products we can afford! There are no practical limits to what we can amass—and currently, no laws forbidding it! The only reason for not being or not becoming prepared is not setting the proper family priority for it to happen.

Get ready now while there are no shortages of foodstuffs, food products, and there are advisory services to support your efforts to become prepared.

Truly, in this country, *...there is plenty, and to spare...*

IF NOT NOW…

Benjamin Franklin said, "*If you fail to prepare, you prepare to fail.*" If you fail to prepare adequately *now* for the unknown future, you will eventually pay the price for your indifference! Remember: you can't buy insurance on a

- Wrecked car;
- Burning barn;
- Sinking ship; or a
- Corpse!

ARE YOU PREPARED TO PAY THE PRICE?

Self-reliance—defined as preparedness with the added scope of sustainability—is akin to the wisdom of buying health, life, fire, or auto insurance. Hopefully you'll never need it, but if you do, the initial cost and subsequent payments will be dwarfed by the multiplied value returned to compensate you for the loss.

Being prepared with provisions for adequate water, food, clothing, shelter, and a safe haven for your family is like providing your family with life insurance for disasters, emergencies, and unplanned events. Every family deserves the increased leverage of *life assurance* protection that family preparedness efforts offer.

The possibility always exists that at some time your family will deal with a disaster or the unexpected. Will it be with or without the protection of the food and supplies, abilities, knowledge, skills, talents, and tools you provide them? *Good fortune favors the prepared.*

Are you prepared to pay the price if you fail to do these things?

Are you prepared to be wrong?

Resource Chart 2–1
Prepper Organizations in US & Canada

American Preppers Network National organization for American Preppers Network	
State/Province Chapter	**Website**
American Preppers Network (National)	http://americanpreppersnetwork.blogspot.com/ Email: *americanprepper@yahoo.com*
Alabama Prepper's Network	http://alabamapreppersnetwork.blogspot.com/
Alaska Preppers Network	http://alaskapreppersnetwork.blogspot.com/
Arkansas Preppers Network	http://arkansaspreppersnetwork.blogspot.com/
Arizona Preppers Network	http://arizonapreppersnetwork.blogspot.com/
California Preppers Network	http://californiapreppersnetwork.blogspot.com/
Colorado Preppers	http://colorado-preppers.blogspot.com/
Connecticut Preppers Network	http://connecticutpreppersnetwork.blogspot.com/
Delaware Preppers Network	http://delawarepreppersnetwork.blogspot.com/
Florida Preppers Network	http://floridapreppersnetwork.blogspot.com/
Georgia Preppers Network	http://georgiapreppersnetwork.blogspot.com/
Hawaii Preppers Network	http://hawaiipreppersnetwork.blogspot.com/
Idaho Preppers Network	http://idahopreppers.blogspot.com/
Illinois Preppers Network	http://illinoispreppersnetwork.blogspot.com/
Indiana Preppers Network	http://indianapreppersnetwork.blogspot.com/
Iowa Preppers Network	http://iowapreppersnetwork.blogspot.com/
Kansas Preppers Network	http://kansaspreppersnetwork.blogspot.com/
Kentucky Preppers Network	www.kentuckypreppersnetwork@gmail.com
Louisiana Preppers Network	http://louisianapreppersnetwork.blogspot.com/

State/Province Network / National organization for **American Preppers Network** (continued)	
Maine Preppers Network	http://mainepreppersnetwork.blogspot.com/
Maryland Preppers Network	http://marylandpreppersnetwork.blogspot.com/
Massachusetts Preppers Network	http://massachusettspreppersnetwork.blogspot.com/
Michigan Preppers Network	http://michiganpreppersnetwork.blogspot.com/
Minnesota Preppers Network	http://minnesotapreppersnetwork.blogspot.com/
Mississippi Preppers Network	http://mississippipreppersnetwork.blogspot.com/
Missouri Preppers Network	http://missouripreppersnetwork.blogspot.com/
Montana Preppers Network	http://montanapreppersnetwork.blogspot.com/
Nebraska Preppers Network	http://nebraskapreppersnetwork.blogspot.com/
Nevada Preppers Network	http://nevadapreppersnetwork.blogspot.com/
New Hampshire Preppers Network	http://newhampshirepreppersnetwork.blogspot.com/
New Jersey Preppers Network	http://newjerseypreppersnetwork.blogspot.com/
New Mexico Preppers Network	http://newmexicopreppersnetwork.blogspot.com/
New York Preppers Network	http://newyorkpreppersnetwork.blogspot.com/
North Carolina Preppers Network	http://northcarolinapreppersnetwork.blogspot.com/
North Dakota Preppers Network	http://northdakotapreppersnetwork.blogspot.com/
Ohio Preppers Network	http://ohiopreppersnetwork.blogspot.com/
Oklahoma Preppers Network	http://oklahomapreppersnetwork.blogspot.com/
Oregon Preppers Network	http://oregonpreppersnetwork.blogspot.com/
Pennsylvania Preppers Network	http://pennsylvaniapreppersnetwork.blogspot.com/
Rhode Island Preppers Network	http://rhodeislandpreppersnetwork.blogspot.com/
South Carolina Preppers Network	http://southcarolinapreppersnetwork.blogspot.com/
South Dakota Preppers Network	http://southdakotapreppersnetwork.blogspot.com/
Tennessee Preppers Network	http://tennesseepreppersnetwork.blogspot.com/
Texas Preppers Network	http://texaspreppersnetwork.blogspot.com/
Utah Preppers Network	http://www.utahpreppers.com/
Vermont Preppers Network	http://vermontpreppersnetwork.blogspot.com/
Virginia Preppers Network	http://virginiapreppersnetwork.blogspot.com/
Washington Preppers Network	http://washingtonpreppersnetwork.blogspot.com/
West Virginia Preppers Network	http://westvirginiapreppersnetwork.blogspot.com/
Wisconsin Preppers Network	http://wisconsinpreppersnetwork.blogspot.com/
Wyoming Preppers Network	http://wyomingpreppersnetwork.blogspot.com/

The American Preppers Radio Network

The American Preppers Radio Network plans to grow to become a premier Ham Radio network	http://www.taprn.com/

Canadian Preppers Network

National organization for **Canadian Preppers Network**	Email: *kymber@novascotiapreppersnetwork.com* http://canadianpreppersnetwork.blogspot.com/
Alberta Preppers Network	http://albertapreppersnetwork.blogspot.com/
New Brunswick Preppers Network	http://newbrunswickpreppersnetwork.blogspot.com/
Newfoundland and Labrador Preppers Network	http://newfoundlandpreppersnetwork.blogspot.com/
Northwest Territories Preppers Network	http://northwestterritoriespreppersnetwork.blogspot.com
Nova Scotia-Nunavut Preppers Network	http://novascotiapreppersnetwork.blogspot.com/
Ontario Preppers Network	http://ontariopreppersnetwork.blogspot.com/
Prince Edward Island Preppers Network	http://princeedwardislandpreppersnetwork.blogspot.com
Quebec Preppers Network (*Reseau de Preparation et de Prevention du Quebec*)	http://quebecpreppersnetwork.blogspot.com/
Saskatchewan Preppers Network	http://saskatchewanpreppersnetwork.blogspot.com/
Yukon Territory Preppers Network	http://yukonterritorypreppersnetwork.blogspot.com/

Inclusion does not indicate endorsement, nor does exclusion indicate rejection!

This is an interim listing; frequent updates at http://www.americanpreppersnetwork.com/.

Consider that being prepared is a practical, prudent, and when needed, a providential decision having been given action to completion. When you change your paradigms, then your actions will change. Change your actions to create better attitude and habits, and your life will change! However for things to change, <u>you gotta change!</u>

Chapter 3
Preparedness Lifestyle

Because no one knows for sure what's in store beyond the distant horizon, the individual who takes responsibility for his life and those of his family not only expects the unexpected—but prepares accordingly. When *you* understand the importance of self-reliance and being prepared, it's as if you hear the "*wake up call*" and begin taking responsibility for managing your own life and the lives of your family members in relationship to unplanned events. In so doing, you understand—paradoxically—that there are many facets of your life which cannot be managed or "*controlled*."

Though you may sincerely desire to stay in control of your life, even the most responsible, the wealthiest, or the strongest person can't control certain types of life events.

What is preparedness?

Preparedness is the state of *being prepared* or put in proper condition of readiness *before* an approaching event, something expected, thought possible, or *unexpected*; to put *things* or *oneself in readiness*.

If you think preparedness is a worthwhile concept for you and your family, a question you might wish to ponder is: to what degree do you wish to be prepared?

Minimally, these possibilities exist:

- Emergency level;
- Survival level; and
- Preparedness lifestyle level.

Emergency Level

Let's consider the **emergency level**. An *emergency* is a short term, possibly life-threatening situation. A list of emergencies would probably be endless. You might wish to name your own.

In our particular living circumstances, for example, we face the potential emergency of wildfire. We live in an area that is a forest of trees. We are in a major drought at this time. We are experiencing day upon day of triple-digit temperatures. Our volunteer fire department is on duty now it seems almost 24/7. We need to be able to leave quickly if fire should threaten our area. What is required to deal with such an emergency?

Several years ago a nearby propane plant suffered a fire and an explosion like wartime. It rocked our house noticeably and we live several miles away—even as the crow flies! The neighborhoods nearest to the depot were evacuated. Would it have been valuable to have emergency preparations for such an event?

We moved from the city to the country for peace and quiet. We have learned that even in such a desirable setting as ours the potential for emergencies exists.

Survival Level

Next, let's consider the **survival level**. *Survival* means remaining alive or in existence. In survival mode, all resources are focused toward remaining alive, living through the experience, day-to-day, over a period of time.

To achieve survival the most basic provisions are essential, but are not necessarily in the same order for every area or person:

- Shelter;
- Fire for food and warmth;
- Clothing;
- Sanitation;
- Water;
- Essential medications;
- Nutrition; and
- Of an intangible nature, it would also be of great value to have faith and hope.

Both my wife and I have experienced bouts with cancer. When one receives such a medical diagnosis, the truly lower priorities of life go way into the background. Once your existence is threatened, your perspective on what's important has a way of dramatically changing and your priorities shift dramatically.

Can you imagine not having even the most basic provisions in the event of a situation completely out of your control? Of course, many have had this experience. Remember Hurricanes Andrew, Rita, and Katrina?

Having basic survival supplies does not guarantee that in a crisis they will be useable or that you will survive. You still may need assistance from the outside world. When that's the case, your hope will be that others care enough to help.

Fortunately the true nature of mankind is that we are charitable in times of need.

Preparedness Lifestyle Level

This brings us to the **preparedness lifestyle level.** The *preparedness lifestyle* requires the family to be proactive, self-reliant, and have a high level of readiness for circumstances beyond the family's control.

A **Preparedness Lifestyle** is:

- The practice of being aware and alert to the possible and probable reality of a disaster/unplanned event that could happen to you and your family.
- Knowing how to ascertain potential disasters to which your family is vulnerable.
- Knowing how to eliminate or minimize your risks (and therefore, the negative effects) of any disasters, to the degree possible.

What defines a *preparedness lifestyle*?

- Ability to adapt to changing circumstances.
- Being educated in skills not necessarily taught in traditional school curricula.
- Being ready with appropriate skills, knowledge, and supplies when outside conditions demand.
- Being self-reliant so as to diminish the potential for having to depend on others for basic needs.
- Living providently, practically, and sustainably—regardless of external conditions.
- Having some normalcy when all is in disarray around you.
- Having peace of mind because you have some assurance that you can deal with problems that may arise.
- Being able to face with a degree of confidence and certainty *the potential problems of an increasing demand for and a decreasing supply of basic commodities.*

The only way you can achieve this level of preparation is by deciding now to take control of your own destiny, make a plan, and commit to accomplish the plan. Although you can't control externally-caused, life-changing events, you *can* organize a plan and implement it for times when such events occur.

IN-HOME STORAGE

The strategy for having adequate supplies to minimize the effects of disasters and unplanned events is having In-Home Storage—a real in-home convenience store!

In-home storage is how you can minimize the negative impact of an unexpected event by having stored—in your possession and under your control—adequate resources of:

- **Shelter**
- **Clothing**
- **Sanitation**
- **Fuel for heating (wood / gas / fuel oil / propane / diesel / other)**
- **Water**
- **Medications and medical supplies**
- **Food**
- **Money**
- **Bedding**
- **Transportation / fuels**
- **Anything your family would need to be self-reliant during a disaster, or an extended period of time subsequent to an emergency or disaster-caused situation**

There are no emergencies for those who are truly prepared!

There is a powerful, secure feeling in knowing that you have chosen to take charge of your personal readiness and that your family will be able to eat and sustain a relatively stress-free rebound period after a disaster—because together, under your leadership, you made the effort to plan ahead and have under your control the life-saving essentials your situation demands.

If you've prepared for your family's self-reliance and security with both emergency and long-term provisions, *you can turn what could have been a life-threatening situation into a manageable problem.*

DISASTERS CAN HAPPEN TO ANYONE…ANYTIME…ANYWHERE

An interesting story …One of the medical doctors treating me in post-cancer care several years ago was a specialist. I had spent weeks searching for a this type of specialist, and I was tickled to find the consummate professional. As is customary for me, I gave him a copy of my book upon meeting him for the first exam—I found it's a great calling card and a way to spread the message of preparedness! Also, those getting a book remember me better.

He said he had been raised on a ranch, and grew up tending the family garden until he was old enough to join his older brothers riding herd. He said he understood the need for a large pantry, and had plenty of space in the large farmhouse on his horse property, but just hadn't got around to "*putting some food by.*"

When I had been in treatment for almost a year, I went into the office for the required health check a week after commencing the program for medication detox. To my surprise, he was not there. Upon inquiry, his Physician Assistant told me he had been hurt in a serious accident the previous Saturday morning and had received a serious concussion. The irony of it all was that he had no doctor "*friend*" for the delicate surgery required.

Later, after six long months, my doctor was back on the job, and I was ready for my release from a 13 months post-medication regime. He related how he had done the same thing I had done—spent a lot of time looking for well-qualified specialists for his own treatment. He had the further handicap of not being able to drive himself to appointments! His wife spent hours each week driving him and helping him navigate the parking lot curbs, steps, building doorways, elevators, hallways, and getting himself unclothed and clothed in tiny dressing rooms.

But the part of his story that meant so much to me was that he had followed the ways and wisdom of his parents and had invested some serious time and money in his family's welfare, "*just in case.*"

Normally, there would have been serious financial, emotional, and mental angst within the family given such an experience. No one in his family was worried though, because the pantry had been full of canned goods, the freezer full of beef from his dad's ranch, and the children never missed a meal!

His wife was grateful she didn't need to shop except for a few fresh things—as he said—"*some weekend pleasure foods, a few seasonal veggies and fruits, and occasionally fresh milk.*"

Fortunately, there was some continuing income from his practice during his forced semi-retirement. The money from the dwindling practice covered the office rent, employee payroll, and other overhead expenses, but he never had to borrow money for living expenses.

I was touched by his experience and he was tearfully grateful for the "*reminder*" to do his fatherly duties that I had given him many months before.

How dramatically this story illustrates the value of choosing a preparedness lifestyle and emphasizes the following points:

- Your **head of family (patriarchal or matriarchal) responsibility** demands you protect your family.

- You can more fully **exercise a higher level of personal freedom**. Unexpected changes in circumstances do not have to force an individual or family to be dependent on others.

- You would be **prudent and wise to be prepared** because **providential** (fortunate, advantageous, beneficial) things happen as a result of advance preparations. Remember the *Parable of the Ten Virgins*!

A PARADIGM SHIFT

If you have had a difficult time in the past with the thought of amassing supplies for impending disasters, what if you shift your thinking to another level, away from the mentally and physically tiring activity of ***food storage***?

What if you embrace the concept of accumulating an adequate supply of food, clothing, and shelter as a *way of everyday life*—**a preparedness lifestyle?** Suddenly it's neither so daunting nor so burdensome—it becomes *your* routine—the way you live on a daily basis! Then you can do it step by step.

Let's take to heart what Lt. General Russell L. Honoré (Ret.), former commanding general of the U.S. First Army and the Commander of Joint Task Force Katrina, said in the aftermath of that great devastation:

> *"Each of us has a personal responsibility to be ready. We need to prepare our families and our homes. In many cases, family and personal preparations can be fairly simple. All it takes is a shift in our thinking… In this new normal, we have only two options:*
>
> 1. ***We can exist in a culture of fear and dependency****, or*
>
> 2. ***We can do the responsible thing****: Live comfortably in a culture of preparedness and readiness—a culture where individuals can save themselves and empower their local, regional, and national governments to better respond to any disaster. It's time for America to adopt this **culture of preparedness**."*

NOTES FOR YOUR LIFESTYLE CHANGES

WHAT YOU KNOW IS YOUR ULTIMATE SURVIVAL TOOL—and you must get it RIGHT!

Hi, my name is Jim Phillips. Being an engineer keenly interested in how things work, and having learned countless lessons from numerous survival experiences, has placed me on a path it seems I was destined to follow; helping others become prepared. **This has become my passion!**

More than 45 years ago my father and I developed a cold weather clothing system that is key to survival when you cannot heat your home, when fuels run out, or when you are without shelter. Even below zero, this clothing **dries itself while being worn!** It performs significantly better than other clothing insulation, wicking materials, layered systems, and everything else!

Some preparedness enthusiasts provide lists of things to purchase and information based on theories or conjecture with little or no real testing. Such advice can put your life in peril during a crisis.

I take a different approach. I am committed to teaching only what I have **tested** and **proven by personal experience!**

Training Based on Solid Principles and Proven Methods

We offer a variety of in-depth preparedness courses on the topics that are most vital to your survival. Whether you are a beginner or an expert, we guide you in the right direction and help you to not feel overwhelmed in the process.

Jim Instructing in a Classroom

> Start from where you are. Do all you can with what you have. Keep at it day after day. Each day learn something or acquire something that leaves you better prepared today than the day before!

With Knowledge Comes Peace of Mind, when you

- Can stay warm in the winter, even without heat or shelter—no matter how cold the temperature.
- Can secure water and know multiple techniques for making water safe to use.
- Can maintain a clean, healthy, sanitary environment that is vital to wellness.
- **Know you can "MAKE IT NO MATTER WHAT!"**

We have the experience and the skills to help families and groups become better prepared than ever before.

Our training is available on DVD and in live classes. Begin this valuable instruction today with **the "Self-Reliant Series PART 1 - THE FOUNDATION (Your True Needs and Priorities)";** it's available free with this book by download at **www.beprepared101.com.** Get a DVD for the cost of S&H by sending a $5.95 check or money order to the address below. Mark the envelop, "Attention: MTBOB DVD Offer".

Jim Teaching a Winter Class

Safe Harbor Alliance
PO Box 628
Lehi, Utah 84043
www.safeharboralliance.com

If you do not take care of yourself and your family, who will take care of you?
You must lay the foundation for being able to feed, clothe, and shelter your
family and yourself. It is often said the Lord helps them who help themselves.
Another way to say it is that chance favors the prepared!

Chapter 4

The Path to Family Preparedness

So you've heard the wake-up call and are considering that it might be advantageous
to do something to prepare yourself and your family for the unknown future.
Where do you begin? Well, it's like any good effort. You start with the intangible
aspects first. You might think of this as being the "*spiritual*" side of preparedness. What
does that mean?

Well, before anything is created in the physical, we know that it is first created in the
mind (though some call it in the heart)—that is the spiritual part of mankind.

Consider how a high-rise building, a bridge, or a house is built. Most of us are just concerned with the finished product. But before the bricks, mortar, lumber, metal, and glass
are put in place to complete a structure, architects and designers are involved in much
envisioning, studying, measuring, drawing, and planning to the minutest detail. In a like
manner for your family preparedness to be solid, sturdy, and lasting, you may wish to
approach it first as an architect would. You don't want to just jump into "*piling up bricks
and mortar, lumber, metal, and glass*"—and then discover your building is built on sand!

SPIRITUAL FOUNDATION

First, let's look at the qualities that are the foundation for building your preparedness program:

- a deep and abiding love for your family;

- a strong desire to protect them;

- acceptance that yours is a sacred duty to responsibly prepare your family physically, mentally, and practically for an uncertain future;

- courage to make the tough decisions—the first one being to commit to protecting your family;

- ability to act on your decisions and keep taking the next step;

- gratitude for your opportunity to do something now before you need it;

- fortitude to keep going when the going gets tough;

- faith in your abilities;

- trust in your Maker—to guide you in what to do, where to go, and how to proceed—and humility to ask for help;

- willingness to sacrifice the less important expenditures of time, money, and focus for those things that will provide the long term feeling of the peace of preparedness;

- readiness to do what it takes;

- charity to act not only in the best interest of your own family but to share the knowledge and skills you acquire with your extended family, neighbors, and co-workers; and certainly,

- hope for a bright future.

Evaluate yourself in relation to these qualities stated above. Are you ready to move forward?

Know that one of the advantages of choosing a preparedness lifestyle is that you continue to mature in these qualities as you step forth in faith. One of the great benefits that accompanies your choice to prepare is the on-going personal growth. Each time you learn a new skill, see the accomplishment of goods acquired, or have the ability to respond to new challenges, you grow in your confidence to be able to handle the emergencies that life throws your way.

Before you begin, it is essential to have already made the commitment that nurturing and protecting your family is a priority. You already protect them with such things as health and life insurance, do you not? When you prepare them to be able to eat, no matter the circumstances, you are protecting them with "*life assurance*."

You're reading this book because you are, at the very least, <u>concerned</u> about protecting your family. The real question is: are you <u>committed</u> to protecting your family?

Many people make the choice to become prepared. But there is a big difference between making a **choice** and making a **commitment**!

This story illustrates the magnitude of difference between *choosing* and *committing*:

Three frogs are sitting on a lilypad in a small pond. One hungry frog ponders for a moment after looking at some ants on the shore. He then tells his two frog friends he's going to jump from the lilypad and onto the bank of the pond to get some ants for lunch.

How many frogs are then left on the lilypad?

Everyone assumes the answer to be 2 frogs—but the fact is that only a **<u>decision</u>** was made—and all 3 are *still* sitting on the pad.

<u>Don't confuse **decision** with **action**</u>! A decision is not an actual <u>**commitment**</u>!

A **choice is a <u>first step</u> to commitment—not the commitment!**

Do not procrastinate the day of implementing your family's preparedness plan. You can make it become a reality only when you put your **decision** into **action**!

IF YOU ARE COMMITTED, READ ON

In this chapter we are going to introduce you to the **Path to Family Preparedness**. This is a visual outline of steps, a map of sorts, to remind you that this is a journey and re-member that your preparedness program does not happen overnight. The **Path** is an exer-cise to help you focus your effort. This tool will not tell you specifically what to do for your family. You are always responsible for choosing your level of preparedness based on your means and needs.

<u>Remember</u>: anything you do to prepare is commendable and each success will en-courage you to do more.

To understand this **Path**, imagine yourself to be standing on a road looking toward the horizon ___ ✳ ___ . The horizon represents your chosen <u>**desire**</u> —your <u>goal</u>—your <u>**priori-ty**</u>—that to which you wish to direct your attention and effort. In line with what Dr. Ste-phen Covey has taught us in his best-selling "**7 Habits of Highly Effective People**," fo-cusing on the horizon is a means for us *"to begin with the end in mind."*

Though we cannot see beyond the horizon or even what life will have for us tomorrow on the path we choose, at least we can proactively choose what we would like to create for ourselves to address the unexpected. Being able to choose is a gift to us from our Maker. Let us use that to our advantage in relationship to being ready for the uncertainties of life.

A wise teacher once said, *"What you focus on is what you get."* Consider the truth of that.

So, to use the **Path** exercise, first, you put your goal on the **Horizon**. Then what? You <u>think</u> in terms of the goal having already been accomplished.

You ask yourself these questions:

- How would the accomplishment of this desire manifest in my life? In other words, how would I know that the goal had been accomplished?

- What things about my life would demonstrate that this goal had been achieved?

- How would my life be different because I realized my goal?

Now, given the specific ways you see the accomplishment of this goal manifesting in your life, you will consider:

- Current resources you have on hand to support this accomplishment.

- The investments you must make to bring this goal into reality.

- Obstacles that potentially block your path.

Once you have done your analysis, you are ready to use your imagination (creative think-ing) to balance your effort. You first <u>imagine</u> what it is like to have this desire fulfilled. (Before, you were just *thinking* about it!) Stepping into an imaginary place of fulfillment where you can see yourself as if your goal is already achieved, walk around in the expe-rience of it, feel the feelings, and <u>feel the power</u> of this completed objective as if it al-ready exists. And it does already exist—in the *"spiritual"* realm. The *"blueprint"* has been created.

Next you create a mental picture. (It also helps to make a physical representation of this picture that you can look at.) Its role is to help you stay focused on your target. The pic-ture is whatever comes to your mind that represents the completed goal with its asso-ciated positive feelings. The feelings are a necessary part of this step. Having a goal with no passion, enthusiasm, or dedication makes the fulfillment of it more challenging.

With these steps completed, it is time to make a commitment to move forward. Imagine that you have a "*blueprint*" that details what needs to be done. You just have to decide what to do first. Then you must take action to accomplish your goal.

Hang your picture (or other representations) where you can see it. When you look at it, step back into that place of fulfillment you created. Feel the good feelings. Then stay open to inspiration about your next step.

Success will build on success. Celebrate your victories. Keep taking the next step and let the reality of your preparedness plan unfold to match or even exceed your horizon goals.

MY PERSONAL PATH STORY

This **Path** model is useful for preparing the mind and heart for whatever you desire to create in your life. It is this kind of preparation that provides the real fuel to keep you moving on your path when obstacles pop up, as they will, when you become sidetracked, discouraged, or just tired.

To give you a little background on this **Path** exercise, I will share a personal story.

I was introduced to this exercise by my wife many years ago. When we first met, I told her I had written a book in 1974, that it had been out of print for 8 years or so, and that I would like to get it back into circulation. Several years later when it was actually the time for me to once again work on **Making the Best of Basics**, she suggested I start with this path exercise so that I might really target my desire and energize my planning before I just jumped in to "*doing*" without any direction.

At the time we did this exercise, I had no adequate computer, no publisher, nor any money to do the things I felt were required to get the book re-published. Yet, three years later **Basics** was published by a major publishing company. During 1998 and 1999 the book became very popular with people seeking ways to be better prepared for Y2K and was #1 on **Amazon.com** for weeks and in their top 10 non-fiction category for weeks and weeks and weeks…

The **Path** exercise helped me to identify rationally what it would mean in my life to have **Basics** published. Once I had accomplished that I used my imagination and my heart to create a picture that would help me stay focused on the goal. You know what they say about a picture being worth a 1000 words!

Once I had created the "*picture*" that represented the 9th edition of **Basics** as my focus, my project began to take off. I even attracted some investors which allowed me the opportunity to have the money to acquire the equipment I needed. Support for new content, relevant information, and a new direction for this revised edition of the book began to show up in unusual ways.

My wife says I am a good example of how the process works once you do the exercise. She often recalls that I would follow my <u>inner promptings</u>. For example, I would be driving through town *en route* to appointments for my "*daytime job*" (**Basics** only received my attention from about 10 p.m. to 2 a.m.) when I would be inspired to go in one of the computer/electronics stores. Invariably there would be a sale on a piece of equipment I needed for working on the book. This is an illustration, she says, of being aware of inspiration once you have experienced this exercise.

My story also points out <u>discipline</u> and <u>sacrifice</u>, she tells me. The re-publishing of the book was important enough to me that I was willing to stay up nights, after customers stopped calling, to put in the time required to get the re-writing job done. I learned once again in my life that your heart's desire will not come about without your <u>appropriate efforts</u>.

We offer the path experience to you as the **Path to Family Preparedness** that you, too, might benefit.

BEFORE WE EMBARK ON THE PATH

Before we embark on the **Path** worksheets there are a few ideas that might be of help to you in "*walking the path*."

I mentioned earlier that you create a mental picture in the **Path** exercise to represent your goal. You may also wish to consider creating a family paradigm—a written belief statement that unites your family in your effort.

Let me share my family's model as an example. This helps our family to share a common perspective and thus know our objectives in terms of our preparedness efforts:

> **We hope for the best;**
>
> **We fear for the worst; and**
>
> **We prepare to deal with what happens!**

3 More Reasons to Become Prepared:

1. We have been **advised** to be prepared... (Remember the **story of Noah**, **Joseph in Egypt**, and the *parable of the Ten Virgins*?)
2. You would be **prudent and wise** to be prepared—**providential** things happen as a result of being prepared.
3. As the **head of your family (patriarchal or matriarchal) responsibility,** all reason demands you protect your family

It's unfortunate that food storage gets such a bad rap in this Nation. When I lived out of the U.S., I was able to see that whoever controlled the food supply controlled the people!

We've been advised to save for the future—so many times for so long…

What if you shift your thinking to another level, away from the mentally and physically tiring activity of *__food storage__*?

What you achieve bit-by-bit is to comprehend the concept of accumulating a supply of food, clothing, and shelter as a *way of everyday life*—**a preparedness lifestyle**—and suddenly it's neither so daunting nor so burdensome. You'll actually get the attitude it doesn't matter what others say or do!

What is a preparedness lifestyle? ***To become self-reliant—to be able to live providently regardless of external conditions!**￼*

May I suggest serious consideration that you make some **Paradigm Shifts** about your preparedness responsibilities? We spent many years in the activity of trying to stay prepared as we raised our 6 children.

Here are the guiding principles that ultimately govern our family's preparedness activities:

1. **We'll bloom where we're planted.**

    We made a conscious decision to live on a rocky hilltop. When those below us may need to evacuate due to flooding, we plan to stay in our home. We have reduced and continue to reduce our belongings so as not to be owned by an allegiance to our material things. If moving in the future seems important, fewer possessions will make it easier for us to move on.

    - **Planning Action Item:** *We chose to build our house on the rock!*

2. **Our home will be our personal convenience store.**

    We've created and continue to maintain a very selective mini-grocery store—an *in-home convenience store*—stocked with the things we like to eat and know we can enjoy during a crisis situation—no matter how long it lasts! We set it up where we have unique access to it and can utilize it as our family needs it!

- **Faith Action Item:** *As others may do without, we can continue to eat—and be able to give help to others in their afflictions!*

3. **Our family will be able to camp out within the walls of our home.**

   In case of a disaster or emergency situation, our family will be able to maintain an **acceptable level of comfort** within our house and on our property. We're prepared *now* to be able to live within our comfort zone in the future when others can't live in theirs. We have equipment that will allow us to continue to function regardless of the status of the normal utilities that we depend on normally.

   - **Works Action Item:** *We got the gear and lost the fear!*

4. **Get out of debt.** The only allowable debts are for purposes of education, our home, or a sound business venture to produce income for the family.

   My father was very wise about most things—he often told me: *"Jimmy, there are only 2 kinds of people, those who earn interest, and those who pay it!"*
   Grow your savings, not your stuff!

   - **Paradigm Action Item:** *We can sustain our lifestyle without too much further reduction of "creature comforts."*

There's a popular national talk radio show host, Dave Ramsey, who proclaims with vigor: *"Live now like no one else, and in the future, you can live like no one else!"* *Spot on, Dave!*

If you fail to prepare adequately *now* for the unknown future, you will eventually pay the price for your disobedience! Benjamin Franklin (and a lot of others, also) said, *"If you fail to prepare, you prepare to fail."*

Remember: you can't buy insurance on a:
- Wrecked car
- Burning barn
- Sinking ship

We are so fortunate to have the capability to buy any products we want in this great country! There is no excuse for not being or becoming a self-reliant family.

There is no shortage of products and services to aid us in becoming self-reliant.
Truly, in this country, *"…there is plenty, and to spare…"*

- **There are no emergencies for those who are truly self-reliant!**
- **If you are truly self-reliant, you have no need to fear!**

With all your getting, get wisdom. The happiest people don't have the best of everything––they just make the best of everything they have!

It is human nature to have both beginnings and progress that has fits and starts—and starts and restarts. There are always problems with any venture into difficult, yet necessary, arenas of change. So what? Keep your spiritual mind on the physical tasks…

Thinking and planning—while virtually essential to eventual success—are too often the culmination of one's efforts.

The genius of any success is found in the execution and implementation—*and they are often left undone!* Don't forget the frog story—it's not the decision—it's the **action**!

Another example of the necessity of action is found in nature—the **centipede syndrome.**

A centipede, when finding itself upside down, goes into extreme action—violently arches its back, wiggles its body, kicks its feet, and strives unceasingly to get some traction with its feet to turn itself right side up. Eventually, it gets a foothold (traction) and flips itself upright.

The centipede had lots of **motility** (meaning: *capable of or demonstrating movement*) but the challenge was to gain **mobility** (meaning: *movement or action; the ability to move about*).

These actions may be perceived the same, but they are definitely not the same!

Have you ever said to yourself that you were going to make more money this year? Was that all it took to achieve earning more money—just saying it? Most likely—not!

Don't confuse *movement* with *action*! Coach John Wooden counseled his players at UCLA, **"Never mistake activity for achievement."** If you recall his success, you can only imagine what his practice drills were like!

The **Path** steps which follow will help you become mentally ready (having made the decision) and spiritually ready (to take action) for the task(s) of becoming prepared for the uncertain future.

Though you have no control over most disasters occurring in your life, you can train yourself to be able to deal with them positively.

"If you are truly prepared, there is no need to fear."

Many years ago, in the 10th edition of **Making the Best of Basics — *Family Preparedness Handbook***, this motto was introduced. It could have been stated as:

If you are truly prepared, you probably will deal with the pain of loss a great deal better!

This is not a guarantee offering complete safety for those who've prepared for every contingency imaginable, but it does reinforce the adage,

Good fortune favors the prepared mind....

You are not in control of natural disasters, nor of most people-caused disasters, and can only respond or react to the personal disasters occurring in your life. When you are unprepared, you often make serious judgment errors due to loss, grief, or just being in a confused and/or unfamiliar state of mind due to the circumstances.

Removing the fear from any uncontrollable situation makes it more acceptable and easier to deal with it—**for deal with it you must—prepared or not!**

Fear causes you mental anguish—pain that can freeze you into complete inaction and total indecision. On the other hand, the prepared mind will be galvanized into positive response because it's able to sort out the problem and reduce it to its more resolvable, or concomitant, parts—dissolving the seemingly complex situation into what-to-do-next simplicity.

All experts study, learn, practice—and do it again and again until their responses are virtually automatic for a given event—whether physical, mental, or moral.

The promise here is that you can increase your ability to deal with problems by being prepared.

Do your homework now. Read, study, learn, and step up to meet the challenge: **make sure your family can eat.**

Food truly is power when normal supplies are unavailable, whatever the reason. As I've said before:

Don't Get Caught with *Your* Pantry Down!

The Path to Your Family Preparedness

Hear the wake-up call!

Commit to make the protection of your family a priority

ASSESS, EVALUATE, RESEARCH

Assess potential risks and vulnerability to emergencies / disasters

Think of the goal as already accomplished

Specify how the completion of your goal will be demonstrated in your life

Determine what resources you have on hand to achieve your goal

Identify the investment you must make to achieve your goal

Name the obstacles blocking the path to your goal

REALITY CHECK

Evaluate your goal; modify if needed

IMAGINE

Imagine your goal fulfilled

Enjoy the "*experience*" of having completed your goal

Create a "*picture*" to represent your completed goal

COMMIT TO MOVE FORWARD

MAKE A PLAN

DECIDE WHAT TO DO FIRST

Take the first step

Have family meetings

Take the next step

Celebrate your victories

Choose your family preparedness goal; put your goal on the Horizon

Manage your resources; keep taking steps!

Goal!

OUR FAMILY PREPAREDNESS PATH WORKSHEET

☑ We have heard the wake-up call.
☑ We are committed to the protection of our family as a priority.

IN THIS SECTION, YOU WILL "ASSESS, EVALUATE, & RESEARCH"

Risk Assessment

Our family is vulnerable to and/or at risk for the following emergency situations and disasters:

Natural	People-Caused	Personal
1.	1.	1.
2.	2.	2.
3.	3.	3.
4.	4.	4.
5.	5.	5.

Current Family Goal

Our current family goal is to become prepared to live at the:

☐ Preparedness Lifestyle Level
☐ Survival Level
☐ Emergency Level
☐ Other

Sample "Horizon" Statements

- *"Our Home is a Safe Haven"*
- *"Our Family is Prepared for the Uncertainties of Life"*
- *"We live a near-normal lifestyle regardless of external conditions"*
- *"We will get out of debt."*

Our Family "Horizon" Statement

REALITY CHECK

Yes	No	Is our goal reasonable, manageable, and achievable?
Yes	No	Does our goal support our highest good?
Yes	No	Will our goal harm anyone in any way?

When Our Family Goal Is Achieved, We Will Have the Following Available to Us:

Preparedness Level	Knowledge / Skills & Education	Tools and Equipment	Food /Supplies	Other Resources
Emergency Level:				
Survival Level:				
Preparedness Lifestyle Level:				
Other Levels				

When our family goal is achieved, our lives will be improved in these following ways:
(State specifics!)

The Resources We Have On-Hand To Support Our Goal Are:

Financial	Knowledge/ Skills/Abilities	Tools/Supplies	Food	Supplies

The Investment Of Time, Money, Resources, Focus, and Talent That We Must Make To Accomplish Our Desired Preparedness Goal Requires:

	Notes
Financial · purchases · savings · planning	
Resource management	
Education · research	
Training · new skills	
Changes	
Sacrifices (What do we give up to get something better?)	
Use of living space	
Other	

The Major Stumbling Blocks In Our Path To Family Preparedness Are:

1.
2.
3.
4.
5.

REALITY CHECK

| Yes | No | Given our level of desire, the investment required, the resources we have, and the obstacles we perceive, are we willing to proceed? |

| Yes | No | Do we need to modify our goal to be more reasonable, manageable, and achievable? |

Set yourself up for success.
If you need to modify your "Horizon," return to previous charts and do it now.

Move On To the Next Step
⬇

FOR THIS SECTION YOU WILL USE YOUR "IMAGINATION"

For this step, take time to daydream a little. In school you usually got in trouble for daydreaming. Here it is an essential part of your spiritual preparedness.

Imagine

1. Imagine your preparedness goal is already completed. Your program is in place in your home.

2. Now picture a "*fitting room.*"

3. Use this fitting room to "*try on*" your completed family preparedness plan as you have described above.

4. Walk around in this imagined experience.

5. Delight in your achievements.

6. Tour your home. How have you integrated your preparedness efforts into your living space, your routine, your financial management, etc.?

7. Observe: What fits? What doesn't fit? What works?

8. How does it feel?

9. What modifications do you recognize?

REALITY CHECK

| Yes | No | Do we need to modify our plan to be more reasonable, manageable, and achievable? |

Set yourself up for success.
If you need to modify your "Horizon," do it now!

<u>Create a Picture</u>

1. Create a mental picture that represents the fulfillment of your family preparedness goal.

    The best way to find your picture is to follow the positive feelings that come with the imagined completion of your goal. As you allow yourself to enjoy the accomplishment of your goal, invite a picture to show up in your mind's eye.

    The picture might be represented by a familiar photograph, a picture from a magazine, a scene from a movie, or even your own creative invention.

2. Actually find or create a picture to hang up and look at it each day to remind you of your goal.

    If you do this as a family, create a collage with all of the pictures.

3. You can create a family paradigm—a written model, a belief, a statement—that also unites you in your effort.

4. Hang it where all family members can see it.

☐ We Are Committed To Move Forward

Our Planning Includes:

Our First Step Is:

We Have Taken Action!

CONGRATULATIONS!
YOU ARE ON THE PATH TO FAMILY PREPAREDNESS…

KEEP TAKING THE NEXT STEP(S)—*One at a time!*

-
-
-
-
-
-
-
-
-
-
-
-
-
-
-
-
-

Personal/Family Assignment

1. Meet with your spouse/family and determine your current self-reliance level, then determine he goals you're willing to set to become self-reliant.

2. Determine the potential disaster or emergency situations to which you are vulnerable—whether natural, people-caused, or personal.

3. Determine the paradigm shifts(s) required to ignite your launch into a self-reliance lifestyle.

4. Determine the actions you must take to get from where you are to where you want/need to be.

5. Determine your willingness to make the commitment to take action steps to become self-reliant.

6. Determine your level of commitment to become self-reliant.

7. What would prevent you from doing what is not only wise, but necessary, to achieve self-reliant?

8. Will you exercise the faith to become self-reliant?

9. Will you focus on the cans, not the can'ts?

10. Are you honest with yourself in feeling the exigency of the financial, economic, and political situations our society faces today?

Now, it's Your Turn to Write the Story of Your Path!

Notes For Your Wake-Up Call

Section II

Starting Your
Preparedness Lifestyle

Chapter 5: 72-Hr.$^+$ *E/PAK*
        <u>E</u>mergency/<u>P</u>reparedness <u>A</u>ction <u>K</u>it

Chapter 6: Getting Your Household in Order
        Family Preparedness Household Notebook

You cannot prepare for everything.
However, that for which you prepare, you should prepare superbly well.

72-Hr.⁺ *E/PAK*

<u>E</u>mergency/<u>P</u>reparedness <u>A</u>ction <u>K</u>it

This chapter provides you an opportunity to become prepared for the unexpected occurrences in your life—as well as for the expected ones! If you're reading this information, then you're showing some interest in becoming more prepared. The information in this chapter is to help you achieve the following purposes:

1. Be a survivor;
2. Be prepared; and eventually,
3. Become self-reliant.

You have been forewarned often by federal. State, and local government leaders that you should be ever vigilant and prepared for the unexpected, the unusual, and the unfortunate realities of life. Though you cannot see over the horizon, you know that beyond it is the unknown future, and that therein lie challenges, making your future uncertain.

> History is a better guide than good intentions.
>
> *Jeanne Kirkpatrick, US Ambassador to the UN*

3-DAY SURVIVAL KIT

The purpose of the 72-hour personal preparedness pack or *3-day survival kit*—as it is commonly called—is to provide emergency protection, rations of water and food, and necessary medical supplies for your struggle with events and forces beyond your control.

Preparedness has its roots in protecting people and their treasures, and is borrowed from the concept of military readiness. Soldiers carried survival supplies when involved in military operations to protect themselves, take care of their personal needs, and allow them to complete their assigned mission.

For the average citizen, it's a ready-to-use, portable package containing supplies, food and water rations, as well as other vital supplies and equipment for maintaining personal well-being—or, at least, staying alive when forced into extremely dangerous or uncontrollable circumstances.

The idea of individuals and families having survival kits is based on the firm—and confirmed—belief that natural disasters and personal emergencies are not a matter of *whether* they will happen, but *when*. Having a few basic categories of supplies and provisions on hand can mitigate that helpless feeling caused by emergencies.

Being prepared reduces the panic associated with the occurrence of seemingly uncontrollable events.

In a complete personal or family readiness plan, a wise family leader would have either a number of survival kits—one for each member of the family—and/or one complete kit available for application in all possible situations, whether:

> | Planning will assure you've considered your needs in case of an emergency, disaster, or life-threatening situation. |

- at home
- at play
- traveling by boat / bus / plane / train
- when on vacation / hotel / overnight
- at work
- in the car / truck
- at school / college
- other: _____

DEVELOP YOUR OWN 72-HOUR⁺ EMERGENCY PREPAREDNESS ACTION KIT

Use the information in this chapter to organize your own **Emergency Preparedness Action Kit**, or *E/PAK*, as we have nicknamed our 72-hour+ kit. Or you can purchase one that meets your needs from any number of preparedness vendors.

Whether designing your own or purchasing your survival kit, consider the level of preparedness you wish to achieve for yourself or your family. A most important aspect of a survival kit is that it be able to keep you alive and well when you are confronted with an emergency or survival situation beyond your control.

Consider the following issues in relationship to 72-hour kits:

- ■ Experience in recent incidents of natural disasters, such as hurricanes Katrina and Rita, the Indonesian tsunami, and the California wildfires, have proven that a 72-hour kit is not normally enough reserve for the duration or privation following a disaster. Depending on the severity of a disaster event, the length of time it lasts, the geographic breadth, and the population at risk, it may take local, state, and federal rescue and repair personnel much longer to provide resources needed for rescue and relief.

- ■ No one kit would resolve all possible disaster scenarios in any part of this nation, and is therefore probably not a viable option to consider for most families. This suggests some deep consideration should be give to all potential disasters that might affect the family. Once that determination is made, then it would be imperative to complete a kit to meet the most likely needs of the threats perceived.

Whether designing your own or purchasing your survival kit, consider the level of preparedness you wish to achieve for yourself or your family.

A most important aspect of a survival kit is that it be able to keep you alive *and* well when you are confronted with an emergency or survival situation beyond your control.

The most important guideline for planning and developing your own ***Emergency/Preparedness Action Kit*** (***E/PAK***) is this:

Your level of preparation should exceed your level of risk!

Here are some useful government and non-government websites for disaster preparedness issues:

Chart 5-1
U. S. Government Websites & Resources

U. S. Government Websites & Resources	
 http://www.usa.gov/	
 www.dhs.gov/	**Department of Homeland Security** Provides a broad range of information relating to homeland security, including the national threat level, travel alerts and procedures, emergency preparation guidelines, immigration policies and border initiatives, school safety, and other security-related topics.
US Dept of Homeland Security's READY Business	Tips for small and medium sized businesses
 http://www.ready.gov http://www.fema.gov/areyouready http://www.fema.gov/plan/index.shtm	**Be Ready Campaign** Provides information to help people prepare for and respond to emergencies. Offers advice on assembling a simple emergency supply kit and creating a family emergency plan. **Furnishes links to state and local emergency management services.**
 Prepare. Plan. Stay Informed. http://www.ready.gov/america/index.html	**Ready America** This division of the U.S. Department of Homeland Security provides helpful preparedness information to help respond to all kinds of emergencies. Recommendations for a Basic Emergency Supply Kit; Making a Plan; and Being Informed.

U. S. Government Websites & Resources (cont.)

http://www.fema.gov/

Federal Emergency Management Agency

This agency's mission is to support citizens and first responders to ensure that as a nation we work together to build, sustain, and improve our capability to prepare for, protect against, respond to, recover from, and mitigate all hazards. Also provides extensive information about preparing for and recovering from numerous types of emergencies and disasters. Gives instructions on applying for disaster assistance; displays flood maps and declarations of disaster areas.

 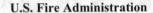

www.usfa.dhs.gov

U.S. Fire Administration

Manages programs relating to fire fighting and fire safety, and collects statistics on incidents and deaths. Also provides fire safety and prevention information.

www.noaa.gov

National Oceanic and Atmospheric Administration (NOAA)

Focuses on ocean and atmospheric conditions. Provides links to forecasts and weather alerts, atmospheric research, conservation activities, and environmental concerns.

www.weather.gov
www.nws.noaa.gov/os/severeweather/

National Weather Service

Provides up-to-date weather forecasts, warnings, radar, air quality, flooding, and weather safety information, including hazard assessments, and weather radios.

http://noaawatch.gov

NOAA Watch — All-Hazards Monitor

Site allows you to insert your city and state data and provides you with a 7-day forecast for your specific area.

http://CDC.gov/

 Centers for Disease Control and Prevention
Your Online Source for Credible Health Information

http://www.bt.cdc.gov/disasters

Natural Disasters & Severe Weather

U. S. Government Websites & Resources (cont.)

Diseases & Conditions	**Centers for Disease Control and Prevention** Information on many health safety topics, including diseases, healthy living, injuries, travelers' health, and environmental health; ADHD, Birth Defects, Cancer, Diabetes, Fetal Alcohol Syndrome, Flu, Hepatitis, HIV/AIDS, STDs.... Provides weekly updates of influenza outbreaks and publications that discuss infectious diseases.
Emergency Preparedness & Response	Bioterrorism, Chemical & Radiation Emergencies, Severe Weather, and other public health issues.
Environmental Health	Air Pollution, Carbon Monoxide, Lead, Mold, Water Quality, Climate Change, and other environmental health issues.
Life Stages & Populations	Infant & Child, Men, Minorities, Pregnancy, Seniors, and Women data.
Healthy Living	Food Safety, Bone Health, Physical Activity, Immunizations, Genetics, Smoking Prevention.
Injury, Violence & Safety	Brain Injury, Child Abuse, Falls, Fires, Poisoning, Suicide, and Youth Violence problems.
Travelers' Health	Destinations, Outbreaks, Travel Vaccinations, Yellow Book of Resources and health information for traveling abroad, travel resources, etc.
Workplace Safety & Health	Asbestos, Chemical Safety, Construction, Mining, Office Environments, Respirators...

U. S. Government Websites & Resources (cont.)

ATSDR Agency for Toxic Substances & Disease Registry **www.atsdr.cdc.gov**	**Agency for Toxic Substances and Disease Registry** Information regarding toxic substances, including exposure registries, medical education, emergency response, risk assessments for contaminated sites, and comprehensive information about toxic substances of all types.
Centers for Disease Control and Prevention 1600 Clifton Rd Atlanta GA 30333 **(800) CDC-INFO or (800) 232-4636** **TTY: (888) 232-**6348 24 Hours/Every Day **http://www.cdc.gov/nceh/**	**National Center for Environmental Health (NCEH)** Plans, directs, and coordinates a national program to maintain and improve the health of the American people by promoting a healthy environment and by preventing premature death and avoidable illness and disability caused by non-infectious, non-occupational environmental and related factors. NCEH is especially committed to safeguarding the health of populations that are particularly vulnerable to certain environmental hazards—children, the elderly, and people with disabilities.
Centers for Disease Control Emergency and Preparedness Response	Information about Natural Disasters, Chemical, Biological, and Radiological, events, etc.
Centers for Disease Control and Prevention (CDC Business Home)	**Resources on Flu, Travel, Safety, etc.**
PandemicFlu.gov **www.pandemicflu.gov/**	**FluGov (Centers for Disease Control)** CDC epidemiologists work with states to collect, compile and analyze reports of flu outbreaks. Annual outbreaks of the seasonal flu usually occur during the late fall through early spring. Most people have natural immunity, and a seasonal flu vaccine is available. In a typical year, approximately 5 to 20 percent of the population gets the seasonal flu and approximately 36,000 flu-related deaths are reported.
FIRE CORPS **http://www.citizencorps.gov/partnersandaffiliates/firecorps.shtm**	**Fire Corps** Promotes the use of citizen advocates (volunteers) to support and augment the capacity of resource-constrained fire and emergency service departments at all levels: volunteer, combination, and career. Fire Corps is funded through the Department of Homeland Security and is managed and implemented through a partnership between the National Volunteer Fire Council and the International Association of Fire Chiefs, and with direction from the National Advisory Committee, a group of 15 national organizations representing the fire and emergency services, to provide the program with strategic direction and important feedback from the field.

U. S. Government Websites & Resources (cont.)

www.usgs.gov	**U.S. Geological Survey** Provides scientific information about the country's landscape, resources, and natural hazards, including earthquakes, floods, droughts, wildfires, climate change, volcanoes, and invasive species.
www.usgs.gov/pubprod/	Purchase maps directly from the **USGS:** • topographical maps • aerial photographs • satellite images • publications • locate and download maps
USGS Earthquake Hazards Program	Tracks US and worldwide tremors, etc.
USGS Volcano Hazards Program	Tracks US and worldwide volcanic activity, mitigation tips, etc.
 www.airnow.gov	**Air Now** Displays air quality index ratings, ozone, and particulate levels for every state in the United States.
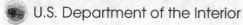 U.S. Department of the Interior www.doi.gov	**Department of Interior** Responsible for the conservation and management of federal land and administration programs relating to native Americans, Alaskans, and Hawaiians. Provides many useful links, including **USGS**, National Park Service, and US Fish and Wildlife Service.
 www.justice.gov	**Department of Justice** Provides information on federal law enforcement, including the country's Most Wanted and Missing Persons lists. Furnishes links to report a crime, report or identify a missing person, locate an inmate or sex offender, or provide a tip to the FBI.

U. S. Government Websites & Resources (cont.)

...for the safety and security of Americans with disabilities **www.disabilitypreparedness.gov**	**Disability Preparedness** **Provides information targeted to the physically disabled. Has discussions regarding evacuation, preparedness, and emergency planning.**
 **www.epa.gov**	**Environmental Protection Agency** Discusses environmental issues, including water, air quality, climate, waste/pollution, and ecosystems. Provides regional and national environmental news, and a listing of environmental laws and regulations. Contains links to report environmental violations or spills.
  www.fda.gov	**Food and Drug Administration** Provides information concerning food safety, nutrition, bioterrorism, food bacteria outbreaks, animal-related illnesses, drug approvals and alerts, radiation-emitting products, and vaccines.
 **www.foodsafety.gov**	**Food Safety** Lists information pertaining to food handling, cooking temperatures, food illnesses, inspections, and product recalls.
  www.nrc.gov	**Nuclear Regulatory Commission** Oversees issues relating to nuclear energy production and safety, including reactors, materials, and waste. Provides recommendations for radiological emergency preparations, and maps of active nuclear reactors and waste disposal sites.
U.S. Department of Transportation **Federal Highway Administration** **www.fhwa.dot.gov/trafficinfo**	**National Traffic and Road Closure Information** Displays maps and associated links to traffic conditions and road closures across the United States.
USDA **www.usda.gov**	**U.S. Department of Agriculture** Develops and executes policies on agriculture, farming, and food. Topics include pest control, weather, animal health, food aid, a plant database, food and nutrition, farm bills, and agricultural news.
U.S. OFFICE OF PERSONNEL MANAGEMENT Recruiting, Retaining and Honoring a World-Class Workforce to Serve the American People **www.opm.gov/emergency**	**U.S. Office of Personnel Management** Maintains disaster preparedness information specifically targeted to federal employees.

U. S. Government Websites & Resources (cont.)

www.whitehouse.gov	**The White House** The official government website details policy, achievements, and challenges facing the United States. Also includes press briefings, presidential addresses, proclamations, and cabinet appointments.
National Database of State and Local Wildfire Hazard Mitigation Programs www.wildfireprograms.com	**National Wildfire Programs Database** A national database of state and local wildfire mitigation programs.
National Safety Council www.nsc.org	**National Safety Council** Making our world safer.
citizen★corps UNITING COMMUNITIES PREPARING THE NATION http://www.citizencorps.gov/	**Get Prepared. Get Trained. Get Involved.** Citizen Corps is FEMA's grassroots strategy to bring together government and community leaders to involve citizens in all-hazards emergency preparedness and resilience. Citizen Corps asks you to embrace the personal responsibility to be prepared; to get training in first aid and emergency skills; and to volunteer to support local emergency responders, disaster relief, and community safety.
DisasterAssistance.gov ACCESS TO DISASTER HELP AND RESOURCES DisasterHelp.gov	Disaster related news, resources for citizens, First Responders, Officials, etc.
FloodSmart.gov The official site of the NFIP FLOODSMART.GOV	Official site of the National Flood Insurance Program
NASA **NASA's Earth Observatory**	Natural Disasters observed by NASA satellite imagery
SBA **US Small Business Administration Disaster Recovery**	Information on Disaster Loans, tips, etc.
ACTIVE FIRE MAPPING **USDA Forest Service Active Fire Maps**	For tracking large incidents reported by the **NIFC**

U. S. Government Websites & Resources (cont.)

USDA Forest Service National Avalanche Center	Information and tips for consumers
DisasterHelp.gov	Disaster related news, resources for citizens, First Responders, Officials, etc.
U.S. State Department	Travel section with Emergency info, Warnings, Resources, Travel assistance, etc.
www.dhs.gov/files/resources/editorial_0306.shtm	Links to homeland security and public safety Web sites from the States and the District of Columbia.
www.ready.gov/america/local/index.html	State and local resources and information on preparedness in your community.
www.ready.gov/america/other/links.html	Many links, mostly government agencies, by **www.Ready.gov**.
Indian Health Service	Mission is to raise the physical, mental, social, and spiritual health of American Indians and Alaska Natives to the highest level. Assure that comprehensive, culturally acceptable personal and public health services are available and accessible to American Indian and Alaska Native people. Uphold the Federal Government's obligation to promote healthy American Indian and Alaska Native people, communities, and cultures and to honor and protect the inherent sovereign rights of Tribes.
National Institutes of Health	**National Institutes of Health (NIH)** As part of the U.S. Department of Health and Human Services, **NIH** is the nation's medical research agency—making important medical discoveries that improve health and save lives.
US Food and Drug Administration	Research, safety, and recall information on food, prescription drugs, medical devices, etc.

U. S. Government Websites & Resources (cont.)

www.weather.gov/om/severeweather/index.shtml	Severe weather forecasts, warnings, and reports.
earthquake.usgs.gov/	Real-time earthquake and seismic event monitoring and reporting by the **USGS.**
www.hhs.gov/disasters/emergency/naturaldisasters/index.html	**HHS**-provided information on the major sources of natural disasters as they relate to emergency planning.
earthquake.usgs.gov/prepare/	Earthquake preparation information by the **USGS**
spaceweather.com	News and information about meteor showers, solar flares, auroras, and near-Earth asteroids
www.prh.noaa.gov/ptwc/	**NOAA Pacific Tsunami Warning Center** Site for NOAA, NWS, PTWC, Tsunami, Warnings, Watches, Advisories, Bulletins, Earthquakes, Pacific, Hawaii, Indian, and the Caribbean.
www.earthquakecountry.info/roots/sevensteps.html	7 Steps to Earthquake safety detailed.
www2.nict.go.jp/y/y223/simulation/realtime/index.html	**National Institute of Information and Communications Technology (NICT)** Real-time Magnetosphere Simulation
www.swpc.noaa.gov/alerts/index.html	**NOAA / Space Weather Prediction Center** Alerts and warnings for sun storms, solar flares/bursts, and other celestial events.
www.ready.gov/america/publications/allpubs.html	The **Federal Emergency Management Agency** has made files for the **Ready Campaign**'s publications available to the public to download at no cost.
www.fcc.gov/pshs/services/eas/handbooks.html	EAS handbooks with instructions for following Emergency Alert procedures by the FCC

Chart 5-2
Non-Government Websites & Resources

Non-Government Websites & Resources

American Red Cross Greater Salt Lake Area Chapter — Train. Prepare. Invest http://www.redcross.org/	**American Red Cross** Lists links to disaster preparation, including for children, elderly, and disabled with special needs. Also, provides information on how to receive assistance after a disaster, and take first aid or other training classes.
AccuWeather.com	**AccuWeather®** U.S. and international weather reports.

Non-Government Websites & Resources (cont.)

www.Weather.com	**The Weather Channel** Weather-related information; local, regional, & national; travel; storms forecasting & reporting
**www.DisasterNews.net**	**Disaster News Network** Tells the story of disaster response and suggests appropriate ways the public can help survivors. It also facilitates information sharing among disaster responders and connects disaster survivors with those who are able to assist them. In addition to its primary focus of telling the story of disaster response, DNN also covers related special topics such as preparedness and mitigation, public violence, environmental hazards, and terrorist disasters.
**www.EarthWeek.com**	**Diary of the Planet**
**www.nemaweb.org**	**National Emergency Management Association (NEMA)**
**http://www.who.int/en/**	**World Health Organization (WHO)**
google.org Flu Trends **www.google.org/flutrends/**	**Google Flu Trends** Tracks influenza outbreaks around much of the world. Compares current year flu activity to previous year.
**www.disastersafety.org**	**Institute for Business and Home Safety** Offers practical information on preparing for earthquakes, floods, freezing weather, hail, high winds, hurricanes, tornados, and wildfires.

Non-Government Websites & Resources (cont.)

 www.avma.org/disaster/saving_family.asp	**American Veterinary Medical Association** Offers emergency preparedness information relating to pets and livestock.
 ww w.kidshealth.org/parent	**Kids Health** Provides medical and first aid information relating specifically to children's needs. Contains useful instruction sheets for dealing with a host of medical and first aid issues.
National Fire Protection Association The authority on fire, electrical, and building safety www.nfpa.org	**National Fire Protection Association** Provides fact sheets and safety tips regarding prevention, fire proofing your home, and evacuation.
 Better information. Better health. www.webmd.com	**Web MD** An online resource that offers medical condition information, symptom-based diagnoses, and health-related news.

Chart 5-3
Additional Non-Government Websites & Resources

Additional Non-Government Websites & Resources

www.operationhope.org/pdpg/pdpg_english.pdf	Personal Disaster Preparedness Guide from HOPE Coalition America
ScienceDaily: Natural Disaster News	Stories, reference articles, science videos, etc.
Reuters AlertNet	news for relief professionals and the public on global humanitarian crises
Red Jeans Ink	Publication on large animal rescue
National Voluntary Organizations Active in Disaster (NVOAD)	Coordinates planning and response to disasters.
National Disaster Animal Response Team	Learn about Humane Society's **N-DART**
International Federation of Red Cross and Red Crescent	Click Directory to find offices worldwide.
International Association of Emergency Managers	Professional org for Emergency Managers
Humane Society of the United States Disaster Center	Tips for all types of critters
Homeland Security Foundation of American (HSFA)	Child safety and protection programs, disaster preparedness efforts, etc.
Hacker Safe	McAfee's website security service
Google News	Opens to the **Google** home page.
Gentillalli and Associates	Criminal Investigation and Intelligence agency
Disaster Resource Guide	News and resources on Business Continuity
CPM Online	News and resources on Business Continuity

Additional Non-Government Websites & Resources (cont.)

Center for International Disaster Information (CIDI)	Information , updates and links for relief workers, consumers and others
AVERT, Inc.	Develop and promote CERT programs and teams, etc.
ARRL (American Radio Radio League)	the National Association for Amateur Radio.
Americares	Information and news about domestic and international disaster relief efforts
AlertsUSA	Terrorism alert and event notification system
1-800-VOLUNTEER.org	Locate local Volunteer Centers in the U.S.
Command School TTX	Provides training and exercises for use of **NIMS**, ICS, etc
Counterterrorism Inc.	Publications and links to products for Security Professionals
www.Depiction.com	Mapping, simulation and collaboration software used in emergency preparedness and response by professionals, volunteers and families
Emergency Services Directory	Directory of sites with information, goods and services
Oregon Institute of Science and Medicine	**OISM** offers a **FREE** online book titled **Nuclear War Survival Skills,** by Cresson Kearny
PreparednessYellowPages.com	Comprehensive directory of preparedness, survivalist, and self-reliance resources.
SurvivalCD.com	Seller of CDs containing Civil Defense documents, resources, etc.
WeAreSafeAndSound.com	Mass notification service for family and friends to share mutual well-being and whereabouts before, during, or after a disaster
Counterterrorism and Security Education and Research Foundation (CTSERF)	Provides educational programs, research, scholarships, aid and training for the general public, security professionals, military/government personnel, etc.
DERA International	Provides support, resource sharing, and networking for Emergency Management disaster preparedness professionals, volunteers and organizations
Doctors Without Borders	Volunteer doctors and nurses who provide urgent medical care in countries to victims of war and disaster regardless of race, religion, or politics
Global Incident Map	Global display of Terrorism and other Suspicious Events
Homeland Civil Defense.org	Disaster preparedness DVDs, printable books and newsletters
Institute for Business and Home Safety	Information and news for businesses, consumers, and insurers.
International Association for Counterterrorism and Security Professionals	Provides education and information to the public and promotes international cooperation in counterterrorism
National Rifle Association	Learn about gun safety, state laws, and training programs for all ages
Natural Hazards Center	Information for groups working to reduce disaster damage and suffering.
NetEOP	Web-based Emergency Operations Planning Tool.

Additional Non-Government Websites & Resources (cont.)

Radmeters4u.com	Radiation detection devices and **free** resources for nuclear preparedness.
Salvation Army	International site with links to worldwide locations and sites.
Save the Children's Children in Emergencies Planning Guide	**FREE** 32-page guide helps Emergency Management professionals plan for the needs of children in times of disaster.
Southern Baptist Disaster Relief	NAMB's national network of volunteers and units, preparedness tips, State office contacts, etc.
Southern California Earthquake Center	Free **Putting Down Roots in Earthquake Country** booklet [in English and Spanish] and other related resources.
TACDA (The American Civil Defense Association)	Provides education, products and resources to help members, families and communities prepare for disasters and emergencies.
TAO Emergency Management Consulting	Provides services for all levels of government, businesses, etc.
United States First Responders Association (USFRA)	Non-profit network of Firefighters, EMS, Rescue, Law Enforcement, Military, and Civilian Support Teams.
United States Water Patrol (U.S.W.P)	Uniformed all-volunteer organization helps guard against terrorism and assists in safeguarding national waterways for **Homeland Security** and aids in public safety on and around waterways.
WebEOC	**ESi's** web-enabled emergency management communications system.
www.globalsecurity.org/military/library/policy/army/fm/index.html	Comprehensive repository of Army Field Manuals for download by Global Security.Org
www.survivalistboards.com/	Survivalist Forum Survival Gear Reviews and Self Sufficiency Articles
DNN Volunteers	*Disaster News Network's* volunteer opportunities, resources, etc.
Emergency Management magazine	Online and traditional magazine by *Government Technology.*
Firehouse magazine	Online and traditional magazine with news, forums, jobs, events, etc for Fire, Rescue, and EMS.
Griffith Colson Intelligence Service	News and updates on global and national security situations.
In Case of Emergency Read Blog	John Solomon edits discussions, research, and guidance on preparedness issues.
National Terror Alert Response Center	News and updates on national and homeland security.
REACT International	Radio Emergency Associated Communications Teams worldwide.
Salvation Army USA	Learn about relief efforts, contact military personnel, join **S.A.T.E.R.N.**, find loved ones, etc.
SOS International	Helps organizations manage health and safety risks facing their travelers, global workforce and customers.
Stratfor	Source of accurate global intelligence, analysis, and forecasting.

Additional Non-Government Websites & Resources (cont.)

USA Freedom Corps	Informational site for AmeriCorps, Citizen Corps, Fire Corps, Freedom Corps for Kids, and the Senior Corps, etc.
www.cd3wd.com/CD3WD_40/CD3WD/index.htm	Extensive listing of links for methods and practices for livestock, farming, housing, clean water and more provided by CD3WD for use as a resource to the third world.

Chart 5-4
Canadian Government Websites & Resources

Canadian Government Websites & Resources

Canadian Resources

🇨🇦 Environment Canada   Environnement Canada

Disasters Resources	Government Website (Cont.)
🇨🇦 Public Safety Canada Sécurité publique Canada **Public Safety and Emergency Preparedness Canada**	**Public Safety Canada** Alerts and information on safety and disaster topics.
Environment Canada - Weather Office	**Environment Canada** Canadian national weather information in English & French.
Getprepared.ca	Public Safety Canada's family preparedness site.
Public Health Agency of Canada	Information on Bioterrorism, Emergency Preparedness, etc.
World Travel Protection Canada, Inc	Monitor and reports health, medical, and travel safety risks around the world to subscribers.

STATE-BY-STATE NATURAL DISASTERS VULNERABILITY

Check your **Sate** listing in the **Potential Natural Disasters by State** chart to ascertain the Natural Disasters types to which you might be vulnerable in your specific location.

For additional local information, contact Homeland Security/FEMA, State Emergency, or County Disasters Management offices, or go to their respective websites for free downloads. The website information is found in the following listing.

The state-by-state chart on the following page details the types of disasters most usually encountered, but you can get additional information from The Weather Channel, local news and weather radio and television stations, and local newspapers, whether print or digital.

Chart 5-5
Potential Natural Disasters by State[i]

STATE	Earth-quake	Flood	Hail Storm	Hurricane	Land Slide	Mud Slide	Severe Storm	Tornado	Tsunami	Volcano	Wildfire	Wind Storm	Winter storm
AL				X			X	X			X		X
AK	X	X			X		X		X		X		X
AZ		X					X	X			X		
AR	X	X		X			X	X			X		X
CA	X	X			X	X	X		X		X		X
CO	X	X			X	X	X	X			X		X
CT	X	X		X			X	X			X		X
DC		X										X	
DE		X		X			X				X		X
FL		X		X			X	X			X	X	
GA	X	X		X			X	X			X	X	
HI	X	X		X		X	X		X	X	X		
ID	X	X			X	X	X				X		X
IL	X	X					X	X			X		X
IN		X					X	X			X		X
IA		X	X				X	X			X	X	X
KS		X					X	X			X	X	
KY		X					X	X					
LA		X		X			X				X		X
ME	X	X		X		X	X				X	X	
MD		X		X			X	X			X	X	
MA	X	X		X			X				X	X	X
MI		X					X	X			X	X	X
MN		X	X				X	X			X	X	X
MO	X	X		X			X	X			X		X
MS		X	X	X			X	X			X		X
MT	X	X			X		X				X	X	X
NE		X					X	X			X	X	X
NV	X	X			X	X	X				X		X
NH	X	X		X			X	X			X	X	X
NJ	X	X		X			X	X			X		X
NM		X					X				X		
NY	X	X		X	X		X				X		X
NC	X	X		X			X	X			X		X
ND		X					X	X			X		X
OH		X				X	X				X		X
OK	X	X					X	X			X		
OR	X	X			X	X	X				X		X
PA	X	X		X			X	X			X		X
RI	X	X		X							X		X
SC	X	X		X			X				X		
SD		X					X	X			X		X
TN		X					X						
TX		X		X			X	X			X		
UT	X	X			X		X				X		X
VT	X	X			X		X				X		X
VA	X	X		X		X	X	X			X		X
WA	X	X			X	X	X			X	X		X
WV	X	X		X		X	X				X		
WI		X					X	X			X		
WY		X					X	X			X		X

MOTHER'S WISDOM

I learned about preparedness and survival kits from my mother. She was wisdom personified and always seemed to know what to do, no matter what the occasion! I truly regret it took me so long to realize it. As a fledgling Boy Scout—*less* than a Tenderfoot, actually––the troop was going on a long-awaited and unprecedented early spring camping trip. At last, I was going to join the older guys whom I not only admired, but secretly revered. The last thing I wanted was to be embarrassed by being unprepared—*imagine not being prepared at a mere 12 years of age!*

When I asked Mother what to take on my extended outing, she replied in her soft-spoken manner, practically without a moment's hesitation, *You need to wonder what could happen and be willing to pay the wages of going into the wilderness. Take some water, Wranglers®, weenies, wipes, warm clothing, weather protection, a weapon, a wayfinder, whatever, and keep a watchful eye...*

Did she ever have a way with words! Let me elaborate on her guidance. Evaluate these points in relationship to your own emergency preparedness.

Wonder: Mother was suggesting I ponder what part of my intended experience I might not be able to control. It was the beginning of my education to learn to assess what problems might occur in the field (or in my life), such as:

    – to which wonders of nature (*read*: disaster) I'd be vulnerable,

    – to what other creature—man or beast—I might encounter, and/or

    – to the kinds of personal problems I might have in the *wilderness...*

She wanted me to plan for the worst, hope for the best, and be able to deal (eventually) with whatever happened. I've never forgotten that prepared or not, I have to deal with the future—as it becomes the present!

Wages: that meant that I must be willing to pay the price to make this trip—time, effort, and risk. From the available alternatives, was this the most practical, prudent, and provident undertaking for me? I had to decide if it was the most intelligent thing to do at that moment—and what about the longer-term consequences and implications of my actions? Even at that early age, I had already been made aware—sometimes painfully—of the consequences of being unprepared to deal with those consequences. Mother was indicating the price of *not* being prepared for the future eventualities in my life.

Water: Mother told me to ta*ke* water. She knew you can't live very long without drinking water. Just a few hours without it and you're in deep trouble! (Of course, that's not necessarily true of taking a bath in times of emergency. But it is one of those things a young boy can learn to do without, at least during a weekend or an emergency.) She told me I wouldn't live three days without water because I'd get weaker every hour without it.

She made sure I carried extra water and told me how important clean drinking water was to camping health. My **WWII** metal canteen my Uncle Jimmie brought back from the Army was my fountain of trail health. Mother made me repeat to her the information about how to obtain and purify additional water for drinking and cooking. She was very certain I understood that daily water consumption was necessary for health and sanitation purposes. She made sure I would have enough water to accommodate additional requirements due to weather conditions, physical stress, exertion, or emergency.

Wranglers®: that meant having appropriate clothing for the occasion, depending on the environment. In my youth, jeans (we could afford the name brand ***Wranglers®*** *only* after the harvest was in the barn) were the working-class clothes in our ex-urban community. They were sturdy clothing, longwearing, tough, easily maintained, and could be worn for man's work—and that certainly included camping out, too. This admonition was also meant to include a regular change of underwear. (How embarrassing to be wearing dirty underwear in case of an accident!)

Weenies: that was a reference to the need for nourishment. My mother knew my penchant for hot dogs, potato chips, and pork and beans. Her instruction to me was to take food that I:

(1) would eat even under the stress of being away from the well-spread table she prepared for the family;

(2) could easily prepare in the boonies; and

(3) would normally enjoy.

Personally, I would have opted for her barbeque pork and creamy Cole slaw—but that would have been totally impractical for the camping environment—as it would be for most emergency situations!

Mother packed a supply of extra food *just in case* of some unexpected emergency—bad weather, getting separated from the others, injury, or other reason for any delayed return. It was food that required no cooking, was comforting and familiar, easily digestible, and stored well without great care for a fairly long period under adverse conditions. She included some homemade beef jerky, nuts from our backyard trees, hard peppermint candy, homemade granola, and home-dried fruits. There were also packets of hot chocolate, instant soup, and canned Vienna sausage.

We are capable of doing without a lot of things when we're stressed. However, having familiar food to eat when everything is going badly gives us comfort far beyond the cost of the food. Food is such an important part of creating and maintaining a positive attitude, especially when all else is falling apart, that it bears repeating: *don't take anyone else's opinion about your emergency food supply—store what you like to eat and you'll eat what you've stored—and you won't lose it!*

Wipes: intimated that if I ate during this camping trip, eventually the natural necessity for wipes would occur. Not to mention tissues for a runny nose from staying out overnight in the humid wilderness! Wipes were indeed essential then for any trip away from home—and still are! This was also meant to remind me about the need for good personal hygiene and grooming—a little soap and elbow grease to remove the dirt and smoke odor from my body. There is no such comfort as being our best self—putting our best foot forward—handling whatever we encounter with panache and style.

Warmth: how can anyone be prepared if the elements are ignored? Back then, the job of finding both small and effective means of keeping warm was more difficult. Today we have modern technology—so many new fabrics for clothing and camping gear, equipment for and supplies to help in this life-saving necessity.

The term *extra clothing* meant having additional layers that might be needed to survive the long, cold hours of an extended weather surprise. Knowing where you're going and the expected—and unexpected—weather conditions meant having the necessary extra clothing for those conditions.

Of course, let us not forget the need for fire to cook food, purify water, and provide warm water for bathing. I carried the supplies for starting an emergency fire in virtually any weather. Mother had some handy fire-starters: candles, chemical heat tabs, and some canned heat from her chafing dish. Fire-starters were essential for igniting wet wood quickly to make a campfire—especially in an emergency situation.

Today, a butane lighter, wax-coated matches in a waterproof container, a magnesium match, some lint from the lint collector in the dryer, some blocks of wax-impregnated fire-starter, and you could start a fire anywhere!.

Weather protection: this was the need for adequate shelter from the unpredictable spring weather in North Carolina—a tent and some waterproof matches. For today's considerations it includes the provision of living space that precludes a family from suffering the effects of inclement weather—whether it's intemperate climate, moisture, or wind-driven forces.

Besides the tent, mother insisted on some kind of poncho or plastic cover to protect me from the rain and wind.

Today, you'd probably opt for a large plastic trash bag with holes cut in the sides for your arms. Or, you could buy foil-like *space blankets*, those reflective emergency blankets that are never large enough to cover your arms and legs!

It also meant having sunglasses, sunscreen for the lips and skin, and clothing for protection against the hot sun.

Weapon: that meant a brand-new Swiss knife attached to my belt for all to see—talk about proud! Nobody was going to mess with me and the complete arsenal at my fingertips. I was prepared for even a bear! Besides, it was a miracle-making tool just waiting to be unleashed, whether for opening a can of weenies, beans or soup, shaving a stick for fire tender, or carving an **X** on a tree to mark the trail (forgive me, tree-lovers—I was only 12 years old!)

It was absolutely important—a veritable rite of passage—that every Scout have his own knife—for first aid, food preparation, minor repairs, and a sense of proud ownership. Even then, the need to carry other tools was obviated by the multi-purpose knife, with its selection of knife blades, can/bottle opener, finger nail file, saw blade, pliers, screwdriver, awl, scissors, even a toothpick!

This is the stuff dreams are made of...!

Because they occupied little space, mother put extra shoelaces, safety pins, needle and thread, fine baling wire (did you forget we lived on a farm?), extra adhesive tape (before duct tape!), a hank of small rope, and some razor blades in an old aspirin tin—just in case.

Wayfinder: meant having the appropriate equipment, such as a wrist compass and a local area road map. At least, I could find my way back to the camp, home, or anywhere on that map, should I be the victim of a *snipe hunt* with the senior scouts. Make sure you have maps of local streets, as well as maps of your destination, if you must depart from your home.

Today, you can go online and get a detailed topographic map of the area you plan to visit—and carry it in a plastic freezer-grade zipper bag. Add to your compass other navigational tools, such as a GPS receiver. At <u>www.earth.Google.com</u> you can see it all from satellite—virtually live!

This category included the need to have a flashlight of some type, and because batteries and bulbs wouldn't last forever, mother put spares of both in a little sealed plastic bag.

Today, technology has made it much simpler—cheap battery-, solar-, and crank-powered lighting devices, so kerosene and propane are no longer the only lighting choices.

Watchful eye: this part of the communication was a little bit trickier because it was somewhat more philosophic, but I know it meant being prepared for any emergency. I practiced until I was compass-trained and ready to take the fifty-mile hike. I was also required to learn all the first aid information, up to and including how to cut the **X** for snakebite treatment. Thank heaven that treatment has been superseded since then! Actually, upon reflection, I couldn't have cut the snake, much less cut an **X** on my own body!

It is indeed fortunate the Scouting programs put particular emphasis on first aid and emergency treatment. We always carried—and were trained to use—a first-aid kit. Likewise, we were also advised not to be lulled into an attitude of having a false sense of security. Mother was quite clear about staying away from danger instead of flaunting our bravery. Her take on that was a rule of ABC's she repeated often, ***Avoid Bravado Constantly!*** That meant that I should do whatever was prudent to avoid injury or sickness in the first place.

Today, a personal or small family first-aid kit should include gauze pads in various sizes, rolls of gauze, adhesive, butterfly, triangular, and Carlisle bandages, rolls of adhesive tape, surgical scissors, wound cleansers or anti-bacterial soap, latex gloves, and pencil and paper for recording details so you can further improve your *E/PAK*.

Whatever: this category was for anything I wanted to take that wasn't in the proscribed categories previously mentioned—like my genuine silver-plated ***Duncan*** yo-yo!…or the latest ***Marvel*** comic book… or jacks and marbles—whatever was important for my comfort and pleasure!

Watchcare: meant caring about the others on the camping trip. This was a quality my mother had in bountiful supply—she really cared about others, constantly on the lookout for someone who needed a lift. Her *good neighbor* policy was in full force at all times. She practiced the true spirit of caring about the community at large, the neighbors, and her family.

So, my mother's instructions sent me scurrying enthusiastically throughout all three floors of the house (including the dark basement where all those veggies grew in Mason jars!), looking for the equipment I needed to impress the older Scouts in the troop. As the seemingly essential items were located, I placed all the pieces of equipment and supplies into little piles on my upper bunk, and then called her for approval.

This is where I learned how to choose what is essential, and how to focus on economy, efficiency, and personal well-being. Mother regarded all the gear and paraphernalia I had assembled. I remember her saying quietly, *All that pep without purpose is piffle!* She gently (well, not so gently that I soon forgot!) instructed me to sort all of my stuff into three piles. I was to place in the first pile the items I *couldn't* do without, a second pile for stuff I *thought* I might need, and a third pile for the things I'd *like* to take with me.

After I had arranged my piles as instructed, mother looked at the three piles carefully and made a couple of corrections in my selection. She then told me to return the stuff heaped in the second and third piles to the drawers and closets—and to place in the camp bag only the items in the first pile.

You know, even years later, mother's words were my guidance when I traveled more than a million miles as an international business traveler. What I eventually learned is that the quality of any trip is being able to do without a great deal of non-elemental stuff.

DESIGNING YOUR EMERGENCY/PREPAREDNESS ACTION KIT (*E/PAK*)

On the following pages are the detailed listings to help you personalize your own 72+-hour kit—the **E**mergency/**P**reparedness **A**ction **K**it (*E/PAK*.)

Use the following charts to determine what you have in your household inventory already for your family *E/PAK* and to define the needs for each member of the family – items, quantities, and selections of foods, foodstuffs, and equipment. Keep items for a family evacuation in easy-to-carry containers.

You decide whether a large, covered trash container, camping backpack, your old college footlocker, a plastic chest (with wheels!), or your military duffel bag suits your needs best.

If you have the resources, also keep a vehicle version of *E/PAK* in the trunk of your car or behind the seat of your truck. You may want one at your place of business, too. It's cheap insurance for saving your life—the life of a family member, a friend, or co-worker!

Rotation

The rules of rotation are not suspended for your *E/PAK*! Every 90 to 180 days the *E/PAK* should be inventoried and re-provisioned. Exchange water, food, and clothing for current supplies. Consume the goods to assure yourself of the effectiveness and quality of your choices. After provisioning your *E/PAK* with its new inventory, place it in its pre-determined storage location.

Enjoy this requirement for rotation. Buy some really good gourmet-type foods for your *E/PAK.* Get some really good gourmet- and picnic-quality foodstuffs you'd find at a high-class business party, classy brunch, or invitation-only social event. When the rotate date comes and you haven't had an emergency, have an *emergency picnic* with your rotate-out foods. These emergency preparedness *trial runs* will provide occasional practice for the time(s) when disasters for which you've prepared actually occur. It'll further prepare you mentally for the eventuality of a disaster, and make the event's foreboding nature a little more bearable.

E/PAK Categories

The *E/PAK* supplies categories are as follows, with relative correlation to Mother's categories:

E/PAK Categories	Mother's Categories		
1. Drinking water	Water		
2. Familiar foods	Weenies		
3. First aid supplies	Watchful eye		
4. Personal care items	Whatever	Wipes	Wranglers®
5. Utensils, tools, and emergency supplies	Warmth	Wayfinder	Weapons
	Weather protection		

Your *E/PAK* Checklist

There are a lot of selections from which to choose. You, too, might elect to sort your stuff into three piles, as my mother suggested to me! Details of the *E/PAK* categories are listed in the following chart. Items in **boldface** type are considered essential.

There are many blanks for you to add the things that are important to you and your family. There are unlimited versions of 72-hour[+] kits available from preparedness providers. Indeed, they should all be customized to your needs, or to whomever the kit belongs.

The charts on the following pages will help you create your own customized and specialized 72-hour⁺ or 72⁺-hour kit. Remember that the minimum is a 3-day supply. Prudence and planning would generally dictate a much longer period of time would be required before utilities, merchant services, and related operations achieve normalcy. That's why we call it the 72⁺-hour kit!

Chart 5-6
Personal *E/PAK* Checklists

Category 1—Drinking Water Items

Water should be stored in durable, food-quality plastic containers. Do not use containers that may decompose or burst. Do not ration water—drink what you need now and find more later. Know how to find and treat water for drinking purposes.

Rotate stored water supplies every 6 months.

Personal *E/PAK* Items	Required	Have	Need	Acquired
❏ **Water / per person per day**	**1 gal. min.**			
❏ **Water treatment unit / portable / chemicals**	**30-day system**			
❏ 2-Bucket / stainless or galvanized metal	1			
❏ 5-gal. collapsible container	1			
❏ Fuel supply for boiling water	30-day amt.			
❏ Water / sterilized pkg.	24 pkg.			
❏				
❏				
❏				
❏				
❏				
❏				
❏				
❏				

Category 2—Familiar/Comfort Foods

The 3 basic rules of food storage also apply to the 72+-hr. personal **E/PAK**:

1. *Store what you eat!*	2. *Eat what you store!*	3. *Use it or lose it!*

Store at least a 72+-hr. supply of non-perishable food for each person. Select foods that require no refrigeration, little or no cooking, and minimal energy-consuming preparation. Select wholesome, pleasurable, compact, and lightweight food items that you currently eat.

All food items should be rotated every 3-6 months.

Personal *E/PAK* Items	Required	Have	Need	Acquired
❏ **Energy foods—peanut butter, trail mix, etc.**	**12 servings**			
❏ **Juices—canned / powdered**	**Selection**			
❏ **Pleasure foods / candies, treats, chips, etc.**	**Select 1 lb.**			
❏ **Ready-to-eat meats, fruits, and veggies**	**9 meals**			
❏ Milk—powdered or canned	optional			
❏ Mixes / meals in pouches / cans / etc.	optional			
❏ Seasonings: sugar, salt, pepper, etc.	optional			
❏ Smoked and dried meats / poultry / fish	optional			
❏ Soups: bouillon / soup cups / ready-to-heat	optional			
❏				
❏				
❏				
❏				
❏				
❏				

Personal *E/PAK* Checklists (continued)

Category 3—First Aid Items				
Personal *E/PAK* Items	**Required**	**Have**	**Need**	**Acquired**
❏ **Antiseptic or hydrogen peroxide**	**1 small bottle**			
❏ **Cleansing agent / sterile soap**	**1 bar**			
❏ **First aid book / instructions**	**1**			
❏ **Rubbing alcohol**	**1 pint**			
❏ **Sterile adhesive strips / asstd.**	**1 dozen**			
❏ 2-in and 3-in sterile roller bandages/ 3 ea.				
❏ 2-in sterile gauze pads (8-12)				
❏ 3-in sterile gauze pads (8-12)				
❏ Activated charcoal				
❏ Antiseptic spray				
❏ Eye wash				
❏ Hypoallergenic adhesive tape				
❏ Latex gloves				
❏ Moistened towelettes (12 pkg.)				
❏ Needle				
❏ Safety pins / asstd. sizes				
❏ Safety razor blade / sharp knife				
❏ Scissors / surgical				
❏ Thermometer / armpit / oral / electronic (ear)				
❏ Tongue blades / wooden applicators				
❏ Triangular bandages (3)				
❏ Tube petroleum jelly / other lubricant				
❏ Tweezers				
❏				
❏				

Category 4—Personal Care Items				
Personal *E/PAK* Items	**Required**	**Have**	**Need**	**Acquired**
Prescription Drugs and Items				
❏ **Prescription drugs—as required**				
❏ **Supplements: vitamins, minerals**	**optional**			
❏ Allergy / asthma				
❏ Cardiac and high blood pressure				
❏ Contact lenses and supplies				
❏ Dentures / replacement parts				
❏ Extra eye glasses or contacts				
❏ Insulin / supplies				
❏				
❏				
Non-Prescription Drugs				
❏ **Anti-diarrhea medication**				
❏ **Aspirin / Acetaminophen**				
❏ *Neosporin*® ointment				
❏ Antacid				
❏ Emetic (to induce vomiting)				
❏ Insect repellent / ammonia (for insect bites)				
❏ Laxative				
❏				
❏				
Special Needs Items				
This listing is for those with special needs: infants, children, adults, elderly, disabled individuals, and pets.				
❏				
❏				

Personal *E/PAK* Checklists (continued)

Category 4—Personal Care Items (continued)				
Personal *E/PAK* Items	**Required**	**Have**	**Need**	**Acquired**
Infants				
❑ **Baby foods**				
❑ **Bottles / nipples**				
❑ **Diapers**				
❑ **Formula / powdered milk / juices**				
❑ **Medications**				
❑				
❑				
❑				
❑				
Children				
❑ **Prescription Medications**				
❑ Dental care supplies				
❑ Glasses / contact lenses / supplies				
❑ Grooming supplies				
❑				
❑				
❑				
❑				
Adults				
❑ Cane / walker / prosthetic device				
❑ Dental care needs				
❑ Glasses / contacts / supplies / replacements				
❑ Grooming supplies				
❑ Health support equipment				
❑ Sunglasses				
❑				
❑				
❑				
❑				
Pleasure and Entertainment				
❑ **Children's games / toys / books**				
❑ **Radio/tape/CD/DVD/AM-FM / batteries**				
❑ Adult books / games / puzzles				
❑ Battery-operated games / toys				
❑ Food / treats and snacks / fruit roll-ups				
❑				
❑				
❑				
❑				
Important Family Documents (see **Chapters 5 and 6** for more details) Keep all records in a waterproof, portable container with adequate protection. Originals of these items should always be stored in a safe deposit box—keep only **copies** in your home storage container.				
❑ **Bank account numbers**				
❑ **Credit card account numbers & companies**				
❑ **Family records: birth, adoption, marriage**				
❑ **Passport, SS card, and vaccination records**				
❑ Bible / other spiritually-oriented materials				
❑ Important telephone numbers list				
❑ Inventory / valuable household goods				
❑ Will, insurance, contracts, deeds, securities				
❑				
❑				
❑				
❑				

Personal *E/PAK* Checklists (continued)

Category 4—Personal Care Items (continued)				
Important Family Documents (continued)				
❑				
❑				
❑				
❑				
❑				
❑				
❑				
❑				

Category 4—Personal Care Items (continued)				
Clothing and Bedding				
❑ **Blankets / sleeping bag**				
❑ **Complete change of clothing**				
❑ **Poncho / folding plastic**				
❑ **Rain gear / rubber shoes**				
❑ **Sturdy shoes / work boots / hiking**				
❑ Blanket / thermal				
❑ Hat / gloves / ear muffs / scarf / bandana				
❑ Hot weather clothing / protective gear				
❑ Thermal underwear / cold-weather gear				
❑				
❑				
❑				
❑				

Category 5—Utensils, Tools, and Emergency Items				
Personal *E/PAK* Items	**Required**	**Have**	**Need**	**Acquired**
❑ **Flashlight / extra batteries**				
❑ **Matches / waterproof container**				
❑ **Mess kit / cooking gear / eating utensils**				
❑ **Pocket knife / utility**				
❑ **Cell phone and solar charger for battery**				
❑ **Walkie-talkie system (short-range)**				
❑ **Radio, AM-FM-SW-Weather / multi-powered**				
❑ **Stove and fuel**				
❑ **Toilet paper**				
❑ **Bio-degradable detergent**				
❑ Aluminum foil				
❑ Axe / hatchet / camp				
❑ Bags / leaf and lawn				
❑ Can opener/ non-electric				
❑ Chlorine bleach @ 5.25% (w/o scent)				
❑ Disinfectant / chemical / lime powder				
❑ Dust mask / work gloves				
❑ Feminine hygiene supplies				
❑ Fire extinguisher: ABC portable type				
❑ Fishing gear / rod / reel / lures / bait digger				
❑ Folding steel shovel (to dig latrine, etc.)				
❑ Heater / tent / space				
❑ Lantern / fuel / light sticks / signal flares				
❑ Maps—waterproofed / compass				
❑ Mirror / signal				
❑ Needles / thread				
❑ Pack for carrying items				
❑ Paper / pencil				

Personal *E/PAK* Checklists (continued)

Category 5—Utensils, Tools, and Emergency Items (Cont.)				
Personal *E/PAK* Items	**Required**	**Have**	**Need**	**Acquired**
❏ Paper cups and plates / plastic utensils				
❏ Personal hygiene items / treated towelettes				
❏ Plastic / sheet / rolled				
❏ Plastic bucket / tight-fitting lid				
❏ Plastic garbage bags / ties				
❏ Plastic storage containers / lids				
❏ Pliers / multi-purpose tool				
❏ Sunglasses / sunscreen / sun hat				
❏ Tape / duct / nylon filament				
❏ Tent / one-man / tube / ground cloth / pad				
❏ Tissues / box / 12 pkg.				
❏ Towel / washcloth / soap /shampoo				
❏ Whistle / plastic / safety				
❏				
❏				
❏				
❏				
❏				
❏				
❏				
❏				
❏				
❏				
Miscellaneous Emergency Items				
❏ **Cash—bills ($1, $5, $10) /**				
❏ **Cash—coins (5¢, 10¢, 25¢)**				
❏ **Extra keys / house / vehicle / safe deposit**				
❏ **Wrench, utility (shut-off / gas and water)**				
❏ Camera / film				
❏ Hunting / gun / ammunition / game bag / knife				
❏ Notebook / pencils				
❏ Tape recorder / tapes				
❏ Watch / alarm clock				
❏				
❏				
❏				
❏				
❏				
❏				
❏				
Helpful Emergency Assistance Items				
❏ Wheeled dolly for rolling bag on hard surfaces				
❏ Wagon or wheelbarrow for rougher terrain				
❏ Bicycle with trailer				
❏ Personal protection (properly licensed!)				
❏ N95 masks (pandemic flu / respiratory situations)				
❏ **Depiction® Mapping Software/Prep Add-On (www.depiction.com)**				
❏				
❏				
❏				
❏				
❏				
❏				
❏				
❏				

Keep these telephone numbers handy in case of a localized disaster or emergency situation. The 911 system may be overwhelmed by calls by other people who aren't prepared!

Reminder List		
Measures to take in case of emergency (when time permits)		
Action to take	Telephone	Telephone
❏ Dial-direct telephone # for **Police Dept.**		
❏ Dial-direct telephone # for **Fire Dept.**		
❏ Dial-direct telephone # for **Ambulance**		
❏ Dial-direct telephone # for your **Doctor**		
❏ Dial-direct telephone # for local **CDC**		
❏		
❏		
❏		

72-Hour⁺ Emergency Kit… or Not ?[ii]

There is no intent in this chapter to discuss *all* the causes and solutions for emergencies and disasters. There are, however, numerous books in the **Preparedness Library** chapter which can help you prepare for natural or people-caused disasters, or for any disasters that might occur to you and your family.

For all the minute details of 72-hour⁺ emergency preparedness issues, there are two books I suggest you read and understand. The best overall book I've read on the subject is Barbara Salsbury's **PLAN …NOT PANIC**, *72-Hour Survival/Emergency Evacuation.*[ii]

Ms. Salsbury defines an evacuation as *…a localized occurrence which forces residents out of their homes on a moment's notice.* It only takes being forced from your home one time to convince the wise person of the need for an emergency kit that is prepared and available. In this book, originally published in May 1994, Barbara provides step-by-step instructions, something missing from other emergency publications.

As I read her book from cover to cover, the following points became clear to me as being critical to know and understand:

❏ It's a fact of life—sooner or later you may need to be evacuated from your home!
❏ Panic takes over if practical preparation has been ignored—that's why I call it the emergency/preparedness action kit!
❏ *Lag-Time*—not the disaster—is the reason for a 72+-hour kit! This is probably the least understood point in emergency preparedness preparations.
❏ *Lag-Time* is the *villain* of most evacuations. It is imperative to understand its impact on all facets of preparation for an evacuation.
❏ The more severe the disaster, the greater the corresponding impact of *Lag-Time*.
❏ *Lag-Time* is why you can't rely on the government or emergency disaster organizations to come to your aid immediately.
❏ When individuals are prepared to take care of themselves, they feel they have greater security.
  ❏ Properly prepared people are a tremendous help to those who arrive to assist and support in disaster situations.

According to Barbara, the critical parameters of a well-planned, well thought-out 72+-hour evacuation and survival plan are:

❑ Understanding the two categories of emergency preparedness and how they affect not only your preparation, but also your ultimate survival.

❑ Using a *Neighborhood Evaluation Form* to determine if there is a potential evacuation lurking in your future.

❑ Creating a 72+-hour kit economically to meet your personal needs.

❑ Including more than three *energy bars* and a flashlight in your 72+-hour kit!

❑ Knowing why the right kinds of foods are vital in an emergency situation—and are very different from those typically kept on the emergency shelf.

❑ Having an emergency water supply is essential.

❑ Designing your own *security blanket*.

❑ Establishing a ***Care-In-A-Crisis*** plan is critical to all of your family members.

❑ Knowing what you must do about shelter, heat, and warmth.

❑ Don't ignore the need for personal sanitation!

❑ Preparing properly with the exclusive *Personal Planning Pages* can make the difference between panic and the ability to cope with an emergency situation.

Your ***E/PAK*** is a collection of foodstuffs, supplies, and equipment you'll place in a backpack, closed and watertight container—or even a paper box as a makeshift carrier. You should have it close to your safest exit from your home, at your place of work, or in your vehicle—wherever you spend the most time! If you are so inclined, keep your ***E/PAK*** or some variation of it in each of several locations. Truly, it's better to be safe than sorry—when those unexpected emergencies hit!

TO LEAVE… OR NOT TO LEAVE? THAT'S A GOOD QUESTION!

Hopefully, you won't ever need your ***E/PAK.*** However, being prepared for such an eventuality is good for easing your mind. My personal desire is that I'll never need my ***E/PAK*** for an emergency. Yet, it will always be in a special location in my home near a protected exit, filled with all the things I'd need for *hunkering down* when a natural disaster, such as a wind, ice, or snowstorm, or a people-caused disaster causes a power outage.

Lots of people tell me they plan to *bug out*. Personally, I plan to stay at home unless a life-threatening disaster requires my departure. There is no place I want to go—except maybe to an expensive hotel. However, with my personal 72+-hour kit, I could even endure a public shelter, if necessary.

I've spent a weekend in a church recreation hall during an ice storm with several other families—it wasn't too bad, except for the lack of privacy. I've also spent a few days at my parents' home—all the kids, grandkids, and all their collective dogs.

But heading for the unfamiliar hills, living in the wilderness fraught with unknown dangers, chasing wild animals with switches, fending off others in a similar plight to mine, while trying to maintain an urban lifestyle, does not seem a good option to me. The very thought of getting on the freeway or city streets during or following a disaster, competing for space with all those folks carrying handguns (even if they do have permits) and other nefarious weapons, is just a little frightening. On the streets I cannot defend myself adequately. At home, I can maintain my independence as long as I have my personal provisions to sustain me until the crisis period is past.

My personal plans in the case of a local disaster—such as an electrical failure—are to make the best of a bad situation, enjoy the intervention in my normally extra-long workday, and spend it with my wife (and the dogs) in the ensuing peace and quiet. It would be a moment to have another honeymoon, savor the quiet, and listen to all those archived short-wave radio programs I've wanted to listen to for ages…

BUT IF YOU MUST LEAVE...

However, if you must leave home unexpectedly (perhaps like those in California who were forced to evacuate due to wildfires), be sure to have the following information ready to go with you:

- ❑ daily contact details for family members
- ❑ local reunion points
- ❑ out of area contacts
- ❑ pertinent family operating data

Chart 5–7 below provides you the opportunity to record information about the daily whereabouts of family members and how they can be contacted. It might be appropriate to keep this information on the family bulletin board (in our house it's the refrigerator), in each *E/PAK*, and even in your wallet. Remember to update as contacts or locations change.

Keep in mind that during times of natural or people-caused disasters, local telephone service is often disrupted. Therefore, each member of the household should carry the name, phone number, and address of a person who is designated as an out-of-area contact. (**Note**: long distance lines often remain useable during emergencies. Additionally, the phone company's emergency network is the pay phone system. It will be restored before residential lines.)

If separated, each family member should call the designated out-of-area contact and communicate his particular situation within a certain period of time, reporting his physical condition, his location, and other information as previously agreed upon. Keep adequate change in your **E/PAK** for making pay phone calls. Use **Chart 5–7** on the following page to identify this out-or-area contact information.

Don't let this picture illustrate your family's legacy because you failed to prepare!

Chart 5-7
Emergency Family Contact Information

My Name:		
My Address:	Street No. / Apt. #	
	City / State / Zip	

My Telephone(s):	Home: ( )	Work: ( )

Daily Contact Information for My Family Members:

Family Member Name	Daytime Location	Daytime Phone Number	Evening Location	Evening Phone Number
Father				
Mother				
Child				
Child				
Child				
Child				
Child				
Child				
Child				
Child				
Other				

Out-of-Area Contacts

Name	
Phone #	( )
Address	
Name	
Phone #	( )
Address	
Name	
Phone #	( )
Address	

Additionally, determine at least 2 alternate locations for family members to reunite if it is unsafe to return home or to the neighborhood. One location should be just outside your home and the other away from the neighborhood. Use **Chart 5–8** below to put this information in writing for all family members.

Chart 5-8
Emergency Reunion Information

Neighborhood Reunion Location

In case of fire or any condition requiring immediate escape from our home, go to the following agreed-upon nearby location as soon as practical and await the other family members.

Place to meet:	
Phone #	
Address	
Alternative:	
Phone #	
Address	

Out-of-Neighborhood Location

In case it is not possible to return home due to imminent danger in our neighborhood area, go to the following agreed-upon location and await the other family members.

Place to meet:	
Phone #	
Address	
Alternative:	
Phone #	
Address	

Also, consider keeping a summary of pertinent family operating information available in your *E/PAK* and wallet. What identification numbers, etc., would be helpful should you have to leave home without notice?

Use **Chart 5–9** below to record the information significant to your family.

Chart 5-9
Pertinent Family Information

Item	Number or Account	Telephone #	Cell phone #	Other
Health insurance	Policy #			
Bank account	Account #			
Life insurance	Policy #			
Identification Card	Issued by:			
Credit card	Account #			
Credit card	Account #			
Credit card	Account #			
Credit card	Account #			
Phone card	Account #			
Social Security #	SS #			
Birth date / certificate				
Driver's license	State #			
Auto insurance	Policy #			
Homeowner/Renter Ins.	Policy #			

Worksheet 5-1
Important Emergency Telephone Numbers

Emergency Telephone Numbers

What?		Who? Person / Resource	Where?	How? Call This Number	When? As Directed
Nearest Relative *(other than family)*			Local Address		
Local Contact *(other than family)*			Local Address		
Out of Area Contact	**Day**	Name	Address	( )	
	Night	Name	Address	( )	
Fire			Local		
Emergency				**911** *or* **1-911**	
Ambulance or Paramedics		**Ambulance**	Local		
Police / Sheriff			Local		
Hospital		Name	Local		
Family Doctor		Name	Address		
Pharmacy		Name	Address		
Poison Control		Local	Regional		
Red Cross		Name	Address		
Utilities / Providers					
Electric Power		Name	Address		
Gas		Name	Address		
Water/Sanitation		Name	Address		
Telephone		Name	Address		
Insurance Agent		Name	Local		
Babysitter		Name	Local		
		Name	Local		

Chart 5–10
Additional Contact Data for Family Members

Parent/Guardian Name:	
Employer	
Work Address	
Work Phone #	
Cell Phone #	
Other	
Parent/Guardian Name:	
Employer	
Work Address	
Work Phone #	
Cell Phone #	
Other	
Dependent's Name:	
Company / Employer	
Work Address	
Work Phone #	
Cell Phone #	
Other	
Dependent's Name:	
Company / Employer	
Work Address	
Work Phone #	
Cell Phone #	
Other	
Dependent's Name:	
Company / Employer	
Work Address	
Work Phone #	
Cell Phone #	
Other	
Dependent's Name:	
Company / Employer	
Work Address	
Work Phone #	
Cell Phone #	
Other	
Dependent's Name:	
Company / Employer	
Work Address	
Work Phone #	
Cell Phone #	
Other	

Chart 5-11
Additional Dependent-at-School Information

Dependent's Name:	
School Name	
School Address	
Main Phone #	
School Contact	
Dependent's Name:	
School Name	
School Address	
Main Phone #	
School Contact	
Dependent's Name:	
School Name	
School Address	
Main Phone #	
School Contact	
Dependent's Name:	
School Name	
School Address	
Main Phone #	
School Contact	
Dependent's Name:	
School Name	
School Address	
Main Phone #	
School Contact	
Dependent's Name:	
School Name	
School Address	
Main Phone #	
School Contact	
Dependent's Name:	
School Name	
School Address	
Main Phone #	
School Contact	
Dependent's Name:	
School Name	
School Address	
Main Phone #	
School Contact	

Be sure to get the answers to the following questions for each dependent child at each school:

- Does the school hold or release your child(ren) in case of an emergency situation?
- To what location does the school intend to move your child(ren) in case of an emergency situation?
- Does the school have a communication plan to advise parents/guardians in case of an emergency?
- Does the school store adequate water, food, and medical supplies to deal with emergencies?
- Does the school have an approved disaster plan?

  In effect, are there any disaster policies you need to be aware of (i.e. emergency pick-up plan)?

EMERGENCY PREPAREDNESS BEGINS AT HOME

Responsibility begins in your own home. You are responsible for protecting yourself, your family, and your property to the best of your capability. This entails planning and preparing your own resources to:

(1) Respond to,

(2) Mitigate the effects of, and

(3) Recover from natural and people-caused disasters that can become your personal disaster(s).

The preparation level should exceed the risk level of the expected and unexpected emergencies or disasters in a particular geographic location.

Being prepared requires learning about potential disasters and emergencies, knowing first aid, CPR, and other life-saving skills.

Adaptability and independence are critical qualities to develop in one's preparation efforts. Unfortunately such self-reliance skills are not taught in most schools. Usually they are learned at the hands of bad experience—a tough taskmaster, indeed!

There is no easy way to become self-reliant. It requires work, meaningful efforts in self-education, and often a large measure of self-denial.

Utilize all the knowledge you can gain to prepare for the disasters which could cause you and your family more than the loss of your car, your property, or your crops.

When designing your *E/PAK*—**regardless of the number of days you build it for**—remember this essential point of preparedness:

There are no emergencies for those who are truly prepared!

SOME FINAL THOUGHTS ABOUT YOUR 72-HR.[+] KIT

- Teach your family about the dangers of disasters and emergencies. Assure family members you have a plan in place. Share the plan and teach your family **who**, **what**, **where**, and **how** to deal with disasters and emergencies—be assured that natural, people-caused, or some personal disaster will provide the **when**!
- Be spiritually prepared to deal with disasters and emergencies—in the aftermath of every disastrous situation, counselors are sent to help you deal with the chaos.
- Get training and know how to offer basic life-saving techniques.

- Make the investment in your family's peace of mind. Use the information in this chapter to teach, train, and outfit your family for the uncertain future.
- The kit should be able to give you emergency and life-saving capability. It could be the difference between your life—or the life of a loved one—because you chose to be prepared!
- Don't try to make your short-term kit into a gourmet dining experience! It's designed to sustain life with the least amount of stress possible. You needn't do anything weird! Include some comfort foods to make things seem normal.
- Don't expect to prepare 3 square meals a day—you probably don't fix 3 meals a day now!
- Make planning a 3⁺-day kit an imaginative journey.
- Rotation of edibles and other supplies should be made frequently—especially if your kit is not stored in cool environment. This is an important key to being able to have the constant security the kit offers.
- Use your imagination to determine your vulnerabilities, and to design the complement of supplies to deal with them. One expert said that your imagination is the extension of your kit!
- Keep notes of your experiences utilizing your Emergency Kit. It will help you continually improve you're your kit and your security.
- Practice using your kit. When you need to rotate supplies, call a drill and enjoy utilizing your supplies. Eliminate the things—foodstuff, equipment, and supplies that didn't meet your standards.
- The overarching rule of food storage and emergency preparedness is:

Store what you eat; Eat what you store. Use it or lose it!

It's the ***prime directive*** of storing edibles—***you must never violate the prime directive***! **Just do it!** Or as Captain Jean-Luc Picard might have said, *So let it be done!*

---

[i] Courtesy: **FEMA,** 2006.

[ii] **Barbara Salsbury** is a nationally-recognized consumer specialist, author, and lecturer. Barbara is a long-time friend, a family preparedness and emergency preparedness expert. Her books and videos are available at her website **www.solutionsforpreparedness.com**. She is one of the premier personas of preparedness! I've known Barbara for more than 35 years! She is the author of many preparedness books, a consumer consultant, and a lecturer throughout the Western states. Bestselling author, Barbara is one of America's leading authorities on self-reliance. For more than 25 years, she has been teaching, researching, and developing personal preparedness solutions.

Barbara has been an emergency preparedness consultant for several major cities, including personal preparedness consultant for the city of Sandy UT. She is the author of 2 national newsletters, producer of 3 videos, and has authored 12 books, including: **Just Add Water, Beating the High Cost of Eating, It's Time to Plan Not Panic,** and her latest, a 365-page resource guide, **Preparedness Principles**. The information in her latest book has been the basis for workshops and seminars presented throughout the nation to groups including The American Red Cross, University Special Courses, corporate *Brown Bag* lunch workshops, Adult Continuing Education classes, civic groups, clubs, churches, and service and professional groups. She was a member of the *1984 Consumer Congress* for the State of Utah, by invitation of the State Attorney General'. She is also a member of the *International Platform Association* and the *American Biographical Research Association.* She is listed in many directories including *The World's Who's Who of Women, Distinguished Americans*, and *Who's Who of American Women*.

[2] The name is derived from representations that in the aftermath of natural or people-caused disasters, 3 days (72+ hours) lapses between the actual occurrence of the emergency and the arrival and availability of competent help. You alone may be responsible for the provision of adequate food, water, shelter, etc., for your very survival! Be aware that the 3 days is a *talking point*—neither a promise nor a guarantee!

The most important thing to know about preparedness is that you can become prepared to deal with practically any situation! The saddest commentary on any preparedness problem would be to discover the problem wasn't as much the enemy as was your reluctance to deal with it responsibly when the opportunity to resolve it was within your control.

Getting Your Household in Order
Family Preparedness Household Notebook

Equally important as having water, food, clothing, and some money stored for present and future use is the need to have a copy of the family's financial matters documented and located in one place for instant access. Take the time *now* to organize your family's papers and records—it may well be the *second* best investment you can make in your family's total preparedness activities. The ability to prove ownership of your bank account(s), safety deposit box, and business, brokerage, and/or investment accounts may be necessary after a natural disaster or other calamity destroys the bank, credit union, brokerage or other financial records. Also, since having proof of ownership will allow you to maintain your real property rights, provide qualification for your earned benefits, or provide continuing rights to the use of physical property, it is well worth the effort it takes to amass the information and organize it so it's readily available.

It is most important that all members of the family know where the family's personal records, documentation of ownership, and other financial papers and records are kept. They must also know to whom to turn for advice in case the primary responsible individual becomes incapable of directing family activities. Planning ahead by having these

What can I actually do?...

We can, each of us, work to put our own house in order.

Small is Beautiful,
by
E. F. Schumacher

forms and papers readily available can save a great deal of agony, anguish, time, and money—especially when an emergency or other unpleasantness causes debility, disablement, or death in the family.

Keep the originals of all your family's important forms in a safe deposit box at the bank or in another secure, private, accessible, safe place *away* from your home. The following pages detail how you can establish a system for safeguarding your family's personal and financial information. ***This information may be invaluable to prove your ownership, provide access to earned benefits—and maybe even protect your life!*** This is an exercise of prudence, practicality, and providence![1]

THE FAMILY PREPAREDNESS HOUSEHOLD NOTEBOOK

Make up a *Family Preparedness Household Notebook* using the worksheets provided in this chapter to collect and maintain your family's critical information in a single volume. This notebook provides a designated place to keep *copies* of important and updated records. It's available on short notice to be carried with the family in the event of an emergency. Make certain each responsible family member knows where it's kept, and that it's a most important item to retrieve on a moment's notice!

Prepare a safe place to keep this *Notebook* with its documents and papers. This *Notebook* will help you keep all your updated records in one place. Use top-loading plastic sheet protectors for the documents, with index dividers to identify the categories. Insert sheets of data and documents in a well-organized loose-leaf notebook, so extra pages can be added as needed. Revise all information as needed to keep your data current.

Supplies for the *Family Preparedness Household Notebook* are available in office supply stores. The cost should not exceed $10 to $20, depending on the amount of supplies and quality of materials selected, and should include these items and accessories:

- Loose-leaf notebook
- Top-loading sheet protectors
- Index dividers
- Waterproof, portable container

Use the forms provided in this chapter to collect and maintain family vital statistics, ancestor history (*genealogy*), and financial records. Examples of important documents you will want to *copy* for your *Family Preparedness Household Notebook* include:

- ❑ Family documents—birth, adoption, marriage, and death certificates
- ❑ Relatives to contact (local and out of area)
- ❑ Social Security cards and entitlements
- ❑ Passports
- ❑ Medical records (and prescriptions for medications, eyeglasses, and prosthetics)
- ❑ Immunization records
- ❑ Driver's license
- ❑ Military records
- ❑ Academic certificates
- ❑ Tax returns (3 years)
- ❑ Wills
- ❑ Emergency Care documents
- ❑ Durable Power of Attorney
- ❑ Living Will
- ❑ Medical Surrogate Designee
- ❑ **HIPPA** Release
- ❑ Guardianship Appointment Form (if available in your state)
- ❑ Personal insurance policies
- ❑ Retirement accounts
- ❑ Contents of safe deposit box
- ❑ Property and household items inventory (photographs and videotapes)

- ❑ Banking and money accounts (3 years)
- ❑ Record of credit / debit cards (3 years)
- ❑ Titles to equipment and property
- ❑ Property insurance policies
- ❑ Contracts
- ❑ Deeds to properties and equipment
- ❑ Stocks, bonds, certificates, and other financial instruments
- ❑ Additional documents relative to your personal needs
- ❑ Stash of cash— bills in small denominations and silver coins

Should you have an emergency need for any of these documents in the future, they'll be easily found and immediately available to help resolve problems and give you peace of mind. This is a vital part of being prepared. It requires discipline and often as not, attention to detail. It is the summation of your life's work, so do this task with a view of protecting your estate for the future.

Additionally, keep a small amount of money in small bills and quarters, dimes, and nickels inside a pocket of this *Notebook*—at least enough to make a few telephone calls or perhaps *influence* someone to do what they would have done under *normal* conditions.

Three Rules of Preparedness:

1. Chance favors the prepared mind.

2. Reality rewards the truly prepared.

3. Hope for the best, prepare for the worst, and be able to deal with what comes.

SUGGESTIONS FOR GETTING ORGANIZED

Resolve to get organized—get started and just do it—now! It's really much easier than searching for lost records in mountainous piles of old bills, tax forms, receipts, and hand-me-down recipes!

Chart 6–1
Records Retention & Storage Chart[1]

Period of time to retain	Item or description
Discard upon expiration or disposal of asset	☐ loan agreements ☐ notes due you or owed ☐ bank account passbooks ☐ lease agreements ☐ auto registration
Short term (1 - 3 years)	☐ household bills ☐ expired insurance policies
Medium term (4 - 7 years)	☐ tax returns and supporting data ☐ bank statements and account information ☐ canceled checks / check registers (except for major purchases) ☐ cash receipts journals ☐ paid loan documents
Period of time to retain	**Item or description**
Long term (permanently)	☐ marriage license ☐ adoption papers ☐ divorce documents ☐ checks and receipts for major purchases ☐ brokerage statements ☐ home purchase documents ☐ home improvements receipts ☐ business (self-employment) records ☐ income property documents ☐ wills and trusts ☐ gift tax returns ☐ inheritance documents

---

[1] Federal, state, and local jurisdiction tax laws change often! This information is for reference only. Seek the advice of a qualified tax professional in your local area for current requirements.

The following ideas and suggestions are intended to help you accomplish the task of organizing your vital information:

- ❏ Keep only *copies* in your *Notebook*. Always protect originals in a safe environment. Moisture, temperature, exposure to light can cause deterioration of paper, cloth, and wood items.

- ❏ Rent and use a safe-deposit box in a bank, credit union, savings and loan, or privately operated business. Place in the safe deposit box the originals of important individual and family documents, inventory lists, and photos/videos of property and possessions. Use the box to store copies of wills and trusts, partnership agreements, and other legal documents. Store valuables, including certificates for stocks and bonds, infrequently used jewelry, and a list (photos are better, videotapes are best!) of expensive and rare jewelry, antique furniture, silver dinner sets, or works of art, also.

- ❏ Waterproof *all* documents and other items subject to water damage. Sprinklers can go off accidentally, and floodwaters can rise—even in a vault!

- ❏ Fireproof your vital information. You can find used fireproof safes at most places where safes are sold or repaired. Used safes may cost as little as 10% of new units— and are just as safe!

- ❏ Review and discard outdated documents periodically. How long should you keep those voluminous records? In the table following are guidelines to help you determine periods of recommended storage for various forms and documents.

- ❏ Create an in-home business center for your family preparedness endeavors. In addition to organizing your household information and records, you will find that the effort of planning, budgeting, searching, shopping, and aggregating a year's supply of foods and other items will itself be a sizeable in-home business.

The difference between having your financial records neat and well maintained on the one hand, or what might be called a natural (or perhaps a personal) disaster on the other hand, is usually a matter of simple organization. No genius is required—just a moderate amount of meaningful work.

The benefit is that you'll spend less time looking for a canceled check, anxiety over misplaced receipts, or perhaps an important stock certificate, or days gathering information for your annual tax return.

The real work is in the creation of the system. Once you've created the system, you'll save many hours in the day-to-day management of your business and financial matters. So, create a system, get a system from a business supply house, get a computer program, or modify the one we recommend. Here are some basic organizing tips utilized as we have tried to gain better control of the paperwork flow in our own lives.

If you haven't established an in-home business center, get a small desk, some office supplies, and at least a 2-drawer file cabinet for your family preparedness *business*.

Keep in this desk the materials that you use almost daily:

- • stationery
- • bills to be paid
- • documents to be filed
- • a record of cash receipts and cash disbursements
- • office supplies—pencils, paper, file folders, paper clips, stapler, and staples, etc.

Use the file cabinet to store materials and documents you use less frequently. Use folder systems with tabs in both the desk and the file cabinet.

It makes filing and finding records easier. Set up folders with categories for the types of items you need for reference and follow-up with an alphabetical file and a *1-31 date* file for your important events.

Typical folders to keep in your desk:

- ☐ Bills to pay
- ☐ Cash receipts journal
- ☐ Income from investments
- ☐ Stock transactions
- ☐ Documents to be filed
- ☐ Income documents
- ☐ Gifts received
- ☐ Tax planning and financial planning information
- ☐ Records of children's financial matters–1 for each child in separate folders

Typical folders to keep in your file cabinet:

- ☐ Household bills paid (*by year*)
- ☐ Personal financial statements
- ☐ Home and home improvement records
- ☐ Tax returns (*by year*)
- ☐ Canceled checks and bank statements (*by year*)
- ☐ Investment account statements
  - IRA / Keogh / Roth plans
  - 401(k) plan documents
  - Other long-term investments
- ☐ Bank passbooks and certificates
- ☐ Copies of wills or trusts
- ☐ Medical documents
- ☐ Durable Power of Attorney
- ☐ Living Will
- ☐ Medical Surrogate Appointment
- ☐ **HIPPA** Release
- ☐ Guardian Appointment Form (if available in your state)
- ☐ Employment contract
- ☐ Partnership/business investments
- ☐ Record of company benefits
- ☐ Investment prospectuses and quarterly reports
- ☐ Insurance policies:
  - Life
  - Health
  - Disability
  - Long-Term Care
  - Auto
  - Homeowner's or renter's coverage (including umbrella policy for business)
  - Other insurance policies

❏ Have a cash disbursements journal—you probably already have one as your checkbook is a record of what you've disbursed (paid) for goods and services. Your disbursements journal can be as sophisticated, complicated, or as simple as you like. There are a number of computerized programs for recording and organizing financial data, and it is well worth the price to have one and use it to analyze your financial position on a timely basis.

❏ Also, keep a record of cash receipts, or at least a cash receipts journal. Why would you want to keep a record of receipts? A record allows you to look back at any time and determine who paid you how much, what, and when. At the end of the year, you can use the journal to double-check, for example, that you received all your dividend checks from a particular mutual fund, or all interest payments on a certificate of deposit. You could also, if you wanted, add a series of columns for the types of receipts you anticipate during the year: dividends, interest, rent, bonuses, etc.

To be aware of what income you receive, record these minimum details:

- date income received
- payor or from whom received
- amount received
- amount deposited
- deposit date

As part of your family's preparedness efforts, take the time **NOW** to organize your family's records. Recognize the importance of being able to access your information while the federal, state, and local governments, financial, legal, and educational systems are functioning normally to assist you in your documentation.

For those who have accomplished some of this, be grateful it is done—but stay in pursuit until you're satisfied you're free of the threat of lost information. For those who haven't begun, start gathering this data now, because it will require maximum persistence and dedication as the demand for this type of information increases. Also, agencies will have limited time and personnel to handle both the system failures and the request for information overload.

WORKSHEETS FOR ORGANIZING INFORMATION

The following chart identifies the worksheets available for use in organizing your entire family's information, if you have not done so already. These worksheets will guide you in accounting for your individual and family information, as well as the family's financial assets and liabilities. They are grouped to help you organize your collection of valuable documents and facilitate their safeguarding. Please take time to review these worksheets, and then begin to enter the requested information in an orderly manner.

Chart 6–2
Directory of Household Preparedness Notebook Worksheets

Work Sheet	Worksheet Description	Page #
Category 1. Emergency Information		
1	Important Emergency Telephone Numbers	6–8
Category 2. Family Information		
2A	Family Members	6–9
2B	Individual Family Member Records	6–10
2C	Location of Family Documents	6–11
Category 3. Personal Insurance		
3A	Life Insurance	6–14
3B	Health & Hospitalization Insurance	6–15
3C	Accident & Disability Insurance	6–16
Category 4. Financial Records		
4A	Banking Accounts	6–17
4B	Financial Advisors	6–17
4C	Contents of Safe Deposit Box	6–18
4D	Record of Credit & Debit Cards	6–19
4E	Debts	6–19
4F	Money Owed Us	6–20
4G	Personal Property Loaned to Others	6–20
4H	Equities in Stocks, Mutual Funds, Treasuries, & Corporate Bonds	6–21
4I	Precious Metals & Other Investments	6–22
Category 5. Real Estate & Property		
5A	Real Estate & Property Insurance	6–23
5B	Property & Household Inventory	6–24
5C	Photos / Videos of Property & Household Items	6–26

The gathering of information suggested in these charts is more than an exercise of prudence and practicality. It might very well prove to be providential—if not critical to protect your hard-earned savings and ultimate net worth!

Legal Disclaimer: This chapter contains the authors' own personal experiences and expert legal resources. It is designed to provide general, though accurate and authoritative information. It is published with the understanding that the author, consultants, and/or publisher have no control over the laws, orders, and types of possible changes in such over a period of time. Choices and decisions remain the sole responsibility of the user.

Notes

CATEGORY 1. EMERGENCY INFORMATION

Worksheet 6–1
Important Emergency Telephone Numbers

Important Telephone Numbers

Who? Person / Resource		What?	Where?	How? Call this Number	When? As Directed
Nearest Relative *(other than family)*			Local Address		
Local Contact *(other than family)*			Local Address		
Out of Area Contact	**Day**	Name	Address	( )	
	Night	Name	Address	( )	
Fire			Local		
Emergency				**911** *or* 1-911	
Ambulance or Paramedics		**Ambulance**	Local		
Police / Sheriff			Local		
Hospital		Name	Local		
Family Doctor		Name	Address		
Pharmacy		Name	Address		
Poison Control		Local	Regional		
Red Cross		Name	Address		
Utilities / Providers					
Electric Power		Name	Address		
Gas		Name	Address		
Water / Sanitation		Name	Address		
Telephone		Name	Address		
Insurance Agent		Name	Local		
Babysitter		Name	Local		

CATEGORY 2. FAMILY INFORMATION

Worksheet 6–2A
Family Members

Name of Family Member	Date of Birth	Place of Birth & Where Recorded	Social Security #

Notes

Worksheet 6–2B
Individual Family Member Records

Record or Document	Location of Records					
	Father	Mother	Child	Child	Child	Child
Birth Certificate						
Adoption Records						
Marriage License						
Citizenship Records						
Social Security Card						
Passport & Visas						
Driver's License						
Military Records						
Retirement Accounts						
Settlements						
Academics						
Awards / Prizes						
Health Records						
Immunization Record						
Disability Awards						
Medications						
Eyeglasses						
Church Records						
Will						
Other						

Worksheet 6–2C
Location of Family Documents

Record or Document	Location / Details
Abstract of title for home or properties	
Automobile / title / bill of sale	
Automobile registration	
Other vehicle titles & registrations	
Birth certificates & adoption records	
Canceled checks / bank statements	
Church records: • baptism • confirmation • membership	
Cemetery plot / deed	
Citizenship papers	
Contracts	
Death certificates	
Guarantees / warranties	

This Chart is continued on the next 2 pages…

Location of Family Documents (cont.)

Record or Document	Location
Health records	
Income property records	
Insurance policies • life • pension plan • disability • health • other insurance	
Keys / properties	
Keys / safe deposit box	
Keys / storage facility & other places	
Marriage / divorce records	
Military service records	
Mortgage documents	
Passports & visas	
Pedigrees for livestock & pets	

Location of Family Documents (cont.)

Property / deeds	
Receipts / tax records	
Savings accounts & passbooks	
Social security records	
Stocks & bonds / certificates	

Tax records:
   current year   20____
   previous year 20____
   previous year 20____
   previous year 20____
   previous year 20____
   previous year 20____
   previous year 20____
   previous year 20____
   previous year 20____
 	
See Chart 6-1 for details	

Trusts records & information	
Unemployment benefits records	
Wills	
Other documents	

CATEGORY 3. PERSONAL INSURANCE

Worksheet 6–3A
Life Insurance

Insurance Company & Local Agent	Insured Name	Policy No.	Beneficiary	Type of Coverage	Premiums		Maturity Date
					Pay On	Amt.	

Other Life Insurance Information

Worksheet 6–3B
Health & Hospitalization Insurance

Insurance Co. (Local Agent)	Insured Name	Policy No.	Type of Coverage	Premium Pay On	Amt.	Benefits

Worksheet 6–3C
Accident & Disability Insurance

Insurance Company & Local Agent	Insured Name	Policy No.	Policy Type	Premium Date	Premium Amt.	Benefits & Coverage

CATEGORY 4. FINANCIAL RECORDS

Worksheet 6–4A
Banking Accounts

Account Name	Bank / Credit Union Address & Phone	Account ID	Account Type	Account Manager	Signatories

Worksheet 6–4B
Financial Advisors

Name	Address	Phone #
Accountant		
Attorney		
Banker		
Executor of Will(s)		
Life Insurance Agent		
Health Insurance Agent		
Stock Broker		
Other		

Worksheet 6–4C
Contents of Safe Deposit Box

Item or Article	Description and / or Details	Property Of:

Additional sheets may be added as needed. A copy should be made for each responsible member of the family.

Worksheet 6–4D
Record of Credit & Debit Cards

Account in Name of:	# Cards Issued & to Whom	Account Number	Company Issuing Card	Address & Telephone	Expiration Date

Worksheet 6–4E
Debts

Person or Company Owed	Address & Telephone #	Amount Owed	Payment Due Date	Final Payment Date

Worksheet 6–4F
Money Owed Us

Due From	Address & Telephone No.	Amt.(s) Due	Payment Due Date	Final Payment Date

Worksheet 6–4G
Personal Property Loaned to Others

Item Loaned / Description	Name / Address / Telephone	Notice Date	Due Date

Worksheet 6–4H
Equities in Stocks, Mutual Funds, Treasuries, & Corporate Bonds

Company / Instrument	Certificate Serial #(s)	Pur-chase Date	# of Shares	Cost per Share	Registered in Whose Name

Worksheet 6–4I
Precious Metals & Other Investments

Account in Name of:	Account Type	Name & Address of Institution (Bank / Depository / Security Company)	Account Number

CATEGORY 5. REAL ESTATE & PROPERTY

Worksheet 6–5A
Real Estate & Property Insurance
(automobiles, trucks, boats, & any personal property requiring title or insurance as a condition of use or ownership)

Insurance Company & Address (Name of Local Agent)	Property Insured (Home/Apt., Furnishings, Auto)	Insurance Type	Coverage Amount	Premium	
				Due	Amt.

Worksheet 6–5B
Property & Household Inventory[2]

Item / Description	Date Acquired	Cost Basis	Market Value	Source of Valuation

Additional sheets may be added. Copy this page as needed to complete your inventory.

[2]A property and household inventory will be extremely helpful in determining how much insurance coverage is needed to protect your investments. The inventory also furnishes a valid record on which to base claims should a loss occur. One method of inventorying your household goods is by going through the house, room by room, closets, bathrooms, attic, basement, and any other storage space, and tagging all possessions with a *sticky label*, item by item, until everything you own is accounted for, identified, and all values determined.

Another method is to take photographs, identifying with details on the back of the photos, appropriate inventory and purchase dates, costs, or current price, and/or value at time of purchase. It's easier to make an audio recording to describe the photos.

An easier method is to record your possessions on video. Include everything on the walls, in the closets, items in the garage, and personal jewelry—anything that has value. It is so easy to do—if you don't own a video system, you can borrow or rent one for a weekend. Include verbal descriptions and personal details as you record the items. Where known, clearly state the date of purchase and cost of each item.

Estimate values if exact figures are not known. Keep sales receipts for substantial purchases. Record current market value and the current date. Current market value is the amount you could get if you sold the item now to a willing buyer. Be sure to include food storage and preparedness items in your household inventory. If you detail what you own, and have the facts duly recorded, you have proof of ownership.

Regardless of method used to inventory your possessions, place either the recorded original or a copy in a safe deposit box, if possible.

Property & Household Inventory (Cont.)

Copy this page as needed to complete your property & household inventory.

Item / Description	Date Acquired	Cost Basis	Market Value	Source of Valuation

Worksheet 6–5C
Photos & Videos of Property & Household Items

Album, Tape, or Videotape No.	Property Record (Write or Record Details on Tape)	Room or Property	Photos / Tapes Stored at:

Worksheet 6–5D
Real Estate & Property Descriptions

Type of Property (Personal / Business)	Real Estate / Property Description	Location	Documentation Located at:

Worksheet 6–5E
Real Estate Financials

Owner(s) & Type of Ownership	Date of Purchase	Original Cost	Mortgage Amount	Payments			
				Interest	Principal	Escrow Acct.	Date Due

Additional Notes on Real Estate Financials

Worksheet 6–5F
Major Home Improvements

Date	Description of Major Home Improvements (Proof of purchase price and receipts required)	Cost

Proof of purchase price and receipted bills for improvements are located at: _____

_____

_____

_____

CATEGORY 6. BUSINESS INFORMATION

Worksheet 6–6A
Business Interests

Employer: _____

  Address: _____

  Telephone: _____ **Fax:** _____

  Date of employment: _____ **Name of immediate supervisor:** _____

Sole Proprietor/Partner/Owner of Business:

Name of business: _____
Type of Business: Sole proprietorship _____ **Partnership** _____ **Corporation** _____
Business partner(s): _____
Home address: _____ **Tel.** _____
Partnership agreement? Yes_____ No _____ Date Filed: _____
Partnership (Buy-sell agreement) insurance? Yes _____ No _____ Date Filed: _____
Copies of contracts & policies location: _____
Instructions for supervision or sale of business are located at: _____
_____
_____

ACCOUNTANT: _____ **Tel.** _____
Address: _____

ATTORNEY: _____ **Tel.** _____
Address: _____

BUSINESS CONSULTANT: _____ **Tel.** _____
Address: _____

BUSINESS ASSOCIATE: _____ **Tel.** _____
Address: _____

ASSOCIATE: _____ **Tel.** _____
Address: _____

ASSOCIATE: _____ **Tel.** _____
Address: _____

ASSOCIATE: _____ **Tel.** _____
Address: _____

ASSOCIATE: _____ **Tel.** _____
Address: _____

ASSOCIATE: _____ **Tel.** _____
Address: _____

Worksheet 6–6B
Business Property Insurance

Insurance Company & Address (Local Agent)	Property Insured (Office, Equipment, Furniture, Personal Computers & Software, Trucks, Autos, etc.)	Type of Insurance	Coverage Amount	Premium Due	Amt.

Additional Notes on Business Documents

CATEGORY 7. GUIDELINES FOR SURVIVORS

Worksheet 6–7
Final Disposition Information & Guidelines

My name is: _____
                first   middle/maiden   last

When I die, please contact: _____
                                 name   relationship

_____
                        address   phone #

My important papers are located at _____

_____

_____

_____

_____

Information for Death Certificate & Filing for Death Benefits

My address is _____
                        street   city   county   state   zip code

Citizen of _____ **Birthplace** _____ **Date of Birth** _____

Social Security Number _____-_____-_____ **Occupation/type of business**: _____

Veteran of: _____
                  branch of service   serial number   rank

_____
       date & place entered service   date discharged   benefits/entitlements

I am/was: ☐ married ☐ never married ☐ widowed ☐ separated ☐ divorced ☐ remarried

Spouse's full (maiden) name: _____

Name of next of kin (other than spouse): _____

Relationship: _____ **Address:** _____

_____

Father's full name and birthplace: _____

_____

Mother's maiden name and birthplace: _____

_____

_____

Final Disposition Information & Guidelines (Cont.)

Preferences After Death:

Disposition of Body

☐ **Autopsy** if doctor or family deems it necessary.

☐ **Donate my body's organs:** ☐ arrangements made on _____ with _____
                                          date   organization
_____

☐ **Cremation**   ☐ scatter ashes:_____

☐ **Burial container:** _____
                                          location

☐ **Funeral Arrangements:** ☐ simple   ☐ no embalming   ☐ no public viewing
☐ least expensive burial or cremation container   ☐ immediate disposition ☐ burial at:_____
_____

☐ **Services:**   ☐ memorial (after disposition)   ☐ funeral (before disposition)   ☐ graveside ceremony at:

☐ my church   ☐ mortuary _____   ☐ other _____

_____

Memorial gifts to: _____ ☐ omit flowers

I have made pre-arrangements with: _____
                                                              name/address of mortuary

_____

Signature: _____ **Date:** _____

Witness: _____ **Date:** _____

Witness: _____ **Date:** _____

Additional Disposition Instructions (Pallbearers, etc.)

_____
_____
_____
_____
_____
_____
_____
_____
_____
_____

Additional sheets may be added as needed. A copy of this form should be completed for each member of the family.

i This chapter has been vetted and approved by Ruth Sebastian, J.D. I appreciate her keen eye for detail and the thoroughness she exhibited as she eagerly edited and re-edited this chapter to make it as complete as possible. Ruth is a 1986 graduate of the University Of Kentucky College Of Law. She practiced private law in Lexington KY until 2006, and was also a financial planner from 1992-2006. Ruth is now an Estate Planner, Elder Law Advisor, and Veterans Advocate. Her passion for helping elders has recovered millions of dollars for elderly who have been victims of financial exploitation. Ruth serves as a consultant on topics such as life, financial, and estate planning, with a focus on avoiding financial exploitation and identity theft. She also speaks to educate groups about the prevention of financial exploitation in their families and communities. Ruth may be reached for consultation on these matters through her website: **www.ruthsebastian.com**, or by E-mail: *ruth@ruthsebastian.com*.

Section III

Setting Up Your In-Home Convenience Store

Family preparedness is more than provisions, prudence, and practicality. It's a passion for being in control of your own life that is so intense that no force can stop you from becoming prepared.

Chapter 7

In-Home Storage
A Basic Strategy for Family Preparedness

If you are unfamiliar with in-home storage, the following pages provide a general idea of what you might expect if you choose to pursue your own *Basics* program. The chapters that follow will provide you with the details of in-home storage. Remember that this is a lifestyle choice. Being prepared through in-home storage requires a commitment to learn new skills and use resources in ways perhaps never before considered.

YOUR PERSONAL IN-HOME GROCERY STORE

Think of your home, apartment, or other safe living/storage place as your personal in-home grocery store. That's right, a virtual personal shopping center, stocked with the things you need and like to eat—set up where you have unique access to all of it when needed!

Imagine having supplies of food and other necessary items on hand from which you can draw continuously for 1 week, 1 month, 3 months, up to a year—or longer—if you so choose.

Imagine everything in constant stock rotation—items consumed are replaced and new items added as they are eaten and enjoyed. Think about having quality foodstuffs to utilize in the preparation of wholesome and nourishing meals when there is no surplus of foodstuff available to you.

Making the Best of Basics was compiled to help you and your family develop just such an *in-home convenience* store. This ***Handbook*** provides:

- guidelines for establishing your own *in-home convenience store;*

- tools to help personalize your *in-home convenience store* and provision it for dairy, bakery, produce, medications, personal care, and meat departments, with additional storage for water and fuel;

- general guidelines for quantities and quality specifications, including listings of what foods, supplies, and equipment to stock;

- charts for listing, prioritizing, and budgeting the orderly acquisition of supplies; and

- recipes for utilizing your *in-home convenience store* provisions.

COMMITMENT—THE MAJOR REQUIREMENT OF IN-HOME STORAGE

Your ***Basic*** in-home storage requires thoughtful planning and review because family resources will need to be re-allocated in new and perhaps unfamiliar ways.

Achieving the goal of preparedness demands personal change; change requires commitment.

Essential resource demands will be:

- sacrificing immediate gratification for long-term objectives;
- setting aside time to establish and maintain a home storage program;
- investing financial resources in purchasing adequate food and supplies;
- designating and using living space for storage of food and supplies;
- using stored foods as a regular part of daily food preparation; and
- rotating foodstuffs and supplies on a fixed schedule.

Though establishing a basic in-home storage program is not easy, it's worth it. You must accept that there is:

- no security without labor;
- no progress today without the experiences of yesterday; and
- no future prosperity without adhering to sound advice.

> ***Wealth and security seem to increase whenever people exert energy in the right direction and in the right causes.***

ADVANTAGES OF IN-HOME STORAGE

If you've only considered food storage necessary for ***natural disasters*** and major catastrophes, then consider the following possibilities supporting the wisdom of being prepared with an in-home food storage program:

- more economical way to live—allows more disposable income for other needs;

- simpler lifestyle—more time for other activities;
- feeling of security—confident because you've made preparations for the unexpected;
- healthier lifestyle—reduce processed foods in the diet;
- new skills for living—survival of the fittest;
- sharing responsibilities in the home—increasing stewardship & maturation of family members; and
- discipline of mind and body.

THREE METHODS FOR ESTABLISHING YOUR PLAN

There are three (3) methods for building an in-home storage program. The following charts outline some major considerations for each of the methods described. Keep these methods in mind as you use the information in the next chapters.

Choose the method or combination of methods that work most effectively for you!

1. The *Pioneer* Method

By far, the **Pioneer Method** is the most difficult method, requiring the most dedication and commitment—but has the greatest benefits for the family striving to achieve family preparedness.

The **Pioneer Method** requires such skills as *scratch* production and gardening. At-home production and preservation skills have been lost, however, because the *pioneer* proficiencies have not been passed to the younger generations.

Additionally, most people either don't have the personal discipline, won't take the time, can't provide the space, neglect developing abilities to master the skills, or refuse to implement the plan in which they've invested.

The **Pioneer Method** is the most difficult because it requires continual effort and serious modification to your current lifestyle to achieve it! However, it's the basis for *sustainable preparedness*. Some refer to this as the **survivalist method**.

Pioneer Method	
Advantages / Requirements	**Disadvantages / Requirements**
• become adept in all aspects of at-home production and preservation skills	• learn how to work and share responsibility within the family
• produce large part of year's supply every growing season from an urban homestead	• need at least a 50' X 100' garden area; without adequate land & zoning, difficult to be a self-sufficient pioneer
• gardening is healthy for the mind & body	• work and sweat
• learn new skills: canning, drying, freezing, pickling, root cellaring, etc.	• generally cannot supply everything from *urban homestead* activities
• own tools of production: canning and drying equipment	• expenditure of time and effort
• knowledge of food production	• cost of tools and equipment
• food tastes homemade	• may cost more to produce at-home at onset of program; however, economies of scale and collection of seeds provides *profit*
• lowers cost of foods and foodstuffs	

2. The *Package* Method

The **Package Method** is the easiest and most often utilized. Some people buy a package program which may be someone else's idea of a complete food storage plan because it seems simple, easy, and quick!

Then the buyer neglects to learn how to use all those stored bulk-packed cans, sacks of wheat, and barrels of untried and therefore unused products, eventually throwing out the stuff without ever trying to learn how to use it and angry for not having made a better investment. The dismaying truth is that the buyer (now perceiving himself a victim!) is then turned off to the wisdom of preparedness because of his own lack of education and application. This is the reason for the motto: ***Store what you eat, eat what you store—use it or lose it.***

The **Package Method** requires little thinking or planning—with consequential results—because no lifestyle modifications are required or implemented. You need to determine what you want to eat or you could starve in the midst of plenty!

Package Method	
Advantages / Requirements	**Disadvantages / Requirements**
• "package deal" of highly processed canned, dried or dehydrated, freeze-dried, home-canned, pickled, frozen, and MREs (meals ready to eat)	• expensive per serving, requires cash outlay immediately
• long-life storage of bulk products	• break open large container of wheat, rice, or beans!
• guaranteed storage for many years	• unlikely you would use this food on a regular basis
• quick, simple, and effortless	• no pain—what did you gain?
• easy way to acquire food: cans, vacuum-packed, cases, individual servings	• not enough food choices for average family
• most likely what you normally consume	Can you subsist on it; enjoy it; and know how to use it?

3. The *Pantry* Method

The **Pantry Method** is perhaps the most-used of all the methods, whether your existing *pantry* is adequately provisioned, or merely a pass-through for your daily bread. This method is also known as the: *eat what you store—store what you eat* system. Most people forget the 3rd part of the equation: *use it or lose it* to prevent resources waste.

Pantry Method	
Advantages / Requirements	**Disadvantages / Requirements**
• most economical and practical method—you can start this method on your next grocery shopping trip	• requires extended period of time to build reserves
• buy foods and foodstuffs more effectively—quantity for discounts and / or on sale	• must shop more effectively—constant attention to detail; cooperation of entire family required
• eat better, improve diet	• knowing what to eat and quantities consumed
• become more practical	• prepare familiar foods with unfamiliar ingredients
• commitment and passion	• sacrifice of non-essentials
• start small, and grow as your budget permits	• financial commitment
• always have the necessary foods / ingredients for meals	• requires attention to detail
• become urban self-reliant	• may not be able to keep up with Jones'
• simplest, easiest, and generally, the healthiest approach • budgeting of resources	• 4 *M* values: — *m*inutes (time) — *m*anpower — *m*oney — *m*aterials

The **Pantry Method** requires only a moderate lifestyle modification and some thoughtful analysis of the family's diet to accommodate its effective implementation. Most people are comfortable starting with reasonable change in their lifestyle, then increasing their immersion into other methods as they increase their intensity in preparedness activities.

SUMMARY OF ADVANTAGES AND DISADVANTAGES / REQUIREMENTS

- The optimum solution for family preparedness is an intelligent combination of all 3 methods discussed previously—utilizing a *mix-and-match* approach to in-home storage.

- It's effective to have some package or program foods with your in-home storage supplies—they're lightweight, less expensive, compact, and fairly portable.

- Learn how to preserve foods from your own garden, your neighbor's, or from the store—gain experience with in-home production and food preservation.

- The single most important thing is to get started now—and *just do it*!

WHAT'S THE BOTTOM LINE?

As you gain knowledge and confidence and determination in your goal of family preparedness, these are the questions you must ask yourself:

- **Which method(s) best fit *our family's* lifestyle?**

- **What am *I* going to do to feed my family?**

- **When will *I* do it?**

Notes

If you are truly prepared, you need not fear!

Food is power!
If you don't need to beg, borrow, or steal, you won't need to bow!
It is the most useful, practical, and life assurance policy available.

Chapter 8

In-Home Convenience Store

Almost everyone accepts the concept of being prepared for emergencies. However, when it's time to do the actual planning and acquiring the necessary items, most *people are simply overwhelmed by the enormity of it all*. Let's face it, most of us have a difficult time getting organized for a Saturday afternoon barbecue, much less planning for and procuring adequate foodstuffs and supplies to feed ourselves for an entire week, month—or longer!

Your thoughts may be like mine: *It could take years to acquire all that stuff…* and *Even if money weren't an issue, where and how can I store food and supplies so they can be used and not go to waste*? More basic than that are the details of *what* to store, *how much* of each, and *which* items to buy first. The solution to the problem is found in an age-old saying: *A journey of a thousand miles begins with the first step.*

Take the first step by using the ***Family Preparedness Handbook*** as your workbook. The answers to the questions of *what* to acquire first, *how much* to store, and *how long* items should last on the shelf are addressed in the **Quick-List** tables in this chapter.

"A meaningful life is not a matter of speed or efficiency. It's much more a matter of what you do and why you do it, than how fast you get it done."

Stephen R. Covey

Don't count on this *Handbook* to bail you out after a disaster unless you've applied some of your personal energy and resources to planning and implementing the concepts and principles that will help you meet your storage needs. This *Handbook* is *not* printed on rice paper with vitaminized ink—you won't be able to boil it and eat it if you've otherwise failed to prepare!

PREPAREDNESS AND IN-HOME STORAGE

The *basic concept of being prepared* is having the resources located in your home (or at least on your property) to be able to live in a near-normal manner for up to a year when natural, people-caused, or personal disasters impact your geographical area, your neighborhood, or your own home. This effort is a choice you make to become self-reliant far in advance of need. Once you make this choice, the negative impact of any disaster is mitigated by your preparedness, and you can provide your family continuing security.

The goal is to be prepared in excess of the potential risk!

Creating a one-year inventory of foods and nonfoods from which a family can live without need of constant replenishment is no small undertaking. We recognize that the average American family may not be financially capable of having a full-fledged, one-year supply of foods and nonfoods, but every family can do a better job of utilizing its resources to attain security—it's simply a matter of choices.

If you are overwhelmed by the magnitude of what it would take to sustain you for a year, then think more in terms of what it would take to keep you alive for a few days, weeks, or months in case you didn't have anything else to eat except what's on hand. Be honest with yourself in both your expectations and the reality of what resources you can commit to creating an in-home store.

There are only three things to remember about building your in-home storage program with the *Basic* concept:

1. **Store what you eat!**
2. **Eat what you store!**
3. **Use it or lose it!**

The biggest challenge in procuring an in-home storage supply is financing its acquisition. Creative use of current household items, wise budgeting in accordance with the family's income, and smarter shopping will help maximize your ability to accomplish your goal.

But, until the in-home storage program is established as a primary financial priority—*after planning the repayment of current debt, of course*—it will not become a reality.

We've found that creating an in-home convenience store is both a journey *and* a destination. Begin planning your journey by determining:

1. when you want to start your journey to preparedness,
2. where you want to be in your progress of achieving preparedness, and
3. how you plan to arrive there.

Once you identify where you are now, commit to move consistently towards your destination, and learn as you progress, you'll get where you're going.

You don't have to do it all at once, just tell yourself, *I just have to begin, and then I can continue from there.*

Most importantly, get everyone in the family involved in the family's food storage program, particularly in decisions about food purchases, because you want to buy only those items your family will consume. As family funds, living and play space, family work as-

Seize this very moment.

What you can do or dream you can do,
Begin it.

Boldness has power and magic in it.

Begin it,
and the work will be completed.

Goethe

signments, and many other assets may require redistribution, indeed, family discussions about change and agreement to changes are important.

A family food storage program is an opportunity for family members to have a common destination and be on a joint journey—generating shared enthusiasm, building family unity, and instilling a feeling of self-reliance for the entire family.

In the remainder of this chapter, we give you practical ways and means, as well as some methods and tools to set up your own in-home storage plan. In this chapter you'll discover the following things:

How to:
- build a *Basic* in-home convenience store;
- know what items to store for best nutrition, health and morale maintenance; and
- select a balance of food and nonfood items and the appropriate quantities of each.

Tools to:
- chart inventory quantities needed
- compute a simple numerical value to determine storage quantities
- prioritize storage selections and budget your money for purchases
- use time units to make your storage program more manageable

What's Important to Store

The *Basic in-home storage program* recommended by the **Family Preparedness Handbook** is comprised of fifteen foods and nonfoods categories.

Six of the categories, called the **Basic Categories**, are the foundation upon which the other categories, or **Building Block Categories**, are added—forming the structure for a viable *Basic in-home storage program*.

The food and nonfood items in the six **Basic Categories** are capable of sustaining life while providing a reasonable healthy and varied diet.

Then, adding **Building Block** foods and nonfoods enhances the utility and enjoyment of your in-home food storage by increasing the variety of recipes and menus and ultimately bringing a higher quality of life to your *Basic* lifestyle.

Chart 8–1
Basic In-Home Storage Categories

Basic Categories—the Foundation Categories	
1. **Water—emergency supplies & treatment**	• 2nd in importance only to the air we breathe • we can survive only a few days without it • simplest *Basic* category to store
2. **Wheat, other whole grains, flours, & beans**	• considered an essential item for any food storage program • assumes family will have other *Basic* foods in storage
3. **Powdered milk, dairy products, & eggs**	• stored as whole dried milk or skim (nonfat)
4. **Sweeteners—honey, sugar, & syrup**	• essential sugars for many food preparations
5. **Cooking catalysts**	• salt, oil, & leavenings essential to food preparation • category essential to body development • least expensive category to store
6. **Sprouting seeds & supplies**	• fresh, green, live whole foods—any time of the year—for pennies per day

The nine **Building Block** foods and nonfoods categories are briefly described in the following chart. Listings in the chart are organized arbitrarily. In practice, each family must choose how to prioritize its own categories, purchases, and the details of which items to acquire for a workable preparedness plan.

Chart 8-2
In-Home Storage "Building Block" Categories

"Building Blocks" Categories	
7. Medical care, medications, & first aid kits	• medications without which a person's life or health is in jeopardy • 30-day supply of all essential medications in an emergency kit • first aid supplies for emergencies or in the event of a disaster
8. Basic supplementation: vitamin, mineral, and herbal supplements	• essential for storage diet to maintain adequate nutrition • processed foods are depleted in vitamins and minerals • additional nutritional losses are incurred from long-term storage of foods • necessary to support the body during stressful times generally accompanying a food storage diet
9. Fuels, energy, & camping gear	• when there are no available public utilities, these commodities will provide the means for cooking your food, as well as heating and lighting your living space • emergency commodities, such as bedding, cooking equipment, other necessities for away-from-home living, if required
10. Personal, family, infant, & pet care essentials	• clothing, personal items, and body care items • necessities for individual special needs • necessities for babies, infants, or children • food and care items for any pets
11. Canned & dried fruits, vegetables & soups	• selection of the family's favorite and familiar fruits, vegetables, and soups in quantities adequate to provide regular meals
12. Kitchen staples— condiments & seasonings	• all the meal accessories the family needs to make meals as tasty and normal as possible
13. Meats & seafood	• selection of meats—fresh, frozen, or canned
14. Domestic maintenance & preparedness	• items needed to maintain the home, yard, garden—all the important things needed for continuing repair and maintenance
15. Pleasure foods—snacks, beverages, sweets, & treats	• morale-lifting, familiar, and convenient foods that would give the family a "lift" when all else seems to be going awry

All fifteen categories together represent a variety of foods and nonfoods that, when stored in your *in-home pantry*, would support family life in a near-normal manner.

Each category has an associated **Pantry List** (found in the last section of this chapter) which identifies suggested storage foods and nonfoods. You are encouraged to personalize the listings and add any other items your family chooses.

Some items in the **Pantry Lists** have been designated as *essential* and are noted in boldface type. For example, in the **Water** category **Quick-List 8–1**, **potable water**, **aseptic water**, **bleach,** and **treatment tablets** have been selected as essentials. *Essential* items are recommended as first purchases within each category because of their contribution to sustaining life in a reasonably healthy and normal manner, enhancing variety in menu and meal selection, and increasing the utility of your storage.

The other food and nonfood items (not in boldface type) on the **Pantry Lists** are referred to as *supplemental* or additional items. They are included to offer greater choice and to fulfill personal needs. That means that even though I don't consider *Twinkies*® a personal choice, it doesn't preclude your family from making that choice!

It is each family's challenge and opportunity to decide which foods and nonfoods to store based on individual preference, age, sex, health needs, finances, available storage space, living conditions, job(s), etc.

The storage categories and **Pantry Lists** are provided as a framework of suggestions from which you make choices to plan your in-home storage program.

The Basic Categories

The first six categories are considered the *Basic* categories. Water, wheat, powdered milk, honey, salt, and sprouting seeds are the real foundation of in-home storage. Each of these items is relatively inexpensive to purchase for storage, stores easily for long periods, and provides adequate nutrition to sustain life—though most people wouldn't get fat from them. The true worth lies, however, in their combination because they work synergistically—each adding greater value to the others.

The advantages of using the *Basic* categories as the foundation of in-home storage are that they maximize:

- family dollars available for storage purchases,
- available household storage space,
- utility of other stored foods, and
- life-sustaining capability with least number of stored foods and least expense.

The following chart illustrates the significance of the *Basic* categories—individually and in relationship to each other. Note that as each *Basic* category is added, nutritional value, diet selection and versatility are increased.

Water by itself will sustain life but offers no nutrition.

Wheat adds nutrition to the diet. Each additional *Basic* category multiplies the value of the others.

This **Building on Basics** concept is what makes the *Basic* categories so fundamentally important to in-home storage.

Many of the remaining chapters in this *Handbook* focus on the *Basic* foods. The information in these chapters will provide you with greater detail about the foods, instructions for utilizing them, and some *Basic* recipes to enhance these stored foods.

Frequently people tell us that their old copies of **Making the Best of Basics** are worn out because of the use they received while raising their families on limited resources.

Using the *Basic* foods offers tremendous opportunities to experience a lifestyle that supports personal growth. Integrating *Basics* foods into your present diet is a way to put new skills into operation, develop greater self-reliance, and improve your ability to adapt to change.

The time to begin using *Basics* is now. Practice new skills and adjust to unfamiliar foods *before* the necessity of living on stored supplies arises. These new skills are not acquired overnight and eating *Basics* foods requires acclimation—the body must adjust gradually to these different foods.

Incorporating *Basics* into the modern lifestyle is a worthy challenge for any family—the rewards will eventually speak for themselves.

Chart 8–3
Building on Basics

A person can live on water alone for many days; add treatment system to assure continuing supply of drinking & cooking water.	Whole-grain cereal (bulgur); soups & stews; side dish; use instead of potatoes. Make primitive breads; boil whole berries for crunchy and chewy cereals; roast for hot drinks; substitute for rice; sprout as substitute for green vegetables; dry sprouts for sugar; use a grinder and crack grain for cereals, whole-wheat flour for gluten (a substitute for meat); make more advanced non-yeast breads such as sourdough & tortillas.	Enhances water and wheat use; expands utility of cracked grains and whole wheat flours. Provides milk and dairy products such as yogurt, cottage cheese, & hard cheeses; makes creamy topping when whipped.	A catalyst for food preparation; essential to chemical action in certain foods; enhances recipes and all foods; sweet preservative for fruits & vegetables.	Cooking catalysts enhance recipes; also essential to chemical action in dough; saline preservative for meats and vegetables; pickling & brining; yeast makes finer breads; oils essential to frying, baking, & general cooking.	Fresh green vegetables provide live whole food year round for excellent nutrition; use alone or with other foods; excellent in salads, soups, sandwiches, add to baked breads, casseroles, etc.
Water (+ treatment device)	**Wheat / whole grains (+ grinder or mill)**	**Powdered milk**	**Sweeteners**	**Cooking catalysts (salt, oil, & yeast)**	**Seeds & Sprouting**
Absolute *Basic*; has fairly short storage life (6-12 mo—depending on original quality and container); heavy, bulky to store, but cheap to acquire; treatment device small & not expensive.	Addition of wheat to water provides a quantum leap for nutrition and survivability; nutritious & versatile grain; has indefinite (15$^+$ years) storage life; grinder provides ability to increase utility of wheat.	Stores well (up to 48 mo.); allows in-home production of yogurt, cottage cheese, and hard cheese when yogurt-maker and cheese press added.	Store indefinitely; enhance taste of foods; honey is preferred sweetener due to higher nutritive content, more healthful attributes, & sweeter than sugar.	Cooking catalysts are essential to cooking; salt stores indefinitely; critical to body cell functioning; very little storage space required for this entire category; oil & yeast essential to baking.	Easiest method of gardening—requires only small space in kitchen cabinet or windowsill. Utilizes simple equipment: quart jar, piece of gauze, & rubber band; inexpensive seed & equipment; requires very little storage space.

GUIDELINES FOR STOCKING YOUR PANTRY

After reviewing the **Pantry Lists** on the following pages and using them as a reference, walk through your home taking a *fresh* look at your household goods as being supplies for your in-home convenience store. Maybe you don't have a year's supply of food yet, but you might have a considerable supply of seasonings and lots of certain canned goods or packaged mixes.

Check out your equipment. What tools do you have for cooking and baking? Do you have camping gear—equipment that might be used for emergencies?

An old lunch box makes a very good container for first aid supplies. What items do you have in the bathroom drawers and in the kitchen cabinets that might go into a first aid kit? Remember the last time you had fast food and threw away the plastic utensils in the plastic sleeve without a care?

What about keeping those for your in-home storage in case you don't have enough water for washing dishes. Picnic supplies may come in handy, too. Emptied plastic soda bottles work well for storing emergency drinking water for short periods of time.

Get boxes and begin sorting storage items as you find them. Make the best use of things you already have. Most people are surprised to find how much they have on hand already. You'll soon realize that preparedness is really a matter of awareness of what you have on hand to solve the problem when the need arises.

Store What You Eat

The most important part of an in-home storage plan is knowing what you eat now and buying what you'll most likely eat in the future. Having a store full of items you don't use or need makes your In-home convenience store somewhat of an inconvenience store! It's truly wasted time, money, and effort if the food stored does not appeal to the family's taste.

This is an excellent time to review carefully your eating habits—becoming even more aware of the "good" foods your family eats as well as the snacks, treats, drinks, and other "junk" foods to which they've become attached. It is also a great teaching moment for parents to urge children (of all ages!) to cut back on all sorts of unhealthy foods, especially since they don't usually store well, as a general rule. It's a good idea to begin to limit your purchases of prepared foods, too.

You manage your in-home pantry in a similar fashion to the local grocery store—as items are stocked, place them behind the goods already on the shelf. As you acquire items for your in-home convenience store, date them so you'll know which was purchased first. Items with shorter shelf life may be noted and dated *"Use by: _____"* to assure utilization within their useful shelf life period. Restock as items are used. Obviously, you will not restock food items not favored by your family. Managing the rotation of all food items will be much easier if you have stored foods that family members are interested in eating.

Inventory management for *Basic* in-home convenience store is very simple—and hopefully, by now, very familiar:

> **Store what you eat.**
> **Eat what you store.**
> **Use it or lose it!**

It's really as simple as that!

It's the *Basics* **K.I.S.S.** theory: <u>**K**</u>eep <u>**I**</u>t <u>**S**</u>uper <u>**S**</u>imple!

Re-order your priorities…

Rebuild, recycle, redo, refinish refurbish, relock, remake, renew, repair, resole, reupholster, and rewire!

Get back to the basics!

Purchase the "Essentials" First

Realistically, given the need to allocate your financial resources to more areas of your life than just purchasing storage supplies, it becomes critically important to have a way to determine what to buy first, so in this edition we provide you some guidelines with a series of **Shopping Lists**–or **Quick-Lists** that eliminate the guesswork and facilitate your decision-making.

The **Essentials Foods & Nonfoods Shopping List** at the end of this chapter identifies selected items from each **In-Home Storage Category** that are recommended as *essential* needs or purchases. As noted, *essential* items have been selected because of their contribution to sustaining life in a reasonably normal and healthy manner, for enhancing variety in meal selection, and to supporting greater utility of the other stored items.

Use the **Shopping List** as a guide to the most useful purchases for your storage supply. If the only items acquired for in-home storage were the *essentials*, you would have a life-and health-sustaining diet.

The advantages of employing the **Shopping List** are that the lists:

- provide you with a ready-made plan until you gain experience to design your own

- allow you to acquire storage items in an orderly and systematic manner—one at a time—and consistent with your income

- facilitate storing supplies from all categories—insuring greater self-sufficiency

- permit flexibility—can be modified to meet your personal needs

Determine Manageable Time Units

The process of gathering a year's supply can be accomplished more easily if the effort is broken into smaller parts. Do this by setting up *time units* in which to accomplish certain interim objectives or stopping places on your journey. Determine the block(s) of time in which you function most comfortably.

If you're oriented to a week-at-a-time schedule, then plan to store 52 one-week quantities. If you organized on a monthly basis, then plan for 12 one-month quantities—or as we call it in today's parlance—*installments*.

Time units are a good method to relate to your acquisition plan. Once you've decided what to buy, merely divide the family's storage requirements by whatever time unit(s) your family chooses, then buy the item(s) in installments. Make the calendar and time work for you!

Chart Your Progress

There are no deadlines other than those you establish for yourself, and they are only in relationship to your own circumstances. ***Any progress you make is success—defined as progressive realization of a worthy goal!*** Put a chart on your wall for your family to see the progress being made.

This chart can also serve to display the range and balance of items stored, helping avoid imbalances (for example: 6 week's/month's worth of powdered milk, only 1 week/month of wheat, and no water for making milk or bread!)

Chart 8-4 is an example of a chart you could make and place on a wall or on the most noticeable place—the refrigerator door! Use colored pens or crayon to show your on-hand position versus your storage needs**.**

Charting your progress will remind you of your family's achievements in your in-home convenience store acquisition plan and gives you encouragement on your journey.

Borrowing money to acquire in-home food storage items is not recommended!

Chart 8–4
Sample Family Progress Chart

Family Progress Chart						
Weeks or Months	**Storage items balance sheet**					
12					■	
11					■	
10		■			■	
9		■			■	
8		■			■	
7		■	■		■	
6		■	■		■	
5	■	■	■		■	
4	■	■	■	■	■	
3	■	■	■	■	■	
2	■	■	■	■	■	■
1	■	■	■	■	■	■
Time Period	**Water**	**Wheat**	**Powdered milk**	**Honey**	**Salt**	**Vitamins**

Start In-Home Storage with a *"Safety Net"* Supply

Having an in-home food storage supply is not an "all or nothing" situation. All food storage is ever-changing and transitional. As you begin your family's in-home food storage project and establish your plan, you may want to experience some immediate progress by starting with the **safety net supply** purchasing concept. This acquisition concept may help you gain momentum immediately by obtaining some items without destroying your overall budget.

Every family should have a few weeks' supply of canned goods and staples, such as flour, sugar, salt, vegetables, soup mixes, cooking oils, spices, canned soups, canned meats, condiments—all the things you'd want to buy now if you couldn't when you really need them!

Safety net purchases should be food and supplies which would sustain life should an emergency occur before your total preparations are completed—at least you would have some food in your pantry. Buy for your storage program those items consumed in your present diet through a process called *planned copybuying*—a purchasing plan you probably already utilize, you just hadn't it formalized with a name.

Planned copybuying means buying extra cans, jars, or packages of foodstuffs, medicines, and household products you routinely use.

Safety net purchasing might include either of the following methods of *planned copybuying*:

- **Dupli-buying:** As you buy food items for immediate use—*buy another for your in-home food storage program*. Do this *every* time you shop. This doesn't include buying extra perishable and low-priority items, of course.

  This method allows you to acquire foods you normally use, while eventually building a reservoir of foodstuffs. Perhaps for the budget-limited, this is the only way to get some foods in the *safety net*.

Please write your notes in the margins—that's why they're so wide!

- **Multi-buying:** *Buy a large supply of anything you use when it's on sale*. As seasonal food and product specials are offered by the stores, you'll maximize your purchasing power through bulk buying.

This is the preferable way to acquire food storage items more quickly, but it requires a greater financial commitment and resources to accomplish.

In essence, *copybuying* is the easiest and simplest method to balance your purchases—you're buying what you eat and eating what you buy!

Maximize Your Purchasing Power

Here are some hints to help remind you to use all techniques at your disposal to minimize costs and maximize value as you implement your in-home storage plan:

- Learn to use coupons effectively when shopping at grocery stores.
- Discover food wholesalers, buying clubs, or establish cooperative grocery clubs with a group of friends. Get into a group-buying plan, learn to master the feed and grain stores, and even haunt the farmer co-ops or open-air markets—whatever it takes to get lower prices and expand your purchasing dollars.
- Find or establish barter or exchange organizations. If there are no organizations of these types in your area, start one. Consider starting with your extended family, neighbors, church group, or other organizations with which you are familiar.
- Join or start a *shared resources* group. Find others who are willing to share the costs and use of expensive equipment, a grains grinder, for example. The equipment then is owned collectively and no one family must bear the entire cost of expensive non-foods items.
- Utilize mail order for those storage items that you cannot obtain locally or are more costly when bought locally. Use Internet resources. i.e., food storage dealers, **eBay**, **Craig's List**, and now **Amazon.com!** Local sources provide great buys on new and used equipment. In a down economy, bargains abound!

Capitalize on the Wide Variety of Resources Available

Planning your in-home convenience store requirements is essential to your budget, space, and eventual welfare. The best knowledge about what your family requires for its subsistence during a time of need—whether it's a short or long period of time—seems always to come *after* your bad experience. That could be far too late to help you get organized.

Knowing how to organize, maintain, and fully utilize a sensible, continuing, workable in-home food convenience store becomes a matter of self-education and implementation for each family in advance of a natural, man-caused, or personal disaster.

Thankfully, there are numerous public and private resources available for those who want to do more homework before launching their journey. Draw on the experience and knowledge of others to establish and maintain proactively your own preparedness and in-home food storage program. In some chapters of this **Handbook** you will find **Resource Directories** which provide listings of publications and other resources you may want to utilize.

PLANNING YOUR ONE-YEAR STORAGE

The kinds of foods and nonfoods and the amounts to be stored for a one-year supply are recommended in this section of the *Family Preparedness Handbook*. This information is compiled from knowledge available as of publication date and intended to provide generic guidelines. These guidelines should be varied according to each family's tastes, situation, and circumstances.

A good in-home storage program is based on knowledge of your own and your family's eating habits. You'll also need to take into account the ages, occupation(s), nutritional state, health, climate, and other factors which may alter the kinds of foods desired, supplies needed, and the amount(s) of each to be stored for an entire family.

Quick-Charts

To help you make your one year in-home storage a reality, this *Handbook* provides an organized framework for stocking your pantry. This chapter includes detailed charts which will enable you to determine the economic impact on your financial resources through a ready-made inventorying, prioritizing, purchasing, and budgeting system.

Amounts are based on living exclusively on your in-home storage for an entire year—without business lunches, dining out, or eating at the parents or kids. By assessing your on-hand supplies, you know where you are currently and how far you must go to reach your one-year supply requirements.

Quick-Guide 8–1. Provides an overview of the **In-Home Storage Categories** and recommended one year storage quantities for the average adult male (**Adult Quantity**.)

Quick-Lists 8–1 through **8–15**. **Pantry Lists** detail for each **In-Home Storage Category** the recommended *essential* and *supplemental* foods and nonfoods, expected **Shelf Life** of these recommended storage items, and the recommended one year storage quantities for the average adult male (**Adult Quantity**.)

Quick-Shop 8–1 Essential Foods and Nonfoods Shopping List. This listing of *essential* foods and nonfoods from all **In-Home Storage Categories** repeats the **Shelf Life** and **Adult Quantity.** In addition it provides worksheet space for figuring family storage requirements. Use this chart to identify *essential* items needed in your in-home storage.

Quick-Shop 8–2 Supplemental Foods & Nonfoods Shopping List. This blank chart provides worksheet space to write down needed *supplemental* storage items and to determine family storage needs. Refer to the **Pantry Lists** for **Shelf Life** and **Adult Quantity** of needed items.

Quick-Plan 8–1 Planning & Budgeting Worksheet. This blank worksheet provides worksheet space to prioritize all of your needed storage items, write down sources and suppliers of storage items, and figure costs of the needed items.

Family Factor

Over the years, our experience in communicating the concept of *Basic in-home food storage and preparedness* has grown. In this edition, we're sharing our easier, simpler method of computing the food and nonfood quantities needed for storage. This method uses a numerical value, based on points assigned to each member of the household.

Once derived by simple math, this numerical value is used as a multiplier for the quantity of each recommended storage item, thus determining the family quantity of that item. To help you derive this numerical value, named the *Family Factor,* you use the *Family Factor Formula.*

The *Family Factor Formula* assigns each family member food consumption points. These food consumption points are percentages (*points*). These are numbers relative to the average adult male consumption level.

Using 100 points for the male adult as the base or index number, the consumption points for other family members are lesser or greater percentages, depending on age, sex, and appetite. See **Chart 8-5** for other family member *points*.

Assume you're part of a family comprised of:
- an average adult male, consumption level @ 100 points (or 100%),
- an adult female @ 85 points (85% or 0.85 consumption of adult male),

- 2 male teenagers @ 140 points each (140% per male teenager or 40% more than adult male),
- a female teenager @ 95 points (95% or 0.95 of adult male),
- a female child @ 75 points (75% or 0.75 of an adult male), and
- an infant @ 50 points (50% or 0.50 of adult male).

The *Family Factor Formula* uses these *consumption points* (converted to percentages) to determine the *Family Factor.*

Use **Chart 8–5** to derive a **Family Factor** by the following steps.

1. Identify the *Number (#) of People* in each *Family Members* category. (i.e., 1 male adult, 1 female adult, 2 male teenagers, etc.)

2. Multiply the *Number (#) of People* in each category by the assigned *Consumption Points* to obtain *Total Points.*

3. Add together the *Total Points* to determine the *Family Total Points.*

4. Divide the *Family Points Total* by 100 to determine the **Family Factor.**

Chart 8–5
Sample <u>Family Factor</u> Computation

Computing Your Family Factor					
Family Members	# People	X	Consumption Points	=	Total Points
Male adult	1		100		100
Female adult	1		85		85
Male teenager	2		140		280
Female teenager	1		95		95
Male child			95		
Female child	1		75		75
Infant (1-3 yrs.)	1		50		50
Family Total Points					685
Divide total points by 100					÷ 100
This is the Sample *Family Factor*:					6.85

Below is a chart for determining *your* own **Family Factor.**

Chart 8-6
My <u>Family Factor</u>

Computing Your Family Factor					
Family Members	# People	X	Consumption Points	=	Total Points
Male adult			100		
Female adult			85		
Male teenager			140		
Female teenager			95		
Male child			95		
Female child			75		
Infant (1-3 yrs.)			50		
Family Total Points					
Divide total points by 100					÷ 100
This is your *Family Factor*:					_____

To derive the maximum benefit from the *Family Factor,* use the experience and knowledge of your family's consumption habits to make adjustments to the *Consumption Point* values, if necessary. Our figures are based on a male adult's average rate.*

For example, say your teenage son can't live without potatoes at every meal. He even rushes home from school to eat a cold boiled potato or heats it in the microwave oven, then drenches the hot potato with 2 tablespoons of butter and dollops on a quarter-pound of sour cream—just so he doesn't starve before suppertime! In such an instance, you'd need to adjust the *Family Factor* in the line item for potatoes in the vegetable section of **Chart 8-11** listings following in this chapter.

Assume for a moment your *Family Factor* is 6.85, just as the **Sample** family. Merely "bump up" the *Family Factor* to **7.0** for this food item in **Chart 8-11**.

Let's also assume no one in the family likes dehydrated potatoes.

Here's what the potato section would be for your family:

Chart 8-11

Fresh, Canned, & Dried Fruits, Vegetables, & Soups Pantry List							
Multiply Adult Quantity by your Family Factor to determine your Family Total							
Quantities rounded to nearest 5 lb., except where noted ↘			Family Multiplier	Food Storage Requirements			
Storage Item	Shelf Life in months	Adult Quantity	Family Factor	Family Total	On Hand	Needs	Quick-Chart Worksheets (✓)
potatoes & yams (fresh equivalent)—200 lb. minimum assorted from this listing							
potatoes, all dried	36-48	25	0	0	0	0	
potatoes, all, fresh—see Chapter 3	1-6	150	7.0	1050	150	900	✓

* Recommended storage quantities are indexed to the yearly requirements for the average adult male.

The *Family Factor Formula* is based on a collection of federal data (*U.S. Department of Agriculture*, *U.S. Required Daily Allowance* (**USRDA**—now the **USDRI**), and other U.S. Government publications) which establish average yearly consumption levels of most foods for the average adult male.

Temper this government information with the knowledge and many years of accumulated experience through testing and learning of food storage consultants, food, and dietary experts, medical doctors, even holistic medical practitioners—and the result is this simplified formula.

Perhaps the most beneficial result of working through these charts will be that you will take the time to consider carefully the details of requirements to provision your family. Then, the budgeting and prioritizing of your future purchases—indeed an investment in your family—will make more sense and have more parameters for positive action in preparing your family.

Step-by-Step Planning

1. Review each **Pantry List** for the recommended storage items; checkmark items needed in your personal pantry. Remember, not every item recommended may be suitable for your family.
2. Transfer the check marked items to the **Shopping Lists. (**The *essential* items are already listed for you.)
3. On the **Shopping List** calculate the **Family Total** (amount needed for one year) by multiplying the **Adult Quantity** by your **Family Factor**. Remember to adjust your "**Family Factor**" to meet your needs.
4. Inventory your current supplies. Fill in amounts in the **On Hand** category of the **Shopping Lists.**
5. On the **Shopping List**, subtract **On Hand** from **Family Total** to determine **Needs**.
6. List needed items on the **Budget Sheets** by priority of need.
7. Identify suppliers and cost of each item on **Budget Sheets**.
8. Total the costs of all items on the **Budget Sheets**.
9. Use this information to plan your shopping.

Quick-Guide 8–1

Storage Item ①	Shelf Life (Months) ②	Adult Quantity ③	Family Factor ④	Family Total ⑤	On Hand ⑥	Needs ⑦	Quick-Plan Worksheets (✓) ⑧
Quantities rounded to nearest 5 lb., except where noted ↘			**In-Home Storage Requirements**				
In-Home Storage Categories							
Water—emergency supplies & treatment (14 gal.)		14 gal.	see Chapter 10 for details ⑨				Quick-List 8–1⑩
Wheat, other whole grains and flours; legumes		700 lb.	see Chapters 14–19 for details				Quick-List 8–2
Powdered milk, dairy products, & eggs		200 lb.	see Chapter 11 for details				Quick-List 8–3
Sweeteners—honey, sugar, & syrup		100 lb.	see Chapter 13 for details				Quick-List 8–4
Cooking catalysts		75 lb.					Quick-List 8–5
Sprouting seeds & supplies		10 lb.	see Chapter 12 for details				Quick-List 8–6
Medical care, medications, & first aid kits		per need					Quick-List 8–7
Basic supplementation		per need	see Chapter 23 for details				Quick-List 8–8
Fuels, energy, & camping gear		per need	see Chapter 22 for details				Quick-List 8–9
Personal, family, infant, & pet care essentials		per need					Quick-List 8–10
Canned & dried fruits, vegetables & soups		2,750 serv.	see Chapter 20 for details				Quick-List 8–11
Kitchen staples—condiments & seasonings		per need					Quick-List 8–12
Meats & seafood		700 serv.	see Chapter 21 for details				Quick-List 8–13
Domestic maintenance & preparedness		per need					Quick-List 8–14
Pleasure foods—snacks, beverages, sweets & treats		2,000 serv.					Quick-List 8–15

Notes for Quick-Guide 8–1

This is an overview sheet for the **In-Home Storage Categories**. **Quick-Lists** (*Pantry Lists*) and **Quick-Shop Charts** (*Shopping Lists*) follow which suggest quantities for many items to help you get started with a *Basics in-home convenience store* plan.

Use the key information noted on the **Quick-Guide** marked with a numbered indicator and explained below to understand the corresponding details on the other **Quick-Charts**.

    ① **Essential and supplemental storage items** for your in-home storage program are listed in this column.
    ② **Shelf Life** or maximum period of time an item is edible is detailed in this column.
    ③ **Adult Quantity** suggested is the recommended storage amount for one year for the average adult male.
    ④ Insert your **Family Factor** previously computed from the *Family Factor Formula*.
    ⑤ Multiply the **Adult Quantity** amount by the **Family Factor** to derive the **Family Total** amount needed for each item.

⑥ Determine how much of this item you have **On Hand** and enter in this column.

⑦ Deduct **On Hand** amount from **Family Total** amount to determine **Needs** (needed amount.)

⑧ Transfer needed items to the **Quick-Plan Worksheet.**

⑨ Refers to chapters in **Making the Best of Basics** – *Family Preparedness Handbook* regarding this category.

⑩ Refer to this **Quick-List** for recommended storage items in this category.

Quick-List 8–1

	Water—Emergency Supplies & Treatment Pantry List						
	see Chapter10 for additional information						
	Multiply Adult Quantity by your Family Factor to determine your Family Total						
✓	**Storage Item**	**Shelf Life (Months)**	**Adult Quantity**	✓	**Storage Item**	**Shelf Life (Months)**	**Adult Quantity**
	water				**containers**		
	water, potable	*6–12*	14 gal.[1]		5-gal. collapsible canvas	*indefinite*	
	water, 4 & 6 oz., aseptic pkg	*indefinite*	2 gal.		6-gal. Mylar bag w / box	*indefinite*	
					15-gal. container	*indefinite*	
					25+ gal. canvas bag	*indefinite*	
					cups, drinking, 6-oz.	*indefinite*	
					canteen / cup	*indefinite*	
	commercial bottled water				50-gal. drum/barrel	*indefinite*	
	1-gal. bottle	*6–12*					
	2$\frac{1}{2}$-gal. bottle	*6–12*					
	5-gal. bottle	*6–12*					
	tools				**water treatment equipment & supplies**		
	barrel pump	*indefinite*			portable treatment unit	*indefinite*	1 unit
	barrel spigot	*indefinite*			bleach, 5.25% sodium hypochlorite	*6*	1 gal.
	bung wrench	*indefinite*			tablets, water treatment	*36–60*	1 pkg.
					iodine tincture, 2%	*indefinite*	2 oz.
					pot with lid (*for boiling water*)	*indefinite*	
	testing kits						
	testing kit, water quality	*indefinite*					

A person may be able to live on water for many days. A water treatment system can assure a continued supply of drinking & cooking water.

Note: From the very beginning, the intent of this *Family Preparedness Handbook* has been to guide each family to examine its own needs, and then act responsibly to provide themselves with the appropriate amount of supplies they have determined. If a family chooses to you have too little, it's their decision. If a family chooses to over-stock their in-home convenience, they'll have the opportunity to not only bless their own family, but perhaps some of their friends, and even their community.

With abundance, others can be given help and support to someone in need. This series of charts will facilitate the organization and accomplishment of your family preparedness plan. Modify anything anyone says anytime to get the job done to your satisfaction. It's your choice, your plan, your life!

Nobody knows it all now, nobody has it all now, and nobody will ever have it all—not now, not ever!

---

[1] This meets the **FEMA** emergency guideline for one gallon per person per day for two-week *subsistence-level* storage.
   Maintenance-level storage guidelines are two gallons per person per day.
   However, you should always store as much water as feasible.
   See **Water, Chapter 10** for water treatment and storage details.

Quick-List 8–2

Wheat, Other Whole Grains, Flours & Beans Pantry List
select 700 lb. minimum from this category
see Chapters 14-19 for additional information

Multiply Adult Quantity by your Family Factor to determine your Family Total

✓	Storage Item	Shelf Life (Months)	Adult Quantity	✓	Storage Item	Shelf Life (Months)	Adult Quantity
wheat—select 350 lb. assorted from this list				**other whole grains—select 100 lb. minimum**			
	wheat, whole grain (berries)	*indefinite*	350		barley	*60*	
	Dark Hard Winter Wheat	*indefinite*			**corn**	*60*	**10**
	Dark Turkey Red Wheat	*indefinite*			oats	*60*	
	Golden 86 Hard White Spring	*indefinite*			popcorn, whole kernels	*12–24*	20
	Montana White Wheat	*indefinite*			Quinoa	*60*	
	Spring Wheat	*indefinite*			rye	*60*	
	wheat, mill prepack	*indefinite*			triticale	*60*	
flours, fresh-ground or commercial—select 35 lb. minimum assorted from this list							
	barley	*1–2*			rice	*1–2*	
	beans (from dried beans)	*3–6*			rye	*1–2*	
	buckwheat	*1–2*			wheat / bran	*1*	
	cornmeal / flours	*60*	**10**		wheat / gluten flour	*6–12*	
rice, whole grain—select 45 lb. minimum assorted from this list							
	rice, white, enriched	*24–48*	10		**rice, wild**	*24–36*	**5**
	rice, white pre-cooked	*36*	25		brown	*1–3*	
pastas (fresh equivalent)—select 35 lb. minimum assorted from this list							
	lasagna	*18–24*			noodles, egg	*6–9*	
	macaroni	*18–24*			spaghetti	*18–24*	

Quick-List 8–2 (continued)

Wheat, Other Whole Grains, Flours & Beans Pantry List

Multiply Adult Quantity by your Family Factor to determine your Family Total

✓	Storage Item	Shelf Life (Months)	Adult Quantity	✓	Storage Item	Shelf Life (Months)	Adult Quantity
	cereals, whole grain—select 50 lb. minimum assorted from this list						
	barley, pearled	12			kernel, whole grains	1–3	
	buckwheat (kasha)	6–12			oats, groats	1–3	
	granola (*see Chapter 7*)	1–3			oats, rolled (oatmeal)	12	
	hominy & hominy grits	12			Quinoa	1–3	
	cereals, processed & prepared—select 25 lb. minimum assorted from these lists						
	ready-to-eat, dry				**ready-to-heat, pre-cooked**		
	corn	12			corn / hominy / posole	12	
	rice	12			oatmeal	12	
	wheat, shredded	12			wheat / rice, creamed		
	legumes, variety of dried beans & peas—select 75 lb. minimum assorted from this list						
	bottled & canned, all	24–36			navy	varies	
	dried, all	60+			peas, black-eyed	varies	
	Anasazi	varies			peas, green or split	varies	
	kidney	varies			pinto	varies	
	lentils	varies			soybeans	varies	
	lima, large & small	varies					
	textured vegetable protein (TVP)—select 10 lb. minimum from this list						
	TVP, unflavored	24–36	5		flavorings—ham / beef / chicken / vegetable.	24–36	1
	equipment & supplies needed for storage—see Chapter 5 for details						
	grain mill / grinder	*indefinite*	1 / family		**mixer / bread making**	*indefinite*	1 / family
	dry ice	*hours!*	depends		containers / tight-fitting lids	*indefinite*	
	diatomaceous earth	*indefinite*	depends		liners, plastic, food-grade	*indefinite*	

Quick-List 8–3

Powdered Milk, Dairy Products & Eggs Pantry List
select 200 lb. minimum assorted from this category
see Chapter 11 for additional information about powdered milk & Chapter 9 for refrigerated item listing details

Multiply Adult Quantity by your Family Factor to determine your Family Total

✓	Storage Item	Shelf Life (Months)	Adult Quantity	✓	Storage Item	Shelf Life (Months)	Adult Quantity
	dairy products, dried & powdered—150 lb. minimum assorted from this list						
	milk, non-instant powdered	*24–48*	100		buttermilk powder	*24–36*	
	butter, dehydrated	*60–96*	20		milk, aseptic packaging	*pkg. date*	
	cheese, dehydrated	*60–96*	25		non-dairy creamers	*24–36*	
	eggs, powdered—25 dz. minimum (fresh equiv.)				**milk, canned—select 24 cans from this list**		
	eggs, dehydr. / freeze-dried	*60–96*	25 dz.		**evaporated milk**	*24–36*	6 cans
	cheese-making items				condensed, sweetened	*24–35*	12 cans
	cheese press (see **Ch. 11**)	*indefinite*			**yogurt-making items**		
	cooking thermometer	*indefinite*			yogurt starter / wet type	*1–2 wk.*	
	cheese cloth, fine mesh	*indefinite*			cheese bag / cheese cloth	*indefinite*	
	Rennet / Junket tablets	*indefinite*			yogurt maker (see **Ch. 11**)	*indefinite*	

Quick-List 8–4

Sweeteners—Honey, Sugar & Syrup Pantry List
select 100 lb. minimum assorted from this category
see Chapter 13 for additional information

Multiply Adult Quantity by your Family Factor to determine your Family Total

✓	Storage Item	Shelf Life (Months)	Adult Quantity	✓	Storage Item	Shelf Life (Months)	Adult Quantity
	honey—select 70 lb. minimum from this listing				**sugar—select 15 lb. minimum from this listing**		
	honey, unfiltered	*indefinite*	65		sugar, white	*indefinite*	10
	comb, pure & unprocessed	*indefinite*			brown	*indefinite*	
	creamed	*48–60*			confectioners	*indefinite*	
	diluted	*36–48*			maple sugar	*48–60*	
	syrup / equivalents—as needed				substitutes, non-sugar	*indefinite*	
	corn syrup	*indefinite*			**equipment for storage**		
	maple syrup	*indefinite*			containers / tight-fitting lids	*indefinite*	
	molasses	*18–24*			plastic bags, food-grade	*indefinite*	

Quick-List 8–5

Cooking Catalysts—Salt, Oils & Leaveners Pantry List
select 75 lb. minimum assorted from this category

Multiply Adult Quantity by your Family Factor to determine your Family Total

✓	Storage Item	Shelf Life (Months)	Adult Quantity	✓	Storage Item	Shelf Life (Months)	Adult Quantity
	salt—select 5 lb. minimum from this list						
	iodized salt	*indefinite*	5		salt, ice cream	*indefinite*	per need
	salt, pickling	*indefinite*	per need		seasoning, herbs, no-salt	*12–18*	
	leaveners, dry & moist—select 1 lb. minimum from this list				**oils, fats & shortening—15 gal. (60 lb.) minimum assorted from this list**		
	yeast, cake, moist	*pkg. date*	4 oz.		vegetable oil, liquid	*12–24*	10 gal.
	yeast, active dry powdered	*12–24*	12 oz.		lard, commercial rendering	*3–6*	
	sourdough starter	*1–3*			olive, extra virgin	*12–24*	
	powder, baking	*6–9*			sesame	*2–4*	
	soda, baking	*18–24*			shortening, vegetable, all	*12*	

Quick-List 8–6

Sprouting—Seeds & Supplies Pantry List
select 10 lb. minimum assorted from this category
see Chapter 12 for additional information

Multiply Adult Quantity by your Family Factor to determine your Family Total

✓	Storage Item	Shelf Life (Months)	Adult Quantity	✓	Storage Item	Shelf Life (Months)	Adult Quantity
	select 10 lb. minimum assorted beans, grains & seeds						
	for best results, use only untreated or organic beans, grains & seeds						
	alfalfa	*24–36*	1		soybean	*24–36*	
	barley, unhulled	*24–36*			vegetables—your selection	*24–36*	
	mung	*24–36*			wheat	*24–36*	
	peas—your preference	*24–36*					
	equipment for sprouting						
	quart jar w / screw ring	*indefinite*			cheese cloth	*indefinite*	
	sealing ring, canning	*indefinite*			rubber band	*indefinite*	
	colander or strainer	*indefinite*			nylon netting	*indefinite*	

Quick-List 8–7

Medical Care—Medications & First Aid Kits Pantry List

Multiply Adult Quantity by your Family Factor to determine your Family Total

✓	Storage Item	Shelf Life (Months)	Adult Quantity	✓	Storage Item	Shelf Life (Months)	Adult Quantity
	personal life-preserving medications[2]						
	cardiovascular conditions medication				**nervous conditions medications**—for those being treated for emotional, psychological or psychiatric disorders & those whose "normal" functioning is dependent upon medication		
	nitroglycerin—all forms	*pkg. date*			anti-anxiety medications	*pkg. date*	
	sub-lingual	*pkg. date*			anti-depressants	*pkg. date*	
	patches	*pkg. date*			tranquilizers	*pkg. date*	
	digitalis preparations	*pkg. date*			**respiratory and allergic conditions**		
	blood thinners	*pkg. date*			allergy medications	*pkg. date*	
	diuretics	*pkg. date*			asthma "puffers"	*pkg. date*	
	heart / blood pressure pre-scriptions	*pkg. date*			bite & sting medications for severely allergic persons	*pkg. date*	
	diabetic conditions medication				cortisone	*pkg. date*	
	insulin—all types used	*pkg. date*			oral med. / "breathing" relief	*pkg. date*	
	injectables	*pkg. date*			**seizure conditions medications**		
	oral dosages	*pkg. date*			epileptic seizure preventives	*pkg. date*	
	syringes / needles	*pkg. date*			seizure medication	*pkg. date*	
	"stomach" and intestinal medications						
	colitis / irritable bowel medications	*pkg. date*			ulcer medications	*pkg. date*	
	gastritis medications	*pkg. date*					
	Other critical conditions medication(s)						
	Prescription medications for preventive care ask your physician for a prescription & refills if you are allergic to **Keflex**, substitute "**Zithromax**", a new & often more costly medication						
	twenty (20) tabs or caps 500 mg **Cephalexin** ("**Keflex**")	*pkg. date*			six (6) caps 250 mg **Azithromycin** ("**Zithromax**")	*pkg. date*	
	Recommended non-prescription health maintenance medications & supplies the following items are useful and helpful in treatment of minor illnesses, aches, pains, and general personal well-being:						
	acetaminophen (reduce fever)	12–24			bicarbonate of soda	12–24	
	antacid medication (for upset stomach)	12–24			syrup of Ipecac (to induce vomiting)	12–24	
	anti-diarrhea medication	12–24			hydrogen peroxide	6–12	
	aspirin (for headaches)	12–24			eye drops	9–12	
	hay fever / cold / sinus tablets	12–24			laxative	*indefinite*	
	ibuprofen (to reduce pain)	12–24			mineral oil	*indefinite*	
	alcohol / rubbing	*indefinite*			moleskin (for foot blisters)	*indefinite*	

---

[2] This information courtesy of Carlin G. Bartschi, MD, who invested a great deal of his limited spare time to prepare, review, and edit the medical material. He also consulted on several other related issues addressed in this edition, especially the water chapter and charts. Dr. Bartschi has worked more than 18 years in the medical profession beginning with his general practice, then specialized in accident and emergency medical & trauma treatment. He practiced family medicine in Yuma, AZ, for 14 years. For many years he devoted his medical expertise exclusively to Emergency Medicine in emergency rooms in 4 southeast Texas hospitals, even while he continued to practice as an emergency room specialist in a suburban Phoenix hospital. Carlin was born and raised in Montpelier ID, completed his undergraduate studies at Utah State University, in Logan UT. He attended medical school at the Universidad Autonoma de Guadalajara (Mexico), and then completed post-graduate training in Saskatoon, Saskatchewan (Canada). Carlin and his wife, Joyce, are parents of 10 children and several grandchildren. He and his family strive to manage a lifestyle of preparedness, both philosophically, and in real-life.

Quick-List 8–7 (continued)

Medical Care—Medications & First Aid Kits Pantry List (continued)

✓	Storage Item	Shelf Life (Months)	Adult Quantity	✓	Storage Item	Shelf Life (Months)	Adult Quantity
	recommended non-prescription health maintenance medications & supplies (continued)						
	anti-itch medication	indefinite			saline solution	indefinite	
	emergency medical care—first aid kits						
	*If you choose to develop your own first aid kit, see itemized listing below*						
	family first aid kit / pre-pack	indefinite	1		Individual 1st aid kit / pre-pak	indefinite	1
	first aid kit itemized listing						
	*If you'd prefer to develop your own first aid kit, here are the essentials. Add any other items specific to your needs.*						
	absorbent cotton / balls	indefinite			manual, first aid	indefinite	
	applicator sticks, cotton-tip	indefinite			medicine dropper	indefinite	
	bandage, finger-tip	indefinite			oatmeal (mixture stops itching)	indefinite	
	bandage, knuckle	indefinite			ointment, anti-bacterial	12	
	bandage, stretch	indefinite			pad, adhesive, sterile strips	indefinite	
	bandage, triangular	indefinite			pharyngeal airway	indefinite	
	bedpan	indefinite			safety pins / assorted sizes	indefinite	
	blades, single-edge razor	indefinite			shaving supplies	indefinite	
	clippers, fingernail / toenail	indefinite			snake-bite kit	indefinite	
	closure, butterfly	indefinite			soap, surgical / cleansing	indefinite	
	cold pack / ice pack	indefinite			splinting material	indefinite	
	contact lens cleaner	indefinite			sunscreen / sun lotion	indefinite	
	cornstarch	indefinite			surgical scissors	indefinite	
	dental emergency kit	indefinite			suture kit, emergency surgery	indefinite	
	douche equipment	indefinite			syringe / needles / injection	indefinite	
	ear drops	indefinite			syringe, irrigation	indefinite	
	eye pads	indefinite			tape, adhesive, medical, assorted 1" / 2" / 3"	indefinite	
	gauze pads, assorted large sizes 18" / 24" / 72"	Indefinite			gauze, rolls, assorted sizes 1" / 2" / 3"	indefinite	
	gauze pads, asstd. 2" / 3" / 4"	indefinite			thermometer	indefinite	
	gloves, rubber / surgical	indefinite			tongue blades / wood	indefinite	
	hand lotion	indefinite			tourniquet	indefinite	
	knife, pocket / multi-blade	indefinite			tweezers	indefinite	
	knife, surgical / blades	indefinite			vinegar	indefinite	
	lubricant, tube, lubricating jelly	indefinite			water, sterile	12	

Quick-List 8–8

Basic Supplementation[3] for Food Storage Pantry List
select items of choice from this category
see Chapter 23 for additional information

Multiply Adult Quantity by your Family Factor to determine your Family Total

✓	Storage Item	Shelf Life (Months)	Adult Quantity	✓	Storage Item	Shelf Life (Months)	Adult Quantity
	herbs & whole food supplements				**live whole food concentrates**		
	aloe vera	6–9					
	apple cider vinegar	36–48					
	bee supplements	12–24			**minerals**		
	beet root powder	pkg. date					
	bladderwrack	pkg. date			boron	12–24	
	blue-green algae	12–24			chromium picolinate	18–24	
	fo-ti	pkg. date			copper	24–36	
	ginger	pkg. date			selenium	pkg. date	
	ginkgo biloba	pkg. date			zinc	24–36	
	Hawthorne berries	pkg. date			**vitamins**		
	saw palmetto	pkg. date			beta carotene	12–24	
	white willow	pkg. date			bioflavonoids	12–24	
					vitamin C	12–24	
					vitamin E	12–24	

Quick-List 8–9

Fuels, Energy & Camping Gear Pantry List
see Chapter 22 for additional information

Multiply Adult Quantity by your Family Factor to determine your Family Total

✓	Storage Item	Shelf Life (Months)	Adult Quantity	✓	Storage Item	Shelf Life (Months)	Adult Quantity
	light & heat equipment—as needed				**family camping equipment & supplies—per need**		
	flashlight / "D" type, 2- or 3-battery	indefinite			camp cooking set	indefinite	
	"D" batteries	12–24			utensils, camp / kitchen	indefinite	
	lamp, kerosene	indefinite			lantern, two-mantle	indefinite	
	kerosene (gal.)	6–12			lantern fuel (gal.)	12	
	perfumed fuel (qt.)	24–36			mantles, replacement set	indefinite	
	candles, tallow or wax	indefinite			fire starter / magnesium kit	indefinite	
	emergency type	indefinite			matches (waterproof)	indefinite	
	camp stove, 2-burner	indefinite			charcoal cooking unit	indefinite	
	stove fuel (gal.)	12			charcoal / briquettes (lb.)	24–36	
	stove accessories	indefinite			starter (qt.)	indefinite	

[3] Thanks to Zoltan P. Rona, MD, MS, for this information on vitamins, minerals, and herbal supplements in the food storage program. Dr. Rona is a graduate of McGill University Medical School and has a master's degree in biochemistry and clinical nutrition from the University of Bridgeport in Connecticut. He is the author of the Canadian bestseller *The Joy of Health, A Doctor's Guide to Nutrition and Alternative Medicine* and is a past president of the Canadian Holistic Medical Association. He is currently in private medical practice in Toronto and had regular columns in *Alive Magazine*, *Health Naturally*, and *The Toronto Star*. Dr. Rona is also known for his many public lectures and media appearances. He also authored *Return to the Joy of Health, A Doctor's Guide to Nutrition and Herbal Medicine*, published by Alive Books, Vancouver, BC, Canada.

Quick-List 8–9 (continued)

Fuels, Energy & Camping Gear Pantry List
Multiply Adult Quantity by your Family Factor to determine your Family Total

✓	Storage Item	Shelf Life (Months)	Adult Quantity	✓	Storage Item	Shelf Life (Months)	Adult Quantity
light & heat equipment (continued)				**family camping equipment & supplies** (continued)			
	portable heater	*indefinite*			stick matches (box)	*indefinite*	
	heater fuel	25			shovel / multi-purpose	*indefinite*	
	canned fuel (lb.)	12–24					
personal camping equipment—per preferences				**overnight gear—family preferences**			
	air mattress	*indefinite*			bag, sleeping	*indefinite*	
	ax	*indefinite*			blanket(s)	*indefinite*	1/ person
	camp shovel / multi-purpose	*indefinite*			cloth, ground, waterproof	*indefinite*	1/ person
	poncho	*indefinite*			pad, sleep, cushioning	*indefinite*	1/ person
	cot	*indefinite*			pillow	*indefinite*	1/ person
	rake	*indefinite*			tent	*indefinite*	per need
	hatchet	*indefinite*					
	ice chest, insulated, 1-gal.	*indefinite*					
	5-gal size	*indefinite*					
	portable heater / fuel	12-24					
				family heat items			
					coal (ton) / stove	36–60	
					firewood (cord)	*indefinite*	
					wood saw, 1-man	*indefinite*	
					wood saw, 2-man	*indefinite*	
safety items					hatchet / ax	*indefinite*	
	carbon monoxide / gas alarm	*indefinite*			wedge	*indefinite*	
	fire / smoke detectors	*indefinite*			sledge hammer	*indefinite*	
hygiene & sanitation—as needed							
	potty, portable	*indefinite*			disposable plastic bags 1 / 3 / 5-6 / 20 / 30-gal.	*indefinite*	
	supplies, sanitary	*indefinite*			pails or buckets	*indefinite*	
	disinfectant aerosols	*indefinite*			chemicals for toilet	*indefinite*	
communications equipment—as needed							
	AM / FM radio	*indefinite*			citizens band radio	*indefinite*	
	batteries	12			batteries	12	
	cell phone(s)						

Quick-List 8–10

Personal, Family, Infant & Pet Care Essentials Pantry List

Multiply Adult Quantity by your Family Factor to determine your Family Total

✓	Storage Item	Shelf Life (Months)	Adult Quantity	✓	Storage Item	Shelf Life (Months)	Adult Quantity
personal essentials				**infant & child care**—*special needs of infants & children*			
	toiletry / travel kit	*indefinite*	personal		formula	*12–18*	per need
	toilet paper	*indefinite*	60 rolls		juices, strained	*12–14*	per need
	feminine needs / sanitary napkins	*indefinite*	per need		foods, strained	*6–12*	per need
family essentials				**supplies**			
	soap, bath	*indefinite*			diapers, disposable	*indefinite*	per need
	soap, hand / face	*indefinite*			clothing	*varies*	per need
	sunscreen	*12–18*			medications	*indicated*	per need
	toothbrush	*indefinite*			sleepers	*varies*	
	toothpaste	*12–24*			cornstarch	*indefinite*	
	shampoo	*indefinite*			talcum powder	*indefinite*	
household essentials					toys	*indefinite*	
	soap, laundry	*indefinite*			games	*varies*	
	cleanser, scouring	*indefinite*			bedding, special sizes	*indefinite*	
	soap, cleaning, liquid	*indefinite*			waterproof sheets	*indefinite*	
	towels, bath	*indefinite*			blankets	*indefinite*	
	wash cloths				**infant safety items**			
	kitchen towels				restraints	*indefinite*	
	dish cloth				bicycle	*indefinite*	
pet care					automotive	*indefinite*	
	food	*6–12*			carrier, back frame	*indefinite*	
	equipment, handling	*indefinite*		**other essentials**			
	immunization / medications	*indicated*					
	maintenance equipment	*per vet*					
	treats	*varies*					

Quick-List 8–11

Fresh, Canned, & Dried Fruits, Vegetables & Soups Pantry List
2,750 assorted servings (fresh equivalent) minimum from this category
see Chapter 20 for additional information about drying fruits & vegetables

Multiply Adult Quantity by your Family Factor to determine your Family Total

✓	Storage Item	Shelf Life (Months)	Adult Quantity	✓	Storage Item	Shelf Life (Months)	Adult Quantity
fruits—1250 servings minimum assorted				**vegetables—1000 servings minimum assorted**			
canned, all, except citrus	*12–18*			beans, green—cut / whole	24–36	
	citrus products	*6–12*			beans, pinto / kidney	24–36	
bottled, all, except citrus	*18*			beans, red / yellow	24–36	
	citrus products	*18*			beets, diced / sliced	12–24	
	jam, jelly & preserves	*12–18*			carrots, diced / sliced	24–36	
	fruit cocktail	*12–18*			corn, cut / creamed	24–36	
potatoes & yams (fresh equivalent)—200 lb. minimum assorted from this list (see Chapter 9)				greens, all	24–36	
	potatoes, all dried	*36–48*	25		peas, all	24–36	

Quick-List 8–11 (continued)

Canned & Dried Fruits, Vegetables, & Soups Pantry List
Multiply Adult Quantity by your Family Factor to determine your Family Total

✓	Storage Item	Shelf Life (Months)	Adult Quantity	✓	Storage Item	Shelf Life (Months)	Adult Quantity
	potatoes & yams (continued)				**vegetables** (continued)		
	potatoes, all, fresh	**3–6**	**100**		tomato, paste / stewed / sauce	24–36	
	potatoes, canned, all types	24–36			vegetables, all mixed	24–36	
	soups—250 servings minimum assorted selected from this list or your preference						
	bean & bacon	24–36			mushroom		
	beans & chili	24–36			onion	24–36	
	cheese	24–36			potato	24–36	
	chicken—cream / noodle / rice / vegetable	24–36			vegetable	24–36	
	other selections—100 servings from this list or your preference						
	macaroni & cheese	24–36			spaghetti & tomato sauce	12–24	

Quick-List 8–12

Kitchen Staples—Condiments & Seasonings Pantry List
select assortment as needed from this category to suit your taste
Multiply Adult Quantity by your Family Factor to determine your Family Total

✓	Storage Item	Shelf Life (Months)	Adult Quantity	✓	Storage Item	Shelf Life (Months)	Adult Quantity
	mixed condiments—as preferred				**nuts & nut butters—select 50 lb. minimum from this list**		
	relish, sweet / dill	indefinite			**nut butters**		
	pickles, cut or whole	indefinite			peanut butter	**12–24**	**15**
	olives, canned, all	12–24			almond butter	12–24	
	mayonnaise	9–12			pecan butter	2–3	
	salad dressing	9–12			**nuts, raw**		
	salsa	12–24			shelled	6–9	
	salad dressings, bottled, all—as preferred				unshelled	12–24	
	bleu cheese	9–12			**nuts, roasted**		
	French	9–12			shelled, bulk, all	3–6	
	Italian	9–12			shelled, canned, all	12–24	
	ranch	9–12			unshelled, bulk, all	6–12	
	other	9–12			unshelled, canned, all	12–24	
	bouillon cubes, granules & liquid—select 1 lb.				**seeds, raw**		
	beef / chicken / ham	12–24			pumpkin	1–3	
	onion / vegetable	12–24			sunflower	1–3	
	chocolate—select 5 lb. from this list				sesame butter	12–15	
	baking, unsweetened	12–24			walnuts	2–3	
	chips, baking	18–24					
	liquid	12			**seeds, roasted**		
	syrup	12–18			pumpkin	1–3	
					sunflower	1–3	
	thickeners, liquid & powder—select 5 lb.				**crackers, table—select 6 lb. from this list**		
	arrowroot	12–24			saltines / lite salt	6–12	
	cornstarch	12–24			seafood	6–12	
	gelatin, dry	12–18			stone ground	8–12	

Quick-List 8–12 (continued)

Kitchen Staples—Condiments & Seasonings Pantry List
Multiply Adult Quantity by your Family Factor to determine your Family Total

✓	Storage Item	Shelf Life (Months)	Adult Quantity	✓	Storage Item	Shelf Life (Months)	Adult Quantity
	gravy mixes—as preferred				**crackers, specialty**		
	liquid	*12–24*			graham	*12–24*	
	powder	*24-48*					
	flavored	*24-48*			**other items—as preferred**		
					tapioca	*24–36*	
	liquid condiments—as preferred						
	catsup	*24–36*			vinegar, apple cider	*indefinite*	
	soy sauce	*indefinite*			Worcestershire sauce	*indefinite*	
	steak sauce	*12-24*					
	**seasonings & spices, whole & ground—select 2 lb. minimum from this listing**						
	herbs & spices				**seasonings, mixed**		
	ground, all	*6–9*			Italian	*12–18*	
	whole, all	*12–15*			Mexican	*12–18*	
	celery, salt	*depends*			*bouquet garni*	*6–12*	
	dill	*depends*			*herbes fines*	*6–12*	
	garlic, flakes or powder	*depends*					
	mustard	*depends*			**flavorings & extracts**		
	onion, flakes or powder	*depends*			almond	*12–24*	
	parsley, flakes or powder	*depends*			banana	*12–24*	
	pepper, black, ground	*indefinite*	**8 oz.**		lemon	*12–24*	
	pepper, cayenne	*depends*			maple	*12–24*	
	peppers, bell—all	*depends*			orange	*12–24*	
	pepper, jalapeño	*depends*			vanilla	*12–24*	
	savory	*depends*					
	sesame seed	*depends*					

Quick-List 8–13

Meats & Seafood Pantry List
select 700 minimum servings assorted (fresh equivalent) from this category
see Chapter 9 for additional information about refrigerator & freezer storage
Multiply Adult Quantity by your Family Factor to determine your Family Total

✓	Storage Item	Shelf Life (Months)	Adult Quantity	✓	Storage Item	Shelf Life (Months)	Adult Quantity
	beef—120 servings minimum from list				**luncheon meats—250 servings min. from list**		
	chipped, dried	*12–24*			spreads, sandwich	*12–24*	
	corned, canned	*12–24*			deviled meats	*12–24*	
	jerky, dried	*6–9*			sausage, Vienna	*12–24*	
	imitation, flavored	*1–3*			pepperoni	*12–24*	
	ground meat	**12–24**	**75**		**seafood—100 servings minimum from this list**		
	poultry—select 75 servings minimum from list				clams, all	*12–24*	
	chicken	*12–24*			crab, chopped / imitation	*12–24*	
	turkey	*12–24*			fish—halibut / mackerel / tuna	*12–24*	
	pork—select 50 servings minimum from list				fish—salmon / sardines	*24–36*	
	bacon	*12–24*			shrimp	*12–24*	
	sausage	*12–24*					
	other cuts	*12–24*					

Quick-List 8–14

Domestic Maintenance & Preparedness Pantry List

Multiply Adult Quantity by your Family Factor to determine your Family Total

✓	Storage Item	Shelf Life (Months)	Adult Quantity	✓	Storage Item	Shelf Life (Months)	Adult Quantity
	garden seeds / plants for growing season				**tools**		
	seeds, garden	*12–24*	**per need**		automotive	*indefinite*	
	supplies, chemicals & mulch	*12–24*	**per need**		general	*indefinite*	
	tools, gardening	*indefinite*			household	*indefinite*	
					yard	*indefinite*	
	kitchen equipment						
	cooking utensils	*indefinite*	**per need**		**food preparation equipment / supplies**		
	meat grinder, hand-operated	*indefinite*			bottling	*indefinite*	
					canning	*indefinite*	
					drying / dehydrating	*indefinite*	
					freezing	*indefinite*	
	storage containers—*use only food-grade plastics approved by USDA & FDA*				pickling	*indefinite*	
	1-gal. pail / lid	*indefinite*					
	5-gal., plastic / lid	*indefinite*			smoking / curing	*indefinite*	
	55-gal. drum / metal / lid / locking ring	*indefinite*					
	#10 can, sealed	*indefinite*					
	cleaning equipment & supplies—*expand your current inventory of supplies by copybuying purchases*				**clothing**—*a year's supply of clothing and supplies should be in your storage program*		
	rubber gloves	*indefinite*			clothing, seasonal	*indefinite*	
					shoes, boots	*indefinite*	
	sewing—*sewing equipment & items should be stored*						
	sewing supplies	*indefinite*			sewing equipment	*indefinite*	
	bedding—*a year's supply of bedding should be maintained*						
	sheets	*indefinite*			comforters	*indefinite*	
	blankets	*indefinite*			pillowcases	*indefinite*	
	quilts	*indefinite*			pillows	*indefinite*	
					inflatable beds	*indefinite*	
	additional gardening items						
	seeds, slips & plants catalogs				**seed or plant requirements for next growing season**		
	fruit, plant catalog				fruit, plants		
	fruit, tree catalog				fruit, trees		
	fruit, vine catalog				fruit, vines		
	vegetable catalog				vegetable plants, nursery		
	soil amendments						
	composted material / mulch				fertilizer, organic / chemical		
	gardening tools & equipment						
	hoe				rake		
	mattock				shovel		
	poles, 6' for beans & tomatoes				spade		
	72-hour emergency kits				**other emergency provisions**		
	family	*12*	**1 kit**		emergency clothing kit	*seasonal*	**as needed**
	individual	*12*	**1 kit**		MREs	*36–48*	selection

Quick-List 8–15

Pleasure Foods—Beverages, Snacks, Sweets & Treats Pantry List
2,000 servings minimum assorted from this category
Multiply Adult Quantity by your Family Factor to determine your Family Total

✓	Storage Item	Shelf Life (Months)	Adult Quantity	✓	Storage Item	Shelf Life (Months)	Adult Quantity
	**beverages—750 servings minimum assorted from this category**						
	juice, fruits				**chocolate & cocoa**		
	aseptic cartons, all	pkg. date			chocolate, regular	18–24	
	canned & bottled, all	12–24			instant mix	12–18	
	apple	12–24			candy, filled	3–6	
	prune	12–24			milk chocolate	6–9	
	grape	12–24			syrup	12–18	
	grapefruit	12			cocoa, regular	18–24	
	orange	12					
	cranberry & mixtures	12–24					
	pineapple	12			**coffee**		
	apricot nectar	12			canned, ground or instant	12–15	
					freeze-dried	6–9	
					chicory	12–18	
	non-caffeine hot drinks				**tea**		
	Pero	12–24			regular		
	Postum	12–24			instant	6–12	
	tea, herbal	9–12			leaves, loose & bagged	6–12	
					herbal, black	12–24	
	canned beverages						
	soft drinks	6–12			**other beverages**		
	bottled sodas	6–12			mixes, powdered	36–48	
	water, carbonated	12–24			liquid concentrates	24–36	
					root beer concentrate / bottle	48–60	
	**snacks: cakes, candy, & chips—750 servings minimum assorted from these listings**						
	cake mixes				**popcorn**		
	chocolate	12–24			popped	2–3	
	lemon	12–24			microwave	pkg. date	
	white	12–24			pre-seasoned	pkg. date	
	candy				**puddings, dry mix**		
	bars	12			vanilla	24–36	
	hard sugar	12			lemon	24–36	
	mixed candies, vacuum-pk.	24–36			banana	24–36	
	gum, chewing				chocolate	24–36	
					gelatin	36–48	
	chips & filled crackers						
	corn chips	12–18			**puddings, pre-mixed (non-refrigerated)**		
	potato chips	12–18			banana	12–18	
	wheat snacks	12–18			chocolate	12–18	
	crackers, snack	12			topping, whipped / sweet	12–24	

Quick-Shop 8–1
Essential Foods & Nonfoods Shopping List

Quantities rounded to nearest 5 lb., except where noted ↘				In-Home Storage Requirements			
Multiply Adult Quantity by your Family Factor to determine your Family Total							
Storage Item	Shelf Life (months)	Adult Quantity	Family Factor	Family Total	On Hand	Needs	Quick-Plan Worksheets (✓)
Quick-List 8–1: Water—Emergency Supplies & Treatment							
water, potable	6–12	14 gal.	per person				
water, 4 or 6 oz. aseptic pack	indefinite	2 gal.	per person				
portable treatment unit	indefinite	1	1 unit				
bleach, 5.25% hypochlorite	6	1 gal.					
tablets, water treatment	36–60	1 pkg.					
Quick-List 8–2: Wheat, Other Whole Grains, Flours & Beans							
wheat, whole grain (berries)	indefinite	350					
grain mill / grinder	indefinite	1 / family					
mixer / bread making	indefinite	1 / family					
yeast , cake, moist	pkg. date	4 oz.					
yeast, active dry powdered	12–24	12 oz.					
cornmeal / flours	60	10					
rice, white, fortified / enriched	24–48	10					
rice, white pre-cooked	36	25					
rice, wild	24–36	5					
Quick-List 8–3: Powdered Milk, Dairy Products & Eggs							
milk, non-instant powdered	24–48	100					
butter, dehydrated	60–96	20					
cheese, dehydrated	60–96	25					
eggs, dehydrated / freeze-dried	60–96	25 dz.					
evaporated milk	24–36	12 cans					
Quick-List 8–4: Sweeteners—Honey, Sugar & Syrup							
honey, unfiltered	indefinite	65					
sugar, white	indefinite	10					
Quick-List 8–5: Cooking Catalysts—Salt, Oils & Leaveners							
iodized salt	indefinite	5					
yeast, cake, moist	pkg. date	4 oz.					
yeast, active dry powdered	12–24	12 oz.					
vegetable oil, liquid	12–24	10 gal.					
Quick-List 8–6: Sprouting—Seeds & Supplies							
alfalfa	24–36	1					
Quick-List 8–7: Medical Care—Medications & First Aid Kits							
personal life-preserving medications							
cardiovascular conditions medication							
diabetic conditions medication							
nervous conditions medications							
respiratory and allergic conditions							
seizure conditions medications							

Essential Foods & Nonfoods Shopping List (continued)

Quantities rounded to nearest 5 lb., except where noted ↘			Food Storage Requirements				
Multiply Adult Quantity by your Family Factor to determine your Family Total							
Storage Item	Shelf Life (months)	Adult Quantity	Family Factor	Family Total	On Hand	Needs	Quick-Plan Worksheets (✓)
personal life-preserving medications (continued)							
"stomach" and intestinal medications							
other critical conditions medication(s)							
prescription medications							
emergency medical care—first aid kit							
family first aid kit, commercial pre-pak	*indefinite*	1					
Individual first aid kit, commercial pre-pak	*indefinite*	1					
Quick-List 8–8: Basic Supplementation							
herbs & whole food supplements							
minerals							
vitamins							
live whole food concentrates							
Quick-List 8–9: Fuels, Energy & Camping Gear							
flashlights / "D" type, 2- or 3-battery	*indefinite*						
"D" batteries	12–24						
lamp, kerosene	*indefinite*						
kerosene (gal.)	6–12						
candles, tallow or wax	*indefinite*						
emergency candles	*indefinite*						
camp stove, 2-burner	*indefinite*						
stove fuel (gal.)	12						
stove accessories	*indefinite*						
camp cooking set	*indefinite*						
utensils, camp / kitchen	*indefinite*						
lantern, two-mantle	*indefinite*						
lantern fuel (gal.)	12						
mantles, replacement set	*indefinite*						
fire starters	*indefinite*						
magnesium/steel kit	*indefinite*						
matches (waterproof)	*indefinite*						
portable heater	*indefinite*						
heater fuel	25						
Quick-List 8–10: Personal, Family, Infant & Pet Care Essentials							
feminine needs / sanitary napkins	*indefinite*	per need					
toilet paper	*indefinite*	60 rolls					
toiletry / travel kit	*indefinite*	personal					
infant care							
clothing	*varies*						
diapers, disposable	*indefinite*						
medications	*indicated*						
formula / infant	12–18						
juices, strained / infant	12–14						

Essential Foods & Nonfoods Shopping List (continued)

Quantities rounded to nearest 5 lb., except where noted ↘			Food Storage Requirements				
Multiply Adult Quantity by your Family Factor to determine your Family Total							
Storage Item	Shelf Life (months)	Adult Quantity	Family Factor	Family Total	On Hand	Needs	Quick-Chart Worksheets (✓)
pet care							
food	6–12						
equipment, handling	indefinite						
Quick-List 8–11: Canned & Dried Fruits, Vegetables & Soups							
potatoes, all dried	36–48	25					
potatoes, all, fresh	3–6	100					
Quick-List 8–12: Kitchen Staples—Condiments & Seasonings							
peanut butter	12–24	15					
pepper, black	indefinite	8 oz.					
Quick-List 8–13: Meats & Seafood							
ground meat	12–24	75					
Quick-List 8–14: Domestic Maintenance & Preparedness							
seeds, garden	12–24	per need					
storage containers	indefinite	per need					
72-hour emergency kit							
family	12	1 kit					
individual	12	1 kit					
emergency clothing kit	seasonal	as needed					
Quick-List 8–15: Pleasure Foods—Beverages, Snacks, Sweets & Treats							
Add your personal & family needs here							

Quick-Shop 8–2

Supplemental Foods & Nonfoods Shopping List

Storage Item	Shelf Life (months)	Adult Quantity	Family Factor	Family Total	On Hand	Needs	Quick-Plan Worksheet (✓)
Personal & Family Supplemental Needs Quantities rounded to nearest 5 lb., except where noted ↘				**In-Home Storage Requirements**			
Multiply Adult Quantity by your Family Factor to determine your Family Total							

Quick-Plan Worksheet 8–1

Planning & Budgeting Worksheet

	Foods & Nonfoods Priority List				
R A N K	**Item or Description**	**Source of Supply**	**Need Am't.**	**Cost Each Unit**	**Total Cost**
1					
2					
3					
4					
5					
6					
7					
8					
9					
10					
TOTALS: Basic In-Home Storage Items					

Inventory Date: _____ ❖ **Projected Purchase Date:** _____ **Budgeted Amount:** _____

Notes for Your In-Home Convenience Store

If you are properly prepared, there is no need to fear.

What about Noah? It certainly wasn't raining when he began to build the ark. That was a situation in which an amateur was given the responsibility—by divine appointment—to build an Ark. More recently, professionals were given the responsibility to build the Titanic—with divine appointments. Which ship would you choose for your trip into the unknown waters of the future?

Chapter 9

Managing Long-Term Storage
Basics of Storage Problems & Solutions

Food storage has some destructive *enemies* constantly working on it at different rates with different effects. The net effect of these food enemies is they reduce or destroy food quality, taste, nutritional values, and create morale problems when you realize your investment of time, energy, and money has become garbage!

The major enemies causing the loss of quality and nutrition in stored foods are:

1. poor quality of foods selected;
2. improper or inadequate packaging and poor storage techniques;
3. high storage temperatures;
4. moisture and microbial infiltration;
5. insect and rodent infestation; and
6. storage period exceeding useful shelf life

Time is the single greatest enemy of in-home storage—the other factors increase in probability as time passes. This chapter outlines some of the problems caused by these food enemies and suggests solutions for their effective resolution as summarized in the following charts.

Quick-Guide 9–1

Summary of In-Home Storage Problems and Solutions

1. Poor Quality of Food Selection Problems

• Lost investment of time, money, & food if food deteriorates or is not acceptable to family tastes.

Solutions	Hints

• Select high-quality, storage-grade foods for in-home storage
 	
• Choose foods with consideration for nutritional value, storage qualities, and in most cases, the taste buds
 	
• Store what you normally eat
 	
• Eat from stored supplies regularly as part of the daily diet to help maintain or develop a taste for the foods available in the storage program
	• never purchase outdated, broken, or dented goods of any kind for food storage
	• damaged, canned, or packaged foods will be contaminated if the airtight seal has been broken
	• especially avoid bulging cans—they're already suspect and dangerous
	
	• these are the common-sense reasons for storing what you normally eat:
	   –eliminates food spoilage
	   –minimizes food deterioration
	   –stabilizes diet during stressful situations
	   –provides insurance against malnutrition
	   –your year's food supply will not exceed original investment
	   –the one factor of food storage that's entirely under your control is buying what you eat [1]

2. Improper Packaging and Poor Storage Techniques Problems

• **Contamination is made easier when foods are not maintained in proper containers.**
• **Rancidity results when airtight seal of a container is broken.**

Solutions	Hints
• Foods must be clean at the time they are purchased • Foods must be clean at time of packaging • Foods must be placed in clean containers free from insects • Foods must be sealed so insects, pests, and moisture cannot gain entrance	**Storage** • rates at which foods deteriorate depend upon the particular food, its purity, the way it's stored, and especially upon its environmental temperature • when a package or can has been opened, the useful life of its contents is greatly shortened **Rancidity** • the warmer the ambient air, the more rapidly rancidity develops • small amounts of natural fats in foods become foul smelling and slightly toxic when the food's protective shell is breached by oxidants • foods which have their natural structure broken up, such as cracked wheat and flour from whole wheat, meal and flour from corn, polished rice, etc., may become rancid when stored unsealed • many dried vegetables, including corn, green beans, and green peas are subject to rancidity when kept in unsealed containers • rancidity may be minimized by storing in properly sealed containers and storage in a cool, dry, and dark location

---

[1] The belief that a person will eat anything under emergency situations has been proven faulty. Dr. Norman Wright, of the British Food Ministry, after experiencing living conditions in England and war-torn Europe following World War II stated, *"A sudden emergency is no time for introducing untried novelties."* He indicated people were more likely to reject unfamiliar or distasteful foods during times of stress than under normal conditions. Isn't this the usual response in times of trouble—reverting to type or habit? When we are frightened, upset, and insecure, don't we tend to return to things with which we are acquainted or familiar? The only way to be certain stored foods will be acceptable to the palate during times of need is to assure our tastes are acquainted with them and tolerate them during normal times.

2. Improper Packaging and Storage Techniques Problems (continued)

Container Suggestions

Glass containers:
- glass bottles and jars are good storage packages; however, they break, don't stack well, let in light, are generally quite expensive, and are always heavy
- when using glass containers, take precautions to place them in a stable position near the floor
- when storing foods in glass containers, store in dark location; some foods deteriorate more rapidly when exposed to light
- as a further precaution for glass containers, hot wax may be poured over the contact point of friction-type lids to ensure protection; with other types of lids, masking tape may be used for sealing cracks where corrosion could begin
- save all glass bottles from salad dressings, pickles, even odd-shaped jars and use them for storage containers
- save gallon jugs and jars for storing rice, beans, powdered milk, etc.
- pack empty bottles with fruit, vegetables, or water
- keep a supply of glass jars and lids on hand for bottling
- some fruits will keep longer in glass containers than in metal cans due to the relatively high acidity of their contents; these include foods and drinks such as pineapple, orange, lemon, lime, apple, and tomato
- fruits, vegetables, and meats properly processed in glass bottles and stored properly will store as well as canned goods

Plastic containers:
- rigid, round plastic containers protect contents better than square ones
- make sure containers are rodent-proof
- bulk-packaged foods, especially flour, granulated sugar, and powdered milk should be immediately repacked in either clean and dry metal, glass, or plastic containers, then sealed with airtight lids
- small, round plastic buckets can be chewed through by rats, but mice will not generally attack plastic buckets

Metal containers:
- food-grade, heavy-duty, sealable plastic liners in new galvanized steel drums provide good storage space capable of excluding both rodents and insects

3. High Storage Temperature Problems

- **Chemical reactions and changes occur in foods which may not be apparent & could be dangerous.**
- **Storage at higher temperatures diminishes shelf life.**
- **Food quality is lost at increased rates at high temperatures.**

Solutions	Hints
• Locate food storage in dry, cool place, below 70°F • Foods should be stored as close to 40°F as possible • The cooler and drier foodstuffs are kept, the longer they remain tasty and nourishing	• generally, changes in color, flavor, or texture are accompanied by loss of nutritional value • for every 20°F increase in storage temperature, the shelf life of stored food is decreased by almost 50% • canned fruits and vegetables may soften and become mushy and have an offensive odor

4. Moisture and Microbial Infiltration Problems

- **Moisture accumulates inside food containers and increases incidence of microbial infiltration.**
- **Chemical reactions in food caused by moisture result in food quality loss and nutritional deterioration.**
- **When both moisture and temperature are high, probability of contamination is greatly increased.**

Solutions	Hints
Storage must be properly sealed and located in a dry, cool place •	• moisture hardens and spoils all forms of stored foods, whether dried in-home or dehydrated commercially, crystallized (such as sugars, salt, desserts, and drink mixes), powdered products (such as baking powder, flours, cornstarch, baked

4. Moisture and Microbial Infiltration Problems (continue)

Solutions	Hints
• Moisture is excluded only by maintaining an airtight seal • Place food on shelves when possible • Avoid placing metal cans directly on concrete or dirt surfaces—use plywood or thick cardboard sheets in layers to prevent cans from direct contact with concrete floors Be observant, and you'll become aware of the indicators of deterioration when you use stored foods	goods, and boxed mixes), processed foods (such as cereals, chips, and crackers), and canned or bottled vegetables, meats, soups, fish, etc. **Molds:** • mold grows in a very low moisture environment and is the prime cause of spoilage in stored foods • mold spores are abundant in the air, and they can live on almost any type of food • molds produce the most poisonous toxins known • in seeds, cereals, and nuts, molds are known to produce toxins which can cause permanent damage to internal organs • *moldy foods should always be discarded* **Rust prevention:** • metal containers often rust through and spoil food • prevention is best achieved by keeping storage containers away from moisture-inducing surfaces by placing cardboard, plywood, or pieces of lumber beneath metal cans to prevent direct contact with concrete floors see following instructions for **wax coating treatments**

Wax Coating Treatments

Shelf life of foods in metal containers is extended by coating containers with wax or paraffin to minimize corrosion in high-humidity areas. Following are two treatment methods:

• **Paraffin method**: Paraffin is heated and the container is either dipped into the wax or a brush may be used to spread the wax onto all surfaces, especially at the joints.

• **Wax method:** Make a solution of 2 oz. jelly wax and 1 qt. mineral spirits by warming the minerals spirits in its container in a bucket of hot water—*don't use an open flame!* Stir the jelly wax into the mineral spirits until dissolved. Then, dip the can—including label—into the solution, making certain the entire can is covered. Place on wood blocks to dry, then place in storage. Choose low-humidity days for this task, and be sure to do this project *outside* the house!

5. Insect and Rodent Infestation Problems

• **Infestation of insects and rodents causes dangerous food contamination.**

Solutions	Hints
• Utilize proper packaging to protect contents • Use metal cans with heavy-duty, food-grade, waterproof, plastic containers and airtight lids for all powdered products	• four-legged critters and pests generally contaminate more food than they eat • rats, mice, cockroaches, and beetles are "dirty" and carry disease • insects packaged in food products feed and multiply easily in captivity of a container • when evidence of pest or critter presence is seen, the foods they've spoiled must be discarded • weevil found in stored grains and some processed grain products, including flours, are "clean" and edible without harm to the human system
• All glass and crockery containers should have air-tight seals • Fumigate with one of *basic* methods of treatment detailed in the section following • The addition of chemicals ought to be according to the best information available from local County Extension agents or food storage experts	**Commercial Packaging:** • most commercial foods are intact and are generally free from insects • in paper packaging such as a paper flour sack, even a very tiny hole may permit pests to enter and lay their eggs; the newly-hatched larvae will infest the foods quickly • normally, packaging protects foods during shipping and storage on market shelves • no matter what precautions you take after placing most commercial packaging in storage, paper packaging alone will not preclude pests for very long • pests may already be in the creases and recesses of packages and with time will enter the paper packaging enclosure

Fumigating Foods for Storage

Basic Dry-Ice Treatment Method

One of the most difficult facets of food storage is repacking or packaging bulk foods into smaller containers while either preventing entry of new or eliminating existing bugs and pests.

Dry ice will eliminate bugs and pests requiring oxygen by replacing the storage atmosphere in the container with carbon dioxide. This is a very simple and easy method of treatment—the most difficult part is finding dry ice and getting it home and into the containers in a timely manner.

Use **Container Requirements Estimator Chart** to determine the number and sizes of containers needed for your bulk storage foods. The **Basic Dry-Ice Treatment Chart** details how much dry ice you'll need to fumigate containers of different sizes. See charts on page 44.

Basic Dry-Ice Treatment Instructions

- Make sure all equipment, containers, and tools are clean and free of dirt before starting.
- Break dry ice into approximate weight as indicated in the **Basic Dry-Ice Treatment Chart**, using a hammer or a big knife, chisel, or flat-blade screwdriver.
- Wipe frosty crystals from dry ice with a clean cotton towel to prevent addition of moisture into container.
- Wrap dry ice in newspaper or butcher paper to prevent direct contact with hands and foods. Grain germination or sprouting may be affected by being in contact with dry ice, but will still have the same baking quality.

Notes on Handling Dry Ice

- Use caution when handling dry ice—dry ice burns, or rather, freezes skin almost instantly!
- Don't use dry ice in glass containers—glass may break if sealed too soon or shatter when dry ices comes in direct contact with glass not designed for subfreezing temperatures.

Caution: keep children away from your work area—dry ice is a temptation for them!

There are two methods for fumigating with dry ice. Each is effective. It's generally a matter of preference, depending on whether you're working with new or existing stored foods.

- For re-fumigating existing foods, use the *Basic on-top method*.

Basic on-top treatment method:

- on top of almost-full container, place required amount of dry ice on folded paper cut from grocery bags or other nonconductive (insulating) material
- press lid down gently, leaving an exit for air to escape
- after 20-30 minutes, check to see if dry ice has completely evaporated
- if not, wait another 5 minutes, then check again
- when dry ice has completely evaporated, remove material and seal container

- When dividing bulk foods into smaller containers, use the *Basic on-bottom method*.

Basic on-bottom treatment method:

- on bottom of 5-gal. metal storage bucket, place $^1/_4$ lb. dry ice wrapped in heavy paper (butcher paper will do nicely, or cut paper grocery bag) or other non-conductive (insulating) material that can be left in bucket
- add storage contents
- press lid down gently, leaving only a small opening for escaping air (lid will bulge if gas can't escape)
- after 20–30 minutes, check to determine if dry ice has evaporated by sealing container (if lid pops off or container bulges, crack seal and wait another 5 minutes, then check again)
- when dry ice has completely evaporated, seal container

Container Requirements Estimator for Dry-Ice Treatment Chart

Stored Item / 100 lb.	5-Gal. Containers Required
Beans	3
Corn, dried	3
Flours—all	4
Lentils	3
Oats, rolled	4
Pasta products—large (large macaroni, noodles, ravioli, spaghetti, etc.)	5
Pasta products—small (elbow, alphabet, etc.)	4
Peas, dried	3
Soup mixes	3-4
Sugar—all	3
TVP	4
Whole grains—wheat, rice, etc.	3

Basic Dry-Ice Treatment Chart

Container Size	Food Quantity (lb.)	Dry Ice Required (oz.)	Expansion Space Required (in.)
Metal Containers			
#10 can	3-5$^1/_2$	1	$^1/_4$
5 gal.	15-35	2-3	$^1/_2$
25-30 gal.	100	8	$^1/_2$
Plastic Containers			
1 gal.	3$^1/_2$-7	1	$^1/_4$
4 gal.	13-30	4	$^1/_2$
5 gal.	15-35	4	$^1/_2$

Other Fumigation Methods

There are several other methods utilized to fumigate stored bulk foods. Some of the commercial pesticides, even though food grade and approved for use, often require more skills and equipment than most of us have. The other do-it-yourself methods recommended include the following three (3) methods described—(1) **freezing, (2) heating, or (3) organic.**

(1) Fumigation by Freezing

The freezing method will kill all live bugs—but not necessarily the eggs—over an extended period of time.

The advantage of the freezing method is its simplicity. Its major disadvantage is that the pest eggs are not usually killed by freezing—that's what makes it difficult to have foolproof storage conditions.

It's always best to refreeze the previously frozen grains after 30 days to assure eggs hatched are killed.

Basic freezer method:

Place small quantities in either chest or upright freezer (*not freezer section of refrigerator*) for 72 hours at 0°F or lower.

(2) Fumigation by Heating

The heating method also has the advantage of killing all forms of animal life in foods.

The disadvantage is that it also kills the food if overheated or left in the oven too long!

Basic heating method:

- pour infested foods in shallow baking pan to depth of one-half inch
- place in pre-heated 150°F oven for *only* 15-20 minutes

Foods will scorch if kept in heat too long. Oven door may be left open to allow moisture and heat to escape.

(3) Organic Fumigation Method

Diatomaceous earth is an organic method to eliminate the hungry little critters feeding on your stored grains. It will rid the container of all bug and critter life. It works best with whole grains, beans, dried items, and processed grains such as rolled oats, TVP, and cereals.

This organic treatment is not harmful to humans or animals. It's also relatively inexpensive and simple to use.

Diatomaceous products are available at most lawn & garden shops, building supply centers, and hardware stores.

Basic organic method:

- for each 5-gallon container of food, put 1$^1/_4$ C. diatomaceous earth into container
- shake vigorously or roll container until all the grains are dusted.

6. Storage Period Exceeding Useful Shelf Life Problems

- Food quality & nutritional values deteriorate continually over time.
- Loss of food value is approximately 2–5% each year.

Solutions	Hints

• Store what is already enjoyed by your family and the problem of storage period exceeding the useful life of stored food simply ceases to exist
 	
  • **Store what you eat.**
  • **Eat what you store.**
  • **Rotate!**
  • **Rotate!**
  • **Rotate!**
	• one of the fundamental tenets of a successful storage program is the rotation of supplies to
	  —prevent spoilage
	  —minimize loss of food value and flavor
	  —keep taste buds acquainted with foods upon which one would depend to sustain life
	• rotation is a "mechanical" method of keeping your inventory edible and nutritious while preventing spoilage
	• rotation of storage foods is a continuous process
	• always place the oldest canned goods in front and mark them so they will be consumed first
	• chemical reaction with metal containers occurs more rapidly with certain foods
	• canned foods will remain usable, if not wholesome, as long as the container seals remain intact and cans are not bulged
	• canned goods should be rotated and replaced with new food as used
	• solids tend to settle if not rotated
	• old, out-of-date food is edible but is not as palatable or nutritious
	• the next section details the typical shelf life of selected canned fruits and vegetables; note shelf life differences in foods: colored fruits, rhubarb, pickles, and sauerkraut have shorter shelf life
	• **Quick-Guide 9–2** following details additional pantry, refrigeration, and freezing information about meats, vegetables, dairy products, baked goods, fish, and other foods

Storage Life of Canned Fruits & Vegetables[2]

Canned Fruits (Western U.S. at 70°F)[3]	Shelf Life (Months)	Canned Vegetables (Western U.S. at 70°F)	Shelf Life (Months)
Apples & applesauce	36	Asparagus	36+
Apricots	36	Beans—black-eyed, lima, navy or pinto	96+
Blackberries	12+	Beans—green, snap or stringless	36+
Blueberries	12+	Beets	48+
Cherries, maraschino	12+	Brussels sprouts	48+
Cherries, sweet	12+	Cabbage	48+
Cherries, black	12+	Carrots	96+
Cranberry sauce	12+	Cauliflower	48+
Fruit salad	36	Corn	96+
Grapes	12+	Hominy	96+
Grapefruit	36+	Peas	96+
Peaches	36	Pickles	12+
Pears	36	Potatoes, sweet	48+
Pineapple	36	Potatoes, whole white	48+
Plums	12+	Pumpkin	48+
		Rhubarb	12+
		Sauerkraut	12+
		Spinach	36+
		Squash	48+
		Tomatoes	48+

[2] From "*Progress in the Tin Plate Industry*," **Food Technology**

[3] Note these shelf life projections are based on western U.S. locations, where humidity is not the problem it is in other areas of the country. Depending on where you live, you may need to factor in shorter shelf life periods and higher incidence of inventory turnover.

Quick-Guide 9-2

Fresh & Processed Foods Shelf Life Table[4]

NOTES ON REFRIGERATED & FROZEN FOODS

When buying frozen foods:
- Be sure all refrigerated and frozen foods items are bagged separately so they will be stored first when you arrive home. Always place refrigerated items in the coolest area of the car for the trip home from the grocery store, especially during warm months.
- It is important when grocery shopping that refrigerated and frozen food items be selected last. This can help prevent spoilage and safeguard against risk of temperature loss.
- Always check frozen food labels for preparation and serving instructions. Unless otherwise stated on container, do not refreeze.
- Always select items in display cases that are below the "*frost line*" or "*load line*" (the line marked on commercial freezer cabinets which indicates the safety level)

Leftover foods:
- Refrigerate leftovers immediately to prevent bacterial growth—do not let them sit unrefrigerated for an extended period.
- Leftovers should be taken from the proper serving temperature (140°F-180°F) to the proper refrigeration temperature (40°F) as quickly as possible.
- Break large food items into smaller portions before refrigerating to promote faster chilling—leaving leftover foods out "to cool down" is not wise as it will promote bacterial growth.
- To prevent contamination in refrigerator, always place cooked food above raw items in the refrigerator. Make sure all food is covered when stacking so particles from the shelf above don't fall onto foods below.

Thawing frozen foods:
- Never thaw frozen food at room temperature! Either thaw in the refrigerator or under cold running water. It's best to let food thaw in a covered container overnight in the refrigerator.

Basic tip: Put your frozen product—fillet of fish, beefsteak, or chicken breast—in a sealed plastic bag, eliminating as much air as possible. Thaw under cold running water.

Food	Pantry (50°–70°F)	Fridge (40°F)	Freezer (0°F)	Special Handling Notes
Average Storage Time in Weeks unless otherwise indicated				
Fresh baked goods				
Breads, fresh	3-5 days	1-2	3-6	keep cool & dry; for maximum storage time when opened, store in airtight container; refrigeration generally extends shelf life; homemade breads may have shorter shelf life due to lack of preservatives
Refrigerated biscuit / cookie dough		pkg. date	26-52	
Rolls, fresh	2-5 days	pkg. date		
Tortillas, corn & wheat flour	5-10 days	3-6	26-52	
Fresh dairy products				
Butter		4-12	24-36	• butter will keep up to 1 year if melted enough to separate the whey from the pure butterfat • pour off the fat and seal in sterile bottles for pantry storage • the remaining whey can be refrigerated and used in cooking

---

[4] Contributors to this section include: USDA; Peggy Gentry-Van Laanen, Assoc. Prof. & Extension Nutrition Specialist, Texas A&M University; Delsa Wilson, food storage consultant; & lecture notes.

NOTES ON REFRIGERATED & FROZEN FOODS (CONTINUED)

Fresh dairy products (continued)

Cheese				
Cream / Neufchatel		12-16		
Hard / wax-coated / opened & unopened		12-24		• mold growing on the surface of cheese can be cut off rather than discarding the entire piece of cheese • cheese bricks will not mold if wrapped in vinegar cloth • change vinegar cloth wrapping every 6 months • ***Basic alternative:*** rub the entire cheese with a cloth moistened in white vinegar to kill and remove the moldy formation
Hard / Parmesan / opened		12-24	24-36	
Hard / Parmesan / unopened	52	96	see notes	freezing not recommended
Processed cheese products	26	96	see notes	freezing not recommended
Soft / ricotta		1-2	see notes	freezing not recommended
Cream, sweet				
Half & half / light or heavy		4-12	see notes	freezing not recommended
Cream, sour				
Sour cream		1-3	see notes	freezing not recommended
Dips, mixed		1-3	see notes	freezing not recommended
Ice cream / ice milk / sherbet				
Ice cream			1-2	
Ice milk			1-3	
Sherbet			1-3	
Milk products, fresh				
Milk, fresh / pasteurized		1	3-4	freezing not recommended
Buttermilk, fresh / pasteurized		1-2	12-16	
Milk-based prepared foods		1		freezing not recommended
Milk, nonfat / powdered / dry / opened		1-2	12	
Milk, nonfat / powdered / rehydrated		1		freezing not recommended
Yogurt, regular & nonfat		pkg. date	4-6	
Yogurt, frozen			36-52	
Milk products, pantry				
Infant formula	52-78	see notes		after opening, maximum refrigeration period is 48 hours
Margarine				
Regular & soft		36-52	52	
Diet		36-90	see notes	freezing diet varieties not recommended
Canned milk				**all:** turn canned milk upside down every other month to prevent lumps from forming due to fats separating; use evaporated, condensed sweetened, and other canned milks within one year; no need to refrigerate until opened; keeps refrigerated 3 days to 1 week after opening
Evaporated / whole	12-24	see notes		
Condensed, sweetened	9-12	see notes		
Non-dairy products				
Whipped topping, aerosol can		18-52		do not freeze pressurized aerosol products
Whipped topping, carton / tub			12	
Creamers, powdered	12-24			refrigeration not necessary
Creamers, frozen / liquid		1	12-24	
Fresh eggs				
In-shell		1-2		
Frozen			36-52	

NOTES ON REFRIGERATED & FROZEN FOODS (CONTINUED)

Food	Pantry (50°-70°F)	Fridge (40°F)	Freezer (0°F)	Special Handling Notes
Average Storage Time in Weeks unless otherwise indicated				
Fresh fish & shellfish				
Fish, fresh / fat types		1 day	12-16	includes bluefish, bonito, eel, grunt, herring, kingfish, mackerel, mullet, porgy, salmon, sardines, sea bass, striped bass, sturgeon, swordfish, lake trout, rainbow trout, tuna, whitefish, whiting & yellowtail
Fish, fresh / lean types		1 day	24-30	includes bluegill, carp, catfish, cod, crappie, croaker, dabs, fluke, flounder, grouper, haddock, halibut, monkfish, ocean perch, octopus, pike, pollock, red snapper, rockfish, sand dab, scrod, shark, sole, snapper & squid
Fish, cooked		3-4 days	12-16	
Fish, smoked / whole		1-2		freezing not recommended
Fish, smoked / cut up		3-5 days		freezing not recommended
Clams, shucked		1-2 days	12-16	
Crabs		1-2 days	12-16	
Oysters, shucked		1-2 days	12-16	
Scallops		1-2 days	12-16	
Shrimp, raw		2-3 days	24-30	do not refreeze previously frozen shrimp
Shrimp, fresh		1-3 days	16-26	
Shrimp, frozen				do not refreeze previously frozen shrimp

NOTES ON STORING FRESH MEATS

Refrigeration

- Prepackaged fresh meats from the meat self-service counter can be stored, unopened, in the refrigerator for 2-7 days.
- Properly wrapped, refrigerated or frozen meats will store well *in the refrigerator* for up to 7 days.
- Unopened vacuum-packed, processed (lunch or table-ready) meats will store in the refrigerator for up to 7 days, depending on cut(s), additives (cheese, pork, etc.), and fat content. Always check the freshness date on these packages when buying. Unopened packages can be kept frozen up to two months without rewrapping or overwrapping.
- For optimal refrigerated storage, temperatures of 28°-32°F are best. However, most refrigerators are equipped to maintain temperatures of 36°-40°F, so this chart is based on 36°-40°F.

Freezing

- Rewrapping, overwrapping, or sealing meat in foil, freezer paper or a heavy plastic wrap (a moisture- and vapor-proof material) will prepare it for freezer storage and extend storage time dramatically.
- Properly wrapped and frozen, fresh meat will store well in the freezer from several months up to a year, depending on cut, as indicated below.
- When freezing meats, label all packages with details about contents, weight, number of servings, or pieces.
- Date should be the date each package was placed in the freezer. Be sure to rotate frozen foods with the same dedication with fresh or canned foods—use oldest packages first.

Cooking fresh & frozen meats

- Meats should be cooked to a minimum internal temperature of 140°F.
- Poultry and stuffed meat items should be cooked to a minimum of 165°F.
- Pork should reach an internal temperature of 150°F.
- Cold meats should be served at a temperature of 40°F or lower.

Food	Pantry (50°-70°F)	Fridge (40°F) Days	Freezer (0°F) Months	Special Handling Notes
Beef / cuts		3-5	6-12	
Beef / ground		1-2	3-4	
Lamb / cuts		3-5	6-9	
Lamb / ground		1-2	3-4	
Leftover cooked meat		4-5	3-4	

NOTES ON REFRIGERATED & FROZEN FOODS (CONTINUED)

Food	Pantry (50°-70°F)	Fridge (40°F) Days	Freezer (0°F) Months	Special Handling Notes

Organ meats
  Brains
  Heart
  Kidney
  Liver
  Sweetbreads
		1-2	3-4	

Lunch meats		3-5	6-12	
Pork / cuts		3-5	6-9	
Pork / ground		1-2	1-2	
Pork / sausage		2-3	1-2	
Tongue		6-7	3-4	
Veal / cuts		3-5	6-9	
Veal / ground		1-2	3-4	

NOTES ON STORING FRESH VEGETABLES

This section briefly describes how fresh vegetables may be stored to preserve their flavor and nutrition. The following information details storing fresh vegetables in the kitchen, pantry, and refrigerated cold storage. Freezing and canning are not a part of this **Quick-Guide.**

Follow these general suggestions to enjoy the results of your selection of fresh vegetables:

- when possible, eat fresh vegetables raw, in salads, in relishes, or sliced as a side dish
- use vegetables as soon as possible after harvesting (or acquiring) to ensure maximum texture, flavor, and food value; cook vegetables in skins when possible, or peel very thinly, since the highest concentration of minerals and vitamins lies near the skin
- when storing a vegetable for only a short time, wash thoroughly, then refrigerate in the refrigerator vegetable drawer or in a heavy-duty, food-grade, freezer-quality, sealable plastic bag
- cook vegetables in a minimum amount of water or use none at all, as many nutrients are water soluble
- start fresh vegetables in boiling water, reduce heat so they boil gently, keeping cooking utensil tightly covered to shorten cooking time and preserve nutrients
- do not stir vegetables more than necessary—air brought in contact with food allows vitamin deterioration and stirring also breaks up the vegetable
- cook only until tender, since overcooking destroys color, texture, and flavor
- cream vegetables in their own cooking liquid to minimize the amount of fat by adding a small amount of milk or yogurt, or thicken with a blend of flour and milk, or cornstarch and water or milk (use *arrowroot* instead, if you're growing your own)
- salt lightly *after* cooking or sprinkle herbal mixes on foods for a healthy taste treat
- use any water from cooking vegetables as soup, sauce base, or put into stock pot
- lemon juice enhances vegetable flavor, making it possible to reduce margarine, butter, or spicy seasonings for a healthy taste treat

Fresh Vegetable Storage without Refrigeration

Food	Pantry (50°-70°F) (Weeks)	Fridge (40°F)	Freezer (0°F)	Special Handling Notes
Beans, all dried; see separate listings	52			
Garlic	3-8			
Lentils	52			
Onions–white or yellow	1-2			
Onions, pearl or globe	2-3			
Onions, sweet, white or yellow	1-2			
Peas, dried	52			
Peppers, chili	2-3			

Fresh Vegetable Storage without Refrigeration (continued)

Food	Pantry (50°-70°F)	Fridge (40°F) Days	Freezer (0°F) Months	Special Handling Notes
Potatoes, new, red	2-3			
Potatoes, white, Russet, Baker	1-2			
Squash—winter (acorn, butternut, spaghetti)	1-2			
Sweet potatoes	5-7			
Tomatillo (Mexican tomato)	1-2			
Tomatoes, green	1-2			
Tomatoes, unripe	1			
Turnips	4-6			
Yams	5-7			substitute in any recipe for sweet potatoes

Fresh Vegetable Storage Requiring Refrigeration

Fresh Vegetables—this listing includes vegetables which may be stored only when refrigerated.

- cold storage in refrigerator at 40°F in heavy-duty, food-grade, sealable plastic bags
- some vegetables should not be refrigerated—check listings of vegetables above
- properly processed and frozen vegetables have shelf life of 10-12 months when stored at 0°F in freezer-quality, food-grade, heavy-duty, airtight plastic bags

Food	Pantry (50°-70°F)	Fridge (40°F)	Freezer (0°F)	Special Handling Notes
Arrowroot		7-14		dishes with arrowroot thickening cannot be reheated
Artichokes		7		
Asparagus		4-6		
Beans—lima, fava		2-3		
Beans—green, snap or string, yellow wax, all long beans		3-5		
Beets		7-10		
Broccoli		3-5		
Brussels sprouts		3-5		
Cabbage—red		7-14		
Cabbage—green		7-14		
Carrots		7-14		
Cauliflower		4-7		
Celery		7-14		
Chard—Swiss		4-5		
Cilantro (Coriander)		7-10		
Corn—white or yellow		1		
Cucumber		4-5		
Dandelion		3-5		substitutes for spinach in any recipe
Eggplant		3-4		
Endive		3-5		
Ginger root		14-21		
Jicama		10-14		
Kale		2-3		
Kohlrabi		4-5		
Leeks		7-14		
Lettuce—butter		3-4		
Lettuce—iceberg & romaine		7-14		
Mushrooms		4-5		
Okra		7-14		okra will turn black if cooked in copper, brass, tin pots or pans

Fresh Vegetable Storage Requiring Refrigeration (continued)

Onions—green (scallions)		7-14		
Onions—sliced		2-3		
Onions—whole		—		do not refrigerate whole onions
Parsley		10-15		
Parsnips		7-10		
Peas—black-eyed		3-4		
Peas—green		3-4		
Pepper—green bell		2-3		
Pepper—red bell		2-3		
Pepper—yellow bell		2-3		
Potatoes	4-8			potatoes should never be refrigerated after purchasing
Radish		10-14		
Rhubarb		4-7		don't eat leaves—they are poisonous to humans
Rutabaga		3-7		
Salsify—oyster plant		7-14		
Snow peas		4-6		
Spinach		2-3		
Sprouts		7-10		see **Chapter 15** for more details
Squash—acorn, banana, buttercup, butternut, Kahoona, Hubbard		4-5		
Squash—crookneck		4-5		
Squash—spaghetti		4-5		
Swiss chard		2-3		
Taro (Dasheen)		2-3		
Tomato – ripe or sliced		1-2		
Turnip		5-7		also stores well in kitchen or pantry
Zucchini		7-10		

Note: One of the best bags I've used for preserving fruits and vegetables in the refrigerator is an "anti-fogging" and "breathing," re-useable plastic storage bag. It seems effective in prolonging storage life of many vegetables by absorbing and removing "ethylene" gas released after harvesting. It is available in several different sizes. Contact: **Evert-Fresh Corp.,** P.O. Box 590974, Houston TX 77254 (713) 529-4593 or 529-4594. I purchased mine at **Whole Foods Market.**

LOCAL AREA RESOURCES

Check with your local County Extension Service or County Extension agent for additional information on fumigating techniques, preparation, and other problems with your in-home storage plan. Rather than list all the local/county resources here, go to the Internet and search for State and local government listings in your geographical area. There are so many growing zones and microclimates in the US that it would be wasteful to try to list them all here! Go to the Internet for latest information—for your area, down to your ZIP code!

FEDERAL GOVERNMENT RESOURCES

The U.S. government provides bulletins about many special subjects to aid in food storage. Again, it would be faster and wiser to go online and search for particular problems you may encounter as you implement your *Basic in-home storage* program.

A word or phrase search in any Internet search engine will deliver an unbelievable number of resources from which to choose a broad range of solutions on most problems.

RESOURCE DIRECTORIES

There are many sources of information and resources for family preparedness, in-home storage, self-reliance, and survivalism. Knowing how to organize and maintain a sensible, continuing, workable, in-home storage program is a matter of constant self-education for each family.

The Internet is a virtual resource directory for providing products and services supplier information in your area. By having access to a larger selection of vendors, shopping for competitive prices will help you combat today's increasing prices and decreasing worldwide food availability.

The Multi-Jar, *Non-Electric* Vacuum-Sealing Pump!

VACUUM-SEALS ALL SIZES OF JARS, EVEN 5-GALLON BUCKETS!

Put up your own food reserves in-home at minimal cost.

Of all the country's many distribution systems, none is more delicate than its *food* distribution system. We live in a unique time in history—similar to Noah's flood and Joseph's famine.

Both of these individuals were directed by God to store several years' supply of food in preparation for the crises they would face. It was an act of faith and obedience toward God and a work of love toward those whom they sought to save.

These are the major factors causing the destruction of foods: time, moisture, air and gases, radiation of heat, and light. Eliminate these factors and food's shelf life is greatly extended.

First, eliminate the problem of liquids by storing dried, freeze-dried, or dehydrated foods.

Additional benefits of using dried foods include: lighter and more compact storage; less heat applied to food, resulting in lower loss of enzymes; reduces incidence of jars bursting due to either falling from shelves or freezing; prevents nutrients from being leached away; emulsification by the liquid; and microbes cannot thrive in an environment without moisture!

Second, use the multi-jar, *non-electric*, vacuum-sealing pump to eliminate the gases. Bugs are destroyed! Microbes are affected by vacuum as if frozen—entering a state of stasis and therefore do not multiply.

Because heat is not used, jar lids can be sealed again and again!

Third, put your food storage in a cool, dry, dark place. Seal foods in glass or metal. Plastic bags allow mice to sample every food in your cellar! If you have dried foods in sacks, transfer them to jars or cans as you open them to maintain nutritional value, taste, and texture.

I have used my homemade unit for more than 10 years, and it works just fine! JTS

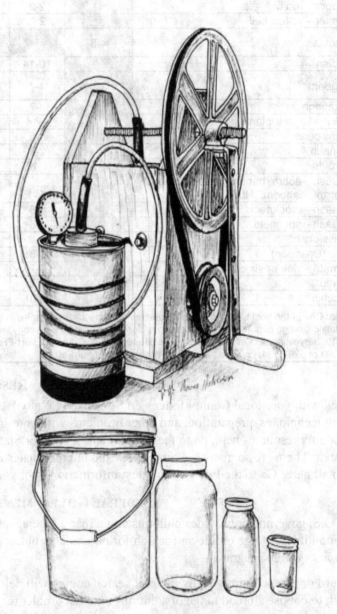

Section IV

Beginning Basics

Preparedness requires faith—not money. It's a matter of choices. Everyone can do something about preparedness. How difficult is it to store some water, a little extra food, or have a plan for emergencies? Put more of your effort into what you need or you'll eventually be constrained to put more extensive effort into dealing with what you get. If you sacrifice little, you gain little. If you would achieve much, you must sacrifice much.

Chapter 10
Water—the Absolute Basic

The most necessary element of your preparedness program is safe drinking water! For all its necessity, water has rather simple beginnings—atoms of hydrogen and oxygen combine. Then, rain and snowfall, snow melts in the high mountains, and water bubbles up from the ground. All together, a network of freshwater creeks is created—streams and rivers, then ponds, lakes, and eventually the great oceans—until water covers 70% of the earth's surface! Then, evaporation occurs, and the cycle repeats itself.

All living things—both plant and animal life—consist mostly of water. In fact, most of the living tissue in the human body—comprising 92% of the blood plasma, 80% of the muscle mass, 60% of red blood cells, and 50% of the rest of the body—is comprised of water! Water is simply the most common substance on earth and is basic to life itself.

However, fresh water, available for human use and management, makes up less than 3% of the earth's total water volume. Most of the fresh water supply—more than 80%, in fact—is in the form of glacial ice and is unavailable for our use. Of the remaining fresh water supply, most is underground, with only 5% present as surface water such as lakes,

> *"Water, water, everywhere… but not a drop to drink."*
>
> *From "Rime of the Ancient Mariner," Samuel Taylor Coleridge*

ponds, rivers, streams, etc. In the 10th edition, we noted the 1994 worldwide water withdrawal[1] from available fresh water supplies to be approximately 2400 cubic kilometers (or 1.7×10^{12} gallons) per day. Projections for the middle of the 21st century were almost 10 times as great, nearly 20,000 cubic kilometers (14.5×10^{12} gallons) per day!

The volume of fresh water withdrawn for human use is increasing dramatically. At the same time, the major nations are facing increasing problems with pollution of their water supplies.[2]

The global rate of consumption more than doubled between 1997 and 2005. Purified water is currently the leading global seller, with U.S. companies dominating the field, and natural spring water, purified water and flavored water being the fastest-growing market segments.[3]

The global bottled water market grew by 7% in 2006 to reach a value of $60,938.1 million (60.9 billion). The market grew by 8.1% in 2006 to reach a volume of 115,393.5 million liters. In 2011, the market is forecast to have a value of $86,421.2 million (86.4 billion), an increase of 41.8% since 2006. In 2011, the market is forecast to have a volume of 174,286.6 million liters, an increase of 51% since 2006.[4]

The clear message: *fresh water is a diminishing resource*. It will require astute management if it is to support us at our accustomed quality of life in the next few decades.

IMPORTANCE OF STORING WATER

We are so accustomed to turning on the tap and having fresh water immediately available that it is difficult to imagine turning on the tap and having nothing come out! That is exactly what can happen when there is a natural disaster. Since the average person in the U.S. uses about 65 gallons of water each day, life changes dramatically when there is no water coming through the pipes.

The human body can only survive a few days without water. It is critical to plan so you can always count on having safe drinking water. You will also need water for cooking and sanitation—although you will have to make do with far less than the 65 gallons you normally use!

When a severe natural disaster such as a flood or major earthquake occurs, water supplies are usually interrupted. Even if the main water lines remain intact, raw sewage may flow into supply sources and distribution systems, exposing drinking water to life-threatening contaminants. In the aftermath of a disaster when services are restored, the public water supply might still be contaminated for several weeks—or even months.

Secure knowledge of how to store safe drinking water and how to obtain, disinfect, and purify contaminated water may save your life. If your water supply is cut off, chances are good that there may also be no power, and no police or medical assistance. In extreme emergencies, you'll need to rely on your own resources until community services are restored, which may be 2-3 days, or even several weeks! You will be responsible for the quality of your own drinking water until safe water is again flowing through the pipes in your home.

A stored supply of safe water is the best alternative. Treatment of polluted water cannot guarantee the same quality as a properly stored water supply. However, if you have not stored water, or your supply is lost, then you will need to treat whatever water is available. You have a variety of treatment options, from very poor quality to very good quality. If you think and plan, you can assure the highest quality water for your family.

In some disasters, you may be required to leave your home and go to an emergency shel-

[1] **Water Resources Research**, J. L. Napier and Donald Scott.

[2] Americans drank more than 2 billion gallons of bottled water in 1994—it is the beverage industry's fastest-growing segment. That fact alone tells us something about the importance of water!

[3] **Wikipedia**, July 2009.

[4] **Wikipedia**, July 2009 @ http://en.wikipedia.org/wiki/Bottled_water - cite_note-0

ter. Depending on the type, time, and severity of the disaster, emergency shelters may not have adequate, if any, supplies of food or water, or even basic sanitation. If possible, it would be advisable to bring water (or the means to purify it) with you.

Impact of Disasters on Water Availability

Different kinds of natural disasters can impact a water utility's ability to deliver potable water to the community. Flooding causes water treatment systems to be overloaded to the point that normal disinfection processes are ineffective. An earthquake or ice storm can damage water and sewer system infrastructures so that water cannot be delivered to customers. It may take weeks or months to rebuild damaged systems.

Hurricanes and tornadoes play havoc with water and sewage distribution, leaving citizens with unsafe water for long periods. A city may be unable to get its water system working quickly. A terrorist has the ability to contaminate a city's water supply. A chemical spill or accident may make a city's water undrinkable.

Your Body's Need for Water Increases under Stress

Water is necessary for every system in your body. An adult's body is 60% to 75% water, and in infants, water comprises up to 80% of its body's composition.

Here are some guidelines for water consumption:

- A healthy 160-pound adult needs a minimum of ten (8-ounce) glasses of water a day to keep body systems functioning optimally. That's ½ ounce per pound of body weight.
- Pregnant women should be drinking for two.
- Infants and children need proportionately as much as adults, and under stress, they may require more.
- A 40-pound child requires a minimum of approximately 20 ounces of water each day.

Physical activity, stress, climate, and body weight can alter these minimum water requirements.

Each individual's requirements for water will vary. It is best not to ration water and allow each person to determine his need for water during a stressful situation.

If you find yourself in a situation without stored water or the means to treat it, you may be forced to drink contaminated water. It only takes 3-5 days without water to cause death. If you have no other choice, it is better to drink tainted now and worry about recovering from a waterborne illness later!

Disasters and emergencies, such as natural disasters, are emotionally and physically traumatic. The extreme stress brought about by these kinds of emergencies increases your body's water requirements just to carry out its normal functions. In disaster situations, your body is going to be doing things it doesn't do on a regular basis. Injuries are less likely to occur in a well-hydrated body. You'll have the energy you need to do difficult things when your body has enough water and you won't tire as easily.

Be aware of the increased water requirements of the elderly, the very young, and the disabled or ill during a disaster situation. They may not be able to communicate their needs to you during this stressful time.

You will also want to use disinfected water for cooking, making prepared drinks, and for brushing your teeth.

STORING WATER

Since safe drinking water may not be available during emergencies, stored water can be of tremendous value. The first thing shipped into a disaster area is usually drinking water, but it may not arrive for several days or weeks. If you have planned properly, your stored water may literally save your life.

Sources of Water for Storage

Municipal Water Systems

Public water supplies are regulated by the **EPA** (Environmental Protection Agency). Public water utilities regularly test water for bacteria and you can expect that city water meets the **EPA** drinking water standards.

To understand the guidelines that the **EPA** has for drinking water and an analysis of the lack of funding for clean drinking water, visit **www.ewg.org**. The **Environmental Working Group**, a non-profit organization, has done a comprehensive study of water quality across the U.S.

Private Wells/Springs

If you get your water from a private well, there are no regulations except when the property is purchased. Prior to purchasing, private wells must be tested and proven to be free of bacteria. They may contain other contaminants however, and it's very expensive to test for multiple contaminants—and the levels of contaminants can vary even with the time of year and rainfall.

If you are presently drinking the water and not getting sick from it, you probably can store it.

It would be advisable to purchase a good quality **NSF**-certified water filter if you are on a private well, which may be subject to agricultural pollutants such as nitrates (from fertilizers) or pesticides and herbicides.

What is the NSF?

NSF International is an internationally recognized, not-for-profit, third-party organization with more than 50 years experience in testing and certifying products to ensure that they meet strict public health standards.

For a system to become **NSF** certified, it must meet 5 basic requirements:

1. The contaminant reduction claims must be true
2. The system must not add anything harmful to the water
3. The system must be structurally sound
4. The advertising, literature, and labeling must not be misleading
5. The materials and the manufacturing process cannot change

NSF annually conducts unannounced inspections of manufacturing facilities[i]. If a filter is not **NSF**-certified, the consumer has no guarantee that the manufacturer is being truthful in its claims. Be wary of any products that are labeled "***Tested to NSF Standards***." This is no guarantee that the product is a valid one or that it really does what the manufacturer says it does.

Community Water Systems

Community systems should be tested for bacteria at least quarterly. The **EPA** requires regular testing of any system that services at least 25 individuals, or has 15 service connections. The only testing requirement is for bacterial presence. Community water systems may have some of the same risks as private wells, especially if they are located in agricultural areas.

Bottled Water

Bottled water is regulated by the **FDA** and may or may not have contaminants reduced. There is a wide range in the quality in bottled water. To find out how pure bottled water is, call the bottling company and ask what kinds of processing methods are being used. A reputable bottler will have test results and be willing to disclose them to the public—if they won't, choose another brand!

The shelf life for bottled water depends on how the water is conditioned:
- **filtered** (if at all),
- **sealed**, and
- **sanitized** or **sterilized** after bottling.

The plastic containers used in bottled water have been known to leach polymers into the bottled water after an extended period.

Bottled water is generally safe to drink for 1-2 years, depending on how the water was sanitized. If water has been disinfected using ultraviolet (**UV**) light or ozonation, it generally will last for 2 years. It may have a "*best if used by*" date on it.

How Much to Store

One gallon per person per day for two weeks (14 gallons) is the bare minimum quantity (***subsistence level***) of water you should store. A 160-pound adult should have at least one half-gallon for drinking, plus at least another half-gallon for food preparation, washing, and sanitation. If space allows, more is always better. You may have thirsty neighbors. Also, do not forget to store adequate water for your pets.

You will need more water in hot weather. Cooking and bathing will require more. In addition, you cannot forget water to flush—presuming you are still in your home.

Children, nursing mothers, the elderly and ill people will need more water.

Food preparation and unforeseen events will require even more water. Always give yourself more than you think you will need. It is better to have more than not enough.

If you can figure out a convenient way to store it, it would be great to store a month's supply, or about 60 gallons per person. A small portion of your stored water should be easy to access and transport. Stackable containers may be a danger if you have children, so use care in planning where and how your water is stored.

Pre-Moistened Towelettes

To minimize the water you may need, "*baby wipes*," or pre-moistened towelettes. They are very effective for cleaning and cutting through grime and grease.

Basic Subsistence-Level Water Storage Requirements

Basic subsistence-level water storage is defined as the amount of water required to sustain human body functions normally. This is considered a minimum daily amount of drinking water—any less will eventually create physical stress and possible ill effects.

A normally active person needs to drink 2 quarts of water per day—and more is better during emergency periods. To meet the minimum *Basic subsistence-level* storage requirements plus basic personal needs—cooking some food, brushing teeth, washing face, hands, etc.—**store at least 1 gallon for each family member per day for a two-week period.**

Note the following about the *Basic subsistence-level* quantity of water:
- This amount includes no allowances for washing dishes or the body.
- High-temperature environments require greater water intake.
- Active children, nursing mothers, and sick people will usually need to drink more than two quarts of water each day.
- Most survival experts agree that when water supplies begin to run low, it should not be rationed (except, perhaps, at sea). The reasoning is there's nothing more demoralizing for the average person than being thirsty when under stress!

- The best rationing plan is to drink a reasonable amount of water daily, then find more! Rather than rationing drastically, minimize the amount of water the body needs by reducing activity and staying cool. In the next section you'll discover how to find emergency water sources in and around the house so you won't need to ration water too sharply.

Chart 10–1

Basic Subsistence-Level Water Storage

Number of family members $\Rightarrow$		
Number of gallons to store for each family member	**X**	**1**
Subtotal for family members	**=**	
Multiply by 14 (for two-week supply)	**X**	**14**
Total minimum gallons of water storage required for your family $\Rightarrow$	**=**	

Basic Maintenance-Level Water Storage Requirements

Basic maintenance-level water storage requirements differ from *Basic subsistence-level* requirements by the addition of water reserves to do some of the normally water-intensive chores—cooking and preparing food, cleaning utensils/equipment, and washing the body—without taking a bath! It's only slightly above *Basic subsistence-level* water storage requirements.

The recommended amount of water for *Basic maintenance-level storage requirements* is 2 gallons for each family member per day for a two-week period.

Chart 10–2

Basic Maintenance-Level Water Storage

Number of family members $\Rightarrow$		
Number of gallons to store for each family member	**X**	**2**
Subtotal for family members	**=**	
Multiply by 14 (for two-week supply)	**X**	**28**
Total minimum gallons of water storage required for family $\Rightarrow$	**=**	

Clearly Label Stored Water Products

Mark all containers with *drinking water* or *washing/flushing water* and the date. If water has been filtered prior to storing, mark it *filtered*.

How to Store Water

Containers for Storing Water

Ideal storage containers are the polycarbonate bottles used in the bottled water industry. They do not leach chemicals into the water, will not impart any undesirable taste, are lightweight, virtually unbreakable, do not leak, and many have handles, which make them easy to carry. They also come in a three-gallon size, which is convenient for an emergency kit.

You can store water in any durable and food-safe container—they are impermeable to vapors and gases. All containers should have a tight-fitting lid to prevent evaporation and entering of contaminants.

Glass is heavy and breakable, However, glass is also impermeable to vapors and gases, does not transfer chemicals or give the water a bad taste. Metal tends to corrode and impart an unpleasant taste.

Plastic is lightweight, but it should be a food safe plastic. Polyethylene and polycarbonate are the most common plastics used to store water and are approved for food and water contact. Polycarbonate containers are usually clear and polyethylene is usually cloudy. The hard clear polycarbonate used for many juices and soft drinks is a good choice for water storage. Empty 2-liter polycarbonate pop bottles are convenient in size and shape and usually will not break if dropped. They also can be frozen without bursting, providing some head or air space is left in the bottle. Thick-walled plastic containers are significantly less permeable to hazardous vapors than are thin-walled containers.

Restaurants and other food service establishments may have plastic containers that can be acquired for the asking and used to store—just be sure they have not been used for spicy, pickled, or highly flavored food products.

Some plastics should not be used for storing water. Vinyl plastic waterbeds are not made of food-safe plastic. Trash containers and other plastic bins may leach undesirable chemicals into stored water. Plastic milk bottles are thin-walled and tend to develop leaks in a short period of time—and it's virtually impossible to remove all the milk from the cheap plastic utilized. Bleach bottles or other plastic bottles that contain hazardous substances are not safe for storing drinking water.

The 55-gallon polyethylene drums are a good option for storing utility water for sanitation and washing purposes. The only problem is weight—50 gallons of water weighs more than 400 pounds! Drums cannot be easily moved, so make sure they are stored in an accessible and protected location, preferably in a place where they can be easily drained.

Siphon pumps are available to draw the water out of large containers. An inexpensive siphon pump is available which allows you to drain a 55-gallon drum in less than 10 minutes. However, the cheap plastic pumps are not very durable and very inefficient.

If stored outside, allow about 20% of the container's space for expansion in case of freezing weather. Polyethylene drums are also available in 5-gallon containers, and come in a variety of other sizes, styles, and colors, including models with spigots on the top. Though safe for food and water, these may impart an off-taste to the water.

Some of your water should be easily transported. If your water is in 55-gallon drums or in a cistern, make sure that they are protected so that they cannot shift during an earthquake or tornado.

Cleaning and Sanitizing Water Storage Containers

Clean and sanitize both new and used containers with hot soapy water before filling them with water:

1. Thoroughly clean lids and handles as well as the containers.
2. Rinse well with clean water.
3. Disinfect using a solution of ½-teaspoon bleach per quart of water. Shake well.
4. Rinse with clean water.

Storage Containers to Avoid

Polyethylene is a cloudy plastic and is used for milk containers and some bottled water. It is not as durable as polycarbonate and tends to impart a flavor to the water. These containers tend to spring leaks over time because they are biodegradable plastic. Plastic milk bottles contain protein and fat residues, which may allow bacteria growth.

Do not use any container not labeled for food or beverage storage. Avoid containers that have stored toxic materials like cleaning solvents, gasoline, paint, antifreeze, or bleach. Small amounts of these toxic materials have leached into the plastic, and will be released into stored water. These containers may be useful for storing water for flushing.

Mylar plastic bags inside cardboard boxes are sold by some emergency supply outfitters. These are awkward and will occasionally break. They are pretty messy when they leak.

Beware of Frauds

Beware of products that claim to safeguard stored water for up to five years. The only active ingredient is 5.25% sodium hypochlorite—common household bleach. One of the products claiming to safeguard water for such a long time currently (Aug. 2009) costs $18.00 or more per ½ ounce. That comes to $576.00 for a ½ gallon of bleach—which normally costs less than $2.00/gallon at the grocery store.

Another stabilized oxygen product claiming to prolong water storage is not proven safe for disinfecting water or keeping it safe longer than recommended storage times.

Storage Reservoirs

•Flow-Through Supply

If your plumbing system can be adapted, you may want to add a water storage reservoir. It could be a large tank or hot water heater to which the heat is disconnected. There are manufacturers of bladder-type and rigid-wall systems. The rigid-wall system has the advantage of being less liable to puncture.

The advantage of a flow-through storage reservoir is that it prevents the necessity to change the water.

The disadvantage is that if the incoming water is contaminated, the reservoir will likewise become contaminated. Installing a shut-off valve may prevent incoming contaminated water—if you are able to close it in time.

Another problem is that broken water mains can create a negative pressure, which can drain household lines, including a plumbed-in water storage reservoir. As soon as any emergency occurs, shut off the main water valve to your house, both to prevent inflowing contamination and outflowing water reserves.

•Cistern

A cistern may be a large storage tank filled with water, perhaps collected from the water gutters on your house. In the old days, cisterns were commonplace and filled the need for water when supplies were short. For those of us who have a well, a cistern is a large rock, cement, or plastic above-ground structure for storing water and creating water pressure.

Our cistern is a number of concrete pipes, 12 feet in diameter and 5 feet tall each, and with 4 of them stacked, is 20+ feet tall, holding thousands of gallons of potable water. We located it on higher ground so there's pressure in the system when there is no electricity. We also have a second tank holding 1500-gallon boiler tank for additional water storage, and flow water through that system for emergency needs.

Today, a cistern can be a good source of water for non-drinking use, for watering a garden during a long-term disaster, and for drinking water when you have the appropriate disinfection and filtering available. The key to installing a cistern is where you live and the amount of annual rainfall!

•Well

If you have your own well and pump, you should know how to get water from the well if power is lost. A small generator can be used to keep the pump working.

Several models of gasoline-operated water pumps are available. Look for a heavy duty, self-priming, centrifugal pump that is ideal for emergencies.

Where to Store Water

Secure water containers to the floor or wall to prevent them from tipping over in an earthquake. If you are using the 5-gallon polycarbonate bottles, the ideal way to store them is in plastic crates. They are stackable up to eight crates, so occupy minimal floor space. They interlock, are sturdy, and will not tip over. These crates are available through the bottled water industry and used crates are often available from the dairy industry.

If you store water containers on shelves, placing them on lower shelves is best. Make sure the shelving material will hold the weight of the water without breaking. Water weighs a little over 8 pounds per gallon. A 5-gallon container of water weighs approximately 44 pounds.

Keep water containers off the floor by placing them on wooden pallets. Keep stored water away from direct sunlight. Light will increase the growth of algae and bacteria over time—and cause plastics to deteriorate more quickly.

If you store water in plastic containers, do not store them in the same location as gasoline, kerosene, pesticides, or other hazardous substances. Vapors can permeate the plastic and affect the water's taste dramatically.

If you store water in 55-gallon drums, put them in an area that does not require moving them. Drums full of water weigh almost 500 pounds when full! Also, remember that freezing water can rupture any container! If you live in an area with long cold spells, take care to place containers in a location protected from the cold.

It is a good idea to store water in several different places. If one location is damaged, another may not be. If you have a convenient place outside your house, it might be a good idea to have some containers there. You might survive the disaster—your house might not.

Treating Water before Storing It

Storing Tap Water

If you are storing tap water, which is treated with *chlorine* or *chloramines*[5] from a city supply, there is no need to add additional chlorine prior to storing it. Boiling is generally not recommended either.

Storing Water from a Public Source

If your emergency storage water comes from a public source, no additional chemical disinfection is required. An exception to this is if an emergency "boil water" notice has been given, in which case you would need to disinfect the water before it is stored.

---

[5] An unstable colorless liquid with a pungent odor. Use: manufacture of hydrazine. Formula: NH_2Cl

Sterilized Water

Water can be sterilized for long-term storage in glass canning jars. If possible, run water through a solid-carbon block filter prior to canning water to remove non-microbiological contaminants. Fill clean canning jars with filtered water, leaving 1 inch of headspace at the top of the jar. Place new lids and screw bands on each jar and process in boiling water bath—20 minutes for quart and 25 minutes for ½-gallon jars. Remove the screw bands, label, and store in a convenient place. If the seal is unbroken, sterilized water should last 5 years or longer when bottled and sterilized by this method.

Shelf Life of Stored Water

Just as water quality varies from location to location, shelf life can also vary. Most tap and filtered water stored in suitable containers is fine for drinking for at least 6-12 months. Shelf life will depend on the quality of the water, storage temperature, exposure to light, fuel-based contaminates, and the type of container utilized. Check stored water every 6 months. If any undesirable characteristics in appearance, taste, and/or odor are detected, replace the water.

If the water has an odor or you question its quality, you can disinfect it before filtering. You will still need to replace filtered water every 6-12 months. It's common sense to rotate water out of your storage and use it on the garden or plants so it is not wasted.

If stored water is several years old or of questionable quality, you can disinfect it and pump it through an **NSF**-certified water filter[ii] to remove the chlorine and other contaminants and refresh the water's taste.

WATER IN EMERGENCY SITUATIONS

Protect Water Sources in an Emergency

If local authorities issue a disaster warning and you have time, fill your bathtub, sinks, and any spare containers with water. In some disasters, water may not be immediately shut off or contaminated and you will have some time to store a reserve—use clean containers for drinking and cooking water.

Everyone in your family should know the location of the incoming water valve so it can be shut off to stop contaminated water from entering your home should water or sewage lines be damaged. As soon as the initial trauma of a disaster is over, immediately shut off the main line water valve, as well as the gas line into your house—and don't forget the electrical power shut-off!

Water can be drained from the highest location in your home. Open a valve on the top floor to prevent a vacuum from forming and allow water to flow more freely from faucets on lower levels.

Where to Obtain Water When Your Water Supply Is Cut Off

Hit the faucets!
After the valve has been shut off, you can still access the remaining water in your pipes. Turn on the faucet at the highest level. Water will remain in the pipes. Turn on the water faucet at the lowest level of the house and drain remaining water from the pipes.

Do you know the location of the water valve in your home and do you have a "*water key*" to allow you to shut off water from the street? You will need to shut it off to prevent contaminated water from entering your home if the city supply is polluted from broken water or sewage lines.

Check tanks and heaters!
Toilet tanks and hot water heaters can be used in an emergency. Do not use your toilet tank if chemical agents or bluing are in the tank.

Your hot water heater may have up to 50 gallons of water. You can access it from the drain valve at the bottom front of the water heater. If your hot water heater is intact and the glass liner is not broken, turn off the valve above the hot water heater. You can have a good supply of water by opening the drain valve on the bottom of the water heater. More water will come out of the water heater if a hot water faucet is turned on before starting to drain water from the water heater.

Drain your hot water heater once a year to remove accumulated sediment in the bottom, thereby having the full capacity of the container readily available and usable. Draining it will also prevent buildup in the bottom of the tank, thus increasing the tank's heating efficiency.

Be sure to turn off the gas or electricity to the hot water tank when the tank is empty.

Garden hoses!
Water remaining in coiled garden hoses may taste like the hose, and may contain lead and other chemical contaminants—better to use that water for flushing.

Other sources of potable water!
- Ice cubes
- Beverages, such as soft drinks, juices, and milk
- Water-packed foods, such as canned fruits or vegetables

Pools and tubs!
Swimming pools or hot tubs may contain salts and acids used in pool maintenance and may be used for washing, but should not be used for drinking. Waterbeds usually have chemicals in the plastic and added to the water to prevent algae, fungal, and bacterial growth. Use this water for hand washing and laundering in an emergency, but do not drink it.

Creeks and springs!
If you are fortunate enough to live near a creek or spring, you may be able to divert that water simply by piping it to your home. An electric pump may be used, possibly powered by a small generator. You must clarify and disinfect water from any origin if you're not sure it's safe, and filter it and treat it before drinking.

When it rains, it pours!
Rainwater can be another source of water during an emergency. Collecting rainwater can save you considerable time and energy trying to find extra water in a pinch. There are several ways to catch rainwater:

- You can use a simple rain barrel to collect rainwater directly and economically. If you choose to collect rainwater as simply as possible, use a rain barrel to gather the water *before* it hits the ground. Rainwater will retain its soft, high quality only if it does not come into contact with soil and rocks where it dissolves salts and minerals.
- You can install a contractor-designed system for your house. Installed systems can be costly because they involve in-ground storage and water treatment tanks to collect and filter the water before it enters your house.

An important tip: Even when your collected rainwater does not touch the ground, it could still have airborne pollutants from local industries—also, never forget it cascades down a dirty rooftop to the gutter (did I mention gutters can be filled with all types of detritus? Be safe–always boil and filter rainwater before using it for drinking or cooking.

Let It Snow!
In an emergency, Ol' Man Winter may also be one of your best friends if your water supply is cut off in the winter. Snow is easy to collect and melt for an extra water supply.

However, you should only gather snow that is clean and free of any dirt, slush, and obviously, animal urination. Snow is easy to scoop into buckets, bowls, pots, and pans. If your other utility services have not been disrupted, you can melt the snow on top of your stove or heater. If you have a fireplace, you can easily melt it by the fire. Transfer it to other containers for boiling, filtering, and storage.

Since snow is collected from the ground, you'll definitely want to boil and filter it before using it for **ANY** drinking, cooking, bathing, and laundering. Try to avoid any snow that has had direct contact with the ground.

Lakes, Ponds, Streams, Rivers!

When a natural disaster occurs, no water source can be presumed safe due to the earth changes that occur during floods, earthquakes, hurricanes, and other pollution. If no other water is available, you will need to get it from lakes, ponds, streams, and rivers.

If you choose to obtain water from one of these sources, you will need to weigh your survival with the risks of drinking unsafe water. If you are prepared ahead of time, you can lessen the risks for yourself and your family. A thorough search of **NSF**-certified filters revealed that none could be used on microbiologically unsafe water[iii].

CONTAMINATED WATER

In emergency situations, you'll need to know how to identify additional water sources. As you consider locating and using unfamiliar emergency water sources, it is important that you become aware of the dangers of ingesting contaminated water. When normal water supplies are interrupted, you may need to use water of unknown quality.

Emergency water sources may be muddy, stagnant, brackish, foul-smelling, or otherwise obviously contaminated. Even clear- and clean-looking water may be contaminated. In addition to having bad odor and taste, contaminated water usually contains microorganisms that can cause serious diseases.

Using contaminated water for drinking or cooking can lead to problems which range from a minor upset stomach to life-threatening illnesses, such as amebic dysentery, viral infection, cholera, typhoid, hepatitis, or even death.

TREATING CONTAMINATED WATER

When you get water from unreliable sources, there are several steps you should take to make sure the water is safe and drinkable. These are the 3 steps:

1. **Clarification**. If the water is cloudy or has a lot of debris and particulate matter in it, the first step is to clarify it. When water is clear, it is easier to kill the disease-causing microorganisms.

2. **Disinfection**. The second step is to disinfect it, which kills microorganisms such as bacteria and viruses. Disinfecting can be accomplished by either heat or chemicals such as chlorine or iodine.

3. **Filtration**. The third step is filtration, which removes other contaminants and possibly the after-taste and chemicals used in the disinfecting process. This step makes it taste good, as well as safer to drink. Filtration of contaminants is extremely important because, during a disaster, it is likely that additional contaminants may have invaded your water supply. Contaminants could include fecal matter, chemicals, asbestos, herbicides, parasites, and pesticides.

How to Clarify Water from Impure Sources

During disasters such as earthquakes, tornadoes, or floods, water becomes contaminated with lots of debris as well as higher levels of disease-causing organisms. Such water resources must be disinfected to kill the microorganisms, but very cloudy or turbid water gives many places for these microorganisms to hide.

Prior to disinfecting discolored water, you will need to clarify it to remove most of the sediment or cloudiness so that the disinfecting process can be effective. There are several ways to do this.

- Allow sediment to settle to the bottom of a container and dip off the clear top portion.
- Pour water through several layers of clean cloth, paper towels, or coffee filters.
- Make a capillary siphon. This method allows water to be transferred from one container to another, using a cloth as a siphon. The solid particles and debris are left behind in the first container and in the cloth, while clarified water drips into a catch container. It works very slowly, but produces fairly clear water. You will need two large containers, a 2 foot length of clean cloth (such as a sheet or towel), and rubber bands or thread.
- Roll the fabric into a long roll.
- Secure the roll with rubber bands or thread.
- Elevate the container of cloudy water a foot or so above the catch container
- Place one end of the roll in the container of cloudy water, draping the other end over the edge so it hangs free from the outside wall of the container.
- Place a clean container below the free-hanging end to catch the clarified water.
- Make a hose siphon. You will need two large containers, a six- or eight-foot section of RV hose, and several pieces of cotton fabric. RV hoses are white and do not contain the same contaminants that are found in garden hoses. RV hoses are marked "*safe for drinking water*."
- If water is very muddy, let it settle first and dip off the top water to prevent the cotton from being clogged with the mud.
- Stuff a piece of cloth in one end of the hose. Elevate the container of cloudy water a foot or so above the catch container. Place the end of the hose with the cotton fabric stuffed into it into the container of cloudy water. Suck on the other end of the hose until water begins to flow through. Place the other end of the hose in the catch container to catch the clarified water. Replace the fabric when it becomes clogged.

How to Disinfect Water

Disinfection is the term used to describe killing waterborne pathogens or microorganisms. You can kill microorganisms with heat or chemicals. Chemicals used to disinfect water are chlorine and iodine.

Disease-causing microorganisms are present in all surface water and some groundwater. Water utilities have disinfected tap water with chlorine since 1908, which has eliminated the majority of waterborne diseases such as cholera and typhoid.

Chlorine kills pathogens such as bacteria and viruses, which are present in all water. In emergencies, the normal system for chlorinating water is disrupted.

In disasters, sewage may overflow into water supplies and the level of turbidity may be so high that normal chlorine levels are ineffective for killing microorganisms. Water utilities generally increase the chlorine considerably when this occurs.

All water that comes from unsafe sources may contain one or more of these infectious microorganisms. Bacteria and viruses can be killed by heat or by chemical disinfecting.

However, parasites such as *cryptosporidium* and *giardia* are not killed by chemical disinfection. They either must be killed by heat or be mechanically filtered out with a water treatment device certified by **NSF** to remove *cysts*.[iv] (See **Point-of-Use Filters.**)

Heat Disinfection or Sterilization by Boiling

Boiling is always an effective way to kill all microorganisms, but it requires access to fuel and some type of heating device. You may or may not have gas or electricity to heat water, depending on the nature of the disaster. If you are well equipped with camping gear, extra fuel, or have a well-stocked emergency kit, then boiling water may be practical for you.

Boiling Water Method for Killing Microorganisms

- Bring water to a rolling boil and boil it for 5 to 10 minutes.
- Add 1 more minute of boiling time for each 1000 ft. above sea level.

Boiling does not reduce contaminants such as volatile organic chemicals, pesticides, herbicides, or inorganic contaminants such as lead, mercury, and asbestos. These substances are actually concentrated by boiling.[v] If you have an effective drinking water system and an emergency pump, you can pass the water through it after disinfecting to reduce these other contaminants.

Chemical Disinfecting

When water is cloudy, the effectiveness of chemicals in killing microbiological organisms is reduced. The water must be clarified first through one of the methods described earlier.

If you cannot clarify cloudy water, add twice the amount of chemicals. Add the chemicals, stir, and allow the water to stand for at least 30 minutes before drinking. The ideal is to use a filtration device[vi] to remove the chemicals before drinking.

•Chlorine—Household Bleach

Common household bleach may be used to disinfect water, as long as it contains Hypochlorite 5.25% as its only ingredient. Do not use granular or powdered forms of household bleach.

To chlorinate 50 gallons of water, add 1 ounce (2 tablespoons) of liquid chlorine bleach, which contains Hypochlorite 5.25%, stir, and allow the water to stand for an hour or more. It only requires ½ teaspoon of bleach to disinfect 5 gallons of water. For smaller containers, add 10 drops per gallon. If the water is cloudy, double the amount of bleach.

Follow these guidelines if you use bleach of differing strengths:

Chart 10–3
Using Liquid Bleach of Differing Strengths

Available chlorine	Drops per quart of clear water
1 %	10
4-6%	2
7-19%	1

Ideally, you should use household bleach that is less than one year old. Dating bleach with the purchase date helps you to keep track of how old it is—although it does not take into account how long it has been on the supermarket shelf.

If your bleach is more than a year old, double the amount. Bleach that is more than two years old has lost its effectiveness as a disinfectant. A slight chlorine odor should be detectable in the treated water. If you cannot smell chlorine, repeat the treatment and let it stand for an additional 15 minutes before using.

Chlorine loses its effectiveness in very alkaline water with a pH of 8 or more. Increasing water temperature speeds disinfecting action and lower temperatures slow the action.

Allow the water to stand exposed to the air for a few hours to dissipate the chlorine odor.

You can also pour it from one container to another several times to reduce the chlorine taste.

Ideally, you would filter it afterwards. If you do not have a solid-carbon filter, use a simple pour-through filter pitcher, which will reduce the chlorine taste and odor.

Basic Bleach Method

For emergency treating of water of unknown quality, use any household bleach containing sodium hypochlorite (5.25% solution) *without* soap additives or phosphates.

By using common household bleach as a chemical treatment method, large amounts of safe drinking water can be provided quite inexpensively.

Follow these simple instructions for treating small quantities of water:

- add bleach per **Chart 10–4** below to water in container
- thoroughly mix bleach in water by stirring briskly

Chart 10–4
Basic Bleach Water Treatment Method

Water Quantity	Water Condition	5.25% Sodium Hypochlorite
1 qt.	Clear	2 drops
	Cloudy	**4 drops**
¹/₂ gal.	Clear	4 drops
	Cloudy	**8 drops**
1 gal.	Clear	8 drops
	Cloudy	**16 drops**
5 gal.	Clear	¹/₂ tsp.
	Cloudy	**1 tsp.**
120 gal.	Clear	2 oz.
	Cloudy	**4 oz.**

Disinfecting Large Quantities of Water with Chlorine

The following table shows how much chlorine bleach is needed to disinfect large quantities of water.

Chart 10–5
Liquid Bleach as Disinfectant for Large Quantities of Water

Gallons	5ppm	10 ppm
400	¾ C.	1½ C.
500	1 C.	1¾ C.
1000	1¾ C.	3¼ C.

•Chlorine Tablets

Chlorine tablets are available from drug and sporting goods stores. Follow instructions on the package. Generally, use 1 tablet for each quart or liter of water to be disinfected.

•Granular Calcium Hypochlorite

Granular calcium hypochlorite (**HTH**) can also be used to treat water. Use ¼ ounce for each 2 gal. of water.

To disinfect water, add the chlorine solution in the ratio of 1 part chlorine solution to 100 parts of water to be treated.

<u>**Disinfecting Large Quantities of Water with Calcium Hypochlorite**</u>

The following table show how much calcium hypochlorite you would need to disinfect large quantities of water.

Chart 10–6
Calcium Hypochlorite as Disinfectant for Large Quantities of Water

Gallons	5ppm	10 ppm
400	1 tsp.	2 tsp.
500	1¼ tsp.	2½ tsp.
1000	2½ tsp.	5 tsp.

•Iodine

Iodine is lightweight, easy to use, and is effective in disinfecting water containing micro-biological organisms. For short-term use, iodine consumed in the quantities required for disinfecting water does not have adverse health effects.

However, some people may have an allergic reaction to iodine and people with thyroid conditions or pregnant or nursing women should not use it.

Iodine comes in tablet, crystalline, or concentrated liquid forms. It is more effective against amoebic dysentery cysts and intestinal parasite cysts such as Giardia than chlorine-based disinfectants.

Iodine is not effective against the parasite Cryptosporidium.

A popular and convenient brand to use is **Potable Aqua**. Iodine's main advantage over chlorine is that iodine will disinfect until the pH gets as high as ten.

Chlorine loses its effectiveness when water reaches a pH of eight or more.

One disadvantage with iodine is its cost—as much as 20 times more than chlorine!

Water treated with iodine has a slight iodine taste and smell, which may be objectionable, although **Potable Aqua** has neutralizing tablets which remove the iodine taste and color.

Iodine has a shelf life of 3 to 4 years unopened and a year after opening. It loses effectiveness with age, so be sure to check the expiration date.

<u>Note:</u> Follow the manufacturer's instructions, allowing adequate "*contact time*."

When using liquid iodine, follow these guidelines:

Chart 10–7
Basic Iodine Water Treatment Method

Water Quantity	Water Condition	Quantity of 2% Iodine
1 qt.	Clear	5 drops
	Cloudy	**10 drops**
½ gal.	Clear	6 drops
	Cloudy	**20 drops**
1 gal.	Clear	12 drops
	Cloudy	**24 drops**

For **clear water**, add 5 drops of 2% iodine solution to 1 quart of water and allow it to stand for at least ½ hour before drinking.

For **cloudy water**, add 10 drops and allow to stand for 30 minutes before drinking.

Filtering the water after disinfecting with iodine will greatly improve the taste, just as it does when using chlorine to disinfect.

How to Filter Water

Now That Your Water Has Been Clarified and Disinfected

Once your water has been clarified and disinfected, it should be filtered. The minimum filtration would be to remove the chlorine, which could be done with a simple granular activated filter such as a pour-through carafe. The best filtration would be a filter made of solid carbon which would remove a wide range of contaminants. Remember that chemical disinfection with chlorine does not kill cysts such as *giardia* and *cryptosporidium*. They must be mechanically filtered out by a filter that is .5 micron or less pore size or killed by heat disinfection (boiling).

Filtration Devices

Filters are in two main categories—backpacking filters and point-of-use filters that are designed for use on (or under) your kitchen sink.

●Backpacking Filters

Most backpacking filters are suitable for two to four people, but could not provide enough water for a large family or group of people.

Backpacking filters mechanically strain bacteria, parasites, and some other contaminants, depending on the type and quality of the filter. Unless they contain a solid carbon block filter, they only marginally reduce chemicals, lead, herbicides, pesticides, or asbestos.

Some filters are combined with a disinfectant such as iodine to kill microorganisms that are too small to be physically filtered. Other filters are designed to be used only on microbiologically safe water, which means that the water has to be disinfected prior to passing it through the filter.

●Point-Of-Use Filters

A point-of-use filter may be used to filter water after it has been clarified and disinfected. This type filters a much larger volume of water than a backpacking filter.

There are over 5,000 point-of-use filters available. The majority are designed to make the water look and taste better, but do little to reduce the greatest contaminants causing serious health concerns. These filters are usually made out of granular activated carbon and do a fair job of reducing chlorine. Filters that are attached to the faucet or installed under the sink cannot be used conveniently in an emergency because there is no way to get the water through them without the standard household water pressure.[vii]

If you plan to use a point-of-use filter, either for household use or in an emergency, be sure to look at the ***NSF Standard 53 Health Effects*** to find out what contaminants it reduces. The pour-through filters reduce chlorine, which will make the water taste better, but most do not reduce lead, parasites, pesticides, herbicides, and volatile organic chemicals. For short-term use, a simple pour-through filter would make disinfected water taste better, but you would still have the exposure to other contaminants.

When there is a disaster, far more contaminants are present in water and you probably do not have water flowing through the tap. In this case, you may have to rely on rivers, lakes, or streams—and they will probably have a very high level of pollution.

The only way you can be assured that a filter does what the manufacturer says it does is to read the **NSF** certification that should be in the documentation.

Using a Drinking Water Filtration System in an Emergency

It is useful to treat water at the tap for everyday use, and in an emergency to filter stored water, or filter water from other sources. If your public officials recommend that you boil water to make it safe for drinking[viii], you must disinfect it with chlorine before or after you pass it through a water treatment system. Chlorine is recommended over iodine because it is easier to remove chlorine and iodine is problematic for many people.

You will want to pass it through the filtration system **after** you have disinfected it to remove the taste of chlorine. If you are boiling your water (*heat disinfection*), boil it **before** passing it through the filtration system. Allow it to cool before filtering.

SOME FINAL THOUGHTS ON EMERGENCY WATER

Water indeed is a precious commodity, both globally and personally. It is *second* only in priority to having air to breathe. You could probably live for two weeks—perhaps as long as four weeks—without food, but you can live only a few days without water.

Water is required to digest food; lubricate the body's organs, joints, and membranes; and to maintain the electrical balance in the body's cells. Water also keeps the body cool in summer and warm in winter.

Beyond its life-sustaining function, water is used to wash the body, cook food, and clean cooking utensils. Water is indeed a very important item to have in ready supply!

Therefore, your first priority in preparing for either an emergency situation or for a long-term in-home storage program is to store an adequate reserve of water.

This preparation must be done in a combination of **three** steps:

1. **Store a subsistence-level or maintenance-level supply of water now and keep it fresh!**
2. **Learn how to treat contaminated water so it's safe to drink.**
3. **Learn to identify alternative sources of potable water to avoid deprivation during emergencies**

The quality of water you have available during an emergency is up to you. If you plan, you can have good water readily accessible. If you do not, you will be at the mercy of government or community sources or your own resources for drinkable water.

If you do not have enough stored water and must rely upon other sources, at least you can disinfect it using chlorine or iodine—and drink it. The next best treatment would be to chlorinate it and remove the chlorine by pouring it through a granular activated charcoal filter.

Ideally, the best-case scenario would be to reduce not only the chlorine, but the other contaminants as well. You can do this if you have planned well and have an **NSF**-certified water treatment system and an emergency hand pump or siphon.

The bottom line is this:

Do what you can now to avoid having to use contaminated water later. You can lessen the health risks for yourself and your family, and know that you will have good, clean, safe drinking water should a disaster or emergency occur.

STORE YOUR EMERGENCY WATER SUPPLY NOW!

Water is generally the cheapest preparedness item to acquire and the easiest to store. It also weighs the most and takes up more space—you can't dehydrate water and reconstitute it without water! The difficulties of a water storage program can be easily overlooked when you realize that in times of greatest need, water will be worth its weight in gold!

Usually, the first emergency supply item brought into a disaster area to aid victims is the water wagon. If you've ever been a victim of a hurricane or flood, you understand the mariner's plight when he lamented, *"... water, water, everywhere...but not a drop to drink!"*

RESOURCES FOR WATER INFORMATION

North Carolina Cooperative Extension Service
Emergency Drinking Water Supplies
Attn.: Dorothy L Miner, Extension Water Quality Associate Specialist
http://www.bae.ncsu.edu/programs/extension/publicat/wqwm/emergwatersuppl.html

Water Supply Management Program
U.S. Army Center for Health Promotion and Preventive Medicine
5158 Blackhawk Road, Aberdeen Proving Ground MD 21010-5403
(410) 436-3919

Washington State Department of Health
Environmental Health Programs
Division of Drinking Water
DOH Pub. #331-115 (Revised October 2001)

Environmental Working Group http://www.ewg.org/tapwater/findings.php
Headquarters, 1436 U Street. NW, Suite 100, Washington DC 20009 | (202) 667-6982
California office, 2201 Broadway, Suite 308, Oakland CA 94612 | (510) 444-0973
Midwest office, 103 E. 6th Street, Suite 201, Ames IA 50010 | (515) 598-2358
Sacramento office, 1107 9th Street, Suite 340, Sacramento CA 95814 | (916) 333-0566

Print Information

"*Food and Water in an Emergency*," FEMA preparedness document
http://www.fema.gov/pte/foodwtr.htm

Boy Scout Handbook, Boy Scouts of America

Drink Water for Life, Deanna DeLong, 3450 SW 108th Avenue, Beaverton OR 97005-1831 (503) 641-1916 *deanna@drinkwaterforlife.net* or www.dwflonline.com $25.00 + $4.95 S&H

Plan…Not Panic: The 72-Hour…Manual, Barbara Salsbury

Testing Facilities

National Testing Laboratories, Inc. (NTL), 6151 Wilson Mills Road, Cleveland OH 44143
Naturally Pure Alternatives (NPA), 575 Live Oak Avenue, Ukiah CA 95482 (800) 825-3227

<u>**Note:**</u> This chapter was submitted by **Deanna DeLong**, an expert in dehydrating foods and rehydrating people! There is so much to tell, but the publisher has limited the pages of this edition or I would continue with more—an expert in so many areas of the preparedness industry!   Here are some of the basics:
Deanna Delong, 3450 SW 108th Ave., Beaverton OR 97005-1831 Bus. (503) 641-1916 cell (503) 720-0355 Fax: (503) 644-9236. email: *deanna@drinkwaterforlife.net* or website: **www.dwflonline.com**. Education: University of New Mexico, *BS Home Economics Education;* Portland State University, *MS Education.* Created curriculum and taught high school, community college, and university classes. **International Teaching***:* ACDI/VOCA, SUSTAIN, USAID, Mellon Foundation, International Executive Service Corps in areas of Central America, Hungary, Poland, Africa, Republic of Georgia (*1985 to 2009):* Seminars and consulting in domestic & small-scale industrial food dehydration. **Author***:* **How To Dry Foods, Revised**, Penguin Group, Inc., ©*2006;* **How To Dry Foods**, Penguin Putnam, Inc, ©*1979 [2.5 million copies in print (45th printing);* **How To Dry Foods Easily**, (DVD & video), **Preservation Pantry** ©*1995;* **Drink Water For Life**, (DVD & book) ©*1998.* PUBLIC **Seminars***: 500+ seminars on* **How To Dry Foods***; 300+ seminars—***Drink Water for Life***.* **Television/Radio***: 200+ appearances—How To Dry Foods, (including* **Oprah***);* **Newspaper/Magazine***: 100+ articles.* **Consultant:** Nesco/American Harvest, Two Rivers WI (*1979 – 1997*), Product testing & development, special projects, Television production, onsite expert, developed Owner's manual & newsletter; Waring Products, New Hartford CN (1993) Seminar for marketing, sales, & engineering departments, owner's manual; TILIA—Foodsaver Vacuum Packaging System, San Francisco CA (*1986 – 1995*) Technical consultant & Talent for infomercials, commercials for television, and wrote Owner's manual.

Quick-Guide 10–1
Emergency Water Resources Guide

Water Source	Guidelines for Use
Interior Water Sources	
Plumbing system	Best water to use in emergency. Everyone familiar with taste, odor, mineral content & quality of water. Know where to find main water valve for cut-off. Have proper valve key.
water lines	Contain several gallons of water, depending on house. Easiest water to access. Turn on faucet at lowest point in line. If water doesn't flow, then open faucet at highest point in line.
hot water heater	Contains 15-40 gallons potable water, depending on size. Open drain faucet at bottom of heater. You may need to screen or filter out sediment before drinking or cooking with it.
tubs & sinks	Fill ahead of time when possible to have additional water on hand.
toilet tanks *(not bowls!)*	Contain 5–7 gallons in tank. Always treat (boiling is preferred method) before using. ***Caution: Not potable if commercial disinfectants or cleaners are used in tank.***
Appliances	Use appliances for emergency water storage.
refrigerator and/or freezer	Consume cooled and frozen drinks & liquid sources (fruits, vegetables, etc.) first—they become less palatable over time during power outage. Ice cubes provide some drinking water; may also be important for first aid or to preserve food longer.
water cooler	,Also clothes washer, tubs, buckets, large pots & pans. Fill to capacity for additional reserves.
Water beds	*Controversial storage source.* **To use water bed water for emergency purposes, follow these requirements**: (1) use only a new mattress (2) fill mattress with fresh tap water (3) add 2 oz. bleach per 120 gallons of water ***(do not use toxic algae inhibitor solution!)*** (4) rotate water at least yearly (5) test 3–4 times yearly for algae & toxins (6) all water bed water must be boiled *before* using it
Exterior Water Sources	
Yard	Water hoses, buckets, barrels of rainwater, puddles, ditches, and troughs may contain water.
water hoses	Suspect contamination if hose end is in bucket, barrel, ditch, or puddle. Hoses lying on the ground may have siphoned contaminated water.
hot water spa or swimming pool	*Controversial source.* Could provide both emergency source and long-term storage. Use for nondrinking purposes. If required for drinking or cooking, treat and boil as contaminated.
Precipitation rainwater	Rain and snow provide water. If caught in clean containers, may be used without treatment. Otherwise, treat as contaminated water. Collect in bowls, pans, buckets, barrels & storage cisterns. Treat *all* water not caught in clean containers.
Surface water lakes streams ponds rivers	Collect water and process: (1) find a sandy spot within 1' –6' of water's edge; (2) dig hole 12" below the water level; (3) wait for water to seep into hole; (4) let suspended particles (mud) settle; (5) dip out clear water carefully to avoid transferring mud. Water may be filtered through sand, grass, charcoal, field filtration unit, or use several layers of cloth to remove larger debris. Treat all surface water as contaminated.
Groundwater	Puddles, ditches, and any ground depression can contain water. All groundwater sources must be treated as contaminated.
well water	Unless used as primary water source, test before using. Check for contamination after any unusual disturbance to area.
natural spring	Normally potable unless inundated by floodwaters or recharge zone contaminated by oil, chemical spills, dead animals, etc. However, if water is not tested, treat as contaminated.

[i] In a thorough canvassing of **NSF**-certified filters, this author found only one company (**Multi-Pure**) whose products could be conveniently used in an emergency and reduces the broadest range of contaminants of any **NSF**-certified filter and are in use homes across the nation. **Multi-Pure** water filters accomplish the following:

[ii] **NSF**-certified to remove contaminants. See specifications in the sales literature or online (**www.multipure.com**) or call (800) 622-9206.

[iii] Markets a clever hand pump and siphon that can be effectively used in an emergency. When using any water purification device in an emergency, you must ***clarify*** and ***disinfect*** the water first, then pass it through the filter for use.

[iv] Certified to remove cysts.

[v] With drinking water system and an emergency pump, you can pass the water through it after disinfecting to reduce these other contaminants.

[vi] Removes chemicals.

[vii] We have whole-house system in our 2nd home the seems to be an exception.

[viii] Reduces the broadest range of contaminants of any **NSF**-certified filter.

Chapter 11
Basics of Dairy Products from Powdered Milk

Few foods are as valuable as milk and milk products. For food storage purposes, powdered milk is a versatile milk derivative with numerous applications. Most dairy products can be made from rehydrated powdered milk: cottage cheese, yogurt, cream cheese, and even hard cheeses. For those who really want to be able to produce their cheese by learning home cheese making, you will find recipes for making homemade cheddar, farmer, and Italian-style cheeses. This chapter provides instructions for making a wide range of basic dairy products and has additional main meal recipes for use with your stored powdered milk.

POWDERED MILK NUTRITION

Dry powdered milk, whether whole or skim (nonfat), provides many of the USDRI (formerly USRDA) (United States Dietary Reference Intakes/United States Recommended Daily Allowance) minerals and vitamins—most notably calcium. Realize, however, that rehydrated dry milk is not the equivalent of raw milk.

The heating, pasteurizing, and drying processes destroy not only the bacteria but also some of the essential enzymes. Therefore, if you use powdered milk exclusively for an extended period of time, you should supplement your diet with an appropriate selection of vitamins and minerals your body needs.

Within several months after processing, all processed foods, including powdered milk, begin to lose nutritional value. The nutritional shelf life of powdered milk is relatively short when compared to its useful shelf life. Powdered milk can still be utilized in recipes and will act acceptably as an ingredient even when no longer nutritious. Since that's true for virtually all stored foods, two things become evident: the need for a nutritional supplement program and rotation through utilization.

PURCHASING POWDERED MILK

Use the following guidelines when purchasing powdered milk for your home storage program:

- non-instant, nonfat powdered milk (made from skim milk)
- less than 4% moisture
- *extra* grade, low-heat, spray-processed
- no artificial color, flavor, or preservatives added
- fortified with vitamins A and D

It is important to select the best quality product for storage because it will be more nutritious and actually store longer. The best grade is labeled "extra" and should contain no more than 4% moisture. Low moisture content is very important, as the moisture factor determines the period of time powdered milk may be stored and still remain nutritious.

Be aware that some brands of dry milk are made from *grade B* milk sources. That's one reason some off-brand products are cheaper than the "extra" grade powdered milk.

Instantized or instant powdered milk has been processed more than non-instant and therefore has a shorter shelf life.

Buy non-instant powdered milk for long-term storage.

When buying powdered milk for storage, check quality, age, moisture content, warranty provisions, and whether the product is being sold by reputable persons and companies.

Always check expiration dates when buying dry milk products.

POWDERED MILK STORAGE

The *extra* grade dry skim milk should be purchased in double-sealed 5-pound cans or in double-wrapped, foil-lined, and paper-reinforced bags. This higher-grade powdered milk will store for up to 60 months if kept dry and cold (40°F).

Storage at temperatures of 60°-70°F will reduce effective (nutritional) storage time to 12-24 months. However, it is possible to use it in recipes and benefit from the stored milk.

REHYDRATING POWDERED MILK

There are many brands of powdered skim milk on the market. Each brand has instructions on the package indicating how much water and milk powder to use for rehydration. The following recipe is a general guideline for rehydration—don't be afraid to experiment with quantities to formulate the best mixture for your own palate.

You can improve the flavor of powdered milk by mixing it half-and-half with whole milk. Add honey, nondairy creamers, fruit juices, sugar, powdered sugar, vanilla flavoring, or any flavoring of choice the family likes to improve the somewhat flat taste of rehydrated dry milk.

Foods made with powdered milk instead of whole milk have fewer calories and less cholesterol. Adding extra powdered milk to a recipe enhances the nutritional value of the recipe. You'll find it easy to experiment with the amounts you can add. Powdered milk is fairly forgiving in its use in soups, sauces, gravies, and especially when rehydrating for drinking. My children never complained because of the richness of the flavor.

Basically, both instant and non-instant milk are normally interchangeable. There are differences in the consistency of different brands, so you may need to note the results with the different brands when substituting for whole milk.

TIPS FOR SUBSTITUTING POWDERED MILK IN RECIPES

- In recipes using milk, add the dry milk to the other dry ingredients. Sift to blend, and then add water in place of the milk called for in the recipe.
- Mashed potatoes are excellent when ¼ to $^1/_3$ C. dry powdered milk per C. of potatoes is added to the mashed potatoes. Use either a rich mix of powdered milk or the water in which the potatoes were cooked to bring to consistency desired.
- Make your ground meat—whether beef, chicken, turkey, or other—recipes richer and more nutritional by adding ¼ to ½ C. powdered milk per lb. of meat.
- Add a thick paste of dry powdered milk and water to soups, stocks calling for milk, and sauces to make them tastier and richer in nutrition.
- For dry cereals, mix extra thick to enhance the taste. (What's the difference in adding honey or sugar to the milk instead of the cereal?)
- For cooked cereals, add ¼ to ½ C. dry milk to the water before adding the dry cereal grain. (I add butter, too!)

RECIPES FOR BASIC POWDERED MILK

BASIC REHYDRATED POWDERED MILK

| 4 C. cold water | $1^2/_3$ C. powdered milk |

Beat ingredients with beater or mixer until smooth. *Yield: 1 qt. milk.*

BASIC BUTTERMILK

| 1 C. non-instant (or 1¾ C. instant) milk | 3 C. gently warm water |
| ½ C. buttermilk (or pkg. butter milk powder) | |

Beat well until blended. Cover. Allow to stand at room temperature for 6-12 hours or until mixture clabbers to desired consistency. Refrigerate to stop clabbering process.

Always save ½ C. for next batch. When mixture doesn't clabber, it's time to get a new start from a commercial brand or more buttermilk mix.

BASIC SOUR BUTTERMILK

Add 1 tsp. lemon juice or white vinegar to *Basic Buttermilk* recipe. Stir well until thoroughly blended. Chill!

This is my favorite summer cooler!

BASIC EVAPORATED MILK

    1 C. water   2/3 C. powdered milk

Mix together thoroughly and chill.

BASIC VITALITY COOLER

    1 C. *Basic Rehydrated Milk*   2 C. water
    $^1/_2$ C. sugar (or honey)   ice
    6 oz. frozen orange juice concentrate

Put milk, sugar, and orange juice in blender; blend until mixed. Add water and ice, blending until mushy. Serve with snacks or for breakfast. May be thinned with additional water and ice, then sweetened to taste. *Yield: approximately 1 qt.*

BASIC SOFT ICE CREAM

    1 C. non-instant dry milk   3 T. honey
    3 C. water

Mix in blender, put in shallow tray and freeze until solid. To serve, break into small chunks and stir with whip or beat with mixer at slow speed until soft. Serve with chocolate syrup, jams, jellies, or other flavorings.

BASIC YOGURT FROM POWDERED MILK

Yogurt is a very flexible food—it can be a drink when thinned with milk, buttermilk, fruit juice, or water; mixed with fruit for a dessert; set in Jell-O®; or used in place of sour cream in stroganoff, sauces, chip dips, and fruit salads. *Basic Yogurt* is a tasty, healthful food with all the advantages of milk. However, it is lower in lactose for those who don't tolerate milk products. It has proven helpful to children and adults with diarrhea. Yogurt is a great way to vary the daily diet and adds a gourmet touch to many recipes.

In-Home Basic Yogurt Production

In France and Switzerland, I knew families who had inherited yogurt starter from their grandparents.

Yogurt is a cultured milk product made from enriched milk to which a yogurt culture, or *starter,* has been added. The milk must be concentrated from one-half to two-thirds of its original volume. Since powdered milk is already concentrated, it is particularly easy to use in making *Basic Yogurt* at home.

Basic Yogurt is very simple to make. All that is required is some warm water, powdered milk, and a little yogurt starter—which is available in the grocery store! The milk with yogurt culture added is kept at a temperature of 100°-120°F for approximately 3-4 hours.

When the *Basic Yogurt* sets up, it can be eaten immediately while warm or refrigerated for later consumption when it's cold. Remember to save a little bit of the *Basic Yogurt* as the starter for the next batch, and you are literally set for life!

To maximize storage of fresh-made *Basic Yogurt*, chill immediately as soon as set-up occurs.

Basic Yogurt may be stored in refrigerator up to one week—then you can make it into cheese to give it a whole new life!

The section following **Suggestions for Making Basic Yogurt Successfully** gives you details for further use of basic yogurt—not a spoonful need be wasted!

Suggestions for Making Basic Yogurt Successfully

Ingredients

The most important advice relative to ingredients for *Basic Yogurt* is:
- Use the best grade powdered milk available.
- Procure a yogurt starter from a reliable source.

Rehydrating powdered milk: when using any powdered milk for yogurt, whether instant or non-instant, *rehydrate it just a little short of being double in strength.*

Yogurt starter: in *Basic Yogurt* recipes, use unflavored commercial yogurt for the starter or use yogurt from the last batch (it shouldn't be more than a week old). Pure yogurt culture can be obtained from health food stores. Most authorities recommend a fresh start every month or two if you are not using it at least weekly.

Use two tablespoons yogurt starter for every three cups of doubly rehydrated milk. Using this rule of thumb, make as much or as little *Basic Yogurt* desired.

Temperature

The lower the set-up temperature, the longer *Basic Yogurt* takes to set. Temperatures of 110°-120°F will produce firm yogurt in approximately three hours. There are several methods for keeping the *Basic Yogurt* mixture at the correct temperature. Perhaps the easiest way to maintain the proper temperature is to buy a commercial yogurt maker, available at most grocery, retail, and health food stores. Alternatively, the yogurt mixture can be placed over a heat register, pilot light, or hot plate—we've even used a heating pad! In using any of these methods, test the temperature by setting a covered pan of warm water over the heat source for several hours, checking the temperature periodically to assure maintenance of temperature in the 110°-120°F range.

Storage

Yogurt will keep in the refrigerator for a week or longer. However, *the longer yogurt sits in the refrigerator the more pronounced the flavor becomes.* Make a batch of yogurt at least once a week to keep the starter fresh.

RECIPES FOR MAKING BASIC YOGURT

The recipes on the following pages will get you started with in-home production of yogurt, utilizing either powdered, commercial, or whole milk. The best part about homemade *Basic Yogurt* is that the flavor can be varied from very mild to quite strong. Customize *Basic Yogurt* to your individual taste as you experiment with homemade products. This is a distinct advantage over buying commercial yogurt, and it's cheaper, too!

Should a batch fail to set up, there is a section later in this chapter titled **"If Yogurt Fails" Check-List** to help resolve *Basic Yogurt* production problems.

BASIC YOGURT FROM POWDERED MILK

2 C. warm water   2 T. yogurt starter (unflavored)
1 C. non-instant powdered milk

Pour warm water (100°F) in the blender and turn on low speed; add powdered milk slowly. Blend until smooth. Add yogurt and blend a few more seconds. (This whole process can be done by hand, but be sure to beat until all the lumps are out.) Pour into jars or glasses. Place jars neck-deep in a pan in warm (100°F) water. Cover pan with lid.

(Cont.)

Place on yogurt maker (or any place a temperature of 100°-200°F can be maintained) for 3-4 hours. Check after 3 hours to see if *Basic Yogurt* mixture has set up. If not set up, check each 20 min. until set. *(If not set up in 4 hours, you probably have a failure.)*

BASIC YOGURT FROM FRESH MILK

> 4 C. fresh raw milk   2 T. yogurt starter (unflavored)
> ¹/₂ C. non-instant powdered milk

Boil (180°F) fresh, raw milk in a saucepan for five seconds. Cool until warm (100°F). Stir in powdered milk. Thoroughly mix yogurt starter with a little warm milk in a small bowl, then add to the rest of the warm milk, stirring in well. Pour mixture into jars or glasses and let stand neck-deep in yogurt maker at 110° until set (usually about 3 hours). Chill immediately after yogurt sets. Keeps in refrigerator approximately one week.

"If Basic Yogurt Fails" Checklist

If yogurt doesn't set up properly, check the following indicators to ascertain what may have caused the failure:

☐ Yogurt was disturbed or stirred while setting up.

☐ The start was added to hot instead of warm milk.

☐ Temperature was too hot (kills yogurt bacteria) or too cool (causes ordinary sour milk bacteria to develop).

☐ Yogurt start was too old or was inactive for some other reason.

☐ Jars or other equipment were not clean.

☐ Fresh, raw milk was not boiled.

☐ Yogurt was in yogurt maker too long (indicated when yogurt is bubbly and starts to separate).

Constructing a Basic Yogurt Maker

If you are truly converted to in-home yogurt production, you can make your own yogurt maker for a few nickels and dimes. On the following page is **Illustration 12–1**, detailing how to make the *Basic Yogurt Maker* from a #10 can, a light socket, and a light bulb:

- Completely remove one end of the can.
- Punch a hole in the remaining end of the can.
- Secure the lamp socket.
- Punch holes in the base and top to provide a draft to heat the pan of water.
- Vary the wattage of the light bulb and its distance from the bottom of the pan to stabilize temperature between 110°-120°F.
- Generally, 25W to 50W bulbs will maintain the proper temperature. An in-line dimmer provides additional heat control.

Illustration 11–1 shows how to make a simple *Basic Yogurt Maker* from a #10 can.

Illustration 11–2 shows how to use the *Basic Yogurt Maker*.

> **Note:**
>
> *At first you might forget to use yogurt freely, but in time you'll find uses for it every day. And remember, if at first you don't succeed in getting the family to use yogurt readily, keep trying. It's certainly worth the effort.*

Illustration 11–1

Basic Yogurt Maker

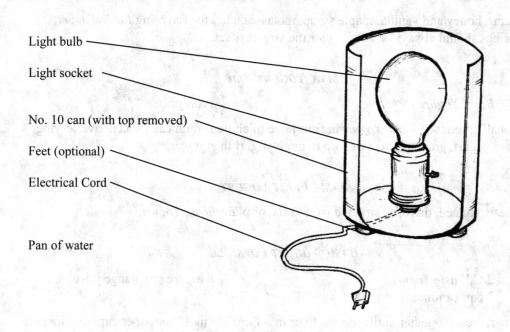

Light bulb

Light socket

No. 10 can (with top removed)

Feet (optional)

Electrical Cord

Pan of water

Illustration 11–2

Using the *Basic Yogurt Maker*

Jars in water

RECIPES FOR BASIC YOGURT

FLAVORED BASIC YOGURT

Use jams, honey and vanilla, maple syrup, molasses, etc., for flavoring *Basic Yogurt*. Flavorings should always be added *after* the yogurt is set.

When adding any flavoring to yogurt, stir lightly; the more yogurt is stirred, the thinner it becomes.

BASIC YOGURT FLIP

Basic Yogurt   Fruit juice

Mix small amount of *Basic Yogurt* in fruit juice of choice. With each successive serving, increase yogurt, gradually working up to more yogurt than juice.

These recipes will help reluctant children learn to like yogurt.

BASIC FRUIT YOGURT

Use fresh, canned, dried, or strained fruit to flavor plain *Basic Yogurt*.

BASIC YOGURT POPSICLE

2 C. *Basic Yogurt*   6 oz. frozen orange juice
2 tsp. vanilla

Mix ingredients together until smooth. Pour into Popsicle molds or paper cups and insert ice cream sticks. Freeze until firm.

BASIC YOGURT PARFAIT

1 C. *Basic Yogurt*   1 C. fruit

Cover bottom of dessert dish with fruit, then add layer of *Basic Yogurt*. Repeat layers, topping with fruit. Chill and serve.

BASIC YOGURT BUTTERMILK

1 C. *Basic Yogurt*   1 C. water

Mix equal parts *Basic Yogurt* and water in blender. *Basic Yogurt* mixed in this manner will replace buttermilk in most recipes. Makes a good drink, too!

BASIC YOGURT JELL-O

Jell-O, partially set   1 C. *Basic Yogurt*

When mixing Jell-O, leave out $1/4$ C. water. Add 1 C. *Basic Yogurt* to partially set Jell-O. Fruit may be added. Lemon-lime and orange Jell-O are especially good with yogurt added.

BASIC YOGURT CREAM SAUCE

Warm (115°-120°F) *Basic Yogurt* and use as a cream sauce on vegetables or in stroganoff recipes. *Do not heat Basic Yogurt above 120°F.* Heat will kill the yogurt bacteria that are beneficial to good health.

BASIC YOGURT SOUR CREAM

Basic Yogurt can be used to replace commercial sour cream in most recipes. Use plain, or add chives, bacon bits, onion flakes, onion or garlic salt, seasoning salt, or ground pepper to flavor *Basic Yogurt*. Use as a base for chip dips or gourmet dressings by adding herbs and spices.

BASIC YOGURT AVOCADO DIP

$^1/_2$ C. *Basic Yogurt*   garlic powder
1 large avocado   salt to taste
3 T. lemon juice

Mash avocado, add lemon juice and seasonings; add *Basic Yogurt* and beat well. Serve with fresh crisp vegetables. (Cauliflower, carrots, turnips, celery, green peppers, jicama, broccoli, etc., are excellent.)

BASIC YOGURT HEALTH DIP

2 C. unflavored *Basic Yogurt* $^1/_2$ tsp. celery salt
2 C. skim milk cottage cheese   garlic powder
$^1/_4$ tsp. garlic powder   salt
$^1/_4$ C. toasted sesame seeds $^1/_4$ C. wheat germ

In a medium bowl blend *Basic Yogurt* and cottage cheese thoroughly. Sprinkle in sesame seeds, wheat germ, celery salt, and garlic powder. Blend well. Salt to taste. Chill. *Yield: 4 cups.* Serve as a dip accompanied by vegetable relishes or crisp crackers.

Vegetable relishes: Raw cauliflowerettes, carrot and celery sticks, jicama, sliced cucumber, and green, red, and sweet pepper chunks.

BASIC YOGURT ROQUEFORT DRESSING

1 C. *Basic Yogurt*   Cracked or ground pepper
$^1/_2$ C. cottage cheese, fine curd   4 oz. Roquefort cheese
Fresh finely chopped garlic or garlic salt   Salt to taste

Mix *Basic Yogurt* and cottage cheese, adding crumbled cheese. Season to taste, then chill to allow seasonings to mingle. Serve cold. (See *Basic Cottage Cheese* information in the following section for directions for your own homemade cottage cheese!)

BASIC YOGURT & HONEY DRESSING

dash salt   1 T. sugar
dash pepper   2 T. honey
dash dry mustard   1 C. *Basic Yogurt*
1 T. lemon juice

Blend salt, pepper, dry mustard, and sugar into a bowl with honey. Add *Basic Yogurt*, stirring lightly. Then gently stir in lemon juice. Goes well with crisp salads, grilled chicken and turkey strips, and any of the popular salad greens.

BASIC YOGURT GREEN GODDESS DRESSING

soft, ripe avocado $^1/_2$ tsp. salt
1 C. *Basic Yogurt* $^1/_2$ tsp. seasoned salt
1 T. parsley flakes $^1/_4$ C. mayonnaise
2 tsp. instant minced onion

Put all ingredients into mixing bowl. Blend ingredients with wire whip. Mix thoroughly. *Yield: approximately 2 C.*

BASIC YOGURT BEEF STROGANOFF

1 lb. ground beef	dash of pepper
5 slices of bacon, diced	$^1/_2$ tsp. sweet basil
$^1/_2$ C. chopped onion	1 tsp. garlic salt
$^1/_2$ tsp. salt	$^1/_4$ tsp. paprika
1 #303 can cream of mushroom soup	1 C. *Basic Yogurt*
hot buttered noodles of choice	

In skillet, brown ground beef with bacon. Add onion and cook until tender but not brown. Drain off excess fat. Add salt, basil, paprika, garlic, and pepper. Stir in cream of mushroom soup and cook slowly, uncovered, 20 min., stirring frequently. Stir in *Basic Yogurt*. Keep hot, but *do not boil*. Serve meat sauce over hot buttered noodles. *Yield: 4-6 servings.*

BASIC YOGURT WHEAT GERM ROLLS

1 C. warm *Basic Yogurt*	1 egg
1 envelope active dry yeast	$^3/_4$ C. wheat germ
$^1/_4$ C. butter or margarine	$2^1/_2$ C. whole-wheat flour
$1^1/_2$ tsp. salt	$^1/_3$ C. powdered milk
3 T. blackstrap molasses	

Before preparing other ingredients, stir dry yeast into *Basic Yogurt*. Add butter, salt, egg, molasses, and wheat germ and stir briskly. Sift in flour and powdered milk. Stir until all ingredients are combined, then beat 200 strokes (10 min. in electric mixer). Cover bowl and set in warm place until double (about 1 hr.). Make into rolls at once or stir and chill in refrigerator 1-8 hr. before using. Bake at 350°F for 20 min. *Yield: twenty 2" rolls.*

BASIC YOGURT RYE BREAD

1 envelope active dry yeast	2 tsp. salt
2 C. warm water	$1^1/_2$ C. rye flour
2 T. honey	7-9 C. whole-wheat flour
1 C. plain *Basic Yogurt*	

In a large mixing bowl combine the yeast and water and allow the yeast to dissolve (takes about 5 min.). Stir in the honey, yogurt, salt, and rye flour. Slowly add wheat flour until the dough pulls away from the sides of the bowl. Turn dough onto a floured breadboard and knead until it feels smooth and elastic, about 5-7 min. Divide the dough into two equal parts; shape and place in greased 9" x 5" x 3" pans. Cover with a clean dishtowel and set in a warm place (85°F) to rise. Preheat oven to 350°F. Bake for 45-50 min. or until done. *Yield: 2 loaves.*

BASIC YOGURT CREAM CHEESES

Basic Yogurt Cream Cheese

Simply pour *Basic Yogurt* into a cheese bag and let drain for an hour or two. A thicker consistency than ordinary yogurt is obtained by draining off the excess water. This drained yogurt can be used in recipes for dips, spreads, sauces, and dressings. This is perhaps the simplest cream cheese method. The result is tangy and delicious.

Alternate Method for Basic Yogurt Cream Cheese

Dump a cup of *Basic Yogurt* into a piece of sheeting or fine cheesecloth and hang it above the sink to drain overnight. The following morning there will be a white ball of the most tender, creamiest cream cheese with no fat. To give this cheese more flavor, season with salt and a little brown sugar. Make a delicious sandwich spread by mixing chopped olives or nuts into cheese. Let your imagination run a little wild!

Sharp Basic Yogurt Cream Cheese

For sharper cream cheese, use *Basic Yogurt* that has aged in the refrigerator for several days. Add some kelp powder or salt to taste. Mix with either minced green onions, chives, caraway seeds, pimentos, olives, or crushed pineapple to make tantalizing spreads and sandwich fillings.

Ricotta Basic Yogurt Cream Cheese

Squeeze *Basic Yogurt* until whey (liquid) is expelled, and the result is a cheese much like ricotta. It can be used as cream cheese in most creamed cheese recipes—try these recipes made with *Basic Yogurt Cream Cheese:*

BASIC YOGURT LEMON CREAM CHEESECAKE

Filling:

12 oz. *Basic Yogurt Cream Cheese*
2 eggs, beaten
$^1/_2$ C. lemon juice
$^1/_2$ C. sugar

Vanilla Wafer Crust:

1 C. vanilla wafer crumbs
1 T. sugar
2 T. melted butter or margarine
pinch salt

Topping:

1 C. sour cream
1 T. grated lemon rind

1 T. sugar

Filling: blend *Basic Yogurt Cream Cheese* and lemon juice thoroughly. Add eggs and sugar and beat until smooth. Pour into vanilla wafer crust. Bake at 350°F for 15-20 min. or until firm. Remove from oven and cool 5 min.

Crust: mix ingredients until butter is absorbed; place crumbs in round 9" baking pan and spread in even layer.

Topping: mix topping ingredients and pour over pie filling. Bake 10 min. longer. Cool. Chill in refrigerator 5 hr. before serving. *Yield: 6 to 8 servings.*

BASIC YOGURT BLEU CREAM CHEESE DRESSING

$^1/_2$ -1 C. buttermilk
1 C. *Basic Yogurt Cream Cheese*
4 oz. bleu cheese, crumbled

1 T. chives
1 T. Worcestershire sauce

Put $^1/_2$ C. buttermilk and all other ingredients in bowl. Mix well, adding more buttermilk until desired consistency is attained. Chill in refrigerator. Serve cold with vegetable slices or strips. *Yield: approximately 2 C.*

BASIC COTTAGE CHEESE FROM POWDERED MILK

> *Cottage cheese is generally interchangeable with yogurt in most recipes and "softens" the taste of the recipe.*

Cottage cheese is made commercially from skim milk, rehydrated concentrated skim milk, or nonfat dry milk solids. The only reason it's not made from whole milk is the cost. However, you can make cottage cheese at home from any type of milk available.

Cottage cheese is full of body-building protein and calcium, but low in butterfat. This makes it filling without the attendant high-calorie intake problems. Cottage cheese makes food taste rich and fattening—without being either.

BASIC COTTAGE CHEESE

To make your own delicious and nutritious *Basic Cottage Cheese*, use the easy directions which follow. This recipe utilizes rennet or Junket tablets to help produce low-acid cottage cheese with minimal effort:

1 rennet tablet (or Junket tablet)   1 pt. buttermilk or *Basic Yogurt*
1 gal. *Basic Rehydrated Powdered Milk*

☐ Dissolve rennet tablet in warm water.

☐ Pour *Basic Rehydrated Powdered Milk* into a large heavy pot and heat to 90°F.

☐ Add buttermilk or *Basic Yogurt*, stirring to mix. Then add dissolved rennet. Cover pot and leave overnight in a warm place.

☐ Next day, a gelatinous, almost solid mass, like firm yogurt, has formed in the pot. This is the curd. With a silver knife cut through this curd to break it into small pieces.

☐ Set the bowl with the curd into a pan of warm water and bring the curd up to 110°F. Shake the bowl gently while it is being heated to help distribute the heat more evenly throughout the curd.

☐ When the curd temperature reaches 110°F, turn off the heat, leaving the cheese bowl in the water for about 30 min. Then pour the cheese into a cloth bag or several layers of cheesecloth and hang it up to drain.

☐ When the curds have drained, mash the cheese with a fork, work in a little sweet or sour cream if you used skim milk, or moisten it with a little *Basic Yogurt* if you don't want the extra fat. You now have a delicious *Basic Cottage Cheese*!

Seasoning alternatives: season *Basic Cottage Cheese* with a little (or lots!) kelp, salt, caraway seeds, chopped chives, dill, or parsley to vary the flavor and taste.

Alternate *Basic Cream Cheese* method: put *Basic Cottage Cheese* in a blender, chop for a few seconds, and it makes a delicious cream cheese—with or without seasonings.

RECIPES FOR BASIC COTTAGE CHEESE

If you're stumped for ways to get highly nutritional foods into the family's diet, try the following recipes using BASIC COTTAGE CHEESE. Substitute BASIC COTTAGE CHEESE for BASIC YOGURT in any of the recipes prior to this section.

BASIC COTTAGE CHEESE CORNBREAD

1 C. cornmeal (yellow or white)	1 tsp. salt
$^1/_2$ C. skim milk	1 tsp. baking powder
$^1/_2$ C. *Basic Cottage Cheese,* creamed	$^1/_2$ tsp. baking soda
1 egg	1 T. sugar

Stir together well all ingredients and spoon into an 8" square greased cake pan. Bake in preheated 425°F oven for 20-25 min. Cut into squares.

BASIC COTTAGE CHEESE CLAM DIP

1 C. *Basic Cottage Cheese*	1 T. grated onion
1 tsp. lemon juice	dash of garlic salt
$^3/_4$ tsp. horseradish	paprika
1 can ($7^1/_2$ oz.) minced clams, drained	parsley
1 T. cream	

Combine *Basic Cottage Cheese*, lemon juice, horseradish, clams, cream, onion, and garlic salt. Mix well; whip. Pour into serving bowl, sprinkle with paprika. Garnish with parsley.

BASIC COTTAGE CHEESE CORNCAKES

$^1/_2$ C. flour	$^1/_2$ tsp. baking soda
$^1/_2$ C. cornmeal	1 egg
1 tsp. baking powder	1 tsp. salt
$^1/_2$ C. *Basic Cottage Cheese,* creamed	$^3/_4$ C. water

Stir all ingredients together; add more water if needed. Use a Teflon-coated fry pan or griddle for cooking. Preheat griddle until a drop of water "dances."

Pour batter to make 4" diameter hot cakes. Turn with a spatula when bubbly.

Serve with syrup, jam, or powdered sugar topping.
Yield: 10-12 hot cakes.

BASIC CHEESE FROM POWDERED MILK

Heating milk and adding rennet, an enzyme found in the stomach of suckling calves, is virtually all that is required to produce cheese. The heat and enzyme applications result in the milk's separation into a liquid portion, the whey, and a solid portion, the curd. The milk "curdles" when the lactic acid level is raised.

This section describes how to make *Basic Cheese* from powdered milk in 25 simple steps. This *Basic Cheese Making* method utilizes buttermilk to achieve the higher acid level required to produce cheese. Heat is applied to cause coagulation.

The coagulate is cut into small pieces, causing the curd to separate from the whey. The heat is then raised to cook the curd. This process, called *cheddaring*, reduces the curd to a consistency which allows for compression into familiar balls or blocks of cheese.

Basic Cheese Making Requirements

Equipment

This equipment is necessary to make *Basic Cheese* with powdered milk:

☐ 4-qt. pan (for 1 batch)   ☐ thin spatula or long knife
☐ cheesecloth, fine mesh   ☐ thermometer, dairy
☐ large strainer or colander   ☐ press for cheese
☐ clock for timing   ☐ wooden spoon for stirring
☐ plastic wrap

Temperature control is critical in *Basic Cheese Making*. This *Basic Cheese* method requires a thermometer—be sure to have one. Accurate temperature control can be enhanced by using a double boiler. If you don't have a large double boiler, place the pan with the milk mixture in a cake or biscuit pan partially filled with water. You may have difficulty finding a cheese press, but you can make a *Basic Cheese Press* by assembling the parts detailed in **Illustration 12-3**.

Ingredients

These ingredients are necessary to make one batch of *Basic Cheese:*

☐ 1 gal. milk   ☐ 1 rennet tablet
☐ 3 T. buttermilk   ☐ 3 tsp. salt
☐ 6-12 drops yellow coloring (optional)

Nonfat dried, regular homogenized, or fresh raw milk may be used.

However, when using powdered milk, you must add 1 C. whipping cream to bring the butterfat content to the required level.

Also, nonfat dried milk coagulates faster when mixed several days before using in the *Basic Cheese Making* process. Keep it refrigerated until ready to use.

Coagulation times differ, based on which type milk is used. Homogenized and fresh raw milk coagulate in approximately 30 min. Nonfat dried milk may take up to 3-4 times longer and must be kept at 88-90°F during the coagulation period.

Directions for Basic Cheese Making

Check off the steps as they are completed, and it should be simple to make some of the best cheese you've ever tasted! Season, color, and shape cheese to your personal taste.

☐ 1. Pour 1 gal. milk into the 4-qt. pan.

☐ 2. Add and stir in 3 T. buttermilk.

☐ 3. Cover and leave at room temperature at least 4 hr. Mixture can safely remain at room temperature as long as 12 hr. *Keep out of direct sunlight.*

☐ 4. Place pan of prepared milk mixture over low to medium heat. Slowly raise the temperature of the mixture to 86°F.

☐ 5. Add coloring to obtain desired tint. *(Coloring is optional—if you desire white cheese, omit this step.)*

☐ 6. Place rennet tablet in 2 T. cold water. Dissolve by stirring. (Hot water will destroy the rennet's enzymatic action.)

☐ 7. Raise the temperature of the milk mixture to 88°-90°F.

☐ 8. While stirring mixture, add the rennet solution. Continue stirring 1-2 min.

☐ 9. Cover the pan, remove from heat, and allow to stand undisturbed for at least 30 min. (If you use nonfat dried milk in this recipe, you must leave the mixture on the heat, maintaining 88°-90°F, to facilitate coagulation.)

☐ 10. When coagulation is completed, use the thin spatula to cut curd to bottom of pan in parallel lines approximately $^1/_2$" apart.

☐ 11. Turn pan 90° and repeat cutting of parallel lines, forming $^1/_2$" squares.

☐ 12. Turn pan 45° and cut diagonally through the curd, intersecting the cuts previously made.

☐ 13. Turn pan 90° and repeat cutting procedure.

☐ 14. Stir the curd gently with your hand, using long slow movements around and up through the curd. Stir and sift the curd by hand for 15 min. Carefully cut up any larger pieces that come up from the bottom, but do not squeeze the curd. You will see and feel the curd begin to separate from the whey. The curd will begin to shrink in size. Stirring keeps the curd from sticking together too soon in the cheese making process.

☐ 15. To cook the curd, slowly apply heat over a 20-30 min. period to raise the temperature of the developing curds and whey to 102°F. Hold at 102° for another 30-40 min. Continue to stir gently with a spoon every 3-5 min.

☐ 16. To firm the curd, remove from heat and let the curds and whey stand for 1 hour, stirring every 5-10 min.

☐ 17. To drain the curd, line a large strainer with a doubled piece of cheesecloth. Pour curds and whey into the cheesecloth. Thoroughly drain off the whey.

☐ 18. Flavor the cheese by sprinkling salt over the curd.

☐ 19. Wrap the cheesecloth around the curd, making a ball. Squeeze out as much whey as possible and drain for 10 min. over bowl or sink.

☐ 20. Put ball of cheese into cheese press, pressing firmly. Apply pressure until curds begin to show through drain holes.

☐ 21. Increase pressure about every 5 min. for the next 30 min. The harder the cheese is pressed, the firmer it will be when removed from the press.

Cooking is complete when the curd holds its shape and readily falls apart on your hand without squeezing. The curd will look like scrambled eggs. Curd will be about the size of small-curd cottage cheese.

Note:

Wrapping the fresh cheese is necessary to prevent drying out or bacterial and odor contamination. Wrapping will prevent mold from forming for a considerable length of time.

☐ 22. Remove cheesecloth and allow cheese to remain at room temperature until the surface is dry. Drying usually takes 4-8 hr.

☐ 23. Cheese is ready to eat or store. The *green* cheese is rather bland and approximates pot cheese in consistency. Cheese spreads can be made at this point.

☐ 24. To *age* the cheese, wrap the cheese tightly in plastic wrap. Be sure to mark the production date on wrapper.

☐ 25. Store cheese in the crisper section of the refrigerator at 35°- 40°F. The flavor will strengthen as the cheese ages.

Yield: 1-2 lb., depending on butterfat content of milk ingredients.

How to Vary Basic Cheese Flavor

Once you've acquired the knack for making *Basic Cheese*, the challenge and thrill of flavor variation lies ahead. The fun begins as you learn to make creative changes to achieve the taste and consistency you want. Sometimes, even minor variations will produce rather significant results in flavor, texture, moistness, and consistency.
The following paragraphs detail how the *Basic Cheese Making* method may be altered to produce different kinds of cheeses. Basically, flavor and appearance variations result from variations in two general areas—ingredients and techniques.

Ingredient Variations

The resulting taste will depend on the ingredients and the mixture of these variables:

Milk base: one of the first ways to change the end result is by changing the milk base. Milk base for cheese comes from fresh raw milk, regular milk, 2% milk, evaporated milk, powdered milk, cream, or even goat's milk. By combining any two or more of the milk base possibilities, there will be a resultant taste difference in the final product.

Starter: there are two starters for *Basic Cheese Making,* either buttermilk or yogurt. By increasing the percent of starter, or by combining them, there will be some change in the coagulation time and also the final taste.

Seasoning: perhaps the most startling taste differences may be achieved by adding salt, herbs, spices, and molding agents to the *Basic Cheese* method. Salt, onion and garlic salt, seasoning salt, parsley, chives, caraway or sesame seeds, hot pepper, olives, pimiento, or Roquefort, bleu, or other cheese molds heighten flavor and give each cheese *personality*. The flavor determines the range of each cheese's use.

Experimentation is the key to full enjoyment of this fascinating and money-saving facet of home storage basics. The following sections explain how to produce two favorite types of cheeses.

Coloration: even though coloring will not generally affect the final taste, it will heighten the visual appeal of the final product.

Technique Variations

If any of the techniques—or a combination of these—is varied, a different consistency will result.

Curd development: consistency and compression of the final cheese product is determined by

- how the reduction of the gelatinous curd is handled
- temperature level of the curd while cooking
- amount of time the curd cooks

Pressure: the amount of pressure applied while the cheese is in the press determines whether a cheese will be moist or dry, soft or hard. Again, these variables, in tandem with other technique variations, will produce different results, depending on the combination used.

Aging: the *tang* or *bite* of a cheese may be enhanced by longer aging periods. The molds which create the strong-flavored cheeses require weeks to expand throughout the cheese. Storage temperature of aging cheese will determine the *curing time* of cheese. The higher the temperature, the faster the cheese ages. However, the cheese will sour or spoil in temperatures in excess of 50°F. As in all other phases of cheese production, you decide what you like—then produce your own favorite cheeses by adjusting the variables.

Directions for Basic Cheddar Cheese

Basic Cheddar Cheese is different from *Basic Cheese* in the method of firming the curd. Follow the steps in the *Basic Cheese* method through step 15, then follow these directions:

☐ A. Drain whey from curd by straining through double layers of cheesecloth in a sieve, colander, or strainer. Save the whey for later use, if desired.

☐ B. Spread cheesecloth on broiler pan rack, spreading pile of curd on the cheesecloth about $^3/_4$"- 1" thick.

☐ C. Place rack over broiler pan on stove top burner, maintaining 98°-100°F temperature. Curd will mat into a rather solid, rubbery mass within 30 min.

☐ D. Slice curd mass into $^3/_4$"- 1" strips.

☐ E. After 15 min., turn the strips over once, then once again each 15 min. for 1 hour, maintaining 98°- 100°F constant temperature.

☐ F. Remove cheddar from heat and cut into cubes. Sprinkle salt lightly over cheddar cheese, allowing to cool to room temperature.

☐ G. Press cheddar cheese into mold or press into a ball or block with hands.

☐ H. Cheese may be eaten immediately or aged, according to your taste.

Directions for Basic White Cheese

To make a smooth *Basic White Cheese*, much like Italian mozzarella, vary the *Basic Cheese* method as follows:

☐ A. Prepare milk mixture, doubling buttermilk starter. (Steps 1, 2, 3, 4)

☐ B. Do not add coloring. (Step 5)

☐ C. Continue with directions. (Steps 6, 7, 8, 9)

☐ D. After the curd forms, use your *hands* to break up the mass, squeezing firmly.

☐ E. Add 1-2 tsp. salt to curds while squeezing through hands. (If you want a sweet, bland cheese, leave out salt.)

☐ F. While squeezing curds in whey, raise temperature until hot as your hands can tolerate. Then, gather curds, pressing them in cupped hands until a large firm ball is formed. Line the interior of the cheese press with cheesecloth.

☐ G. Remove cheese ball from whey and place in cheese press. Press firmly to tighten the ball. You may want to pour whey over ball to get remaining curds, but capture whey in a container for use later in soups and gravies.

☐ H. Put pressed cheese back into whey, bringing temperature to approximately 200°F (just below the boiling point).

☐ I. Remove pan from heat and let cheese stand in whey until cool. Take pressed cheese from whey, hang to dry for 8-24 hr. in cheesecloth, then it's ready to eat!

RECIPES FOR BASIC CHEESES

BASIC CHEDDAR CHEEZ-O-LETS

Basic Cheez-O-Lets are a cross between a pancake and a cheese omelet.

4 oz. *Basic Cheddar Cheese*, grated	1 T. grated onion
3 eggs	1 T. dried parsley
2 heaping T. whole-wheat flour	salt and pepper
$^1/_2$ tsp. baking powder	vegetable oil for frying

Blend all ingredients together. Heat oil in skillet and drop mixture in by spoonful. Fry until crisp and golden brown. Turn to brown other side. Drain well on absorbent paper. Serve hot. *Yield: serves 2-3.*

BASIC WHITE CHEESE LASAGNA

18 oz. pkg. lasagna noodles, cooked per directions

Meat Sauce:

$^1/_4$ tsp. sweet basil	2 cans pizza topping mix
1 lb. ground beef	1 can (6 oz.) tomato paste
1 clove garlic, minced	salt and pepper
1 med. onion, finely chopped	

Brown beef in saucepan, and cover with lid. Add garlic, onion, basil, pizza topping, tomato paste, salt, and pepper to taste. Simmer for 20 min., stirring occasionally till done.

Cheese Filling:

2 lb. *Basic White Cheese*, grated	2 eggs
1 tsp. parsley flakes	salt and pepper

Mix all ingredients together, salt and pepper to taste.

Topping:

6 oz. mozzarella, grated or slices	$^1/_2$ C. Parmesan cheese
(or use more *Basic White Cheese*)	

Lightly grease baking dish and spoon in enough meat sauce to cover the bottom. Top with strips of noodles, then spread layer of cheese with part of the cheese filling mixture. Repeat layers, with meat sauce on top.

Sprinkle with Parmesan cheese and top with mozzarella cheese, grated or sliced. Bake in oven at 350°F for 30 min. Let stand 5-10 min. so all layers set before serving. *Yield: 6 servings.*

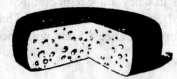

Illustration 11-3

Basic Cheese Press

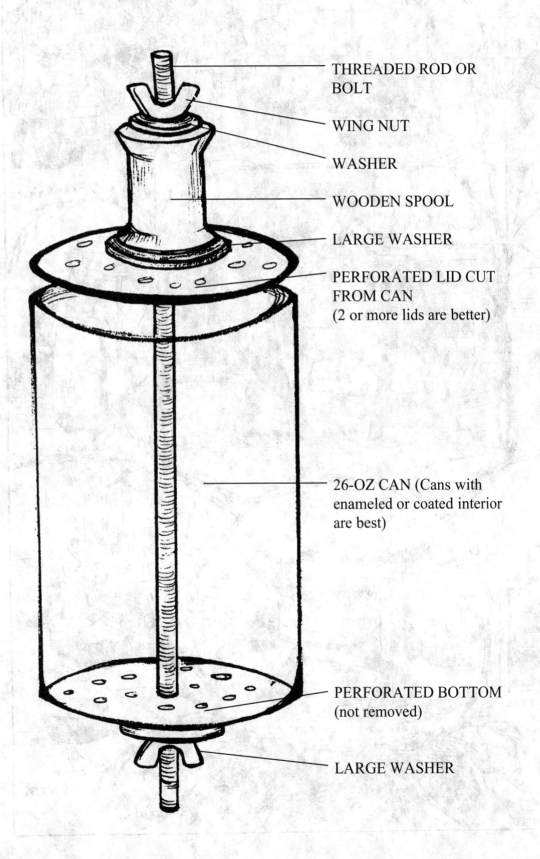

THREADED ROD OR
BOLT

WING NUT

WASHER

WOODEN SPOOL

LARGE WASHER

PERFORATED LID CUT
FROM CAN
(2 or more lids are better)

26-OZ CAN (Cans with
enameled or coated interior
are best)

PERFORATED BOTTOM
(not removed)

LARGE WASHER

The future is as bright for us as is our preparedness—prepared or not, we will live in the future. How you live in the future depends on how well you plan, take action, and prepare now.

Chapter 12

Basic Sprouting Guide
Healthy Kitchen Gardening

My friend Richard tells this story[1] from his youth: *"I remember when I was a very young boy, and during all my growing-up years, each year Dad would buy one hundred baby chicks. Like all the other farmers in the area, he fed them starter mash and then growing mash until they reached their mature stage. Then most of them would be killed, dressed, and put into the freezer for our winter meat, leaving a few of the best layers to provide fresh eggs for the winter.*

"I distinctly remember my dad putting those chickens on the scales, one at a time. He'd say, 'Yep, this one's five pounds! Yep, five pounds!' Occasionally he'd say, 'OOPS! This one didn't eat enough, it's not five pounds.' I also remember the large streaks of yellow fat on the fatter chickens when they were being dressed and wrapped before freezing.

"Now I have a large family of my own. We've also raised our hundred baby chicks to five pounds with lots of fat on their bodies, too. A few of years ago, my then

> Sprouts are live whole food, providing great nutritional value to the diet.

---

[1] This story was told to me by Delsa Wilson, a long-time friend and food storage consultant. Richard is currently president and owner of one of the largest sprouting equipment and seed businesses in the Intermountain West—he's certainly committed to the concept of sprouting! Richard can be contacted at **Life Sprouts**.

eight-year old son and I decided to experiment on a recommendation from a friend, who said we could increase the chickens' growth with sprouts. So, we decided to feed at least half of our chickens a diet of three-day sprouted wheat and other sprouts and check them against the regular-diet chickens.

"That year our sprout-fed chickens reached 6 to 6½ pounds with very little fat in the same amount of time it took the others to reach 5 pounds! The next year we decided to go all the way and feed all the chickens a sprout diet uniquely. Every bite of food we fed them was 'live food,' as opposed to 'dead food' of dried ground grains. Much to our surprise, not one chicken was less than 8 pounds, and some were as much as 8½ pounds—with absolutely no fat at all!

"We had kept track of how many hundreds of pounds of grain it normally took to raise those chickens. The big surprise was that with the live sprouts, we used 25% less food by sprouting the same amount of grain—and yet those chickens were much bigger, heartier and had less fat!"

When we tell people about Richard's experiment, sometimes we hear older folks say they don't want to grow that much bigger!

They're missing the point: *the importance of sprouts has nothing to do with adults growing to be giants, but being healthier and having less body fat at any age!*

Live sprouts have live enzymes, vitamins, minerals, and amino acids we need for everyday healthy living. The truth is we could live on *live* sprouts for a very long time and remain very healthy.

It doesn't take too much effort to sprout seeds for food—*Quinoa seeds sprout in as little time as twelve hours!*

Reasons for using sprouts are so plentiful and so important it's usually only a matter of listing them to convince you to try this very special kind of in-home gardening—accomplished in the comfort of your own kitchen. Increasing numbers of families find sprouting nutritious, delicious, and far less expensive than buying them at grocery store prices.

NUTRITIONAL ADVANTAGES OF SPROUTING

Nutritionally, dried seeds, grains, and legumes provide only a small portion of the total nutrients the body requires. However, once they are sprouted, seeds provide the largest relative amounts of nutrients per unit of intake compared to other food sources.

Sprouting multiplies the content of minerals and vitamins in the seed many times because a wealth of nutrients is released to aid the development of the seed during its growth process.

There is no doubt more nourishment contained in a plant's sprout than at any other time in its life cycle. Often, new nutrients occur where there were none before. Vitamins A, B complex, C, and E are increased—sometimes as much as ten times!

Both the quantity and quality of the protein in most sprouts are dramatically increased. New amino acids form as the seeds sprout, resulting in increased digestibility.

Sprouts are biogenic—alive and capable of transferring their life energy to your body.

They contain enzymes which aid in digestion of foods, provide a good source of fiber, and slow the aging process. They are also an excellent multipurpose vegetable.

Using sprouts greatly increases vitamin content of dishes, provides a *live food*, and in general supports better health for the body.

To add to all of their nutritional plusses, untreated and organic sprouts are free of pesticides and are pest-free, too.

Watching your weight? An additional benefit of sprouts is the low carbohydrate, fat, and cholesterol content—a real plus for weight-watchers.

SOME HEALTH ADVANTAGES OF SPROUTING

Why should you eat more sprouts? Here are some positive reasons:

- A tablespoon (T.) of organic sprouting seeds will generally fill a quart jar when peak sprouting is reached. A pound of seeds could make many bowls of sprouts!
- Sprouts are healthy, nutritious vegetables that cost less than store-bought vegetables.
- Organic sprouts are chemical-free, generally taste as sweet as baby vegetables, and are fresh and at their nutritional peak, not to mention undamaged by handling.
- Sprouting is easy—even a child can sprout! Children enjoy seeing the growing cycle and marvel at the veggies growing in a jar. In minutes each day, sprouts can be grown and harvested.
- No soil, fertilizer, weeding, or as in our case in the Hill Country of South Texas––keeping the deer and other 4-legged critters from eating our crops!
- Sprouts grow practically anywhere in the house, in any season, and require only a small amount of space.
- Sprouts can be easily taken on camping trips and outings. The equipment is so simple, inexpensive, and easy to clean that you can take them anywhere.
- A kitchen garden grows in a very short period, ranging from overnight to approximately 3 days—though there are some seeds may take at 5-7 days at the most. You can control the growth period to accommodate your taste.
- Sprouts store well in the refrigerator—when properly maintained—sprouts will keep several days to weeks.
- Organic sprouts are a true health food, with the nutritional elements the body needs.
- Sprouts are easily assimilated by the body and are high in bioavailability
- Sprouts can be eaten raw, blanched, fried, stir-fried, baked, boiled, steamed, and grilled!
- Spouts can be utilized in salads, on sandwiches, in omelets, ethnic dishes, soups, casseroles, and baked in bread. We add sprouts to fresh-popped corn with salad dressings (I particularly like *bleu cheese*!) to make a great snack!
- Sprouts contain amino acids that make the protein much more digestible.
- Sprouts provide good fiber for better digestive tract health.
- Sprouts have many minerals, trace elements, and enzymes, too.
- Sprouts are low in calories and low in fat.
- Sprouts provide the body with simple sugars, delivering quick energy without the "*sugar drop*" later.
- Sprouts contain no cholesterol and provide some essential fatty acids the body needs.
- Sprouts are practically a perfect weight-loss food.
- Sprouts exposed to the sun during final hours of sprouting will produce chlorophyll, which helps cleanse and oxygenate the blood.
- Sprouts have enzymes to aid in the digestion and assimilation of nutrients.
- Sprouts provide fiber to help the waste elimination process.
- Sprouts produce lecithin to help the body get rid of bad cholesterol.
- Sprouts consumed as a part of a raw food diet will accelerate the body's detoxification.
- Sprouts provide antioxidants to protect the body from internal and external toxic chemicals and environmental factors.
- Sprouts are effective in helping the body rebuild its damaged tissue and heal itself.
- Sprouts help build the immune system.

STORAGE ADVANTAGES

It really doesn't matter how sprouts are utilized in food preparation, they will sustain good health and stamina. If you had only a supply of sprouting seeds in your food storage, you could live a full year or more, eating only from your kitchen garden. The best part is that sprouts are also the least expensive fresh vegetables you can procure and store!

It is virtually impossible for a family to store enough fresh vegetables to last a long period of time—or to have them available in times of extreme duress, whether due to people-caused or natural disasters. By sprouting seeds, fresh vegetables are only 2-3 days away—year-round!

Sprouts substitute for green vegetables and replace lettuce and other greens when they become expensive or unavailable. Get a variety of seeds and learn to use them and you will have fresh green vegetables year-round, even when there is no way to grow vegetables in soil. This makes sprouting seeds a high-priority acquisition item for your family's preparedness plan.

The amount of food value stored in such a small space is a boon to a family's foods storage program. Sprouting is a very easy way to increase the utility of many types of grains, seeds, and legumes or beans. Sprouts are easy to prepare and utilize. Both equipment and supplies are easily found and readily available almost anywhere.

The effort required for a batch of sprouts is minimal. Bringing sprouts to the table, ready to eat, *takes less than 10 minutes* during the entire 3-day (average) growth period.

Compared to vegetable gardening, kitchen gardening with sprouts is *easy*. There is little fuss and bother. Sprouts require no fertilizer. In fact, all that's required is some water, air, and a small nook where they can grow. Sprouts conserve energy, too. They require few resources for their sprouting cycle. You can eat sprouts without cooking them, and any sprouted beans or grains cook much quicker. Sprouts save money—all of the above, and this, too! Sprouting inexpensive seeds can help support your family's overworked budget!

BASIC SPROUTING

This chapter is designed solely to help readers realize the importance of sprouting in their food storage program—and now is the time to start learning how to sprout! It summarizes the basic information needed to either become an accomplished sprouter or to improve your sprouting acumen.

Experiment! Don't be afraid to try something new—there's not much you can do to hurt sprouts! After a few tries, you'll discover at which stage of sprout development your family prefers different sprouted seeds. Some like sprouted seeds best after they have sprouted just 48 hours, others when 4–5 days old, when the sprout has more *chewiness* and has a more substantially developed flavor.

Past this point, as the sprout is actually becoming a plant, they tend to become bitter and woody. Actually, sprouts may be used any time after the shoot emerges from the seed, but with some seeds, it's better to wait until the shoot is longer. ***Sprouts are best when they taste best to you!***

BASIC SPROUTING EQUIPMENT

Sprouting is, without a doubt, the simplest process in the kitchen. Children delight in taking responsibility for sprouting seeds—even small children can sprout most seeds. The worst thing that can happen is losing a batch from too little moisture.

BASIC SEED SPROUTER — Generally, the only equipment needed for sprouting can easily be found in your home. Here's the short list of equipment:

    ☐ Quart, half-gallon, or gallon threaded wide-mouth jar;

☐ Piece of cotton gauze, nylon net, or pantyhose top—any clean, durable fabric;

☐ Strong rubber band (or sealing ring for quart jar); and

☐ Voilà! a basic and inexpensive tool for sprouting.

Sprouts require no fertilizer. All that's required is some moisture, some air, a small place in a kitchen cabinet, a small spot on the windowsill, or place on the countertop under a kitchen towel. An occasional rinse during the day—as indicated in the **Basic Sprouting Guide**—and you have rich, nutrient-dense food at very low cost.

The utilization of a jar is by far the oldest and most popular method of sprouting, as well as one of the easiest. All you need is a threaded quart, half-gallon, or gallon glass jar having either a standard or wide mouth.

One technique is to cover the mouth of your sprouting jar with muslin, cheesecloth, or nylon fabric. Plastic or stainless mesh screens will work, but the screens are subject to mold and mildew build-up and are not as easy as using special sprouting lids designed specifically for this purpose.[2]

Whichever method or type used, the idea is to rinse away the unnecessary hulls for cleaner, fresher sprouts.

STEP-BY-STEP BASIC SPROUTING METHOD

There are only a few general rules for sprouting—it's practically foolproof! Almost all seeds are sprouted the same way, with a few exceptions. The **Basic Sprouting Guide** points out some special handling requirements for particular seeds, grains, and beans. Check the **Guide** for specifics when sprouting.

To utilize the ***Basic sprouting method***, follow these general directions:

☐ Measure the appropriate amount of beans, grain, or seeds for batch, removing broken seeds and foreign objects.

☐ Place measured amount of seeds in jar half-full of warm water. Cull out *floaters* or *sinkers as follows*:

— when majority of seeds sink, throw out all the *floaters*

— when majority of seeds float, throw out all the *sinkers*.

☐ Secure gauze (or nylon fabric) over the mouth of the jar with the rubber band (or jar ring).

☐ Soak 6–8 hours—or as directed in the **Basic Sprouting Guide** at the end of this chapter—in a warm location in the kitchen.

☐ Then drain seeds well by turning bottle upside-down. Leave it angled to one side in the sink or dish drainer for a few minutes. Rinse them again gently in warm water to remove contaminants. Allow to drain once more, and then place in kitchen cabinet, on the counter, or in the window covered with a dark towel so germination may begin. (Be sure to place jar where it's warm—not hot!)

☐ Drain and rinse seeds 2–3 times each day—or as directed by the **Basic Sprouting Guide**—always draining well to prevent souring of sprouts.

☐ When sprouts attain desired length, eat the whole thing—seed, sprout, and roots—for a healthier meal or snack.

☐ Store unused sprouts in refrigerator to retard further growth. The **Basic Sprouting Guide** gives the recommended sprout length for each seed. Sprouts generally achieve peak palatability, highest vitamin content, and potency within 2-3 days.

---

[2] Many preparedness dealers offer a number of jar sprouters in both plastic and glass—some have seeds included. The polyethylene screen cap can be added to your own choice of wide mouth jar.

IDEAS FOR USING SPROUTS

Using sprouts varies the menu, adds bulk to recipes, and improves the flavor of many ordinary dishes. Sprouts are versatile—they can be used in so many ways. Eat them as fresh sprouts, in salads, teas, sandwiches, soups, gourmet entrées, casseroles, pancakes or breads; raw, boiled, sautéed, steamed, or stir-fried—you're limited only by your imagination!

In fact, you can create your own *designe*r or *gourmet* sprout combination by mixing and matching your favorite grains, seeds, and beans in the same batch. This allows customization for your eating pleasure and maximizes your inventory of sproutables, too.

There is no waste in preparation, no fuel required to prepare them, and once you get the hang of it, practically no failures. Sprouting is not only one of the keys to nutritional stability—a potential lifesaver—but is also a great money-saver.

Children especially like to help with this kitchen duty. In fact, most elementary schools teach sprouting as part of the curriculum. A child's natural inquisitiveness will help him master sprouting in a very short time, leaving more of your time for the more complicated and time-consuming household and kitchen duties.

There are so many ways to utilize sprouts, they would fill many cookbooks! Before going to the cost and effort of buying other books on sprouting, try some of the following ideas first.

Should you need additional information about advanced sprouting techniques, you can find information either by a search in your favorite Internet browser for **Sprouting** or find a book in chapter 27. Once you locate a title you like, search on Google or **Amazon.**

Suggested Uses for Sprouts

Use In	Suggestions
Stir-fry	Add any of these sprouts to vegetables— alfalfa, clover, mung, or radish sprouts—or all simultaneously!
Mashed potatoes	Grind or chop very fine either: alfalfa, chia, or clover sprouts—for taste and color, too!
Vegetable juices	Make **Basic Sprout-8** with sprouts—tomato juice, ground chia, barley, cabbage, clover, lettuce, radish, and/or watercress! If you get too much flavor, start with any one sprout, making additional sprout combinations until you get the taste you prefer.
Sautéed vegetables	Add cabbage, corn, garbanzo, lentil, mung, pea, radish, or watercress sprouts for *zingggg*! These intensely flavored sprouts are especially good with sliced onion, a clove of garlic, and/or some green peppers—try these in a game-time snack bowl over white rice that is steamed to perfection!
Steamed vegetables	Add whole alfalfa, chia, clover, corn, garbanzo, lentil, mung, pea, radish, or wheat sprouts during the final 2 min. steaming time.
Rice	Add whole, chopped, finely chopped, or whole sprouts — alfalfa, barley, chia, pea, radish, or watercress, to rice dishes and to steamed rice after cooking—but just before serving!
Soups	For flavor or thickening, add chopped or whole sprouts—corn, garbanzo, lentil, mung, pea, radish, or wheat. See **Soup Recipes** section on the next page for specifics.

Bean sprouts are even more palatable and digestible when cooked before eating, and any anti-nutrients in the bean family are nullified when cooked.

Baking

Home-baked goods: Enhance by adding whole or chopped sprouts.

Baked beans: Add any sprouted bean with short sprout—*best when bean has just split open by plant growth*—try lentil, mung, lima, pinto, or navy bean sprouts.

BreadMaking

Breads: Ordinary homemade breads become more eye-appealing with sprouts peeking through the crust and seen throughout the loaf. Sprouts add great taste and greater nourishment in each delicious slice! Some care is required when adding or substituting sprouts in bread recipes.

The basic rule for substituting sprouts in any bread recipe is:

> **Substitute 1 C. sprouts in any bread or flour recipe for**
> **$^1/_2$ C. flour and $^1/_2$ C. liquid.**

Breadmaking Notes:

Exercise care when using sprouts in breadmaking. Sprouts are an abundantly rich source of enzymes. Some of these enzymes have the ability to digest protein, so yeast action will be inhibited and often results in heavy bread.

NOTE: When substituting sprouts in bread recipes, be aware of these potential problems:

☐ *If the yeast does not fully react in the dough, the dough will produce heavy bread.*

☐ *When adding sprouts to yeast goods, add them as late as possible in the mixing process, and then be sure dough is warm and working.*

☐ *Do not allow dough to sit too long with sprouts added—the dough may sour.*

Breakfast Treats

Try some of the following to add zest and nutrition to a sedate breakfast:

Omelets & scrambled eggs — Add chopped or whole alfalfa, chia, clover, mustard, or radish sprouts for a bright-eyed start to your day.

Pancakes and waffles — Ground or finely chopped buckwheat sprouts enhance nutrition in an ordinary breakfast.

Casseroles

When using sprouts in casseroles, add them just a few minutes before serving, either in the pan or sprinkled on top. Sprouts add vitality and flavor to any casserole.

Casseroles — Add $^1/_2$ C. to 1 C. whole or chopped sprouts—adzuki, barley, cabbage, chia, clover, corn, lentil, mung, spinach, or wheat.

Salads

Eat sprouts fresh and uncooked for a taste treat. Create your own combinations. Get creative with sprouts, and you'll certainly be healthier and less harassed in preparing nutritious meals.

Basic sprout salad — Perhaps the easiest sprout salad to make: mix a handful of chilled sprouts, whether one kind or a combination, in a bowl. Then pour French, Italian, Russian, bleu cheese, or plain homemade mayonnaise over them, then stir gently until sprouts are lightly covered.

Deluxe salad — Add sprouts to your lettuce salad—alfalfa, mung, chia, radish, or wheat—or combine them!

Lettuce substitute — Use sprouts as a substitute for lettuce altogether in your favorite salad.

Coleslaw — Substitute chopped cabbage sprouts for cabbage. For a different taste, add some radish sprouts!

Potato salad — Add alfalfa, lentil, mung, or radish sprouts to "*liven up*" your potato salad recipe.

Sandwiches

Improve the flavor and nutrition of your favorite sandwich(es) by adding sprouts. Try these additions to your sandwich and improve your diet:

Chicken salad or tuna salad: Alfalfa sprouts are better than lettuce—cheaper, and more easily available!

Lettuce substitute: Use any sprout or combination of sprouts to replace lettuce—alfalfa, chia, clover, lentil, mung, or radish.

Avocado (mashed): Spread thickly on fresh, home-baked whole-wheat bread. Top with alfalfa, barley, clover, or chia sprouts.

Super sandwich spread: Add to salad spread mixture chopped or ground alfalfa, chia, clover, lentil, mung, and/or radish sprouts.

Sprout cheese filling (or dip): Add ground or chopped alfalfa, clover, lentil, mung, or radish sprouts to softened cream or Neufchatel cheese.

Grilled cheese: Top hot sandwiches with alfalfa, chia, clover, lentil, lettuce, mung, sesame, or watercress sprouts for added flavor.

Sprout Soups

If you like the flavor of any particular bean, seed, or grain, you can make it into a sprout soup. Simply sprout your selection, add 1 C. sprouts into boiling water slowly, then cover and simmer. Cook till tender or to your preference. Season to taste. Serve hot.

BASIC SPROUT SOUP

1 C. sprouts (your choice of vegetable)	$^1/_2$ C. sour cream
1 C. water	1 tsp. soy sauce
pinch of parsley	salt & pepper to taste

Add sprouts to boiling water. Reduce heat, simmer 3–5 min., and then stir in sour cream. Season to taste with soy sauce. Sprinkle parsley on top just before serving.

EGG-SPROUT SOUP

2 C. bean sprouts	2 eggs, beaten
4 C. vegetable broth or soup	1 T. soy sauce
Salt to taste	

Add sprouts to broth. Simmer 8–10 min. Remove from heat and stir in beaten eggs. Season to taste with soy sauce.

Sprout Vegetables

Sprouts are vegetables. They may be boiled, baked, or sautéed as any other vegetable, served alone, or in combination with other vegetables. The number of recipes for sprouts is endless because they can be added to almost any vegetable or meat dish to improve taste and nutritional value. The secret to gaining the most nutritional value from sprouts is to cook them as little as possible. The following recipes will guide you in utilizing sprouts as vegetables.

BASIC SPROUT VEGETABLE SOUP

1 C. sprouts of choice	pinch salt
2 C. water	$^1/_2$ T. butter

Add sprouts to boiling salted water, reduce heat, and simmer 3–5 min. Remove from heat, add butter, and cover for 20 min. Serve hot. Serve alone or with bacon, cheese—whatever!

*Note: **BASIC SPROUT VEGETABLE SOUP** recipe may be used as a basic ingredient for many other recipes.*

SPECIAL INSTRUCTIONS

What *Not* to Sprout

Caution — Here are the two most important things *not to sprout*:
- ■ Don't sprout seeds *intended for agricultural use*. They are generally treated with poisonous insecticides and may not be safe for human consumption.
- ■ Don't sprout *tomato* or *potato* seeds—they are generally poisonous to humans.

Jar Sprouting Method[3]

Step One: Soaking

For a quart-sized jar, start with 1½ tablespoons or more of seeds as indicated in the **Basic Sprouting Guide**. Place the seeds inside the jar, screw on the fabric or fine mesh lid and partially fill the jar with warm water—not hot! Swirl it around to clean the seeds, then pour it out. Then, refill with warm water to cover the seeds to approximately three (3) times the seed depth and let the seeds soak overnight, or for the time indicated in the **Basic Sprouting Guide**. To protect from light, keep jar covered or place in cabinet overnight.

Step Two: Draining and Starting

Drain off the soak water. Find a location that is not exposed to direct sunlight. Place drained jar—propped at an angle—to allow any extra water to drain out. Turn the jar to over in your hands to help spread out the seed. Cover the jar with a dishtowel and leave for 3 to 4 hours.

Step Three: Rinsing

Rinse the sprouts with cool, fresh water 2 or 3 times each day until they are ready to eat or refrigerate. When they begin to throw off the seed hulls, let the jar overflow with slowly running water and the hulls will float out the top through the screen. Be sure to turn the jar to spread out the seed each time you rinse.

Step Four: Harvesting

Pour the sprouts into a pan, bowl, or clean sink and rinse with clean water. Skim off any remaining hulls that float to the surface. Some hulls will fall to the bottom of the container. A few stubborn hulls may need to be removed individually by hand. This does not apply to seeds, such as wheat berries, which have no hulls.

Pull out the sprouts, gently shake off excess moisture and drain in a colander, When fully drained, either use them or place in a sealed, airtight container such as a sliding or zipper lock plastic bag which leaves some room for air circulation.

For chlorophyll and carotene-developing sprouts, there is the added step of greening, one day before the final harvest, and that is described in **Step Five**. It's optional, but I recommend greening to gain nutritional improvement in sprouts.

Step Five: Greening

Remove the sprouts and clean the jar and lid. Place sprouts for greening back into the jar. Place in indirect sunlight—near a kitchen window is just fine, After the sprouts have greened with chlorophyll and carotenes for a day or so, rinse, drain and eat or refrigerate,

Step Six: Refrigerating

Refrigerate after 4 days! Sprouts will stay fresh and hearty for a week or more when refrigerated, if you rinse them every day or two. You can even give the green sprouts an extra hour or two of sunlight after rinsing to keep them at their nutritional peak.

Caution:
Since sprouts are frost sensitive, do not place stored sprouts near the freezer compartment.

---

[3] Many preparedness suppliers offer a number of jar sprouters in plastic and glass to choose from (seeds included), as well as the single polyethylene screen cap to add to your own wide-mouth jar. There are many dealers carrying their line of seeds and supplies.

Tray Sprouting Method

This method is equally easy and simple as the **JAR SPROUTING METHOD**. It is also the best way to sprout several kinds of seeds such as beans and grains at the same time. The one I use is the plastic *Sprout Garden.* I've had one for years, and it still works fine!

The bottom of this sprouting tray is molded with holes for good drainage, and keeps the smallest seeds from falling through the holes. The dividers give an advantage over the jar method by allowing you to sprout different seeds separately in each compartment.

The depth of the tray, combined with the array of holes, promote good air circulation— essential to a healthy crop of sprouts. The snap-on protective lid keeps out dust, mold spores, and insects.

Another popular use is to plant an indoor garden with soil (such as forest mulch). Mine has been quite handy for quick production of crops of wheatgrass, sunflower, or buck-wheat lettuce in just a few days.

Here's how easy it is to utilize the **sprouting tray**:

Step One

Start with 2 to 4 tablespoons of small seeds (or 4 to 6 tablespoons of large seeds). Rinse as described in the **Jar Method** and then soak in the provided sprouter covers. When sprouting different kinds of seeds, it's best to use different covers. Be sure to cover to protect from light.

Step Two

Spread the soaked and swollen seeds over the *seedbed* in a tray compartment. Rinse under the faucet gently and allow the seeds to spread evenly.

Step Three

Use the cover to protect from light and possible airborne contaminants. Use the extra sprout cover as a drain board on the bottom and stack them, if you have more than one sprouter. Place the tray(s) in a suitable warm location.

There are pre-mixed salad combinations available in the preparedness marketplace:

- There is a 3-part salad mix that contains alfalfa, broccoli, and radish seed. When sprouted, they fluff up together into a delightful, tasty combination. They are good alone, together, or mixed with other salad fixings.

- There is a 5-part salad mix that contains mung beans and lentils besides the above three. This creates a nutritionally denser, higher-fiber salad. Or this mix can be added to soups for a hearty flavor and nutritional boost.

- There is a bean salad combination that contains mung and adzuki beans with lentils and radish seed. Adzuki beans are high in fiber, protein, calcium, iron, vitamins A, B_1, B_2, and niacin. This combination is good by itself, or added to various vegetable dishes. The salad mixes can be sprouted using either the jar or tray method.

Step Four

Rinse sprouting seeds 2-3 times daily. Check the bottom of the tray for signs of mold. If you find any, wipe it off with a paper towel and rinse again.

Step Five

In a day or two, tiny leaves will begin to appear on sprouts such as alfalfa, cabbage etc. Uncover any compartment containing these to allow indirect light to enter, but do not place in direct sunlight. Use each cover of each sprouter tray as a drain board underneath and pour out any excess drainage each rinsing.

Step Six

Harvest by cleaning to remove hulls and drain well. Hulls may rinse out easily by pouring the water through the exit ports on the side of the trays.

Special Treatment for "Reluctant" Sprouting Seeds

There are some seeds that need special treatment to achieve sprouting. There are two methods for success with the following categories of *reluctant sproutables*.

1. "Paper Towel" Sprouting Method

Use this method when the seeds are large or have thick skins, such as nuts.

☐ Use a large glass baking dish or metal pan that won't rust.

☐ Place a baking or cooling rack in the dish or pan.

☐ Spread two layers of *dampened* paper towels on the raised rack to make a sprouting *bed*.

☐ Place pre-soaked seeds on moist—not sopping wet—towels.

☐ Cover seeds with another two layers of moist (with all excess water squeezed out) paper towels, leaving ends and sides open so air can circulate.

☐ Rinse frequently as indicated in the **Basic Sprouting Guide.** Remove seeds from between damp towels when rinsing. Use a sieve, strainer, or colander to contain them while rinsing in running water, then return seeds to the damp paper towels. Thoroughly moisten paper towels by re-soaking, then wringing them out during each rinsing cycle.

☐ Keep the seeds moist between rinses by sprinkling *only* the top layer of paper towels.

☐ Remove sprouted seeds from sprouting bed when ready to eat. Store sprouts tightly covered in refrigerator to preserve their freshness.

2. "Sprinkle" Sprouting Method

This method of sprouting reluctant seeds is for mucilaginous seeds such as chia, flax, and watercress. Here's how to deal with these seeds:

☐ Eliminate the normal pre-soaking of these seeds. Instead, cover with just enough water to wet seeds. Pour off excess water. Allow seeds to sit for an hour. If seeds appear to dry out too quickly, sprinkle them lightly with a little water every few hours.

☐ Seeds will form a jelly-like, gelatinous mass. Do not remove the *jelly*. The seeds will sprout in the jelly, and there is no need to rinse them if you keep the jelly moist by sprinkling the seed mass regularly.

☐ When the seeds have reached the edible stage, rinse the seeds in cold running water until the jelly is washed away. Use soon, as these seeds are prone to drying out and/or molding quickly.

BASIC SPROUTING GUIDE

Step 1	Step 2	Step 3	Step 4	Step 5	Step 6
Selection of Sprouting Seeds	**Measure Quantity**	**Prep & Soaking Hours**	**Days to Sprout**	**Recommended Daily Rinsing & Special Handling Requirements**	**When Best for Eating**
Use only <u>untreated</u> or <u>organic</u> grains, seeds & beans	*Qty. of Seeds Needed for 1 qt. harvest*	*Thoroughly* • *Wash* • *Cull* • *Soak* • *Drain*	*Typical days required to mature*	• *Recommend daily rinses under cool, clean, running water* • *Always drain thoroughly after rinsing* • *Special treatment required for selected seeds* • *Some precautions required when consuming raw sprouts*	*Mature length range for best eating flavor*
Adzuki	1 C.	8 – 12	4 – 5	• rinse 3 – 4 times	$\frac{1}{2}$" – 1"
Alfalfa	3 T.	4 – 8	3 – 5	• rinse 2 – 3 times; *may be sprouted in window* • rinse vigorously on last day to remove hulls	1" – 2"
Almond— shelled	$\frac{1}{2}$ C.	8 – 12	3 – 5	• rinse 2 – 3 times; can be difficult; "sprinkle" method	when split
Amaranth	12 T.	none	2 – 3	• rinse 3 – 4 times	$\frac{1}{4}$"
Anise	6 T.	8 – 12	2 – 3	• rinse 5 – 6 times	1"
Barley— unhulled	2 C.	4 – 8	3 – 4	• rinse 3 – 4 times; can be difficult to sprout • use dried barley sprouts to make **diastatic malt** • steam prior to eating	seed length
Beans- general (*see listings*)	1 C.	8 – 24	3 – 5	• rinse 3 – 5 times, depending on bean • *larger bean + shorter sprout = sweeter taste* • steam cook to destroy anti-nutrients & toxins	$\frac{1}{4}$" – 1$\frac{1}{2}$"
Black-eyed Peas	1 C.	12 – 18	3 – 5	• rinse 3 – 4 times • steam prior to eating to destroy toxins	$\frac{1}{2}$" – 1"
Broccoli	3 T.	6 – 12	5 – 6	• always drain thoroughly; stir to prevent clumping • keep in sealed container for storage	when leafy
Buckwheat— unhulled hulled	1 C. 1$\frac{1}{2}$ C.	15 – 30 min. 8 – 12	2 – 3 3 – 5	• rinse both 4—5 times 1st day; 2 – 3 times thereafter • unhulled seed somewhat difficult to sprout • hulled seeds are easier to sprout	$\frac{1}{4}$" – $\frac{1}{2}$" 1" – 3"
Cabbage— Savoy Chinese	3 T.	8 – 12 6 – 8	3 – 4 4 – 5	• rinse 2 – 3 times; *also sprouts in kitchen window* • stronger flavor when longer & older • use soon after sprouting	$\frac{1}{2}$" – $\frac{3}{4}$" 1" – 1$\frac{1}{2}$"
Canola	3 T.	6 – 8	2 – 3	• rinse 2 – 3 times; *also sprouts in kitchen window*	1" – 1$\frac{1}{2}$"
Chia	2 T.	none	1 – 4	• mucilaginous seed—must use "sprinkle" method • usually very difficult to sprout	$\frac{1}{4}$" – 1"
Clover—red	1$\frac{1}{2}$ T.	8 – 12	3 – 5	• rinse 2 – 3 times; *also sprouts in kitchen window*	1" – 2"
Corn— regular popcorn	2 C. 1$\frac{1}{2}$ C.	4 – 8 8 – 12	2 – 3	• rinse 2 – 3 times • *longer sprouts have stronger flavor* • best when steamed; may be eaten raw	$\frac{1}{4}$" – $\frac{1}{2}$"
Fenugreek	1 C.	4 – 8	3 – 5	• rinse 1 – 2 times; *longer sprouts = bitter taste*	1" – 2"
Flax	4 T.	none	4 – 5	• mucilaginous seed—use "sprinkle" method • usually very difficult to sprout	1" – 1$\frac{1}{2}$"
Garbanzo (*chickpea*)	1$\frac{1}{2}$ C.	8 – 12	3 – 4	• rinse 4 times; can be difficult to sprout • lightly steam prior to eating to destroy toxins	$\frac{1}{2}$"
Kidney Bean	$\frac{3}{4}$ C.	8 – 12	2 – 4	• rinse 3 – 4 times • lightly steam before eating to destroy toxins	$\frac{1}{2}$" – 1"
Lentil	$\frac{2}{3}$ C.	6 – 12	2 – 4	• rinse 2 – 4 times; eat when sprout is visible • lightly steam before eating to destroy toxins	$\frac{1}{4}$" – 1"
Lettuce	3 T.	4 – 8	3 – 5	• rinse 2 – 3 times; *may also sprout in window* • longer sprouts have stronger flavor	1" – 1$\frac{1}{2}$"

BASIC SPROUTING GUIDE
(CONTINUED)

Step 1	Step 2	Step 3	Step 4	Step 5	Step 6
Selection of Sprouting Seeds	Measure Quantity	Prep & Soaking Hours	Days to Sprout	Recommended Daily Rinsing & Special Handling Requirements	When Best for Eating
Use only <u>untreated</u> or <u>organic</u> grains, seeds & beans	Qty. of Seeds Needed for 1 qt. harvest	*Thoroughly* • Wash • Cull • Soak • Drain	*Typical days required to mature*	• *Recommend daily rinses under cool, clean, running water* • *Always drain thoroughly after rinsing* • *Special treatment required for selected seeds* • *Some precautions required when consuming raw sprouts*	*Mature length range for best eating flavor*
Millet, hulled	2 C.	4 – 8	3 – 4	• rinse 2 – 3 times • best when steamed before using (*tastes like barley*)	$1/4$"
Mung	1 C.	8 – 12	3 – 5	• rinse 3 – 4 times vigorously to remove hulls • steam cook to destroy anti-nutrients & toxins	1" – 2"
Mustard	$2^1/_2$ C.	8 – 12	3 – 4	• rinse 2 – 3 times; *also sprouts in kitchen window*	1" – $1^1/_2$"
Oats, unhulled	2 C.	2 – 6	1 – 2	• rinse 1 – 2 times—excess water causes souring • use "sprinkle" method	seed length
Peanut	$1/_2$ C.	8 – 12	2 – 3	• rinse 2 – 3 times • steam for 10 – 15 min. prior to eating to destroy toxins	$1/4$" – 1"
Peas— general	3 C.	8 – 12	2 – 3	• rinse 2 – 3 times; split peas will not sprout • steam for 10 – 15 min. to destroy toxins	seed length
Pinto Bean	1 C.	8 – 12	3 – 4	• rinse 3 – 4 times • steam for 10 – 15 min. to destroy toxins	$1/_2$" – $1^1/_4$"
Pumpkin— hulled	2 C.	8 – 12	3	• rinse 2 – 3 times • *light toasting = better-tasting sprouts*	$1/4$"
Quinoa	$1/_4$ C.	4 – 6	1 – 2	• rinse 2 – 3 times; sprouts very quickly	$1/4$" – $1^1/_2$"
Radish	3 T.	6 – 8	3 – 6	• rinse 2 – 3 times; *also sprouts in kitchen window* • gets "hotter" with increasing length	$1/8$" – $1^1/_2$"
Rice—brown, whole grain	$1^1/_2$ C.	8 – 24	3 – 4	• rinse 2 – 3 times • short-grain brown rice will sprout best • best when steamed before using	seed length
Rye	1 C.	8 – 12	2 – 3	• rinse 3 – 4 times; eat within 3 days	$1/4$" – $1/_2$"
Sesame	$1^1/_2$ C.	8 – 12	$1^1/_2$ – 2	• rinse 3 – 4 times; only unhulled seeds will sprout	seed length
Soybean	1 C.	18 – 24	4 – 6	• rinse 5 – 6 times; difficult to sprout; don't keep too long after sprouting, beans ferment very quickly • steam cook to destroy anti-nutrients & toxins	$1/_2$" – 2"
Spinach	2 T.	6 – 8	3 – 5	• rinse 2 – 3 times; *also sprouts in kitchen window*	$1/_2$" – 2"
Sunflower— Shelled	1 C.	2 – 8	1 – 2	• rinse 2 – 3 times; edible in 12 – 36 hours • sprouts taste bitter when more than 2" in length	1" – 2"
Triticale	2 C.	8 – 12	2 – 3	• rinse 3 – 4 times; eat within 3 days; ferments easily—even in refrigerator • use same as wheat sprouts	seed length
Vegetable seeds (*see listing*)	2 – 3 T.	6 – 12	2 – 3	• rinse at least 2 times • best when eaten raw • use soon after sprouts reach suggested length	1" – 2"
Watercress	2 T.	none	3 – 5	• mucilaginous seed—use "sprinkle" method • usually very difficult to sprout	$1/_2$"
Wheat	1 C.	8 – 12	3 – 6	• rinse 2 – 3 times; *long & old sprouts = bitter taste*	seed length

Notes For Your Sprouting Guide

(CONTINUED)

Honey comes out of the air....At early dawn the leaves of trees are found be-dewed with honey.... Whether this is the perspiration of the sky or a sort of sali-va of the stars, or the moisture of the air purging itself, nevertheless it brings with it the great pleasure of its heavenly nature. It is always of the best quality when it is stored in the best flowers.

Pliny (A.D. 23-79)

Chapter 13
Basics of Honey Use

The history of mankind's relationship to honey is an indicator of its importance in food storage. References to honey are recorded on the walls of post-Ice Age cave-dwellers, depicting their honey-gathering expeditions. The Old Testament mentions the Promised Land flowing with milk and honey—symbols of abundance. Honey was discovered in the Egyptian tombs unspoiled—even after being in storage for more than 2,000 years!

The Egyptians held honey in high esteem and approached its use reverently, feeling it had almost magical properties. Jars of honey found in the Pharaohs' tombs date from as early as 1400 BC.

It was also used to preserve and embalm! Alexander the Great was embalmed in a large jar of honey! If you've received raw honey direct from the hive, you may have found an occasional worker bee embalmed in the container.

Besides being used as food, it was used as medicine—more than half the remedies pre-scribed by Egyptian doctors contained honey. Ancient Egyptians, Greeks, and Romans

"For he on honey-dew hath fed, And drunk the milk of Paradise."

from "Kubla Kahn," Samuel Taylor Coleridge

Caution:

When buying honey directly from the farm, always ask about the processing method used—if the answers don't make sense, don't buy large amounts.

spread honey on wounds to hasten their healing—so did the German field medical personnel during World War I!

Even as late as 1970 in England, a surgeon announced he was using honey on open wounds after surgery—and had fewer bacterial infections than similar wounds treated with antibiotics. Honey proved to be an effective disinfectant; it hastened healing; and bacteria did not develop resistance to it, as often happens with antibiotics.

When the early settlers brought bees to America, the Indians called them *"White Man's flies."* The white-blossomed clover which was provided for the bees was called *"white foot."*

During the settlement of America, until the development of the maple syrup industry, honey was the only source of sweetening for the hardy pioneers.

Honey is the oldest known sweetener. Concentrated from the natural nectar of flowers, honey usually tastes like its major source of nectars. Bees in orange-grove country produce orange-flavored honey; bees in garden areas produce honey with a more complicated array of flavors, depending on the mixture of flower types.

The most common sources of honey are clover and alfalfa crops.

Since the early settlers arrived, generations of Americans have grown up on mild-tasting and light-colored honey. Today, blended honey is typically what we find in retail stores.

Though blended honey is not necessarily any lower in quality, it does provide the sameness we've come to expect when we buy processed foods.

Unfortunately, honey has 64 calories per tablespoon—18 more calories per tablespoon than table sugar.

However, depending on its source, honey may also have as much as 25%–40% more sweetening power. This usually means smaller amounts of honey than sugar are required to achieve the same level of sweetness.

Honey contains very small amounts of trace minerals and vitamin nutrients, making it a better choice than sugar. Honey is a whole food, and since no chemicals are utilized in its production, honey is an organic choice, also. Whether honey is a *better* sweetener than sugar is your choice.

BUYING HONEY

Buy and store honey labeled **U.S. Grade A** or **U.S. Fancy** if buying in retail outlets. Be apprised, however, there are no federal labeling laws governing the sale of honey, so only honey labeled *pure* is entirely honey and not a blend.

Unfortunately for the consumer, honey grading is currently a matter of voluntary compliance—with very lax interpretations by some producers. This lack of standardization causes consumers particular grief when manufacturers selectively use misleading words such as *organic, raw*, *uncooked*, or *unfiltered* on labels.

However, the FDA[1] investigates producers and distributors engaged in fraud or acts which put the honey consumer at risk.

---

[1] The FDA takes a great deal of interest in "sticky" problems related to honey purity. Adulteration of honey by adding syrups from cheaper sugar sources are investigated rigorously by the FDA. More proof that nothing's perfect, however—the FDA does not regulate the drugs used in raising bees. Drugs are used because bees are susceptible to a number of diseases. *Fumagillin* is the drug of choice for a parasite that attacks the digestive tract of the bees; *oxytetracycline* is used to control European foulbrood disease which destroys the young bees in the hive.

Local honey producers normally are very careful about the quality of their products, and their supplies are usually safe. However, always use caution when purchasing any farm product from unknown sources.

HONEY SELECTION CRITERIA

Commercial honey quality is judged by these **four** factors:
1. mild flavor;
2. clean aroma;
3. absence of defects (bits of honeycomb, critter body parts, etc.); and
4. light to clear color

Honey ranges in color from almost clear, to nearly white, and on to nearly black. Honey can have tints of yellow, amber, orange, green, and even blue. Honey is considered more valuable when its color is lighter and costs even more when it's almost colorless.

The lighter-colored honey usually has a more delicate flavor and aroma. In fact, honey grading, and therefore its pricing structure, is based on its appearance relative to color and clarity.

Use these parameters of quality when selecting honey for long-term in-home storage:

- **whole-comb honey** is the least processed form of honey, but be sure to verify it came from the hive without going through some processing.

- **unfiltered** honey is usually heated some to allow the impurities to be removed by a screening process, but most of the nutrients remain in the honey.

- **raw (uncooked)** honey may contain some spores of botulism[2], generally harmful only to children less than 1 year old.

- **liquid** honey is heated to higher temperatures to allow it to be filtered more easily and to remove bee parts, hive intruders (dead, of course!), bits of honeycomb, etc.; liquid honey is usually lighter in color, has greater clarity, is easier to package, resists crystallization longer—but destroys many of the beneficial nutrients inherent in natural whole-comb honey.

- **crystallized honey** is a creamy, smooth spread, often used for spun, creamed, or aerated forms of retail honey. The honey crystals are mixed in or blended in to give body to the liquid honey base.

STORING HONEY

For best storage capability, store pure, unprocessed honey. It does not normally support growth of bacteria and requires no refrigeration to prevent yeast and mold populations.

Store all forms and varieties of honey in containers with tight-fitting lids to prevent:

- absorption of moisture, which could alter the texture, and

- environmental exposure, which could alter the taste.

As with all stored products, honey should be rotated, even in view of its seeming long life.

The secret to storage and use is to store it in small quantities. Even though stored honey usually gets darker in color and stronger in flavor, it's still effective as ever in sweetening foods.

> *Pure honey stores extremely well—it is the only storage food that will not spoil!*
>
> *However, it will become darker and have a stronger taste, and eventually crystallize when stored for years.*

---

[2] According to the Center for Disease Control, in Atlanta, GA, infants less than a year old should not be fed raw honey because of the danger *of clostridium botulinum*, which transmits "infant botulism." An adult's immune system would kill the botulism bacterial spores before infection set in.

Storage Considerations

There are many different kinds of honey available. However, there are only **three** considerations for its storage—that's what makes it such a favorite sweetener in food storage:

1. **Contamination**
2. **Temperature**
3. **Length of storage**

Contamination

As long as honey is kept sealed in a cool, dry, and dark place, it has virtually no storage limitations, as proven by the ancients. Avoid storing honey in plastic buckets or pails near petroleum products (including the power lawnmower), chemicals, or any other fume- or gaseous odor-producing product.

Temperature

Both high and low temperatures affect honey storage, though neither will destroy its usefulness. Lower temperatures cause honey to become very dense. Higher temperatures will cause honey to be runny. However, in either case, as long as the honey is tightly covered, no damage should result.

Length of Storage

Usually the worst thing that happens to older honey is *crystallization*—which is easily cured by warming the honey container gently in warm water. Crystallization is a natural aging process and does not affect the honey's food value, although it darkens the color and intensifies the flavor. Refrigeration only increases the rate of crystallization.

How to de-crystallize honey: Simply place the container of honey in a pan of warm water until the crystals disappear. If more heat is required, keep the container from touching the bottom of the pan by putting a rack under it and set the pan over low heat, at approximately 150°F. Be careful not to overheat crystallized honey, since too much heat causes the honey to change color and flavor. It's easier and less frustrating to de-crystallize small amounts of honey as needed, as it will subsequently return to crystal form quickly.

Storage Differences

Pure, unprocessed comb honey: keeps best in covered containers in a cool, dark, and dry place. It is the purest form of honey and requires no preservatives. Pure honey usually becomes crystallized as it ages or if stored at cold temperatures.

Creamed honey: may be stored at room temperature or in the refrigerator. Freezing or refrigeration will not harm creamed honey, but may speed its crystallization. This crystallization can be *cured* by warming as explained in the previous section. Creamed honey may partially liquefy if stored at too high a temperature. There are a number of creamed mixtures made from honey. These mixtures are created by adding water, air, and / or flavorings and are generally *spreads* used as toppings or desserts. You can make your own with a blender or mixer, some butter or margarine, a little peanut, almond, or cashew butter—the combinations are endless!

Diluted honey: when diluted with water or any other liquid, honey should be kept tightly covered in the refrigerator. As with other syrups, diluted honey may ferment or mold quickly if not kept cold. Usually the label on the honey container will indicate the best means of storage.

USING HONEY

Honey has several advantages over sugar:

- Honey is sweeter, measure-for-measure, than sugar. Honey weighs 12 ounces per cup, but 1 cup of sugar weighs only 7 ounces—that's why honey has more sweetening power than sugar.

- Honey is a natural food—it's much better for your health than refined sugars.

- Baked products stay fresher longer when honey is used. Honey absorbs and retains moisture, thus retarding the drying out and staleness associated with home-baked items. This is especially important when you want to bake in advance or save baked goods for any length of time.

When honey is utilized even in small amounts, it adds a slightly heightened flavor to the recipe. Adding too much honey, on the other hand, will make the recipe too sweet, and the possibility of recipe failure is increased.

You'll have new tastes to surprise and delight you as the experimentation process of substituting sugar with honey develops.

Note:
If the honey flavor is too strong, use up to $^1/_4$ teaspoon of baking soda per cup of honey to neutralize the acidity of the honey and to make the flavor more mellow.

SUBSTITUTING HONEY FOR SUGAR

Honey may be used, measure-for-measure, in place of sugar in the following preparations:

- baked apples
- baked ham
- candied vegetables
- cinnamon toast
- custards
- dressings for salads
- glazes
- lemonade
- pie fillings
- puddings
- punch drinks
- sweet & sour dishes

Note:
Honey does not replace sugar, measure-for-measure in recipes.

When baking with honey as a substitute in regular recipes, these are ***three steps you must take*** to make the substitution of honey work:

1. *Use only 75% liquid honey for sugar*—*¾ C. honey* for each *1 C. sugar* required.

2. *Reduce the total liquid ingredients by 25%*—eliminate ¼ C. liquid for each C. of sugar replaced by honey.

3. *Reduce oven heat approximately 25°–35°F.* Honey caramelizes, becoming darker and/or burning at a lower temperature than sugar.

The following chart illustrates a formula for substituting honey for sugar in most recipes:

Chart 13–1

Sugar-to-Honey Recipe Conversion Chart

Sugar to be Replaced	Honey Amount Substituted	&	Recipe Liquid Decreased		Option: instead of decreasing liquid, add following ingredients with honey:		
					Flour	+	Soda
1 C.	$^3/_4$ C.	&	$^1/_4$ C.	or	4 T.	+	$^1/_4$ tsp.
$^1/_2$ C.	6 T.	&	2 T.	or	2 T.	+	$^1/_8$ tsp.
$^1/_3$ C.	$^1/_4$ C.	&	$1^1/_2$ T.	or	$1^1/_2$ T.	+	$^1/_{12}$ tsp.
$^1/_4$ C.	3 T.	&	1 T.	or	1 T.	+	$^1/_{16}$ tsp.

Basic Hints for Honey Use

General

These tidbits of kitchen wisdom about using honey in the place of sugar have evolved over the years:

- Measure all ingredients carefully—accuracy is very important when using honey. All measurements are level—*do not overfill measuring utensils.*
- Unless noted specifically in the recipe, use liquid honey *only.*
- Use mild flavors of clover-type honey in most recipes.
- Stronger-flavored honey is best utilized in spice cakes, gingerbread, brownies, fruit punches, and oven-baked ham where its pronounced flavor is not overpowering.
- Honey should always be used at room temperature, or even slightly warmer, so it will flow easier and combine better with the other ingredients.
- When preparing oven-baked recipes, mix honey thoroughly with other ingredients before pouring mixture into baking pans. This prevents a too-moist, oversweetened layer from collecting on the top of the baked item.
- Combine honey with liquid ingredients to assure complete distribution in the mixture.
- Sauces will be smoother when made with honey instead of processed sugar.
- Honey will come out of a measuring utensil much better when a coating of oil is placed on the utensil prior to putting honey in it.
- A rubber or flexible plastic spatula is useful in getting all the honey out of the bowl or off the utensil.

Cakes

Honey can generally replace up to one-half of the required sugar required in standard recipes without changing the proportions of the other ingredients in the recipe.

Cookies

The amount of honey used to substitute for sugar in standard cookie recipes is directly related to the hardness or crispness desired in the final product.

- **For hard cookies:** substitute no more than $^1/_3$ of the required sugar. Keep in mind that hard cookies will probably lose their crispness if not eaten in a short time. Most honey cookies, candies, and frostings become too soft during high-humidity weather.
- **For soft cookies:** substitute up to $^1/_2$ the required sugar with honey.
- **For moist-type fruit bars and soft, "gooey" mixtures:** substitute up to $^2/_3$ of the required sugar with honey.

Bread

Freezing bread with honey as sweetening is not advised, since honey deteriorates when frozen, causing the thawed bread to be *mushy.*

RECIPES FOR HONEY

BASIC HONEY-BUTTER MIX

$^1/_2$ C. butter   1 C. bland honey

Combine ingredients with electric mixer until creamy and smooth. Store in refrigerator in tightly closed container.

BASIC CINNAMON BUTTER

1 C. *Basic Honey-Butter Mix*   1 tsp. cinnamon

Combine ingredients with electric mixer on high speed. Store in tightly closed glass or plastic container with tight-fitting lid.

> **Note:**
>
> *Some honey-flavored cakes and other baked goods improve in flavor and texture when aged a few days.*

BASIC HONEY-BUTTER CINNAMON BUNS

$^2/_3$ C. very warm water	2 T. nonfat dry milk
1 T. yeast	$^1/_4$ C. raisins
$^1/_2$ C. *Basic Cinnamon Butter*	$^1/_4$ C. chopped pecans
1 egg	2 C. sifted flour
$^1/_2$ tsp. salt	additional cinnamon, if desired

Measure very warm water into large mixing bowl. Sprinkle or crumble yeast over water; stir until dissolved. Combine *Basic Cinnamon Butter*, egg, salt, and dry milk. Add to yeast mixture; blend well. Add fruit, nuts, and flour. Stir to mix; then beat until batter is shiny and smooth, about 2 min. Scrape sides of bowl. Let rise in warm place, free from draft until doubled, about 30 min. Roll out in long "snakes" and coil into 3" to 6" circles. Bake at 350°F for 20–25 min. Remove from pan, serve warm. *Yield: 12 buns.*

BASIC FRENCH TOAST

2 eggs, slightly beaten	8 slices bread
$^1/_4$ C. milk	butter or oil for frying
$1^1/_4$ C. *Basic Honey-Butter Mix*	2 T. lemon juice
$^1/_4$ tsp. salt	

Combine beaten eggs, milk, $^1/_4$ C. *Basic Honey-Butter Mix* and salt. Dip bread in mixture and fry in butter until golden brown. Combine remaining *Mix* and lemon juice. Heat and serve over toast. *Yield: 4–6 servings.*

BASIC HONEY CHIPPEES

$^1/_2$ C. butter	$^1/_2$ tsp. baking soda
$^1/_2$ C. honey	$^1/_2$ tsp. salt
1 egg	1 C. chocolate chips
$1^1/_4$ C. sifted flour	$^1/_2$ C. chopped pecans

Cream butter and honey together; add egg and beat well. Sift together dry ingredients and add to creamed mixture. Stir in chocolate chips and pecans. Drop by rounded teaspoons onto greased cookie sheet. Bake at 375°F for 12–15 min. *Yield: 3 dozen cookies.*

BASIC HONEYOAT BREAD

1 C. rolled oats (regular)	$^1/_4$ C. vegetable oil
2 C. boiling water	$^1/_2$ C. dry milk
2 T. yeast	6–$6^1/_2$ C. sifted wheat flour
$^1/_3$ C. lukewarm water	$2^1/_2$ tsp. salt
$^1/_2$ C. honey	

Place rolled oats in large bowl or pan and add boiling water. Let stand until lukewarm (about 20 min.).

Dissolve yeast in lukewarm water and let stand 5 min., and then add to mixture. Add honey and oil.

Sift together dry ingredients twice and then add to mixture. Knead well for 5 min.

Let rise until double in bulk, then knead again. Shape into two loaves. Let rise 10 min. and bake in well-greased loaf pans at 325°F for 1 hr. Turn out and brush tops with butter.

BASIC HONEY-BUTTER COOKEES

2 C. butter	8 C. sifted flour
1 C. honey	$1^{1}/_{4}$ tsp. baking powder
2 eggs, separated	2 T. lemon juice
1 T. grated lemon peel	1 C. almonds, chopped

Cream butter and gradually add honey. Beat in egg yolks and lemon peel, flour, baking powder, and lemon juice. Stir well and chill.

Shape into small balls and flatten. Brush with beaten egg whites and sprinkle with almonds. Bake at 350°F for 10–15 min. *Yield: 7–8 dozen cookies.*

BASIC HONEY CRISPEES

$^{1}/_{2}$ C. butter	$^{1}/_{4}$ tsp. salt
2 T. milk	1 C. coconut
1 C. flour	1 tsp. vanilla
$^{3}/_{4}$ C. honey	2 C. **Rice Krispies**® cereal

Combine all ingredients except vanilla and cereal in saucepan.

Cook over medium heat, stirring constantly until dough leaves sides of pan and forms a ball. Remove from heat. Cool.

Add vanilla and cereal. Shape into balls; roll in additional coconut. If not eaten at once, store in refrigerator.

BASIC BUTTER PECAN COOKEES

1 C. butter	2 tsp. vanilla extract
$^{1}/_{4}$ C. honey	2 C. finely chopped pecans
2 C. sifted flour	confectioners' sugar
$^{1}/_{2}$ tsp. salt	

Cream butter; gradually add honey and beat well. Stir in flour, salt, and vanilla. Mix well. Add chopped nuts. Form into very small balls and place on greased baking sheet.

Bake at 300°F for 40–45 min. Roll in confectioners' sugar while still hot. *Yield: 6 dozen cookies.*

BASIC HONEY CUSTARD

2 eggs	$^{1}/_{4}$ C. honey
2 C. milk	$^{1}/_{8}$ tsp. salt

Beat eggs slightly. Add milk, honey, and salt. Pour into individual molds and set in a pan of water.

Bake at 350°F for 30 min. Allow to cool and chill in refrigerator. *Yield: 6 (4-oz.) cups.*

BASIC PEANUTTY CHOMPERS

1 C. honey
1 C. peanut butter

1–1$\frac{1}{2}$ C. nonfat dry milk
(noninstant)

Add peanut butter to warm honey and mix well. Stir in 1–1$\frac{1}{2}$ C. dry milk. (The amount of powdered milk depends on the peanut butter's oiliness.) Form into small balls.

BASIC FRUIT CUP MIX

4 C. mixed fruit
$\frac{1}{2}$ C. honey

1 T. chopped candied ginger
1 T. lemon juice

Place fruit in serving bowl or refrigerator dish. Combine honey, candied ginger, and lemon juice; pour mixture over fruit and chill for 2 hr. before serving.

Yield: 4–6 servings.

- A typical winter mix could include grapefruit and orange sections, fresh pineapple, bananas, red grapes, etc.

- A summer mix might include melon, berries, peaches, pears, etc.

BASIC SWEET PEARALILLI

7 C. firm ripe pears
$\frac{1}{2}$ C. diced green pepper
1 can (4 oz.) diced pimiento
2 C. golden raisins
4 C. mild-flavored honey
$\frac{1}{2}$ C. lemon juice

1 T. grated lemon peel
1 tsp. salt
$\frac{1}{4}$ tsp. ground ginger
$\frac{1}{4}$ tsp. whole cloves
$\frac{1}{2}$ tsp. ground allspice
4 sticks cinnamon

Put unpeeled, cored pears through food grinder, using coarse blade (or use food processor). Combine with balance of ingredients in a pot. Tie whole spices in a cloth so they may be easily removed. Stir well to blend. Over medium heat, bring to boil, stirring continually. When rolling boil is reached, reduce heat and simmer, stirring often to prevent sticking, until relish is thick enough to spoon into sterilized pint jars. Remove spice bag. Seal lids at once.

Yield: approx. 4 pt.

NOTES FOR YOUR HONEY USE

Section V

Wheat Basics

It seems as if a lot of people aspire to getting something for nothing. The ancient evils of greed and covetousness seem to show their face today in the form of entitlement—which is generally a selfish act. Entitlement takes much from some and gives little to many. Whatever happened to the "earning our bread by the sweat of our brow…" that epitomized our forefathers?

Chapter 14

Wheat—the Great Grain

Wheat is referred to as the staff of life because it is the most widely grown and consumed grain in the world. Wheat is utilized in many forms by different cultures, but the form of wheat most widely used is flour, whether for pastas, breads, or other baked goods. Flours are available from the minimally processed whole-wheat flours, such as graham and bread flour, to the highly processed white flours, unbleached or bleached, such as bread, pastry, cake, all-purpose, self-rising, and semolina flour.

Perhaps less known are other types of wheat available for our use. Among them are the unprocessed forms of whole-grain wheat. These include whole or cracked kernels of the *wheat berries*. Slightly more processed forms include bulgur, couscous, wheat germ, wheat bran, rolled and flaked wheat (similar to oatmeal), and the wheat meals. The most recognized forms are the higher processed forms such as farina, semolina, and white flour.

With such a wide range of uses, wheat is considered by many experts to be one of the most basic food storage items. It is certainly easy to store and has high value in the daily diet. Wheat can be prepared easily in an extremely wide variety of dishes—from breakfast cereals to breads to main dishes to desserts.

Wheat is also very nutritious, containing high amounts of protein, calcium, niacin, riboflavin, and thiamin. When sprouted, vitamins A and C are also present in increased amounts.

As interest in wheat storage and in-home storage and use has increased, equipment for in-home processing and food technology for its use and enjoyment have kept pace with the demand. Commercial resources for producing, milling, storing, grinding, and preparing wheat have increased at ever-lower costs. Grinders, grinding mills, storage containers, widespread delivery systems, and availability are working for the wheat devotée.

This chapter contains many helpful ideas for storing and preserving whole-wheat grains. The following chapters have recipes for utilizing wheat from whole kernel to white flour. Virtually every form of preparing wheat in-home is covered.

By the way, here is an early warning message—***don't try to start a whole-wheat diet all at once!*** You would suffer digestive problems an antacid won't resolve! The normal digestive system cannot adapt immediately to the extreme dietary change a diet of whole wheat would cause.

Small children would probably have digestive and elimination problems when commencing a high-level wheat consumption diet. A diet with a few ounces per day of processed flour products is a far cry from a diet of *cracked whole-wheat cereal* at breakfast, *whole-wheat bread sandwiches* for lunch, then a *wheat sprout salad*, a *whole-wheat bulgur casserole*, some more *whole-wheat bread,* and a *wheat-based dessert* at dinner! Living on *Basic foods* is a lifestyle unto itself.

Wheat causes allergic reactions in some people, and a whole-wheat diet will be very difficult for them. Many persons who at lower levels of wheat intake may not be aware of their allergy to wheat may discover their latent sensitivity when they ingest more wheat more often.

If you aren't using whole-wheat food daily, start utilizing it at some meal soon. Get accustomed to whole-wheat foods by using some whole-wheat flour in white flour recipes the family already likes. Once you've cleared that hurdle, start on the next one. Eventually you'll be able to utilize whole-wheat flour exclusively when flour is required in a recipe. Then, and only then, are you ready to use only your own wheat flour produced in-home for wonderful dishes, including all those delightful whole-wheat casseroles you'll create!

Let reason prevail—start now in your goal of utilizing wheat in every form. Break into the whole-wheat lifestyle with a gentle, guiding effort. Don't wait for a cataclysm—you'll have more than *one* serious problem with which to deal!

BASIC STORAGE GUIDELINES

This storage plan suggests how much whole wheat to purchase and has guidelines for storing wheat. These are the suggested criteria for purchasing wheat for storage:

• **Variety**	• **Protein content**
• **Moisture content**	• **Quantity**
• **Containers**	• **Storage techniques**

In the following pages are the major criteria for purchasing, treating, and preserving bulk whole wheat as well as how to utilize it effectively in your preparedness lifestyle.

Purchasing Whole Wheat

Varieties to buy include Dark Hard Winter, Spring Wheat, Dark Turkey Red, and Montana White Wheat because they store best. Grain should be cleaned for human consumption and free from all foreign matter possible.

Note:

When buying whole-wheat flour from the store, buy it only if it has been refrigerated. Be sure to keep it refrigerated until utilized.

Buy *Grade #1* for food storage. Always buy the best grade(s) available—the quality of your results in cooking, baking, and realizing the full health benefits whole wheat offers depends on your choice of grain!

Protein content should be 13% or higher. There are wheat varieties available to the consumer with as much as 18% protein.

Moisture content should not exceed 10% in the grain. This will inhibit microbial infiltration and insect infestation.

Quantity to buy varies according to age, weight, size, sex, and appetite of each person. See the **Quick-Guides** in **Chapter 8** for details of suggested quantities for your family.

Containers for Storing Whole Wheat

Use crushproof, waterproof, and moisture-proof containers.
All food storage products must be protected to prevent infiltration, infestation, and contamination. The better a container meets these requirements the better condition stored wheat will be in when needed.

Store wheat in round cans.
When storing wheat in square cans, allow several inches open space on all sides of the cans to allow air to circulate more freely.

A round, 5-gallon metal bucket, enamel-coated interior, with an airtight lid and waterproof seal is the best option for storing bulk whole wheat. These containers are generally available from restaurant suppliers, barrel, container, or used-container dealers.

This type of container will hold approximately 35 pounds of wheat and is convenient for both transporting and long-term storage purposes. These containers will stack safely, allow better ventilation, protect the contents, and require less storage space.

A 5-gallon polyethylene bucket with tight-fitting lid and waterproof seal is a good alternative to the metal can.

Plastic buckets are usually available at the same businesses where you find metal cans. The same cautions that apply to a metal container's former contents applies equally to plastic buckets.

Always use a heavy-duty, food-grade, sealable, plastic liner in any container for bulk wheat.
With any container, a food-grade plastic or Mylar® liner is necessary to prevent infiltration of contaminants, infestation, and moisture.

Properly processed, treated, prepacked, and factory-sealed wheat can be purchased from reputable mills and food storage dealers.
Commercially sealed wheat usually requires neither turning nor aerating when properly stored.

Caution:

Attention to previous contents of any used container is important. Make sure no chemicals, odorous food, or non-food products were stored in food containers.

Basic Storage Techniques

There are a few critical things about bulk wheat storage we bring to your awareness. Properly stored wheat will store indefinitely. Improperly stored wheat will neither store for very long, due to spoilage, nor have any food value left when used, even if it doesn't spoil.

Temperature Range

Temperature range for storing bulk wheat is 45°-65°F.
Edible and sproutable wheat was discovered in the pyramids after centuries of storage. Wheat will keep indefinitely when properly stored. However, since ideal storage condi-

tions are difficult to maintain, always rotate stored wheat. Use older wheat first and re-place it annually with new wheat at harvest times, when prices are generally lower.

Moisture Protection

Always store wheat in a dry environment.
Bulk wheat must be kept dry to prevent infestation and contamination. Moisture provides an environment for molds, bacteria, and a multitude of bugs to grow.

Wheat draws moisture, so take precautions to protect stored wheat from exposure to high humidity and high temperatures.
Use boards or wooden platforms under metal cans to prevent bottoms of cans from touch-ing or being in direct contact with concrete, earth, or any moisture-conducting surface. The bulk wheat draws moisture, so it must be isolated by the wood and air buffer to prevent spoiling.

Ventilation

Leave air space around stored wheat containers.
Ventilation is necessary because the ambient air provides a buffer zone for the stored wheat as it gains and loses heat.

When storing wheat in square cans, allow several inches open space on all sides of the cans to allow adequate ventilation.
Wheat stored in square cans stacked too closely together does not allow the heat generated to escape. The increased temperatures cause sweating inside the containers.

Use boards or wooden platforms under all storage containers, especially metal cans, to prevent bottoms from rusting from sweating.

Light

Avoid storing wheat in bright light.
Some light, however, will discourage molds from growing in small containers.

Fumigating Wheat for Storage

Dry-Ice Methods
Carbon dioxide released from evaporating dry ice will kill all animal life in the container. There are two different ways to fumigate wheat with dry ice.

Basic on-top method:
- on top of almost-full 5-gal. container, place $^1/_4$ lb. dry ice on non-conductive (insulat-ing) material such as Kraft paper
- press lid down gently so some air can escape
- after 20-30 min., check to see if dry ice has completely evaporated
- if not, wait another 5 min., then check again
- when dry ice completely evaporated, remove material and seal container

Basic on-bottom method:
- on bottom of 5-gal. metal storage bucket, place $^1/_4$ lb. dry ice under non-conductive (insulating) material, such as Kraft paper, that can be left in bucket
- press lid down gently, leaving only a small outlet for escaping air (lid will bulge and will eventually blow off if air can't escape)
- after 20-30 min., check to confirm if dry ice has evaporated by closing the lid; if it bulges, loosen lid and wait another 5 min., then check again
- when dry ice is completely evaporated, seal container

Caution:

Do not put dry ice directly on wheat. The wheat will be frozen and be-comes useless as food.

Freezing Method

The freezer will kill all live bugs—but not necessarily the eggs—over a period of 72 hours in the freezer. The advantage of the freezer is its simplicity. Its major disadvantage is that the eggs may not be killed by freezing. It's always best to refreeze the previously frozen wheat after 30 days—assuring eggs hatched since the 1st treatment are killed.

Basic freezer method: place small quantities in either chest or upright freezer (*not* freezer section of refrigerator) for 72 hours at 0°F or lower.

Heating Method

The heating method has the advantage of killing all forms of animal life in the wheat. The disadvantage is that it will also kill the wheat when overheated or left in the oven too long!

Basic heating method: pour infested wheat in shallow baking pan to depth of $^1/_2$". Place in preheated 150°F oven for *only* 15 - 20 min. Wheat will scorch if it gets too hot for too long. Oven door may be left open to allow moisture and heat to escape.

Organic Method

Diatomaceous earth is an organic method to eliminate the hungry little critters feeding freely on your storage supply. It will rid the container of all bug and critter life. This organic treatment is not harmful to man or animals. It's also very cheap and simple to use.

Basic organic method: for each 5-gal. container, put in 1¼ C. diatomaceous earth, shake vigorously, or roll closed container until all the wheat grains are dusted. To use wheat after treatment, rinse grain before using, then blot dry with towel using a massaging action to wipe off powder. Or use it with dust on it—it's treated with an organic compound!

Local Area Guidance

Local County Extension Service agents will have additional information on the best storage techniques and details for your geographical area.

What Not to Do with Storage Wheat

Here's a short list of things to avoid when storing bulk wheat—or when storing any food products:

- Do not pack wheat tightly into any storage space that is not optimal for storage.
- Do not store wheat directly on dirt or cement floors, as wheat draws moisture from these surfaces.
- Do not store wheat in a container which holds more than two bushels or 100 lb. The large containers are difficult to move. Any infiltration, infestation, spoilage, or exposure will contaminate the entire contents.
- Do not store wheat near:

  hot or cold water pipes, heating ducts, or steam pipes;

  washing machine or clothes dryer (*vented or not*); and

  where laundry is hung to dry.
- Do not store wheat in any of these locations:

  in an unheated garage or non-insulated space;

  in a basement or underground space not completely dry; and

  in any uninhabitable space.
- Do not put salt in wheat when storing it.
- Do not use aluminum garbage cans for wheat storage since an airtight seal is generally impossible to achieve due to the loose-fitting lids.

• Garbage cans are not designed for storing edible food—even when with food-grade plastic liners. Don't risk your food to bad container selection.

Grinding Wheat

If you store wheat in bulk, you must have access to a wheat grinder. There are many models on the market, both hand-operated and electric models. The electric models are great but quite expensive.

It makes good sense to have a hand-operated, foot-, or bicycle-powered model before purchasing an expensive electric model.

The more a wheat grinder is utilized, the better it grinds the wheat into flour—the stones literally grind themselves to a perfect fit. All motorized grinders normally ship with instructions, so be sure to follow the operating instructions of the manufacturer for best results.

Keep fresh-ground or commercially-ground (store-bought) flours in the refrigerator or in an equivalently cool, dry place. Refrigeration at 40°F will extend shelf life of ground wheat by approximately six months.

BASIC WHOLE-WHEAT BULGUR

One of the most basic and interesting forms of whole cooked wheat is bulgur, used worldwide and ranks as one of the most versatile and utilized whole-wheat foods in many Middle Eastern countries. Bulgur is easily made from whole-wheat kernels as they come naturally from the field, with only the chaff stripped off.

Sometimes called *wheat berries*, these whole kernels need soaking or steam cooking to become tender. When cooked, they have a sweet, nutlike flavor and a slightly chewy texture.

Bulgur is probably the easiest whole-wheat food to prepare. None of the measurements are critical, and there's no fussing with stirring, continual watching, etc., as with flour recipes.

Bulgur can be made from whole-wheat kernels and cracked wheat kernels—or many other grains, too. It can be used as a very nutritional breakfast cereal, to replace rice in most dishes, as a substitute for mashed potatoes, or it can be baked with selected seasonings to make a delightful, nutritious, crunchy TV snack, and it is great in stuffing for meats and fowl.

There are many known ways to prepare dishes with wheat bulgur and many ways that haven't been discovered yet.

DIRECTIONS FOR MAKING BASIC BULGUR

Wheat kernels can be made into *Basic Bulgur* quite simply. This recipe is an in-home method for processing the whole-wheat grain—called *wheat berries*—for easy and quick use whenever needed. *Basic Bulgur* exists in two forms, whole grain or cracked.

BASIC BULGUR

1 part whole-wheat kernels   ½ - 1 tsp. salt
2 - 3 parts water

Basic Bulgur is easy because the measurements are not critical! This is how to make a batch of *Basic Bulgur*:
- Cover wheat with water, approximately 2" above level of wheat in an appropriately large, heavy pot.
- Bring ingredients to boil, then turn off heat and let mixture stand for $1^1/_2$ - 2 hr.
- Repeat cycle by bringing mixture to rolling boil, adding water if needed. Turn off heat, let stand for 15 - 30 min.
- Stir in salt to taste.
- Drain all remaining water from cooked wheat berries.

DIRECTIONS FOR MAKING BASIC CRACKED BULGUR

Cracked bulgur can be made from scratch more quickly and easily than whole-berry bulgur. This is the simple recipe for making *Basic Cracked Bulgur*:

BASIC STEAMED CRACKED BULGUR

Combine 2 C. cracked wheat and 4 C. water in an open-top pan or metal bowl. Elevate pan or bowl (use small bowl or jar lid) inside a larger, covered pan. Add water in the larger pan to 2" below the rim of the smaller pan. Cook over high heat, covered, for 15 min., then reduce heat to very low. Steam until tender and water in small pan is absorbed, about 3 hr. This is *Basic Cracked Bulgur*.

BULGUR BASICS

These are the additional things you need to know to complete the *Bulgur Basics* course: storage of moist and dried bulgur, drying and rehydrating bulgur, cracking whole-wheat kernels and dried bulgur, and how to make bulgur by alternative methods.

Storing Moist Bulgur

Refrigerator: put moist bulgur in a tightly covered bowl, plastic airtight container, or heavy-duty, self-sealing, plastic freezer bag. This provides storage for about two weeks.

Freezer: for longer-term storage of moist bulgur, package as above. Effective storage period is approximately one year. For longer storage periods, see the following section.

Drying Basic Bulgur

Basic Bulgur can be dried for long-term storage. It dries quickly and easily in either the oven or in an electric drier.

Air drying is not recommended: since bulgur is so water laden it tends to spoil before drying completely. Here are the two best methods for drying *Basic Bulgur*.

Oven drying: spread *Basic Bulgur* in a thin layer on cookie sheet. With oven temperature set at 200°F, allow to slow cook until crispy. Stirring and turning with a spatula decreases drying time. Leave oven door slightly ajar to permit moisture to escape.

Allow *Basic Bulgur* to cool completely before packaging.

Electric dryer: cover drying tray with plastic film or Kraft paper. Spread cooked bulgur in a thin layer. Dry until crisp and brittle. Cool completely and package for storage.

Cracking Dried Basic Bulgur

Barely crack the dried *Basic Bulgur* in a blender or grain mill. In most *Basic Bulgur* recipes, either cracked wheat or whole berries may be used equally well. However, the *Basic Cracked Bulgur* will be less coarse and have a more delicate wheat taste.

Storing Dried Basic Bulgur

Place dried *Basic Bulgur* in an airtight package. The best packaging for small quantities is the freezer-quality, heavy-duty, food-grade, sealable plastic bag. The large size holds just enough dried bulgur for a meal. Several bags may be placed in a larger metal or glass container to further protect them. Store in a cool, dry, and dark location.

Rehydrating Basic Bulgur

Use the following chart as a guideline for rehydrating *Basic Bulgur*.

Note:

When a recipe calls for cooked whole wheat, measure equal amount of dried BASIC BULGUR instead.

Add liquid to cover. Bring to a boil until rehydrated to your taste or recipe directions.

Chart 14-1
Basic Bulgur Rehydrating Method

Yield	Ingredients		
1 C. = 1 serving	Water	Salt	Bulgur
1 C.	$^3/_4$ C.	$^1/_4$ tsp.	$^1/_3$ C.
2 C.	2 C.	$^1/_3$ tsp.	$^2/_3$ C.
6 C.	4 C.	1 tsp.	2 C.

Rehydrate 15–30 min. in any liquid, or combination of liquids, until suited to your taste.

Alternate Methods for Making Basic Bulgur

Use one of the following alternate recipes or methods to make *Basic Bulgur*. With all these choices, there's bound to be one *Basic Bulgur* which will become your favorite.

BASIC MICROWAVE BULGUR

1 C. whole-wheat kernels $^1/_2$ - 1 tsp. salt
3 C. water

Put water in a large microwave-safe bowl. Cover with Kraft or waxed paper loosely folded over top of bowl. Heat water for 5 min. on high power setting. Stir in rinsed wheat kernels, cover, and heat again on high power for 5 min. Reduce to medium ($^1/_2$ - power), continue covered heat for 1 hr. until soft and chewy. Allow to stand covered 5 min. Remove cover, test for doneness, then stir in salt to taste. This is a batch of *Basic Microwave Bulgur*.

BASIC ALL-NIGHT BULGUR

Combine ingredients for *Basic Microwave Bulgur*, except salt, in a covered pan. Bake about 5 hr. or overnight in a warm oven (150°- 200°F degrees). Stir in salt to taste.

BASIC BOIL & WAIT BULGUR*

Combine ingredients for *Basic Microwave Bulgur*, except salt, and bring to boil. Then immediately cover and remove from heat. Let stand overnight or at least 10–12 hr. Stir in salt to taste. May be eaten then or warmed later, when desired.

* Some folks make *Basic Bulgur* by this method the night before, warm it in the microwave oven, and eat it on the way to work the next morning. Or, you can take it to work and warm it for a healthy hot snack.

BASIC BOIL & SIMMER BULGUR

Combine ingredients for *Basic Microwave Bulgur,* except salt. Bring to a boil, reduce heat, and simmer gently for 4–6 hr. or until tender. Add water as needed to prevent sticking. Stir in salt to taste.

BASIC STEAM BULGUR

Combine ingredients for *Basic Microwave Bulgur,* except salt, in an open-top pan or metal bowl. Elevate pan or bowl inside a larger, covered pan with water 2" below the rim of the smaller pan. Cook over high heat, covered, for 15 min., then reduce heat to very low. Steam until tender and water in small pan is absorbed, about 3 hr. Stir in salt and eat.

BASIC SLOWCOOK BULGUR

Cook ingredients, except salt, in a crock pot or slow cooker. Cover; cook 4 - 6 hr. Add salt.

BASIC BACHELOR BULGUR

> 1 C. whole-wheat grain   2 C. boiling water
> $^1/_2$ tsp. salt

Even a bachelor can make this *Basic Bulgur* recipe! Combine ingredients with *boiling water* in 1 qt. thermos at night. Screw lid on lightly and leave until morning. Grab it on your way out the door to work! Leave out salt, if you prefer salt-free bulgur.

RECIPES FOR BASIC CRACKED BULGUR

These recipes utilize *Basic Cracked Bulgur.* The whole-wheat berries are cracked in a grinder or blender prior to processing. The cracking process makes a finer, more delicate tasting food than the classic *Basic Bulgur.*

BASIC BULGUR SAUSAGE

> 1 C. *Basic Cracked Bulgur,* cooked   1 tsp. Worcestershire sauce
> 1 tsp. sage   1 egg
> 2 dashes onion salt   1 tsp. brown sugar
> 2 dashes garlic salt   5 drops liquid smoke
> dash cayenne pepper   1 tsp. beef base or bouillon cube

Combine all ingredients, mixing vigorously. Form patties and fry in small amount of oil.

BASIC BULGUR SEASALAD

> 5 C. *Basic Cracked Bulgur,* cooked & cooled   1 C. shrimp (or crab, tuna, etc.)
> $^1/_4$ C. green pepper, diced $^1/_2$ - 1 C. mayonnaise
> $^1/_2$ C. green onion, diced   2 T. pickle juice or vinegar
> 1 C. celery, diced   salt to taste

Combine and chill. You may substitute cooked and cooled rolled grain instead of bulgur.

Note:

BASIC CRACKED BULGUR, as well as many other kinds of grains, may be cooked as described here by decreasing the cooking times.

The only part of the cooking process that could possibly go wrong with making *BASIC BULGUR* is to cook it without water!

RECIPES FOR BASIC BULGUR

BASIC BULGUR CEREAL

2 C. *Basic Bulgur*   2 C. water

Crack *Basic Bulgur* in grinder or blender. Heat in steam 10–20 min. or boil 5 min. in water or other liquid. Serve hot and sweeten to taste.

BASIC SWEET BULGUR

3 C. *Basic Bulgur*   milk
$^1/_2$ C. water   sugar or honey

Heat cooked bulgur in water. Serve hot with milk and sweeten to taste. Makes a chewy breakfast cereal. Add dried fruit for additional flavor and nutrition.

BASIC BULGUR PORRIDGE

6 C. *Basic Bulgur* $^1/_2$ C. sugar
$^1/_4$ C. raisins   honey
1 C. milk

Heat bulgur and raisins to boil, reduce heat. Stir in milk and sugar, simmer approximately 3–5 min. Serve porridge hot, with additional milk and honey to taste. Brown sugar or maple syrup may also be used to sweeten porridge.

BASIC CRUNCHYSNAX

2 C. *Basic Bulgur*   seasonings of choice

Spread *Basic Bulgur* thinly on cookie sheet. Bake at 325°F, stirring occasionally, until very dry and crunchy. Add seasonings to taste. Serve as snacks.

BASIC BOSTON-BAKED BULGUR

4 C. *Basic Bulgur*   1 C. water
½ - 1 C. catsup or BBQ sauce $^1/_2$ C. molasses
1 onion, sautéed   3 - 4 tsp. prepared mustard
salt and pepper   3 slices bacon, cooked & diced

Mix together and bake 30 min. at 325°F.

RECIPES FOR BASIC BULGUR SOUPS & SALADS

BASIC BEEF & VEGGIE SOUP

$1^1/_2$ lb. ground beef $^1/_4$ C. chopped parsley
1- 2 lb. beef knuckle bones   2 - 3 tsp. pepper
$2^1/_2$ qt. water $^1/_8$ tsp. powdered cloves
1 C. *Basic Bulgur* $^1/_4$ tsp. salt
1 C. diced or shredded carrots   1 can tomato soup
$^1/_2$ C. chopped onions or leeks $^1/_2$ tsp. fresh herbs (*fines herbes*[1])
1 C. sliced celery

---

[1] Fresh herbs (*les fines herbes* is the French name) are usually proportionate measures of fresh parsley, chives, tarragon, and chervil—when and where available. Sometimes marjoram and thyme, and even basil, may be added to the mixture. The essence of fresh herbs is achieved by mincing them together with a sharp knife, then adding at the last minute to the pilaf—thus imparting the essential oils to the food.

Brown ground beef and pour off grease. Remove fat from bones. Simmer together water, ground beef, and bones for 2–3 hours. Add remaining ingredients. Cover and continue cooking until vegetables are tender, 15 - 20 min. Remove meat from bones, dice, and return to soup mixture. Heat to boiling.

Yield: 6 - 8 servings.

BASIC BULGUR SALAD

$^1/_2$ C. *Basic Bulgur*	1 C. chopped parsley
water to cover	1 C. chopped green onions
4 tomatoes, cubed	1 green pepper, cut in strips
1 C. fresh mint (chopped)	

Cover *Basic Bulgur* in water and soak for 30 min. Squeeze out water and transfer to a bowl. Combine remaining ingredients, add salad dressing, and toss. *Yield: 4 servings.*

BASIC SEAFOOD SALAD

1 C. *Basic Bulgur*	1 tomato, cut in wedges
2 - 3 T. mayonnaise	$^1/_4$ C. chopped green pepper
2 T. diced green pepper	1 C. tuna or cooked shrimp
$^3/_4$ C. diced celery	

Marinate *Basic Bulgur* in mayonnaise for 20 - 30 min. Add remaining ingredients. Arrange greens around a bowl, pile seafood mixture on top. Sprinkle paprika over seafood.

RECIPES FOR BASIC BULGUR MAIN DISHES

BASIC BAKED CHICKEN

$^1/_2$ C. *Basic Bulgur*	2 T. vegetable oil
1 can of mushroom soup	1 pkg. chicken thighs
1 C. chicken broth	(skins removed)
$^1/_4$ tsp. sage	1 clove garlic
$^1/_2$ tsp. poultry seasoning	$^1/_2$ C. chopped onion

Put *Basic Bulgur* in casserole dish. In separate bowl combine soup, broth, and seasonings. Pour $^1/_2$ of the soup mixture into the casserole and mix with the wheat. In a skillet, heat oil and brown chicken. Remove and arrange on top of *Basic Bulgur*. Add garlic and onion to skillet, sauté until tender. Remove with a slotted spoon and stir in remaining soup mixture, then pour over chicken. Bake at 350°F for 1 hr.

BASIC CHEESE CASSEROLE

$2^1/_2$ C. *Basic Bulgur*	2 cans cream of chicken soup*
1 C. milk	$^1/_2$ tsp. dry mustard
$^3/_4$ C. grated cheese	

Combine ingredients, reserving $^1/_4$ C. cheese to sprinkle on top of mixture. Bake at 375°F for 30 - 40 min.

* Substitute tomato soup and add $^1/_4$ tsp. oregano for Mediterranean flavor.

BASIC BEEF CASSEROLE

1 lb. ground beef	1 large onion, diced
1 clove garlic, crushed	1 C. *Basic Bulgur*
1 T. parsley flakes	2 cans tomato soup
1 tsp. celery flakes	$\frac{1}{2}$ C. catsup or tomato sauce
salt and pepper to taste	grated cheese

Sauté meat and seasonings with onion. Combine *Basic Bulgur* with meat mixture, soup, and catsup, then pour into casserole dish. Sprinkle with cheese. Bake at 350°F for 30 min. *Yield: 6 - 8 servings.*

BASIC TOMATO CASSEROLE

3 C. *Basic Bulgur*	3 C. tomato juice
1 tsp. salt	$\frac{1}{4}$ small onion, finely chopped
6 slices bacon, diced & fried	1 C. grated cheese
4 T. flour	bread crumbs (optional)

Place salted *Basic Bulgur* in buttered baking dish. Fry diced bacon; add flour, tomato juice, and onion to make a sauce. Remove from heat and add $\frac{1}{2}$ C. grated cheese. Pour over *Basic Bulgur*. Top with remaining cheese. Sprinkle bread crumbs or crushed saltine crackers over cheese to add crunch, if desired. Bake 45 min. at 350°F.

BASIC TUNA CASSEROLE

2 T. chopped onion	$\frac{1}{8}$ tsp. pepper
1 T. butter or margarine	2 eggs, slightly beaten
2 C. *Basic Bulgur*	$\frac{1}{3}$ C. crisp cracker crumbs
1 C. cream of mushroom soup	1 T. butter or margarine
1 can (6 oz.) tuna	paprika
$\frac{1}{2}$ tsp. salt	

Sauté onion in butter over moderate heat until onion is straw colored. Mix in baking dish with *Basic Bulgur*, soup, tuna, salt, pepper, and egg. Top with mixture of crackers and melted butter. Sprinkle with paprika. Bake in moderate oven (350°F) for 30 min. *Yield: 6 servings.*

BASIC MUSHROOM CASSEROLE

4 C. *Basic Bulgur*	1 can cream of mushroom soup
$\frac{1}{2}$ C. milk or water	$\frac{1}{2}$ C. chopped onion, sautéed

Mix together in a casserole. Bake at 350°F for 20 - 30 min. For variety add chopped celery, green pepper, or fresh mushrooms. Use in place of rice or potatoes.

BASIC POULTRY CASSEROLE

$\frac{1}{4}$ C. butter or margarine	$\frac{1}{8}$ tsp. pepper
$\frac{1}{2}$ C. chopped celery	$\frac{1}{2}$ tsp. poultry seasoning
$\frac{1}{4}$ C. finely chopped onion	$\frac{1}{2}$ C. *Basic Bulgur*
$\frac{1}{4}$ C. flour	5 C. cooked & cubed
2 C. chicken broth	turkey or chicken
1 C. milk	1 C. grated cheddar cheese
1 tsp. salt	buttered bread crumbs

Melt butter, add celery and onions. Cook until tender, but not brown. Blend in flour. Stir in chicken broth and milk. Cook over low heat, stirring constantly until thickened. Add seasonings, *Basic Bulgur*, poultry, and cheese. Pour into buttered 2-qt. casserole. Sprinkle with buttered bread crumbs and bake 35 - 40 min. in 350°F oven. *Yield: 10 -12 servings.*

BASIC BULGUR JAMBALAYA

8 oz. sausage link, cut in $^1/_2$" rounds	2 T. chopped parsley
2 lb. ground beef	$^1/_4$ tsp. thyme
1$^1/_2$ C. diced ham	$^3/_4$ C. salt
$^1/_2$ C. chopped onion	$^1/_4$ tsp. pepper
$^1/_2$ C. chopped green bell pepper	dash of cayenne
$^3/_4$ C. thinly sliced celery	$^1/_8$ tsp. powdered cloves
2$^1/_2$ C. *Basic Bulgur*	$^1/_4$ tsp. chili powder

Sauté sausage, ground beef, ham, onion, bell pepper, and celery in heavy skillet until lightly browned. Drain grease. Add remaining ingredients. Cover and bring to boil; reduce heat and simmer. Stir occasionally until mixture thickens, about 45 min. *Yield: 5- 6 servings*.

BASIC ITALIAN CASSEROLE

$^1/_4$ C. salad oil	$^1/_2$ tsp. basil leaves
1 onion, chopped	$^1/_4$ tsp. pepper
$^1/_2$ lb. mushrooms, sliced thin	3 C. *Basic Bulgur*
2 tsp. beef stock base	2 med. zucchini, sliced thin
$^1/_2$ C. water	

Heat salad oil in large frying pan over medium heat. Sauté onion and mushrooms until limp and liquid has evaporated. In a small cup, stir together beef stock base and hot water. Add liquid to the pan with basil leaves, pepper, and cooked, drained *Basic Bulgur*. Cover and bring to simmer. Add zucchini. Cover and simmer until heated throughout and liquid is absorbed, about 10 min. *Yield: 6 servings*.

BASIC ChiliBULGUR

1 lb. ground beef (optional)	1 qt. tomatoes, cut up
1 large onion, chopped	1 tsp. Worcestershire sauce
2 tsp. garlic powder	1 T. flour
2 tsp. chili powder	2 beef bouillon cubes
1 tsp. salt	3 C. *Basic Bulgur*

Sauté meat and onions until meat is browned. Add all ingredients except *Basic Bulgur*. Bring to boil, reduce heat, and simmer gently for 30 min. Add *Bulgur* and heat thoroughly.

BASIC SPANISH CASSEROLE

4 slices bacon, cut into thin strips	$^1/_2$ tsp. salt
1 large onion, chopped	1 tsp. seasoned salt
$^1/_2$ C. chopped celery	$^1/_4$ tsp. pepper
$^1/_2$ C. chopped green bell pepper	1 tsp. sugar
1 clove garlic, finely minced	1 tsp. Worcestershire sauce
1 lb. can tomatoes	1 C. *Basic Bulgur*
2 C. water	

Sauté bacon in heavy skillet over moderate heat. Add onion, celery, green pepper, and garlic. Continue cooking until onion is straw colored. Blend in tomatoes, water, salts, pepper, sugar, Worcestershire sauce, and *Basic Bulgur*. Cover and simmer over low heat until most of liquid is absorbed, 20 - 25 min.

RECIPES FOR BASIC BULGUR PILAF

Pilaf is normally prepared as a rice dish. It is made of rice combined with seasonings, vegetables, meat, fish, or poultry. There are as many variations of rice pilaf as there are cooks. Pilaf made from wheat is economical and certainly more nutritious than rice pilaf. These pilaf recipes demonstrate the usefulness of wheat as *Basic Bulgur Pilaf.*

BASIC PILAF MIX

2 T. butter (margarine or oil) $^1/_2$ tsp. salt
3 T. chopped onion $^1/_8$ tsp. pepper
1 C. *Basic Bulgur* $^1/_4$ C. water

Heat butter in heavy skillet; add onion and sauté until straw colored. Add *Basic Bulgur*, water, salt, and pepper. Cover and simmer over low heat until all liquid is absorbed. Use this *Basic Pilaf Mix* to make flavored variations described below. *Yield: 4 servings.*

BASIC CHICKEN-FLAVORED PILAF

1 batch *Basic Pilaf Mix*   2 C. chicken bouillon or stock

Prepare *Basic Pilaf Mix*. Add *Mix* to boiling bouillon or stock. Cover and simmer over low heat until added liquid is absorbed. To save cooking time, use less liquid. *Yield: 4 - 6 servings.*

BASIC FRESH HERBS PILAF

1 batch *Basic Chicken-Flavored Pilaf*   1 T. fresh herbs *(fines herbes)*

Prepare *Basic Chicken-Flavored Pilaf*. Stir fresh herbs into bowl just before serving for a fresh taste. *Yield: 4 - 6 servings.*

BASIC BEEF-FLAVORED PILAF

1 batch *Basic Pilaf Mix*   1 T. Worcestershire sauce
2 C. beef bouillon or stock

Prepare *Basic Pilaf Mix*. Add *Mix* to boiling bouillon or stock, then add Worcestershire sauce. Cover and simmer over low heat until added liquid is absorbed. To shorten cooking time, use less liquid. *Yield: 4 - 6 servings.*

BASIC MEDITERRANEAN PILAF

1 batch *Basic Pilaf Mix*   1 C. tomato juice
1 C. chicken bouillon or stock

Prepare *Basic Pilaf Mix*. Add *Mix* to boiling bouillon or stock and tomato juice. Cover and simmer over low heat until added liquid is absorbed. To save cooking time, use less liquid. *Yield: 4 - 6 servings.*

BASIC PARMESAN PILAF

1 batch *Basic Chicken-Flavored Pilaf* $^1/_3$ C. Parmesan cheese
$^1/_4$ C. chopped onion   1 T. chopped parsley flakes
$^1/_4$ tsp. garlic salt

Prepare *Basic Chicken-Flavored Pilaf*. Add onion and garlic salt. After cooking, stir in cheese and parsley. *Yield: 4 - 6 servings.*

BASIC TAIWAN PILAF

1 batch *Basic Chicken-Flavored Pilaf*   2 T. soy sauce

Prepare *Basic Chicken-Flavored Pilaf.* Add soy sauce just before serving. *Yield: 4 - 6 servings.*

BASIC CANTONESE CHICKEN & TAIWAN PILAF

1 batch *Basic Taiwan Pilaf*	$^1/_2$ tsp. salt
3 T. oil	$1^1/_8$ tsp. white pepper
1 C. Chinese pea pods, cut $^1/_2$"	$^1/_2$ C. sliced water chestnuts
2 T. cornstarch	$1^1/_2$ C. sliced mushroom
$^1/_2$ C. water	$^1/_3$ C. slivered almonds
2 C. sliced cooked chicken	$1^1/_2$ C. chicken stock

Prepare *Basic Taiwan Pilaf.* In another heavy skillet, heat oil, then add pea pods, chestnuts, mushrooms, and almonds. Sauté over moderate heat 2 min., then add chicken stock, salt, and pepper. Cover and cook 6 min. Make a paste of cornstarch and water. Stir into pea pod mixture. Add chicken and return to heat. Stir frequently until mixture thickens and reaches boiling for 2–3 min. Serve over *Basic Taiwan Pilaf. Yield: 4 - 6 serving.*

The best things in life are nearest: breath in your nostrils, light in your eyes, flowers at your feet, duties at your hand, the path of right just before you. Then do not grasp at the stars, but do life's plain, common work as it comes, certain that daily duties and daily bread are the sweetest things in life.
Robert Louis Stevenson

Chapter 15

Basics of Whole-Wheat Flour Cookery

Versatility is one of the most important benefits of storing whole wheat. What makes wheat an essential storage food is that its range of applications increases beyond the basics of the wheat berry by processing the wheat berries to whole-wheat flour. This processing requires merely grinding the berries with a hand-operated grinder, an electric grinding mill, or a blender. The necessity of such equipment becomes apparent if you store whole wheat. An alternative is to store purchased whole-wheat flour—but store-bought has no equal to your own home-ground flour!

The obvious advantage of the home-ground products is its freshness—you make it when you need it—there are no date codes or possible contamination due to distribution problems. The entire wheat kernel is ground into flour, allowing the freshness—as well as the health benefits—to really come through in the finished recipe!

By using your own home-ground whole-wheat flour and supplemental storage foods you can make pancakes, waffles, snacks, pretzels, pasta, tortillas, pie crusts, muffins, cakes, and cookies. This adds tremendous variety to your *Basic* diet. Recipes are included in this chapter for these wheat-based foods.

Of course with whole-wheat flour you can also make bread and bread stuffing. Directions for *Basic* breadmaking are provided in this chapter. This is a more advanced use of wheat flour and requires a little more effort than the previously mentioned foods, but certainly bread is a significant addition to a *Basic* diet. As an extra in this chapter, there is a recipe for making *wheat sugar* which can be used in bread recipes.

A few of the recipes call for *stone-ground* whole-wheat flour. Home-ground flour is usually equal to coarser commercial stone-ground flour. Both home-ground and stone-ground are coarser than whole-wheat flour bought at the grocery store. Almost always you may substitute one for the other without problems in most recipes.

RECIPES FOR PANCAKES, WAFFLES & MORE

BASIC QUIXMIX

This recipe introduces *Basic QuixMix,* a simple and easy *Basic* mix for quick-to-fix recipes to help you enjoy whole-wheat flour products. It's a quick mix to have on hand for preparing whole-wheat biscuits, pancakes, waffles, crackers, sweet breads, loaf breads, pretzels, and a number of other home-baked items.

Use *Basic QuixMix* in any *Basic* recipe calling for *biscuit mix*.

8 C. whole-wheat flour	$^1/_2$ C. sugar
$^1/_3$ C. baking powder	2 C. powdered milk
4 tsp. salt	2 C. shortening or margarine

Mix dry ingredients well. Cut in shortening until texture resembles cornmeal. A mixer may be used. Store *Basic QuixMix* in an airtight container in the refrigerator or freezer.

BASIC QUIXMIX BISCUITS

1 C. *Basic QuixMix*	$^1/_2$ C. water

Rolled method: prepare *Basic QuixMix*. Mix with water until soft dough forms. Add additional dry mix if necessary. Keep it easy to handle, then roll it into a ball. Knead gently for 30 seconds. Roll out to $^1/_2$" thick. Cut biscuits with 2" round biscuit cutter. Bake on ungreased cookie sheet 8 - 10 min. at 450°F.

Drop method: prepare *Basic QuixMix*. Combine with water. Drop onto greased baking sheet. Bake 12-15 min. at 375°- 400°F. *Yield: 8 - 12 biscuits.*

BASIC QUIXMIX PANCAKES

$1^1/_3$ C. *Basic QuixMix*	1 C. water
1 egg	

Prepare *Basic QuixMix*. Mix ingredients, let stand for 5-10 min. Cook on hot griddle until brown, then turn and brown on other side.

Variation #1: use milk instead of water for better-tasting pancakes.

Variation #2: add 1 egg, thoroughly beaten into batter for richer pancakes.

BASIC QUIXMIX BREAKFAST BREAD

2 C. *Basic QuixMix*	$^3/_4$ C. water
$^1/_4$ C. brown sugar	$^1/_2$ C. raisins
2 eggs, slightly beaten	

Prepare *Basic QuixMix*. Blend in sugar. Combine eggs and water in separate bowl and stir into *Mix*. Add raisins.[1] Pour into greased 9" pan. Bake at 350°F for 35 - 40 min.

BASIC QUIXMIX CINNABREAD

CinnaBread ingredients:

2 C. *Basic QuixMix*	$^3/_4$ C. water
$^1/_4$ C. brown sugar	$^1/_2$ C. raisins
2 eggs, slightly beaten	

CinnaBread topping ingredients:

$^1/_2$ C. brown sugar	$^1/_2$ tsp. cinnamon
$^1/_2$ C. chopped nuts	

Prepare *Basic QuixMix*. Blend in sugar. Combine eggs and water in separate bowl; stir into *Mix*. Add raisins. Pour into greased 9" pan. In separate bowl, combine sugar, cinnamon, and nuts. Sprinkle over top of *Bread*. Bake at 350°F for 35 - 40 min. Serve hot. Check bread during last 5 min. to make sure topping doesn't burn.

BASIC "SCRATCH" BATTER

$1^1/_4$ C. sifted whole-wheat flour	2-3 eggs, well beaten
3 tsp. baking powder	$1^1/_4$ C. milk
3 T. brown sugar	3 T. oil
$^3/_4$ tsp. salt	

Sift together dry ingredients (flour, baking powder, sugar, salt). Combine liquid ingredients (eggs, milk, oil) in separate bowl. Stir liquid mixture into flour mixture. Bake on greased hot griddle until golden brown.

> **Note:**
>
> *Experiment with* BASIC "SCRATCH" BATTER *to determine which kind your family likes best. Then, add bananas, nuts, apple cubes, or any other fruit or flavoring for a taste treat.*

BASIC OATCAKES

1 C. oats	1 T. honey
1 C. whole-wheat flour	2 eggs
$^1/_4$ tsp. baking soda	2 C. buttermilk
$^1/_4$ tsp. salt	$^1/_4$ C. melted butter

Stir dry ingredients (oats, flour, soda, salt) to mix well. Add remaining ingredients and stir. Aging several hours or overnight in refrigerator improves flavor. Add $^1/_4$ C. wheat germ to dry ingredients for extra nutrition and flavor. Cook on greased, hot griddle until brown.

BASIC BLENDER PANCAKES

$1^1/_2$ C. buttermilk*	2 eggs
$^3/_4$ C. whole-wheat flour	$^1/_4$ C. margarine
2 T. cornmeal	$^1/_2$ tsp. baking soda
2 T. brown sugar	1 T. baking powder

Blend buttermilk and whole-wheat flour on high speed for 3 - 4 min. Add cornmeal, brown sugar, eggs, and margarine and blend till combined. Add soda and baking powder, blend briefly. Using large spoon or small measuring cup, pour batter onto hot griddle. Turn when steam no longer rises from pancakes. Brown on both sides. Serve hot with favorite syrup.

* Substitute: 1 C. yogurt and $^1/_2$ C. milk.

---

[1] To prevent raisins and other fruits from going to the bottom of the pan during baking, dust fruits with flour before stirring them int the batter or dough.

RECIPES FOR BASIC SNACKS

BASIC WHEATNUTS

3 C. whole-wheat flour	2 T. baking powder
2 T. malted milk powder	1 C. brown sugar
$\frac{1}{2}$ tsp. salt	1 C. buttermilk or sour milk
$\frac{1}{2}$ C. wheat germ	

Combine all ingredients and mix. Dough should be sticky. Press onto greased cookie sheet to $\frac{1}{2}$" thickness. Bake at 350°F for 30 - 35 min. Cut into strips and put through a meat grinder. Return to oven and dry.

BASIC GRAINOLA

4 C. rolled oats (uncooked)	$\frac{1}{2}$ tsp. salt
1 C. wheat germ	$\frac{3}{4}$ C. honey
1 C. coconut (shredded)	1 C. vegetable oil
$\frac{1}{4}$ C. sesame seeds mixed	2 C. dried fruit and nuts,

Combine dry ingredients (oats, wheat germ, coconut, sesame seeds, salt) in a large bowl. Mix honey and oil together and heat until honey is thinned. Stir into dry mixture. Spread on 2 greased cookie sheets or two cake pans. Bake at 300°F until lightly browned (15 - 20 min.). Stir every 5 min. during baking and several times while cooling.

Add mixed dried fruits and nuts using any of the following: raisins, dried apples, dried bananas, dried apricots, toasted sunflower nuts, walnuts, pecans, almonds, etc.

BASIC GRAINOLA #2

1 C. soy flour	1 C. sunflower seeds
1 C. dry powdered milk	1 C. wheat germ
5 C. rolled oats	1 C. shredded coconut
1 C. sliced almonds	$1\frac{1}{4}$ C. honey
1 C. sesame seeds	1 C. warm vegetable oil

Combine dry ingredients (flour, milk, oatmeal, almonds, seeds, wheat germ, coconut) in large bowl. Mix honey and oil together and heat until honey is thinned. Stir into dry mixture. Spread on 2 greased cookie sheets or 2 cake pans. Bake at 300°F until lightly browned (15 - 20 min.). Stir every 5 min. during baking and several times while cooling.

BASIC GRAINOLA #3

4 C. oatmeal	$\frac{3}{4}$ C. honey
1 C. coconut	1 tsp. vanilla
1 C. wheat germ	$\frac{1}{2}$ C. chopped nuts
1 C. sesame seeds	$\frac{1}{2}$ C. raisins
1 C. vegetable oil	

Mix all ingredients together, except nuts and raisins; spread thin on 2 cookie sheets. Bake at 300°F for 20 min. Stir every 5 min. to avoid burning. When cool, add chopped nuts and raisins. Cool before taking off cookie sheet.

BASIC GRAINOLA #4

8 C. rolled oats	$\frac{1}{2}$ tsp. salt
1 C. nuts (pieces)	1 C. vegetable oil
1 C. wheat germ	$\frac{1}{2}$ C. water
1 C. shredded coconut	$\frac{1}{2}$ C. date nuggets

$^1/_2$ C. brown sugar

Mix all ingredients together and place on large tray. Bake at 250°F for 2 hr., stirring approximately every 30 min.

BASIC HAWAIIAN GRAINOLA

$^1/_3$ C. margarine or vegetable oil	$^1/_4$ C. wheat germ
$^1/_2$ C. brown sugar	$^1/_4$ C. sesame seeds
$^1/_4$ tsp. salt	1 C. sunflower seeds
$^1/_4$ C. water	$^1/_2$ C. coconut
$^1/_4$ C. honey	1 C. chopped nuts
1 tsp. cinnamon	1 C. dried fruit bits
3 C. rolled grain	

Melt margarine; add brown sugar, salt, water, honey, and cinnamon. Mix remaining ingredients except dried fruit. Pour margarine mixture over dry ingredients. Mix well and spread in a 9" x 13" inch baking pan. Bake at 350°F for 15 - 20 min., stirring occasionally. Cool; add dried fruit. Store in an airtight container.

Low-fat, low-sugar variation: omit margarine/vegetable oil, brown sugar, and honey. Add $1^1/_4$ C. apple juice concentrate.

BASIC GRAINOLA COOKEES

3 C. *Basic Grainola*	1 tsp. baking soda
1 C. butter (margarine)	1 tsp. salt
1 C. brown sugar	2 tsp. vanilla
2 eggs	12 oz. chocolate morsels
2 T. water	1 C. chopped nuts or coconut
$1^3/_4$ C. flour	

Prepare *Basic Grainola*. Cream butter, brown sugar, and eggs until fluffy. Add water and blend well. Sift flour, soda, and salt together and add to creamed mixture. Stir in *Basic Grainola*, vanilla, chocolate morsels, nuts, or coconut. Mix until well blended. Drop by teaspoon onto greased cookie sheet and bake at 350°F for 12 min.

RECIPES FOR BASIC PRETZELS

Pretzels are usually made from regular white flour, but the following recipes use whole-wheat and wholesome rye flours. Before baking, dip each pretzel in boiling salted water, to give the familiar shiny crust to the pretzel, then sprinkle with coarse salt. Soft pretzels are delicious with a soup or salad lunch, or with sausages and cheese for a late supper. Serve them hot, warm, or at room temperature, spread with butter. Or, my favorite, the hot pretzel with cold mustard! Pretzels can be refrigerated or frozen, then reheated for serving.

BASIC SOFTWHEAT PRETZELS

1 T. active dry yeast	$^1/_2$ C. warm water
3 C. stone-ground whole-wheat flour (approx.)	$^1/_2$ C. sugar
3 C. all-purpose flour, unsifted $1^1/_2$ tsp. salt	$^3/_4$ tsp. baking powder
2 C. milk, scalded, cooled to room temperature	4 T. coarse salt, kosher style
2 qt. boiling water	$^1/_4$ C. vegetable oil
1 egg white, slightly beaten	

In a large bowl, dissolve yeast in the warm water. Then stir in sugar, $1^1/_2$ tsp. salt, milk, and vegetable oil. With a wooden spoon gradually mix in $1^1/_2$ C. stone-ground whole-wheat flour and 1 C. of the all-purpose flour.

Cover and let rise in a warm place until bubbly, about 40 min. Sift $1^1/_2$ C. more of the all-purpose flour with baking powder; add to dough with remaining $1^1/_2$ C. of stone-ground whole-wheat flour. Mix with wooden spoon, then turn out dough on a lightly floured board.

Knead for about 5 min. or until dough is no longer sticky, adding a little more all-purpose flour if necessary. Roll out and pat dough into a 9" x 15" rectangle. Press a long-blade knife straight down through dough to cut into strips $^1/_2$" wide and 15" long.

With your palms, roll each strip back and forth on the board into a strand about 20" long; twist each into pretzel shape. Let rise, uncovered, for 30 min.

Dissolve 3 T. coarse salt in boiling water. With a slotted spoon, lower 1 pretzel at a time into boiling water; after about 2 seconds, lift out, wipe the bottom of the spoon on paper towels to drain briefly. Set pretzels on a liberally greased baking sheet, arrange $^1/_2$" apart. Brush with egg white and sprinkle lightly with remaining coarse salt.

Bake at 400°F for 20 min. or until crust is golden brown.

Serve warm or transfer to a rack to cool. Wrap airtight for storage. To reheat, set pretzels directly on oven rack at 350°F for about 5 min. (8 min. if frozen) or until crusty.

Yield: *approx. 18 pretzels.*

BASIC SOFTRYE PRETZELS

Follow directions for *Basic SoftWheat Pretzels*, substituting rye flour for whole-wheat flour.

Add 3 T. crushed dill seed for extra good taste, if desired.

RECIPES FOR BASIC CRACKERS

BASIC SALTCRAX

4 C. whole-wheat flour	1 T. honey
2 tsp. salt	1 T. active dry yeast
$^2/_3$ C. dry powdered milk	$^1/_3$ C. vegetable oil
$1^1/_2$ C. warm water	

Mix together flour, salt, and powdered milk. In 1 C. warm water dissolve honey and yeast. Add to the dry ingredients along with vegetable oil. Add remaining (or a little more) warm water. Form into a ball. Place in a greased bowl, cover, and let rise $^1/_2$-1 hr.

Knead for a few minutes. Return to bowl. Take a lemon-sized piece of dough at a time, keeping the remaining dough covered. Roll out the dough on a lightly floured board. Roll each piece as thin as possible.

Bake on ungreased cookie sheet in a 350°F oven about 6 min. Turn pan around, turn crackers over and bake 2 - 3 min. more. Watch browning very carefully. Cool slowly. Break by hand into irregular shaped crackers.

BASIC GRAMMACRAX

$^1/_2$ C. butter or margarine	$^1/_2$ tsp. baking powder
$^2/_3$ C. dark brown sugar, firmly packed	$^1/_4$ tsp. ground cinnamon
$2^3/_4$ C. whole-wheat flour	$^1/_2$ C. water

Cream butter or margarine and sugar well. Mix remaining ingredients and add to creamed mixture, alternating with $^1/_2$ C. water. Mix well. Let stand 30 min. Roll out dough on floured board to $^1/_8$" thickness, cut in 1" squares, and put on oiled cookie sheet.

Bake in preheated 350°F oven for 20 min. or until slightly browned.

BASIC HONEY GRAMMACRAX

$2^1/_4$ C. whole-wheat or graham flour	$^1/_3$ C. margarine or shortening
$^1/_2$ tsp. salt	$^1/_4$ C. warmed honey
1 tsp. baking soda	3 T. water
$^1/_3$ C. brown sugar	

Combine dry ingredients (flour, salt, soda, sugar) and cut in margarine or shortening. Combine honey and water and add to dry ingredients. Blend well. Roll out $^1/_2$ the dough on an ungreased cookie sheet to $^1/_4$" thickness. Prick dough with a fork. Repeat with remaining dough.

Bake at 375°F for 8 - 10 min. or until golden brown. Remove from oven and cut into squares. Cool.

BASIC SESAME WHEATCRAX

$1^1/_2$ C. whole-wheat flour	4 T. sugar
$1^1/_2$ C. all-purpose flour	$^1/_2$ C. vegetable oil or shortening
$^1/_4$ C. wheat germ	$1^1/_2$ C. milk or water
$1^1/_2$ tsp. salt	$^1/_4$ C. sesame seeds
2 C. rolled oats	

Mix dry ingredients (flours, wheat germ, salt, oats, sugar) with oil and milk or water. Add sesame seeds and knead until a smooth dough is formed. Roll out thin and cut into desired shape. Put on lightly greased cookie sheet. Bake at 375°F until golden with brown spots.

RECIPES FOR BASIC PASTA

Everyone loves pasta, and everyone will love whole-wheat pasta even more! Use the following recipe to make *Basic Pasta Mix*, then expand your pasta skills and meals with it.

BASIC PASTA MIX

$^3/_4$ C. egg (measure exactly)	2 T. vegetable oil
2 T. + 1 tsp. water	$3^3/_4$ C. whole-wheat flour

Mix ingredients together until the size of popped corn. Shape according to pasta maker directions or roll $^1/_8$" thick and cut into thin noodles and hang or lay flat to dry.

Use *Basic Pasta Mix* for any pasta, noodles, lasagna—even dumplings!

BASIC NOODLES

6 eggs	2 C. whole-wheat flour
$^1/_2$ tsp. salt	boiling broth or salted water
1 tsp. vegetable oil	

Beat eggs thoroughly, add salt, oil and flour. Mix well. Roll mixture out on floured board with wax paper between rolling pin and dough. When $^1/_8$" thick, cut with sharp knife, large needle, or cutter, roll up, and put into boiling broth or salted water.

BASIC NOODLE CASSEROLE

1 batch *Basic Noodles*	1 can tuna
1 can peas, #303	$^1/_4$ tsp. salt
1 can mushroom soup, undiluted	

Mix ingredients in greased casserole dish. Bake at 350°F for 30 min.

Yield: 6 servings.

RECIPES FOR BASIC TORTILLAS

BASIC WHEATORTILLAS

4 C. whole-wheat flour	$^1/_2$ C. shortening
$1^1/_2$ tsp. salt	water

Mix flour and salt. Cut in shortening. Mix in enough water to make a pliable dough. Knead until soft and stretchy. Form balls, cover with a cloth. Let rest 30 min. Roll paper thin.

Cook in ungreased, medium-hot, cast-iron skillet until high spots turn dark brown.

BASIC CORNY WHEATORTILLAS

$1^1/_2$ C. cornmeal	$^3/_4$ tsp. salt
$1^1/_2$ C. whole-wheat flour	6 T. shortening
$^1/_2$ tsp. baking powder	$^3/_4$ C. water

Combine cornmeal, flour, baking powder, and salt. Cut in shortening. Add warm water and stir until mixture is moistened. (A teaspoon or more additional water may be added if dough is too stiff.) Turn out onto a floured surface and knead 5 min. or until mixture is no longer sticky. Shape into 14 balls. Roll each into a thin 6" circle.

Bake on a hot, ungreased griddle for 1 min. each side.

RECIPES FOR BASIC PIE CRUSTS

BASIC PIE CRUST MIX

2 C. whole-wheat flour $^3/_4$ C. vegetable shortening
1 tsp. salt   4 - 8 tsp. ice water

Mix whole-wheat flour and salt. Cut $^1/_2$ C. of the shortening into flour mixture until fine as meal. Cut remaining shortening into mix until mixture resembles the size of green peas. Sprinkle 4-8 tsp. ice water on mixture, stirring in lightly with a fork. Then mix well, shaping into a ball. Roll out to fit pan.

Bake at 400°F for 8-12 min.

BASIC PIE SHELL

1 C. stone-ground whole-wheat flour $^1/_3$ C. vegetable shortening
$^1/_4$ tsp. salt   cold water

Mix stone-ground whole-wheat flour and salt in bowl. Cut in vegetable shortening until mixture resembles coarse meal. Mixing with fork, add enough cold water to hold ingredients together. Gather into ball and roll on floured board to fit pie pan. Trim edges and flute.

Bake at 400°F for 8 - 12 min.

RECIPES FOR BASIC MUFFINS & QUIXBREAD

BASIC WHEATBRAN MUFFINS

3 C. wheat bran* $2^1/_2$ C. whole-wheat flour
1 C. boiling water $2^1/_2$ tsp. baking soda
1 C. brown sugar   1 tsp. salt
$^1/_2$ C. margarine   1 pint buttermilk
2 eggs

Combine 1 C. wheat bran and 1 C. boiling water, stir, and let steep. In a separate bowl, cream sugar and margarine. Beat eggs. Combine flour, soda, salt. Combine the 1 C. of steeped bran with remaining 2 C. bran, eggs, flour mixture, buttermilk, margarine, and sugar. Mix. Store in tightly covered plastic container. Let stand at least 12 hr. before baking. Batter will keep in refrigerator for 6 weeks. When preparing to bake, preheat oven to 400°F. Stir batter well and spoon into lined muffin tins, $^2/_3$ full.

Bake 20 - 22 min.

* Substitute oat bran, if preferred.

BASIC OATBRAN MUFFIN MIX

1 C. dry buttermilk powder   1 T. salt
    or powdered milk   1 C. brown sugar
3 C. whole-wheat flour   6 C. oat bran*
2 T. baking soda   6 T. molasses

In a large bowl, combine buttermilk powder, flour, baking soda, and salt. Stir to blend. Add brown sugar, making sure there are no lumps. Add oat bran whole or process dry in a blender. Stir into flour mixture. Slowly pour molasses over mixture while mixing until evenly distributed.

Keep in an airtight container in the refrigerator or freezer.

* Use all or part of the oat bran.

BASIC OATBRAN MUFFINS

3 C. *Basic OatBran Muffin Mix* ¹/₄ C. vegetable oil
³/₄ C. water 4 egg whites (or equivalent)

Prepare *Basic OatBran Muffin Mix*. Combine egg white, oil, and water in separate bowl. Add *Mix* and stir just until moistened. Bake in paper-lined muffin tins for 15-20 min. at 400°F or until wooden pick inserted in the middle comes out dry.

Yield: 12 large muffins.

Variation: Omit 2 egg whites and add 1 C. mashed or shredded fruit such as bananas, apples, pineapple, carrots, etc.

BASIC ZUCCHINI BREAD

2 C. sugar 1 tsp. salt
1 C. vegetable oil 1 tsp. baking soda
3 eggs, beaten 3 tsp. cinnamon
2 zucchini (unpeeled and grated) ¹/₄ tsp. baking powder
3 tsp. vanilla ¹/₂ C. chopped nuts
3 C. whole-wheat flour

Mix sugar, oil, eggs, zucchini, and vanilla in large bowl. Sift together in separate bowl flour, salt, soda, cinnamon, and baking powder. Add dry ingredients to first bowl, stirring to combine well. Add chopped nuts.

Bake at 350°F for 45 - 60 min.

Yield: 2 loaves.

RECIPES FOR BASIC CAKES

BASIC WHEATCAKE MIX

²/₃ C. vegetable shortening (margarine) 3 C. whole-wheat flour, sifted
1¹/₂ C. brown sugar (packed tightly) 1¹/₂ tsp. vanilla
4¹/₂ tsp. baking powder 3 eggs
1 tsp. salt 1¹/₂ C. milk

Cream together shortening, brown sugar, and vanilla. Add eggs and beat thoroughly. Sift together whole-wheat flour, baking powder, and salt. Combine wet and dry mixtures, adding milk. After thorough mixing, pour into greased 11" x 17" pan.

Bake at 350°F for 25 - 30 min. (In 9" x 9" pans or for cupcakes, bake 20 - 25 min.

Yield: 24- 28 cupcakes.

BASIC SPONGE WHEATCAKE

6 eggs, separated ¹/₂ tsp. salt
¹/₂ C. water ¹/₂ tsp. lemon juice or extract
1¹/₂ C. sugar 1 tsp. cream of tartar
¹/₄ tsp. almond extract 1¹/₂ C. stone-ground whole-
  wheat flour

Use mixer to beat yolks, water, sugar, and flavoring 5-7 min. until very thick and creamy. Sift flour and salt twice, then add to bowl of liquid. Beat egg whites until stiff and fold into batter. Add remaining ingredients gradually, continuing to beat. Pour into cake pans.

Bake at 325°- 350°F for approx. 1 hr. until top springs back from touch.

BASIC APPLECAKE

4 fresh, diced apples	2 eggs
2 C. sugar	2 C. whole-wheat flour
$\frac{1}{2}$ C. vegetable oil	2 tsp. cinnamon
2 tsp. vanilla	1 C. nuts (optional)
2 tsp. baking soda	1 C. raisins (optional)
1 tsp. salt	

Place diced apples (not grated) in bowl. Add sugar, oil, vanilla, soda, salt, and eggs and mix thoroughly. Sift dry ingredients (flour, cinnamon, nuts, raisins) together, then add to wet mixture. Pour into greased 9" x 13" pan. Bake in 350°F oven for 60 min. or until cake shrinks from sides of pan. Frost with frosting recipe.

Frosting:

2 C. powdered sugar	4 oz. cream cheese
$\frac{1}{2}$ C. butter	1 tsp. vanilla

Combine ingredients and beat well. Spread topping with knife or spatula.

BASIC APPLESAUCE CAKE

$\frac{1}{2}$ C. shortening	$\frac{1}{2}$ tsp. cloves
1 C. sugar	1 tsp. cinnamon
1 egg	1 C. chopped nuts
2 C. sifted whole-wheat flour	1 C. raisins
$\frac{1}{4}$ tsp. salt	1 C. thick unsweetened
$\frac{3}{4}$ tsp. baking soda	applesauce (warmed)

Cream shortening and sugar until light and fluffy. Add egg and beat thoroughly. Add sifted dry ingredients (flour, salt, soda, cloves, cinnamon), then nuts and raisins. Warm applesauce and stir into batter. Pour into well-greased and floured 8" x 8" pans. Bake 50 min. at 350°F.

BASIC ANGELCAKE

1 C. + 2 T. whole-wheat pastry flour*	$1\frac{1}{2}$ tsp. cream of tartar
12 large egg whites ($1\frac{1}{2}$ C.)	$1\frac{1}{2}$ C. sugar
1 tsp. vanilla or almond extract	$\frac{1}{2}$ tsp. salt

Combine flour and $\frac{3}{4}$ C. sugar and stir. Set aside. Combine salt and cream of tartar with egg whites and whip until whites stand in peaks. With mixer on low speed, gradually add the remaining $\frac{3}{4}$ C. sugar and flavoring. When sugar blends, stop mixer and sprinkle $\frac{1}{3}$ of the flour mixture over the beaten egg whites and blend briefly. Add another $\frac{1}{3}$ of flour mixture and blend briefly. Add final $\frac{1}{3}$ of flour and *blend only until mixed.*

Pour into ungreased angel food cake pan. Bake for 1 hr. at 350°F. Invert pan to cool. *Do not remove cake until cool.*

* Substitute: $\frac{3}{4}$ C. flour and $\frac{1}{4}$ C. cornstarch for pastry flour.

BASIC FRUIT COCKTAIL CAKE

1 egg	$\frac{1}{4}$ tsp. salt
1 C. sugar	1 tsp. baking soda
2 C. fruit cocktail, not drained	$\frac{1}{2}$ C. brown sugar
1 C. whole-wheat flour	$\frac{1}{2}$ C. chopped nuts

(See next page)

Beat egg and add sugar; beat together well. Stir in fruit cocktail along with the juice—*do not drain.* Mix flour, salt, and soda together. Combine mixtures. Put in greased 7" x 12" or 8" x 13" pan and sprinkle with brown sugar and nuts. Bake at 350°F for 50 - 60 min. *Yield: approx. 8 servings.*

BASIC QUIKCAKE

1^1/$_2$ C. whole-wheat flour	5 T. vegetable oil
3 T. cocoa or chocolate	1 T. vinegar
1 tsp. baking soda	1 T. vanilla
1 C. sugar	1 C. cold water
^{1}/$_2$ tsp. salt	

Sift together first five items into a greased 9" x 9" x 12" pan. Pour next three ingredients into hollow of dry ingredients. Pour cold water over all ingredients and mix with spoon until nearly smooth and flour is not visible in mixture. Bake at 350°F for 30 min.

BASIC CARROTCAKE

3 C. finely shredded carrots	^{1}/$_2$ tsp. salt
1 C. vegetable oil	2 tsp. baking powder
4 eggs	^{1}/$_2$ tsp. baking soda
2 C. sugar	2 C. whole-wheat flour
1 tsp. cinnamon	

Mix together carrots, oil, and eggs. Mix in sugar, cinnamon, salt, baking powder, and soda. Mix on medium speed for 2 min. Add whole-wheat flour and mix just until moistened. Bake in a 350°F oven for 35-40 min.

Cream Cheese Frosting:
Combine 8-oz. cream cheese, softened, 2 T. milk & 4 C. powdered sugar. Add 1 tsp. vanilla. Beat until smooth.

RECIPES FOR BASIC COOKEES

These "cookee" treats made with whole-wheat flour are as nutritious as they are delicious. They are good for quick energy and help children adapt to whole-wheat cookery. These particular *Basic Cookees* recipes have proven to be favorites for children of all ages. These are classified as *s'more* cookies—that's short for *I want some more Cookees, Mom.*

BASIC YOGURT COOKEES

1 C. margarine	1 tsp. baking powder
1 C. white sugar	^{1}/$_4$ tsp. salt
1 C. brown sugar	^{1}/$_2$ tsp. nutmeg
1 tsp. vanilla	4 C. sifted whole-wheat flour
2 eggs, beaten	1 C. yogurt

Cream margarine and sugars. Add vanilla and beaten eggs. Sift dry ingredients (baking powder, salt, nutmeg, flour) together twice and add, alternately with yogurt, to the egg mixture. Working with half the dough at a time, roll out on floured board to ^{1}/$_8$" thickness. Cut in small rounds with cookie cutter. Place on greased cookie sheet and bake at 400°F for 8-10 min. *Yield: 24-30 cookies.*

BASIC MOLASSES COOKEES

^{1}/$_4$ C. butter or margarine	1 tsp. cinnamon
^{1}/$_4$ C. sugar	1 tsp. ground ginger
^{1}/$_2$ C. molasses	^{1}/$_4$ tsp. cloves
^{1}/$_2$ tsp. salt	1^1/$_2$ C. whole-wheat flour

2 tsp. baking soda   2 T. vinegar

Melt butter or margarine with sugar and molasses in small saucepan over low heat, then cool. Combine salt, baking soda, cinnamon, ginger, and cloves with whole-wheat flour in mixing bowl. Stir in molasses mixture. Add vinegar and stir in. Drop by teaspoon onto greased cookie sheets. Bake in moderate oven (350°F) for 7 min. or until cookies are set. Remove carefully with spatula. *Store in covered jar.*

BASIC CHOCKEES

$^1/_2$ C. **Nestle's Quik® Cocoa**	$^1/_2$ tsp. baking soda
$^1/_4$ C. warm water	2 C. milk
$1^1/_2$ C. margarine	2 tsp. vanilla
2 C. sugar	2 C. raisins
2 tsp. salt	1 C. chopped nuts
6 C. whole-wheat flour	

Mix cocoa with enough warm water to make a medium-thick paste. Cream margarine and sugar together in separate bowl. Sift together all dry ingredients (salt, flour, soda). Add to sugar mixture alternately with milk. Finally, add cocoa mixture, vanilla, raisins, and nuts. Drop onto greased cookie sheets.

Bake at 350°F for 10 min.

As an added treat and to heighten eye appeal, dust with powdered sugar.

BASIC SUGAR COOKEES

1 C. shortening	$3^1/_2$ C. whole-wheat flour
2 C. powdered sugar	1 tsp. baking soda
2 eggs	1 tsp. salt
$^1/_2$ C. buttermilk	

Mix shortening, powdered sugar, and eggs together thoroughly. Stir in remaining ingredients. Drop rounded teaspoonfuls about 2" apart on lightly greased baking sheet.

Bake at 400°F for 8-10 min. *Yield: approx. 6 dozen cookies.*

BASIC CHOCOCHIP COOKEES

$2^1/_4$ C. whole-wheat flour	1 tsp. vanilla
1 tsp. baking soda	$4^1/_2$ T. powdered dry milk
1 tsp. salt	1 T. water
$^1/_2$ C. soft butter or margarine	$^3/_4$ C. chopped peanuts
1 pkg. chocolate or carob chips	$1^1/_2$ C. brown sugar (packed)
3 eggs, beaten	1 C. sunflower seeds, unsalted

Stir together dry ingredients (flour, soda, salt). Cream the butter and sugar. Add to eggs, vanilla, powdered milk, and water. Beat until fluffy. Add flour and blend well. Stir in chocolate chips and nuts. Drop onto greased cookie sheet.

Bake at 375°F for 10-15 min.

BASIC APPLESAUCE COOKEES

1 C. brown sugar	$^1/_2$ tsp. salt
$^1/_2$ C. vegetable shortening	$^1/_2$ tsp. nutmeg
1 egg, beaten well	$^1/_2$ tsp. cinnamon
1 C. applesauce	$^1/_4$ tsp. cloves
1 tsp. baking soda	1 C. raisins
2 C. whole-wheat flour	$^1/_2$ C. chopped nuts

Cream brown sugar and vegetable shortening. Add beaten egg; mix well. Add apple-sauce and soda, mixing thoroughly. Add remaining ingredients, mixing well. Drop spoonfuls onto greased cookie sheet. Bake at 375°F for 15-20 min.

BASIC WHOLE-WHEAT BREAD COOKERY

The whole breadmaking scene these days is made more attractive by the use of a commercial bread mixer. There are many on the market, and we suggest every family eventually buy one—but only after the basic food items are in the larder!

If you already have one of these new countertop, automatic loaf bread makers and don't want more than a really basic 1-$1^1/_2$ pound loaf when you bake, your worries are probably over. The rest of this section on breadmaking is superfluous for you—just read the instructions with your bread maker. If you don't have a bread baking machine or a bread mixer yet, read on!

Don't let the prospect of making homemade bread by hand deter you from enjoying a wonderful and rewarding experience in creativity. Added to the personal growth is the money saved by making bread from your stored wheat. It does take extra time to make your own fresh-baked bread—what accomplishment doesn't have its price or skill its apprenticeship?

In this chapter, you'll discover why it takes more time to make whole-wheat bread than bread made with all-purpose flour. You'll learn that whole-wheat flour is coarser and heavier. You'll understand why whole-wheat dough must be kneaded for 10-15 minutes to produce loaves with an even texture and that each rising also takes longer.

In the following paragraphs you will find what you need to know about basic bread-making—the how-to's, the whys, and the wherefores of certain breadmaking steps—to succeed in making every bread recipe in this section.

Directions for Basic Breadmaking

Mixing

The yeast and flour manufacturers have discovered that equally consistent quality and even quicker preparation will result when half the flour and all the undissolved yeast are stirred together in the mixer bowl. By eliminating the additional step of dissolving the yeast in warm water separately, the preparation time is significantly shortened.

Most *Basic* recipes work either way, though. If you prefer the separate steps method, then continue. Only a few recipes in this *Handbook* are not modified to mixing yeast and flour initially—but you can convert them easily; merely choose the better way for you.

Next, add the warm liquid ingredients and beat with an electric mixer. This beating stage begins the important process of developing the gluten—the bread's framework. Now stir in as much flour as necessary, by hand, to make a moderately stiff dough that comes out of the bowl in a mass. There should be some flour left over for the next step.

Kneading

Turn the dough out on a lightly floured surface. The flour used for kneading is part of the measured amount. You will want to flour your hands, since a moderately stiff dough is still rather sticky.

To knead dough, curve your fingers over the dough, pull it toward you, then push it down and away from you with the heel of your hand. Then give the dough a quarter turn, fold the dough toward you, and push it down again. Add flour till the dough loses its stickiness.

Notes:

When a recipe gives a range for the amount of flour needed, start with the smaller amount, adding only enough extra flour to make the dough easy to handle.

Using more flour than necessary makes the dough stiff and less manageable during kneading and shaping, thus producing heavier bread.

Note:

On high-humidity days, dough takes more flour.
Keep repeating the kneading motions until the dough is smooth.

Kneading is the key step to a good loaf of bread. This process develops the gluten in the flour into long, thin strands. In the dough, firm kneading strokes develop long strands of gluten, giving bread small uniform holes and a fine texture.

Rough or too vigorous kneading breaks and shortens the gluten strands, causing large holes in the bread. This results in poor rising.

Knead till the dough develops a *life* of its own. It will feel elastic and respond to your touch. Kneading usually takes about 8-10 minutes. Don't worry about too much kneading; you won't knead dough too long—it'll wear you out long before you overdo the kneading.

Rising

A constant temperature of 80°F is ideal for the rising of yeast bread. During rising, the yeast grows and gives off carbon dioxide which is trapped in the gluten strands, causing the mass of dough to stretch. This gives the bread its fine texture.

Place dough in a warm place for rising. Place it on the top rack of a cold oven and put a pan of hot water on the lower rack. Or, if you prefer, just set the bowl of dough on your kitchen counter, making sure the rising dough is protected from drafts.

Rising times given in recipes are approximate—actual rising time depends upon temperature and humidity in your kitchen.

To prevent the surface of the dough from becoming dry and hard as it rises, place dough in a lightly greased bowl, turning once to completely coat its surface. Cover the coated dough loosely with waxed paper or a dampened kitchen towel.

Rising is completed and the dough is ready for shaping when it has doubled in bulk and two fingers pressed lightly $\frac{1}{2}$" into the dough leave an indentation. Punch the dough down by pushing your fist into the center once. Then, pull the edges of the dough to the center, turn the dough over, and place it on a lightly floured surface.

Shaping

Various methods can be used to shape dough, but first let the dough rest covered for about 10 minutes after it has been punched down and divided into manageable portions. This resting period allows the gluten strands to relax, making the dough less elastic and much easier to handle.

Handling the dough during shaping bursts the large air bubbles and produces bread with a smooth, even exterior. To shape dough into a loaf, roll into a 12" x 8" rectangle. Be sure to roll to outer edges to pop any air bubbles. Roll rectangle up tightly, starting with the 8" edge.
As you roll, seal with fingertips. Seal the seam completely by pinching the dough together. Also seal the ends by pinching each into a thin sealed strip. Fold strips under the loaf into the seam side.

Place loaf seam-side down into a greased baking pan. Grease and cover the surface and let rise again till it's almost doubled in size. When checking the second rising, press fingers lightly against the edge of the loaf. The dough should feel light and spongy. It will have lost its elasticity and won't bounce back.

If you prefer, you can shape loaves into empty fruit juice cans or bake them in layer cake pans or on cookie sheets—or make great dinner rolls. Braided bread is popular, but be sure to braid the bread very loosely so the interwoven effect is not lost as the bread doubles in bulk while rising again.

Baking

Bake bread at the temperature specified in the particular recipe. During the first few minutes of baking, the leavening gas in the dough expands rapidly, giving the bread its greatest volume. This is the reason the oven should be preheated to the correct temperature before putting the raised loaf in to bake. As bread bakes, the gluten framework is set, the yeast is destroyed, and this in turn stops the rising action. At this point, the flavor of the bread is fully developed. That's also when the family starts hanging around the kitchen!

After the suggested time for baking has elapsed, test the bread for doneness by tapping the top crust with your finger. When there is a hollow sound, the bread is thoroughly baked, and the crust should be nicely browned. If the bread browns too quickly, cover the loaf with aluminum foil while baking to prevent the crust from burning. Use the foil cover also after the top has browned but sides are still light.

Remove yeast breads from baking pans immediately after taking them from the oven. This prevents the crust from being "steamed" in the pan. Place bread on a wire rack to cool, or be devoured, whichever comes first.

How to Keep Bread Fresh

Note:

If you consistently have problems with crusts browning too quickly, check oven temperature with an oven thermometer to make sure the oven reading is correct.

Hopefully, the instructions and guidelines in the previous paragraphs will help elevate you above the level of a *Basic bread maker*. Now that you're on your way to homemade breads, rolls, and other treats, here are some suggestions for storing homemade bread dough and breads:

- Wrap cooled breads in foil or clear plastic wrap. Store in a well-ventilated breadbox.
- Do not unnecessarily refrigerate baked yeast breads or rolls—refrigerator temperatures cause breads to go stale.
- Refrigeration prevents mold from forming in the short range. During hot weather, it may be a better choice—depending on how fast bread disappears in your house.
- Store crisp-crusted bread and rolls unwrapped. Try to use them the same day.
- For "*just-baked*" freshness when life is hectic, freeze your baked bread. The fresh quality is retained up to 3 months in fully-baked products.
- To use frozen bread, thaw first, then unwrap.
- Unbaked homemade dough will freeze well for only a few weeks.
- Slice bread before freezing—it's not convenient to use if entire loaf must be thawed.
- There's no need to thaw bread before toasting or when making sandwiches to eat later in the day.
- Reheat bread and rolls to restore their crispness.
- Dinner rolls and sweet rolls will freeze for up to three months satisfactorily.
- Apply toppings after breads or rolls are thawed. Glazes, icings, and frostings with powdered sugar do not freeze well.

RECIPES FOR BASIC BREADSTUFFS

The previous section provided suggestions for *basic breadmaking* techniques. These recipes will help you bake some *Basic* breads, as well as our favorite *advanced Basic* breads.

BASIC ONE-RISE WHEATBREAD

2 T. active dry yeast	3 T. shortening
$^1/_2$ C. warm water	$1^1/_2$ T. salt
$5^1/_2$-6 C. whole-wheat flour	4 T. honey
$2^1/_2$ C. white flour	2 T. molasses
$^1/_4$ tsp. sugar	
$3^1/_2$ C. scalded milk (powdered, 2%, or diluted canned)	

Dissolve yeast in warm water and sugar. Add salt, honey, molasses, and shortening to scalded milk and allow mixture to cool to lukewarm. Stir 2 C. flour into liquid and beat with mixer until thin batter stage. Add yeast and beat well. Add remaining flour, 1 C. at a time, mixing or stirring until dough will not absorb more flour. Knead 15 min. Put into pans and let rise 45 min. (doesn't need to rise twice). Bake at 425°F for 15 min., then reduce to 325°F for 45 min. *Yield: 3 small loaves.*

BASIC WHEATBREAD

$3^1/_4$ C. warm water	1 T. salt
2 T. brown sugar	1 C. powdered milk
2 T. active dry yeast	1 to 2 C. white flour
2 T. honey	6 to 8 C. whole-wheat flour
2 T. molasses	2 T. vegetable oil
2 tsp. butter or margarine	

In a large bowl, mix $^1/_2$ C. warm water with sugar, add yeast, and let stand about 5 min. Add honey, molasses, butter or margarine, salt, powdered milk, and $2^3/_4$ C. warm water. Stir in white flour, then stir in wheat flour until dough is easy to knead—not too stiff and not too sticky. Knead 10 min., using oil.

Divide into loaves, shape, and place in greased pans. Let rise 45-60 min., then bake 45 min. in 350°F oven. Let cool slightly, then brush tops of loaves with butter or margarine.

Yield: 2 large loaves.

BASIC WHEATROLLS

2 T. yeast	2 eggs, beaten
$^1/_2$ C. warm water	$^1/_2$ tsp. salt
$^1/_3$ C. vegetable oil	$^1/_2$ C. dry powdered milk
$^1/_3$ C. brown sugar	$4^1/_2$-5 C. whole-wheat flour

Mix yeast and warm water, set aside for 5 min. Mix together oil, brown sugar, eggs, and salt. Then add powdered milk, mixing well. Add enough flour to make a soft dough which leaves the side of the bowl. Turn onto well-floured board. Turn dough over to coat with flour and knead 10 min. or until smooth and satiny. Place in a greased bowl, cover, and allow to rise until almost double in bulk (1-2 hr.) Shape as desired and place in greased pans. Let rise again.

Bake at 400°F for 15 min.

BASIC ONION BUNS

3 T. butter or margarine	$^3/_4$ C. finely chopped onion
3 C. all purpose flour (unsifted)	3 T. sugar
3 C. whole-wheat flour	$1^1/_2$ tsp. salt
2 T. active dry yeast	2 C. hot water

In fry pan, sauté onion in butter until golden. Set aside. In large mixer bowl, blend 1 C. regular flour, 1 C. whole-wheat flour, sugar, salt, and yeast. Add onion mixture (saving 2 T. for topping buns) and the hot water. Beat at low speed 2 min. Add 1 C. whole-wheat flour and beat at high speed 2 min. Stir in remaining whole-wheat flour and enough regular flour to make a soft dough. Sprinkle $^1/_3$ C. regular flour on a board; turn dough out and knead until smooth and elastic, about 5 min., adding more flour as needed.

Place in greased bowl, turning over to grease top. Cover. Let rise in warm place until double, about 1 hr. Punch down and divide into 2 equal pieces. Roll each into a ball and place 4" apart on greased baking sheets. With greased fingers flatten each into a 4" circle. Spread some of the reserved onion mixture on each. Let rise until double, about 50 min.

Bake at 375°F for 20-25 min.

BASIC TOMATOBREAD

3 T. active dry yeast	1 C. honey
1 T. sugar	$^1/_2$ C. molasses
1 C. lukewarm water	$^1/_2$ C. shortening
$1^1/_2$ qt. tap water	18-20 C. whole-wheat flour
1 C. tomato juice	butter or margarine
4 T. salt	

Add yeast and sugar to lukewarm water. Set aside while mixing the other ingredients. In a large mixing bowl beat together water, tomato juice, salt, honey, molasses, and shortening. Add yeast mixture. Beat in 10 C. whole-wheat flour.

Knead in 8-10 more C. whole-wheat flour. Cover and let rise until double in size. Knead down again and shape into loaves.

Place in well-greased loaf tins. Let dough rise to top of pans.

Bake at 350°F for 40 min. Cool slightly and grease tops of loaves with butter, then turn loaves on sides to cool.

Yield: 7 medium loaves.

BASIC PUMPERNICKEL BREAD

4 T. active dry yeast	$^3/_4$ C. cornmeal
$3^1/_2$ C. warm water	2 tsp. caraway seeds
$^1/_2$ C. molasses or honey	$^1/_2$ C. sunflower seeds
1 T. oil	2 T. carob or cocoa powder
2 T. salt	3 C. rye flour
2 C. mashed potatoes	9-10 C. whole-wheat flour

Sprinkle yeast over water and allow to activate. Add the remaining ingredients and mix well. Knead 10-12 min. Let rise until double. Shape into 4 loaves. Let rise to double again.

Bake in a 350°F oven for 50 min.

Yield: 4 small loaves.

BASIC DILLYBREAD

1 T. active dry yeast	1 T. dehydrated onion flakes
4 tsp. sugar	2 tsp. dill seed
$^1/_4$ C. warm water	2 C. whole-wheat flour
$^1/_3$ C. powdered milk	$^1/_8$ tsp. baking soda
$^1/_2$ C. water	1 tsp. margarine
1 egg, unbeaten	1 tsp. salt

Dissolve yeast and sugar in warm water. Combine powdered milk and water to make thick milk. (*Basic Cottage Cheese* may be substituted.) Add egg, onion flakes, dill seed, and yeast; beat well. Mix flour and soda. Add flour $^1/_3$ at a time, beating well after each addition. Cover. Let rise in warm place until doubled in bulk.

Stir down dough. Turn into well greased $1^1/_2$ qt. casserole dish. Let rise in warm place until light, about 30-40 min. Brush with butter, sprinkle with salt.

Bake at 350°-400°F for 50-60 min.

Yield: 1 loaf.

BASIC CARROTRAISIN BREAD

1 T. active dry yeast	$^1/_2$ C. honey
$^1/_3$ C. warm water	$6^1/_2$ C. stone-ground whole-
2 C. milk, scalded and cooled	wheat flour (approx.)
5 T. melted butter or margarine	1 C. finely shredded carrots
1 tsp. salt	1 C. raisins

Dissolve yeast in water in large bowl. Add milk, 3 T. of butter, salt, honey, and gradually stir in 5 C. flour to make a soft dough. Stir in carrots and raisins. Spread about $^3/_4$ C. of the remaining flour on breadboard.

Turn out the dough, and knead until dough is elastic and not sticky, for 10-15 min. Sprinkle additional flour on the board and hands as needed to prevent sticking. Place dough in a greased bowl. Turn dough over to grease the top, cover with a towel, and let rise in a warm place until almost doubled. Let rise another 45 min. more, then punch down. Let rise another 20 min., then punch down; let rise 10 min., then punch down. Squeeze dough to release air bubbles. Divide dough in 2 equal portions. Knead each for about 30 seconds on a lightly floured board and shape into a smooth round loaf. Place each loaf on a greased cookie sheet. Cover and let rise until almost doubled—about 1 hr. Brush tops with the remaining butter.

Bake at 350°F for about 30 min. or until browned and the loaves sound hollow when tapped. Let cool on racks. Wrap airtight. May be stored at room temperature for up to three days. Freeze for longer storage.

Yield: 2 loaves.

BASIC SPROUTBREAD

1 C. scalded milk	1 C. wheat sprouts
$^1/_2$ C. warm water	1 tsp. salt
2 T. oil	4 C. whole-wheat flour
2 T. honey	1 T. active dry yeast
1 egg	

Put scalded milk, water, cooking oil, honey, egg, and sprouts in blender and blend. Pour into mixer bowl, add salt and 2 C. flour, and then blend. Add yeast and 2 C. flour and knead for 10 min. Form dough into a loaf and place in a greased 5" x 9" bread pan. Let rise until double.

Bake at 350°F for 60 min. *Yield: 1 loaf.*

BASIC STONEBREAD MIX

2 T. dry active dry yeast	2 T. salt
5-6 C. lukewarm water	5 C. dry powdered milk
$^1/_2$ C. honey	$^1/_3$ C. shortening or margarine
20 C. stone-ground whole-wheat flour	

Make yeast mixture with yeast, $^1/_2$ C. warm water, and 1 tsp. honey and let stand for 10 min. Mix dry ingredients (flour, salt, milk) in large mixing bowl, making a well in the center. Pour in remaining liquids and yeast mixture. Stir with spoon as long as possible, then continue mixing with hands. Mix until stickiness begins to leave the dough.

Grease the sides of the bowl and your hands with shortening or margarine and continue to work the dough, kneading it very thoroughly. Use considerable pressure when forming the loaves in order to remove all air bubbles. Place loaves in well-greased pans and cover with wax paper. Allow to rise until almost double in size.

Place in a preheated oven at 300°F and bake for $1^1/_4$ hr. Remove loaves from pans and leave uncovered for 15 min., then cover with wax paper and a heavy towel to finish cooling.

Yield: 5 loaves.

BASIC RAISINBREAD

1 batch *Basic StoneBread Mix*	$1^1/_2$ C. raisins
1 tsp. ginger	

Prepare *Basic StoneBread Mix.* Add raisins and spices to *Mix* before first mixing of dough. Then follow remaining directions in *Basic StoneBread Mix* above.

BASIC CINNAROLLS

1 batch *Basic StoneBread Mix*	$^1/_2$ C. brown sugar
1 tsp. ginger	1 T. cinnamon
1 tsp. grated orange peel	1 T. soft butter

Prepare *Basic StoneBread Mix.* Add ginger and grated orange peel to batter before first mixing of dough.

When shaping rolls, sprinkle surface of dough with mixture of sugar, cinnamon, and soft butter before rolling. Place on greased baking pans.

Bake at 400°F for 30-40 min. Serve piping hot.

BASIC STUFFING & DRESSING COOKERY

Perhaps your family enjoys stuffing or dressing with their favorite entrées. Stuffing is a great taste addition to any meal. It's a good way to utilize all those bits and pieces of vegetables, meats, seasonings—whatever's on hand.

When you're really hungry for some stuffing, the *Basic EasyBread* recipe is designed to provide homemade bread for the stuffing base. It is also a great bread for slicing, too!

Directions for Making Basic EasyBread

BASIC EASYBREAD

1 T. dry active dry yeast	1 T. salt
3 C. warm water	9+ C. whole-wheat flour
$\frac{1}{4}$ C. honey	

Dissolve yeast in $\frac{1}{4}$ C. of the warm water and 1 tsp. of the honey. Let stand 5 min.

Stir in remaining water, honey, and salt.

Add flour. Knead 10 min.

Put dough in lightly greased bowl. Cover with damp cloth and place in unheated oven over large pan of hot water until double in bulk.

Divide and form into loaves. Place in greased pans. Let rise until double.

Bake at 350°F for 1 hr.

After allowing to cool fully, cut into $\frac{1}{2}$" slices, then cut into cubes. Dry bread thoroughly in oven, let cool.

Then, place dried bread cubes and crumbs into sealed plastic bags. Store in refrigerator or freezer till needed.

> **Note:**
>
> This is **BASIC EASYBREAD**—it's easy to make and economical besides.
>
> **BASIC EASYBREAD** is used as the filler base for stuffing & dressing recipes.

Basic EasyBread is the base for *Basic StuffMix*. The chart following provides information to help mix and match ingredients to have the most taste variations with the least ingredients. It should help determine the amount of stuffing or dressing needed to fill the poultry neck and body cavities.

Measurements are not particularly critical; consider them guidelines in developing creativity.

Any of the ingredients or all of them may be used interchangeably.

No two stuffings or dressings should ever be made the same. Stuffings should be a pleasure to prepare and a joy to eat!

Chart 15-1
Basic StuffMix Ingredient Measures

Ingredients for *Basic StuffMix*	Poultry Weight (Uncooked)			
	3-6 lb.	10-12 lb.	16-18 lb.	22-24 lb.
Basic EasyBread, cubed and dried (see recipe above)	4 C.	6 C.	12 C.	16 C.
stock: broth, milk, or water	$^3/_4$ C.	$1^1/_2$ C.	$2^1/_4$ C.	3 C.
egg, beaten	1	2	3	4
butter (margarine)	$^1/_2$ C.	$^1/_2$ C.	1 C.	$1^1/_2$ C.
celery, chopped	$^1/_2$ C.	1 C.	$1^1/_2$ C.	2 C.
onion, chopped	$^1/_2$ C.	C.	$1^1/_2$ C.	2 C.
salt	1 tsp.	2 tsp.	3 tsp.	4 tsp.
pepper	1 tsp.	2 tsp.	3 tsp.	4 tsp.
thyme	$^1/_8$ tsp.	$^1/_4$ tsp.	$^1/_2$ tsp.	1 tsp.
sage	$^1/_8$ tsp.	$^1/_4$ tsp.	$^1/_2$ tsp.	1 tsp.
parsley flakes	$^1/_2$ tsp.	1 T.	$1^1/_2$ tsp.	2 T.
MSG (optional)	1 dash	2 dashes	$^1/_2$ tsp.	1 tsp.

RECIPES FOR BASIC EASYBREAD STUFFING

BASIC STUFFMIX
(3-6 lb. poultry or fowl)

4 C. *Basic EasyBread*, cubed and dried
1 tsp. pepper
$^1/_8$ tsp. thyme
$^1/_8$ tsp. sage
$^1/_2$ T. parsley flakes
1 tsp. salt

$^1/_2$ C. celery
$^1/_2$ C. chopped onion
$^1/_2$ C. butter (margarine)
$^3/_4$ C. stock
1 egg, beaten
1 dash MSG (optional)

Prepare *Basic EasyBread* in advance. Slice, then cube and dry in oven. Mix lightly all dry ingredients (bread, pepper, thyme, sage, parsley, MSG, salt). Sauté celery and onion in butter, pour over dry mix. Add stock and egg, tossing lightly to prevent crushing bread cubes.

Spoon *Basic StuffMix* into salted body cavity of any fowl. Do not overstuff. Close openings, bake according to poultry roasting directions. *Yield: approx. 1 qt. stuffing or dressing.* (See **Chart 15-1** above for other amounts.)

Basic StuffMix Variations

Basic StuffMix can be used to stuff wild poultry (duck, goose, Cornish hen, rock hen, etc.), as well as pork chops, ham slices, leg of lamb, lamb chops, fish, or even bell peppers.

By varying the liquid and dry ingredients, there are literally thousands of possible stuffings for any conceivable purpose.

Liquid ingredients: use poultry or fowl drippings or giblet stock, diluted with water, milk, or dry powdered milk to change the flavor.

Dry ingredients: heighten flavor of *Basic StuffMix* and embellish the stuffing by adding chopped nuts, sliced raw apples, sausage (cooked and crumbled), chopped green or red bell peppers (sautéed), chopped pineapple, canned or frozen oysters, mushrooms, dried prunes or apricots (chopped or sliced), wild rice, and of course giblets (cooked and chopped).

Try these variations for *Basic StuffMix:*

BASIC STUFFMIX DRESSING

Spoon *Basic StuffMix* into greased covered dish.

Bake at 350°F for 30-40 min. To make top crisp, remove cover during final 5 min. of cooking.

BASIC STUFFMIX MEATLOAF

Crush dried bread in the ingredients before making *Basic StuffMix.*

Then substitute mixture for breadcrumbs and herbs in your favorite meat loaf recipe.

MAKING SUGAR FROM WHOLE-WHEAT BERRIES

Diastatic malt is the European bread bakers' secret ingredient. It's made from sprouted and roasted grain, usually barley. Fortunately for us, sprouted wheat berries work equally well. The malt's enzymes mellow and soften the gluten in flour, converting some of the flour's starch into sugar. This helps create bread with a better flavor, more delicate, and with a slightly nutty taste. Bread texture is improved, also.

Wherever diastatic malt is found, both powdered and liquid forms are usually available.

Diastatic malt is very easy to make at home by drying sprouted wheat berries. When sprout is about the same length as the wheat berry, rinse and dry on a cloth towel.

Spread $^1/_2$" thick on dryer tray, or on cookie sheet if you're using the oven as a dryer, and allow to dry until crispy. Then, grind dried sprouts in a grain mill or pulverize in a blender until powdered.

Stored in the refrigerator, diastatic malt will retain its enzymes for up to two years. When properly stored in freezer, it will last as long as stored wheat.

BASIC WHEAT SUGAR
(Diastatic Malt or Malt Extract)

2 C. sprouted wheat or barley

Sprout wheat berries or barley seed until sprout is same length as grain. (See chapter on **Basic Sprouting. Chapter 12**).

Dry wheat sprouts at 140°-150°F until crispy. Do not allow temperature to exceed 170°F, or the enzymatic action will be killed.

Grind or pulverize in blender at high speed until powdered.

May be used to replace up to one-fourth (¼) of the sugar called for in most bread recipes.

Recommendation for use:

Use 1 tsp. per batter for 2-4 loaves of bread.

Note: using a little diastatic malt is good, but using too much is bad. Too much always makes breads dark and sticky, and sometimes either too sweet—or just plain bitter!

Talk of joy; there may be things better than beef stew and baked potatoes and homemade bread—there may be.
David Grayson

Chapter 16

Basics of "WheatMeat" Cookery

Grains of wheat add another menu dimension to your food storage when ground into whole-wheat flour and used to prepare a meat substitute. Whole-wheat flour combined with water in a three-step process results in *Basic Gluten*, a gluey vegetable protein substance that causes the whole-wheat dough to become sticky and dense.

When gluten is dried, cooked, and flavored with meat, meat juices, bouillon, or other seasonings, it can be used as a meat replacement.

Basic Gluten is fairly easy to make, and the task can be delegated to a younger member of the family, since no subtle or delicate handling is required. In fact, the success of a gluten batch depends on the thoroughness of the beating it gets—the rougher the better.

Experimentation is the key to gluten's success. There are many ways to use it in the family's diet.

Try the recipes for *Basic flavorings* and *Basic Gluten Beef Flavoring* included in this chapter. Then create your own "*wheatmeat*" specialties.

DIRECTIONS FOR BASIC 3-STEP GLUTEN

This is a simplified and improved *Basic Gluten* recipe. Instructions are designed for beginning gluten making. The best gluten is made from freshly-ground, hard, whole-wheat flour. [1] Merely add some water to stone-ground wheat flour to make the glutinous mass. Then rinse the dense, gooey mass under hot running water for a batch of *Basic 3-Step Gluten*. Simple!

BASIC 3-STEP GLUTEN

16 C. stone-ground whole-wheat flour   3 C. water (approx.)

1. Combine flour and water into a ball-like mass. Then knead, pound, or beat the ball (or mix in bread mixer if you have one) for 10–15 min.

2. Cover glutinous mass with cold water and let it set for 1 hr. Then, wash out the starch by holding the soft dough in your hands under water as hot as your hands can tolerate. When the dough is firm, starch has been removed. Continue rinsing until the bran, which feels like sand, has been washed out. Drain in a colander or straining basket 30 min. more for easier handling. If too wet, dry in 200°F oven approximately 30 min.

3. The final step cooks and flavors the *Basic Gluten*. If you've decided what you'll make with the gluten, both can be done simultaneously. Any seasoning may be used.

FLAVORING BASIC GLUTEN

Basic Gluten can be flavored by either of two easy methods. Flavoring can be done in small batches or as needed when you're at the stove preparing a meal.

"Frying-in" flavoring: cut *Basic Gluten* into strips or rolls, or shape into patties. Fry in bacon, sausage, or beef juices until enough flavor for your taste is absorbed.

"Boiling-in" flavoring: cut *Basic Gluten* into strips, rolls, or patties as above. Drop shaped gluten into simmering stock, juices, or any flavoring of your choice.

After flavoring, allow to drain in a colander, *Basic Gluten* may be stored in refrigerator for up to two weeks.

> **Note:**
>
> *Successful gluten-making depends upon a very thorough beating of the dough mass.*

---

[1] The best available book about preparing gluten I know is **The Amazing Wheat Book,** by LeArta Moulton. Her website is **http://learta.com/**, *LM Publications*, *885 East 900 North, Mapleton UT, 84664* TOLL FREE: (888) 554-3727. She is one of the few consummate professionals remaining in the preparedness industry. LeArta has authored a number of books, manuals, and videos about healthy foods, herbs, making 100% whole-wheat breads, and working with gluten and seasonings for meat substitutes. She teaches innovative cooking techniques and creative recipes for preparing wheat and other wholesome foods that rival fast foods for taste and speed—but win in nutrition! Her books will teach you how to enjoy nutritious popular main dishes, breakfasts, and great snacks at ¼ the cost of commercially-prepared foods. She publishes the only up-to date guide on the market today, to my knowledge, for making and cooking with **Wheat-Meat...** spicy sausage, tender chicken-fried steaks, jerky, tasty wheat balls, and great veggie burgers. Perfect for replacing meat in spaghetti, Mexican dishes, chili, sauces and for any recipe calling for cooked hamburger

LeArta's books are a **must** if you are storing wheat! Hundreds of fast, delicious, and easy recipes in her book guide you in healthy and nutritious utilization of wheat in its many uses. She has time-saving techniques for making bagels, pocket bread and perfect whole wheat breads with all of the popular tastes of the day—plus other wheat firsts, *i.e.,* chips (like potato chips), crackers, and trail mixes. Find instructions on how to sprout, make wheat grass for optimum health. You can learn her proven techniques and recipes to steam, pop, crack, and cook the wheat kernel, plus methods for cooking wheat with very little heat.

The following flavoring recipes will help make *Basic Gluten* a tasty menu addition.

BASIC GLUTEN "LITE" FLAVORING

7 C. water	$^1/_2$ C. lite soy sauce
1 #303 can consommé or beef broth	salt and pepper to taste

Bring water to boil, reduce heat, then add soup and soy sauce. Roll out *Basic Gluten* and cut into $^1/_2$" strips with sharp knife or heavy scissors. Drop strips into broth. Simmer 30 min. Use chicken, ham, turkey, onion, garlic, mixed vegetable—any flavoring of your choice—in lieu of the consommé in the ingredients above. The flavoring can be as subtle or intense as you'd like. Perhaps you'll get some ideas from these *Basic* recipes:

BASIC GLUTEN BEEF FLAVORING

2 T. beef base granules*	$^1/_4$ T. pepper
1 T. soy sauce	4 tsp. seasoned salt
$^1/_2$ C. chopped onion	7 C. water

Mix all ingredients and bring to a boil. Add *Basic Gluten* strips and simmer 30 min.

* Substitute 12 beef bouillon cubes.

RECIPES FOR BEEF-FLAVORED BASIC GLUTEN

BASIC STEAKETTES

Form *Basic Gluten* into steak-shaped forms and season with *Basic Gluten Beef Flavoring*. Then follow these directions for delicious meat substitutes.

BASIC PAN-FRIED STEAKETTES

Basic Steakettes	1 C. sliced mushrooms
$^1/_2$ C. butter (margarine)	salt and pepper to taste

Prepare *Basic Steakettes*. Sauté *Steakettes* in butter. Reduce heat to low. Sprinkle sliced or rehydrated mushrooms over *Steakettes* and cover with lid for 5 min. Serve hot.

BASIC SKILLET STEAKETTES

Basic Steakettes	6 slices bacon
1 egg, beaten	1 C. butter (margarine)
2 C. bread crumbs, crushed fine	1 can mushroom soup, undiluted

Prepare *Basic Steakettes*. Dip *Steakettes* in egg, then roll in bread crumbs. Fry bacon in pan, remove, and chop fine. Return bacon to pan, add butter. Brown *Steakettes* in bacon grease. Pour mushroom soup over *Steakettes* until simmering. Serve hot over rice or noodles. (This dish may be baked in the oven for 15 min. at 425°F.)

BASIC GROUND BEEF

After simmering or frying *Basic Gluten* in beef flavoring, grind gluten in meat grinder and substitute in recipes calling for ground beef. See following recipe for using *Basic Gluten Ground Beef* in a burger.

BASIC GLUTENBURGER

1 batch *Basic Ground Beef*	all-purpose flour
1 egg	$^1/_2$ C. butter (margarine)
1 medium onion, chopped fine	salt and pepper to taste

Prepare *Basic Ground Beef.* Stir egg and chopped onion into *Ground Beef.* Add just enough flour to make patties. Fry in butter, browning both sides. Cover and steam 5 min. to bring out full flavor.

BASIC PATTIES IN MUSHROOM SAUCE

2 C. *Basic Ground Beef*	dash garlic salt
2 eggs	2 tsp. sage
1 medium onion, chopped	2 C. cooked rice
$^1/_2$ C. soy sauce	1 can mushroom soup, undiluted

Prepare *Basic Ground Beef.* Mix egg, onion, soy sauce, garlic salt, and sage together, then add *Ground Beef* and rice. Form into patties. Fry in oil slowly until browned. Add undiluted mushroom soup, simmering 10–15 min.

BASIC SAUSAGE

1 batch *Basic Ground Beef*	1 T. flour
sausage seasoning to taste	$^1/_2$ C. butter (margarine)
1 egg	

Season *Basic Gluten Ground Beef* with sausage seasoning until the flavor suits you. Then stir in egg and flour. Form into patties and fry in butter, browning both sides.

Acorns were good until bread was found.
Francis Bacon (1561-1626)

Chapter 17
Basics of Sourdough Cookery

Sourdough is mentioned in Egyptian history more than 4,000 years ago. Its history is replete with the salvation of generations. What could be simpler than mixing flour with water, then leaving it covered in a warm place overnight? The wild yeast in the air will find a home in the mixture, and they start working their magic to form a sourdough—talk about your first "convenience" food! It's difficult to feel sorry for the ancient civilizations when you realize how easy it was for them to earn their bread!

More recently, when America was in its formative and early growth years out in the Old West, sourdough was known as the frontiersmen's survival kit. Later, it was such a major part of prospectors' diets that the nickname *Sourdough* became a complimentary and hard-won title for the hardy souls who *won the West*.

Sourdough cookery is yet another way to use the whole wheat in your food storage. Sourdough starter, a form of leavening like yeast, when added to whole-wheat flour and water makes a batter which can be used to prepare pancakes, breads, rolls, cookies, and cakes. To help you use your stored wheat in sourdough cookery, this chapter offers you recipes for *Basic Sourdough Starters* and a *Basic SourBatter Mix* which is used to make breads and other sourdough delights. Directions for sourdough breadmaking and a yeast recipe conversion table are included.

HINTS FOR SUCCESSFUL BASIC SOURDOUGH COOKERY

Basic Sourdough Cookery can be fun and often provides more satisfaction than any other type of baking. The only limits to the use of sourdough are the limits of your imagination. Keep these points in mind when cooking with sourdough:

- Sourdough is a form of yeast, reacting to the same conditions as all other yeast.

- Sourdough is slower-acting and always needs more warmth for a longer period of time to ensure best results. With reasonable care, and allowing enough time and warmth to provide proper fermentation, there are no mysteries to sourdough cookery.

- Allow sufficient time for preparation and follow directions until you feel comfortable with the difference in sourdough leavening.

- By saving a cup of sourdough from each batch, you have your *starter* for the next time. *(Remember: take out a cup, put in a cup!)* If you protect your *Basic Sourdough Starter*, it will become your true kitchen friend and could ultimately make a billion pancakes—if you have the time and patience.

- Most flour in grocery stores today is all-purpose flour—good enough for ordinary pancakes, cookies, and cakes, but not good enough flour for *Basic Sourdough Cookery*. Grind fresh flour from your wheat storage to get the best results. If you must buy flour, you'll get better results using *unbleached hard winter wheat flour*. It makes a better-tasting and more nutritious loaf of bread. This flour may not be available at your local grocery stores. However, whole-food, health, and natural food stores may have a better selection of flours for *Basic Sourdough Cookery*.

> **Note:**
>
> *Most beginner failures are the result of the starter being too cool at night, preventing the sourdough leavening action from occurring normally.*

BASIC SOURDOUGH STARTER

There are a variety of *Basic Sourdough Starters* for *Basic Sourdough Cookery*. On the following pages are a number of ways to initiate your own *Basic Sourdough Starter*. One of the easiest things about all sourdough recipes is that *any* sourdough item can be prepared with *any* sourdough starter.

Obtain a starter from someone who has one *working*—in fact, the genealogy of an aged starter can be as prestigious to the cook as the prepared food is to the delight of the person eating it! If you don't have an acquaintance with a sourdough starter, there are 5 different *Basic Sourdough Starter* recipes on the following pages—now you can have it all!

If you're just beginning with sourdough cookery, here are a few bits of information you might want to know when you're utilizing *Basic Sourdough Starters*:

- Storing sourdough starters at room temperature invites the growth of undesirable bacteria and molds.

- Get a crockery pot (ceramic cheese pots are perfect) for your sourdough starter. Scald the pot before adding the starter. Always keep some sourdough starters "going" in your sourdough pot in the refrigerator.

- Storing sourdough starter at cold temperatures is important because the starter is not a sterile yeast culture. The cold temperature does not harm the yeast, it merely reduces its reproduction rate.

- If your starter becomes too sour, add just a pinch of baking soda to sweeten it.

- A good sourdough starter has a strong, sour milk odor. The sour smell is a part of normal *aging*.

- Sourdough starter is most effective for mixing and rising when between 78° to 85°F.

- Liquid separates from sourdough starter that goes too long without being used and replenished. To restore the sourdough starter, just use it and replenish it with a cup of batter, or "sweeten" it by stirring in a teaspoon of sugar.

- If starter develops any abnormal discoloration or odor or has mold growing in it, discard it immediately. The presence of fuzzy mold indicates the starter should be discarded.

- If replenished (by using) regularly, sourdough starter stays fresh. If starter is not to be used for several weeks, freeze or dry it to keep it from spoiling.

- Avoid spoilage by washing starter crock weekly. Wash it with detergent in hot, soapy water. Rinse and dry carefully before returning sourdough starter to starter crock.

- To carry sourdough starter to camp or for backpacking, add enough flour to shape the starter into a ball and place it in a sealable, heavy-duty, food-grade plastic bag with flour.

- Starter can be dried by following directions in the next section. Just mix the dried starter with the appropriate amount of liquid the night before you intend to use it so it can reactivate. Combine with recipe ingredients next morning for great sourdough cooking—like prospectors and pioneers of the Old West did!

RECIPES FOR BASIC SOURDOUGH STARTER

Make your own *Basic Sourdough Starter* by preparing one of the following recipes:

BASIC WATER-BASE SOURDOUGH STARTER

2 C. flour of your choice	1 pkg. active dry yeast
2 C. water	

Mix ingredients well. Keep in a warm place overnight. Next morning, you have *Basic Sourdough Starter*. If you prefer, allow to *age* up to 48 hours for a stronger, more robust sourdough taste.

Put 1 C. of this *Starter* mixture in a scalded (**but cooled**) container with a tight cover. Store in the refrigerator for future use. The remaining batter can be used immediately for pancakes, muffins, bread, or cake.

When replenished every week with flour and water in equal amounts, *Basic Sourdough Starter* will last years—if not a lifetime.

BASIC MILK-BASE SOURDOUGH STARTER

1 C. buttermilk	1 C. flour of choice

After mixing ingredients, let stand for 48 hours or until fermentation begins. To expand the *Basic Milk-Base Sourdough Starter*, add equal amounts of flour of your choice and condensed milk.

Be sure to save 1 C. of the mixture in a ceramic cheese pot for future use.

BASIC RYE SOURDOUGH STARTER

$1^1/_2$ C. rye flour $^1/_2$ T. active dry yeast
$^1/_2$ C. water

Mix ingredients together well. Place in warm spot for 24 hours to ferment.

Place 1 C. *Basic Rye Sourdough Starter* in a ceramic cheese pot and refrigerate for future use.

BASIC SAN FRANCISCO SOURDOUGH STARTER

$3^1/_2$ C. unsifted whole-wheat flour   1 package active dry yeast
1 T. sugar   2 C. warm water

Combine flour, sugar, and undissolved yeast in a large bowl. Gradually add warm water to dry ingredients and beat until smooth. Cover with transparent wrap and let stand in warm place for two days. *Basic San Francisco Sourdough Starter* is usually somewhat more sour than other *Basic Sourdough Starters.*

Put 1 C. *Basic San Francisco Sourdough Starter* in ceramic cheese pot and refrigerate for future use.

To replenish *Basic San Francisco Sourdough Starter*, add $1^1/_2$ C. whole-wheat flour and 1 C. warm water. Beat until smooth, then place in warm spot to ferment. Stir before using. Remember to save 1 C. for future use.

BASIC HONEY SOURDOUGH STARTER

3 C. water   1 tsp. honey
3 C. flour

Mix ingredients in blender or stir very well. Let stand in warm room in open crock-pot or large bowl for three days or until it smells yeasty and is full of bubbles. Stir often during aging process.

Save 1 C. *Basic Honey Sourdough Starter* in a tightly covered ceramic cheese pot in the refrigerator. This *Starter* will keep for several weeks.

Freeze *Basic Honey Sourdough Starter* if not used often. Reactivation requires 24 hours after freezing.

To activate refrigerated *Starter,* add 3 C. water and 3 C. flour (for making up 2 loaves of bread). Stir often and keep in warm room. It will be ready to use in about 6 hours.

Drying Basic Sourdough Starter

If you're not going to use your prized *Basic Sourdough Starter* immediately, or if you want to preserve it for posterity, you can dry it just as vegetables are dried for storage. In the dried form, the yeast goes into a spore stage, with the ability to stay inert for a lengthy period of time.

Follow these instructions for drying *Basic Sourdough Starter:*

- Spread *Basic Sourdough Starter* in a thin layer on plastic wrap or Kraft or butcher paper (not wax-coated paper!).
- Set electric drier or oven at 120° - 130°F. *Never allow temperatures to exceed 140°F.* Temperature control is critical. *Basic Sourdough Starter* yeast culture is destroyed for baking purposes at temperatures in excess of 143°F. Open-air drying is a possibility in climates where sun drying is successful, but the problem of unfriendly mold and bacteria is too great for my personal gambling instincts.

- Dry until thoroughly dry on top. Peel from sheet of plastic or paper, turn over and dry the other side thoroughly. Continue turning and drying until extremely dry and brittle.

- Break into pieces and pulverize in blender.

- Pack in heavy-duty, food-grade, sealable, waterproof plastic bags. Mark on package the original liquid amount of the now-dry starter. You'll need that information when you rehydrate it for use later or to inform anyone receiving it as a gift. Store in refrigerator or freezer.

- *Basic Sourdough Starter* properly dried and sealed in an airtight, heavy-duty, food-grade, sealable plastic bag will store for up to 6 months. Always store in a dark, dry, and cool location. *Starters* will keep up to 2 years in the refrigerator and indefinitely in the freezer.

- To reactivate dried *Basic Sourdough Starter*, merely add enough water or milk to obtain the original consistency of the starter. Enzyme reactivation begins at 50°F. Water and warmth bring the yeast in the *Starter* back to the active stage. *Starter* mixture should remain at room temperature for 8 - 12 hours to allow cultures to activate fully.

Yeast Recipe Conversion for Basic Sourdough Cookery

Virtually every regular yeast recipe can be converted to *Basic Sourdough Starter* leavening. To accomplish this, **two** factors must be kept constant in the recipe conversion:

- **leavening quality and quantity,** and

- **moisture and dough consistency**

Recipe conversion is tricky, requiring practice, patience, and effort—not to mention a good bit of luck, sometimes! The results are worth the effort in taste alone, if you're a true *devotée* of sourdough cookery.

The following chart interprets some of the ground rules for conversion from regular yeast recipes to *Basic Sourdough Cookery*:

Chart 17–1

Exchanges for Converting Yeast Recipes to Basic Sourdough

Yeast Recipe	Exchanges for Conversion to *Basic Sourdough*	
If Ingredients Require:	**Add &**	**Delete**
yeast*	1 C. starter	yeast
baking soda	1 tsp.	
baking powder (if required)		1 tsp.
baking powder (if not required)	$^1/_4$ tsp. (if bread is too *heavy*)	
flour		$^1/_2$ C.
milk	may substitute equal buttermilk	
rising time	more time—rises more slowly & requires slightly more warmth	

* 1 tsp. active dry yeast or $^1/_3$ oz. compressed dry yeast in regular yeast recipe requires 1 C. *Basic Sourdough Starter.*

DIRECTIONS FOR BASIC SOURBATTER

Basic SourBatter is used in almost every *Basic Sourdough Cookery* recipe. Each recipe can be made from your choice of sourdough starter. You can add water or milk to water-base starter and milk or water to milk-base starter to affect the taste.

Basic SourBatter should be prepared at least the evening before it's needed. That means if you want pancakes for breakfast in the morning or to make bread tomorrow, prepare the starter today or tonight.

BASIC SOURBATTER MIX

> 1 C. *Basic Sourdough Starter* (your choice)   2 C. flour (wheat, rye, etc.)
> 2 C. warm water or milk

> **Note:**
>
> *Don't use a metal container or leave a metal spoon in the batter. The chemical reaction could kill the starter's leavening action.*

Place *Basic Sourdough Starter* of choice in a large mixing bowl (large enough to allow for any expansion that may take place, depending on how warm it is), preferably of glass, pottery, wood, or plastic.

Add the water, milk, and flour. Mix thoroughly. The mixture will be thick and lumpy, but will become thin while fermenting and be lively by morning.

Cover the bowl and put in warm spot overnight. Allow 10 - 12 hours during the night in a warm spot in the kitchen for complete fermentation. In the morning, return 1 C. of the *Basic SourBatter Mix* to the sourdough pot to replenish your starter and keep in the refrigerator until next use. The remaining *Basic SourBatter Mix* is what you use in your recipe.

> **Note:**
>
> *BASIC SOURBATTER is just starter until the other ingredients of the recipe are added.*

To increase the amounts of *Basic SourBatter Mix* for pancakes or waffles to serve a larger number of people, the *Basic Sourdough Starter* (leaven) should be increased proportionally to the amount of flour and water you use. Be sure to increase other recipe ingredients proportionally, too!

Alternate directions: there is an improved way to use sourdough which does not require night-before preparation as when using the traditional method. Make up *Basic SourBatter* as much as a week before need. Allow it to become leavened for a day or so. Store *Mix* in a tightly sealed ceramic pot.

Then, when *Basic SourBatter Mix* is needed for a favorite sourdough recipe, take the batter from the refrigerator and allow it to stand at room temperature for 30 - 60 min. The *Mix* is now ready to use at your convenience without night-before planning.

DIRECTIONS FOR BASIC SOURBREADMAKING

Flour quantities, especially in *Basic Sourdough Cookery* recipes, are approximate because of the many differences in liquid absorption, compactness, and the amount of liquid alcohol present in the batter. The variation in liquid is peculiar to sourdough since the yeast breaks the flour starch down into alcohol and carbon dioxide gas during fermentation. Although this occurs in all yeast breads, the long and variable fermentation period of any sourdough starter produces substantially more liquid alcohol, depending on the starter's strength.

Here are the 10 steps for simplified *Basic SourBreadMaking*:

1. Place *Basic SourBatter Mix* in nonmetal bowl. Stir in required sugar, salt, and flavorings gently. The yeast enzymes are already active and in suspension in the *Mix*.
2. Add the flour a little at a time and stir until the dough pulls away from the sides of the bowl.

3. Turn out dough onto floured board and knead until it feels smooth and elastic. When properly kneaded dough should not be sticky and should spring back when pressed with the finger.

4. Dough may be given one or two risings. Two risings produce a finer texture in the loaf, but one rising produces a highly satisfactory bread, especially when it is well kneaded. If one rising is preferred, skip now to *Step #7*.

5. To let rise twice, shape the dough into a ball and place in a greased bowl. Roll the dough in the bowl to coat entire surface. Cover with clean dishtowel and place in a warm place to rise until dough doubles. Sourdough usually takes $1\frac{1}{2}$ - 2 times longer to rise than other yeast dough.

6. Punch the dough down and turn out onto lightly floured board. Knead gently.

7. When a double recipe or a recipe for two loaves is used, divide the dough into two equal parts. Shape the dough and place in a greased loaf pan.

8. Cover dough with clean dishtowel and put in warm spot to rise. Allow dough to rise until about double in bulk or until top of the dough reaches $\frac{1}{2}$" - 1" above the rim of the pan. The bread will rise slightly more during baking. Preheat oven while dough rises.

9. Brush dough with a glaze of oil or butter just before placing in the oven.

10. Bake at appropriate temperature until done. The loaves will sound hollow when tapped on top crust.

RECIPES FOR BASIC SOURDOUGH BREAD

BASIC SOURBREAD

2 C. *Basic SourBatter Mix*	1 tsp. salt
4 C. sifted flour (more if needed)	2 T. vegetable oil or shortening
2 T. sugar	

Prepare *Basic SourBatter Mix*. Sift dry ingredients (flour, sugar, salt) into a bowl, making a well in the center. Add oil to *Mix* and mix well. Pour *Mix* and oil into the well of flour. Add enough flour to make a soft dough for kneading.

Knead on a floured board for 10 -15 min. Place in a greased loaf pan. Cover and let rise until doubled in size. Bake at 375°F for 1 hr. *Yield: 1 loaf.*

Variations:

Basic Whole-Wheat SourBread: substitute 1 C. whole-wheat flour for 1 C. white flour.

Basic Sourdough Sweet Bread: use honey, brown sugar, or molasses instead of sugar.

Basic Orange SourBread: add juice of 1 orange and grated orange rind.

BASIC SOURBREAD #2

$1\frac{1}{2}$ C. *Basic SourBatter Mix*	2 T. margarine
$\frac{3}{4}$ C. milk	$\frac{1}{4}$ C. warm water, 105°–115°F
3 T. sugar	1 package active dry yeast
1 tsp. salt	5 - 6 C. unsifted flour

Prepare *Basic SourBatter Mix*. Scald milk. Stir in sugar, salt, and margarine; cool to lukewarm. Measure warm water into large warm bowl. Sprinkle in yeast; stir until dissolved. Add lukewarm milk mixture, *Mix,* and $2\frac{1}{2}$ C. flour. Add the remaining flour slowly and mix thoroughly. Turn out onto lightly floured board; knead until smooth and elastic, about 8–10 min. Place in greased bowl, turning to grease top. Cover; let rise in warm, draft-free location until doubled in bulk.

Punch dough down; divide into three equal pieces. Form each piece into a smooth round ball or a 14" tapered roll. Place on greased baking sheets. Take a sharp knife and make several criss-cross cuts on tops of round loaves or make several diagonal cuts on tops of long loaves. Cover; let rise in warm, draft-free location until doubled in bulk again. Bake at 400°F about 25 min. or until done. Remove from baking pans and cool on wire racks.

BASIC SOURHONEY BREAD

4 C. *Basic SourBatter Mix*	2 tsp. baking soda
2 C. milk	$^1/_4$ C. wheat germ
2 T. butter	2 C. wheat flour
2 tsp. salt	4 C. white flour
2 T. sugar	1 package active dry yeast
$^1/_4$ C. honey	

Prepare *Basic SourBatter Mix*. Scald milk, then melt butter and honey in milk. Allow to cool to lukewarm, mix yeast in milk, and stir to dissolve. Add to *Mix*. Sift wheat flour and wheat germ into dough. Blend sugar, salt, and soda in another bowl until smooth, then sprinkle over top of dough, stirring in gently.

Set dough in warm spot for 30 min., covered with cloth. Punch down and sift in white flour until the dough is too stiff to stir with spoon. Turn out on floured board and begin to knead with hands.

Work in the remaining flour, kneading with heels of hands 100 times until the dough is light and satiny to the touch. (***Caution:*** *Do not knead too long or include too much flour.)*

Separate into loaves. Flour lightly, fold over, seal, and place in greased pans. Pans should be half full. Grease tops, set in warm spot, and let double in bulk again.

Preheat oven to 400°F, bake for 20 min., then reduce to 325°F and continue to bake until bread shrinks from sides of pans. If done, bread will give a hollow sound when thumped on top. Remove from oven; turn out onto rack or towel, and butter top and sides.

> **Note:**
>
> *Flour required may vary from quantity indicated—gauge by feel.*
>
> *Rather too little than too much.*

BASIC SOURHONEY BREAD #2

3 C. *Basic SourBatter Mix*	2 T. dry milk
$^1/_2$ C. warm water	1 T. honey
$3^1/_2$ C. whole-wheat flour	2 T. vegetable oil
2 tsp. salt	

Prepare *Basic SourBatter Mix*. Mix ingredients together until satiny and smooth, reserving the oil for the final mixing. Let rise for 1 hr. Mold two loaves or use 46-oz. juice cans. Let dough rise again until double in bulk. Bake 30 min. at 400°F, then 30 min. more at 325°F.

BASIC SOURDOUGH BANANANUT BREAD

1 C. *Basic SourBatter Mix*	2 C. flour
$^1/_3$ C. shortening	1 tsp. salt
1 C. sugar	1 tsp. baking powder
1 egg	$^1/_2$ tsp. baking soda
1 C. mashed bananas	$^3/_4$ C. chopped walnuts

Prepare *Basic SourBatter Mix*. Cream together shortening and sugar; add egg, mixing until blended. Stir in banana and *Mix*. Sift flour, measure, and sift again with salt, baking powder, and soda. Add flour mix to batter, then add walnuts, stirring until blended. Pour into greased loaf pan. Bake at 350°F for 1 hr. or until toothpick comes out clean.

BASIC SOUR-RYE BUNS

1 C. *Basic SourBatter Mix*	$^1/_2$ C. vegetable oil
$3^3/_4$ C. warm water	1 tsp. salt
$^1/_4$ C. all-purpose flour	1 egg white, beaten
4 C. rye flour	coarse salt or caraway seed

Prepare *Basic SourBatter Mix*. In large bowl, combine *Mix* and warm water. Stir in flour. Beat well. Cover and let stand several hours or refrigerate overnight. Add rye flour, oil, and salt. Mix well. Dough will be a bit sticky. *(continued on next page)*

Knead on lightly floured surface about 5 min., adding more all-purpose flour as necessary to make a soft dough. Place in greased bowl; turn once to grease surface. Cover and let rise till double. Punch dough down; divide dough into three portions. Cover, let rest 5 min.

Divide each portion into eight balls. Turn each ball in hands, folding edges under to make circle. Press ball flat between hands. Place on greased baking sheet, pressing into 3"–4" circles. Brush with egg white; sprinkle with coarse salt or caraway seed. Let rise till double. Bake in 375°F oven 25 - 30 min. *Yield: 18 - 24 buns.*

RECIPES FOR BASIC SOURDOUGH BISCUITS, MUFFINS, AND PANCAKES

BASIC SOURBISCUITS

$^1/_2$ C. *Basic SourBatter Mix*	$^1/_4$ tsp. baking powder
1 C. milk	$^1/_2$ tsp. baking soda
$2^1/_2$ C. sifted flour	2 T. yellow cornmeal
1 T. sugar	2 T. salad oil
$^3/_4$ tsp. salt	3 T. melted butter or margarine

Night before: prepare *Basic SourBatter Mix,* then measure $^1/_2$ C. into large bowl. Add milk and 1 C. flour; mix well. Let stand covered overnight.

Next morning: beat in 1 C. flour; mix well. Add sugar, salt, baking powder, baking soda, and remaining $^1/_2$ C. flour in sifter. Sift evenly over dough. With wooden spoon, beat into dough to mix well; beat until dough is stiff enough to clean side of bowl. On lightly floured surface, knead dough about 15 times until light (dough will be soft). Let dough rest, covered with inverted bowl for 10 min.

Roll dough $^1/_2$" thick. Cut biscuits with lightly floured cutter. Sprinkle bottom of 9" x 9" x 2" pan with 1 T. cornmeal. Dip each biscuit into combined oil and butter. Arrange close together in prepared pan. Sprinkle tops of biscuits with remaining cornmeal. Let rise in warm place. When almost doubled, bake in 375°F oven until browned.

BASIC SOURBERRY MUFFINS

$^3/_4$ C. *Basic SourBatter Mix*	1 egg
$^1/_2$ C. whole-wheat flour	1 C. drained blueberries
$1^1/_2$ C. white flour	$^3/_4$ tsp. baking soda
$^1/_2$ C. cooking oil	$^1/_2$ C. undiluted canned milk
$^1/_2$ C. sugar	

Prepare *Basic SourBatter Mix*. Stir the above ingredients into *Mix* in the order of listing, to make the mixture moist and hold together nicely. *Do not beat vigorously.* If necessary, add more *SourBatter Mix*. Bake in greased muffin tins at 375°F for 30–35 min.

Note: this recipe cooks more slowly than other sourdough muffins, so be sure they are done before you remove them from the oven.

BASIC SOURGRIDDLE MUFFINS

1 C. *Basic SourBatter Mix*	6 T. yellow cornmeal
$^3/_4$ C. buttermilk	1 tsp. baking soda
$2^3/_4$ to 3 C. flour	$^1/_4$ tsp. salt

Prepare *Basic SourBatter Mix*. Mix together *Mix* and buttermilk. Combine flour, 4 T. cornmeal, soda, salt and add to buttermilk mix. Stir to combine, using hands when necessary. Turn out and knead until smooth. Roll $^3/_8$" thick. Cover and let rise a few minutes.

Cut muffins with 3" cutter. Sprinkle sheet of waxed paper with 1 T. cornmeal. Place muffins on paper and sprinkle with remaining cornmeal. Cover and let rise 45 min. Cook on medium hot griddle for 30 min., turning often. Cool and split. *Yield: 12 - 14 muffins.*

BASIC SOUROAT MUFFINS

$^3/_4$ C. *Basic SourBatter Mix*	1 egg, slightly beaten
$1^1/_2$ C. sifted flour	$^1/_2$ C. buttermilk
$^1/_2$ C. brown sugar, firmly packed	1 C. rolled oats
1 tsp. salt	$^1/_2$ C. salad oil
1 tsp. baking soda	

Prepare *Basic SourBatter Mix*. Mix together flour, brown sugar, salt, and soda. Make a well in the center. Blend egg, buttermilk, rolled oats, and oil together; stir in *Mix*. Pour this mixture all at once into the flour well. Stir lightly to moisten ingredients. Batter will be lumpy. Grease muffin cups or line with baking cup liners; fill about $^2/_3$ full. Bake at 375°F for 30–35 min. *Yield: 12 - 15 muffins.*

BASIC SOUR-RAISIN MUFFINS

1 C. *Basic SourBatter Mix*	$^1/_2$ C. cooking oil
$^1/_2$ C. whole-wheat flour	$^1/_2$ C. undiluted canned milk
$^1/_2$ C. white flour	1 egg
$^1/_2$ C. sugar	1 C. raisins
$^3/_4$ tsp. baking soda	

Prepare *Basic SourBatter Mix*. Combine dry ingredients (wheat flour, white flour, sugar, soda) in bowl. Make a well in the center and add all of the liquids at once. Stir just to moisten. Add raisins and enough *Mix* to make the mixture moist and hold together nicely.

Stir gently till combined. Bake in greased muffin tins at 375°F for 30 - 35 min. *Yield: 16 - 18 muffins.*

Note: these muffins seem to take a long time to bake completely, so check to be sure they are done.

BASIC SOURWAFFLES

4 C. *Basic SourBatter Mix*	$^1/_4$ C. milk
1 egg	1 tsp. baking soda
4 T. oil or shortening	1 tsp. salt

Prepare *Basic SourBatter Mix*. Add egg, oil, and milk to *Mix*, stirring in well. Blend dry ingredients (soda, salt) in small bowl; sprinkle over wet mixture and stir in gently. Let rest 5 min., then drop or pour onto a hotter-than-normal waffle iron. If mixture appears too thick, add more milk. *Yield: 10 - 12 waffles.*

BASIC GRIDDLE SOURCAKES

3 C. *Basic SourBatter Mix*   1 tsp. salt
1 or 2 eggs   1 T. sugar
1 tsp. baking soda   2 T. bacon grease or salad oil

Prepare *Basic SourBatter Mix*. Add eggs, soda, salt, and sugar. Beat with a fork until
blended. Add melted grease. Cook pancakes on griddle; serve with butter and syrup or
honey. Molasses, jelly, or honey from your storage are also good. *Yield: 10 - 12 servings.*

BASIC CORNY SOURBREAD MIX

1 C. *Basic SourBatter Mix*   2 T. sugar
$1^1/_2$ C. yellow cornmeal $^1/_4$ C. melted butter
$1^1/_2$ C. evaporated milk $^1/_2$ tsp. salt
2 eggs, beaten $^3/_4$ tsp. baking soda

Prepare *Basic SourBatter Mix*. Thoroughly mix the *Mix*, cornmeal, milk, eggs, and sugar
in large bowl. Stir in melted butter, salt, and soda. Turn into a 10" greased pan and bake
450°F for 25 min. Serve hot with butter and honey.

BASIC CORNY SOURSTICKS

Prepare *Basic Corny SourBread Mix* according to directions. Spoon *Mix* into a buttered
cornbread stick pan, filling each cup $^2/_3$ full. Bake at 425°F for 20 min. or until done.

BASIC SOURSCONES

1 C. *Basic SourBatter Mix* $^1/_2$ tsp. salt
1 C. flour   1 T. sugar
2 tsp. baking powder $^1/_4$ C. melted shortening
1 tsp. baking soda   2 eggs, slightly beaten

Prepare *Basic SourBatter Mix*. Combine dry ingredients (flour, baking powder, soda,
sugar) and make a hole in center. Combine shortening, beaten eggs, and *Mix*, then pour
into dry ingredients. Mix and add additional flour, kneading until dough leaves fingers
and is no longer sticky. Tear off pieces of dough, flatten in hand, and pull to thin patty.
Fry in deep hot oil (375°F) until golden on each side. Drain on paper towels. Serve piping hot with butter, honey, or jam.

BASIC DATE SOURLOAF

$^1/_2$ C. *Basic SourBatter Mix*   1 C. undiluted evaporated milk
$1^1/_2$ C. unsifted flour   2 T. sugar

Night before: prepare *Basic SourBatter Mix*. Combine *Mix*, flour, evaporated milk, and
sugar. Set in warm spot to ferment.
Next morning: add the following ingredients to fermenting *Mix*.

$^3/_4$ C. brown sugar, packed $^1/_2$ C. quick-cooking rolled oats
$^1/_4$ C. butter   1 tsp. baking powder
1 C. chopped dates $^1/_2$ tsp. baking soda
$^1/_2$ C. chopped walnuts $^1/_2$ tsp. salt
2 eggs, beaten

Cream brown sugar and butter, add dates and nuts; set aside. Combine eggs, rolled oats,
baking powder, soda, and salt. Stir date mixture into the *Mix*. Turn into a greased loaf
pan (5" x 9") and let rise about 1 hr. Bake at 375°F for 1 hr. Cool for 10 min. in pan, then
remove to cooling rack. *Yield: 1 loaf.*

RECIPES FOR SOURDOUGH CAKES, ROLLS, AND DOUGHNUTS

BASIC SOURDOUGH CINNAROLLS

$^1/_2$ C. *Basic SourBatter Mix*   2 C. unsifted flour
1 C. undiluted evaporated milk

Night before: prepare *Basic SourBatter Mix*. Combine *Mix*, evaporated milk, and flour in large bowl; leave in warm spot overnight.

Next morning: add following ingredients to *Mix*.

$^1/_4$ C. soft butter   1 tsp. salt
3 T. sugar   2 T. butter, melted
1 egg $^1/_4$ C. brown sugar
$1^1/_2$ C. unsifted flour (or more) $1^1/_2$ tsp. cinnamon
$^1/_2$ tsp. baking soda $^1/_4$ C. raisins (optional)
1 tsp. baking powder   melted butter

Beat together butter, sugar, and egg; blend into *Mix*. Combine the dry ingredients (flour, soda, baking powder, and salt); mix with batter. Turn onto a floured board and knead until the surface is satiny and doesn't stick to board (add flour if necessary). Place ball of dough in the center of board and roll out to a rectangle 8" x 16". Brush surface with melted butter and sprinkle with a mixture of brown sugar and cinnamon (and raisins, if you wish).

Roll up dough, starting on one of the long sides; cut roll at $^3/_4$" intervals. Dip top and bottom of each roll in melted butter. Place in a square 9" pan, cover loosely, and let rise in a warm spot for about 1 hr. or until nearly doubled. Bake at 375°F for 30 - 35 min. or until crust is golden brown. *Yield: 9 large rolls.*

BASIC SOURDOUGH CHOCOCAKE

$^1/_2$ C. thick *Basic SourBatter Mix*   1 tsp. vanilla
1 C. water   1 tsp. cinnamon
$1^1/_2$ C. flour   3 squares melted chocolate
$^1/_4$ C. nonfat dry milk $^1/_2$ tsp. salt
$^1/_2$ C. shortening $1^1/_2$ tsp. baking soda
1 C. sugar   2 eggs

Prepare *Basic SourBatter Mix*. Combine *Mix*, water, flour, and dry milk; allow to ferment 2–3 hr. in a warm spot until bubbly and has strong sour milk odor. Cream shortening, sugar, flavorings, chocolate, salt, and soda. Add eggs one at a time, beating well after each addition. Combine with *Mix*. Beat well. Pour mixture into deep cake pan. Bake at 350°F for 25–30 min.

BASIC SOURDOUGHNUTS

$^1/_2$ C. *Basic SourBatter Mix* $^1/_2$ tsp. salt
1 C. lukewarm water   1 tsp. baking powder
1 C. flour $^1/_2$ tsp. nutmeg
2 T. sugar   1 egg
2 T. brown sugar   2 T. melted shortening
1 tsp. baking soda dissolved in 1 T. water $1^1/_2$ C. flour

Night before: prepare *Basic SourBatter Mix* and combine with water, flour, and sugar in bowl and let stand at least 6 hours or overnight.

Next morning: add remaining ingredients to *Mix*. Knead on lightly floured board 25 times. Roll $^1/_2$" thick and cut with doughnut cutter. Drop in hot fat, 380°F, fry until golden brown, then turn on other side.

Drain on paper towels spread over newspaper or paper bag. Roll in powdered or granulated sugar. Serve warm. *Yield: 10 - 12 doughnuts*.

BASIC SOURDOUGH GLAZED APRICAKE

1 C. *Basic SourBatter Mix*   1 tsp. baking soda
$^1/_2$ C. shortening $^1/_8$ tsp. nutmeg
$1^1/_2$ C. sugar $^1/_2$ C. milk
2 eggs $^1/_2$ C. apricots, finely chopped
$1^1/_2$ C. unsifted flour   1 tsp. salt
$1^1/_2$ tsp. baking powder   3 T. apricot jam
powdered sugar

Prepare *Basic SourBatter Mix.* In large bowl, cream shortening and sugar. Add eggs, one at a time, beating well. Add dry ingredients (flour, salt, baking powder, soda, nutmeg) to *Mix* alternately with milk, mixing after each addition. Add chopped apricots, lightly floured, stirring until well blended. Turn into greased and floured $1^1/_2$ qt. tube mold. Bake at 350°F, 50 - 60 min.

Allow cake to cool 10 min., then invert on cooling rack, removing the mold carefully. Allow to cool completely.

Brush on apricot glaze made from 3 T. apricot jam warmed over low heat until soft enough to spread, then dust with powdered sugar.

BASIC SOURALMOND SPICECAKE

1 C. *Basic SourBatter Mix*   1 tsp. baking soda
$^1/_2$ C. shortening $^1/_2$ tsp. cinnamon
$1^1/_2$ C. sugar $^1/_4$ tsp. nutmeg
2 eggs $^1/_8$ tsp. cloves
$1^1/_2$ C. unsifted flour $^1/_2$ C. milk
$1^1/_2$ tsp. baking powder $^1/_2$ C. ground almonds
1 tsp. salt   powdered sugar

Prepare *Basic SourBatter Mix.* In large bowl cream shortening and sugar. Add eggs, one at a time, beating well after each addition. Blend in *Mix*. Combine flour, baking powder, salt, soda, cinnamon, nutmeg, and cloves.

Add dry ingredients to batter alternately with milk, mixing after each addition until well blended. Add ground almonds and mix until well blended.

Turn into a greased and floured $1^1/_2$ qt. tube mold. Bake at 350°F for 50 - 60 min. or until done. Allow cake to cool for 10 min., then invert on cooling rack, removing mold carefully. Cool until slightly warm to touch and sprinkle with powdered sugar.

NOTES FOR YOUR SOURDOUGH COOKERY

*I'm always watching my weight. I don't eat sweets like cookies or chocolate.
But bread is different. I can't even have one piece,
because when I start, I can't stop.*
Daniela Pestova

Chapter 18
Basics of White Flour Cookery

Estimates indicate that at least one-third of all the food we eat is made with white bleached flour. In the grocery store, the baked goods department and the bread aisle have a fairly large percentage of the store's area. Most commercial bakery products are made from white bleached flour. Check the cereal, pasta, and prepared mixes aisles for all the loaves of bread, cake, pancake, and biscuit mixes—all clearly made from white flour. Anyone can see that white flour is a significant part of the American diet.

This section on white flour cookery is included in the *Handbook* because we recognize the broad-scale use of white flour. As long as there's wheat, there will be those who will demand white flour.

One of my college professors told us in class: *Minds are like parachutes—neither functions if it isn't opened!* The following information about white flour is presented so anyone with an open mind can evaluate the value of white flour in an in-home storage program. Some of the readily apparent problems with white flour are that it cannot be made in-home, it costs more to buy at the store than to make home-ground whole-wheat flour, it doesn't store very well, and it has very little nutritional value in and of itself.

THE CASE AGAINST WHITE FLOUR

Whole wheat contains twenty-six minerals and vitamins, plus other trace minerals. These vitamins and minerals are locked in until the outer shell is broken. As wheat is processed at the typical milling operation, the first step in processing is a hot steam wash to soften the outer shell, or bran. This bran layer is a rich source of food fiber, the roughage to help with the body's normal digestive process.

The outside layer is then scarified by tiny, sharp, razor-like blades until it is totally removed. These hull shavings are pieces of bran and are normally sold separately, often to health food stores so they can sell it to people who want to be healthy!

The next layer is called the endosperm, or *middling*, at the mill. It is taken off by the same method as the bran. Middlings are generally sold to farmers to keep their pigs and cows healthy. Finally, the wheat germ and oil are removed. More than 72% of all the nutrition in wheat is in the germ and oil. Wheat germ is the concentrated source of the wheat nutrient—the vitamins, minerals, and proteins. This is the living part of the grain that can reproduce itself when the seed is planted. When the germ and oil are left in the flour, it soon turns rancid. Flour that turns rancid quickly is a bad commercial product, so germ and oil are removed. Removal of the bran, the endosperm or middling, the wheat germ, and the wheat oil decreases the nutritional value of wheat by as much as 85%.

The residue of powder left after milling is called *unbleached flour*. Consumers want white flour, so bleaching agents (chemicals) are added. The bright white color makes us think we have the best quality product—in reality, there is virtually little food value remaining in the flour; it's merely stripped wheat kernels.

The white flour purchased at the grocery store is merely white dust—highly processed, chemically-treated, with added synthetic compounds—and it's called enriched white flour! More than fifty years ago the Food and Drug Administration knew there was no nutritive value left in the processed white flour, so a law was passed that assured all white flour would be enriched with three vitamin Bs—*thiamin, niacin, and riboflavin*—and iron. Perhaps that ruling is a major indicator as to why we should consider the whole-wheat alternative instead of commercial bleached white flour.

A WHITE FLOUR EXPERIMENT

Let me relate a story told me by Delsa Wilson:[1]

Have you ever seen a trail of ants? The next time you see such a trail, gather some children or curious adults and do this scientific experiment. Take a quarter cup of white bleached flour from the sack in your kitchen and make or lay a strip barrier across the ants' trail. As the ants march along their trail, you'll notice they move with great speed. However, when they reach the flour barrier, they'll begin to make crazy little circles in a seeming fit of confusion. Ultimately, an ant scout will find the outer edge of the flour barrier and all the ants will follow the scout back to the other side of the flour strip. They resume their orderly trail speed and continue on their path.

To finish the experiment, use the same amount of fresh-ground whole-wheat flour and make a similar barrier strip 3" to 4" away from the white flour strip. With a magnifying glass, you should be able to see the ants within 12" to 18" turn their heads toward the whole wheat. They'll literally stop in their tracks, turn around, and go back to the whole-wheat flour and devour it!

This experiment indicates that ants, being both industrious and intelligent, dismiss white flour from their diet. Another case in point—it has been proven that no self-respecting cockroach will eat anything made with white bleached flour. If the insect world won't eat white bleached flour, why do humans insist on consuming tons of it?

My son lives in Texas where garden pests are a problem. He told me how proud he was of his organic garden because it had no insect problems. He said they only buy white bleached flour to put in his dust gun to dust his vegetables—and it's the most effective treatment he's found for keeping the pests at bay!

THE CASE FOR WHOLE WHEAT

Our society is so accustomed to the factory-processed, quick-fix, convenience-foods environment that it is taking a toll on our individual and collective well-being and longevity. If one-third of all the food we eat is made with bleached white flour, is it any wonder our population has so many health problems?

At the University of Utah, a test was done with computer technology which identified all the vitamins, minerals, amino acids, and calories of any substance. Equal-sized slices of white bakery bread and homemade wheat bread were analyzed by the system based on the same criteria.

The results of the calculations indicated it would require 150 slices of white bread to equal the nutrition of 1 slice of homemade whole-wheat bread.

The American Cancer Society has stated that we could prevent most of the lower tract cancers, diverticulitis, and infections in the colon if we ingested enough soluble and insoluble fibers which come from vegetables, fruits, *grains*, legumes, nuts, and seeds. Perhaps this is another important argument for the use of whole-wheat flour in a food storage program.

Now that we've completed the treatise on the evils of white flour, here are some *Basic* white flour recipes for your in-home food storage program!

---

[1] Delsa Wilson can be reached by phone only (801) 403-9082, (Salt Lake City UT). Delsa is a forty-five year "veteran" in the preparedness industry. She is an active food storage consultant and a provider of preparedness products. She still teaches, trains, and practices what she preaches—even the choir listens attentively to her sermons!

RECIPES FOR WHITE FLOUR

BASIC WHITE FLOUR BISCUIT MIX

8 C. sifted white flour	4 tsp. salt
1 C. nonfat dry milk	$1^1/_3$ C. shortening
$^1/_4$ C. baking powder	$^1/_3$ - $^1/_2$ C. water or milk

Sift together dry ingredients (flour, milk, baking powder, salt). Cut in shortening with two knives until fine as flour, then add water or milk.

Drop onto greased baking sheet. Bake at 450°F for 12 - 15 min.

BASIC DUMPLINGS

Use *Basic White Flour Biscuit Mix* for excellent dumplings. Drop 'em by spoonfuls into 2 qt. boiling water with 1 tsp. salt. Or, add to boiling liquid in stews, soups, etc.

BASIC VEGGIE-FILLED BISCUITS

Basic White Flour Biscuit Mix	$^1/_2$ tsp. salt
2 C. chopped celery	2 T. margarine
2 C. coarsely grated carrots	$^1/_2$ tsp. melted margarine
1 large onion, finely chopped	

Prepare *Basic White Flour Biscuit Mix*. In covered pan, cook celery, carrots, onion, salt, and margarine for 10 min., stirring occasionally. Roll *Mix* into a square or rectangle and cut in 5" squares. Fill each square with $^1/_3$ C. cooked vegetables. Fold up the corners to meet in the center and pinch edges together to seal. Place biscuits on greased baking sheet. Brush with melted margarine and bake at 400°F for 15 min. or until lightly browned. *Yield: 9 to 12 biscuits.*

BASIC BEEF PIE

Basic White Flour Biscuit Mix	8 oz. sliced mushrooms
1 lb. lean ground beef	1 tsp. salt
$^1/_2$ C. chopped onion	$^1/_8$ tsp. garlic salt
8 oz. tomato sauce	1 tsp. chili powder

Prepare *Basic White Flour Biscuit Mix*. In separate pan or skillet, brown beef, then add onion and cook until tender. Add half of the tomato sauce and mushrooms; then add salt, garlic salt, and chili powder; heat until bubbly. While meat mix cooks, knead *Mix* 8–10 times on floured board. Divide dough in half. Roll out $^1/_2$ dough to fit a 9" pie pan.

Line pan, pour in hot filling. Roll out remaining dough and place over filling. Crimp edge; slit top. Bake at 425°F for 15 - 20 min. or until done.

Heat remaining tomato sauce and mushrooms in saucepan. Serve sauce over wedges of beef pie. *Yield: 4–6 servings.*

BASIC PIZZA CRUST

2 T. active dry yeast	pinch sugar
$3^1/_2$ C. flour	1 tsp. salt
$^1/_4$ C. oil	$1^1/_4$ C. lukewarm water

Crust: mix all ingredients well. Knead until smooth and shiny. Let rise $1^1/_2$ hr.

Pizza: brush top side with olive oil. Spread tomato sauce or prepared pizza sauce to within $^1/_4$" of crust edge, cover with grated mozzarella cheese, then sprinkle parmesan cheese on top. Add any meats or vegetables of your choice. Bake at 425°F for 15 - 20 min.

BASIC FRENCH BREAD

2 T. active dry yeast	6–7 C. flour
2^1/$_2$ C. warm water	cornmeal
2 T. shortening	1 egg white
3 tsp. salt	

Dissolve yeast in ^{1}/$_2$ C. warm water. While yeast is rising, put shortening, salt, and remaining water into bowl and mix. Add yeast mixture. Gradually add flour to form stiff dough. Knead 5–10 min. Cover and let rise until double in bulk (about 1 hr.).

Punch down and let rise again in bowl until double in bulk (about ^{3}/$_4$ hr. longer). Punch down again. Remove from bowl and form into loaves as follows: divide dough in two parts and roll each part into a rectangle about 10" x 14". Roll dough jelly roll fashion to form a loaf about 14" long.

Slash top of bread and place on cookie sheets which have been sprinkled with cornmeal. Cover and let rise until double in bulk.

Bake at 400°F for 15 min. and 350°F for about 45 min. longer. Brush loaves with egg white while baking for a golden brown crust.

BASIC RAISIN BREAD

1 box raisins (6 oz.)	1 tsp. salt
2 C. cold water	1 tsp. lemon extract
2 T. active dry yeast	2 C. scalded milk
^{1}/$_4$ C. warm water	2 eggs, beaten
2 T. butter or margarine	6 C. flour (approx.)
2 T. sugar	melted butter
^{1}/$_8$ tsp. mace	

Soak raisins 1 hr. in 2 C. cold water. Drain well. Dissolve yeast in warm water. Put butter, sugar, spice, salt, and flavoring into a bowl. Pour scalded milk over all. When cooled to lukewarm, add eggs, yeast mixture, and raisins. Gradually, add flour, kneading to make a smooth ball. Cover and let rise until double in bulk. Punch down and form into two loaves.

Put into greased bread pans and let rise until double in bulk.

Bake at 400°F for 15 min., then 350°F for 35 min. longer.

Remove from pans, brush with melted butter. Cool on racks.

BASIC SWEETROLL DOUGH MIX

2 T. (pkg.) active dry yeast	1 tsp. salt
^{1}/$_2$ C. lukewarm water	^{1}/$_2$ C. butter or margarine
^{1}/$_2$ C. scalded milk	4^1/$_2$–5^1/$_2$ C. flour
^{1}/$_2$ C. sugar	2 eggs, slightly beaten

Dissolve yeast in warm water. Put scalded milk, sugar, salt, and butter into separate bowl and mix. When cooled to lukewarm, add yeast. Add 1 C. flour and eggs. Slightly mix. Continue adding flour until a firm ball is formed. Cover and let rise until double in bulk. Punch down and let rise 1 hr. Punch down once again and turn out onto floured board and form as desired.

Bake at 400°F for 25 min.

BASIC CINNAMON-NUT COFFEE CAKE

Basic Sweet Roll Dough Mix
$^1/_3$ C. flour
$^1/_3$ C. sugar

2 tsp. cinnamon
3 T. soft butter
$^1/_4$ C. chopped nuts

Prepare *Basic Sweet Roll Dough Mix*. After second rising of *Dough Mix*, roll $^1/_3$ of it into circle to fit a 9" pan. Sprinkle top with mixture of flour, sugar, cinnamon, butter, and chopped nuts. Cover and let rise until double in bulk.

Bake at 400°F for approx. 25 min. Serve warm.

Yield: 3 pans of 9" round cakes.

BASIC HONEY TWIST

Basic Sweet Roll Dough Mix
$^1/_4$ C. butter, creamed
2 T. honey

1 egg white
1 C. confectioners' sugar

After second rising of *Basic Sweet Roll Dough Mix*, roll into a long cylinder 1" in diameter. Coil into buttered 9" layer pan beginning at outer edge and covering the bottom. Cover and let rise until double in bulk. Bake at 375°F for 20 - 25 min.

While hot, spread with mixture of butter, honey, egg white, and sugar.

MARGE'S "MEAN" BREAD

My friend Marge Means makes this every week and brings it to our group of volunteers. This is really great bread—tasty, crunchy crust, and especially delightful with butter and homemade jam! (She brings the butter and jam, too!)

This is a great bread recipe—and so easy!

2 C. warm water
$^1/_3$ C. oil
¾ -1 C. Brown sugar

½ tsp. salt
1½ T. yeast

Combine the above ingredients together in a large bowl. When properly combined, gradually add flours.

5 - 6 C. flour (any combination of wheat and white flours)
½ C. coarse-ground wheat or oatmeal

Hand mixing—use a wooden spoon to mix. When dough becomes stiff, flour hands and continue to knead until smooth.

Machine mixing—gradually add flour until dough pulls away from sides of bowl.

Let mixture rest 20 - 30 min.

Grease small loaf pans and hands, and then divide dough into equal portions.

Shape dough into smooth loaves and let rise in pans until double in size. (You can speed rising by placing in warm oven.) When rising is double in size, turn oven to 350° F. Bake until golden brown on top.

Remove from oven and brush top with butter.

Serves: 6

Enjoy!

Here is Bread, which strengthens man's heart,
and therefore is called the staff of life.
Matthew Henry

Chapter 19

Basics of Triticale Flour Cookery

Triticale[1] is a grain derived from crossing wheat and rye genetically. Triticale has been touted as an equal or better grain than wheat. As an alternative grain for in-home storage, triticale has good, long-term storage qualities. It is a larger kernel or berry than wheat, has a higher protein efficiency ratio (**P.E.R.**) than wheat, and a higher percentage of protein.

Triticale flour also makes an excellent replacement for wheat pastry flour—and does not taste like rye at all! Gluten strands do not form as in whole-wheat batters; therefore, *wheat flour must be mixed in with any triticale bread recipe to make a high-rising bread.*

Since most cooks haven't developed recipes for triticale in their cookbooks, there are two cautions of which you should take note when substituting triticale in wheat recipes:

---

[1] Triticale (trit-ih-KAY-lee) is a crop species resulting from a cross between wheat (*Triticum*) and rye (*Secale*). The name triticale (*Triticale hexaploide Lart.*) combines the scientific names of the two genera involved. It is produced by doubling the chromosomes of the sterile hybrid that results when crossing wheat and rye. This doubling produces what is called a polyploid.

> • *Triticale cannot be substituted measure-for-measure for wheat because triticale has lower elasticity.*
> • *Substitution of triticale for wheat should not exceed $^1/_2$ the wheat flour required.*

The following recipes have been specially formulated for triticale flour.

RECIPES FOR BASIC TRITICALE BREADS, BISCUITS, AND MUFFINS

BASIC TRITIQUIX BREAD (2-HR. BREAD RECIPE)

3 T. active dry yeast	6 T. safflower oil
5 C. lukewarm water	$^1/_2$ C. honey
1 tsp. sugar	11 C. triticale flour
1 heaping T. salt	1 C. regular wheat flour

Mix dry yeast and $^1/_2$ C. warm water, sprinkle sugar on top, and stir. Mix salt, safflower oil, and honey into $4^1/_2$ C. warm water, mix well, and stir in yeast mixture. Stir in 4 C. triticale flour and $^1/_2$ C. regular wheat flour, mixing well. Add 4 more C. triticale flour and $^1/_2$ C. regular wheat flour, mix well; add remaining triticale flour, mix well.

Knead well for about 5 min., place in pan, and let rise for $^1/_2$ hr.

Cut batter into four even parts and knead each several min. Place in greased loaf pans and let rise to level of rim for approx. 25 min. When bread is ready to bake, place in pre-heated 350°F oven for 45 min. Remove from oven, take bread from pans, and allow to cool. Brush tops of loaves with warm butter. *Yield: 4 medium loaves*.

BASIC BUTTERMILK BREAD

$2^1/_2$ C. triticale flour	$^1/_2$ C. raisins (optional)
1 tsp. salt	$^1/_2$ C. molasses
$^1/_2$ C. cornmeal	$^1/_2$ C. sour cream
$1^1/_2$ tsp. baking soda	$1^1/_3$ C. buttermilk

Combine dry ingredients (flour, salt, cornmeal, soda) with raisins, if used. Mix molasses with sour cream and buttermilk. Combine the two mixtures.

Bake in greased bread pan 1 hr. at 350°F.

BASIC CHERRYANA BREAD

$^1/_2$ C. shortening	$^1/_2$ tsp. baking powder
1 C. sugar	$^1/_4$ tsp. salt
3 eggs	$^1/_3$ C. maraschino cherries
1 tsp. baking soda	1 C. banana pulp
$^1/_2$ C. chopped nuts	2 C. triticale flour

Cream shortening and sugar until light and fluffy. Add eggs one at a time and beat well after each addition. Dissolve soda in mashed bananas, add to creamed mixture. Add dry ingredients (baking powder, soda, salt). Fold in cherries that have been chopped and well drained, then stir in nuts. Pour into greased loaf pan and bake for 1 hr. at 350°F.

Variation: replace cherries with chopped dried apricots for *Basic TritiCotana Bread*.

BASIC TRITIBISCUITS

2 C. triticale flour	6 T. shortening
$1^1/_2$ tsp. salt	$^2/_3$ C. milk
4 tsp. baking powder	

Mix dry ingredients (flour, salt, baking powder); cut in lard or vegetable shortening with a wire pastry blender. Stir in milk, adding just enough to make a soft, light dough, stirring as little as possible. Drop from spoon onto a greased, floured baking sheet. Let stand 3 min.

Bake at 375°F approx. 10 min.

Yield: 12 - 16 biscuits.

BASIC TRITIBRAN MUFFINS

2 C. boiling water	4 beaten eggs
3 C. bran flakes (cereal)	3 C. triticale flour
1 qt. buttermilk	7 C. flour
1 C. shortening	5 tsp. baking soda
3 C. sugar	1 tsp. salt

Pour water over bran cereal, add buttermilk. Cream shortening and sugar; add eggs and mix well. Add mixture to cereal. Sift in flours, soda, salt. *Do not mix too long.* (Batter can be stored in the refrigerator and will keep approx. three weeks.) Spoon mixture into greased muffin pans, filling about $^3/_4$ full.

Bake for 15 - 20 min. at 350°F.

Yield: 4–5 doz.

BASIC TRITICOT BRAN MUFFINS

boiling water	$^3/_4$ tsp. salt
$^2/_3$ C. finely cut dried apricots	1 C. whole bran
2 T. sugar	$^3/_4$ C. milk
1 C. triticale flour	1 egg, beaten
$2^1/_2$ tsp. baking powder	$^1/_4$ C. salad oil
$^1/_3$ C. sugar	

Pour boiling water over apricots to cover, let stand 10 min. Drain well; mix with 2 T. sugar. Sift together dry ingredients (flour, baking powder, sugar, salt). Mix bran, milk, egg, and oil; add to flour mixture, stirring just till moistened.

Gently stir in apricots, fill greased muffin pans $^2/_3$ full. Sprinkle tops with additional sugar.

Bake in 400°F oven about 25 min.

Yield: 1 dozen muffins.

RECIPE FOR TRITICALE MAIN DISH

BASIC TRITIMEAT LOAF

1 lb. ground beef	1 C. triticale flour
$^1/_4$ tsp. oregano	$^1/_2$ tsp. dry mustard
1 tsp. sugar	1 T. Worcestershire sauce
$^1/_4$ C. chopped onion	$^1/_4$ C. green pepper, chopped
$1^1/_2$ C. tomato juice	1 egg

Mix all ingredients well. Place in loaf pan.

Bake 350°F for 60 min.

Yield: 6 - 8 servings.

RECIPES FOR TRITICALE DESSERTS

BASIC APPLECAKE

3 T. butter	$^1/_2$ tsp. salt
1 C. sugar	1 tsp. baking soda
1 egg, beaten	3 C. chopped apples
$^1/_2$ tsp. nutmeg	1 tsp. vanilla
1 C. triticale flour	$^1/_2$ C. chopped nuts
$^1/_2$ tsp. cinnamon	

Cream butter and sugar; add egg and mix well. Sift dry ingredients (nutmeg, flour, cinnamon, salt, soda) together. Add to creamed mixture. Stir in chopped apples, vanilla, and nuts. Pour in greased 8" x 8" pan.

Bake in 350°F oven about 45 min. Serve warm with whipped cream or ice cream.

Yield: 10 - 12 servings.

BASIC APPLESPICE CAKE

$^1/_3$ C. oil	1 tsp. ground cloves
1 C. sugar	1 tsp. salt
1 egg	1 tsp. cinnamon
1 C. sweetened applesauce	1 C. raisins
$1^3/_4$ C. triticale flour	1 C. currants
1 tsp. baking soda	

In a large bowl combine oil, sugar, and egg with electric mixer. Then beat in applesauce. Sift together dry ingredients (flour, soda, cloves, salt, cinnamon). Add flour mixture to the batter gradually, continuing to beat batter until smooth. Stir in raisins and currants. Transfer to greased and floured 9" x 13" cake pan.

Bake in 350°F oven for 40 min.

BASIC GINGER QUIXBREAD

2 C. triticale flour	$1^1/_2$ tsp. baking soda
1 tsp. salt	2 tsp. ginger
1 C. molasses	2 eggs
$^1/_2$ C. sugar	1 C. sour milk
4 T. melted shortening	

Combine all ingredients and beat for 2 min.

Bake 35 - 40 min. at 350°F.

Serve warm or cold, topped with whipping cream.

BASIC FRUITORTE

1 C. sugar	$^1/_2$ tsp. salt
1 egg, beaten	$^3/_4$ tsp. baking soda
1 can fruit cocktail, drained	4 T. brown sugar
1 C. triticale flour	$^1/_4$ C. chopped walnuts

Blend sugar and beaten egg; add the drained cocktail mix and the sifted dry ingredients (flour, salt, soda). Spread in square 9" pan. Mix the brown sugar and nuts and sprinkle on top.

Bake at 325°F for 15 min., then reduce to 300°F and bake another 45 min.

Serve with whipped cream or ice cream.

BASIC NO-CRUST APPLE PIE

8 C. apples, peeled, cored & cut in thin wedges	$^1/_2$ C. brown sugar
	$^1/_2$ C. triticale flour
$^1/_2$ C. sugar	$^1/_4$ C. butter
1 tsp. cinnamon or nutmeg	pinch of salt

Toss together first three ingredients and put in shallow 2-quart baking dish. Mix remaining ingredients until crumbly. Sprinkle over apples.

Bake in preheated 400°F oven about 30 min. Serve with whipped cream or ice cream.

Yield: 6 servings.

BASIC TRITIBROWNEES

4 squares unsweetened chocolate	1 tsp. baking powder
$^2/_3$ C. shortening	$1^1/_4$ C. triticale flour
2 C. sugar	1 C. nuts
4 eggs	1 tsp. salt
1 tsp. vanilla	

Heat oven to 350°F. Grease oblong pan, 13" x 9" x 2". In large saucepan, melt chocolate and shortening over low heat. Remove from heat. Blend in sugar, eggs, and vanilla. Mix in remaining ingredients. Spread in prepared pan.

Bake 30 min. or until brownees pull away from sides of pan. Do not over bake. Cool slightly; cut into bars about 2" x $1^1/_2$."

Yield: 24 - 32 brownees.

BASIC PEANUTTY COOKEES

1 C. raw or brown sugar	2 T. evaporated milk or cream
$^1/_2$ C. shortening	$1^1/_2$ C. triticale flour
1 egg, well beaten	1 tsp. baking soda
$^1/_2$ C. peanut butter	

Cream sugar and shortening, add egg and peanut butter. Add cream and dry ingredients (flour, soda). Form into small balls, about 1" in diameter.

Place on greased cookie sheet and bake at 350°F. for 8 - 10 min.

BASIC CHOCOCHIP COOKEES

$1^1/_2$ C. sugar	6 C. triticale flour
$1^1/_2$ C. brown sugar (packed)	2 tsp. baking soda
2 C. shortening	1 tsp. salt
2 tsp. vanilla	12 oz. pkg. chocolate chips
1 tsp. water	1 C. chopped nuts
4 eggs	

Cream together sugars, shortening, vanilla, water, and eggs.

Add dry ingredients (flour, soda, salt, chocolate chips, and nuts), mixing thoroughly.

Spoon onto greased cookie sheet.

Bake 375°F for 10 - 12 min. or until golden brown.

NOTES FOR YOUR TRITICALE COOKERY

Section VI

Back to Basics

There is no easy way you can become self-reliant.
It requires personal effort—rigorous work in self-education—and often vigor-
ous self-denial.

Chapter 20
Basics of In-Home Drying
Dehydrating Fruits & Vegetables

Drying, bottling, canning, pickling, brining, smoking, fermenting, and root-cellaring are different approaches our forebears used to save and have food for the future. Not having these methods to slow or stop food deterioration would have meant hunger, starvation, and ultimately death. To this already substantial list, we can add more recently developed preservation methods that have proven commercially and economically effective, such as refrigeration, freezing, dehydrating, and freeze-drying.

Today, for most of us city-dwellers, urbanites, and suburbanites, the preservation methods such as *curing, smoking*, and *root cellaring* require more time, space, equipment, etc., than we have available! There's already plenty of stress on our limited resources. In fact, many of us are barely competent in *refrigerating* or *freezing* our food to have for future use!

Fermenting sauerkraut, *brining* and *pickling* tasty relishes, maybe some *canning* ("putting up") jam and jelly in bottles, are methods likely to be within your capability and interest. But the minimal time required and expenses involved in *drying* make it an even more practical preservation method for our times. The drying of fruits and vegetables is the oldest method of preserving foods—it's been around several centuries longer than any other method of food preservation—whether fruits, herbs, vegetables, or meats.

See how many of these food preservation methods meet your resource capabilities and skill levels:

- *Canning* and *bottling* methods use extremely high temperatures to kill all biological activity. They also require some special and fairly expensive equipment, lots of preparation time, a great deal of storage space, and heavy stuff to handle and store.

- *Freezing* uses extremely cold temperatures to slow the spoilage factor through a type of suspended animation. Again, a great deal of time required for processing, cost of the freezer(s) required for adequate storage, ever-increasing energy costs, and the space required for operating equipment.

- *Fermenting, pickling, brining,* and *salting* use chemical solutions to achieve preservation—not good for your health, given what we understand now about high blood pressure and damage to the gastrointestinal tract.

- *Commercial dehydration* is food drying with special equipment to remove water from food at temperatures below normal cooking temperatures. Most in-home storage programs are built around storing dehydrated foods. Purchased thoughtfully and used properly, dehydrated foods are an excellent method for economical in-home storage.

- *Freeze-drying* entails freezing fresh or freshly-cooked foods, then super-dehydrating them by vacuuming off the moisture at sub-zero temperatures.[1] Commercial freeze-dried food is perhaps the ultimate food storage medium. Unfortunately, for most budgets, its higher quality is reflected in its much higher price.

- *Curing* and *smoking* are not particularly difficult, but again there are serious health questions about the curing agents utilized. There are also limited fruits and vegetables that can be appropriately cured or smoked in the typical household. This method of preservation is mostly used in preserving meats and fish. The **Game Meats, Fish, & Fowl** chapter (**Chapter 21**) has instructions for the preservation of various meats.

- *Root-cellaring* of fruits and vegetables requires a good-sized, below-ground level, indoor or outdoor space. Digging a pit or mounding earth and using insulating straw to extend storage of root crops and tree fruits just isn't within the reach of most of us urbanites and suburbanites. If you have the space and the inclination to construct or improvise a root cellar, there are resources at the end of this chapter to help you utilize this method of storage.

Even without a complete analysis of all the food preservation systems, it's fairly easy to conclude that most food preservation methods are neither affordable nor effective in-home methods for the majority of us. Experience indicates the urban dweller can use drying much more effectively and economically. If you're like me, however, you might get passionate about ***Basic in-home drying***. It is the simplest, least expensive and most fascinating method for preparing food today for use tomorrow.

Basic in-home drying is technologically non-threatening and low stress—it can be done while watching your favorite TV show. Storing dried foods is easy and fairly uncomplicated. Another advantage of this method is that some of the dried food can be eaten like snacks now or later, without cooking them before enjoying them.

Dried food products normally keep longer, cost less to prepare, and take less storage space. Most people agree the taste is better, too, when compared to other methods of pre-

---

[1] Contrary to what some may believe, in-home freeze-drying is not a possibility, even though some of the foods found in the bottom of home freezers are so badly freezer-burned they appear to be freeze-dried! Don't try to save freezer-burned foods—and spare your pets by throwing it in the trash, not in the yard!

servation. The real bonus is the ease of preparation and quick turn-around time from both the fresh-to-dried state and back from dried to the ready-to-eat state.

DRYING METHODS

Drying removes the moisture from the food that microorganisms need to remain biologically active. Food deterioration is slowed tremendously by drying. The differences[2] among drying methods are determined by the sophistication of the equipment and technology involved:

- **In-home food drying** removes 80%–90% of moisture.
- **Commercial food dehydrating** removes 96%–97.5% of moisture.
- **Commercial food freeze-drying** removes 98%+ of moisture.

In-home drying is fairly unsophisticated when compared to the commercial facilities specializing in food dehydration and freeze-drying and cannot approach the low levels of moisture attained by commercial establishments. On the other hand, there is a greater loss of nutritional values from commercial methods, as shown in **Chart 20–1**. *In-home drying* compares more than favorably with all of the other drying preservation processes in relationship to nutritional losses.

Chart 20–1
Nutritional Losses by Selected Preservation Processes

Preservation process	Normal loss of nutrition	Processing method
Canning	60–80%	high temperatures and water-logging
Freezing	40–60%	rupturing of cells
Comm'l. Dehydrating	5–15%	moderate heat and moderate air flow
In-home Drying	3–5%	low heat and gentle air flow

IN-HOME DRYING

Advantages of In-Home Drying

In-home dried foods retain more of their nutritive values than hot or cold packing, freezing, or pickling. When compared to *canning,* the most common method of preservation in the United States, *drying* is outstanding in keeping the food values in foods after processing. Drying foods in-home is the least expensive, most nutritious, and most realizable method of preserving foods for most of us. Since time is our most precious and least available resource, in-home drying is the best investment we can make to facilitate an effective method of preserving food.

Because in-home drying does not use extremely high temperatures, almost all the vitamins, minerals, and enzymes are retained intact. The flavors of fruits and vegetables are retained much better because rehydrated dried foods have a concentration of wholesome, real-flavor sweetness and taste that is intensely, delightfully delicious. As a bonus, dried foods are full of fiber, have no refined sugars added, and have concentrated amounts of naturally occurring nutrients, sugars, and flavors.

Basic Reasons for In-Home Drying

Drying foods in-home is one of the best and most basic methods of home storage for these reasons:

Saves space: dried foods can be stored in 40%–50% less space. With such a high percentage of their water removed, dried foods are smaller.

Saves weight: dried foods weigh up to 75% less than their fresh equivalents.

---

[2] See the USDA Agriculture *Family Preparedness Handbook No. 8, Composition of Foods: Raw, Processed, Prepared.* If not available from USDA, try your library or your County Extension Agent.

Convenient: reconstitute in minutes by simply soaking in water or adding to a soup, casserole, or other recipe to which an extra measure of can be added.

Economical:

- allows you to take advantage of seasonal prices of produce
- saves losses from excess production—both market and home (leftovers)
- costs only pennies per hour to operate dryer
- packaging supplies are inexpensive and readily available

Nutritious:

- retains greater percentage of nutrients than other methods of preservation
- food tastes better than when processed by other methods
- dried food is edible as is or can be reconstituted to its natural state by simply soaking in plain water
- there are no synthetic or unnatural preservatives required in the drying process

Secrets to Successful In-Home Drying

The secrets to successful in-home drying are

- choosing the highest quality foods available
- handling foods in each step of the process quickly to prevent deterioration of quality
- keeping all equipment and working surfaces hygienic
- deactivating the enzymatic action in foods
- treating appropriately to preserve color, nutrients, taste, and food quality
- ensuring even drying to extend storage life and reduce decomposition
- drying in the shortest time possible without actually cooking or burning foods
- removing enough moisture from foods to prevent spoilage from growth of organisms and molds:
    - —vegetables should contain less than 10% moisture
    - —fruits should contain less than 20% moisture

BASIC IN-HOME DRYING METHOD

There are only **six** steps to in-home drying of fruits and vegetables, storage, and rehydration for use. A full explanation of each of these steps is found in the following sections. These steps are

1. **Selection of fruits and vegetables**
2. **Preparation for drying**
3. **Preservation treatment prior to drying**
4. **Drying (including doneness testing)**
5. **Post-drying handling to extend shelf life**
6. **Rehydration for use**

The **Basic In-Home Fruit Drying Quick-Guide 20–1** and the **Basic In-Home Vegetable Drying Quick-Guide 20–2** at the end of this chapter detail the requirements for in-home drying of fruits and vegetables.

Preparation, treatment prior to drying, testing for doneness, estimated shelf life, and rehydration use details are also included. Specific instructions and suggested alternatives for each step are noted.

These **Quick-Guides** serve as quick references and summaries for drying the most common fruits and vegetables.

Step 1: Selection of Fruits & Vegetables

Always use fruits and vegetables in their "prime." Select sound, fresh, ripe, but firm fruits and vegetables at their maturity. Keep in mind the axiom used in modern-day parlance, "the best beginning makes the best finish." A low-quality product at the beginning will produce a low-quality product when dried, or prepared in any manner.

The best dried produce will normally come from your own family garden, mainly due to its freshness and your careful handling.[3] When shopping at your grocer's for drying produce, sort out the bruised, overripe, and immature products. Wash all produce carefully, whether homegrown or store-bought, as part of the preparation step.

Step 2: Preparation of Fruits & Vegetables for Drying

Preparation involves washing, drying, peeling, cutting, slicing, pitting, removing seeds, coring, chopping or dicing, mashing, or blending. Do this before treating. The following general suggestions will help you prepare fruits and vegetables for drying:

- Wash all produce to remove dirt, germs, or pesticides that might be on the surface. Put a drop of mild, liquid dishwashing detergent in a clean sink full of warm water. This will remove most pesticides, waxes, dirt, and germs without damage to foods.

- Use a vegetable brush for all root crops or other hard-surfaced produce.

- When produce is to be chopped or diced, wash before *and* after cutting.

- Discard all outer leaves of leafy produce before washing.

- Always wash exterior of fruits and vegetables prior to peeling or cutting. Remove all possible contaminants prior to exposing "flesh" of all fruits and vegetables. This prevents cross-contamination while cutting and slicing, putting pieces on trays, etc.

- Always use a stainless steel knife to prevent discoloration of the fruit or vegetables.

- Turn pitted fruits "*inside out*" to aid treating and drying.

- Cut all pieces approximately the same size. Obviously, the larger the pieces of food, the longer they'll take to treat, dry, and rehydrate. Larger pieces are also a greater risk for spoilage, particularly if careful attention is not given them in the dryer. When all pieces are the same size during drying, the overall quality of the batch will be higher.

Step 3: Pre-Treatment for Fruits & Vegetables
Blanching Pre-Treatment

Blanching is a pre-treatment for some fruits and all vegetables. It was one of the secrets that Clarence Birdseye, as part of his discovery for freezing foods successfully, intro-

---

[3] My personal observation of produce departments in today's markets is that they lack care in handling our already vitamin-depleted, over-processed, and mechanically-mangled foods. I've watched many produce clerks slam fruits and vegetables into bins and forcibly weld fruits together so they stack without rolling off the slanted display shelf or rack. If produce weren't already damaged or beginning to rot in the bins or on the display counters, at the checkout lane, the rolling belt churns the soft produce against the heavy merchandise, especially bottles of milk and cereal boxes, bags of flour, packages of meats, and my favorite tool of destruction, canned goods. Then the checker picks up my prize selections, scans them, and repositions them on the belt or packing counter surface to assure they roll, drop, slam, or otherwise get bruised while passing through the price-scanning process to the bagger. If anything gets past the checker without being thoroughly rolled and damaged, it is the responsibility of the grocery bagger to finalize the process and assure all fruits and vegetables are bruised. I watch with detached wonder as <u>my</u> carefully-selected items are double-dribbled on the surface of the packing bin, thrown into the grocery sack or bag, then dropped unceremoniously into the shopping basket–not unlike a basketball slam-dunk! At last, I can take charge and roll my bruised and hurting possessions to the car—it's the least I can do to protect my investment. Lately, I've asked the grocery personnel to handle my selections as if they were taking them home themselves, and sometime, it actually helps—at least I feel better having mentioned it!

duced in 1924. Blanching foods can be achieved in two ways. Foods can either be steamed in a basket over boiling water or be put directly into the boiling water.

Foods being processed for in-home drying must be blanched—*but not completely cooked!* Successful blanching doesn't cook foods fully but brings them to the point of just being tender. However, if foods are mistakenly left in the steam or water too long, *over-blanching is better than under-blanching.* Most of the vitamin loss in the drying process occurs while blanching. However, it's a small price to pay for the dividends.

Steaming foods is the better blanching pre-treatment method because it adds less water to foods and dissolves fewer nutrients than boiling.

When the blanching process is completed, either blot food or gently roll pieces in a towel to soak up excess moisture. After foods are blanched and blotted dry, no other pre-treatment is required prior to placing them into the dryer.

Blanching fruits and vegetables has these purposes:
- sets color
- stops ripening process (enzymatic action)
- prevents changes in flavor
- facilitates drying process
- reduces drying time
- reduces contamination from molds and bacterial growth

Chemical Solutions for Fruits

Chemical solutions may be used to treat fruit to prevent discoloration, molds, and bacteria. See **Chart 20–2** following for details of treating specific fruits to prevent darkening.

Chart 20–2
Chemical Solutions for Treating Fruits

Solution	Purpose	Mixture Preparation	Time in Mixture
Ascorbic acid	Prevent discoloration[4]	1–1½ tsp. to 1 C. cold water	Soak fruit 2–3 min.
Saline	Prevent molds & bacteria	4–6 tsp. to 1 gal. cold water	Soak fruit 10 min.
Sulfur	Prevent molds & bacteria	1–1½ tsp. to 1 gal. water	Soak fruit 10–20 min.

Ascorbic acid: Darkening will occur with some fruits, such as apples, apricots, peaches, pears, and nectarines. The pre-treatment for reducing the oxidation is an antioxidant chemical in the form of pure crystalline ascorbic acid. This product is generally available in most full-service pharmacies or on grocery shelves. This method is a temporary treatment, helping keep the original color intact while in the dryer.

Either dip fruits in the ascorbic acid mixture or sprinkle onto all surfaces with a sprinkle bottle. Drain thoroughly and dry by blotting with paper or cloth towel.

Saline solution: Formerly a popular method for pretreating fruits, but today's health conscious generation doesn't like the idea of too much salt in their diet.

Sulfuring: The purpose of sulfuring of fruits is to inhibit the growth of molds and bacteria that cause souring. The easiest method for applying sulfur to fruits is to make a mixture of sulfur (available at any pharmacy) and cold water and soak for 10-20 minutes. Commercial dehydrating plants utilize sulfuring as a prime method of treatment.

Alternatives to Chemical Solutions

Nature's own chemical preservatives and some kitchen actions are effective in helping preserve color, facilitate drying, and prevent contamination as explained in the next sections.

---

[4] For apples, use up to 3 tsp. per C. of cold water. Apples darken so quickly they require special handling.

Fruit juice: Many people prefer lemon, lime, or pineapple juice instead of a chemical bath. Simply dip fruit in unsweetened juice of lemon or pineapple, drain in a colander, blot with paper towels, and put into dryer.

Vitamin C: Crush 3–4 vitamin C tablets (500 mg each) into 1 quart cold water. Soak fruits in solution for 10 minutes.

Removing skins or peels: Drop fruits into boiling water for 30–60 seconds, rinse in cold water, and then peel by hand.

Cracking or "nicking" skins or peels: When fruit skins or peels are thick, but not to be removed, put them in boiling water for 15–45 seconds. Immediately dunk into cold water and the skin should crack. If they're too thick to crack, then make several nicks in the skins with a sharp stainless steel knife.

Freezing: Put fruit into freezer overnight, then thaw by dropping into hot water just before processing.

Step 4: Drying Fruits & Vegetables

Warm, dry air is passed over, under, around, and through the food, pulling out the moisture, evaporating it, and reducing the food to between $^1/_6$-$^1/_3$ of its original size. Drying removes as much as 90% of the moisture from vegetables and only slightly less, approximately 80%, from fruits.

Whatever the heat source, all you need is a sustained temperature of 140°–150°F, a number of trays to hold the fruit or vegetable, and several hours of unattended drying time.

Spread one layer of prepared and treated produce on each drying tray. Turn produce often to assure thorough drying.

A temperature of 140°F for at least half the drying time is required to kill the inherent bacteria in drying foods.

The time required for successful drying depends on these variables:

- moisture in prepared and treated foods
- humidity
- temperature inside dryer
- size of pieces of foods
- rotation of trays and stirring of foods

In-home drying effectively preserves food with more flavor, color, appearance, texture, and the highest food value when compared to commercial processes. Little effort is required to perfect *Basic in-home drying*, and equipment and time commitments are small.

Drying may be done in the sun, in an oven, or in an electric home dehydrator. Families without hungry children or nosy pets may be able to use heating ducts or furnace rooms as heat sources, or the tops of counters and open spaces.

In earlier times, the sun was the prime heat source for drying. As I remember, in my youth, picking, selecting, preparing, paring, slicing, dicing, laying out the fruits and vegetables on wood frames with cheesecloth was the family's evening entertainment as we listened to *The Green Hornet, The Shadow,* and *The Gene Autry Show.* I also recall that it was doubly entertaining for my grandmother—she got a kick out of seeing us work! It was indeed worth the work when she cooked up some great vittles from the pantry in the cold of winter!

In today's busy world, however, people buy an electric dehydrator and try to fit drying experiences during half-time or between doing the dishes and washing clothes.

Indoor Drying Methods

There are several in-home methods[5] for drying foods, and each is somewhat different, based on the area's temperature and humidity ranges, food you want to dry, and the time available for processing. The usual locations utilized for indoor drying are listed here.

Space: Hang strands of beans, pods of pepper, and baskets of herbs and flowers in whatever warm space available.[6]

Oven: Most electric and gas stoves will work, even though not an excellent method of drying. Temperature control is a little difficult, and they are inconvenient at times.

Heat register: Registers are not recommended due to the contaminants in the typical home heating ducts.

Commercial dryer: Many models are available. A listing of manufacturers and suppliers is provided at **http://doctorprepper.com/preparedness-resources/**.

Shop carefully before buying any electrical appliance. (In previous editions, a do-it-

If yourself plan for building a dryer was included. Prices of dryers are now less than what the parts formerly cost for a homemade unit. In fact, some of the parts may no longer be available!)

Microwave oven: Except for blanching and boiling foods prior to drying them, this method has proven too difficult to control for most people. Also, cooking often occurs prior to drying. Then, too, there are the dry, hard spot in the foods! It's not a recommended *Basics* drying method. In all fairness, however, there are experts who succeed where others fail.[7] We've tried the system, but haven't perfected it yet. If you're a serious drying devotée, you might want to get the book and try this method.

Outdoor Drying Methods

In some climates, outdoor drying is an easy and natural process. If you don't live in one of those climates or microclimates, contact your State Agricultural Extension Agent. Local agents usually have the best information on local drying methods for their area.

Solar heat: [8] Open-air processing in the heat of the direct sun. This works best where daytime temperatures are high and humidity ranges are low both day and night.

Shade[9]**:** For geographic areas where the temperature, air movement, and humidity range allow food to complete the drying process without direct sun exposure (after an adequate "jump-start" either by solar or artificial heat).

Air: For geographic areas where the movement of air is adequate to complete the drying process (after a "jump start" in an oven or dryer, of course.)

Drying Tips

These tips apply both to indoor and outdoor drying methods.

- Do not mix vegetables and/or fruits while drying. All fruits and vegetables have different drying times and even different tests for doneness.

---

[5] The USDA has another out-of-print brochure which describes these alternatives with explicit details: *Farmers' Bulletin No. 984, Farm and Home Drying of Fruits and Vegetables.* If not available at the library, call your County Extension Agent.

[7] Isabel Webb, author of *Fruit Drying with a Microwave,* Sterling Publishing Co., Inc., 387 Park Avenue South, New York, NY 10016, seems to have a very good system for microwave fruit drying.

[8] The USDA Federal Extension Service has a pamphlet, *Sun Dry Your Fruits and Vegetables (1958),* a step-by-step explanation of drying procedures for the southwestern and south central U.S.

[9] Mother called the last two methods "*porch drying.*" It's how we dried the remainders of "*daddy's garden.*" In those days, we laid butcher paper on the slats of the wood porch swing and used an electric fan to provide enough air to make both shade and air-drying methods work. (That was also prior to air pollution!)

- Rotate trays as needed to assure even drying (or turn trays around in oven).
- Prevent scorching and discoloration by rotating food trays away from the heat source or lower the temperature a few degrees—but not below 140°F.
- Drying temperature for juicy foods should be started at less than 140°F and raised slowly. Too much heat too soon will harden the outer cells and prevent release of internal moisture. This is particularly important with the "juicy" fruits.
- Maintain temperature between 140°–150°F for maximum drying effectiveness and to reduce molds and bacterial growth.
- Check trays occasionally to separate pieces sticking together.
- Turn larger pieces over more often and keep them near the outside of the dryer.
- Move nearly dry pieces to center of trays and pile them up—but continue to turn them from time to time.

Note:
Vegetables must be drier than fruits for home storage purposes.

Doneness Testing

Appearance and feel are the in-home drying tests for determining when dried foods are ready for storage. Fruits are considered dry enough for storage when pieces have these qualities:
- no moisture can be squeezed from a dried sample when it's cut
- pieces are tough and pliable, like leather
- pieces separate after being squeezed together tightly

Vegetable tests for doneness are characterized in terms of
- brittle
- tough-to-brittle
- crispness

See **Quick-Guides** for details for the doneness test for each fruit and vegetable, including any exceptions. Always perform the doneness test with a cooled test piece. When the test piece has passed the doneness test, remove entire batch from dryer and allow to cool thoroughly.

Before packaging foods, check once more for pieces that are not dried properly. Those may be recycled through the dryer or eaten within a few days.

Package only the best quality foods for your food storage.

Step 5: Post-Drying Handling to Extend Shelf Life

There are several techniques that will help both improve the quality of dried foods and extend their shelf life in your food storage program. If you're encountering difficulty with either in-home dried foods or commercially dehydrated food, perhaps there are some resolutions in the following sections.

Conditioning Period

Prior to packaging, certain dried foods, usually fruits with large pits or those with skins left on and dense vegetables, require a "conditioning period"— a day or so in a closed bulk container. Conditioning allows the moisture remaining in some of the pieces to re-distribute more evenly throughout the dried batch. After the conditioning period, too-moist pieces should be removed and eaten immediately or reprocessed in the dryer.

Molds and Bacterial Elimination

Whether you dry food in the outdoor sun or in the kitchen oven, there are two methods you can use to assure that molds, yeast, and bacteria are killed after the drying process prior to packaging. Extreme temperatures above and below the life support range of molds, yeast, and bacteria effectively eliminate them.

Heating: after testing for doneness, spread dried foods on a baking sheet, approximately 2" thick.

- Heat dried foods in warm oven at 165°–175°F for 10–12 minutes to kill any organisms or mold spores that may have developed during the drying process.

- Deadly bacteria, molds, and food yeast can live only in atmospheres having a certain level of moisture and temperature, so this method eliminates them with high heat levels prior to final packaging for storage.

- Attention must be given to assure dried foods are not cooked or burned while heating them at this higher temperature range.

- Allow foods to cool thoroughly before packaging.

Freezing: after putting cool dried foods in food-grade, plastic, re-sealable bags, place them in a chest or upright freezer—*not freezer section of combination unit*—for 48 hours at 0°F or lower.

- When removing from freezer, allow to return to room temperature very slowly to avoid internal sweating.

- Freezing is a very effective method for eliminating molds, yeast, and bacteria because fewer nutrients are lost through freezing than heating.

Packaging and Storing

Dried foods will begin absorbing humidity when removed from the dryer or exposed when opening the packaging for use. To prevent absorption of humidity, as soon as foods are properly cooled, package them immediately in heavy-duty, food-grade, airtight, self-sealing plastic bags.[10]

Here are some general notes to help in packaging and storing in-home dried foods:

- Freezer-weight, zip-lock bags are excellent for packaging dried foods. Force excess air from bags as they are sealed.

- Procure heavy-duty, food-grade, storage-quality, sealable plastic bags from local commercial packaging wholesalers.

- Store dried food products in a cool, dry location out of direct sunlight. Use a Kraft-paper bag inside larger plastic bags to shield dried foods from sunlight. Paper used outside the plastic bags provides nesting places for bugs and spiders.

- Store only one kind of food in each individual package to avoid mixing flavors and possible cross-contamination should molds or spoilage occur.

- Another method for storing dried products is to place dried food in a food-quality, plastic bag, then put it in an airtight glass or metal container.

- Discard moldy food. Don't take chances on botulism or a debilitating sickness over a few pennies or dollars. Don't feed moldy foods to the dog, either!

- The advantage of having small amounts in individual packages will eliminate big losses should a mold or bacterial condition occur.

- The problem of a few bugs in dried foods may be solved by spreading the infested dried food on a cookie pan, placing in a 300°F oven for 25–30 minutes. Bugs and eggs die, and the food is edible again. (Protein content is higher, too!)

---

[10] Packaging wholesalers may also have desiccant (moisture removing chemical) packs for insertion in plastic bags. The desiccant will absorb moisture and may be renewable when heated in the oven.

Step 6: Rehydration for Use

To rehydrate dried fruits and vegetables, cover them with water and soak for approximately 30 minutes, adding more water if necessary. The **Quick-Guides** provide details for rehydrating each fruit and vegetable.

Be aware of results as you rehydrate your dried food so you'll become more proficient in utilizing the fruits of your labors.

There are books on dehydrating and using dehydrated foods, as well as many listings of equipment dealers and suppliers online at **http://doctorprepper.com/preparedness-resources**

Suggestions for rehydrating foods:

- Add hot, boiling water to dried foods, then cover to speed rehydration. *Better rehydration occurs when water is added to foods—not when foods are added to water!*

- Rehydration with boiling water will usually cook dried foods adequately, though this depends on the manner in which the food was prepared, treated, and dried.

- When additional cooking is required, do not boil or simmer, just keep hot at low heat.

- Do not use excess water when rehydrating dried foods—nutrients will be lost.

- Soaking water remaining from rehydration can be used in another recipe.

- Use rehydrated fruits in recipes as if fresh—no extra sugar needed to sweeten them.

- Dried fruits may be eaten dry or chopped and diced for desserts and cereals.

- Always add salt *after* rehydration process is completed.

- Rehydration is not necessary when making soups, stews, or casseroles with dried vegetables. Remember to adjust liquid for their absorption.

- Store small portions in individual packages. Small portions will prevent big losses in your storage should infestation or mold occur.

- Portion control will also reduce waste after opening a package or rehydrating it for use.

Basic in-home drying, whether building a homemade dryer in the garage or buying commercial equipment with today's technology, has literally become an electronic breeze!

Quick-Guide 20–1

Basic In-Home Fruit Drying Guide

Basic directions for selecting, preparing, preservation treatment, drying in electric dryer, doneness testing, storing, and rehydrating fruits:

Step 1: Select quality, ripe, firm, and undamaged fruit. Wash carefully.

Step 2: Prepare fruit for drying. Review listed suggestions as guidelines.[1]

Step 3: Treat to preserve color and taste, if specified.
Then spread fruits in a single layer on dryer tray.

Step 4: Maintain drying temperatures between 140°–150°F.
Turn frequently or change tray positions to dry fruits evenly without scorching.

Step 5: Storage life in months for in-home dried fruits when stored at 70°F.[2]

Step 6: Rehydrating stored dried fruits to use by covering with hot, boiling water.

Step 1 Fruit Selection	Step 2 Preparation for Drying	Step 3 Preservation Treatment[3] Prior to Drying	Step 4 Drying & Doneness Test	Step 5 Shelf Life	Step 6 Rehydration for Use[4]
Apple	Pare, core, and cut in $^1/_8$"–$^1/_4$" slices or rings. Leave peeling on if "chewy" apples preferred.	Immediately after cutting, either treat in ascorbic acid[5] bath @ 3 tsp. to 1 C. cold-water solution or 100% lemon juice. Or, may blanch 4 min. instead.	Leathery to brittle	6	Equal hot water and apples. Soak 10 min. Soft, but holds shape. Dried apples are an excellent chewy snack.
Apricot	Peel, if desired. Cut in halves, remove pits. May be quartered. Turn inside out to speed drying.	Treat in ascorbic acid bath solution @ $1^1/_2$ tsp. to 1 C. cold water. Or, treat with other listed solutions.	Leathery & pliable	8	Equal hot water and apricots. Soak 15 min. Soft and dark. Dried apricots are an excellent snack.
Avocado	Peel, cut in half, and remove seed. Cut into thin strips.	Must treat to prevent from turning black. After slicing, dip immediately in 100% lemon juice.	Leathery & pliable	2	Will not rehydrate well—use equal hot water and avocado. Soak 10 min. Soft and mushy. Good only for guacamole and soup flavoring.
Banana	Peel and slice across or along length, or cut in quarters, halves or dry whole.	No treatment required.	Leathery & pliable, not sticky	4	Equal hot water and bananas. Soak 15 min. Soft, limp, and dark. Dried bananas are an excellent chewy snack.

---

[1] Check with your State Agricultural Extension, County Extension Agent, or local food storage experts for particulars about special needs for drying fruits in your geographic or climate area.

[2] Approximate period before deterioration of food becomes noticeable to the taste. After this period, even though the food quality, i.e., flavor, nutritive value, etc., is declining, fruits will still be edible and useful, as long as they are not contaminated. In-home dried fruits stored at 50°F will have a shelf life approximately 4 times as long as when stored at 70°F! The key to extending storage life of dried fruits is to keep them at the lowest possible temperatures. Freezing dried fruit in airtight packages will provide many years of shelf life.

[3] Treatment process includes the following methods to prevent molds & bacteria, discoloration, loss of flavor (souring), and to extend storage:

- ***Sulfur solution treatment***—bathe fruit in solution of $1^1/_2$ tsp. sulfur to 1 C. cold water, drain in colander, blot dry with paper towels, then put into electric dryer.

- ***Antioxidant solution treatment***—dip fruit in undiluted, unsweetened lemon, lime, or pineapple juice, depending on your preference for taste. Drain fruit in colander and blot dry with paper towels, then put into electric dryer immediately.

- ***Ascorbic acid solution treatment***—dissolve 3-4 vitamin C tablets (500 mg ascorbic acid each tablet) in 1 qt. cold-water solution. Soak fruit in solution for 10 minutes, drain in colander, blot dry with paper towels, then put into electric dryer immediately.

- ***Blanching treatment***—place fruit in basket suspended above boiling water (blanch fruits w/steam instead of boiling water) as required. Remove and blot dry. Place fruits in dryer immediately.

[4] When rehydrating fruits for desserts, allow liquid to be absorbed and the fruit plumps up. Always add any sweeteners after rehydration is completed.

[5] Apples require a stronger antioxidant treatment to prevent darkening and loss of flavor. Use 3 tsp. sulfur to I. C. cold-water solution.

Basic directions for selecting, preparing, preservation treatment, drying in electric dryer, doneness testing, storing, and rehydrating fruits:

Basic In-Home Fruit Drying Guide (continued)

Step 1 Fruit Selection	Step 2 Preparation for Drying	Step 3 Preservation Treatment[6] Prior to Drying	Step 4 Drying & Doneness Test	Step 5 Shelf Life	Step 6 Rehydration for Use[7]
Berries—all with skin, exceptions in separate listings	Leave whole, remove stems. Crack skins by dropping into boiling water for 15–45 sec., depending on toughness. Plunge into cold water immediately to crack skin. Dry thoroughly. (Freezing will also crack skins.)	No treatment required for blueberries, huckleberries, currants, or cranberries.	Hard, without visible moisture when squeezed between fingers	6	Will not rehydrate well—use equal hot water and berries. Soak 10–15 min. Good for purées, drink flavoring, etc. Dried berries are excellent sweet-tart snacks.
Blueberry	See Berries for details.	No treatment required.	Leathery & pliable, like raisins	12	Equal hot water and blueberries. Soak 10–15 min. Dried blueberries are a sweet-tart snack.
Cherry	Remove stems, cut in half, and remove pits. Drain if juicy.	No treatment required.	Leathery & pliable, like raisins	12	Equal hot water and cherries. Soak 10 min. Soft, but holds shape. Dried cherries are an excellent snack.
Citrus peel (zest)	Clean orange or lemon peel thoroughly. Scrape off inner pith to avoid bitter taste. Cut into strips.	No treatment required.	Crispy	12	Use dried only. Prior to use, chop in blender to desired fineness. Use as spice; add to liquid in recipe.
Coconut	Drain milk. Break in half and remove meat from shell. Slice or grate.	No treatment required.	Leathery to crisp	1	Use dried only. Sprinkle on foods. Drop small amounts in blender to flavor drinks.
Cranberry	See Berries for details.	No treatment required.	Leathery & pliable, like hard raisins	6	Equal hot water and cranberries. Soak 10–15 min. Dried cranberries are a tart snack!
Date	Wash thoroughly and dry well. Best dried whole.	No treatment required.	Leathery, but slightly sticky	12	Equal hot water and dates. Soak 15 min. Dried dates are excellent sweet snack.
Fig	Wash thoroughly. Leave whole, dip in boiling water 1 min. to crack skin.	Steam 20 min.	Leathery, but slightly sticky	6	Equal hot water and figs. Soak 15 min. Dried figs are tough but excellent for snacking.
Grape	Use only seedless grapes for drying. Leave whole, but remove stems. Crack skins with sharp knife, blanching quickly or freezing.	No treatment required.	Pliable, dark brown or black color	6	Raisins—will not reconstitute to grapes! Use dried in baking, cooking, and on cereal. Raisins make an excellent sweet snack.
Grapefruit	Peel, break into sections, and pierce with knife.	No treatment required.	Leathery & pliable	6	Equal hot water and grapefruit. Soak 15 min. Soft flesh, but holds shape. Dried grapefruit is a tart and bitter-sour snack.

[6] Treatment process includes the following methods to prevent molds & bacteria, discoloration, loss of flavor (souring), and to extend storage:

- ***Sulfur solution treatment***—bathe fruit in solution of 1½ tsp. sulfur to 1 C. cold water, drain in colander, blot dry with paper towels, then put into electric dryer.
- ***Antioxidant solution treatment***—dip fruit in undiluted, unsweetened lemon, lime, or pineapple juice, depending on your preference for taste. Drain fruit in colander and blot dry with paper towels, then put into electric dryer immediately.
- ***Ascorbic acid solution treatment***—dissolve 3–4 vitamin C tablets (500 mg ascorbic acid each tablet) in 1 qt. cold-water solution. Soak fruit in solution for 10 minutes, drain in colander, blot dry with paper towels, then put into electric dryer immediately.
- ***Blanching treatment***—place fruit in basket suspended above boiling water (blanch fruits w/steam instead of boiling water) as required. Remove and blot dry. Place fruits in dryer immediately.

[7] When rehydrating fruits for desserts, allow liquid to be absorbed and the fruit plumps up. Always add any sweeteners after rehydration is completed.

Basic In-Home Fruit Drying Guide (continued)

Basic directions for selecting, preparing, preservation treatment, drying in electric dryer, doneness testing, storing, and rehydrating fruits:

Step 1	Step 2	Step 3	Step 4	Step 5	Step 6
Fruit Selection	Preparation for Drying	Preservation Treatment Prior to Drying	Drying & Doneness Test	Shelf Life	Rehydration for Use
Kumquat	Peel, break into sections, and pierce with knife.	No treatment required.	Leathery & pliable	6	Equal hot water and kumquat. Soak 15 min. Soft flesh, but holds shape. Dried kumquat is an excellent chewy snack.
Lemon	Peel, break into sections, and pierce with knife.	No treatment required.	Leathery & pliable	6	Equal hot water and lemon. Soak 15 min. Soft flesh, but holds shape. Pulverize dried lemon for lemonade drink mix
Nectarine	Peel if desired. Cut in half, remove pits. Quarter or slice if desired.	Treat in ascorbic acid bath @ 1½ tsp. to 1 C. cold-water solution. Or, treat with any other solution.	Leathery & pliable	6	Equal hot water and nectarine. Soak 5 min. Soft, dark flesh holds shape. Dried nectarine is an excellent chewy snack.
Melon—all kinds	Cut open, remove all rind and seeds, and slice flesh into chunks.	No treatment required.	Leathery, but not sticky	2	Melons will not rehydrate. Dried melon is a sweet and chewy snack.
Orange	Peel, break into sections, pierce with knife.	No treatment required.	Leathery & pliable	6	Equal hot water and orange. Soak 15 min. Soft flesh, but holds shape. Dried orange is an excellent tart snack.
Papaya	Peel, slice, and remove seeds.	No treatment required.	Leathery to crisp	6	Equal hot water and papaya. Soak 5 min. Soft, dark flesh and holds shape. Dried papayas are an excellent chewy snack.
Peach	Peel, if desired, by quick blanching and removing by hand. Cut in half, remove pits. Quarter or slice if desired.	Treat in ascorbic acid bath @ 1½ tsp. to 1 C. cold-water solution. Or, may treat with any solution.	Soft, leathery & pliable	6	Equal hot water and peaches. Soak 5 min. Soft, dark flesh and holds shape. Dried peaches are a chewy, excellent snack
Pear	Pare and remove core and other woody parts. Cut into ⅛", ¼", or ½" slices or rings.	Treat in ascorbic acid bath @ 1½ tsp. to 1 C. cold-water solution. Or, may blanch for 2 min.	Soft, pliable to leathery	6	Equal hot water and pears. Soak 10 min. Soft, dark flesh and holds shape. Dried pear slices are an excellent snack.
Pineapple	Cut away outer skin. Cut into slices or chunks.	Blanch 1 min.	Leathery, but not sticky	8	Equal hot water and pineapple. Soak 10 min. Soft, mushy, but holds shape. Dried pineapple is an excellent tart snack.
Plum	Leave whole or cut into thin slices. Blanching not required, but drying is faster. When using whole, steam for 5 min. to crack skins and speed drying.	No treatment required.	Leathery & pliable	8	Equal hot water and plums. Soak 20 min. Soft, slippery but holds shape. Dried plums are prunes and are an excellent snack. Prunes soaked in water make juice.
Strawberry	Remove stems and leaves. Cut in half or thirds.	Blanch 1 min.	Leathery & pliable	6	Equal hot water and strawberries. Soak 10 min. Soft, mushy, and holds shape. Dried strawberries are an excellent tart snack.
Tangerine	Peel, break into sections, and pierce with knife.	No treatment required.	Leathery & pliable	6	Equal hot water and tangerine. Soak 15 min. Soft flesh, but holds shape. Dried tangerine is an excellent snack, but tart.
Watermelon	Cut open, remove all rind and white lining, slice flesh into chunks, remove seeds.	No treatment required.	Leathery, but not sticky	2	Watermelon will not rehydrate. Dried watermelon is a sweet and chewy snack.

Basic In-Home Fruit Drying Guide (continued)
Basic directions for making fruit leather in the electric dryer:

BASIC FRUIT LEATHER

Fruit leather is made by first making a purée of ripe fruit or fruit combinations, then drying it. You choose whether to leave peeling on as part of the puree. Fruit leather is simple to make and is nutritious, tasty, and fun for kids of all ages. The ingredients are very simple:

1 batch ripe fruit, puréed (after treating for drying)

Pare fruit skins and imperfections, remove seeds, core, and stems. Purée ripe fruit (or fruit combinations) in a blender until smooth. Pour fruit purée onto center of dryer sheets; spread thinly, $1/8" – 1/4"$ with spatula. Use waxed paper inserts for trays or cookie sheets when oven-drying fruits. Keep purée at least $1/2"$ from sides of tray. Dry for 12 hr. or more. When leathery and not sticky, allow to cool fully, roll up in waxed paper or plastic wrap. Leave long or cut into shorter lengths and store in heavy-duty, food-grade, freezer-quality, sealable plastic bags.

Additional Notes:

Quick-Guide 20–2

Basic In-Home Vegetable Drying Guide

Basic **directions for selecting, preparing, preservation treatment, drying in electric dryer, doneness testing, storing, and rehydrating vegetables:**

Step 1: Select quality, ripe, firm, undamaged vegetables and wash carefully.

Step 2: Prepare vegetables for drying. Review suggestions for guidelines.[8]

Step 3: Treat all vegetables by blanching to preserve color and taste and eliminate molds and bacteria. Then spread in single layer on dryer tray.

Step 4: Maintain drying temperatures between 140°–150°F. Turn frequently or change tray positions to dry vegetables evenly w/o scorching.

Step 5: Storage life in months for in-home dried vegetables when stored at 70°F.[9]

Step 6: Rehydrating stored dried vegetables according to chart suggestions.

Step 1	Step 2	Step 3	Step 4	Step 5	Step 6
Vegetable Selection	Preparation for Drying	Blanching Treatment[10] Prior to Drying	Drying & Doneness Test	Shelf Life	Rehydration for Use [11] [12]
Asparagus	Use uppermost 3"–4" of spear.	Blanch 5 min. or steam 15–20 min.	Tough to brittle	2	Barely cover asparagus with hot water. Soak 15–20 min. Stems will remain tough after rehydrating.
Bean—bush varieties	Shell[13] mature beans.	Blanch 15–20 min. or steam until tender.	Shatters when crushed	4	For each C. dried beans use 2 C. cool water. Soak 2½ hr. or until all water is absorbed. Beans must be fully cooked before eating.
Bean—snap	Trim and slice lengthwise, at diagonal, or cut in 1" pieces.	Blanch 6 min. or steam 15–20 min. until tender.	Brittle & crisp, dark green to green-brownish color	4	Use twice the water as beans. Bring to boil, cover, reduce heat, and simmer 30 min. Use as fresh: soups, stews, and casseroles.
Bean—green and yellow	Trim and slice lengthwise, at diagonal, or cut in 1" pieces.	Blanch 6 min. or steam 15–20 min. until tender.	Brittle & crisp, dark green to brownish color	4	Use twice the water as beans. Bring to boil, cover, reduce heat, and simmer 30 min. Use as fresh: soups, stews, and casseroles.
Bean—lima	Shell mature beans.	Blanch 5 min. or steam 10–15 min.	Hard & brittle	4	For each C. beans use 2 C. cool water. Soak until all water is absorbed. Beans must be fully cooked before eating.
Beets	Use small, tender beets, free from wood-like fibers. Trim tops, but leave crown.	Blanch 40–45 min. or steam until cooked through and tender. Cool, trim roots and crown, peel. Cut into 1/8" shoestring strips, ¼" cubes, or thin slices.	Tough to brittle, dark red color	4	Equal hot water and beets. Soak 1 hr. Tender and limp, but good flavor and color.

[8] Check with State Agricultural Extension Division, County Extension Agent, or local food storage experts for particulars about special needs for drying vegetables in your geographic area.

[9] Approximate period before deterioration of food becomes noticeable. After this period, even though the food quality, i.e., flavor, nutritive value, etc., is declining, vegetables will still be edible and useful, as long as they are not contaminated. In-home dried foods stored at 50°F will store for approximately 4 times as long as when kept at 70°F! The key to extending storage of dried foods is to keep them at the lowest possible temperatures. Freezing properly dried and packaged vegetables will extend shelf life many years.

[10] *Blanching treatment*—blanch vegetables in boiling water as suggested to prevent molds & bacteria, discoloration, loss of flavor (souring), and extend shelf life. Some vegetables may be steamed instead.

[11] Dried vegetables can be pulverized into powder in the blender for making baby food, flours, purées, or soup thickeners.

[12] Add salt, sugar, or other seasonings *only after* rehydration is completed.

[13] Try mother's "burlap-bag shelling" method: place mature pea and bean pods in an old pillowcase and tie shut. Insert the pillowcase into a burlap bag or potato sack (we called them "gunnysacks"). Then pop the ensemble into a clothes dryer at low or medium heat. Let them bang around for 25–30 minutes to dry the pods and expel the peas and beans from the pods.

Basic In-Home Vegetable Drying Guide (continued)

Step 1 Vegetable Selection	Step 2 Preparation for Drying	Step 3 Blanching Treatment Prior to Drying	Step 4 Drying & Doneness Test	Step 5 Shelf Life	Step 6 Rehydration for Use
Broccoli	Trim "trees" and cut as if serving fresh. Peel stalk and cut into 1/4" rounds.	Blanch 4-5 min.	Crisp & brittle, dark color	1	Equal hot water and broccoli. Soak 30 min. Tender and limp flowerettes, but good flavor and color. Stem probably tough.
Cabbage	Remove outer leaves. Quarter head, remove core. Shred into shoestring-size strips.	Blanch 4-5 min. or steam 5-6 min. until completely wilted.	Brittle	1	Use 1 1/2 cool water as cabbage. Soak 15–20 min. Flavor good and no strong odor. Best use is sauté or baked. Steam causes dried cabbage to be soggy and off-color.
Carrots	Use crisp, tender carrots, without woody tissue. Peel, trim roots and tops. Cut 1/4" slices or strips.	Blanch 4 min. or steam 8-10 min.	Tough to brittle, deep orange color	6	Equal hot water and carrots. Soak 30 min. Flavor and color good, real carrot texture.
Cauliflower	Remove flowerettes from core. Split stems.	Blanch 3 min. or steam 10 min. until tender.	Crispy, tends to turn brownish	1	Equal hot water and cauliflower. Soak 15–20 min. Flavor and color good, but texture soft.
Celery	Remove leaves and bottom. Cut stalks into small pieces.	Blanch 1 min.	Dry & brittle	2	Equal hot water and celery. Soak 20 min. Flavor and color good, but has soft texture.
Corn—cut	Husk corn. Remove ends and silk.	Blanch 10 min. or steam 20-30 min. to set milk in kernels. Cut off kernels with sharp knife (don't cut into cob) before putting into dryer.	Dry & brittle[14]	4	Use twice water to corn. Bring to boil in saucepan, cover, reduce to low heat and simmer 30 min., adding water if needed. Flavor and texture good as canned.
Corn—whole ear	Use tender, sweet corn. Remove husk and silks.	Blanch whole ear 10 min. or steam for 20-30 min.	Dry & brittle	6	Add corn to boiling pot of water. Cover and reduce to simmer until corn is tender.
Cucumber	Peel and slice thinly.	Blanch 1 min.	Crispy	4	Equal cool water and cucumbers. Soak 1 hr. Color good, but rehydrated cucumbers are tough and tasteless. Use in dip or spread mix.
Eggplant	Peel and cut in 1/2" slices or 1/2" cubes.	Blanch 4-5 min.	Leathery to brittle	2	Equal cool water and eggplant. Soak 30 min. Color darker and texture tough, but tastes like eggplant. Use in soups.
Garlic	Remove outer layers and split buds.	No treatment required.	Brittle	2	Do not rehydrate for cooking. Use dried garlic in recipes. Drop dried bud in vinegar or olive oil, or place in any other food.
Horseradish	Trim off tops and slice thin or grate.	No treatment required.	Brittle	4	Do not rehydrate for cooking. Equal warm water and horseradish 30 min. for use in dip or spread mix.
Kale	Wash and cut into strips.	Blanch 4 min.	Crisp & brittle	2	Steam leaves 5–6 min. Good flavor and tender, but off-color.

[14] For excellent cornmeal, grind dried corn in wheat grinder or blender. Pulverize dried corn for soup thickener.

Basic In-Home Vegetable Drying Guide (continued)

Basic directions for selecting, preparing, preservation treatment, drying in electric dryer, doneness testing, storing, and rehydrating vegetables:

Step 1 Vegetable Selection	Step 2 Preparation for Drying	Step 3 Blanching Treatment[15] Prior to Drying	Step 4 Drying & Doneness Test	Step 5 Shelf Life	Step 6 Rehydration for Use[16] [17]
Leek	Remove outer leaves. Slice, cube, or chop $^1/_8$"–$^1/_4$".	No treatment required.	Brittle	4	Equal hot water and leeks. Soak 15 min. Has appearance and taste of steamed leeks.
Mushroom	Leave buttons whole, slice larger sizes. Use stems if tender.	Blanch 3 min.	Leathery to brittle	2	No rehydration needed. Texture and flavor good. Use in casseroles, soups, and stews.
Okra	Cut off tips and slice $^1/_2$".	Blanch 5 min.	Leathery to brittle	4	Use twice the water as okra. Bring to boil, cover, reduce heat and simmer 30 min.
Onions	Remove outer leaves. Slice, cube, or chop $^1/_8$"–$^1/_4$".	None required.	Brittle	4	Equal hot water and onions. Soak 15 min. Appearance and taste of steamed onions.
Parsnip	Use small, tender parsnips, free from woody fibers. Trim tops, peel but leave crown.	Blanch 5 min. or steam until cooked through and tender. Allow to cool, then trim roots and crown. Cut into $^1/_8$" shoestring strips, $^1/_4$" cubes or thin slices.	Tough to brittle	4	Equal hot water and parsnips. Soak 1 hr. Tender and limp, but good flavor and color.
Pea—green	Shell young, tender sweet peas.	Blanch 3 min. or steam 10 min.	Shatters when crushed	4	Use twice the water as peas. Bring to boil, cover, reduce heat and simmer 30 min. Dried peas are an excellent snack.
Pepper—all "hot" types	Use only mature peppers. Dry whole, diced, slivers, halves, or quarters.	No treatment required.	Pliable to brittle, depending on type	8	Mince, crush, or turn to powder in blender for use as seasoning in recipes.
Pepper—all sweet types	Cut and remove seeds. Cut peppers in $^1/_8$"–$^1/_4$"–$^1/_2$" strips, rings, or diced.	Scald in boiling water 3–5 minutes. Spread 2 layers deep.	Pliable to brittle	8	Equal hot water and sweet peppers. Soak 15–20 min. Flavor and color like steamed. Soft flesh and tough skin.
Potato	Peel and cut into shoestring strips $^1/_8$"–$^1/_4$" or slice $^1/_8$" thick.	Rinse first in cold water. Blanch 5 min. Soak in lemon water ($^1/_4$ C. lemon juice and 1 qt. cold water) for 45–60 min. to prevent turning black during drying process.	Brittle	4	Equal cold water and potatoes. Soak 25–30 min. Texture and flavor of raw potato. Use for mashed potatoes, in soups, and stews.
Pumpkin	Cut and remove seeds. Slice into 1" strips. Peel, then slice strips crosswise $^1/_4$".	Blanch 3 min. or steam 8–13 minutes until slightly soft.	Tough to brittle	1	Equal water and pumpkin. Bring to boil in covered pot. Reduce heat to low, simmer 10 min. Color good, slightly mushy texture.
Rhubarb	Wash and cut into 1" strips.	Blanch 3 min.	Tough to brittle	4	Equal hot water and rhubarb. Soak 15–20 min. Flavor and color good, soft texture.

[15] *Blanching treatment*—blanch vegetables in boiling water as suggested to prevent molds & bacteria, discoloration, loss of flavor (souring), and extend shelf life. Some vegetables may be steamed instead.

[16] Dried vegetables can be pulverized into powder in the blender for making baby food, flours, purées, or soup thickeners.

[17] Add salt, sugar, or other seasonings *only after* rehydration is completed.

Basic In-Home Vegetable Drying Guide (continued)

Basic directions for selecting, preparing, preservation treatment, drying in electric dryer, doneness testing, storing, and rehydrating vegetables:

Step 1 Vegetable Selection	Step 2 Preparation for Drying	Step 3 Blanching Treatment[18] Prior to Drying	Step 4 Drying & Doneness Test	Step 5 Shelf Life	Step 6 Rehydration for Use[19][20]
Spinach and other leafy greens	Choose young, tender leaves. Wash again. Cut into $1/4$–$1/2$" strips.	Blanch 2 min. or steam 4-5 min. until thoroughly wilted. Spread several layers deep.	Brittle	2	Steam leaves 5-6 min. Good flavor and tender, but off-color.
Squash—Hubbard	Cut and remove seeds. Slice into 1" strips. Peel, then slice crosswise $1/4$" thick.	Blanch 3 min. or steam 8-13 min. until slightly soft.	Tough to brittle	1	Equal water and Hubbard squash. Bring to boil in pot. Cover; reduce heat to low, simmer 10 min. Off-color and soft texture.
Sweet potato	Wash and peel. Slice $1/4$" thick or dice.	Blanch 3 min.	Tough to brittle	1	Equal cold water and potatoes. Soak 25-30 min. Texture and flavor of raw potato.
Swiss chard	Wash and cut into strips.	Blanch 2 min.	Crisp & brittle	2	Steam leaves 5-6 min. Good flavor and tender, but off-color.
Tomato—for stewing	Choose red-colored tomatoes. Dip in boiling water to remove skins. Chill in cold water and peel. Cut into $1/2$–$3/4$" sections.	Blanch 3 min.	Leathery & pliable	3	Equal hot water and tomatoes. Soak 30 min. Flavor of tomato paste. Flesh is mushy and skin is tough. Color is darker. Use in soups, stews, casseroles and sauces.
Tomato—for sun-dried	Select small paste tomatoes. Slice in half lengthwise or cut larger ones into quarters.	None required, but watch carefully at end of drying cycle to prevent scorching.	Leathery & pliable	6	Equal hot water, vinegar, and tomatoes. Soak until chewy. Drain and cover with vinegar/olive oil, marinate in fridge 24 hr. Add to Mexican and Italian tomato sauces.
Turnips	Trim tops and roots. Slice into $1/4$" rounds.	Blanch 5 min.	Tough to brittle	2	Equal hot water and turnips. Soak for 1 hr. Good flavor and color, texture soft and limp.
Zucchini & summer squash	Leave peeling on and slice into thin slices across.	Blanch 3 min.	Pliable to brittle, depending on variety	1	Equal hot water and zucchini or summer squash. Soak 15 min., and then steam 8 min. Good flavor and color, but limp and mushy.

[18] *Blanching treatment*—blanch vegetables in boiling water as suggested to prevent molds & bacteria, discoloration, loss of flavor (souring), and extend shelf life. Some vegetables may be steamed instead.

[19] Dried vegetables can be pulverized into powder in the blender for making baby food, flours, purées, or soup thickeners.

[20] Add salt, sugar, or other seasonings *only after rehydration is completed.*

Basic In-Home Vegetable Drying Guide (continued)

Step 1	Step 2	Step 3	Step 4	Step 5	Step 6
Vegetable Selection	Preparation for Drying	Blanching Treatment Prior to Drying	Drying & Done-ness Test	Shelf Life	Rehydration for Use
	BASIC SUNSTYLE DRIED TOMATOES				
	3 lb. tomatoes of choice (plum, sauce, or medium salad) 2 tsp. salt	Wash and dry tomatoes carefully. Cut tomatoes lengthwise, across or in half. Place cut side up on dryer trays, 1 layer deep. Sprinkle salt evenly on tomatoes. Turn every 2–3 hr. As tomatoes near fully dried stage, watch carefully to prevent scorching. Cool thoroughly. Store dry in freezer-quality, heavy-duty, food-grade, sealable plastic bags, or place in jars with oil and garlic. Store in cool, dry and dark location for up to 3 months or refrigerate for 9-12 months.			
			GOURMET SUNSTYLE DRIED TOMATOES		
			2–4 C. olive oil		3–6 garlic buds
			Dry as directed in *Basic SunStyle Dried Tomatoes* recipe. Stuff slices of dried tomatoes into clean storage jars with tight-fitting lids. Peel and cut garlic bucs in half, drop into jars. Pour olive oil into jars to cover dried tomatoes, tighter lids. Leave at room temperature 1-2 weeks for blending of flavors. Either store in cool, dry, and dark location for 2-3 months or put in refrigerator for up to 12 months. For gifts, use decorative jars with rubber gaskets.		

Hunting is a holy occupation.
Old Navajo Indian saying

Chapter 21

Basics of Preparing Game Meats, Fish, and Fowl

My love of country cooking and fixin' game meats and fowl was instilled in me by my Mother's parents. My Granddaddy Pace owned a *gentleman's farm* not too far outside the city limits of Greensboro NC. To get there from downtown, you'd drive northward on Elm Street until it dead-ended at a field, take a hard right turn, drive a few blocks through McAdoo Heights, a small mill village town at a crossroads—with a stop light in the center of town. At the light, then you'd turn left onto Church Street, and go down the steep hill. Then it was a short drive to the city limits.

You could always tell when you were near the line of demarcation where the country started: there was a classic brick church on the NE corner at the turnoff to White Oak, a mill town where all the large Revolution and Cone denim and corduroy mills were located. At that point, the road became Church Street Extension. One of the county schools was on the West side of the road, facing a big church on the East. After passing those landmarks, it was all country! Or so it seemed to a young'un like me!

Down the hill on the left was the large lake which was the city's water reservoir. Before long, Granddaddy's Gulf *fillin'* station would appear to view on the right as the car climbed the hill towards Hamtown and Snoufferville, where we lived. We were just a little farther up the road on the left. After the station, located in the SW corner of the Pace farm was the farmhouse.

Granddaddy was proud to be the owner of the first filling station in the north county! I still remember the oiled floors in the station (a result of all the oil changes!) and the icebox—real ice—chilling down the Nehi grape and orange sodas. Of course, there were Cokes and RC Colas, too! Don't forget the Moon Pies!

Grandmother suspected there were some other libations there also, but she didn't go into the station. She was not happy it was a *jot'em* down store for Granddaddy's friends—but he always said he could afford it. It goes without saying that he was a loved and respected businessman in the community and over at the local church.

My Granddaddy was also a very accomplished hunter, because there was always some wild game hanging on a hook on the beam of the screened-in back porch or out in the smokehouse.

My Grandmother knew how to cook wild as well as domestic animals—she was renowned far and wide for her fabulous Brunswick stew and Southern-style pork barbecue!

Hopefully, in this chapter, I can share some interesting ideas and recipes for using small and large game meats, fish, and game birds and waterfowl. If you're not presently a hunter or fisher, this information probably won't be particularly appealing to you.

However, in the future, there may be a need to hunt—or maybe an opportunity for you to go out into the field. If you're already a hunter or wild game *aficionado*, you've probably devised or concocted your own favorite dishes for your prize catch(es).

We're not dealing here with the subjects of field dressing, skinning, butchering, or preserving big game, fowl, or fish trophies brought home from the hunting or fishing expedition. There are some references at the end of this section for references to books about those skills.[i] This section provides the basics of preparing some tasty meals from your hunting and fishing prowess.

HANDLING GAME MEATS, FISH, & FOWL

Handling instructions for game, fish, and fowl are not complicated. Caution should be exercised when cutting animal flesh to prevent cutting:

1. yourself, and
2. the animal's internal organs which could contaminate the edible meat.

Always work with cold—almost frozen—meat, fish, or fowl. There are several important reasons:

- handling is easier
- odor is practically non-existent
- cutting is easier
- not as *sticky* as when warm
- reduces spoilage
- work surfaces are easier to keep clean
- reduces contamination
- reduces exposure to food bacteria

STORAGE FOR GAME MEATS, FISH, & FOWL

Properly wrapped and stored, wild game meat will keep fresh in the refrigerator for a few days and in the freezer for several months, depending on cut and how well it's prepared for freezing.

Re-wrap or over-wrap and seal the freshly dressed meat in foil, freezer paper or heavy plastic wrap—just be certain to use a moisture-proof and vapor-proof material for both short- or long-term freezer storage. Label all freezer packages, describing contents, weight, or number of servings or pieces and show the date each went into the freezer.

Keep your larder of frozen game meats, fish, and fowl tasting its best by using the oldest packages first.

Storage Periods

The following chart indicates the length of time game meats may be stored in cold storage:

Chart 21–1
Storage Periods for Game Meats

Game Meats Description	Refrigerated* (days)		Frozen (months[1])	
	Raw	Cooked	Raw	Cooked
Venison leftovers—cooked meat	—	4 - 5	—	3 - 4
Venison - ground meat or sausage	1 - 2	4-6	3-4	4-6
Organs - brains, heart, kidney, liver & sweetbreads	1 - 2	3 - 4	3 - 4	4 - 5
Tongue / head	6 - 7	7 - 10	3 - 4	4 - 6
Wild pig – cuts of meat	3 - 5	5 - 7	4 - 6	6 - 9
– ground meat	1 - 2	2 - 5	1 - 2	2 - 4
– sausage	2 - 3	3 - 7	1 - 2	2 - 5
Rabbit, squirrel & other small game	1 - 2	2 - 5	3 - 6	9 - 12

Basic Brine Pickling

There are several methods for preserving game meats, fish, and fowl. Pickling is one of the basic methods of preservation of meats, dating from the earliest days of food preservation.

Simply stated, the food item to be preserved is immersed in a container of salty water and left there until it absorbs all the saline solution it can. It was a particularly effective method for preserving wild game.

It continues an effective basic method when resources are limited and portability is important. It's often a better method than jerking meat, because the brine pickling method allows for large pieces to be preserved, instead of small strips. Most of the salty taste can be removed by cooking.

Chart 21–2
Brine Pickling & Curing Times

Cut	Days in Mixture
Ham	21 - 24
Shoulder	14 - 16
Bacon	8 - 10

The amount of time meat is left in the mixture depends on size(s) and amount(s) of cut(s). When meat is removed from the pickling solution, it must be thoroughly dried, then wrapped in cotton sacking or cheesecloth. Meat is then hung on a wire to protect it from predators while it's draining,

---

[1] Storage periods in this chart are based on 36°F-40°F. temperature storage. Most refrigerators are manufactured to maintain this temperature range. I've stored these items much longer, but there were resultant losses in taste and texture—not to mention the freezer burn!

curing, and during storage. The brine mixture and **Chart 21–2** will guide you in successful brine pickling.

BASIC BRINE PICKLING MIXTURE

4 quarts water	3 C. coarse salt
$2^3/_4$ C. brown sugar	1 bay leaf
1 sprig thyme	12 juniper berries, crushed
12 peppercorns, crushed	

Boil ingredients together in large pot for 5 min. Skim scum from top and discard. Allow brine mixture to cool before using. Place cuts of wild boar, javelina, or any pork meat—actually, any cut of meat—in cooled pickle mixture according to **Chart 21–2**. Take meat from mixture, thoroughly dry, then wrap in muslin, gauze, or cotton cloth bag and store in safe place away from critters.

Corning Meat for Storage

Any tough cut of meat can be corned, whether game meats or birds; beef chuck, flank or brisket; pork Boston shoulder, picnic shoulder, leg or blade end; lamb shoulder or leg. Wild fowl, such as duck or goose can be corned, also. However, birds may only be corned when cut into serving pieces.

The following recipe utilizes the *Basic Brine Pickling Mixture* recipe above to corn meats:

BASIC CORNED MEAT

5 lb. meat or poultry	4 quarts *Basic Brine Pickling*
1 C. coarse salt	*Mixture*

Slice meat 1" thick, or cut poultry into serving pieces. Rub the meat or poultry with the salt. Place a layer of salt in a large glass or ceramic dish.

Lay meat on salt, then alternate layers of meat and salt until all meat is covered with a layer of salt. Place cover on dish, and place in refrigerator for 24 hr.

Rinse meat under cold running water to remove remaining salt and coagulated blood and juices, and then place in a clean glass or ceramic dish.

Pour *Basic Brine Pickling Mixture* through a strainer lined with cheesecloth to remove scum and particles, covering meat with the brine.

Place heavy object on meat to keep it under brine, then cover dish. Place in refrigerator for 24 hr. For the next 10 - 12 days, remove scum from top of brine solution.

Remove from *Basic Brine Pickling Mixture* and wrap or place in plastic bags for refrigerating or freezing.

STORAGE FOR GAME BIRDS & POULTRY

Wild fowl, as well as chicken and turkey, are good meats to store in a food storage program. There are some restraints, however—the major one being their relatively short storage time, even when frozen. The gamy taste in wild game results from the aging process, so all game birds and meats taste better when fresh. Long-term storage accents their gaminess.

Storage Periods

Game birds and poultry may be stored for short periods of time. The following chart outlines the storage capability of various birds, properly moisture/vapor-wrapped and frozen.

Chart 21–3
Maximum Storage Periods for Game Birds & Poultry @ 0°

Poultry / Fowl	Refrigerated		Frozen	
	Raw	Cooked	Raw	Cooked
Chicken & other yard & game birds	1-3 days	2 - 4 days	12 mo. (whole) 6 - 9 mo. (*pieces*)	4 - 6 mo. 2 - 4 mo.
Ducks	1-2 days	2 - 4 days	6 mo. (whole)	4 - 6 mo.
Goose/gosling	1 - 2 days	2 - 4 days	6 mo. (whole)	4 - 6 mo.
Turkey	1 - 4 days	2 - 6 days	6 - 7 mo. (whole) 2 - 3 mo. (*pieces*)	4 - 6 mo. 2 - 4 mo.

Storage of Ground Turkey/Wild Fowl Sausage

To store turkey sausage for later use, there are two options:

1. **Uncooked storage:** form patties, wrap individually without pre-cooking, and re-frigerate (no more than 3 days) or freeze (not more than 12 months) until needed.

2. **Pre-cooked storage:** for a low-fat breakfast, *brown-and-serve* sausage treat, shape *Basic Turkey Sausage* (see recipe in **Wild Fowl** section) into patties or links, wrap separately in foil, then poach in boiling water for approximately 15 minutes. Refrigerate sausage patties or links for no more than 3 days. Use frozen patties and links within 5 months.

GAME MEATS, FISH, AND FOWL PREPARATION

If you can cook a turkey, fry a piece of chicken, cook a hamburger or steak, or bake a fish, you are ready to cook game meats, wild-caught fish, or fowl. The following table indicates some of the temperatures and baking times for selected game.

When pan-frying, grilling, boiling or preparing using other methods, adjust the time and temperature to fully cook the flesh. Wild animals aren't inspected for disease! **Always cook wild animals, birds, and fish adequately!**

Chart 21–4
Baking Times and Temperature Chart

Game, Fish, or Fowl	Oven Temperature	Minutes per Pound
Big Game		
Buffalo	Broil only	Cook to desired doneness
Deer	300°- 325° F	15 - 20
Elk & Moose	325° - 350° F	30 - 35
Fish		
All Fish	325°- 350° F	20
Game Birds		
Ducks	350° F	15
Geese	325°- 350° F	25 - 30
Partridge	350° F	15 - 20
Pheasant	325° F	15
Pigeon	350° F	15 - 20
Quail	350° F	15
Small Game		
Groundhog	300°- 325° F	25
Porcupine	300°- 325° F	25
Squirrel	325° F	20 - 25
Raccoon	300° F	15
Rabbit	300°- 325° F	20

VENISON

Tip:
To help dispel strong odor of wild game when cooking indoors, simmer a pan with a small amount of white vinegar on another burner.

Venison is by far the favorite American big game meat[2]. Venison includes any game from the deer family. The most commonly eaten venison in the US is deer. Elk is the second most popular game meat, and moose follows as a distant third choice. Here are some important points to remember about preparing venison for use and storage:

- Venison from a freshly killed animal should age in a cool place for 1 to 2 weeks, according to your own particular taste.
- For the best flavor from venison, trim off all body fat before aging—it's the aging fat that causes the rancid flavor.
- Venison can be larded just prior to cooking with salt pork, bacon, or beef suet to provide cooking grease.
- Venison's wild game taste can be made more mellow (*sweetened*) while cooking by using butter or beef suet instead of salt pork or bacon, utilizing lower oven, grill or pan temperature to compensate for it.
- Cook venison *medium rare.* when using butter—prevents burning both the meat and the butter.
- Venison steaks, chops and loin cuts, when cut from young animals properly dressed and aged, are especially good either broiled or grilled outdoors.
- Overcooking any deer family meat makes the meat *dry*. Venison has very low fat (as low as 4%) when compared to similar beef cuts (up to 25%). *Overcooking causes drying and toughening of all meats.*
- Salt is not necessary *before* cooking—season with salt and pepper *after* cooking, unless the recipe specifies seasoning prior to cooking.
- Marinate in milk or buttermilk, salt brine, vinegar, solution of water and baking soda or wine to remove the wild or *gamey* taste and to render venison cuts more tender.

Additional Notes

---

[2]Captain James A. Smith's **DRESS 'EM OUT!** gives step-by-step explanations about the skill of skinning and butchering field birds and animals—from rabbits to big game to wild turkeys! Another fine book is **VENISON: FROM FIELD TO TABLE**, by John Weiss. This book also has many recipes for preparing the deer family meats. Additional titles in **Preparedness Library, *Chapter 27, Sec. 2A & 2G; Sec. 3C & 3M*.**

RECIPES FOR VENISON

Directions for Making Basic Venison Jerky

In today's world, neither a smokehouse nor a teepee is needed to make jerky, and you certainly don't need smoke, either! These instructions can be used as given or modified to make jerky from either venison or beef. Just follow the basic procedures at the outset, then experiment a little as you gain experience. Soon, you'll produce *world-class* jerky—and other game meat delights.

Jerky is approximately 75% protein and provides good nourishment. To eat, cut or bite off a piece, and chew like chewing gum. Jerky actually improves in flavor as it's chewed.

- ❑ To produce 1 lb. of beef jerky, take 4 lbs. of lean meat with a minimum amount of connective tissue and fat. The best cuts are from the round or eye of the loin. Trim fat to avoid greasy-tasting jerky.

- ❑ Slice across the grain in thin strips—approximately 1/8". Slicing with the grain requires a wider strip, approximately ½" - 1", and the jerky is not as tender. You may want to use tenderizer on the venison. Be sure to follow the instructions on the container.

- ❑ Soak each slice of venison in your favorite marinade, sauce, or jerky seasoning for 1 - 8 hours or overnight.

- ❑ Then remove excess liquid by laying on cloth or paper towels to drain.

- ❑ Sprinkle meat slices with salt, pepper, and/or sugar to taste. Don't over-season with salt, since jerky tastes saltier and stronger when dried.

- ❑ Place meat in smokehouse, dehydrator, or oven. Heat to 150° - 175°F until meat slices become more *tough* than *brittle*.

- ❑ The drying process cannot be hurried. Drying is greatly dependent on the thickness of the slices, the humidity level during drying, ambient temperature inside the drying device, etc.

- ❑ Allow dried jerky to cool, then place in freezer-grade, self-sealing type, heavy-duty plastic bags, plastic containers with airtight closures or lids, or glass jars with tight-fitting lids. Always store in a cool, dry place.

- ❑ Home-jerked meat must be refrigerated to protect from spoilage. It also extends the shelf life. Freezing also greatly extends shelf life of jerked meats.

The following *jerky recipe* is for any meat you'd like to *jerk*. These are basic instructions for jerking and using beef as the meat of choice.

The jerking method described above and the following recipe may also be used for making venison jerky or any other type of meat, poultry, or fish.

Non-hunters need not despair—this recipe is for you, too!

BASIC BEEF JERKY

3 lb. lean beef roast (or other meat, poultry or fish)

Marinade Ingredients:

1 T. salt	$^1/_3$ C. Worcestershire sauce
$^1/_4$ C. soy sauce	$^1/_2$ tsp. ground pepper

Cut meat into thin strips, approximately $^1/_4$" thick, and place in a baking dish. Mix marinade ingredients and pour over strips. Marinate approx. 24 hr. in refrigerator, turning once or twice. Drain. Place cake cooling racks over cookie sheet and cover with paper toweling. Place strips on rack and let dry in 150°F oven until quite dry and tough, about 3 - 4 days.

Curing period while jerking may be interrupted, since the drying time is not critical—only the end result matters.

BASIC VENISON ROAST

3 - 4 lb. venison roast	$^1/_2$ envelope dry onion soup

Place roast on large piece of heavy-duty foil. Sprinkle dry onion soup on meat. Seal foil tightly on all edges. Bake at 325°F in shallow roasting pan approximately 45 min. per lb.

A moist roast will result because foil seals in juices. Thicken juices to make gravy.

VENISON ROAST à la ROCK SALT (French Style)

2 - 3 lb. venison roast	fresh-ground black pepper
6 - 8 fresh garlic buds	3 - 4 lb. rock salt (ice cream salt)

Preheat oven to 450°F. Trim all fat from roast. Insert garlic buds into top of roast with small incisions about 3" apart. Dust with black pepper. Sear roast on all sides in a dry hot skillet. Immediately place roast in a large roasting pan on a bed of rock salt. Cover roast with remaining salt, using warm water to hold the salt in place on sides, if necessary. Place roast in oven. Cook for approximately 15 min. per lb. Remove roast from oven when done to your taste. Break away hardened rock salt and brush off any remaining salt crystals. Serve hot. *Yield: 4 - 6 servings.*

BASIC VENISON STEW

$2^1/_2$ lb. cubed venison	1 bunch shallots, chopped
$^1/_4$ lb. butter	3 T. flour
2 stalks celery, chopped fine	2 C. water
1 med. bell pepper, diced	bay leaf
$^1/_2$ lb. carrots, diced	thyme
1 large onion, chopped	salt & pepper

Sauté venison cubes in butter in heavy pot until browned. Pour off drippings. Add celery, bell pepper, carrots, onions, and shallots and lightly sauté. Make a paste from hot drippings and flour. Add this to pot, then add water; mix thoroughly. Add seasonings to taste. Cook at medium heat until tender, about 3 hr., adding water as necessary. *Yield: 6 servings.*

BASIC CHICKEN-FRIED VENISON STEAK

Venison steaks	$^1/_4$ lb. saltine cracker crumbs
1 egg, beaten	$^1/_4$ lb. butter

Cut steaks approximately $^1/_4$" thick. Dip in beaten egg, then coat with cracker crumbs. Fry in butter until brown. *Don't overcook!*

BASIC PAN-FRIED VENISON STEAK

Venison steaks (or chops)	salt & pepper
$^1/_4$ lb. melted butter	fresh-ground black pepper

Dip steaks into melted butter, season with salt and pepper. Sauté to medium-rare. Brush with melted butter and add fresh-ground black pepper.

TERIYAKI VENISON STEAK

Venison steaks

Teriyaki marinade ingredients:

$^1/_4$ C. soy sauce	1 clove garlic, crushed
1 tsp. ground ginger	1 tsp. sugar

Mix marinade ingredients. Trim all fat from steaks. Marinade several hours. Broil or barbecue steaks to desired doneness. *Don't overcook!*

BASIC MARINATED VENISON ROAST

3 - 4 lb. venison roast

Basic Marinade ingredients:

$^1/_2$ C. red wine vinegar	6 whole cloves
1 C. water	12 peppercorns
1 med. onion, minced	$^1/_2$ tsp. caraway seeds
1 clove garlic, crushed	$^1/_2$ T. salt
$^1/_2$ C. celery tops, chopped fine	1 carrot, grated
1 T. honey	2 bay leaves

Mix all ingredients of *Basic Marinade* in bowl. Marinate roast 24 - 48 hr. Remove from *Basic Marinade*. Roast meat in 375° F oven until done as desired. Baste with marinade and drippings.

BASIC CREAMED VENISON

$^1/_4$ C. shortening	1 bay leaf
2 lb. venison, cubed	2 C. water
1 clove garlic	4 T. butter
$^1/_2$ C. minced onion	4 T. flour
1 C. diced celery	1 C. sour cream
1 C. diced carrots	1 tsp. salt
pepper to taste	1 can currant jelly
noodles of choice for 6, cooked *al denté*	

Melt shortening in heavy frying pan. Add meat and garlic, brown on all sides. Arrange meat in baking dish. Place vegetables in frying pan with fat; cook for 2 min. Add salt, pepper, bay leaf and water; pour over meat.

Bake in 250°F oven until meat is tender. Melt butter in frying pan; stir in flour. Add meat broth, then boil until thick. Remove from heat. Add sour cream and more salt, if needed.
Pour *Basic Creamed Venison* over meat and vegetables. Serve with noodles and currant jelly.

Yield: 6 servings.

VENISON HAWAIIAN

3 lb. venison (approx.)	1 #303 can pineapple chunks
1 C. water	1 tsp. salt
2 or 3 green bell peppers, cut up	Chinese noodles or rice
Basic Hawaiian Sauce (see below)	

Cut meat into 1" cubes. Brown meat cubes on all sides. Add water and salt, simmer gently until meat is tender, approximately 1 hr. Keep adding water as it evaporates. Clean seeds from green peppers and cut into 1" squares. Add salt to water, boil green peppers for 5 min. in salty boiling water and drain. Add pepper squares and pineapple chunks to browned meat.

Basic Hawaiian Sauce:

4 T. cornstarch	$^1/_4$ C. vinegar
$1^1/_4$ C. pineapple juice (or orange juice)	4 T. soy sauce
$^1/_2$ C. sugar	

Mix cornstarch with a little cool liquid so it doesn't lump, then combine all ingredients and cook until sauce is thick and clear. Pour *Basic Hawaiian Sauce* over meat mixture, simmer 5 min. Serve over Chinese noodles or cooked rice.

Yield: 6 servings.

WILD PIG

Feral Hogs (razorbacks and wild boar) and javelinas (collared peccary, musk hog, desert hog, and wild pig) are especially rich and delicious meats and are easy to prepare—cook them the same way you cook pork. They are especially delicious when prepared Texas-style—barbecued over an open fire, or, my personal favorite, method, Hawaiian-style—cooked right in the ground!

RECIPES FOR WILD PIG

BASIC BARBECUED WILD PIG

any size pig / various cuts	1 large onion, sliced
garlic salt	1 btl. barbecue sauce of choice

Place trimmed meat in roasting pan, sprinkle with garlic salt, use large fork to penetrate meat. Break onion slices into rings, spread rings over meat. Bake meat wrapped tightly in aluminum foil in 350°F oven for 1 hr. Remove from oven and cover with sauce, recover with aluminum foil tent. Cook at 300°F for $1^1/_2$ - 2 hours until done, checking occasionally until meat is separating from bones. Baste with sauce each time inspection is made. *Yield: approximately $^1/_2$ lb. / serving.*

BASIC BOILED PICKLED PIG

5 lb. wild boar, javelina or pork meat / cuts	4 quarts brine (see *Basic Brine Mixture* recipe)

Place meat or cuts in boiling *Basic Brine Mixture* until meat turns gray at the bone or center of the cut. Skim top fatty materials from top of boiling mixture and discard. Serve hot with mixed vegetables and cornbread for a country meal that's delicious!

Salt Pickle for Preserving Domestic Pork

Even though the friendly barnyard porker is not a game meat, this bit of information is best located here. My Grandmother Pace left me this hand-written instruction for curing pork:

GRANDMOTHER PACE'S DOMESTIC PIG PICKLE

10 gal. water	20 lb. salt
1 lb. saltpeter	8 lb. brown sugar

Place cuts of meat in boiling mixture; cook until cooked throughout, skimming off the scum as necessary. Once cooking is completed, leave in brine to cure. See **Chart 2** for soaking times.

SMALL GAME

There are still a few who enjoy hunting squirrels and rabbits, even though the sport seems to have lost some of its appeal. Here are a couple of recipes to help make the best of the hunt.

Note:

Small game can be substituted in almost any recipe calling for chicken!

RECIPES FOR SMALL GAME

FRIED SQUIRREL OR RABBIT

rabbit or squirrel	$\frac{1}{2}$ C. melted butter
$\frac{1}{4}$ C. salt	2 C. crushed corn flakes
1 qt. water	$\frac{1}{2}$ C. shortening

Soak dressed and cut-up game into serving pieces. Soak in salt and water solution 2 - 6 hr. Drain thoroughly. Dip pieces in melted butter, then roll in crushed corn flakes.

Brown in hot fat, then reduce heat. Cook at low temperature for approximately 1 hr. (If game is older, add $\frac{1}{2}$ C. water to pan, cover and cook slowly an additional $\frac{1}{2}$ hr.)

Salt and pepper to taste.

Yield: 3 - 4 servings.

RABBIT STUFFED PEPPERS

1 - 2 lb. rabbit, dressed and cooked	$\frac{1}{2}$ lb. uncooked bacon
1 tsp. oregano	$1\frac{1}{2}$ tsp. salt
$\frac{1}{2}$ tsp. black pepper (freshly ground)	$\frac{2}{3}$ C. cooked rice
$\frac{1}{2}$ can condensed tomato soup	3 small onions, chopped
4 green bell peppers (halved, seeded and blanched)	1 T. lemon juice
parmesan cheese (grated)	catsup

Remove rabbit meat from bones; grind with bacon. Combine rice with ground meat, tomato soup, onions, lemon juice, and seasonings, mixing well. Place pepper halves in baking dish; stuff with filling. Top each with catsup and Parmesan cheese.

Note: if rabbit is smaller, adjust recipe proportionately.

Bake, covered, at 375°F for 35 min. Uncover, then bake for 10 min. longer.

Yield: 6 - 8 servings.

FISH

Almost everyone likes to fish, and almost everyone loves to eat freshly-caught and cooked fish. Here are a couple of recipes for fish you'll probably like. Almost all fish can be cooked with the same seasonings—the family differences will be the most distinguishing characteristic for the taste.

RECIPES FOR FISH

BASIC FOIL-BAKED FISH

fresh fish	$^1/_2$ medium onion per fish
salt and pepper to taste	lemon wedges (if preferred)

Split fish belly, gill to tail, and eviscerate. Rinse fish interior in running water. Salt and pepper interior, laying in sliced or quartered onion.

Wrap in foil and place in coals. Cook only until flesh is white throughout. (May be baked 30-40 minutes at 325°F.)

Serve immediately. There's no need to remove scales or bones—the flesh will fall away from both when cooked properly. Serve with fresh lemon slices or quarters.

BASIC SMOKED FISH

3-4 large fish	2 C. salt

Brine Mixture:

2 C. salt	8 qt. water

Remove fish heads, eviscerate and clean thoroughly. Soak 6-8 hr. in brine mixture. Drain, then rinse in fresh cold water. Drain again, removing all excess moisture.

Put 2 C. dry salt in shallow pan, dip fish, allowing fish to pick up as much salt as will cling to the skin and body cavity. Pack in deep pan, sprinkling remaining salt in pan between layers and over fish. Leave in salt for 6 hr. if split, 12 hr. if whole. Remove from salt, rinse and drain before smoking and drying. Dry in sun or smoker until flesh shrinks and becomes brittle.

MARINATED FISH FILLETS

marinade of choice	butter or margarine
1 - 2 lb. fish fillets or whole (cleaned)	fresh lemon or lemon juice

Marinate fillets for 30 min. In cast iron skillet, melt 2 tsp. butter. Place fish in hot skillet, cooking each side approximately 5 min. Baste with remaining marinade, applying some to each side while cooking and after turning.

Dash juice of lemon on cooked fish when serving.

MARINATED FISH STEAKS

marinade of choice	butter or margarine
1-2 lb. fish steaks	fresh lemon or lemon juice

Marinate fish steaks for 15 - 20 min. Place in baking pan, putting a pat of butter and some of the lemon juice on the top of each fish steak.

Bake at 350°F for approximately 7 - 10 min. each side. Midway through baking time, turn steaks, basting with remaining marinade. Sprinkle lemon juice on fish when serving.

Tip:
Soak fresh or frozen fish in milk or buttermilk to improve the taste.

Note:
Discard milk without using it in other foods or recipes.

GAME BIRDS, WILD FOWL, AND POULTRY

Game birds and wild fowl provide a welcome addition to the basic lifestyle, with a lean and tender source of animal protein. Poultry is a mainstay in many homes, and their wild cousins provide sport as well as food. It may be difficult and expensive to hunt wild fowl, small or large, in some areas of the country. However, wild fowl are available from farm-raised fowl sources in most large grocery stores.

The biggest advantage to farm-raised fowl is the convenience and year-round availability. Farm-raised game is usually more tender, has a more delicate and less gamy flavor, but may have a little more fat than wild game birds.

I suggest you question the farm operator about the diet of the game—it greatly affects the flavor of the meat. There also may be limited breeds of farm-raised birds available, depending on local demand. The most popular fowl breeds are pheasant, quail, woodcock, dove, pigeon, duck, goose, partridge, and chukkar.

Game birds are very low in fat—approximately 5% to 7%—so basting with butter, stock, fruit juices, or your favorite alcoholic beverage will add moisture to the cooking pot or pan. Marinating prior to cooking with one of the bastes previously mentioned will help reduce the gamy taste, as well as tenderize the meat of wild fowl or game.

Using strong-flavored herbs and spices, such as garlic, peppers, rosemary, sage, and thyme will make the flesh more savory to the taste. The same is true of strong-flavored vegetables, such as onions and leeks, for example. Let your imagination run a little "wild" to achieve the best taste for your wild game birds.

Basic Cooking Methods for Poultry & Wild Fowl

Both poultry and wild fowl are considered *birds,* so this section is designed to help with the basics of preparing them for the table. *Follow special preparation instructions in* **Chart 21-5** *for cooking ducks and geese. Stuffing is best made in its own pan—some of the fats from wild birds can be both greasy and slick.*

Poultry & Wild Fowl Cooking Tips

There are some things to remember when cooking game birds and fowl. Remember these tips when cooking poultry and wild fowl:

- The slower and longer game birds are cooked, the better the taste.
- When a wild bird is properly cooked, the flesh will practically fall off the bones.
- Most game birds taste better when cooked with fruits, such as pineapple chunks or slices, orange sections or slices, apples, lemon and lime slices, cherries, and strawberries! Be imaginative!
- When roasting in the oven or in a covered pan, both carrots and potatoes will absorb excess fat. Discard them to avoid ingesting the fats!

•Basic Steaming

Place bird on a rack or in a steaming basket in a pot with at least 1" of boiling water and a tight-fitting lid. Check pot to assure water does not boil away, adding water as necessary. Keep poultry above water level; cover pot and steam whole birds for 1 hour and cut-up birds for 45 minutes.

•Basic Roasting

When oven-roasting poultry, always place bird breast-up in a shallow roasting pan. Rub the body cavity with salt, butter, and herbs—sage, basil, thyme—and add cut-up pieces of celery, onion, garlic, and/or quartered apples to help mask the wild or gamy taste.

When poultry is cut into pieces, turn skin up. Brush skin with a light coating of oil or butter.

Cover bird loosely with foil, and cook at 325° - 350°F for approximately 40 minutes per pound, if bird weighs less than 7 - 8 pounds.

Birds weighing more than 8 pounds need to be cooked for 20 - 25 minutes per pound. Remove foil during last 20 minutes of cooking time. If using a roasting bag, follow manufacturer's recommendations for utilization and cooking times.

•Basic Broiling

Cut bird into halves, quarters, or pieces, leaving skin on. Brush pieces with oil or butter. Place pieces skin-side down on a lightly oiled broiler rack with a drip pan. Position pieces to allow slow cooking. Turn pieces 3 - 4 times, brushing with butter, oil, or sauce of choice. Chicken pieces require 20 - 30 minutes cooking time. Turkey, ducks and geese require 30-60 minutes time.

•Basic Braising

Braising may be accomplished by two methods:

Pan braising: *sear* to brown coating by pouring a small amount of oil into a hot, heavy pan or skillet, then turning bird (whole or in pieces) over until browned on all sides. To complete cooking, add $\frac{1}{2}$ stick of butter to pan, lower heat to medium, cover with a tight-fitting lid and allow heat to steam bird in its own juices for approximately 2 hours, turning occasionally to prevent burning of bottom pieces. (Uncover last 30 minutes to allow outer meat to brown, if not seared prior to braising.) Juices make excellent sauce or gravy!

Oven braising: virtually the same as in a pan or stove, the only difference is using a pot with a tight-fitting lid in the oven. Cook at 350°F until bones separate easily from meat. Brown during last 30 min. of cooking by removing lid and leaving uncovered in oven. Add vegetables, fruits, or herbs during last hour of cooking to add flavor and make a one-pot meal. Add water, salt and pepper, garlic salt, etc., to make a great-tasting soup!

•Basic Stewing and Simmering

Place bird in water to cover in a large pan or pot on top of stove. Season with onions, garlic buds, celery, carrots, and any other vegetable(s) of choice. Bring water to boiling, then reduce heat to simmer. Correct seasonings. Cook for 1½ - 3 hours, until meat falls off bones. Makes a wonderful stew that's both hearty and healthy.

Chart 21–5

Poultry & Wild Fowl Preparation

Type of Fowl	Dressed Avg. Wt.	Wt. per Serving (Uncooked)	Attributes Of Bird	Cooking Guidelines
Home-Raised Chicken				
Broiler or fryer	1½ - 4 lb.	¼ - ½ lb. (bone-in) ¼ - ½ lb. (boneless)	young & tender; all-purpose meat for any chicken recipe	broil, fry, braise, roast, or steam
Capon	4 - 7 lb.	½ lb.	largest chicken; more white meat; tender & flavorful	roast
Roaster	3 - 5 lb.	½ lb.	large, plump and young chicken	roast
Stewing hen	3 - 6 lb.	½ lb.	larger, mature chicken; more fat & less meat	braise or stew; use for ground chicken, soups, stews or stock
Small Chickens and Game Birds				
Grouse Guinea fowl Partridge Pheasant Pigeons Prairie chicken Ptarmigan Rock Cornish hen Squab	1 - 2 lb.	1 bird	small; tender & meaty birds	roast, braise, broil, fry
Wild Turkey				
Fryer or Roaster	4 - 9 lb.	¾ - 1 lb.	smaller & younger bird; tender & meaty	broil, roast, fry
Hen or Tom	10 - 20 lb.	½ - ¾ lb.	larger & older bird; more flavor and fat, traditional size bird	10-19 lb., roast in oven 20+ lb., roast or braise in heavy skillet
Wild Duck				

Special preparations instructions:	
• Remove excess fat from body cavity • Remove wing tips and 1st joint • Prick skin all over body, rub with garlic salt • Boil 10 min. To reduce fat, skim it from the water • Don't coat skin with oil or grease	• Place celery, onion or quartered apples in cavity • Salt cavity, place duck on rack in roasting pan • Roast 400°F. approx. 15 min., then remove • Reduce heat to 325° F., cook 20 to 25 min. per lb. • Pour off accumulated fat for sauce or stuffing

Type of Fowl	Dressed Avg. Wt.	Wt. per Serving (Uncooked)	Attributes Of Bird	Cooking Guidelines
Male or Female	2 - 6 lb.	1 lb.	wild flavor; most often plump and fatty	• less than 3 lb., fry or broil • 3 - 6 lb., roast or braise
Wild Goose				

Special preparations instructions:	
• Remove excess fat from body cavity • Sprinkle salt in body cavity, then parboil 10 min. • Prick skin on legs, wings and chest • Place on rack in roasting pan • Roast at 450° F. for 30 min., turn every 10 min.	• Reduce heat to 325° F. • Remove goose from rack & pour off fat • Stuff and place goose directly in roasting pan • Continue to cook until done, spooning off fat

UPLAND GAME BIRDS

These game birds include the families of dove, pigeon, woodcock, common snipe, quail, partridge, pheasant, grouse, ptarmigan, prairie chicken, and the king of birds—wild turkey!

RECIPES FOR UPLAND GAME BIRDS

All the small birds can be cooked by the same recipe—there will be only a slight taste difference due to family characteristics of each type of bird. There are many books on the subject of cooking in the field and at home.[3]

Here are just a few ideas for preparation of the small upland game birds—whether you bag them yourself or buy them at the market!

BASIC DOVE PIE

10 doves	1 large onion, chopped
2 qt. water	2 T. bacon grease
2 tsp. poultry seasoning	flour
1 tsp. salt	pastry for 2-crust pie
dash of pepper	

Place doves in boiling water, add poultry seasoning, salt, pepper, onion and bacon grease. Simmer for 1 hr. or until doves are tender. Remove doves from broth; remove meat from bones. Return meat to broth; cook for 30 min. longer. Thicken broth with flour. Fit half the pastry into pie pan; pour dove mixture into pan. Cover with remaining pastry. Bake in 400°- 425°F oven until top is browned.
Yield: 4 servings.

BASIC BAKED PHEASANT

1 to 2 pheasants, quartered	$^1/_3$ C. chopped onion
1 can cream of chicken soup	1 clove of garlic, minced
$^1/_2$ C. apple cider	1 (4-oz). can mushrooms
4 tsp. Worcestershire	paprika
$^3/_4$ tsp. salt	

Preheat oven to 350°F. Place pheasant in 9" square baking dish. Blend soup, cider, Worcestershire sauce, salt, onion, garlic and mushrooms. Pour over pheasant. Sprinkle generously with paprika; bake for 1 hr. or longer, or until tender. *Yield: 4 servings.*

BASIC TURKEY SAUSAGE

Fresh turkey or wild fowl sausage is extremely easy to make from the less-desired or bony/tendonous parts. It can even be seasoned to taste like pork—without the fat and grease of pork! Experiment to devise your own special recipe to suit your personal taste.

2 lb. ground turkey/wild fowl of choice	1 tsp. black pepper
1 tsp. sage	1 tsp. salt (optional)

Combine all ingredients and mix well. Refrigerate overnight to allow flavors to develop deep flavor. Shape into 15 - 18 patties. To serve, cook in a lightly oiled skillet over medium heat until done.

Seasoning Variations:
- ☐ Add red pepper (cayenne, jalapeno, or other hot pepper) in place of black pepper.
- ☐ Substitute Italian seasoning for sage.
- ☐ Add garlic to the above recipes.

---

[3] This is where Captain James A. Smith's book, **DRESS 'EM OUT!** excels—he not only gives step-by-step explanations about dressing out field birds and waterfowl, he but he also has recipes for in-the-field preparation!

WATER FOWL

For those who hunt the larger game birds, the most commonly taken are the duck family:

Chart 21–6
Large Water Fowl

Pond ducks including:	bald pates and black duck; teals: blue-winged, cinnamon, green-winged, mallard, pintail, and wood duck
Diving ducks, including:	canvasback, greater and lesser scaups, and redhead ducks
Wild geese, including:	Canada, snow, and white-fronted geese

If you've gone hunting and taken any of the birds listed above, you deserve the honor and recognition you'll get when the entire family enjoys the meal with any of the following entrées:

RECIPES FOR WILD WATER FOWL

GREEK DUCK

8-12 duck breasts	10 whole cloves
$^1/_4$ C. table oil	20 allspice berries
5 small onions, quartered	2 T. wine vinegar
1 can (6 oz.) tomato paste	salt and pepper to taste
1 C. water	2 oranges, cut in quarters
2 bay leaves	1 tsp. cinnamon
1T. orange peel (freshly grated)	

Brown duck breasts in oil over medium heat for approximately 30 min. Add remaining ingredients, sprinkling cinnamon over the top, cover and simmer for 2 hr.
Yield: 2 breasts per serving.

WILD DUCK à l'ORANGE

2 wild ducks	$^1/_2$ tsp. ground ginger
6 bacon slices	$^1/_2$ tsp. salt
1 (6-oz.) can frozen orange juice concentrate	1 T. cornstarch
1 garlic clove	1 C. water
$^3/_4$ tsp. dry mustard	

Clean ducks; tie legs and wings close to body. Place in shallow pan, breast-side up. Lay strips of bacon over ducks. Roast in 450°F oven for 20 - 25 min. per lb. Combine undiluted orange juice concentrate, garlic, mustard, ginger and salt in small saucepan. Heat mixture to boiling. During last 10 min. of roasting, remove bacon and brush sauce over birds generously. Mix cornstarch with a little cold water and stir into remaining sauce; add remaining water. Stir over low heat until thickened. Serve with duck.
Yield: 4 servings.

DUCK PILAF WITH SAFFRON RICE

1 duck, cleaned and dressed	$2^1/_2$ C. water
garlic salt	$^1/_4$ tsp. Spanish Saffron
pepper	3 T. raisins
$^3/_4$ C. brown rice	

Trim fat from duck; disjoint. Sprinkle liberally with garlic salt, and pepper. Place pieces in shallow 9" x 15" roasting pan. Broil for 10 min. each side, or until skin is brown and crispy. Remove pieces from pan; drain off fat. Put remaining ingredients in pan and stir well.

Place duck on top of rice, skin up. Cover pan with foil. Place in 225°F oven for 2 hr. or longer, until all liquid is absorbed by rice. Remove foil and brown 10 min. at 350°F.
Yield: 6 servings.

Note:

For those who are fortunate enough to bag wild fowl, here are some recipes for preparing excellent dishes, and for enjoying them to their fullest. These recipes are not intended for preparation in the field—the equipment requirements are far too serious for that!

Wild fowl can be substituted in almost all recipes for chicken—the taste will vary accordingly!

Quick-List™ 21-1
Game Meats, Fish, & Fowl Preparation Supplies

In-Field Equipment & Supplies : Game Gear

rifle	rifle ammunition	scope	gun case
shotgun	shotgun ammunition	protective glasses	game bag
sportsman's scale	tape measure	nylon rope	orange vest
gambrel to hang game	pack frame for game	block and tackle lightweight	field glasses
flashlight	batteries	duct tape	waterproof tarp

In-Field Equipment & Supplies: Fishing Gear

vinyl sheeting/heavy	hunting knife	carving knife	boning knife
fish hooks	pocket knife	hook remover	hip boots/waders
lures/artificial bait	fishing gear/rod & reel	fishing line	wading belt
fillet knife	lure container	fish net	gaff
fish scaler	bait bucket/bait well	hat	sunscreen
ice chest/48-quart	stringer	cleansing agents	chemical coolant/blocks

At-Home Equipment & Supplies

chopping block	cutting board	boning knife	butcher knife
cleaver	butcher's saw	sharpening steel	rubber gloves
larding needle	basting bulb	scale	spice shakers, lg. alum.
large pans/mixing	sausage casings	sausage seasoning	meat grinder/electric
dish cloths	kitchen towels		meat grinder, hand-op.

Seasonings

salt/table	salt/pickling	rock salt	salt/pickling
pepper/ground	peppercorns	white pepper	ginger
dry mustard	thyme	rosemary	marjoram
paprika	allspice	fennel	coriander
cayenne pepper	mace	sage	cumin/ground
cumin/seed	cloves	nutmeg	bay leaves
jalapeno pepper			

Other Equipment & Supplies

portable heater	fuel	matches	poncho
tent	gas lantern	sleeping bag	air mattress
canteen	camp cooking set		ground cushion

[i] This special list is provided to assure you have all necessary processing supplies on hand!

Chapter 22

Energy and Fuels Storage

You've taken some important steps to assure your family will have food, water, shelter, appropriate clothing, and you're feeling fairly well prepared. Now it's time to resolve one of the ten issues discussed in previous chapters regarding your ability to prepare your food, wash your dishes, and keep yourself clean and healthy. You need to consider what you will use as a backup source of energy for warmth, light, and also for a measure of safety, security, and wellness.

If power is lost for a period of time—for whatever reason—how will you cook your food? What will you use to fuel your camp stove, have light to extend you day, or power your generator? Obviously, when you've stocked up on the proper mix of canned, dried, freeze-dried foods and MREs, you'll probably need less cooking time, effort, and fuel.

From my own experience, eating cold food out of a can in the dark may sound romantic, but it's a difficult adjustment for most people—especially, the aged, the infirm, all children, women, teenagers, and most men!

If you have stored foods your family normally eats without warming, heating, or cooking—consider yourself fortunate! If you can pull that off successfully, you got game!

There is still the need for keeping warm and having a ring of light in which to congregate and share information, news, and to increase communication—an excellent method to dispel the fear and loneliness.

The types and options of primary, secondary, and alternate items of equipment and supplies for heating, lighting, and cooking are practically limitless. With access to the Internet and the knowledge of a name, product, description, or just by entering a single word or a short phrase, *i.e.: flashlight, camp stove,* or *lantern,* you can find an extremely large number of viable solutions to help you acquire the equipment and supplies you need.

Having a stored supply of fuel will be very important for your family's comfort should an emergency arise that eliminates the energy that powers your home. Without electricity you still need to prepare food, wash dishes and clothes, clean, bathe, and stay warm or cool. Electricity, natural gas, and other energy sources could be interrupted by an earthquake, flood, hurricane, or other natural disaster—not to mention rationing of energy-producing commodities due to natural disasters, trucking strikes, economic, or other infrastructure disasters or emergencies.

The family with fuel to provide adequate energy for cooking, cleaning, sterilization, lighting, and warmth will be much better prepared than those families who ignore this important storage category. However, in your eagerness to accomplish this priority, don't forget the essentials of safety which are important in the storage of highly flammable materials.

How fortunate you are to be able to choose—that's a luxury your forefathers never had! *What if the fuel choice I make is the wrong one, and it is no longer readily available?*

There are three (3) solutions to this question for your consideration in storing fuel:

1. Purchase the <u>one most effective fuel</u> for the intended use of the equipment you plan to purchase. The fewer items you store to do the task, the better it will be for your budget and limited storage area.

   For example, if you choose to utilize a number of kerosene (or propane, white gas, butane, etc.) lamps for lighting, why not purchase the entire cooking, heating, and/or lighting equipment set utilizing that one fuel to simplify your fuel storage? This is a simple solution—as long as you choose a fuel that will be easily available when you need additional supplies.

2. Purchase multi-fuel equipment. These cooking, heating, and lighting devices utilize several different types of fuels.

   This is best solution. However, multi-fuel equipment items cost more than their single fuel counterpart.

3. Purchase different sets of equipment for different fuels as a remote third possibility. Equipment redundancy would be the most expensive solution, but would give you the most security.

   Your redundancy might include a kerosene space heater and camp stove for heating and cooking, with a wood burning fireplace, wood stove, or fire pit you dig in the back yard as a back-up.

   There are many non-liquid fuel systems, too. Have you considered a hibachi, charcoal grill, Volcano-type cooker, or solar oven for cooking as part of your redundancy program?

ALTERNATIVE ENERGY SOURCES

Another option to consider is using alternative energy sources such as solar or wind power as a backup for your local power grid. There are many home wind-power kits you can purchase as well as solar-power kits.

You can store extra power in backup batteries and if you want, you can even rid yourself of the need to connect to the local power company's system. Or you can sell your extra energy to the power company.

Some of the benefits of utilizing alternative energy systems include reduced electricity costs and in some areas the power company will actually pay you for providing your extra power to them. In addition to electricity, make sure that you store an adequate supply of fuel for the use of your generator(s) in case of a power outage.

The biggest drawback to using solar or wind power is the high cost of installation, which can at least be partially offset by state and federal incentives and policies that promote renewable energy and energy efficiency.

To find out what financial help is available in your area, visit **http://www.dsireusa.org/**.

Cooking your food, boiling water, washing the body, dishes, and clothes requires lots of heat. What have you considered for those purposes? Go online to find solar water heaters, and energy storage systems, for example.

Check with your local officials for the proper way to store fuel safely. Energy is something most of us take for granted these days. Make sure you are not left without it when disasters strike.

Energy conservation and *energy efficiency* are often used by the uninformed and uninitiated as synonyms. However, there are significant differences.

Energy conservation implies getting by with a lower level of service or utilizing less services—freezing in the dark or sacrificing essential creature comforts—to save resources and money.

Energy efficiency means getting more services with less expense—getting the same energy services while using less energy—therefore saving money and non-renewable resources.

Alternative energy sources replace traditional energy sources to achieve both *energy conservation* and *energy efficiency*, and accepts the trade-offs as essential to the long-term benefits for all concerned.

These are the **<u>Don'ts</u>** of storing your alternate fuel resources:

- Don't store white gas, kerosene, or similar liquids in your home or garage.
- All fuels must be stored where children can't reach them.
- Don't store liquid fuels of any kind in the same storage space utilized for medicines, food, or water—an offensive taste will generally result from the toxic fumes given off by liquid fuels.

The following pages list some typical camping equipment utilizing energy or fuel and their respective consumption rates. This will guide your determination of fuel(s) needed for your storage program.

ENERGY AND FUELS PRODUCTS

Fuels – Gas Detectors

When utilizing any combustible fuel, oxygen is consumed and carbon monoxide or other deadly fumes result from combustion. Also, explosive gases leaking from butane, propane, and natural gas can destroy life and property.

When storing and utilizing these gaseous fuels, it would be wise to have carbon monoxide gas detectors installed in areas of use to protect the family. An alarm with a high-decibel warning will sound when dangerous concentration levels are attained.

Caution:
Use all types of burning fuel _only_ in a well-ventilated space.

Warning: When utilizing any fuels in a closed area of the home other than your contractor-installed appliances, utilize a CO_2 gas detector for safety.

Fire Starters

Fuel storage discussion would be incomplete without including the means for starting a fire. Have a supply of matches, newspapers, and/or kindling to facilitate starting the fire. Store both waterproof and windproof matches for emergencies. Keep them in sealed plastic bags, used pill bottles, or glass bottles with tight-fitting lids to protect from moisture.

Fire-starters include: stick (kitchen/strike anywhere) and book matches, cigarette lighters, and magnesium fire starters.

The best choice is the magnesium starter—it works even when conditions are at their worst and even when materials are wet. Most people need help in starting a fire, and this fire-starting tool is a small item, but a necessary and rugged piece of equipment everyone can afford and should have! There is a large selection of all types of fire-starters.

Use your Internet browser and search for **Magnesium Fire Starters** or **Water Proof Matches**.

There is always the butane fire-starter used for starting your barbecue fire—they just don't store well for long periods of time. Not all of the brands and styles have refillable models. Butane is also very expensive for the utility derived from their short life. The refillable models are preferable, just be sure to have refills on hand.

Lighting Equipment

There are many options for emergency lighting. Note there are significant different values of light, from short-term, battery-operated flashlights to fuel-based lighting of longer duration and greater intensity.

- Candles
- Emergency Candles
- Cooking Oil
- Electric
- Battery-Powered

Candle-Power Lighting

Tallow Candles

Tallow candles burn brighter, longer, and are fairly smoke-free when compared to wax candles. Tallow candles are generally available in specialty stores only, unless you make your own. Store tallow candles in a cool, dry location.

Candles stored in the freezer will burn slower and without dripping. The following chart gives details for approximate burning times:

Height	Diameter	Approx. Hrs. Burn Time
6"	½"	3
6"	1"	8
9"	2"	48

Wax Candles

Wax candles are available almost anywhere housewares are sold. They are available in many types, shapes, and lengths. Candles provide a soft, low light and are normally reasonably priced.

Candles are easy to store and have an indefinite shelf life. Candles must be stored in a cool place.

In use, the candle's open flame presents a fire hazard and consumes a small amount of oxygen when burning.

Size	Approx. Hrs. Burn Time
¾" diameter x 4"	20 hrs.
⁷/₈" diameter x 4"	5 hrs.
2" x 9"	75 hrs.
Tea light	2-4 hrs.

Emergency Candles

There are two types of emergency candles available for camping, storage, and emergency purposes. Both are generally smokeless and odorless when burning.

One type is made of hardened wax in a can has the capability of utilizing several wicks simultaneously.

The other type is a liquid paraffin-filled bottle with a wick for easy lighting. The liquid paraffin burns without odor or smoke, and has no residual wax waste or dripping. This candle has a minimum 100-hour burning time and shelf life in excess of 10 years.

Cooking Oil Candles

Emergency candles can be made with cooking oil or even used grease when other options run out.

Pour oil into jar or small bowl to approx. ¾ full, cut strings and push one end into oil to the bottom of the container, leaving 1" of string lying over the edge of container mouth. Light the dry end of string. If more light is desired, utilize several strings.

This is an emergency lighting solution. Some smoke will be caused by the burning oil.

Enter **emergency candles** in your browser or go to: **http://www.judyofthewoods.net/lamp** to get details for making emergency candles.

Battery-Powered Lighting

When electricity is lost, having alternative sources for lighting will be not only necessary, but providential.

There are many types of equipment available to provide light, and having both short- and long-term solutions is advisable. You should have solutions for localized task lighting to general or area lighting, Note that all sources of light are not equal—each type has its particular and often specific use.

Battery-powered lanterns are very handy for general lighting, and are available in two lamp models:

- Fluorescent lamp models
- LED bulb models, for longer-lasting battery operation.

Also available in manual crank (hand wound) models, but these are not as bright as the gas or kerosene models.

Flashlights

Flashlights

A flashlight with fresh batteries is essential to safety in every home. They provide a quick, reliable source of light and are available in a wide variety of shapes and sizes. A 2-battery flashlight with new batteries will operate approx.6 hours.

Always buy quality—your safety or your life may depend on your choice!

Note: Flashlights should not be stored with batteries installed. Store extra batteries and bulbs where they are easy to find—in the dark!

Features to buy in a flashlight include these:

- Small and lightweight;
- May be carried in a pocket, on a belt, or attached to a backpack, and/or attached to an object for utility;
- Uses a variety of battery types: alkaline, lithium, or rechargeable batteries;
- Fewer batteries to operate is better;
- Simple to operate;

Flashlights (continued)

- Heavy-duty construction with bulb protected, shock resistant, and waterproof;
- Doesn't turn on easily in pocket or backpack;
- Utilizes LED or Cree bulb, with 10,000 hr. life, shock-resistant construction;
- Chargeable units that provide operating time of 8 - 12+ hrs per battery charge; and
- Light beam (wide/spot) for different applications should be considered.

Resources: Search for <u>flashlight</u> in your browser for latest technology, availability, and competitive pricing.

Types of Flashlights

Crank flashlight: Light lasts approx. 30 min. with 1 min. cranking. Acceptable light quality. Some have capability of charging cell phones (3 min. winding = 8 min. talk time—but doesn't fit all phones). The crank flashlight currently is neither waterproof nor capable of producing long-lasting light.

LED flashlight: Utilizes long-lasting LED bulbs which are brighter than filament bulbs. Energy-efficient operation permits long-lasting use. LED flashlights are available in a large selection of size, style, lamp brightness, and durability.

Rechargeable flashlight/automatic night light combination: It plugs in the wall and functions as a nightlight, but when the power goes out it is a fully charged flashlight that automatically turns on. It is easy to find and always ready in an emergency.

Shake flashlights: Essentially magnet flashlights with an LED bulb or bulbs. Shaking the light charges the capacitor, which then provides the electricity to power the bulb.

Technology has improved, but the magnetic flashlight is not a totally reliable flashlight for emergencies or long-term storage, especially when not use frequently. As the flashlight ages, their bright light doesn't last for a long period before getting dim. Most models are water-resistant.

Caution: can damage items sensitive to magnetic fields, such as computer disks, credit cards, etc.

Solar-Powered Flashlights: 8 hr. of sunlight will provide 4-5 hr. of lighting. Some models will even charge well on cloudy days. Some models may last up to 20 years. Buy models that have several LED bulbs, and are water- and shock-resistant.

Types of Flashlights (continued)

A two-battery, D-cell flashlight with standard-life dry cell batteries will provide light for the approx. times shown in the chart below. Long-life batteries have substantially longer usability.

Shelf life of batteries is important. Age, heat (cold temperature actually extends battery shelf life), manufacturer, humidity, bulb size utilized—all these factors affect the length of battery life and, ultimately, the effective performance of the battery. Choose batteries for a flashlight with the same consideration as all other items of basic emergency equipment. Rotate batteries on a planned schedule in your in-home storage or preparedness inventory.

Rechargeable, long-life flashlights are available, as well as rechargeable batteries. Research indicates rechargeable batteries have much shorter life than conventional batteries; however the convenience of recharging makes them a better alternative. Acquire a solar-powered electrical recharging system for long-term emergency use.

There are also self-powered, crank, compact flashlights, making it possible to have light without batteries. Light is produced by means of an internal generator, powered by pulling or squeezing a lever, pulling a trigger, or winding a hand crank.

Enter **flashlights** in your browser for additional information.

Type of Use	Battery Condition	Approx. Hrs. Battery Life
Continuous	new	5 - 6
	old	3 - 4
Intermittent	new	7 - 8
	old	4 - 5

Flashlights for Every Preparedness Purpose!

Kerosene Fuel Lighting
Caution: Lanterns consume good air and exhaust bad air—use only where well ventilated

Kerosene Lantern

Given today's technology, a kerosene lantern seems a bit old-fashioned and out of place! However, a kerosene lantern with a 1" wick will burn approximately 45 hours per quart of kerosene, saving lots of natural resources and utilizing approximately one-fourth as much fuel as a gas lantern. Kerosene lanterns are an effective and fairly safe lighting source. There are now scented lamp oils which replace kerosene. This lamp oil is generally available in retail stores. Make sure the oil is approved for use in your lamp.

There is a difference in lighting quantity and quality, as the kerosene lantern is quite dim when compared to the two-mantle gas lantern. The light output of a kerosene lantern is comparable to a 40W - 60W light bulb.

Kerosene produces some black smoke when burning.

Burning 5 hours each day, the following chart details the amount of kerosene that would be consumed in a given period:

Period	Fuel Consumed in 5 Hr.
Day	$^1/_4$ pt.
Week	1 qt.
Month	1 gal.
Year	12 gal.

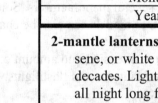

2-mantle lanterns are available in a multi-fuel model, utilizing unleaded gas, kerosene, or white gas fuels. These popular lamps have been a camping favorite for decades. Lighting brightness is adjustable, making them very convenient to use all night long for safety and security.

2-mantle lanterns produce heat, requiring adequate ventilation when using. All fossil fuels produce CO_2 and should never be used inside a closed environment.

Coleman fuel stored in an unopened container in a dry place with a stable temperature has a shelf life of 5 - 7 years. Opened containers of any fuel stored should be used within 1 - 2 years—evaporation is certain! Use caution when storing and using this fuel and the equipment operating on it.

A typical gas lantern produces a high intensity light and lots of heat, too. Light output is approximately the same as a 200W light bulb.

The pressurized gas delivery system has a fairly loud hissing noise when operating.

Assuming an operating or burning time of 5 hours per day, the following approximate amounts of fuel would be consumed:

Period	Fuel Consumed in 5 Hr.
Day	1 pt.
Week	1 gal.
Month	4 gal.
Year	50 gal.

Enter **kerosene lanterns** in your browser for additional information.

Chemical Lighting

Light stick is a chemical mix in a plastic sheath, available in varying lengths and diameters, and in a variety of colors. Activation is by bending the plastic sheath and shaking to mix the contents. A brightly colored, diffused light is emitted for approx. 6 - 12 hrs.

Light sticks are safe for all environments, including where gas vapors may exist. Light sticks are windproof, weatherproof, create no sparks to ignite flammable liquids, and are safe for use by all ages.

Shelf life is limited to 3 - 4 years, depending on manufacturer. Though not a bright light source, it is the safest form of lighting.

Search your browser for **light sticks.**

Solar Lighting

Solar-powered lights are fixtures commonly used along garden walkways, and are relatively inexpensive, weather-resistant, and can be brought indoors to light up interior space. These lights can be purchased in hardware, lighting, discount merchandisers, and discount wholesale stores.

Solar-powered lighting is available from several manufacturers. Some models are charged by normal bright sunlight, other models can also be charged by an auto adapter, or 110VAC house adapter.

Models vary in time required for charging, intensity, and amount of lighting time. There are several models of solar-powered lanterns and flashlights.

Search on your browser for **solar flashlights.**

Cooking Equipment
There are many types of cooking equipment, operated by several fuel options.

Two-Burner Gas Camp Stove

The 2-burner stove is one of the most popular cooking surfaces in use by campers. Easy to use, simple to operate, proven over the years—and very affordable. Available in liquid fuels, propane, and butane models.

Both burners of a Coleman-type gas camp stove in use 4 hours per day will consume approximately the following amounts of Coleman fuel:

Period	Approximate Fuel Consumption per 5 Hours
Day	5 pt.
Week	3 gal.
Month	10 gal.
Year	100 gal.

Canned Fuels

Canned fuels have been utilized for many years as an excellent short-term emergency and utility heating source. Canned fuels have proven essential to the food service industry, the military, the Boy Scouts, and campers.

Most portable buffets and many restaurants utilize canned heat as a warming or heating source for foods, so most people are familiar with this source of heat and fuel.

Emergency Tin Can Stove

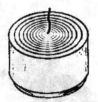

In an emergency situation, you can make a tin can stove by turning a 1-gallon metal can (#10 can) upside-down and inserting a heating unit in it. Any metal container would work.

Make the emergency tin can stove by using a 1-gallon can (#10 can), by completely removing the top, punching several (4 - 8) holes on the sides at both ends (close to the top and bottom seams) to assure air to the heat source and a flow of heat to the cooking surface. Place heating unit on a non-flammable surface, start fire, set tin can stove over the burning heat source and use as a camp stove. Bricks, rocks, or any heat-safe material will assure the flame is at the appropriate height for cooking purposes.

Make a simple heating unit from a 3-oz. tin can, roll a cut length of a corrugated cardboard box sized to the height of the can, coil it tightly inside the can, pour paraffin wax over the coiled corrugate, light the wax and fix your meal. It doesn't get more basic than that!

In a pinch, you can use any paper filler—it only serves as the wick. The wax burns hot and clean, providing adequate heat for emergency cooking. It may require height adjustment with a stone, piece of brick, etc. to get the heat adjusted properly. This heating unit will burn approx. 1 - 2 hours.

Enter **tin can stove** in your browser or go to this site for a 10-minute video: **http://www.wonderhowto.com/how-to-make-tin-can-survival-cook-stove-169431/**

Charcoal Briquettes

Charcoal is a very efficient fuel. It can be made from almost any wood source, including any hardwood twigs, limbs, chips, nutshells, and fruit pits. Charcoal provides a hot fire and produces little or no smoke.

It requires only 3 - 4 commercial briquettes in a small (8" x 8") hibachi or charcoal grill to generate enough heat to cook a simple meal and produce a little warmth as a bonus.

Store enough charcoal to for several weeks' supply—it does not deteriorate in storage. Store only unopened cans of charcoal starter fluid in a safe place.

MAKING BASIC CHARCOAL

There are basically two types of charcoal to choose from:

(1) Lump Charcoal, made directly from various hardwoods. and

(2) the extruded, and most notable, the briquette made from mostly scrap wood and sawdust, mixed with binders to hold their shape.

The length of time charcoal will burn is determined by the amount of oxygen available, so when you can control the air supply, you control the burn time and heat intensity.

Make your own charcoal using the following steps:

- Take a metal bucket or can with lid and punch ½" holes all around and on ends.
- Put wood, sticks, or woody material into can and cover with lid.
- *Cook* over hot fire. The holes in the can allow the gases and flame to escape while reduced oxygen keeps the wood from burning completely to ashes.
- When the flame from the holes in the can turns to bright yellow-red, remove can from the fire and allow to cool.
- Store charcoal in paper bags or cardboard cartons in a dry environment.

Caution:

When using charcoal in an enclosed space, vent the grill by setting it on the fireplace hearth or placing it near a partially opened window.

Death could result if space is improperly ventilated.

Alternative Energy Resources for Heating

There are many types of heating equipment, each operating on different fuels. Here are a few things you can prepare in advance to help you be ready when the public utilities fail to deliver their normal services. This, of course, if these alternatives aren't your basics already!

Firewood

Firewood for heat is important when you have an operating fireplace or stove in the home. Though fireplaces are inefficient, they can provide enough warmth in a limited area to protect from freezing. Stoves are very efficient for warming large spaces.

Energy Content of Selected Woods

Specie	BTUs	Specie	BTUs
Rock Elm	32,000	Black Ash	22,600
Shagbark Hickory	30,600	Green Ash	22,100
White Oak	30,600	Silver Maple	21,700
Bitternut Hickory	29,200	Manitoba Maple	19,300
Sugar Maple	29,000	Large Tooth Aspen	18,200
Beech	27,800	Hemlock	17,900
Red Oak	27,300	Trembling Aspen	17,700
Yellow Birch	26,200	Butternut	17,400
Red Elm	25,400	Balsam Poplar	17,260
White Ash	25,000	White Pine	17,100
White Elm	24,500	Basswood	17,000
Red Maple	24,000	White Cedar	16,300
Tamarack	24,000	White Spruce	16,200
Black Cherry	23,500	Balsam Fir	15,500
White Birch	23,400		

Energy content per air-dried full cord, in 000s for BTUs of selected species. Notice the hardest species are at the top of the list.

Coal

Caution: Coal cannot be utilized safely in pre-built metal or metal-lined fireplaces. Be sure to check the fireplace manufacturer's recommendations for fuel utilization in metal fireplaces.

Two to four tons of coal, sparingly used, normally meets the cold weather needs of a family for a year. While a standard brick-lined fireplace is comfortable during times of plenty, it is not the most efficient way to heat a home when electricity and/or natural gas are not available.

Either a potbelly or *Ben Franklin*-type stove or an old-fashioned coal or wood kitchen range would be more practical for warming large spaces. They also double their value as a means for cooking food. If coal were the only heating source, approximately one ton per month would be consumed in a standard stove or fireplace, depending on the severity of the winter weather, efficiency of stove or fireplace, and temperature maintained in the house.

Coal should preferably be stored in the dark and away from circulating air. After a period of time, air tends to break the coal into small pieces. Smaller pieces are consumed at a faster rate and higher intensity than larger lumps.

The best method for storing coal is in a hole lined with plastic sheeting. After putting coal in the hole, cover with more plastic and then cover with dirt. The plastic helps to keep the air out and also helps prevent loss in recovering it.

If coal is to be stored above ground, place it on the north side of the house where it will be out of the sun. Smaller quantities can be stored in potato sacks or large cans. These types of containers are more convenient when storing coal in a garage or basement space.

Newspaper Logs

Make a substitute for firewood from the daily newspapers—it's like having firewood delivered to the door at no extra cost! There are several commercial newspaper log-making machines which simplify and speed up the process of folding and rolling newspapers.

Four newspaper logs last approximately 1 hour and produce heat equivalent to a comparably sized stick of wood.

Newspaper logs utilized as fuel overcomes problems of smoldering, flying ashes, and popping of wood.

The average daily newspaper will make 2 - 3 logs. The typical city Sunday edition will make up to seven logs.

Newspaper logs provide, pound-for-pound, approximately the same heat as wood and are an efficient energy source—and it's delivered directly to your home!

Type **newspaper logs** into your browser or go to this site for additional information: **http://www.ehow.com/how_4891600_fireplace-newspaper-logs.html**.

MAKING BASIC NEWSPAPER LOGS

- Use 6 sections (five double sheets in each section) for each newspaper log.
- Fold double sheets to single page size.
- Fold each single page section in half width-wise.
- Turn 90° and fold in half again.
- Stack the sections, alternating cut with folded sides. Allow bottom or outside section to extend out from the roll by 3 - 4 inches. This makes a convenient way to light the roll.
- Roll papers very tightly, securing the center and ends of the newspaper roll with a tightly twisted piece of wire.

BASIC NEWSPAPER LOGS — CLEANER-BURNING VERSION

The following method provides a cleaner-burning version of the **Basic Newspaper Log** by using water to help break down the paper, much like *papier-maché*.

This type log burns more effectively because the compressed paper is now expanded. These logs are fatter and will burn more brightly.

INSTRUCTIONS FOR "CLEAN-BURNING" NEWSPAPER LOGS

- Divide the newspaper into sections.
- Fold sections to half size, approximately 12" x 15" x 1/2" thick.
- Fill laundry tub ¾ full with water and add 2 tablespoons detergent to speed saturation. Place newspaper sections in tub and allow to soak in this mixture for approximately 2 hours, or until newspapers have absorbed maximum amount of water.
- While wet, roll the sections individually onto a 1" metal or wood rod, squeezing out the excess water while smoothing down the ends and edges.
- Tie with a metal tie-wrap near ends and middle to hold roll intact while drying.
- Slide the rolls off the rod and stand them on end to dry, tipping the rolls slightly to allow air to circulate through the center of the roll. The *log* should be approximately 12" long and 2" - 4" in diameter. They are ready to use when completely dry.
- Adding the detergent speeds the saturation rate of the newsprint.
- A few crystals of copper sulfate added to the water will create beautiful flame highlights.

Notes For Your Energy and Fuels Storage

Section VII

Basics of
Preparedness Self-Health

Chapter 23

Basics of Supplementation
Vitamins, Minerals, and Herbs

Your body requires vitamins and minerals for its normal functions of growth and maintenance. You probably expect the food you eat to supply those essential nutrients. Today, however, the nutritional value of food diminishes as it is picked, processed, packed, distributed and warehoused, then placed in a retail outlet for the consumer's selection and purchase. This means even a routine diet requires nutritional supplementation.

Most Americans are missing at least one essential nutrient in their bodies. Many are deficient in more than one vitamin or mineral nutrient. A nationwide survey conducted by the University of California at Berkeley confirmed that 70% of the men and 80% of the women reported eating foods containing less than two-thirds of the recommended level of one or more of the 15 vitamins and minerals considered essential for good health.

On top of that, when the excess fat being consumed was added to their food consumption habits, 98% of those surveyed were inadequately nourished. The study reveals the nutrients most often missing are calcium, zinc, folic acid, magnesium, and vitamins A, C, E, and B_6.

This chapter will provide you with guidelines for a supplementation program that will help you maintain good health under normal circumstances and during more stressful times, whether caused by disasters or by a permanent lifestyle change. When your body is under stress due to any changes, you will have an even greater need to support your physical and mental health with the appropriate vitamin, mineral, and herb supplementation.

Supplementation is just what the word means—*supplements* to be taken in addition to an intelligent diet combined with a health/fitness and body maintenance program. Supplementation is not meant to overcome the effects of a diet that is too high in fats or sugars or too low in fiber, nor is it intended to alleviate other abuses of the body from physical inactivity, stress, and other substances generally recognized as harmful to the human body.

There are optimum amounts of each nutrient that one should take. Levels in excess of the optimum daily allowance levels have minimal or even nonexistent benefits or harmful effects—except for the product vendors!

This is the 2nd edition of the *Handbook* in which a preeminent doctor, with great holistic medical and research credentials combined with clinical experience, has suggested a specific supplementation program and explains why each supplement should be a part of your in-home storage program—not to mention its utilization in your daily diet.

ABOUT DR. ZOLTAN RONA

In my efforts to provide the best recommendation possible for this important food storage and emergency preparedness category, I asked Zoltan P. Rona, M.D., M.S., to give his guidance for a valid vitamin, mineral, and herb supplementation selection for a "*typical*" in-home storage program.

Dr. Rona is eminently qualified to provide such guidelines. He graduated from McGill University Medical School, and he also earned MS degrees in biochemistry and clinical nutrition from the University of Bridgeport in Connecticut.

Dr. Rona is a general medicine practitioner with an emphasis on preventive medical counseling, particularly in the field of nutrition and holistic medicine.[1] He has excellent credentials as a recognized expert in holistic medicine, having served as President of the **Canadian Holistic Medical Association**.

DR. RONA: WHY SUPPLEMENTATION?

In one of my early conversations with Dr. Rona, I asked which question was the one most commonly asked of him as a healthcare practitioner. He indicated the question most asked was, "*Does everyone need to take vitamin, mineral, and herbal supplements?*"

His response to this question is an unequivocal **"Yes!"**

I asked him to explain why he recommends supplementation so strongly. The following pages are the result of his discussions with me about the need for supplementation for short-term emergency preparedness, longer-term food storage, and on a daily basis.

---

[1] Dr. Rona regularly has contributed to magazines in the medical field, including his past columns in **Alive Magazine**, *Health Naturally,* and **The Toronto Star**. He is known for his many public lectures and media appearances in Canada and the US. He is the author of an international best-seller, **The Joy of Health—A Doctor's Guide to Nutrition and Alternative Medicine**; also **Fertility Control—The Natural Approach**, and numerous contributions to magazines and medical journals. His second book about natural health and nutrition, **Return to the Joy of Health—A Doctor's Guide to Nutrition and Herbal Medicine,** was also a bestseller.

Vitamin and Mineral Needs Not Met by Food Alone

"The quality of our food grown in mineral-depleted soils is not what the agri-business industry wants us to believe. With over 70,000 new chemicals added to our environment since the 1940s, how could anyone say that our food supply is the best it's ever been? "Studies indicate that our daily vitamin and mineral needs are not met by food alone. Up to 80% of our food's value is lost through spraying crops, processing, transporting, freezing, storing, cooking, and adding chemicals for preservation.

"Have you noticed over the years you've been shopping that the foods found in stores tastes less and less like real food? Since there is a taste difference—what makes you think there isn't a corresponding difference in nutritive values?

"According to some experts, at the present rate of extinction, as many as one-fourth of the world's plant species will be lost within the next 50 years! If you were really aware of the content of the food you buy in any supermarket in the U.S., you'd be surprised to know that almost 90% of your food is now provided by *only* 20 major botanical plants. Where would we be if another blight such as caused the Irish potato famine were to happen?

"It's indeed fortunate that we see more farmland being diversified, crop rotating, and rebuilding of soil without chemicals. However, based on current chemical agricultural practices, eventually there won't be enough fertile topsoil left to grow the food from the plant species remaining!

"Leonardo da Vinci said, "*We know more about the movement of celestial bodies than about the soil underfoot.*" The soil is the crucible of plant life, and in it is the hope and reality of matter and energy for growing food that will not only sustain us but give us both better health and longer lives.

"To derive the same amounts of vitamins and minerals your grandparents did from food alone in the early part of the 20th century, you would need to consume six large meals per day. Since this would overload you with calories, it's far better to take vitamin and mineral supplements.

"The apparent lack of adequate vitamins and minerals in the average diet has prompted some health professionals to conclude that one of the reasons for today's epidemic-like levels of obesity, fatigue, and mental illness is *micronutrient deficiency.*

> The body will handle malnutrition in one of two ways:
> (1) weight loss, or
> (2) weight gain because the body retains fat, hoping to find what it needs from stored body fat!

Protection for the Body

"A primary reason for taking supplemental vitamins and minerals is to protect our bodies against the toxic effects of a polluted environment. Over the past decade, extensive research has been done on the subject of *free radical pathology.* Many reputable scientists and medical doctors believe that free radical pathology is at the root of immune system disorders such as cancer, heart disease, and a long list of degenerative diseases, including aging.

"Free radicals are highly reactive molecules (containing an unpaired electron) which can cause damage to the body. They can be offset by antioxidants—vitamins, minerals, and enzymes. Free radicals contribute to the degradation of any organ or system, leading to such symptoms as hardening of blood vessels, plaque, wrinkles in skin, etc.

"By the way, *free radicals have been damaging our bodies since our first breath!*

"Free radicals come from radiation, hydrocarbons from car exhaust, cigarette smoke, drugs, pesticides, herbicides, food additives, industrial waste products, and many other sources. The gradual deterioration of the ozone layer plays a part.

"All of this necessitates even greater protection with antioxidant nutrients like beta carotene, vitamin A, B vitamins (especially B_3 and B_6), vitamins C and E, bioflavonoids, selenium, zinc, silicon, amino acids, enzymes such as S.O.D. (*superoxide dismutase*), coenzymes, and essential fatty acids."

Basic Self-Health Improvement

Dr. Rona suggests two very easily implemented steps you can take immediately to improve your health:

"1. Eat Healthier Food.[2] Even in the face of less than ideal food quality, eating a healthier diet is possible. Follow these general guidelines to improve your diet:

- most importantly, decrease the intake of saturated fat and cholesterol by eliminating red meats;
- eliminate all refined oil and margarine products from your diet—instead, use high quality organic unrefined seed oils, such as

  - olive oil
  - sunflower oil
  - pumpkin

  - hemp
  - flax
  - walnut

- for your pantry, use instead:

  - coconut oil
  - butter

  - ghee (clarified butter)
  - olive oil

- keep high-fat dairy products, especially cheeses, to a minimum;
- eat cultured dairy products, such as yogurt or buttermilk in small amounts, is fine if they are low-fat products[3];
- reduce coffee and regular tea to one 6 oz. cup;
- consume no alcohol[4];
- eliminate refined sugars and replace with Stevia, Agave, Maple Syrup, Molasses, Brown Rice Syrup, date sugar, or cane sugar;
- add unheated fermented foods, such as:
  - raw unfiltered apple cider vinegar,
  - cultured vegetables,
  - fermented young or green coconut products;
- drastically reduce use of white flour products;
- replace table salt with mineral-rich sea salt; and
- drink 6 8-oz. glasses of pure, high-quality water

It is better to eat whole foods than enriched foods.

In essence, the more vegetarian your food selection...

the better for your overall health and well-being.

---

[2] Authoritative governmental and public service agencies recommend eating a balanced diet containing at least five servings daily of fruits and vegetables rich in antioxidant vitamins. Other self-protective health measures should be included, such as decreasing the intake of fats and salt, not smoking, avoiding excess alcoholic beverages, exercising regularly and reasonably, and having regular checkups.

[3] Vegans and dairy-allergic people should consume cold-cultured veggies and coconut.

[4] Recent studies show that wine—especially red—has great benefit if limited to 1 serving of 4-6 oz. per day.

"2. Take Antioxidants.[5] Take some broad-spectrum antioxidant supplements. The two worry-free supplements Dr. Rona recommends, for a variety of reasons, are:

- **bee pollen**
    and
- a **green supplement**, such as *blue green algae* or *chlorella*.

"This antioxidant combination provides a perfect mixture of maximum-spectrum antioxidants, the richest available in tablet or capsule form. Some scientists have called both bee pollen and green food concentrates nature's most perfect foods. Together they contain a very well-balanced supply of all the essential amino acids, vitamins, trace minerals, essential fatty acids, RNA, DNA, plant enzymes, coenzymes, and prostaglandin precursors.

"Blue green algae and chlorella are vegetarian sources of vitamin B_{12}. These *superfoods* fulfill daily essential vitamin and mineral needs and provide antioxidant protection. Both these products can be used to enhance work and sports performance.

"The use of bee pollen by professional and Olympic athletes for physical endurance and power is well documented. The world medical literature reports benefits from bee pollen extract in a long list of chronic conditions:

- anemia
- depression
- obesity
- prostatitis

- arthritis
- insomnia
- poor memory
  and concentration

- chronic fatigue
- menopause
- premature aging
- senility

"Blue green algae, on the other hand, has been demonstrated to help in both the prevention and treatment of all viral conditions.

Side effects and toxicity from overdoses of either blue green algae or bee pollen, even in children, have never been reported in more than thirty years of broad-scale use.

For those who want a safe and effective way of optimizing health, preventing illness, and living longer, these whole food supplements may very well be the answer."

BASIC SUPPLEMENTATION FOR IN-HOME STORAGE

After discussing the concept of food storage with its concomitant food quality and nutritional deficiency problems, Dr. Rona and I both felt a vitamin, mineral, and herbal supplementation program would be needed in a *Basic* food in-home storage program.

---

[5] The antioxidants discussed here are the vitamins C, E, and the provitamin beta-carotene. They are important to the body's cell-protection systems. Antioxidants have the ability to neutralize free radicals, those highly reactive and unstable molecules that can cause cell damage. The body's billions of cells are continually exposed to these free radicals, which are produced through normal bodily processes as well as external sources, such as air pollution. (And how do we avoid air pollution?) Many scientists believe this cellular damage, along with other factors, may lead to the development of chronic diseases such as cancer, cataracts, and even heart disease.

Many physicians and other scientists now believe vitamin supplements or eating foods that are fortified with vitamins and minerals is a sound health practice—especially for people who don't eat a wholesome diet and for those with special dietary needs, such as pregnant and lactating women and the elderly. The antioxidant vitamins themselves can be obtained through a wide variety of supplements and food products, including breakfast cereals and real juice drinks. (The nutrient contents of foods and supplements can be determined by checking the labels.)

Overwhelming scientific evidence indicates there are virtually no inordinate risks of health problems or reactions to reasonably elevated levels of the antioxidant vitamins C, E and beta carotene. (In fact, all three of these vitamins are officially classified as *Generally Recognized as Safe* (**GRAS**)—but it's always prudent to follow label instructions or the advice of a healthcare professional.)

"These are the major reasons supplementation is recommended for your in-home storage program:

- difficulty of determining the nutritional value remaining in stored foods
- continuing loss of food value, including vitamin and mineral potency
- additional food value losses occurring when food storage items are improperly stored and/or prepared"

"You are urged to do the following **three** things, in consultation with qualified healthcare providers:

1. **Examine your own diet, lifestyle, and potential supplementation requirements.**
2. **Determine your specific needs for supplementation.**
3. **Plan and execute your own personal supplemental nutrition program.**

After your own careful examination of the information presented in this chapter, search other sources to guide your efforts in deriving the best plan for you and your loved ones.

"Use the information contained in both the text and the four **Intake Guides** to plan adequate protection for your biggest investment—your health and personal well-being. Take the time to establish a supplementation program for your family as you implement your in-home storage plan.

"No single plan is perfect for everyone, so your personal homework is essential. Be sure to assess this area of your life as rigorously as any other in preparation for a long-term program of good health maintenance.

Dr. Rona, what vitamin, mineral, and herbal supplements are applicable for a home storage program?

"Here is a listing of possible supplements for in-home storage that are easy and inexpensive to have on hand. These supplemental nutrients can be taken without side effects[6] by most people. The primary reason for the effectiveness of supplementation is due to the deficiency in one or more of these vitamins or minerals. These supplemental items are available at most natural food stores.

"The listings include:

• apple cider vinegar	• hawthorne berries
• aloe vera	• iron[7]
• bee products	• kola nut
• beet root powder	• live whole food concentrates
• beta carotene	• parsley
• bioflavonoids	• saw palmetto
• bladderwrack (a seaweed, *kelp*)	• selenium
• blue green algae and other green foods	• Siberian ginseng
• boron	• vitamin C
• chromium picolinate	• vitamin E
• folic acid	• white willow
• ginger	• yerba maté
• ginkgo biloba	• zinc

---

[6] Care should be exercised with vitamin E; see note on p. 23–15, *Vitamin Supplement Intake Chart*.

[7] Iron (Fe) for bleeding in males; for female use if unable to become pregnant.

Purchasing Supplementation

"Be an informed buyer. Study carefully every supplement you plan to purchase. Compare labels from suppliers. Supplemental product forms include caplets, capsules, gels, liquids, powders, time-release and non-time-release forms, gelled capsules, lotions, ointments, and other forms, such as creams, injections, and patches. Some forms of these supplements provide better bioavailability (absorption in the body) than others, even with the same dosage. Some will be buffered, others chelated. There are many names for processes to enhance absorption into the body with increased effectiveness.

"However, *no form of supplement provides 100% absorption.*

"Generally, except for some of the fat-soluble vitamins, it doesn't matter whether you buy "*natural*" or "*synthetic*" vitamins. Buy with knowledge about which forms of supplements are best suited to your own body's chemistry. Study the products from various companies before investing either your money or your health in *any* supplements plan or program.

The **Yellow Pages**® in virtually every phone book will have local listings for retailers of vitamins, minerals, and herbal supplements. Ask holistic health professionals for their recommendations.

> **"Quality is foremost in buying and utilizing vitamin, mineral, and herbal supplements—as it is in all items on which you're betting your health or your life!"**

Storing Supplements

"Store vitamins, minerals, and herbs in a dry, cool, and dark environment. Supplements will not store for long periods. Potency and flavor diminish when stored too long, in high temperature locations, or in bright light. Supplements must be rotated as other storage items.

"Refrigeration for vitamins, minerals, and herbs is neither normally required nor is it recommended—unless such storage is recommended by the manufacturer. When transferring products from a large container to a smaller one for convenience, be sure caps are tightly closed and the containers are opaque to protect products from diminished potency.

LIVE WHOLE FOOD CONCENTRATES

"Live whole food concentrates might well be the most logical and convenient answer to the deteriorated quality of foods available from supermarkets today. Whenever possible, use whole food concentrates rather than single nutrient tablets or capsules. That's because when one isolates a single component from a given food, a lot of the benefits of the complete food are lost. Supplemental vitamins and minerals cannot duplicate the mixture of nutrients and many yet-to-be-identified substances of value to health found in natural foods.

"Whole foods contain what are called *"phytochemicals"* which are linked to both the prevention and treatment of such major degenerative diseases as heart disease, strokes, high blood pressure, and cancer. *The only way to get these phytochemicals is by eating whole foods or live whole food concentrates.*

"Some of the best-known phytochemicals are
- *Indoles* and *isothiocyanates*: found in cruciferous vegetables like broccoli, Brussels sprouts, cabbage, cauliflower, kale, Bok Choy, rutabagas, and tur-

nips. They help protect against colon cancer. Evidence is also mounting that these phytochemicals help in both the prevention and treatment of other cancers, most notably breast cancer.

- *Isoflavones,* such as *genistein:* found in soybean products like tofu and soy milk. Isoflavones offset the negative effects of excessive estrogen in breast and ovarian cancers.
- *Limonene*: found in citrus fruits, produce enzymes that eliminate cancer-causing substances from the body. Citrus fruits are mostly known for their high content of vitamin C and bioflavonoids, both of which are also vital for optimal immune system function.
- *Phytosterols:* found in soybeans, can lower the absorption of cholesterol from the diet, and help prevent colon cancer.

"Under emergency or survival conditions, when people do not have access to live whole foods, the only option may be live whole food concentrates. Live whole food concentrates are processed and converted from live whole food at temperatures less than 100°F, thereby maintaining the "life" within the food. Temperature during the conversion process is the crucial deciding factor distinguishing a "live" from a "dead" food. Shelf life of live whole food concentrates can be at least 10 years.

"The major advantages of live whole food concentrates are:
- naturally occurring high vitamin and mineral content with highly bioavailable antioxidants
- naturally occurring, highly concentrated phytochemicals
- naturally low in calories, fats, salts, and sugar
- naturally occurring live active enzymes and soluble fiber
- a rapid and convenient way of supplying the vital 5^+ daily servings of fruits; and
- vegetables that are pesticide- and herbicide-free."

VITAMINS

Beta Carotene

Beta carotene is a fat-soluble nutrient that the liver can convert to vitamin A in the body slowly—and only when the body needs it. Beta-carotene is nontoxic in nature, so it is an alternative or substitute for traditional forms of vitamin A. The best source of beta carotene is whole carrots. Equally good is a live whole food concentrate of carrots. Eating carrots or swallowing live whole food carrot concentrate capsules is therefore better than just drinking carrot juice—which is better than just taking a beta carotene supplement.

Carrots and carrot juice are alkaline-forming foods. They lower the risk of cancer, especially smoking-related cancers like lung cancer. They help lower blood cholesterol and are excellent complementary treatments for all skin disorders and respiratory problems like asthma and bronchitis. They may also be of help for gastrointestinal problems like colitis, enteritis, and ulcers.

Fruits and vegetables are rich in beta carotene as well as other carotenoids, which all help boost the immune system against bacterial, viral, fungal, and parasitic diseases as well as cancer. It's far better to eat the whole food and/or its juice—the whole food has much more nutritional value.

Bioflavonoids

Bioflavonoids are special antioxidant compounds found in many fruits, especially berries, vegetables, green tea, and wine. Some better known bioflavonoids include *catechin, hesperidin, rutin, quercetin, pycnogenol, pronogenol,* and *polyphenols*. Bioflavonoids can lower LDL-cholesterol levels and inhibit platelet stickiness. Together with vitamin C in large doses, bioflavonoids are very effective in the treatment of allergies. They also help prevent the rapid deterioration of vitamin C by oxidation. Bioflavonoids are considered essential in the human body because they strengthen the walls of the capillaries and are known to help build resistance to infections. They help increase the effectiveness of vitamin C and aid in prevention of bleeding gums.

Vitamin C

Vitamin C is an antioxidant which helps prevent all degenerative diseases. It lowers high blood cholesterol levels and helps prevent atherosclerosis by directly promoting the breakdown of triglycerides. By regulating arterial wall integrity, vitamin C performs an essential role in collagen formation. Vitamin C regenerates and reactivates the vitamin E used in the body to block oxidation of LDL-cholesterol. It helps resist infection, aid healing, and maintain healthy gums and teeth. Because vitamin C is water soluble, it is flushed away every day by our bodies and must be replenished.

People who smoke, drink alcohol, are under stress, or are elderly may need higher levels of vitamin C. It is also important for the following reasons:

- formation of collagen and the health of bones, teeth, gums, nails, muscles, ligaments, and all other connective tissue
- strengthens blood vessels; prevents bleeding and plaque formation in the arteries
- promotes healing of all body cells
- increases resistance to infection
- aids iron absorption and utilization
- antioxidant which helps prevent cancer and heart disease
- natural antihistamine in high doses

Get your vitamin C from whole food sources. If you don't tolerate citrus, try eating more peppers, garlic, onions, cantaloupe, kale, parsley, turnip greens, broccoli, rose hips, black currants, strawberries, apples, persimmons, guavas, acerola cherries, potatoes, cabbage, and tomatoes. All fresh fruits and vegetables contain vitamin C and variable amounts of bioflavonoids.

Some people have bad reactions to vitamin C, including headaches, gas, nausea, and lightheadedness. Often these symptoms can be overcome by using buffered forms of vitamin C like sodium ascorbate, calcium ascorbate, ester C, and others. In general, vitamin C is a weak acid. Candida, bacteria, fungi, and parasites are often killed off by high-dose vitamin C, and this releases toxins into the system. Stomach gas, headache, nausea, and lightheadedness sometimes result—but this is just a sign of a temporary cleansing or detoxification reaction. These problems can be eliminated by doing a vitamin C flush.[8]

If stomach gas is a problem with a vitamin C supplement and you don't wish to do a vitamin C flush, consider adding sodium bicarbonate to your ester C, sodium ascorbate, or calcium ascorbate supplement. This is available in powdered form and can be taken immediately after taking the vitamin C. Start with low doses of vitamin C and increase gradually as tolerated. Additionally, use a good *lactobacillus acidophilus* and *bifidus* supplement to help control the bowel flora, reducing gastrointestinal toxins and improving digestion.

---

[8] **Vitamin C flush**: This is done by increasing the dose of vitamin C to the point of clear, watery diarrhea which usually results in an effective purge of the majority of these toxins. The vitamin C flush is best done with buffered vitamin C powder. Take 1 tsp. in juice every $1/2$ hour until watery diarrhea is reached. After this bowel tolerance (or intolerance!) level is attained, adjust dosage to where the bowels feel comfortable. The gas and other detoxification reactions should disappear when the bowel movements are again normal.

A supplement of vitamin C (500-1000 mg.) can increase iron absorption by up to 30%. Other good absorption aids include Swedish bitters, betaine or glutamic acid hydrochloride, apple cider vinegar, and lemon juice.

Worsening hay fever and bleeding gums are signs of vitamin C deficiency. They are also a sign of a greater need for bioflavonoids. These can be taken in high doses without side effects and might also help you tolerate vitamin C supplements better.

If you are having trouble tolerating even the buffered forms of vitamin C, consider getting yourself checked out for chronic gastrointestinal dysbiosis. It is possible that you are suffering from a bacterial flora imbalance, candida overgrowth, bacterial infection, or parasites. A natural healthcare practitioner can order a comprehensive stool and digestive analysis with a comprehensive parasitology evaluation to rule out this potential problem.

Vitamin D

Vitamin D is a fat-soluble vitamin that is naturally present in only a very few foods. It is added to other foods and is available as a dietary supplement. It is also produced by synthesis when ultraviolet rays from sunlight strike the skin and is synthesized by the liver and kidneys. Vitamin D is essential for promoting calcium absorption in the gut and maintaining adequate serum calcium and phosphate concentrations to enable normal bone growth, prevent bone loss, and prevent muscle spasms..Without sufficient vitamin D, bones can become thin, brittle, or misshapen. Vitamin D sufficiency prevents rickets in children and bone disease in adults. Together with calcium, vitamin D also helps protect older adults from osteoporosis. Vitamin D has other roles in human health, including modulation of neuromuscular and immune function and reduction of inflammation.

New research[9] indicates the prevalence of vitamin D insufficiency among children in the U.S. is higher than previously thought. Although several small studies had found a high prevalence of vitamin D deficiency in specific populations of children, this new study is the first to examine the issue on a nationwide basis.

A new study in the journal **Pediatrics** magazine reveals a troubling prevalence of low levels of vitamin D among children in the U.S. Researchers evaluated data from over 6,000 children aged 1 to 21 who participated in the National Nutrition Examination Survey (NHANES) between 2001 and 2004. Insufficient levels of vitamin D were defined as 15 to 29 nanograms per milliliter (ng/mL), and deficient levels as less than 15 ng/mL.

Over 60% of the children studied had vitamin D levels defined as insufficient. Outright deficiency occurred in 9% (or 5.4% of those studied) of the subjects. If applied to the U.S. population, these percentages would be equivalent to nearly 51 million children with insufficient vitamin D levels, and 7.6 million children with vitamin D deficiency. Participants who consumed at least 400 IU of vitamin D per day were less likely to experience a deficiency, but just four percent of the children used vitamin D supplements.

In addition to its consequences regarding bone health, vitamin D deficiency can potentially increase the risk of future heart disease and other health conditions. The researchers concluded that physicians should be screening children for vitamin D levels, especially in populations that are considered high risk.

Vitamin E

Whether from a natural or synthetic source, **all** forms of vitamin E supply the body with some efficacy or activity.

Vitamin E is also known as *alpha-tocopherol*. Studies indicate that supplementation of as little as 200 **IU** daily in men can reduce the risk of a heart attack by 46%; in women the risk reduction is by 26%.

---

[9] **Pediatrics** August 1, 2009 (*online*)

- The natural forms of vitamin E are *d-alpha-tocopherol, d-alpha-tocopheryl acetate, d-alpha-tocopheryl succinate* and mixed *tocopherols.*

- The synthetic forms of vitamin E are *dl-alpha-tocopherol, dl-alpha-tocopheryl acetate* or *dl-alpha-tocopheryl succinate.*

Studies indicate that the most biologically active are the esterified natural forms: *d-alpha-tocopheryl acetate* and *d-alpha-tocopheryl succinate.* Both have been found to provide full antioxidant activity in the body and are the ones recommended by the top authorities on vitamin E at the Shute Institute and Medical Clinic in London, Ontario, Canada.

Recent studies indicate that high levels of stored iron in the body (ferritin) are associated with a greater risk of heart disease and diabetes.

High-dose vitamin E supplements can interfere with iron absorption. If you have been prescribed iron to correct iron deficiency, take your iron supplement about 12 hours apart from vitamin E. Iron destroys vitamin E in the body. Iron absorption is enhanced by sufficient acid in the stomach.

Birth control pills, mineral oils, alcohol, pollution, and chlorinated drinking water can possibly deplete vitamin E in the body.

Basic Vitamins for Daily Supplementation[10]

Following is a basic overview of the vitamins you should consider having in your daily supplementation. There are many different kinds of vitamins capable of helping your body achieve a high level of health or to be able to remain healthy—especially under adverse conditions.

These vitamins, along with the essential minerals, also called micronutrients, are elements your body needs, in small amounts, to promote good biochemical reactions within the body and in its individual cells.

Vitamins provide your body with the capability to:

- help it grow effectively,
- digest food efficiently,
- stay mentally alert and more mentally sound,
- be more resistant to infectious diseases,
- use carbohydrates, proteins, and fats more effectively, and
- act as catalysts in your body to initiate or speed up the body's chemical reactions.

The difference between the vitamins and the proteins derived from food is that the body doesn't burn up the vitamins, so you can't use them for energy. Because your body does not make most vitamins and minerals within the body, they must be ingested from food sources or from vitamin supplements.

If you aren't getting enough of certain vitamins or minerals for a long period of time you can suffer from a specific disease or condition.

Basically, there are 12 vitamins the body absolutely needs—four (4) are fat-soluble and nine (8) are water-soluble.

---

[10]Contributed by **Maryel Isham-Allen**, Certified Nutritional Consultant (**CNC**), Homeopathic Therapeutic Consultant, Certified Quantum Biofeedback Specialist, B.S. Human Ecology, University of Texas @ Austin; Investor and contributing columnist/artist to *Enjoy Whole Health Magazine,* San Antonio TX.

The 4 Fat-soluble vitamins that can be stored in the body fat and in certain organs, such as the liver, include:

1. **A**
2. **D**
3. **E,** and
4. **K**

These fat-soluble vitamins are dissolved in lipids[11] and require bile in order to be absorbed. They are also stored in tissues, and if you have too many of them they can become toxic to you.

The 8 Water-soluble vitamins that are not stored in the body in large amounts include vitamin C and 8 of the B vitamins, seven which were mentioned previously:

1. **Vitamin B$_1$,** (*thiamin*) assists in the production of energy and affects enzymes that influence the muscles, nerves, and heart.
2. **Vitamin B$_2$** (riboflavin) assists in the production of energy and affects enzymes that influence the muscles, nerves, and heart.
3. **Vitamin B$_3$** (*niacin*) assists the cells and also helps maintain the health of the skin, nervous system, and digestive system.
4. **Vitamin B$_5$** (*pantothenic acid*) allows the body to grow and develop normally.
5. **Vitamin B$_6$** (*pyridoxine*) helps to break down protein and maintain the health of red blood cells, the nervous system, and parts of the immune system.
6. **Vitamin B$_7$** (*biotin*) also assists in the breakdown of protein and carbohydrates and helps the body make various hormones.
7. **Vitamin B$_9$** (*folic acid*) helps the cells in the body make and maintain DNA and is important in the production of red blood cells. B$_9$ slows aging of the cells.
8. **Vitamin B$_{12}$** (*cobalamin*) assists with growth and development. It also has a part in producing blood cells, the functions of the nervous system, and how the body uses folic acid and carbohydrates.

These B vitamins dissolve in water, so care should be exercised when washing, preparing, and cooking to prevent actually eliminating them in the process. They are easily absorbed and excreted, and are not readily stored in the body's tissues. These vitamins seldom reach toxic levels in the body.

All of these essential basic vitamins are found in food, but if you don't consume the proper foods, the vitamins will need to come from nutritional supplements to assure you are getting all of the vitamins and minerals that your body needs—especially when your diet is substandard due to stress or proper foods privation when living under conditions dictated by natural, people-caused, or personal disasters or emergencies.

---

[11] A biological compound that is not soluble in water, *e.g.* a fat.

Vitamin Supplements Intake Guide

Vitamins are indispensable to our general nutrition and good health. However, they do not directly contribute to energy or bodybuilding materials. Their important work is to form complex chemical compounds that have enzymatic activity necessary to convert food to energy and to build tissue. A prolonged lack of vitamins results in serious health problems.

Most people assume all vitamins are supplied by a well-balanced diet. However, it is difficult under current conditions to eat the necessary variety, quality, or quantity of foods to get all the essential vitamins.

Adequate research has been done to prove the normal consumption of foods detailed in the *four food groups* does not supply these necessary vitamins. This is due mainly to the inadequate processing, distribution, handling, storage, and preparation of food.

Pollutants (oxidants) also put tremendous stress on our immune systems, thereby requiring more vitamins to rid the body of unwanted toxins.

The standard three-meals-a-day diet is lacking in some of the vitamins we need for our body's metabolic competence. The lack of vitamins allows our body's defenses to be more vulnerable to disease.

Also, some of the foods we eat are in reality "*antinutrient*" foods, thus robbing our body of nutrients necessary for digestion and assimilation.

The **Vitamin Supplement Intake Guide (Quick-Guide 23–1)** on the following pages details this specific information in the various columns:

1. The current United States Recommended Daily Allowance (**USRDA**) for selected vitamins.
2. A recommendation for the corresponding *Basic Optimal Health Daily Allowance* (**BOHDA**) based on major studies which differ from the **USRDA's** (*now* **USDRI**) published information.
3. Whether the selected vitamins are fat- or water-soluble.
4. The known function of the vitamins in the body.
5. Food sources which provide the vitamins.

Quick-Guide 23–1

Vitamin Supplements Intake Guide[1]

Dietary Supplement & Solubility	USDRI[2,3] Ch = 12 mo.- 4 yr. Ad = 4 yr.-Adults Fe = Adult Female PL = Pregnant/ Lactating	Corresponding Basic Optimal Health Daily Allowance[4]	Function in Body	Selected Food Sources[5]
Beta carotene	no USDRI established	• Ch @ • Ad @ 5,000-25,000 IU • Fe @ • PL @	• decreases free radical damage to lipoprotein • decreases risk of heart attacks • converted in liver & intestines to preformed vitamin A	blue green algae, spirulina, chlorella, yellow, orange & dark green vegetables, fish liver oil, green leafy vegetables, peach, alfalfa sprouts, sweet potato, papaya
Biotin *B-complex vitamin*	30 mcg	• Ch @ 25 mcg • Ad @ 50-300 mcg • Fe @ 25-300 mcg • PL @	• *water-soluble* coenzyme aids metabolism of carbohydrates-fats-proteins • aids in prevention of nervous system disorders • not a true vitamin (made in intestines)	unrefined whole grains: oats, rice, rye, wheat; all meats; liver; leafy green vegetables; poultry, saltwater fish, eggs, nuts, beans
Bioflavonoids* *(see Vitamin P)*				
Folic acid *(folacin)* *B-complex vitamin*		• Ch @ 200 mcg • Ad @ 400 mcg • Fe @ 400 mcg • PL @ 800 mcg • PL @ 800 mcg / pregnant • PL @ 500 mcg / lactating	• *water-soluble* vitamin helps in formation of hemoglobin and red blood cells • normal growth & reproduction • enhances protein metabolism • treats pernicious anemia & sprue	green leafy vegetables, broccoli, asparagus, okra, parsnips, cauliflower, cantaloupe, nuts, legumes, Brussels sprouts, whole-grain cereals, yeast, oranges, carrots
Niacin *(see Vitamin B₃)*				
Pantothenic acid *(see Vitamin B₅)*				
Vitamin A[6] *(retinol)*	• Ch @ 2,500 IU • Ad @ 5,000 IU • PL @ 8,000 IU	• Ch @ 15,000 IU • Ad @ 10,000-50,000 IU • Fe @ 3,000 IU • PL @	• essential *fat-soluble*[7] nutrient & antioxidant • aids in growth & repair of body tissues • necessary for night vision • essential for the formation of visual purple	eggs, colored fruits & vegetables, fish liver oil, milk & dairy products, beef liver

1 The FDA requires disclosure of certain nutritional values in food products. Shaded rows of the chart indicate which values *must* appear on nutrition labels of foods and drugs—all other ingredients *may* be listed.

2 The U.S. government's evaluation of the minimum daily requirements of a substance is to prevent a deficiency disease or condition in the population.

3 **Dietary Reference Intakes (DRI)** are the most recent set of dietary recommendations established by the Food Nutrition Board of the Institute of Medicine (1997-2001). They have replaced previous RDAs and may become the basis for updating the RDAs. The values shown here are the highest **DRI** for each nutrient.

4 Where there is a distinct difference between the **USRDA** and other major studies.

5 Complete listings available from published literature. Amounts of nutrients and vitamins vary among producers and their respective products. Always check labels of foods to verify contents.

6 Recommended one-half of the requirement be in the form of beta carotene.

7 *Fat-soluble vitamins* are stored in either the fat (lipid) tissues or body organs for longer periods and can cause toxicity only at very large doses. Likewise, minerals, which are stored primarily in the bones and muscle tissue, require extremely large doses to cause toxicity in the body.

Vitamin Supplements Intake Guide (continued)

Dietary Supplement	USDRI Ch = 12 mo. - 4 yr. Ad = 4 yr.-Adults Fe = Adult Female PL = Pregnant/Lactating	Corresponding Basic Optimal Health Daily Allowance	Function in Body	Selected Food Sources
Vitamin B₁ *(thiamin)*	• Ch @ 0.7 mg • Ad @ 1.5 mg • Fe @ 1.2 mg • PL @ 2 mg	• Ch @ 25 mg • Ad @ 50-300 mg • Fe @ 25-300 mg • PL @	• maintains healthy skin, mouth, eyes, hair • helps stabilize appetite • essential for carbohydrate metabolism • essential for normal function of heart, nervous system, digestion, growth, learning capacity	organ meats, pork, nuts, whole wheat, wheat germ, poultry, fish, brown rice, egg yolks, legumes, whole grains, blackstrap molasses, brewer's yeast
Vitamin B₂ *(riboflavin)*	• Ch @ 0.8 mg • Ad @ 1.7 mg • Fe @ 1.3 mcg • PL @ 2 mg	• Ch @ 25 mg • Ad @ 50-300 mg • Fe @ 25-300 mg • PL @	• *water-soluble* vitamin prevents inflammations • helps carbohydrate-fat-protein metabolism • produces antibody & red blood cells • essential for healthy eyes, hair, skin, nails	cheese, milk & milk products, egg yolks, peanuts, brewer's yeast, nuts, organ meats, whole grains, blackstrap molasses
Vitamin B₃ *(niacin & niacinamide)*	• Ch @ 9-16 mg • Ad @ 8 mg • Fe @ 16 mg • PL @ 15 mg	• Ch @ 25 mg • Ad @ 50-500 mg • Fe @ 25-300 mg • PL @	• *water-soluble* coenzyme essential in digestion • dilates blood vessels & helps blood circulation • reduces cholesterol in blood • needed for healthy skin, nervous system & production of sex hormones	lean meats, poultry, fish, peanuts, wheat germ, brewer's yeast
Vitamin B₅ *(pantothenic acid)*	• Ch @ 3 mg • Ad @ 10 mg • Fe @ 5 mg • PL @ 7 mg	• Ch @ 25 g • Ad @ 25-500 g • Fe @ 25-300 g • PL @	• *water-soluble* vitamin aids in resisting stress • aids in formation of fats & provides energy • stimulates growth	eggs, orange juice, brewer's yeast, legumes, liver, whole grains, wheat germ, mushrooms, salmon
Vitamin B₆ *(pyridoxine)*	• Ch @ 700 mcg • Ad @ 2 mg • Fe @ 2.4 mg • PL @ 250 mg	• Ch @ 25 g • Ad @ 50-500 mg • Fe @ 50-300 mg • PL @	• essential *water-soluble enzyme* factor for carbohydrate-fat-protein metabolism • helps in digestion & weight control • enhances healthy skin, nerves & muscles • forms antioxidants	milk, cabbage, cantaloupe, legumes, blackstrap molasses, meats, organ meats, peas, wheat germ, whole grains, brown rice, prunes, leafy green vegetables, brewer's yeast
Vitamin B₁₂ *(cobalamin)*	• Ch @ 3 mcg • Ad @ 6 mcg • Fe @ 1.7 mg • PL @ 8 mcg	• Ch @ 25 g • Ad @ 50-500 mcg • Fe @ 25-300 mcg • PL @	• *water-soluble* vitamin essential to formation & maintenance of red blood cells • enhances carbohydrate-fat-protein metabolism • promotes healthy nervous system	pork, beef, organ meats, cheese, milk & milk products, eggs, fish
Vitamin C *(ascorbic acid)*	• Ch @ 40 mg • Ad @ 60 mg • Fe @ 90 mg • PL @ 60 mg	• Ch @ 1,000 mcg • Ad @ 1,000-10,000 mg • Fe @ 500-10,000 mg • PL @	• *water-soluble* nutrient & antioxidant • essential in formation of skin connective tissue • strengthens body's immune system • helps in wound healing	tomatoes, acerola cherries, sprouted alfalfa seeds, peppers, citrus fruits, papaya, cantaloupe, broccoli, strawberries

Vitamin Supplements Intake Guide (continued)

Vitamin			Description	Food Sources
Vitamin D (cholecalciferol)	• Ch @ 400 IU • Ad @ 400 IU • Fe @ 600 IU • PL @ 400 IU	• Ch @ 400 IU • Ad @ 400-600 IU • Fe @ 600-800 IU (age 60+) • PL @	• *fat-soluble* nutrient essential for proper function of nervous system, heart & normal clotting • aids in calcium & phosphorous absorption to prevent osteoporosis in elderly persons	fat, butter, fish liver oil, oily fish (herring, sardines), egg yolks, salmon, tuna, organ meats, bone meal
Vitamin E[8] (tocopherol)	• Ch @ 15 mg • Ad @ 22 IU • Fe @ 33 IU • PL @ 30 IU	• Ch @ 200 IU • Ad @ 200-800 IU • Fe @ 100-800 IU	• *fat-soluble* powerful antioxidant & free radical scavenger • essential for cell respiration & sustains the efficiency of blood flow • composed of several tocopherols of which the alpha form is most active	margarine, cold-pressed oil, whole wheat & wheat germ, sweet potatoes, molasses, nuts, dark green vegetables, eggs, organ meats, oatmeal, liver, desiccated liver
Vitamin F (lineolic acid)	• Ch @ 10-12 IU • Ad @ 10-17 IU • Fe @ 11 IU • PL @ 13 IU		• unsaturated fatty acid essential to growth • necessary for healthy skin & hair • makes calcium available to body cells • enhances normal glandular activity • destroys cholesterol	butter, wheat germ, vegetable oils, sunflower seed
Vitamin K (phylloquinone)	• Ch @ 35 IU • Ad @ 60-75 IU • Fe @ 90 IU • PL @ 90 IU	• Ch @ • Ad @ 80 mcg males • Fe @ 65 mcg females • PL @	• *fat-soluble* group of similar compounds including: **K-1** from plants; **K-2** made in the intestines by bacteria; **K-3**, a synthetic form • produces blood-clotting factors • helps prevent osteoporosis • not a true vitamin, developed in intestines	widely available in foods such as spinach, green cabbage, tomatoes, liver, lean meats, egg yolk, whole wheat, strawberries
Vitamin P (bioflavonoids)	no USDRI established *(take with equivalent amount of vitamin C)*	• Ad @ 500-10,000 mg • Fe @ 500-5,000 mg	• *water-soluble* vitamin prevents colds & flu • promotes healthy capillary walls • enhances growth of connective tissue • helps prevent bruising	buckwheat, black currants, cherries, grapes, fruits

Notes on Vitamins

Notes on Vitamins

[8] The upper limit of vitamin E is 1,000 mg because of a significant risk of bleeding which may increase the risk of hemorrhaging and premature death (adults over 19 years).

MINERALS OF IMPORTANCE

Boron

Boron is a trace mineral which is essential in the prevention of osteoporosis and arthritis. Many people are deficient in this mineral simply because of poor soil quality. Lack of boron in soils may be one of the reasons for the failure of medical therapies in the treatment of both osteoporosis and osteoarthritis. Boron is a *helper* mineral that helps the body maximize its use of calcium, magnesium, and phosphorous.

Activated Charcoal

Activated charcoal is an antidote for almost all known poisons. It is a natural agent that relieves gas and diarrhea. To use for insect stings and bites (even snake bites while on the way to the hospital), make a poultice (or use cotton or gauze) by mixing the contents of a capsule with enough water to make a moist paste and place over the wound, tape in place, and keep the poultice moist.

Chromium Picolinate

Chromium picolinate is the most bioavailable (best absorbed) form of chromium. It is essential for the prevention and the complementary medical treatment of diabetes, heart disease, atherosclerosis, high blood cholesterol, obesity and other eating disorders. Chromium picolinate is a general tonic which improves energy, cuts the cravings for sweets, and normalizes blood sugar levels by helping in the production of insulin. It plays a vital role in the breaking down of simple sugars in the body. It is also important to the body's enzymes and hormones.

Copper

Copper is an important trace mineral stored in the liver. This vital component of enzymes is necessary to the breaking down of proteins for rebuilding body tissue. It is also required to convert the body's iron into hemoglobin—and is essential in the utilization of vitamin C.

Copper is essential to optimal operation of brain nerves and connective tissues. Copper in the optimal doses controls cholesterol and is vital in the prevention of aortic aneurysms. The zinc-to-copper ratio must be balanced in the body (*8:1 zinc: copper is ideal*) and can be determined through a combination of blood, urine, and hair tests. If testing is not possible, make sure that supplemental zinc and copper are taken in the optimal ratio.

Selenium

Low selenium levels are associated with an increased risk of atherosclerosis. Approximately 80% of selenium content in foods is lost in the processing of food. Selenium is an antioxidant which works in conjunction with vitamin E to protect vascular tissue from damage by toxins. Besides preventing cardiovascular disease, selenium helps in both the prevention and complementary medical treatment of cancer, arthritis, and a long list of degenerative diseases, among which are premature aging and hardening of the tissues. It is generally conceded that men need more selenium than women. Almost half the selenium found in the male body is in the reproductive organs.

Zinc

This essential mineral is needed by everyone! It is found in every cell of the body. Zinc performs many important functions in the body such as converting proteins into energy,

RNA/DNA formation, male prostate gland protection, and, in conjunction with calcium, increasing bone formation.

Zinc is becoming the most frequently prescribed supplement in holistic health centers—and with good reason. It can have a wide range of beneficial effects that include enhancement of wound healing, promotion of a healthy immune system, optimizing sexual performance, and balancing thyroid function.

Zinc is believed to play a vital role in mental functions, the healing process, blood stability, and in keeping a proper alkaline balance in the body. The wound-healing effects of zinc supplementation have been known since 1955. Many double-blind studies since that time have demonstrated zinc's ability to accelerate healing in post-surgical cases, leg ulcers, and gastric ulcers.

Zinc deficiency signs and symptoms are similar to the general signs of malnutrition and include growth retardation, infertility, delayed sexual maturation, low sperm count, hair loss, various skin conditions, diarrhea, weakened immune response, behavioral and sleep disturbances, vitamin A nonresponsive night blindness, impaired taste or smell perception, impaired wound healing, and white spots or horizontal ridges on the fingernails.

A recent study showed that taking about 10 zinc lozenges (containing 23 mg. of zinc) per day reduced the length of recovery from the common cold from an average of 10.8 days to 3.9 days. One of the reasons for this may be because zinc is a cofactor for a number of enzymes involved in the immune response. Zinc deficiency is associated with compromised immune response and is normalized by zinc replacement therapy.

Many skin problems, including acne, boils, some forms of hair loss, and severe body odor, respond favorably to zinc supplementation of 100-150 mg. per day. Topical application of zinc sulfate solution can reduce the length of healing of cold sores caused by both Type 1 and Type 2 herpes virus from 17 days to 5.3 days.

Many over-the-counter ointments advertised for the relief of cold sores, diaper rashes, and hemorrhoids have zinc as one of their ingredients. At least one mouthwash advocated for periodontal disease prevention and halitosis contains therapeutic amounts of zinc. Corticosteroid therapy used for a variety of reasons rapidly depletes zinc stores and causes retardation of tissue healing. A variety of other drugs, alcohol, and tobacco smoke also deplete zinc body stores and require supplementation to prevent skin and immune system problems.

Growth in children, healthy hair, taste perception, and the sense of smell are all related to zinc status. Anorexia nervosa, bulimia, and other eating disorders respond positively to zinc supplementation.

Most recently, ophthalmologic studies have demonstrated that zinc supplementation can prevent macular degeneration, a common cause of blindness that occurs with aging. Memory problems ("*no zinc, no think*"), behavioral disorders, insomnia, depression, and many other nervous system abnormalities have been associated with zinc insufficiency.

Processed foods, stress, diuretics, alcohol, and other factors deplete the body of zinc. The nearly 200 signs and symptoms of the "*candidiasis syndrome*," popularized by a rash of sensationalized books, all recommend the use of zinc supplementation as a part of both its treatment and prevention.

Many authors wonder whether *candidiasis* is really a zinc deficiency problem in disguise. Zinc and copper are both involved in optimal thyroid function, liver function, and cholesterol control. This balance is also essential for the correct metabolism of essential fatty acids and their conversion into various hormones. Balancing these two minerals may be crucial to the prevention of many common diseases, including cardiovascular disease, hypothyroidism, prostatitis, and different forms of arthritis.

<u>Dr. Rona does not recommend the long-term use of zinc supplementation without supervision by a healthcare practitioner.</u> Aside from the potential heart and circulatory problems caused by copper depletion with high zinc supplementation, some individuals have problems with absorption of one or both of these minerals.

For those concerned about being adequately nourished in zinc the safest thing to do is to optimize the diet. Published **RDA** (Recommended Dietary Allowance) for adults is 15 mg. per day. In approximately 1,000 nutritional intake assessments done in Dr. Rona's practice, less than 10% get the minimum RDA zinc intake levels from their diets.

The richest sources of zinc are generally the high-protein foods such as organ meat, seafood (especially shellfish), oysters, whole grains, and legumes (especially beans and peas). Beyond ensuring zinc adequacy from the diet, the best thing to do is see a holistic healthcare practitioner to decide whether or not supplementation for specific therapy is worth trying.

Mineral Supplements Intake Guide

Essential mineral elements normally found in the body are supplied in natural foods. Often, they are lost or destroyed in production, distribution, delivery, storage, and/or during meal preparation. These natural minerals are needed for the body's purifying and cleansing processes. The essential minerals are divided into two categories, *macrominerals,* and *microminerals*. The listings in the chart below differentiate these two types of essential minerals. Those noted in the listing here are detailed in the chart on the following pages.

Macrominerals
- Calcium
- Chlorine
- Magnesium
- Phosphorous
- Potassium
- Sodium
- Sulfur

Microminerals
- Boron
- Cobalt
- Chromium
- Copper
- Fluorine
- Iodine
- Iron
- Manganese
- Molybdenum
- Nickel
- Selenium
- Silicon
- Tin
- Vanadium
- Zinc

Macrominerals are needed in the diet in amounts exceeding 100 mg. per day. Of all the *macromineral* nutrients, only calcium tends to be low in the American diet.

*Micromineral*s are also known as "trace elements" and are needed in the body in extremely small units. Many of the micronutrients are needed in such minute amounts they are rarely a problem, with the exception of iron and zinc.

The **Mineral Supplements Intake Guide (Quick-Guide 23–2)** details the following information for the macrominerals and microminerals indicated above:

1. The current United States Recommended Daily Allowance (**USRDA,** now the **USDRI**) for the selected minerals mentioned in the chapter;
2. A recommendation for the corresponding *Basic Optimal Health Daily Allowance* (**BOHDA**), based on major studies which differ from the **USRDA's** (now **USDRI**) published information;
3. The known function of the mineral in the body; and
4. Food sources which provide the mineral.

Quick-Guide 23–2
Mineral Supplements Intake Guide

Dietary Supplement	USDRI[1] Ch = 12 mo.- 4 yr. Ad = 4 yr.-Adults Fe = Adult Female PL = preg-nant/lactating	Corresponding Basic Optimal Health Daily Allowance[2]	Function in Body	Selected Food Sources[3]
Boron*	**no USDRI established**	• Ch @ • Ad @ 3-6 mg • Fe @ 2-5 mg • PL @	• *micromineral* modulates calcium & magnesium retention in bones & lessens fibromyalgia • helps prevent osteoporosis, rheumatism & arthritis • treats tendinitis, joints & joint deterioration, sciatica, heel & bone spurs • treats skin disease & scleroderma • treats hormone imbalance & raises serum estrogen levels • lessens progression of Alzheimer's disease	fruits, vegetables
Calcium *(highest mineral content in body)*	• Ch @ 800 mg • Ad @ 1000 mg • PL @ 1300 mg	• Ch @ 800-1000 mg • Ad @ 1000-2000 mg • Fe @ 1000-1500 mg • Fe @ 1200-2000 mg (over 52 yr.) • PL @ 1500-2000 mg	• *macromineral* essential to body synthesis • develops and maintains strong bones & teeth • protects against osteoporosis • ensures proper blood clotting • aids vitality & endurance	dairy prod. (8 oz. nonfat milk = 300 mg; 1 C. yogurt = 400+ mg), goat s milk, tofu, oats, brewer's yeast, legumes & dark green vegetables, enriched cereals, citrus fruits, figs, shellfish, liver, nuts, antacids w/o aluminum (Tums® = 200+ mg)
Choline[4]	• Ch @ 250 mg • Ad @ 375 mg • Fe @ 425 mg • PL @ 950 mg	• Ch @ 1000 mg • Ad @ 2000 mg • Fe @ 3500 mg • PL @ 3000-3500 mg	• nerve transmission • aids metabolism • helps regulate liver and gall bladder • precursor to acetylcholine, phospholipids &betaine	egg yolks, organ meats, brewer's yeast, wheat germ, milk, peanuts
Chromium* *(in picolinate form)*	**no USDRI established**	• Ch @ 200 mcg • Ad @ 200-600 mcg • Fe @ 200-600 mcg • PL @	• *micromineral* essential for maximization of glucose • for synthesis of cholesterol & fatty acids • essential part of enzyme systems	whole grains & whole-grain cereals, brewer's yeast, beer, clams, corn oil, dried beans, cheese, potato, brcwn rice, meats
Copper	• Ch @ 1 mg • Ad @ 2 mg • Fe @ 2 mg • PL @ 2 mg	• Ch @ 1 mg • Ad @ 0.5-2 mg • Fe @ 0.5-2 mg	• *micromineral* prevents anemia by controlling storage & release of iron to form hemoglobin • promotes energy and connective tissue metabolism • essential part of tissue covering nerves	nuts, dried peas & beans, dried fruit, raisins, whole grains, leafy vegetables, molasses, organ meats, fish, shell fish, legumes—widely ava lable in most foods

1 The U.S. Government's evaluation of the minimum daily requirements of a substance has been developed to prevent a deficiency disease or condition.
2 Where there is a distinct difference between the USDRI and other major studies.
3 Complete listings available from published literature. Amounts of nutrients and minerals vary among producers and their respective products. Always check labels to verify contents.
* Essential for human nutrition, but no USDRI has been established.
4 Special Considerations: individuals with depression, liver disease, renal disease, or Parkinson's disease may be at risk of adverse effects with intake levels @BOHDA.

Mineral Supplements Intake Guide (continued)

Dietary Supplement	USDRI Ch = 12 mo.- 4 yr. Ad = 4 yr.-Adults Fe = Adult Female PL = pregnant/lactating	Corresponding Basic Optimal Health Daily Allowance	Function in Body	Selected Food Sources
Iodine	• Ch @ 70 mcg • Ad @ 150 mcg • Fe @ 150 mcg • PL @ 150 mcg	• Ch @ 100 mcg / from iodized table salt • Ad @ 150-300 mcg • Fe @ 150-300 mcg	• *micromineral* essential for total body metabolism • essential for normal function of thyroid gland • prevents goiter	iodized table salt, food grown near the ocean, kelp (bladderwrack), mushrooms
Iron	• Ch @ 10 g • Ad @ 10 g • PL @ 18 mg	• Ch @ • Ad @ 15-30 g • Fe @ 15-30 g • PL @ 20-30 g	• *micromineral*, essential part of hemoglobin carrying oxygen to tissues • part of enzyme system of all cells for energy production • important to muscle tone	whole-grain cereal products, nuts, legumes, raisins, molasses, green leafy vegetables, potatoes, yellow vegetables, dried fruits, boiled lentils or kidney beans
Magnesium	• Ch @ 200 mg • Ad @ 400 mg • PL @ 450 mg	• Ch @ 250-500 mg • Ad @ 500-1,000 mg • Fe @ 500-750 mg	• *macromineral* helps develop strong bones & teeth • helps regulate muscle tone • aids in proper functioning of nerves	green leafy vegetables, nuts, seeds, whole-grain cereals, legumes, apples, cherries, figs, raisins, prunes, lemons, alfalfa, celery, cherry juice
Phosphorous *(2ⁿᵈ highest mineral content in body)*	• Ch @ 800 mg • Ad @ 1 g • PL @ 1.3 g	• Ad @ 200-400 mg • Fe @ 200-400 mg	• *macromineral* essential for development of strong bones & teeth • essential to development of enzymes in cells that control storage & release of energy • transports fatty acids in body	whole-wheat grains, nuts, legumes, dairy products, eggs, phosphate additives/carbonated drinks, yellow cheese, glandular meats, poultry, seeds: sesame, sunflower
Selenium*	no USDRI established	• Ch @ 100 mcg • Ad @ 100-400 mcg • Fe @ 150-300 mcg	• *micromineral* required to activate enzyme to combat cell membrane oxidation • preserves tissue elasticity for body's maximum immune response & helps prevent cancer • protects normal cells against radiation damage	broccoli, onions, tomatoes, tuna, nuts, brown rice, grains, nuts, cereals (especially those grown in ND, SD, MT, WY), chicken, turkey, brewer's yeast
Zinc	• Ch @ 8 mg • Ad @ 15 mg • Fe @ 12 mg • PL @ 20/25 mg	• Ch @ 15 mg • Ad @ 30-100 mg • Fe @ 20-50 mg	• *micromineral* aiding digestion & metabolism of phosphorous, carbohydrates & proteins • component of body synthesis for normal growth & development; enhances wound healing • promotes healthy immune system • part of insulin & reproductive processes • increases male sexual potency; elevates testosterone; reduces prostate swelling	organ meats, poultry dark meat, fish, seafood (especially oysters), liver, eggs, legumes (soybeans & peanuts), whole grains, spinach, mushrooms, sunflower seeds

HERBS AND WHOLE FOOD SUPPLEMENTS

Aloe Vera

Many of you know that aloe vera is an ingredient in cosmetics, pharmaceuticals, gels, lotions, shampoos, juices, creams, toothpastes, and nutritional supplements. Some people use aloe topically for its antibiotic properties, others internally for its bowel cleansing action, antioxidant, or anti-aging effects.

Aloe vera contains many free radical scavengers and immune system enhancers. These include beta carotene, vitamin B complex, vitamin C, selenium, silicon, zinc, boron, calcium, chromium, magnesium, manganese, potassium, polyphenols, essential fatty acids, saponins, and large molecular weight polymeric sugars (e.g., acemannan).

Aloe is very effective in the treatment of digestive disorders. One of the many reasons why aloe vera is so effective for digestive problems is its content of natural digestive enzymes and cofactors. Aloe contains amylase, lipase, oxidase, catalase, bradykinase, glucomannan, and fiber. All reduce inflammation; stimulate better digestion of protein, carbohydrate, and fat; and soothe ulcers.

Medical and scientific literature supports aloe vera's primary or complementary use for a long list of conditions. The following chart indicates a partial listing of conditions known to benefit from aloe vera:

Chart 23–1
Selected Conditions Known to Benefit from Aloe Vera Treatment

- Acne
- Allergies
- Amenorrhea (no menses)
- Asthma
- Bites (bee stings/insect bites)
- Bleeding/hemorrhage (anywhere)
- Boils
- Burns
- Bruises
- Cancer[1]
- Canker sores (mouth ulcers)
- Chemical burns
- Chicken pox itch
- Colds and flu
- Colitis and Crohn's Disease
- Constipation[2]
- Coughs
- Denture sores
- Diaper rashes
- Eczema
- Fatigue (often used as a tonic)
- Fever
- Food poisoning
- Headache
- Heartburn/indigestion (from any cause)
- Hemorrhoids
- Hepatitis and jaundice
- Herpes
- Inflammation and infections (anywhere)
- Menopause
- PMS (Pre-Menstrual Syndrome)
- Pain
- Psoriasis
- Scars
- Sunburns
- Stomach problems
- Thinning hair
- Tinnitus (ringing in the ears)
- Ulcers (anywhere)
- Venereal diseases
- Warts
- Wounds (anywhere)

Dr. Rona has often recommended aloe vera be taken internally in juice form. Most patients love the results but hate the taste of different brands of aloe vera juice. Many either try to disguise the taste by diluting it with sweet juices, thus reducing its potency, or just give up because nothing neutralizes the sour/bitter aftertaste. One option may be to swallow capsules containing live aloe vera concentrate.

---

[1] Aloe contains several anticarcinogenic compounds.

[2] Avoid as a laxative during pregnancy unless anthraquinone content of the aloe vera being consumed is known to be low.

The whole leaf cold processing method maximizes the desirable constituents of aloe vera juice, increases the pleasant polysaccharide concentration, eliminates the undesirable anthraquinones, and improves its penetration into the body.

"Dr. Rona, how can aloe vera be effective for so many different conditions?"

The answer lies in the nearly 100 ingredients contained in the leaf of the healthy aloe plant. These include numerous antioxidant vitamins and minerals. A closer look at the listing of reported and suggested uses will give you confidence that aloe vera has withstood the test of time and the scrutiny of cynical investigations.

It is difficult to know how aloe vera works—it has very complex properties:

- It is an excellent nutrient with important proteins, vitamins, minerals, and some substances that are essential to the release of energy in the body of humans and animals alike.
- Its chemical properties allow it to penetrate the skin and body membranes, thus carrying essential nutrients to the living cells of both the skin and internal organs.
- It contains several enzymes necessary to the body but not yet fully understood by science.

Apple Cider Vinegar

Apple cider vinegar is a fundamental health aid that has a multitude of uses and is especially useful in both short- and long-term storage scenarios, whether for cooking or for its medicinal properties. It's made by fermenting the juice of whole, fresh apples. It's high in calcium, potassium, sodium, phosphorus, and other trace minerals. It has an average acetic acid content of 5% and has been used as both a food and a medicine.

A long list of medical conditions can benefit from apple cider vinegar supplementation, including obesity, infections, allergies, arthritis, fatigue, circulatory disorders, and thinning hair. It is true that apple cider vinegar can increase the body's acidity, but in many individuals this produces a beneficial effect. In others, the excess acidity makes their symptoms worse. Some people are allergic to it—in other cases apple cider vinegar has no effect whatsoever. Published research indicates that apple cider vinegar inhibits diarrhea due to its astringent property, helps oxygenate the blood, increases metabolic rate, improves digestion, fights tooth decay and intestinal parasites, and improves blood clotting ability.

Many people over age 60 suffer from a lack of stomach acid. Supplementation of 1 to 2 T. of apple cider vinegar with each meal aids in protein digestion and prevents many vitamin and mineral deficiencies. Add some honey to sweeten vinegar's taste, if necessary. Apple cider vinegar can also be used as a mouthwash and throat gargle for antiseptic purposes. It has no significant side effects and is safe for diabetics. Also, despite its sodium content, apple cider vinegar is suitable for low-sodium diets.

Bee Supplements

Most of you are familiar with bee supplements like bee pollen, royal jelly, and propolis. If not, here is basic information about these bee-produced supplements:

- ***Propolis*** is a rather strong-tasting bee product well known by health advocates for its natural antibiotic properties.
- ***Royal jelly*** is a supplement which must be combined with honey to preserve its potency. Royal jelly has been touted as a natural substance which benefits a wide range of health conditions. This is because it contains all the B complex vitamins,

high concentrations of vitamin B_5 (pantothenic acid), vitamin B_6, acetylcholine, minerals, vitamins A, C, D, and E, enzymes, hormones, amino acids and immune-boosting substances. Most healthy people tolerate it well without any side effects.

- *Bee pollen* contains simple sugars, amino acids, calcium, carotene, copper, enzymes, iron, magnesium, manganese, polyunsaturated fatty acids, sodium, potassium, vitamin C, and plant sterols.

- There is no known toxicity, but the rare individual may be allergic to pollen and experience hay fever-like symptoms. If you are a well-controlled diabetic or have hypoglycemia (low blood sugar), taking any bee supplement should not affect your blood sugars noticeably. If, on the other hand, your sugar level is poorly controlled, these supplements might upset the apple cart for you. Check the label or check with the manufacturer concerning the amount of glucose and fructose in each capsule or tablet before taking bee-produced supplements.

Beet Root Powder

Beet root powder is particularly high in carotenes, iron, calcium, potassium, niacin, copper, vitamin C, folic acid, zinc, manganese, magnesium, and phosphorus. Beet root powder enriches the blood and is also a good general tonic. The most optimal way of deriving the benefits of beet root aside from eating the real thing is to swallow capsules of beet root live food concentrate.

Bladderwrack

Also known as *fucus vesiculosus,* or *kelp*, bladderwrack is high in sodium alginate, calcium, phosphorus, magnesium, iron, sodium, selenium, potassium, iodine, sulfur, vitamins C and B_{12}. It's an alkaline-forming food, replenishing glands and nerves, particularly the thyroid. Bladderwrack is a good source of trace minerals and has traditionally been used in the complementary medical treatment of obesity, goiter, hypothyroidism, anemia, emaciation, impotence, nervousness, a weakened immune system, and hair loss.

Blue Green Algae & Other Green Foods

Blue green algae, spirulina, chlorella, barley green, green kamut, and other concentrated green foods are all excellent sources of high-quality vegetable protein, complex carbohydrates, essential fatty acids, essential amino acids, phytochemicals, chlorophyll, vitamins, minerals and fiber. ***These whole foods plus water provide enough nutrition to help sustain life for years.***

Although there are only minor differences among all these "green food" products, blue green algae seems to have a bit of an edge in some areas, especially with respect to a higher vitamin B_{12} and beta carotene content. All green foods have these qualities:

- natural appetite suppressants
- rich in beta carotene and other carotenoids
- high bioavailability (easily digested and absorbed compared to synthetic vitamins and minerals)
- strong antioxidant properties

Some of the many beneficial effects of green foods include higher energy, greater physical stamina, improved digestion and elimination, allergy relief, and immune system boosting. All green foods are compatible with each other as well as all other supplements on this list.

Cayenne Pepper

Also known as *capsicum frutescens*. Cayenne pepper is best known for strengthening all aspects of the circulatory system, normalizing blood pressure, and heart muscle regulation. It is used as a digestive aid to control gas and stomach upset, as a warming agent for joint and lower back pain, to break up mucus congestion in the respiratory tract, to stop bleeding, and to fight infection.

Cayenne is a stimulant, anti-emetic, expectorant, tonic, vasodilator, homeostatic.

Contains: Vitamin A, C, riboflavin, some vitamin B's and Niacin, Iron, Calcium, Magnesium, Phosphorus, Sulfur, and Potassium.

Available in liquid extract, salves, and creams.

Echinacea Root

Also known as *echinacea angustiflolia,* echinacea root is commonly called "*King of Blood Purifiers*," it is an herb used for the immune system and acts at various sites in the body to enhance immune system function, cleanse the lymph system, support normal white blood cell activity, promote healthy lung function, and support healthy upper respiratory tract tissue. Echinacea supports healthy immune response following sudden environmental changes or stress, as well as other stressors.

Caution: Echinacea should not be taken over a long period of time; it is best used for acute or chronic illness.

Contains: Vitamin A, E, C, Iron, Copper, Sulfur, and Potassium.

Fo-Ti

Fo-ti is a Chinese herb useful for improving deleterious effects of aging, arthritis, rheumatism, atherosclerosis, constipation, senility, gray hair, impotency, and insomnia. Effectively increases blood circulation and energy.

Ginger

Also known as *zingiber officinale*, this herb is best known for its soothing qualities for the gastrointestinal tract. It is particularly effective for nausea associated with pregnancy (morning sickness), anorexia, gas and flatulence, gastric and intestinal spasms, acute colds, painful menstruation, joint stiffness, and cold extremities. Ginger is a cardiac tonic, eases uterine pain, decreases serum cholesterol, and helps poor circulation.

Ginkgo Biloba

Also known as *maidenhair*, ginkgo is a strong antioxidant which can produce relaxation of blood vessels, inhibit platelet aggregation, increase peripheral and cerebral blood flow, and act in general as a cardiovascular and brain tonic. Ginkgo biloba has traditionally been used in the complementary medical treatment of arterial insufficiency, ischemic heart disease, peripheral vascular disease (it affects both arteries and veins), memory loss, other failing mental faculties, almost any neurological condition, tinnitus (ringing in the ears), and high blood pressure.

Hawthorne Berries

Also known as *crataegus oxyacantha*, this herb is best known for its use in cardiac weakness, valvular murmurs, shortness of breath, mitral valve regurgitation, chest/angina pain, anemia associated with heart irregularity, and nervous exhaustion. Hawthorne is high in bioflavonoids which can help heal chronic muscle, tendon, and ligament inflammations. It has traditionally been used in the complementary medical treatment of coronary artery disease, angina pectoris, arrhythmias, arteriosclerosis, and other circulatory weaknesses. Hawthorne berries have a potent synergistic effect with the digitalis cardiac glycosides and should be used with caution by people taking prescription cardiac drugs.

Kola Nut

Also known as *cola acuminata, cola sitida,* and *cola vera*, this herb is a natural anti-depressant, gastrointestinal stimulant, astringent, diuretic, and pain reliever. Kola nut has traditionally been used in the complementary medical treatment of depression, nervous irritability of the stomach, chronic diarrhea, obesity, migraines, tremors, insomnia, and constipation.

Parsley

Also known as *ligusticum porterii*, this common herb has natural anti-viral, anti-bacterial, expectorant, and diuretic effects. It has traditionally been used in the comple-mentary medical treatment of viral infections, sore throats, bronchitis, coughs, infected cuts and wounds, enlarged prostates, and fluid retention. Parsley works well to disguise the odor of garlic and synergistically with other herbal antibiotics like echinacea, golden-seal, and chaparral.

Saw Palmetto

Also known as *serenoa serrulata*, *serenoa repens,* or *sagal serrulata*, this herb works as a diuretic, nerve sedative, expectorant, general nutritive tonic, urinary antiseptic, ga-strointestinal stimulant, muscle builder, and circulatory stimulant. Saw palmetto has tra-ditionally been used in the complementary medical treatment of prostate conditions (benign prostatic hypertrophy, prostatitis), enuresis (bed wetting), stress incontinence, infections of the genitourinary tract, and muscle-wasting diseases of any kind.

Siberian Ginseng

Also known as *eleutherococcus senticosus*, this general tonic is a circulatory stimulant which fights stress, debility, exhaustion, depression, obesity, poor memory, and low sex drive. Studies show that long-term use may increase both physical stamina and IQ.

White Willow

Also known as *salix nigra, salix alba,* or *salix discolor*, this herb is powerful because of its content of salicin and tannins. It has anti-inflammatory, antipyretic, analgesic, antisep-tic, and astringent properties. Studies also indicate that it can boost thermogenesis—the body's natural ability to burn fat. White willow has traditionally been used in the com-plementary medical treatment of pain, obesity, arthritis and rheumatism, connective tis-sue inflammation, headaches, muscle aches, fevers, and infections of all types.

Yerba Maté

Also known as *ilex paraguayensis*, this herb is used as a stimulating beverage throughout much of Latin America.

Yerba maté is a central nervous system stimulant but has some calming properties. It is an antispasmodic, helps control excessive appetite, and, if taken only during daytime hours, helps induce a restful sleep at night. Yerba maté contains caffeine (0.2%-2%), but significantly less than coffee or tea. It also contains iron and may help with alertness and iron deficiency. It has diuretic properties but is nontoxic if used in moderation. Excessive consumption or caffeine sensitivity may be problematic (diarrhea, insomnia, anxiety) in sensitive individuals but far less so than coffee, tea, or soft drinks and well worth using in small amounts for its health-promoting qualities.

Yarrow[3]

Also known as *archillen millefolium*, yarrow is one of our most valuable herbs, and has a wide range of uses including acting as a blood cleanser, helping regulate liver function, toning the mucus membrane of the stomach and bowels, and healing the glandular system. Yarrow opens pores to allow perspiration to flow to eliminate waste and support the kidneys. The leaves are an effective first aid to stop bleeding of cuts and abrasions, and to remove the "*sting*" of mild sunburn. Yarrow is an astringent, diuretic, and a nervine,

Contains: Vitamins A, C, E, F, and some K.

Minerals include: Manganese, Copper, Potassium, Iron, and Iodine.

Available in liquid extract, tea, capsules, and salves.

Adult Dosage: 20 ml X 3 times daily; or

200 ml tea X 3 times daily

Herbal and Whole Food Supplements Guides

There are more than 400 herbs in commerce in the U.S. today. It is neither possible nor needful to review all of them here. However, the next two **Guides** will further explicate those herbs and whole food supplements discussed earlier in this section. The **Basic Herbal Supplement Efficacy Guide (Quick-Guide 23–3)** on the following page lists the herbs referenced in this chapter, classifying them according to the **body system(s) benefited** and **identifying which vitamins and minerals they supply**. The body systems categories are:

> **Caution:**
>
> *Any substance, including the mildest of herbs, can be toxic when used without intelligent and reasonable care.*
>
> *Toxicity and consumer safety are relative—any herb is safe when consumed in reasonable amounts by reasonable consumers.*

1. **Stimulants:** increase system stimulus and increase blood circulation
2. **Diuretics:** increase the urine output to remove harmful substances
3. **Expectorants:** cause the expulsion of mucus and break up congestion
4. **Astringents:** cleansers acting as natural "antibiotics"
5. **Nervines:** relieve nervous irritation caused by strain and tension
6. **Tonics:** strengthen all organs affected by the action of digestion

Some herbs may be listed under more than one category. Most botanical plants contain vitamins and minerals the human body can digest more easily than those from animals or fish. This makes herbs excellent sources of vitamins and minerals our bodies need.

The **Basic Herbal and Whole Food Supplement Intake Guide (Quick-Guide 23–4)** identifies the major function(s) of these herbs in the body, their sources, and the forms available for their utilization. Every family's medicine chest should contain herbal remedies to alleviate the symptoms of simple, everyday health problems. Recommendations for *Basic Optimal Health Daily Allowance* (**BOHDA**) are made for selected herbs, based on major efficacy studies.

---

[3] Many updates and contributions of new material provided by **Maryel Isham-Allen**, owner of **Quantum Light Therapeutics, Inc.**, is a. Certified Nutritional Consultant (**CNC**), Homeopathic Therapeutic Consultant, Certified Quantum Biofeedback Specialist. Located in San Antonio TX. Contact her @ *maryel01@satx.rr.com* or through her website **www.quantumlighttherapeutics.com.** Phone: (210) 731-9111, Fax: (210) 733-3368. Maryel offers a holistic approach to nutritional consulting, working with the body to support better health and guide individuals to a clearer understanding of their personal nutrient needs, suggesting ways to improve food and supplementation selection.

Quick-Guide 23—3

Basic Herbal Supplement Efficacy Guide

The selected body systems categories affected by these herbs are: Stimulants, Diuretics, Expectorants, Astringents, Nervines, and Tonics.

Herb	S	D	E	A	N	T	Available Vitamin & Mineral Nutrients
Aloe vera			X	X	X	X	beta carotene, B complex, C, selenium, silicon, zinc, boron, calcium, chromium, magnesium, manganese, niacin, phosphorous, potassium, polyphenols, essential fatty acids, saponins, polymeric sugars (acemannan), amylase, lipase, oxidase, catalase, bradykinase, glucomannan, crude & dietary fibers, zinc, natural digestive enzymes & cofactors
Apple cider vinegar		X	X			X	calcium, potassium, sodium, phosphorus, other trace minerals (*more than 90 compounds in all*), crude fiber, niacin, riboflavin, thiamin, vitamins A & C
Bee supplements *(Of the 22 elements in the body needing renewal by nutrient intake-- enzymes, hormones, amino acids, etc.—only bee pollen contains them all!)*			X	X	X	X	**Vitamins:** provitamins A, B_1, B_2, B_3, B_6 group, B_{12}, pantothenic acid, biotin, folic acid, choline, inositol, C, D, E, K, rutin **Minerals:** calcium, phosphorous, potassium, sulfur, sodium, chlorine, iron, manganese, copper, iodine, zinc, silicon, molybdenum, boron, titanium **Enzymes:** amylase, diastase, saccharase, pectase, phosphatase, catalase, disphorase, cozymase, cytochrome, lactic, dehydrogenase, succinic, hydrogenase, 24 oxidoreductases, 21 transferases, 33 hydrolases, 11 lyases, 5 isomerases, pepsin, trypsin **Amino Acids:** isoleucine, leucine, lysine, methionine, phenylaline, theonine, alanine, valine, histidine, arginine, cystine, tyrosine, aspartic acid, glutamic acid, hydroxyproline, proline, serine **Other:** nucleic acids, flavonoids, phenolic acids, tarpenes, nucleosides, glucose, fructose, gibberellins **Propolis:** potent natural antibiotic properties kills all types of bacteria, viruses, yeasts, fungi & parasites; natural sterilizer **Royal jelly:** benefits a wide range of health conditions; contains all B complex, high concentrations of B_5 (pantothenic acid), E_6, acetylcholine, minerals, A, C, D, and E, enzymes, hormones, amino acids & immune-boosting substances **Bee pollen:** contains simple sugars, amino acids, calcium, carotene, copper, enzymes, iron, magnesium, manganese, polyunsaturated fatty acids, sodium, potassium, C & plant sterols
Beet root powder	X					X	B_6, carotenes, highest iron available, calcium, potassium, niacin, copper, C, folic acid, zinc, manganese, magnesium, phosphorous
Bladderwrack	X	X		X		X	calcium, phosphorus, magnesium, iron, sodium, selenium, potassium, iodine, sulfur, vitamin A, C, B_{12}, high in sodium alginate, good source of trace minerals, zinc, crude & dietary fibers, protein
Ginger root	X		X	X		X	magnesium, cobalt, dietary & crude fibers, iron, manganese, niacin, phosphorous, potassium, protein, riboflavin, selenium, sodium, thiamin, tin, vitamin C
Ginkgo biloba				X			magnesium
Hawthorne	X				X		trace minerals, zinc
Kola nut	X				X	X	3.5% caffeine
Parsley	X	X	X	X	X	X	A & C, trace minerals, zinc, calcium, crude & dietary fibers, magnesium, manganese, niacin, phosphorous, potassium, protein
Saw palmetto			X	X	X	X	vitamin A
Siberian ginseng	X			X		X	B, copper, zinc, calcium, iron, chromium, manganese, niacin, potassium, riboflavin, thiamin
White willow				X	X	X	calcium, trace minerals, cobalt, crude & dietary fiber, iron, magnesium, manganese, niacin, phosphorous, potassium, protein, riboflavin, selenium, silicon, sodium, tin, vitamin C, zinc
Yerba maté	X	X				X	0.2%-2% caffeine, significantly less than coffee or tea, iron

Quick-Guide 23–4

Basic Herbal and Whole Food Supplements Intake Guide

Dietary Supplement (no USRDA established)	Basic Optimal Health Daily Allowance Ch = 12 mo.– 4 yr. Ad = 4 yr.–Adults Fe = Adult Female PL = Pregnant/Lactating	Complementary Medicinal Properties (Functions in Body)	Plant Source & Forms
Aloe vera	*external use*: apply to all areas generously • Ch @ apply 3X–4X • Ad @ apply 3X–4X • Fe @ apply 3X–4X • PL @ apply 3X–4X *internal use:* • Ch @ ¹/₂ adult dosage • Ad @ 2-4 fl oz 2X • Fe @ 2-4 fl oz 2X • PL @ use not advised	• *externally:* excellent tissue-healing agent: stimulates cell renewal, deters wrinkles, soothes sunburn, burns & cuts, minimizes scarring & relieves pain; radiation burn treatment without equal; hemorrhoid remedy • *internally:* excellent anti-inflammatory, antiviral & immune-enhancing property • effective treatment of digestive system, promotes regularity & soothes stomach ulcers; reduces bowel transit time • reduces mucous membranes infection; reduces allergies • helps facilitate & regulate menstrual flow • antioxidant combats damage by free radicals • combats effects of airborne chemical pollutants & radiation • reduces inflammation; relieves diaper rash	**Source:** 200 varieties, only *Barbadensia Miller* species considered the "true aloe" plant; leaves provide the juice (whole-leaf, cold-processed is most effective liquid form and is 99.5% water) **Forms:** *external use:* cream, gel, lotion *internal use:* gel, liquid, flavored juice, capsules of live whole food concentrate, freeze-dried
Apple cider vinegar	• Ch @ 1 tsp. 2X daily • Ad @ 1-2 T. 2X daily • Fe @ 1 T. 2X daily • PL @ 1 T. mealtime • Adults 60+ 1-2 T at Mealtime	• *externally:* conditions skin & relieves itching; soothes sprained muscles; relieves foot corns, calluses & athlete's foot • *internally:* beneficial in treating obesity, infection, allergies, fatigue, circulatory disorders, stomach disorders, diarrhea & thinning hair • improves digestion; combats intestinal parasites; helps sweeten bad breath; effectively aids protein digestion & prevents many vitamin and mineral deficiencies; fights tooth decay • eases arthritis, aches & pains; relieves nighttime leg cramps • helps lower cholesterol • helps oxygenate the blood; improves blood-clotting ability • increases metabolic rate	**Source:** fermented juice of whole, fresh apples; usually available in 5% acetic acid content **Forms:** organic liquid form @ 5% acidity recommended **Caution:** *Do not use distilled white vinegar as a substitute for apple cider vinegar.*
Bee supplements, including bee propolis	• Ch @ 2-4 gm 3X • Ad @ 3-6 gm 3X • Fe @ 3-6 gm 3X • PL @ 3-6 gm 3X	• completely fulfills essential vitamin & mineral needs • provides antioxidant protection for life extension • enhances work & sports performance • used by professional & Olympic athletes to increase physical endurance • effective in treatment of multiple sclerosis, infections, cancer, bowel disorders, prostate problems, depression, anemia, arthritis, chronic fatigue, depression, insomnia, menopause, obesity, poor memory and concentration, premature aging, prostatitis, senility; helps allergies & allergic conditions • high dosages used to treat coronary artery disease, high blood fats & nocturia (need to urinate at night caused by an enlarged prostate)	**Source:** plant pollen collected by bees **bee pollen**—male germinating cell of plants, collected & used for food & making royal jelly **propolis**—sticky resin gathered by bees for structural components of hive, sealant & microbial inhibitor **royal jelly**—made by worker bees & fed to all bees for first 3 days, then only to queen bee; super-nutrient & whole food **Forms:** granule, liquid, capsule, tablet, extract, tincture, honey-preserved
Beet root powder	• Ch @ ¹/₂ adult dose • Ad @ • Fe @ • PL @	• enriches blood • good general tonic	**Source:** beet root **Forms:** powder of live whole food concentrate, capsule

Basic Herbal and Whole Food Supplements Intake Guide (continued)

Dietary Supplement (no USRDA established)	Basic Optimal Health Daily Allowance Ch = 12 mo.- 4 yr. Ad = 4 yr.-Adults Fe = Adult Female PL = Pregnant/Lactating	Complementary Medicinal Properties (Functions in Body)	Plant Source & Forms
Bladderwrack (kelp)	• Ch @ ¹/₂ adult dose • Ad @ 5-10 gm 3X • Fe @ 5-10 gm 3X • PL @ 5-10 gm 3X	• treatment of immune system & anti-aging • replenishes glands & nerves; treatment of hypothyroidism & goiter • treatment of obesity, anemia, emaciation, hair loss, impotence & nervousness • toxin scavenger for digestive tract	**Source:** *fucus vesiculosus*, or kelp, an ocean plant; whole herb used **Forms:** cut & sifted, powder, capsule, extract
Blue green algae & other green foods	• Ch @ 1-6 gm 3X • Ad @ 4-6 gm 3X • Fe @ 3-6 gm 3X • PL @ 3-6 gm 3X	• nutri-dense concentrated green superfoods strengthen immune system; superior antioxidant source • increases energy, stamina, physical endurance & power of athletes • adds alkalinity to system • cleans cells & tissues of toxins • enhances work and sports performance • prevention & treatment of all viral conditions including Chronic Fatigue Syndrome and AIDS	**Sources:** whole plant of blue green algae, chlorella, spirulina; leaves or sprouts of barley grass, wheat grass, green kamut, spinach, alfalfa; leaves and flowers of broccoli **Forms:** powder, capsule, tablet
Fo-ti	• Ch @ ¹/₂ adult dose • Ad @ • Fe @ • PL @	• improves blood circulation; increases energy & stamina, resistance to disease • strong antioxidant & anti-aging properties for arthritis, rheumatism, atherosclerosis, senility, premature gray hair & impotency • stimulates kidneys; diuretic • reduces pain of sciatica & knee joint pain • reduces constipation; detoxifies liver; tonic	**Source:** Chinese herb *Ho Shou-Wu*, tuberous root of *Polygonum multiflorum* **Forms:** powder, extract
Ginger root	• Ch @ ¹/₂ adult dose • Ad @ 1-3 gm 3X • Fe @ 1-3 gm 3X • PL @ 1-3 gm 3X	• cardiac tonic stimulates circulatory system, lowers serum cholesterol & lessens joint stiffness & cold extremities • relieves sore throat & reduces effect of acute colds • cleansing of kidneys & bowels • soothes gastrointestinal tract; reduces gastric flatulence, & intestinal spasms • effective for nausea associated with pregnancy; morning & motion sickness • lessens effects of anorexia • relieves painful menstruation & uterine pain	**Source:** rhizome (underground stalks) of ginger plant; has good storage qualities due to covering on root **Forms:** fresh juice or minced for tea, cut & sifted, powder, capsule, extract
Ginkgo biloba	• Ch @ ¹/₂ adult dose • Ad @ 40 mg 3X • Fe @ 40 mg 3X • PL @ 40 mg 3X	• cardiac vasodilator helps heart muscle to reduce heart attack risk • increases peripheral circulation in heart & cold extremities • prevents free radical damage; strong antioxidant • enhances brain's ability to metabolize glucose, increases neurotransmission • improves short-term memory & improves mental alertness; improves brain function by increasing blood supply to the brain • relieves impotency when caused by arterial deficiency • improves memory, failing mental faculties, and other neurological conditions • improves alertness & concentration • aids in proper eye & ear function, effective in treating tinnitus & vertigo	**Source:** fruit of oldest tree on earth, tree leaf extract, also known as *maidenhair* **Forms:** powder, extract

Basic Herbal and Whole Food Supplement Intake Guide (continued)

Herb	Dose	Uses	Source / Forms
Hawthorne berries	• Ch @ 1/2 adult dose • Ad @ 250 mg 2X • Fe @ 250 mg 2X • PL @ 250 mg 2X	• complementary medical treatment of coronary artery disease, angina pectoris, arrhythmias, arteriosclerosis, and other circulatory weaknesses; potent synergistic effect with digitalis cardiac glycosides (should be used with caution when taking prescription cardiac drugs), used in treatment of cardiac weakness, valvular murmurs, shortness of breath, mitral valve regurgitation, chest/angina pain & anemia associated with heart irregularity and nervous exhaustion • high level of bioflavonoids helps heal chronic muscle, tendon, and ligament inflammations; stabilizes collagen in joints to reduce arthritis suffering • relieves irregularity; aids in insomnia • prevents "little" heart attacks; works best when taken over long period of time	**Source:** made from berries, flowers & leaves of crataegus oxyacantha plant, thorny shrub native to Europe **Forms:** powder, cut & sifted, capsule, tea, extract
Kola nut	• Ch @ 1/2 adult dose • Ad @ • Fe @ • PL @ use not advised	• natural anti-depressant used in complementary medical treatment of depression, nervous irritability of the stomach, chronic diarrhea, obesity, migraines, tremors, insomnia & constipation • gastrointestinal stimulant; natural diuretic; pain reliever; stimulates brain • increases performance & endurance	**Source:** nut of cola acuminata, cola sitida, and cola vera **Forms:** powder, tea
Parsley	• Ch @ 1/2 adult dose • Ad @ 2-4 gm 3X • Fe @ 2-4 gm 3X • PL @ 2-4 gm 3X	• removes kidney & gall stones • relieves liver ailments • natural antiviral, antibacterial, expectorant, and diuretic effects • used in complementary medical treatment of viral infections, sore throats, bronchitis, coughs, infected cuts & wounds • reduces enlarged prostate; reduces fluid retention • synergistic with other herbal antibiotics: Echinacea, goldenseal & chaparral	**Source:** leaves & seeds of ligusticum porterii plant—leaves have more iron than any other green vegetable; uses whole herb **Forms:** powder, flakes, capsule, tea, extract
Saw palmetto	• Ch @ 1/2 adult dose • Ad @ 160 mg 2X • Fe @ use not advised • PL @ use not advised	• relieves mucus in head & nose • prevents progression of prostate disease & wasting diseases; relief for male & female reproductive systems • works as a diuretic, nerve sedative, expectorant, general nutritive tonic, urinary antiseptic, gastrointestinal stimulant, muscle builder, and circulatory stimulant • complementary medical treatment of prostate conditions: benign prostatic hypertrophy & prostatitis; treatment for genitourinary tract conditions: enuresis (bed-wetting) & stress incontinence • treatment of infections of all muscle-wasting diseases	**Source:** berries (fruit) of serenoa serrulata, serenoa repens or sagal serrulata **Forms:** whole, powder, capsule, tea, extract, concentrate

Basic Herbal and Whole Food Supplements Intake Guide (continued)

Dietary Supplement (no USRDA established)	Basic Optimal Health Daily Allowance Ch = 12 mo.- 4 yr. Ad = 4 yr.-Adults Fe = Adult Female PL = Pregnant/Lactating	Complementary Medicinal Properties (Functions in Body)	Plant Source & Forms
Siberian ginseng	Short-term stress (30 days or less duration): • Ch @ 1/2 adult dose • Ad @ 1-2 gm 3X • Fe @ 1-2 gm 3X • PL @ use not advised Long-term stress (more than 30-day duration): • Ch @ 1/2 adult dose • Ad @ 250-500 mg • Fe @ 250-500 mg • PL @ use not advised	• builds resistance to mental & physical stress • helps in adapting to extreme temperatures • increases efficiency of mental & physical work • enhances cognitive & memory functions by increasing level of neurotransmitters in brain, improving brain cell metabolism, optimizing action of certain enzymes & increasing supply of oxygen to brain cells • slows aging process • stimulates circulatory system & normalizes heart • regulates & normalizes blood sugar levels • helps increase sex drive • increases stamina & endurance • lowers blood pressure & blood fat levels • combats stress, debility, exhaustion, depression, obesity • long-term use increases physical stamina • hair stimulant	**Source:** root of eleutherococcus senticosus, shrub up to 9' tall **Forms:** powder, cut & sifted, capsule, tea, extracted powder
White willow	• Ch @ ¹/₂ adult dose • Ad @ 1-3 gm 3X • Fe @ 1-3 gm 3X • PL @ use not advised	• effective aspirin substitute • powerful pain reliever due to content of salicin & tannins • used in the complementary medical treatment of pain, obesity, arthritis and rheumatism, connective tissue inflammation, headaches, muscle aches, fevers & infections of all types • can boost thermogenesis—the body's natural ability to burn fat	**Source:** bark of *salix nigra, salix alba,* or *salix discolor,* or white willow tree **Forms:** cut & sifted, powder, capsule
Yerba maté	• Ch @ use not advised • Ad @ 1 cup 2X • Fe @ 1 cup 2X • PL @ use not advised	• stimulates central nervous system; helps maintain alertness • antispasmodic; calming effect on nerves • helps control excessive appetite • helps induce a restful sleep (if taken only during daytime hours) • combats iron deficiency • nontoxic if used moderately (*contains less caffeine than coffee, tea, or sodas*)	**Source:** *ilex paraguayensis* **Forms:** tea (*a stimulating beverage throughout much of Latin America*)

Professional References for Supplementation

The following listing provides additional information from recognized professional, medical, and botanical specialists, including their published literature. These writings report the results of their studies regarding the benefits of supplementation. More information about vitamin, minerals, and herbs in **Preparedness Library, Chapter 27, Section 3.I.**

Balch, James F. and Balch, Phyllis A., *Prescription for Nutritional Healing.* Garden City Park NY: Avery Publishing Group Inc.

Goldstrich, Joe D., *The Cardiologist's Painless Prescription for a Healthy Heart and a Longer Life.* Dallas TX: 9-HEART-9 Publishing,

Hamilton, Kirk, *Clinical Pearls in Nutrition and Preventive Medicine. 1990-1995;* & *CP Currents. 1990-1995.* Sacramento CA: IT Services.

Rona, Zoltan P., *The Joy of Health, A Doctor's Guide to Nutrition and Alternative Medicine.* Toronto, ON Canada: Hounslow Press.

Rona, Zoltan P., *Return to The Joy of Health.* Vancouver, BC Canada: Alive Books.

Werbach, Melvyn R., *Nutritional Influences on Illness.;* & *Nutritional Influences on Mental Illness,* Northamptonshire England: Thorsons.

Werbach, Melvyn R., *Nutritional Influences on Illness.* 2ⁿᵈ *Ed.;* & *Botanical Influences on Illness.* Tarzana, CA: Third Line Press.

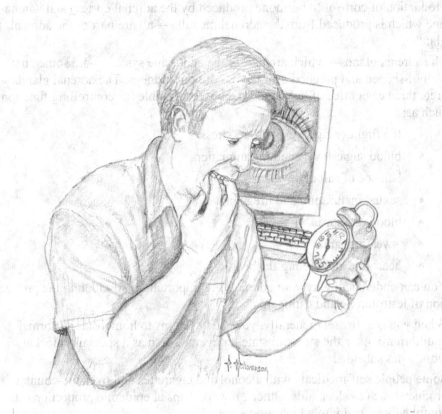

Chapter 24
Basics of Battling Stress
How to Reduce Stress and Pain

There is one certainty about disasters and emergencies: they create stress not only on the environment in which you live, but also on and in your body, impairing your ability to deal with otherwise common decision-making and actions. This chapter could be your conduit to finding the solution to reducing your stress levels in every part of your life.

If you're stressed by just getting through the vicissitudes of daily life, you can certainly imagine how stressful disasters or emergencies could be![i] There are many circumstances impacting your ability to handle stress in your life and they can depend on your:

- attitudes and outlook on life,
- relationships and the quality of those relationships,
- genetic makeup, and
- ability to reason and think through situations.

Even while you have a strong ability to reason and think, stress can still turn on automatic stress responses in your body. Your body is not capable of defining the difference. Your brain activates part of the involuntary nervous system, the autonomic nervous system (**ANS**), which helps you cope, and this controls the production of cortisol (a hormone produced by the adrenal cortex) and adrenaline which is produced from the adrenal medulla —all are part of the adrenal glands.

The adrenal glands—which are part of the endocrine system—are somewhat walnut-shaped and perched near the top of your kidneys. The adrenal glands secrete three categories of hormones and are responsible for controlling functions such as:

- the flight or fight response to stress,
- blood sugar levels and inflammation,
- balance of salt and water,
- sexual maturation and pregnancy,
- blood pressure,
- sweating, and
- heart rate and feeling flushed.

You can understand why your adrenals are important in stimulating the production of testosterone and estrogen.

When you are stressed generally, your body returns to homeostasis (normal equilibrium), once the stressful state, or event—such as a special project at work—has subsided.

Some people self-medicate with alcohol and cigarettes and over-the-counter products, such as sleep aids. Others, now perhaps at epidemic proportions, are continually locked into a high-alert state.

This high-alert state of stress will cause systems in your body to start "*robbing Peter to pay Paul*" by rerouting the blood flow from your skin and other systems such as your digestive system, causing nausea and clammy skin. Stress will actually age your body.

Stress can cause depression, suppress your immune and endocrine systems, and cause adrenal fatigue, chronic fatigue, and fibromyalgia—all which have underlying adrenal malfunction. Some outwards signs to watch for can be pale skin, the lips become pierced, and the eyes and brow bone will slope downward.

It is important to understand the stress factors, whether natural, people-caused, or personal disaster—or just ongoing and unrelenting stress caused by your job, debt, or personal emotional problems. It is equally vital to protect your body and be able to mount a defense with a **Battle Plan** for preparedness.

If you are aware of the potential effects that stress has on your body, you can prepare to assist your body when you are confronted with stress. Start now, by beginning to understand everything you think, say, and do have a direct effect on being locked into a high state of personal alert.

The body and the mind are interconnected. Thought (fear) can affect your body's physiological responses, and temporarily the body cannot distinguish between an actual event and a perceived event—that's why the hair on the back of your neck stands up when you watch a scary scene in a movie.

You are challenged daily, so take the necessary steps to be prepared for the unexpected.

Develop a **Battle Plan** which will put you at ease and will help eliminate your stress.

BATTLE PLAN: SUPPLEMENTATION FOR DEALING WITH STRESS

Supplements are a vital component for sufferers of stress! **While** there may be a wide range of supplements that help you specifically, there are a few that offer benefits to anyone suffering from stress and adrenal fatigue.

Calcium—This mineral helps in many cell functions as well as building strong bones. It also helps provide energy to muscles so when adrenal function lessens; the body leaches its calcium reserves, causing bone loss over an extended period of time.

Adding calcium supplements allows your body to function better and speeds your recovery. Low calcium levels can also cause muscle aches, cramps, and pains which are very common with adrenal fatigue sufferers.

Other functions that calcium aids include heart regulation. Some adrenal fatigue patients can experience their heart racing or a fluttering sensation which can be due in part to low calcium.

Calcium also assists with the transmission of messages through the nervous system. Here again, lack of calcium can cause problems with the nerves which can be experienced as pain. Good calcium levels also help maintain vital enzyme levels.

Magnesium—This mineral works together with calcium and is vital in maintaining a good chemical balance in your body. Magnesium is very important in energy production and, in fact, is involved in over 300 enzyme reactions.

Whereas calcium helps muscles by allowing them to contract more efficiently, magnesium helps your muscles relax. The two minerals team up in many ways.

When plenty of calcium is available, it could flood the cells, but magnesium blocks the excess calcium and helps maintain balance.

Magnesium also helps regulate hormones.

Vitamin C—This vitamin is essential for the creation and maintenance of collagen within the body and is vital for tissue repair. It strengthens blood vessels and is an antioxidant.

Vitamin C also allows the body to utilize carbohydrates and synthesize fats and proteins.

Collagen is the most plentiful tissue in the body and functions as connective tissue. This includes cartilage, tendons, ligaments, and many other types. Vitamin C also plays a large role in the production of antibodies which stave off infections and help you heal quickly.

One common complaint of some adrenal fatigue patients is that they seem to catch every little cold or sniffle that comes along. In many cases, this is true because their immune system is being compromised by a lack of Vitamin. C.

It is important to know that Vitamin C does not stay in the body long, so frequent doses may be necessary—even to the point of several doses per pay.

B Complex Vitamins—There are numerous B vitamins the body needs on a regular basis. This includes the following—I've included their scientific names as sometimes those are used more commonly on supplement labels—*thiamine* (B_1), *riboflavin* (B_2), *niacin* (B_3), *pantothenic acid* (B_5), *pyridoxine* (B_6), *biotin* (B_7), *folic acid* or *folate* (B_9), and *cobalamin* (B_{12}). These vitamins as a group are known as **B Complex Vitamins**. It is widely known that these vitamins affect numerous important systems within the body.

- **Vitamin B_1,** (*thiamin*) and **vitamin B_2** (riboflavin) assist in the production of energy and affect enzymes that influence the muscles, nerves, and heart.

- **Vitamin B₃** (*niacin*) assists the cells and also help maintain the health of the skin, nervous system, and digestive system.

- **Vitamin B₅** (*pantothenic acid*) allows the body to grow and develop normally.

- **Vitamin B₆** (*pyridoxine*) helps to break down protein and maintain the health of red blood cells, the nervous system, and parts of the immune system.

- **Vitamin B₇** (*biotin*) also assists in the breakdown of protein and carbohydrates and helps the body make various hormones.

- **Vitamin B₉** (*folic acid*) helps the cells in the body make and maintain DNA and is important in the production of red blood cells. **B₉** slows aging of the cells.

- **Vitamin B₁₂** (*cobalamin*) assists with growth and development. It also has a part in producing blood cells, the functions of the nervous system, and how the body uses folic acid and carbohydrates.

Deficiency of certain B vitamins can cause anemia, tiredness, loss of appetite, abdominal pain, depression, numbness, and tingling in the arms and legs, muscle cramps, respiratory infections, hair loss, and eczema. Many of these same symptoms are noted by adrenal fatigue sufferers which highlights the importance of getting enough of these vitamins.

Digestive Enzymes—When you are a victim of adrenal fatigue, your body is out of balance, it does not produce enough digestive enzymes to help you fully use the nutrients in your food. For this reason, it is wise to take a high quality digestive enzyme prior to each meal. This will help break down the food faster and allow you to get more nutritional benefit from the food you ingest.

Another digestive aid is HCL (hydrochloric acid), which can aid in the breakdown of protein. (This is not the industrial HCL used as a drain cleaner!) The body naturally produces this substance in the stomach acid to break down meats and complex proteins. HCL is available in capsule form at any health food store or your local pharmacy.

Think of your body as a city with many homes and buildings—each day some catch on fire. Fire trucks are sent to put out the fires, but someone forgot to keep gas and oil in the fire trucks. Eventually, the trucks break down and now there are no more trucks available to put out the fires.

Using supplementation is analogous to maintaining gas and oil in the fire trucks—when your body really needs help to fight stress, the help is there for your body's defense.

ADDITIONAL PREPAREDNESS RECOMMENDATIONS[1]

The following remedies give temporary stress relief to the body and mind:

Bach Rescue Remedy Flower Essence is designed to calm and stabilize following any kind of trauma. This solution is a true first aid. It contains five flower essences, Star of Bethlehem, Rock Rose, Clematis, Cherry Plum, and Impatiens. May be used directly from the bottle or diluted in water. **Rescue Remedy** is available as a liquid, spray, or cream. Place a small amount under the tongue, rub on the lips, on skin behind the ears, or on the inner wrists. This product may be used on animals and plants for stress relief, also.

---

[1] **Maryel Isham-Allen**, Certified Nutritional Consultant (**CNC**), Homeopathic Therapeutic Consultant, Certified Quantum Biofeedback Specialist, B.S. Human Ecology, University of Texas @ Austin; Investor and contributing columnist/artist to *Enjoy Whole Health Magazine,* San Antonio TX.

Topical application is the same for humans and animals.

Dosages:

- Humans—3-5 drops
- Children—½ adult dose
- Plants and large animals—10 drops in water bucket
- Small animals— 3-5 drops on food or in water

ETS: Emergency Trauma Solution from **Perelandra Center for Nature Research**[2] is an advanced remedy for both acute and chronic situations, designed to be used many times during the day when health and well-being are challenged. May be taken following: medications, nightmares, freak-outs from weather conditions (violent thunderstorms), accidents, trips to the vet, dentist, or doctor, following an argument, before a test, caught in traffic, or just feeling overwhelmed anytime.

ETS solutions are also available for animals, plants, and soil.

Activated Charcoal is an antidote for almost any known poison which may have been ingested—which doesn't mean you should not call **Poison Control Center** <u>immediately</u>!

In the meantime this natural agent relieves gas and diarrhea. Simply take as directed.

For bites and stings: make a very moist paste with charcoal and water, then place over the wound, then cover with gauze and tape.

<table>
<tr><td>Caution:
The FDA has not evaluated all of these statements. This information is for educational purposes on-ly. Always consult your own personal doctor or licensed professional for medical advice.</td></tr>
</table>

NOTES FOR BATTLING YOUR STRESS

---

[2] Developed by **Machaelle Small Wright**; available only from: Perelandra Ltd. P.O. Box 3603 , Warrington, VA 20188 (USA (800) 960-8806) (Overseas & Mexico 1-540-937-2153)

NOTES FOR BATTLING YOUR STRESS

---

i This chapter courtesy of best selling author Jennifer Busch. A little about Jennifer: she was recruited early in her career by a national publishing company and a trade journal, *The American Chiropractor*—the leading trade journal for Doctors of Chiropractic. After learning the internal mechanisms of publishing, she was rapidly promoted to the position of National Sales Manager. Jennifer married Dr. Richard E. Busch III in 1996, and together they founded and developed a leading chiropractic clinic that is now nationally recognized for its successful non-surgical treatment of chronic and severe disc conditions, the **DRS Protocol™**. Jennifer is also an international marketing and development consultant for healthcare practitioners.

Jennifer has survived her own journey through the reality of adrenal fatigue, chronic fatigue, and fibromyalgia. With the release of her best-selling, new book, **All in My *Mind? Overcomeing Adrenal Fatigue, Chronic Fatigue and Fibromyalgia***, she provides hope to others suffering from the same conditions. Her book is dedicated to the thousands who are suffering needlessly. Only through her determination and never-ending faith did she discover the truth and uncover first the causes and then the treatments that would help her—once again—lead a normal, active life. For further information, go to **www.jenbusch.com**. Contact Jennifer via email at this address: *jennifer@jenbusch.com*.

Additional information by **Maryel Isham-Allen**, owner of **Quantum Light Therapeutics, Inc. Maryel** is a Certified Nutritional Consultant (**CNC**), Homeopathic Therapeutic Consultant, and Certified Quantum Biofeedback Specialist. Her office is located in San Antonio TX.

Website: **maryel01@satx.rr.com** or **www.quantumlighttherapeutics.com.**

Phone:(210) 731-9111

Fax: (210) 733-3368.

Quantum Light Therapeutics, Inc .is dedicated to supporting body, mind, and sprit to bring more happiness and fulfillment to everyday life. We introduce individuals to a variety of light modalities in order to reduce tension, stress and to reeducate body systems toward balance and harmony.

> *"…Everything man needs to maintain good health can be found in nature…*
> *The true task of science is to find those things…"*
> Paracelsus, the father of modern pharmacology

Chapter 25

Basics of Essential Oils

Plants that create scent produce essential oils[i]. Basically, essential oils are the plant's body odor. The plant creates a volatile chemistry to assist itself in its health and procreation. Essential oils can function for humans in the same manner. A plant produces essential oils for the following reasons:

- to heal itself from injury
- to maintain its health
- to survive stressful times
- to repel or to attract insects

Essential oils have been used for centuries by indigenous cultures all over the world to treat illness, treat and heal injuries, and maintain sacred spaces

Not only do native peoples acknowledge the power of essential oils, but so does modern science. In the last hundred years, science has seriously studied essential oils. A number of Nobel Prizes have been won by those who identify and understand the function of essential oils.

Science has found essential oils to be powerful tools for healing. Doctors in France routinely prescribe them to their patients.

Caution:

The FDA has not evaluated all of these statements.

This information is for educational purposes on-ly. Always consult your own personal doctor or licensed professional for med-ical advice.

Essential oils are easy to store or carry because they are little bottles of liquid that will last for years and years when properly stored in cool, dark environments.

Essential oils increase effectively the human body's ability to:

- provide pain relief and anesthesia
- prevent and relieve disease and infection
- stop inflammation from injury and trauma
- treat and prevent skin conditions
- aid sleep
- de-stress mind and body
- sedate and relax
- repel and relieve insect bites

BASIC ESSENTIAL OILS

When you are ready to acquire essential oils for your in-home convenience store , use **Chart 25-1** as a reference list of oils recommended for storage and use.

Notes on Essential Oils

- All essential oils will be antiseptic, antibacterial, antiviral, and antifungal to varying degrees. They are natural antibiotics and the body does not create immunity to them.
- Herbs grow weak in storage, losing their effectiveness—essential oils will not!
- Essential oils work primarily through the nose—directly to the brain. There is almost an immediate reaction to essential oils within the *limbic system*[1].
- When essential oil vapors are breathed deeply, the oils enter the lungs where they interact with the blood stream.
- Essential oils can also enter the body through the skin unless they evaporate first.

Word of Caution

There are usually warnings against oils being taken internally. This primarily pertains to a class of oils that are high in phenols[2]. Phenols can damage the liver. (For example: *Tylenol*® is a phenol and carries warnings not to be ingested for long periods of time—as are some essential oils. Normally, warnings are clearly marked on such essential oils. Read the **Cautions** in the chart below to know why these essential oils should not be taken internally:

- ***Camphor***
- ***Eucalyptus***
- ***Helichrysum***
- ***Oregano***

Chart 25–1
Essential Oils Recommended for Long-Term Storage

Essential Oil	Use / Remedy	Cautions
Camphor *Cinnamomum camphora*	<ul><li>Reduces scar tissue—rubbing on skin poses no problem; good for the skin</li><li>Mental Stimulant</li><li>Decongestant</li><li>Reduces scarring—regenerates new cells and prevents scarring</li><li>Expectorant</li><li>Arthritis relief</li><li>Muscular aches and pains reduced</li><li>Oily skin conditions</li><li>Cold and flu relief</li></ul>	*Camphor* is almost all *ketonic*[3]—that should be a warning! The way the molecules are bonded in ketones provides very tight bonding and the liver must work over time attempting to break them down to soluble substances for secretion through the kidneys and skin. It's probably best not to ingest them because of this—it's not worth the risk! With ketones, there also needs to be the warning of *neurotoxic*[4]. As aromatherapy research continues, this seems to be less of a problem. *Camphor* is invaluable in its ability to repel ticks and help ease lung congestion.

[1] The **limbic system** is an interconnected system of brain nuclei associated with basic needs and emotions such as hunger, pain, pleasure, satisfaction, sex, and instinctive motivation. The most primitive part of the brain, it is situated close to the inner wall of each cerebral hemisphere and includes the brain system concerned with the sense of smell.

[2] A **phenol** is a poisonous caustic crystalline compound, used in the manufacture of resins, dyes, and pharmaceuticals, antiseptics, and disinfectants. (Formula: C_6H_5OH).

[3] A **ketone** is an organic compound containing a carbon atom connected to an oxygen atom by a double bond and to two carbon atoms. The simplest ketone is acetone, an important industrial solvent.

[4] A **neurotoxic** substance damages, destroys, or impairs the functioning of nerve tissue.

Essential Oils Recommended for Long-Term Storage (continued)

Essential Oil	Use / Remedy	Cautions
Eucalyptus *Eucalyptus Globules*	• Decongestant aids breathing • Inflammation • **More Uses:** Stimulate circulation, Treat sinus infections, Open sinus and breathing passages, Relieve muscular aches and pains, Revive due to nervous exhaustion, Treat acne, Disinfect	Primarily an oxide and tends to interfere with metabolizing of other drugs and can render pharmaceuticals ineffective. This occurs due to the manner in which the oxygen atom connects into the basic hydrocarbon molecule: the oxygen atom hangs away from molecule as if waving in the breeze and can easily interact with other substances. Ingestion of eucalyptus is generally discouraged, but is often mixed in natural medicines to be ingested all the time! Care should be exercised in the ingestion of such combinations.
Helichrysum *Helichrysum italicum* or *Helichrysum augustifolium*	• Stops bruising if applied immediately • Prevents and treats blood clots. Anti-clotting benefit of this oil is miraculous. This was first documented by research in France.	• Contains ketones, though different in nature! • However, it is a miracle worker. • There is research from Australia suggesting the nature of *Helichrysum* ketones is less harmful than other ketones.
Lavender *Lavandula augustifolia*	• Protects the skin from sun and damage, wound healing • Calms, soothes, sedates, • Antispasmodic – relieves cramping, muscle tension, coughing • Promotes skin regeneration • Lifts tension	• Contains camphor, a ketone; all references indicate it is safe. Because ketones can be strong mental stimulants, there is concern of causing seizure—especially people prone to them. • The camphor in lavender partly explains its ability to provide good sun protection.
Lemon *Citrus limon*	• Antiseptic; purifies; cleanses • Lymphatic support • Boosts immune system • Revives skin and relieves signs of aging • Reduce anxiety, calm, feel happier • Nontoxic	• Phototoxic—applying lemon to the skin before going out into the sun can cause serious burn to the skin. • Burns are more like radiation burns and can take many weeks to heal. • Can irritate sensitive skin, so use fatty oil if a problem.
Lemon Eucalyptus *Eucalyptus citriodora*	• Mosquito repellent (Government Approved) • Relieve muscle strain, sports injuries	• Could irritate skin, so use fatty oil if this is a problem. Non-toxic.
Roman Chamomile *Chamaemelum nobile, Anthemis nobilis*	• Relieves spasmodic breathing as in asthma • Calms and relieves stress • Sleep-inducing • Soothes muscular and emotional tension • Relieves rashes, hives, and inflamed skin • Use with hyperactive children	• Safe for children, avoid in early pregnancy if you are allergic to ragweed. • Non-toxic.
Tea Tree *Melaleuca alternifolia*	• Stops sore throat • Protects against viruses • Antifungal for toe and nail fungus • Stops pus from forming in insect/ant bites • Insect bites—relieves itching and defends against infection	• Tea tree helps and will stop the itching, but the sting is totally relieved with green pepper oil. The secret is immediate use—the sooner the better! • To take the sting out of bites, stings and like attacks on the skin, use green pepper oil immediately.
Texas Cedarwood *Juniperus mexicana* or *Juniperus ashei*	• Repels chiggers • Treats respiratory and urinary infections • Acne and skin infections	• Cedarwood oil on the body and cedarwood mulch spread over the ground will stop chiggers.
Oregano *Origanum vulgaris*	• Powerful immune booster • Defends against virus, infection, & fungus	• Always use fatty oil when applying to the skin, as it will burn if you do not. • Do not take internally.

BASIC ESSENTIAL OIL BLENDS

All oils can be added to fatty oils such as coconut, olive, safflower, etc., so the skin is protected from strong irritating essential oils. It also helps spread the essential oils over the skin more efficiently.

Fatty oils are less expensive than essential oils and it makes good sense to use fatty oils to extend your supply of essential oils, protect your skin more effectively, and save money.

Essential oils can be blended together to create even more remedies for special needs:

Chart 25–2

Essential Oils Blends Recommended for Long-Term Storage

Use	Remedy	Blend
Headaches, Minor	Minor headache relief	50% **Peppermint** 50% **Lavender**
Headaches, Severe	Severe headache relief	Add **Roman Chamomile** to **Minor Headache Relief** formula (above)
Antifungal	Apply to toes for severe fungal infections. Breathe it in to protect from mold especially debilitating black mold.	80% **Tea Tree** 20% **Oregano**
Repel ticks	Spray or rub onto skin	50% **Lemon Eucalyptus** 50% **Camphor**
Respiratory infections (Serious)	Rub onto chest front and back. This blend requires a carrier or fatty oil to be added to the blend to protect the skin from irritation and makes the essential oils go further.	50% **Eucalyptus** 20% **Camphor** 20% **Texas Cedarwood** 20% **Peppermint**

AROMATHERAPY[5]

Treating Stress with Essential Oils

Aromatherapy for stress relief is a *holistic*[6] therapy, utilizing natural essential oils in promoting a feeling of physical and emotional well-being. Essential oils derived from natural plants have been shown to have calming effects on the central nervous system.

Commonly used essential oils for stress:

- Chamomile
- Clary Sage
- Eucalyptus
- Frankincense
- Grapefruit
- Lavender
- Lime
- Orange Mandarin
- Orange Sweet
- Rose
- Spearmint
-

Often aromatherapy is used in conjunction with other holistic practices such as acupuncture pressure and therapeutic massage during which essential oils are either massaged into the skin or are placed under the nose for maximum effect.

Using aromatherapy for stress relief is quite common in spas across the country. It is also offered through holistic professionals who practice aromatherapy in combination with other techniques or by itself.

---

[5] Aromatherapy is the use of oils extracted from plants to alleviate physical and psychological disorders, usually through massage or inhalation.

[6] Therapy characterized by the view that a whole system of beliefs must be analyzed rather than simply its individual components; taking into account all of somebody's physical, mental, and social conditions in the treatment of illness.

The following descriptions highlight the use and efficacy of selected essential oils that can help in maintaining or restoring healthy balance resulting from stressful situations:

Chart 25–3

Selected Essential Oils for Maintaining/Restoring Balance

Essential Oil	Use/Remedy	Caution	Comments
Clary Sage (*Salvia sclarea*)	• Calms and relieves stress and/or tension • Promotes restful sleep • Regulates the female reproductive system	• Non-toxic • **Note:** large doses can produce narcotic effect, do not use with alcohol or pregnancy, and avoid if estrogen is a problem	• Calms the nervous system, particularly in cases of depression, stress, insomnia, and deep-seated tension. • Good tonic for the womb and female functions in general, such as painful periods, scanty menstruation, and relaxation during labor, thus encouraging a less painful birth • Necessary for every woman—can balance extreme emotions, reducing stress and restore inner tranquility
Frankincense (*Boswellia carterii*)	• Relaxes, calms, and promotes sleep • Vapors open sinus and breathing passages • Uplifts moods • Creates meditative state • Reduces inflammation • Soothes and heals inflamed skin, bruises, and burns • Use with asthma—especially if there is underlying nervousness; deepens the breath	• Non-toxic • Non-irritating • Non-sensitizing • **Note**: some frankincense can have synthetic or unidentified ingredients—avoid when pregnant	• This oil has an ancient history. • Most famous for being the incense given to the Christ Child. • French translation means "*real incense.*" • Used as incense within churches to uplift and create a meditative state.
Grapefruit (*Citrus paradise*)	• Astringent • Stimulant • General tonic • Antiseptic • For oily skin • Tightens skin • Increases circulation • Nervous exhaustion • Stimulates lymphatic system, obesity, and water retention • Aids in relief of depression	• Phototoxic • Note: do not apply to skin if going outdoors— can burn skin severely • Can irritate the skin— always use with fatty oil	• Grapefruit essential oil does not carry a warning about interfering with medications. • Grapefruit seed extract available. Vapors of grapefruit often helps a person feel more optimistic and hopeful about themselves and life

Selected Essential Oils for Maintaining/Restoring Balance (continued)

Essential Oil	Use/Remedy	Caution	Comments
Lime *(Citrus aurantifo-lia)*	• Antiseptic • Antispasmodic • Astringent • Hypotensive[7] • Excellent oil to erase negative energy and prepare a space for relaxation or meditation • Sanitizes • Treats cold & flu symptoms • Relaxing baths & massages • Diffuse or use in candle meditation • Excellent perfume oil—wear as perfume on skin or around neck in a necklace	• Phototoxic[8] • Do not wear outside in the sun; can cause serious burn • May cause skin irritation; always use with a fatty oil if applying to skin	• Lime brought by Spanish to the New World where it naturalized in the West Indies and Mexico • Both pressed lime and distilled lime available—distilled lime is great for relieving stress and creating a space for meditation • Lime is a higher heart oil and helps to step up ability to express compassion and forgiveness
Orange Mandarin *(Citrus reticulate)*	• Anti-depressant • Anti-spasmodic • Anti-stress • Astringent • Calmative • Sedative • Tranquilizing • Use in lymphatic massage • Stops muscle spasms • Diffuse into air for general relaxation and sedation • Good in baths and perfumes	• Phototoxic—do not wear outside on skin—can be a problem with skin burning • May cause skin irritation--use with fatty oil if applying to skin	• Citrus comes from China; Mandarin oranges could have been called mandarin, as these are the oranges given to mandarins (high-ranking Chinese officials). • This fruit is not an orange, but a tangerine. • Mandarins have been used many 100's of years to treat children—especially with sleeping problems
Rose *(Rosa species)*	• Rose petals have sedative • Antiseptic • Anti-parasitic • Anti-inflammatory • Heart-supportive properties • Psychological studies indicate rose oil can induce "*sweeter dreams*," increase concentration and rate of work capacity • Rose contains natural waxes that are wonderful in keeping skin soft and smooth • Smelling rose helps one feel relaxed and loved	• Non-toxic • Safe	• Rose has been valued for its perfume for 1000's of years • Rose oil deteriorates rapidly with exposure to sun and wind, the content is highest on the first morning when the flower opens • Rose petals picked for distillation are picked manually, day by day, at/or just before sunrise.

[7] Lowers blood pressure.

[8] Makes the skin unusually sensitive to light and subject to damage by light, e.g. by sunburn.

Selected Essential Oils for Maintaining/Restoring Balance (continued)

Essential Oil	Use/Remedy	Caution	Comments
Spearmint (*Mentha spicata*)	• In the Middle Ages, spearmint was used to whiten teeth • Heals animal and insect bites • Prevents milk from curdling • Heals mouth sores • Repels rats and mice • Analgesic • Anti-depressant • Antiseptic • Anti-spasmodic • Restorative • Tonic • Treats colds and flu • For acne and dermatitis • Digestive disorders • Fatigue • Nervous tension • Hyperactivity • Stress relief • Allows one to center and meditate; diffuse into space before meditating • Clears negative energy from the space • Use when there is a need for silence and peace	• Can be irritating to skin as it ages, so use with fatty oil	• Safe • Non-toxic. • USA is the prime grower of spearmint

APPLICATIONS FOR TREATING STRESS

Using Linens and Cotton Balls

Many people find that a few drops on linens will help them de-stress.

Pillowcases are the linen of choice. A few drops of a stress-relieving essential oil may be all you need to relax and sleep the night. Test in an inconspicuous spot of article to avoid staining expensive linen.

Use a few drops on a linen handkerchief. You can keep this in a pocket or purse—a few whiffs when things are stressful will be helpful.

Other than a linen handkerchief, use a cotton ball. The cotton ball can be put into a small plastic bag and easily carried in a purse or pocket.

Misting a dryer sheet with essential oils will add a nice natural fragrance to bed linens.

Warm Bath

Set aside a half-hour at the end of the day. Take a relaxing bath with essential oil or essential oil blend. If there's no time to take a relaxing bath with essential oils, take a shower, put a few drops of a relaxing essential oil or essential oil blend on the floor of shower cubicle and the warm water will vaporize the molecules during the shower.

Take a minute or two to breathe in these molecules deeply to relax and dissipate stress.

Massage

Have a friend, family member, or a professional massage therapist give you a massage. Add the essential oils to a fatty oil, such as fractionated coconut oil or jojoba oil.

Keep in mind that essential oils go a long way—just a few drops will do. For each 1 oz. prepared essential oil, mix with 15 drops of lavender and 10 drops of chamomile for a delightful massage oil.

Meditation

Meditation is an ancient art spanning many centuries and cultures. In today's high-tech, busy world, meditation is practiced to help turn off the mind, rest the body, and feed the spirit.

Breathing is at the very core of meditation and also at the core of aromatherapy.

Meditation is excellent for de-stressing and the addition of essential oils to this practice is wonderful. If you can't or don't have time to meditate just diffuse or mist a relaxing essential oil or blend of essential oils and just sit quietly for a few minutes doing nothing—just enjoying the aroma and the peace.

It's amazing sometimes how little downtime is needed to feel refreshed and ready to face the day's trials again. Put a few drops of the blend on a tissue, cotton ball, or in an aromatherapy necklace and sniff that throughout the day when things start to get hectic.

APPLICATION OF ESSENTIAL OILS

The two most important questions in Aromatherapy:

- **Which oil do I use?**
  and
- **How do I use the oil?**

First, decide *which* essential oil to utilize in a specific situation; **Then** decide *how* to use the oil in one of the following applications:

- Diffusion
- Inhalation
- Compression
- Massage
- Baths
- Skin and Hair Treatments

Diffusion

Several methods are used to diffuse essential oils. The easiest method is to take an enamel or stainless steel pan or glass dish, add some water, then put on the stovetop at low heat. As the water begins to simmer, add an essential oil or blend of oils, when the water gently evaporates, the essential oils will also evaporate into the air, penetrating wherever the air wafts.

There are also special equipment items on the market for diffusion of essential oils. Some of them are described below:

Aroma Lamps are generally pottery shells enclosing a light bulb or a hollow space for a tea candle with a little bowl or cup on top. Add water to the bowl, then the essential oil, and plug in or light the candle. The essential oils will begin to evaporate.

Often the bowls are not big enough, as tea candles burn for approximately 5 hours so the bowl must contain enough water to last. The distance from heat source must be just right:

- too close and the oils are burned or the water boils; and
- too far away and the water does not heat enough and evaporation is stopped.

Bowls can be difficult to clean, the oils can bake onto the bowl and sometimes sticky residues can be left behind. Generally, bowls are not too expensive and very portable.

Aroma Diffusers are usually electrical. They can be complicated or simple and most are made of plastic that will be affected by the oils sooner or later. There are some made of glass, but they can break, and tend to be more expensive—though more convenient. Some models have timers that releases the oils at intervals, though most work like vaporizers. They can be difficult to clean and can use large quantities of oil. Several companies market aroma diffusers, so search on the Internet for best prices.

Aroma Rings are usually ceramic rings for light bulbs in lamps. Place the ring on the light bulb, add the oil, and turn on the lamp. The oils are diffused from the heat generated by the light bulb. Using bulbs with too high wattage will cause the oil to burn and the results will not be satisfactory. For setting the mood, aroma rings are very functional and when used with appropriate bulb wattage, can be effective in diffusing essential oils.

French Diffusers are simply ceramic bottles with corks. The oil is placed in the bottle and corked. Left in the house, or in a window, the heat of the day warms the ceramic bottle and the oil slowly evaporates into the air. This method is not particularly effective.

Perfumes are oils applied to the body to evaporate due to the warmth of the skin. As deodorants, they are applied to areas that perspire—under the arms or on the feet. Perfumes can be used to create a personal signature or special atmosphere around to attract others' attention. These essential oils are usually worn behind the ears, at the wrists, between the breasts, and behind the knees. Often blended oils are fixed with fatty oil or other carriers that are used to dilute the oils, as they may burn the skin if applied directly.

Wearing perfumes can be used therapeutically to relieve stress or create healing.

In *Ayurvedic medicine*, there are times prescribed for different body functions and using oils as a perfume during these times can be most effective. The following chart details some of the concepts of use of perfumes in Ayurvedic medicine:

Chart 25–4
Time of Day Application for Maximum Effectiveness

Perfume Selection	
According to Ayurvedic Medicine[9] Prescription	
Time of Day	Body Function
Midnight (11pm)-1am	Gall Bladder
1am-3am	Liver
3am-5am	Lung
5am-7am	Large Intestine
7am-9am	Stomach
9am-11am	Spleen and Pancreas
11am-1pm	Heart
1pm-3pm	Small Intestine
3pm-5pm	Bladder
5pm-7pm	Kidney
7pm-9pm	General Circulation

Vaporizers or humidifiers add moisture to the air. Essential oils can be diffused to the room or area by the mist created by the vaporizer. Additional moisture can be important in the winter when interior air becomes dry and affects nasal passages. Essential oils can offer protection from flu and colds, too.

---

[9] A traditional Hindu system of healing that assesses somebody's constitution and lifestyle, and recommends treatment based on herbal preparations, diet, yoga, and purification.

Misting or Spritzing is a fast way to get essential oils into the air. It's easy and inexpensive, but the effect does not last for a very long time. Plastic bottles are often used for this, but some essential oils can interact with plastic. Essential oils will last longer in glass bottles. Add water (some have used alcohol) to the bottle and a selected essential oil desired in the area. The essential oils will float on the surface of the water, so shake the bottle prior to each use. Add a drop or two of vinegar or alcohol to help the oils mix with water. Normally, mix 1-oz. water with 30 to 50 drops of essential oil.

Spritz air conditioning filters to disperse essential oils throughout the house. People, plants, and animals can be spritzed to rid them of insects.

Candles can be purchased with essential oils or fragrance already added. Natural oils are preferable in candles. With unscented candles, add essential oils to the well of the candle (where the wick burns a depression in the candle) and the oils will evaporate. Oil candles can be used in the same way. Add essential oil either to the liquid oil or add it to the wick well. Light the candle and the oil evaporates into the room. The oils can burn using this method. Some users disapprove of this method of diffusion, since the chemical composition of the oil is changed when burned.

Potpourri is fresh or dried plant materials usually, though most usually, a combination of flowers or wood shavings. Place the plant material in a large jar with a screw top. Add 8-12 drops of essential oil. Shake well and leave for 1-2 hours before shaking again and emptying into the display container. As the fragrance fades, re-treat the flowers/shavings by replacing into the jar and repeat the process. Natural oils do not last as long as fragrance oils in potpourri mixes.

Inhalation

Inhalation or breathing in of essential oil is one of the quickest ways to affect brain chemistry, since the nose is connected to the limbic or emotional center of the brain. Depression can be easily lifted just by breathing chocolate. *Inhalation is one of the fastest ways to bring change and transformation to thoughts and feelings.*

Use for: colds, flu, depression, sinusitis, cough, fever, congestion, allergies. boost memory, enhance mood, panic attacks, and insomnia.

Hot steaming bowl of water, add 1-3 drops of essential oils and put a towel over your head. Close your eyes and breathe the fumes into your lungs. Do not get too close to the steam—it can cause burns. After a few minutes, stop breathing the vapors and add more essential oils. As the water cools, stop the treatment. Repeat as needed, 3-4 times a day. Also use vaporizers. Supervise small children—hot water can cause burns.

Sauna creates steam heat by pouring water over hot rocks. Oils may be added to the water to create oil inhalations, which are especially good for detoxing and improving respiratory issues. Dry saunas are also available if moisture is a problem. Essential oils are flammable, so care should be exercised when pouring essential oils directly on a hot surface.

Cotton balls with 1-3 drops of essential oil added, then placed into a plastic bag can be carried in a purse or pocket to use as needed when going out. Cotton balls with essential oils can be placed in the outer ear canal. Handkerchiefs with a drop or two can be placed under the pillow or by the bed. This makes it possible to have them when traveling. Pillows can be misted to enhance sleep, help in treatment of colds and flu, respiration difficulty, etc.

Face misters are electric and mist air into the face for breathing in. Just add essential oils to the water and follow directions provided with the appliance.

Rub your hands together, add a drop or two of oil to palms, and rub them together briskly. Cup hands around the nose and breathe in. Assure that only a drop or two of the essential oil is used, as the oil can run down the arms.

There is a controversy about whether to use wet or dry heat with essential oils. The major issue concerns mold or fungus growth due to the presence of water. In selling diffusers, first some made claims that moist heat was bad, and then later, dry heat was attacked with the equal vigor. Common sense should help determine which method to utilize. There may be some evidence that moist air is not good for asthmatics, so dry methods of inhaling the oils need to be considered in the case of asthmatics.

Compress

Compresses are effective when pain and swelling occur, and can relieve the pain. It is important to understand when to use a cold compress and when to use a warm compress.

Cold compresses are for new injuries, and serve to reduce swelling and inflammation, insect bites, some headaches, and fever, or to reduce heat.

Hot compresses are for old injuries to reduce muscular pain, relieve dull aches, varicose veins, asthma, toothaches, menstrual pain, boils, and abscesses.

Alternating cold and hot compresses can help open sinuses, some headaches, and arthritic pain when massage will not help.

To make a compress, mix 5-15 drops of essential oils in a quart of water. Immerse a small towel or wash cloth into the water. Let it soak for 1-2 minutes, and then squeeze most of the water out of the material. Fold neatly, and then cover the folded cloth with plastic wrap or foil to prevent direct contact with the skin. Apply compress to the area needing treatment. After treatment, add an ice bag for cooling or a towel or small blanket for warming. Alternate and repeat as needed.

Massage

Massage is one of the most important uses for essential oils. The full benefit essential oils bring to the massage experience benefits both the person giving and the person being given a massage. Massage formulas can be found in books to relieve muscular aches and pain, relax, reduce stiffness, and ease all kinds of conditions. The essential oil formulas can also be individualized using various methods to select the oils. There is also a need to understand blended (fixed) oils and how they work with and within the body. Many massage therapists mix and match blended oils in combination with other essential oils to achieve the desired results.

There is also a form of massage and essential oil therapy that releases emotional pain. The subject can re-live or remember old wounds and hurts. Crying, anger, fear, and other emotions can arise as the person releases this stored trauma.

Various parts of the body can benefit from massage. The back and shoulders are the most popular, but foot and hand massage can be very effective as well as facial and cranial massage.

There are various techniques, schools, and methods of massage. Explore the ones that seem most promising for the relief needed. Massage schools are available in most areas, and instruction should be readily available virtually anywhere. Try different massage methods and ask the therapist to use essential oils—bring them if needed.

INTERNAL OR ORAL USE OF OILS

Some oils may be taken internally. This is a difficult area for aromatherapists because this feels too much like prescribing pills and practicing medicine—which is not permitted legally. Aromatherapists must be very aware of a person's history to prescribe essential oils to be taken internally. The liver is the organ that breaks down oils. If a person is taking medicines that tax the liver or has a liver disease of any kind, he must not be permitted to take essential oils—even exposure to the oils should be limited. The quality of the

Note:

It is illegal and unlawful to prescribe essential oil for medicinal purposes without a license!

oils must be very high for internal use. Most *expressed*[10] oils, unless organic, are not appropriate for internal use.

Oils can be dropped into the mouth for dental use. *Myrrh* can be added to dental floss to help gums. *Tea tree* and *peppermint* are often found in toothpaste. *Wintergreen* is often found in mouthwashes. *Eucalyptus* is often in cough drops that are melted in the mouth.

If getting the oils into the mouth and swallowing is a problem, then use honey, sugar, bread, or alcohol. Mixing 1-2 drops of oil with 2 teaspoons of honey in hot water is soothing and enjoyable. Many enjoy tea in the morning made with a drop or two of *peppermint*, *spearmint*, *bergamot mint* (*Mentha citrata,* used in Earl Grey tea), *grapefruit*, *lemon*, or *orange*. Essential oils can be added to plain tea to give it variety and added flavor.

Many oils are *carminative*[11] and can have a good effect on the digestive process. A drop or two of *fennel*, *anise*, or *peppermint* can ease an upset stomach and help digestion.

It is generally not expected that a person continue longer than two weeks in the treatment of a condition with essential oils. Medical advice should be sought when dealing with any medical complaint. Assure that all ministrations are given by trained and licensed aromatherapists qualified to deal with these issues—or pass on treating. **Note**: There are laws against prescribing essential oils without a license.

Always use nontoxic, non-irritating, or non-sensitizing essential oils. Formulas should be kept to three oils or less. Administration under the tongue is the best method to get the oils into the body. Oils can be placed in gelatin tablets, mixed with blended (fixed) oils, mixed with food, or mixed in water. Essential oils can be taken 3 to 4 times a day as the oils are rapidly excreted (usually in 4 hr., but as short as 30 min.) through the urinary system, sweat glands, or expired through the lungs.

Dosage usually depends on weight.

The rule of thumb for administration is:

- 1 drop per 50 lb. of weight;
- 2-4 drops of the appropriate essential oil;
- 3-4 times a day treatment;
- two weeks of use;
- stop for a week; and
- repeat cycle, depending on need.

Make sure the administrator of any essential oil(s) is fully qualified to be giving treatment. The phenolic compounds in some essential oils can cause mucus membrane irritation and some oils could cause death when administered without examination and discussion with the patient.

<u>Gargles and mouthwashes</u> are good for bad breath, mouth ulcers, stopping colds from "dropping" into the chest, and sore throats.

For mouthwashes, add 2-3 drops of oil into a half glass of water and swish in the mouth. Spit out when finished. For gargles do the same. Oils float on water, stir or shake before each use.

<u>Douching</u> is used to cleanse, heal, and refresh the vaginal area. Vinegar water with essential oils can be used. Care must be taken on the choice of oils. All authorities do not recommend this treatment, exercise extreme caution in this treatment!

<u>Culinary</u> use of essential oils is mostly for flavor and fun.

Only small amounts of any essential oil are needed in recipes—1 drop or less may be enough for most recipes. Some practice is required to achieve the proper balance in reci-

---

[10] Liquid forced out of something by squeezing or pressing.

[11] Aids in relieving flatulence or colic by expelling gas.

pes. When cooking with essential oils, add them at the last moment so their fragrance remains, as the heat will dissipate them quickly.

Cold drinks, smoothies, salad and salad dressings, teas, and punches are especially good choices in which essential oils can maximize their flavors.

Baths

Using essential oils to relieve stress is an easy method of relaxation and release. The warmth of the water carries the vapors to the nose and a sense of deep relaxation can be achieved. Bath therapy is an essential oil treatment with tremendous positive results. However, special training is required to practice this therapy[12].

There are also baths for general health and well-being. Honey baths, bubble baths, oatmeal baths, milk baths, salt baths, seaweed baths, soda baths, relaxing baths, sensuous baths, cellulite baths, sitz baths, and footbaths.

Essential oils do not mix well in water. An emulsifier[13], to help the oils mix with water is required, such as honey, milk, vinegar, soda, or borax. Merely add a small amount of any of these emulsifier and add the essential oil(s) to them, mix together, and add to the bath.

Honey bath is good for inflammation and can be combined with essential oils that are anti-inflammatory.

Cream, Fresh Milk, Dried Milk, or Egg Yolk bath is good for dry skin

Salt, Vinegar, Sea Weed, and Soda baths are good for cleansing and detoxing.

Foot and Hand baths are good for rheumatism. Use 6-8 drops of oil in a bowl of warm to hot water. Use an emulsifier and swish the oils well into the water. Have a kettle of hot water close by to keep the water hot.

Sitz baths are used to ease hemorrhoids, candida, and ease stitches from childbirth. Use 4-5 drops of essential oil in a large stainless steel basin (a porcelain tub has a porous surface and is difficult to clean for this purpose) of hot water or a bidet (which is made of non-porous vitreous china).

Always prepare your bath water first—the hotter the water the faster the essential oils will be released into both the water and the air. Get into the tub with a bottle of prepared essential oils and your chosen emulsifier, then add some of the hot bath water to your bottle of oil and shake. Then add the contents of the mix to your bath water and vigorously swish it into the water.

Breathe the vapors in deeply, relax, and soak.

Skin and Hair Treatments

Shampoos are used to cleanse the hair. The hair is naturally acidic and can become damaged when it becomes alkaline. Vinegar and lemon rinses are important to the hair for this reason. Usual recipe is 2 oz. concentrated liquid soap to 6 oz. water and essential oils added to treat for normal, oily, dry, or dandruff conditions. A small amount of borax can be used as an emulsifier.

Hydrosols are well-suited to skin and eye care. Hydrosols are a colloidal solution in which the particles are suspended in water remaining from the distillation of essential oils. There are very small amounts of essential oils in the water and can be spritzed onto the face and even into the eyes without causing problems.

Many essential oils can cause stinging and burn the face if use inappropriately. Hydrosols eliminate this concern and are safe.

---

[12] **Gritman Essential Oils** company trains therapists in *Essential Oil Bath Therapy* and can help you if you are interested in this form of therapy.

[13] A chemical agent that maintains or creates an emulsion, which is a suspension of one liquid in another, e.g. oil in water.

Creams and Lotions are used to moisturize, rejuvenate, heal damaged skin, and treat natural creams and lotions tend to separate and may need refrigeration to keep fresh. When adding water to fixed oils, dormant mold spores can be released and start to grow, which is often the reason for creams and lotions spoiling. Many references caution against use of unclean hands or fingers in the oils. Popsicle sticks can be used to get the creams out of their jars, or squeeze bottles can be used for lotions to keep them from becoming contaminated.

Making cream and lotion can be difficult—it's probably easier to add essential oil(s) to a commercially prepared cream. Use this modified cream for massage and skin preparations.

In summary, essential oils have the ability to help in the human body's healing process.

When properly utilized, essential oils have the capability to soothe, comfort, heal, and help preserve the health and vitality of those who utilize them properly.

---

[i] This chapter was originally authored especially for this edition by **Meg Shehad**, owner of **Gritman Essential Oils. Meg** is a Certified Aromatherapist, Certified Intuitive Oil Counselor, and Licensed Professional Counselor in the State of Texas. Meg lives in the greater Houston Area. She certifies specialists and professionals in aromatherapy level 1, level 2, level 3, and level 4 qualification.. She grants the title of *Professional Certified Aromatheraptist* upon completion of class work, projects, and case studies. Meg has 15 years experience as a counselor, and 15 years as owner of Gritman Essential Oils. Meg has given lectures, classes in the USA, Canada, and Europe. She can be reached at **1-(888) GRITMAN** (888-474-8626) or **www.gritman.com**. You contact **Meg Shehad** at *Meg@Gritman.com* or (281) 996-0103.

Meg has written the **Gritman Guide to Essential Oils**, the **Gritman Guide to Sixty Most Popular Essential Oils**, and **The Wise Woman's Aromatherapy—Macerations.** She also appears on the radio program, *Earth 101* on *Pacifica Radio*. Meg is the CEO of Gritman Corporation, and the company is shared with her daughter, Amy, and partner Lou. The company carries a large selection of essential oils and other related products. Gritman distills and grows some of its own essential oils. Gritman also makes *macerations*, an alternative to essential oils. All Gritman employees enjoy talking with customers and answering questions—customers are seen as extensions of the Gritman family.

Meg earned her BA in elementary education and her MA in clinical psychology. Meg was a science and math teacher before becoming a mother. While a mom, she returned to school and obtained the Masters in Clinical Psychology and created a private practice. While working with essential oils, she found they had a profound effect on her clients. She has used her many talents to create a company that can be relied upon for high quality essential oils.

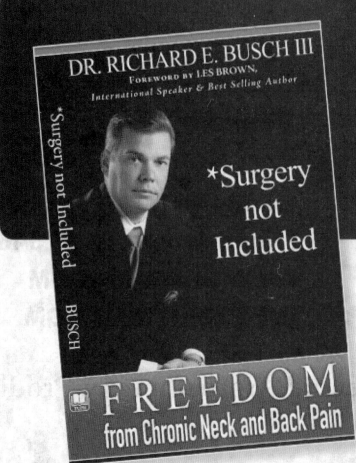

"You are consigned ultimately to live in the future—prepared or not! The choices you make today will determine your tomorrows. The choice is truly yours!"

Chapter 26

Basics of Genetic Engineering

In the late 1980's, a health epidemic struck the United States, killing more than 100 people, and ultimately affected another 5,000 to 10,000 people who became deathly ill, some of whom became disabled. It took more than 4 years to discover the cause of the epidemic. Finally, the source of the epidemic was identified as L-tryptophan, a sixty-year old, well-accepted form of food supplementation. It was determined a certain brand had genetically engineered a new form that resulted in the health catastrophe[i].

Genetic engineering of plants and animals is aggressively and distinctly becoming what could become the most massive challenge yet to human beings because the changes can be self-perpetuating, and any errors will be genetically passed on to the next generation.

The genetically-engineered plants that are the most common in the United States are corn, soy, canola, cottonseed oil, and wheat. It is estimated that 40% of the corn supply and 80% of the soybean supply are genetically engineered. It is practically impossible in the marketplace today to escape genetically altered products—they have become ingredients in the dominant part of the products in our grocery stores—60% of food products in the typical grocery store have genetically modified content, and therefore are inevitably in our kitchens and pantries.

Caution:

The FDA has not evaluated all of these statements. This information is for educational purposes only. Always consult your own personal doctor or licensed professional for medical advice.

In May 2009, The American Academy of Environmental Medicine (**AAEM**) released its position paper on Genetically Modified (**GMO**) foods stating that:

> "*GMO foods pose a serious health risk...*" and calling for a moratorium on GMO foods. Citing several animal studies, the **AAEM** concludes "*...there is more than a casual association between GMO foods and adverse health effects*" and that "*...GMO foods pose a serious health risk in the areas of toxicology, allergy and immune function, reproductive health, and metabolic, physiologic, and genetic health.*[1]"

The **AAEM** called for the following actions to be taken:

- a moratorium on GMO food;
- implementation of immediate long term safety testing and labeling of GMO food;
- physicians to educate their patients, the medical community and the public to avoid GMO foods;
- physicians to consider the role of GMO foods in their patients' disease processes; and
- more independent long-term scientific studies to begin gathering data to investigate the role of GMO foods on human health.

According to Dr. Amy Dean, PR chair and Board Member of **AAEM**,

> "*Multiple animal studies have shown that GMO foods cause damage to various organ systems in the body. With this **mounting** evidence, it is imperative to have a moratorium on GMO foods for the safety of our patients' and the public's health.*"

One of the main reasons for the problems with the GMO's is that as a result of the genetic modification, these crops produce new proteins that have never been present before which, are in effect, truly alien to the earth! As a result of this, our bodies are not capable of properly breaking them down. As a result, the proteins produced and consumed cause the animal or human to have allergic reactions to the "*alien*" protein. This reaction will cause inflammation within the body.

This *inflammation in the system is the true problem* because it has been shown that inflammation is the cause of many of the major health problems today. These include arthritis, heart disease, and even cancer.

The major problem with GMO's is they are part of the content of virtually everything we eat! GMO's started as experimental and it was assumed that they would never enter the food supply. However, that has all changed. Now, unless you are consuming a food that is certified as organic, chances are there is some substance in the product that is genetically modified.

WHY GENETICALLY MODIFIED SEED?

There are several reasons for the development of GMO seeds—they are created to be resistant:

- to pests and
- to herbicides.

GMO seeds are also purported to have better:

- cold tolerance, and
- disease resistance.

The plan was to increase yields and "*feed the world.*" At this point, it is highly questionable if this will be achieved—in fact it appears that the overall production may be diminishing.

In the past, farmers would harvest their crops, sell, and/or save the grain, holding back some grain for seeds for their next year's crops. With the development of GMO's, if the

---

[1] http://www.aaemonline.org/GMOpressrelease.html

farmers buy and plant the GMO seeds it is illegal to hold grain back for seed because legally the seed is owned by companies such as Monsanto. The companies control the distribution and pricing of their patented seed products.

A number of studies over the past decade have revealed that genetically engineered foods can pose serious risks to humans, domesticated animals, wildlife, and the environment.

WHAT ARE SOME SIDE EFFECTS OF RAISING GMO PLANTS?

A reported side effect of raising GMO's is the genetically modified plant are cross-pollinating with non-modified plants and causing a gene transfer in the otherwise normal plant. For example, the GMO plants that are developed to be pesticide-resistant will actually produce their own pesticides, and these genetic modifications may even cause the same types of production through cross-pollination in regular plants. Then it is entirely possible that this production—since it is may be in the form of a virus or bacteria that was introduced into the plant for resistance—could take place in our own intestinal system, which in turn could cause our own body to produce the pesticide or herbicide within the intestinal tract or other organ.

These problems may be some of the causes for the new mystery illnesses that are becoming more abundant, such as chronic fatigue and fibromyalgia, and other health problems which include higher risks of toxicity, allergies, antibiotic resistance, immune-suppression, and cancer.

There are possible effects on the environment:

- biological pollution causing plants and animals to become extinct,
- creation of a strain of super weeds, and the
- possibility of unknown viruses.

Then, too, there is the high probability of contamination of non-altered as well as engineered plants and animals. The problem is that we just don't know:

- Have we opened a Pandora's Box with inherently dangerous alterations?
- Have we created new allergies?

GMO soybeans and corn each contain two new proteins with allergenic properties[2], nutritional related problems, and diseases—and perhaps even poisons. Scientists are arguing for long-term testing.

According to Canadian geneticist David Suzuki, there isn't any scientific evidence to show the GMO plants and food are safe, and he warns,

> "*The experiments simply haven't been done and we now have become the guinea pigs.*" He continues, "*Anyone that says, 'Oh, we know that this is perfectly safe'; I say is either unbelievably stupid or deliberately lying[3].*"

Of equally high concern is an untested and unregulated category of "*nanotechnology*" that also alters food products, nutritional supplements, and packaging. Nanotechnology is also referred to as *molecular manufacturing*—which is the alteration of materials on a *nanoscale* of a millionth of a millimeter (180,000[th] the size of human hair!)[4]

---

[2] *See L Zolla, et al,* **"Proteomics as a complementary tool for identifying unintended side effects occurring in transgenic maize seeds as a result of genetic modifications,**" *J Proteome Res. 2008 May;7(5):1850-61; Hye-Yung Yum, Soo-Young Lee, Kyung-Eun Lee, Myung-Hyun Sohn, Kyu-Earn Kim,* **"Genetically Modified and Wild Soybeans: An immunologic comparison,**" *Allergy and Asthma Proceedings 26, no. 3 (May–June 2005): 210-216(7); and Gendel,* **"The use of amino acid sequence alignments to assess potential allergenicity of proteins used in genetically modified foods,**" *Advances in Food and Nutrition Research 42 (1998), 45–62.*

[3] **"Suzuki warns against hastily accepting GMO's**", *The Leader-Post* (Canada), 26 April 2005.

[4] "**Nanotechnology: More Hazardous than GMO's & Toxic Chemicals?**" **The Ecologist**, 7/23/09 (by Levitt)

According to a definition in a recent report in *Nanotechnology in Agriculture and Food*, May 5, 2006, food is "*nanofood*" when nanoparticles, nanotechnology techniques, or tools are used during cultivation, production, processing, or packaging of the food.

Nanotechnology is promoted on the forecasting of improved food flavor, nutrition and processing. There is to be a category of "*functional foods*" (common, everyday foods that are capable of conveying medications and supplements). This is all promoted, for worldwide approval, on the back of the promise of increased production and economics—that this technology will save the world from starvation.

You will discover in another report, **Out of the Laboratory and onto Our Plates: Nanotechnology in Food and Agriculture**[5]*, Friends of the Earth*, 2nd ed., Apr. 2008, there is a conclusion that nanomaterials are in very popular drinks and packaging. I recommend to all readers they read this report to be aware of major brands and merchandisers selling such products and packaging. They are neither my statements nor necessarily my opinions, but certainly need considering.

> "*Nanotechnology can be very dangerous when used in food*," said report co-author Dr. Rye Senjen. '*Early scientific evidence indicates that some nanomaterials produce free radicals which destroy or mutate DNA and can cause damage to the liver and kidneys. Existing regulations in the US did not require testing or labeling for nanomaterials when they were created from existing approved chemicals, despite major differences in potential toxicity*.'"

There are major differences between genetically engineering or modifying than that of breeding. Breeding does not cross species' barriers and does not create plants and foods that could never naturally occur. Not only are there potential health and environment problems, there are also ethical questions that could be addressed about this technology.

To avoid the genetically altered, engineered, molecularly manufactured plants and products, plant your own garden and preserve your own foods. Buy locally grown meats and fresh organic food. When you must buy processed foods, read the labels thoroughly!

For more information, go to **http://www.safe-food.org/-consumer/shop** for a strong start on **GMO** attributes. Use your browser to find references about **GMO** on the Internet.

Learn to read product labels—however, reading labels is no guarantee you'll get no **GMO** products, because the manufacturers are not required to list all ingredients used in their processes.

In conclusion: There is a long road to travel before these issues are resolved!

Inform yourself on these issues and determine whether you want to continue to support an industry-controlled harvest of genetically modified foods and food products with your food dollars.

---

[i] **Dr. Richard E. Busch III** is a nationally recognized Doctor of Chiropractic, author, speaker, and President Emeritus of *The American Chiropractor* magazine. He founded the Busch Chiropractic Pain Center in 1996 and since, he has successfully treated thousands of patients for chronic and severe disc conditions that traditionally would have required surgery. Dr. Busch is a pioneer in bringing the **DRS Protocol**™, utilizing spinal decompression technology, to the forefront of care for appropriate low back and neck conditions. He has served as a national consultant for the continuing development of this technology and the **DRS Protocol**™. This protocol incorporates unique and proprietary elements of nutrition as a significant element—as is enzyme therapy—in which Dr. Busch is certified. All elements of the protocol contribute to some of the highest success rates for the alleviation of back and neck pain. Dr. Busch trains physicians and chiropractors across the nation in the **DRS Protocol**™ to help patients avoid surgery, and he is a consultant to many physicians and chiropractors. Dr. Busch has published a recent eye-opening book ***Surgery not Included: Freedom from Chronic Neck and Back Pain**. You can visit his website at **www.surgerynotincluded.com**. Dr. Busch's wife, Jennifer, is active in the business and has authored the detailed information (**see Chapter 24**) included in the "*Basic Stress Battle Plan*," and her wonderful book dealing with the results of stress entitled **All In My Mind? How to Overcome Adrenal Fatigue, Chronic Fatigue, and Fibromyalgia.**

---

[5] **Ibid.**

Section VIII

Basics Library

Chapter 27: Creating A Preparedness Library

category

Canning & Preserving

title

Making the Best of Basics: Family Preparedness Handbook

publisher

Gold Leaf Press

author

James Talmage Stevens

You must re-forge yourself and create new paradigms—break out of your mould; study, learn, practice, and gain knowledge until you are comfortable with your new self.

Chapter 27

Creating A Preparedness Library

A **library** of essential and practical books is important to meet information needs when entering the uncharted territory of survivalism, preparedness, and self-reliance. Since most people are neither personally experienced in nor prepared by education for a strict preparedness lifestyle, having the proper books can help save time, effort, expense, and frustration as life changes are introduced.

Many of my best food preparation and preservation books were handed down from my grandparents and my mother. Many others were collected over the years as our family moved from place to place. Our food books were always the first items to be packed when we transferred, much to the despair of employers paying for the move, moving company personnel, and our children.

My mother never discarded a book on food, food preparation, or food storage subjects—nor have I!

The books listed in this chapter are based on either personal reviews or recommendations

The great French Maréchal Lyautey once asked his gardener to plant a tree on the property. The gardener objected, indicating the tree was a slow-growing species, and would not reach maturity for at least 100 years.

Maréchal Lyautey replied, "*If that's the case, there is no time to lose, you must plant it this very afternoon!*"

Story told by John F. Kennedy, US President

of friends, industry experts, business associates, food storage professionals, publishers, editors, and other participants in the survivalist, preparedness, and self-reliance disciplines. In some cases very little information other than the title is available. For those books which have written reviews in the following lists, the descriptions have been kept to a minimum and highlight the main subjects covered. We leave the joy of discovery of additional information in each of these books to the reader.

Some of the books listed in this chapter may now be out of print. If you are willing to expend the effort, you might still find many of the older titles in:

- thrift shops,
- second-hand bookstores,
- discount bookstores,
- online booksellers (There are thousands of them on the Internet—go to the **Amazon.com** used book listings in any category),
- from one of the many book finders in **Chart 27-15, Publishers, Presses, Booksellers, & Catalog-Order Resources** section at the end of this chapter, or go to the
- public library collections.

Today, with Internet, especially—**Amazon.com, Craig's List,** and **eBay**, there is no end to the discoveries possible. The marvel of the Internet will bring you much information, and your browser becomes the greatest tool in finding even more resources. Our lives are truly blessed by the information explosion on the Internet!

Note: My greatest and best successes were gained by copying the title into the Google search engine—it truly epitomizes the value of electronic information! Use these resources to locate the books you want to read or acquire for your personal preparedness library.

Notice: Some information in this directory may be obsolete by the time it is published. It is the natural consequence of publishing any type of list.

HOW TO USE THIS "PREPAREDNESS LIBRARY" OF BOOKS

The following guide will help you utilize the "**Preparedness Library**" listings more effectively:

- ☐ Books have been categorized by subject in **Charts 27-1** to **27-14.** See subject areas included on the following page.
- ☐ Within each subject area, books are listed alphabetically by their title.
- ☐ Title is followed by author(s) and name of publisher, where available.
- ☐ A short summary is included, if we've had the opportunity to review it.
- ☐ **Chart 27-15** provides contact/address information for the book's publisher, where known. All publisher information has been consolidated in **Chart 27-15** to allow more space (and less visual clutter) in the book listings.
- ☐ Listings of other publishers of preparedness-related books, independent presses, and retail vendors of survivalist, general preparedness, and self-reliance books are also found in **Chart 27-15.**

Books in this chapter are categorized in the following subject or knowledge areas:

1. Information and Commercial Directories   **Page 27-5**

Some of these sources include information about equipment, products, and supplies from distributors, manufacturers, and producers. Not all are to be found in bookstores. Typically, public libraries will have these books on the shelves.

2. Emergencies and Disasters Books   **Page 27-6**

Books in these categories provide information and solutions for situations caused by events considered life-threatening in the short term, and usually require immediate handling to assure personal safety or to prevent serious injury—or even death.

A. Outdoor Skills and First Aid   **Page 27-6**

Backpacking, camping, cooking outdoors, emergency medical care, emergency rescue, field medical care, and first aid; fishing, hunting, land and water navigation, staying alive outdoors, and tracking

B. Disasters (natural, manmade, and personal) and Survival   **Page 27-12**

Earthquakes, floods, hurricanes, tornadoes; biological, chemical, or nuclear disaster; civil disorder, general disasters; war, job loss, fire, and financial loss

3. Preparedness Lifestyle Books   **Page 27-16**

These books provide information about activities that sustain life on a daily basis. Often, these activities require skills normally not utilized in today's lifestyle. These skills, though seldom used today, can make life more enjoyable.

C. Homesteading, Building, Maintenance, and Repair   **Page 27-16**

Do-it-yourself skills, animal husbandry, auto repair, bees and honey production, blacksmithing, burying the dead, butchering, electrical wiring/systems, home and outbuilding construction, plumbing systems, small-scale farming, soap making, and woodworking

D. Water   **Page 27-20**

Water purification, storage, treatment, dangers, systems

E. Gardening and Food Production   **Page 27-21**

Backyard gardening, composting, fruits, herbs, irrigation, mulching, mushrooms, organic gardening, pest control, vegetables, greenhouses, small-scale hydroponics, sprouts and sprouting

F. Harvesting and Gathering Wild Foods   **Page 27-26**

Edible wild herbs, plants, roots, mushrooms, foraging, hunting, plant and weed identification, sea vegetables

G. Preserving and Storing Foods   **Page 27-28**

Brining, canning, curing, dehydrating (drying), freezing, pickling, refrigerating, smoking, freeze-drying, storage plans and tips, root cellaring, and using stored foods

This section is devoted to information regarding presses, publishers, and independent vendors of survivalism, preparedness, and self-reliance books reported in this list.

Responsible persons with additional information about other survivalist, preparedness, and self-reliance subjects and related book titles are urged to send us details with a review copy.

Authors of survivalist, preparedness, and self-reliance subjects are invited to send copies of their works for review and submission to these listings, of course!

Our staff is always searching for old and new preparedness titles and library references. Any publications about family preparedness and home storage subjects are worthy of review and inclusion here.

We reiterate: inclusion does not indicate endorsement, nor does exclusion indicate rejection!

This is an ever-increasing listing, and will be updated frequently. Go to www.DoctorPrepper.com for additional information. Please submit any titles and literature information you may have for inclusion in this chapter by clicking on the Contact Me button at the top of the home page and enter the information in the comments block. Preparedness suppliers, books, and additional preparedness information {and product information) also available at http://doctorprepper.com/preparedness-resources/

INFORMATION AND COMMERCIAL DIRECTORIES

The following are information and commercial directories. Some of these sources include information about equipment, products, and supplies from manufacturers, producers, processors, and their distributors and retailers.

Not all directories are to be found in bookstores. Typically, the public library will have most of these books in its non-lending collection.

Chart 27–1
Information & Commercial Directories

Christian Media Directory, The, pub. Christian Media, Box 448, Jacksonville OR 97530 ☎/🖷(541) 899-8888
– listing of all companies known to be in the Christian Media market in the US; includes Christian newspapers, audio, broadcasting, book, music, video, magazine, and support & promotional suppliers; 8000+ listings
Christian Retail Directory, The, pub. Christian Media, Box 448, Jacksonville OR 97530 ☎/🖷(541) 899-8888
– national directory of manufacturing firms involved in the marketing & distribution of products into Christian Booksellers; includes listings of wholesalers, distributors, & retailers; 5400+ listings
Concert Sponsors & Providers Directory, The, pub. Christian Media, Box 448, Jacksonville OR 97530 ☎/🖷(541) 899-8888
– listings of Christian organizations, ministries, & promotion firms that sponsor a Christian event; 4000+ listings
Encyclopedia of Associations, The, pub. Gale Research Associates, Inc., Detroit MI ☎(800) 877-GALE
– multi-volume set, revised and published annually; one of the standard sources of information about most non-profit, not-for-profit associations, & associations in general
Instant Information, Joel Makower & Alan Green, pub. Prentice Hall
– a comprehensive listing of organizations of all types
International Christian Media Directory, The, pub. Christian Media, Box 448, Jacksonville OR 97530 ☎/🖷(541) 899-8888
– firms, organizations, & individuals outside the US involved in Christian media; 1000+ listings
National Directory of Addresses and Telephone Numbers
– designed to help you find the sources for the products and services you seek; available at most libraries
Oxbridge Communications, Inc., 150 5th Avenue #302, **New York** NY ☎(212) 741-0231 or (800) 955-0231 🖷(212) 633-2938
– publisher of directories for periodicals, catalogs, magazines, newsletters, college media; newsletters for publishing trends, print leads, and media leads
Pirate Radio Directory, The, Andrew Yoder & George Zeller, pub. Tiare Publications
– guide to the world of pirate radio is published annually & will quickly become a standard reference; complete listing covers recently active pirate stations, with notes on frequencies, formats, QSL addresses, etc.; extensive introduction to pirate radio listening
Resource Directory for the Disabled, Richard Neil Schrout, pub. Facts on File, Inc., 460 Park Ave. So., New York NY 10016 ☎(212) 683-2244 or (800) 322-8755
– an excellent listing of many of the public and private resources available for the disabled
Tapping the Government Grapevine: User-Friendly Guide to US Government Publications, Judith Schiek Robinson, pub. The Oryx Press
– excellent book about how to get the information you want from the federal government
Thomas Grocery Directory, 🖳www.thomascat
– the *"ThomCat"* of the grocery industry (see **Thomas Register of Manufacturers** above)
Thomas Register of Manufacturers, 🖳**www.thomascat.com**
– popularly known as *ThomCat*, one of the best resources for pure research about US producers; multi-volume resource listings & cross-listings of manufactured items & their manufacturers by name, brand names, and general categories; invaluable reference

When you find errors, please address the correct data to:
Doc@DoctorPrepper.com

EMERGENCIES AND DISASTERS BOOKS

These books provide information and solutions for situations caused by events considered life-threatening in the short term, and usually require immediate handling to assure personal safety or to prevent serious injury or even death.

A. Outdoor Skills and First Aid

This category includes books about backpacking, camping, cooking outdoors, emergency medical care, emergency rescue, field medical care, and first aid; fishing, hunting, land and water navigation, staying alive outdoors, and tracking.

Chart 27–2
Outdoor Skills & First Aid Books

Alaska on Foot, Erik Molvar and Elayne Sears
– wilderness techniques for far northern climates
American Medical Association Handbook of First Aid and Emergency Care, pub. American Medical Association
– comprehensive, step by step guide for emergency care
American Medical Association Pocket Guide to Emergency First Aid, pub. American Medical Association
– concise, clearly illustrated sections for treating emergencies; pocket-size edition
American Medical Association Pocket Guide to Sports First Aid, pub. American Medical Association
American Red Cross Adult CPR, American Red Cross
American Red Cross First Aid and Safety Handbook, American Red Cross and Kathleen A. Handal, MD
– supplement to medical help; focus on preventing, preparing for and coping with emergencies
Baby and Child Emergency First Aid Handbook, The, Mitchell Einzig
– simple step-by-step instructions for most common childhood emergencies
Backcountry First Aid and Extended Care, Buck Tilton
– new edition contains new section with advice to international travelers
Backpacking Basics, Thomas Winnett
– revised edition covering the latest backpacking developments; save money buying equipment and food; pre-trip planning, where to go, getting in shape, how much to comfortably carry, and how to pack it
Basic Essentials of Backpacking, Harry Roberts
– essential knowledge for a safe, enjoyable backpacking trip into the wilderness; beginners skills, starting with the proper preparation; equipment lists and comfort tips
Basic Essentials of Camping, Cliff Jacobson
– increase camping skill level of the general public; gear needed, fire-starting, camp cooking, map and compass skills; basic skills for safer and more enjoyable camping experience
Basic Essentials of Cooking in the Outdoors, Cliff Jacobsen
– the cooking and meal preparation part of a camping trip; unique ideas and simple solutions to typical camp-site dilemmas; meal planning, food procurement, cooking, utensil care, disposal concerns, cooking in the rain or wind, bake using a variety of ovens, and protecting your food from animals; excellent tips for delicious meals
Basic Essentials of Rescue, Buc Tilton
– assess injury situations and plan for evacuation, where possible; improvise a litter, proper carrying techniques
Basic Essentials of Survival, James E. Churchill, pub. ICS Books
– if stranded or lost; survive off the land for two to three days; prepare for the unexpected; necessary survival skills
Best of Woodsmoke, Richard L. Jamison, pub. Horizon Publishing Co.
– manual of primitive outdoor skills
Boy Scout Handbook, pub. Boy Scouts of America
– general preparedness by the group that introduced being prepared
Camper's Companion, Greenspan and Kahn
– for car camping, backpacking, canoeing, etc., a pack-along guide to make outdoor trips better; recipes from basic to gourmet; complete packing and resource list; great outdoor tips
Camper's Pocket Handbook, John Goll
– backcountry traveler's companion
Camping and Survival—Step-By-Step Guide to Wilderness Skills and Outdoor Living, Brice Peterson, pub. Step by Step Publishing
Camping in the '90s—Tips, Techniques and Secrets, Leigh Ellis and Victoria Logue
Camping Secrets, Cliff Jacobsen
– gain an unfair advantage over your camping friends; unique advice and recommendations
Camping's Forgotten Skills—Backwoods Tips from a Boundary Waters Guide, Cliff Jacobson, pub. ICS Books

Outdoor Skills & First Aid Books (continued)

Canteen Cup Cookery, Galen Geer – make survival food taste better
Care and Use Of Individual Clothing and Equipment, Army Field Manual 21-15 – use basic field gear
Cold Can Kill—Hypothermia, Christine B. Hall
Cold Comfort, Glenn Randall, pub. Lyons and Burford – keeping warm in the outdoors
Cold Weather Survival, pub. US Army – survive under the most severe and varying cold weather conditions; survive in any cold weather area of the world
Commonsense Outdoor Medicine and Emergency Companion, The, Newell D. Breyfogle – medical, first-aid, and a survival guide for home or field
Complete Book of Outdoor Survival, Fears – plan for the unexpected; importance of attitude in survival; information about: survival kits, fire building, survival shelters, finding and treating water, food and survival, medicine and safety, and more
Complete Guide to Orienteering in North America, Berndt Berglund
Complete Idiot's Guide to First Aid Basics, The, (Complete Idiot's Guides), Stephen J. Rosenberg and Karla Dougherty
Complete Outdoor Encyclopedia, Sparano – 1-volume library on the outdoors; 1600+ illustrations; hunting and shooting, game animals, fishing and birds, camping, boating, archery and bow-hunting, and hunting dogs; first aid and outdoor information resources
Complete Outdoorsman's Handbook, Jerome J. Knap, pub. Pagurian Press – outdoor living and wilderness survival
Complete Wilderness Training Book, Hugh McManners, pub. Dorling-Kindersley – learn the field skills needed by training for the great outdoors
Cooking with the Sun, Beth and Dan Halacy – build, use and how to cook in solar cookers; harness sun's energy for cooking, 100+ recipes; illustrations & photos; for survival and camping
Delorme's Atlas and Gazetteer of the Western US – full-color maps of most Western States, except Nevada and New Mexico, combine topographic map information from the USGS surveys and more current information about roads and other man-made structures
Desert Hiking, Dave Ganci
Ditch Medicine, Hugh L. Coffee – advanced field procedure for emergencies, war or civil disasters; help for traumatic injuries; advanced medical procedures in a field setting; real-world lessons and step-by-step instructions, for serious first-aid field responders
Dr. Cohen's Healthy Sailor Book, Michael Martin Cohen, MD – hypothermia, dehydration, motion sickness, skin problems, psychological aberrations induced, isolation, and fatigue; mix rehydration solutions for diarrhea victims using commonplace ingredients
Emergency Book—You Can Save a Life!, The Bradley Smith and Gus Stevens, pub. Simon and Schuster – put this book—or one like it—in your first aid storage, but only after reading several times
Emergency Care and Transportation of the Sick and Injured, pub. American Academy of Orthopedic Surgeons – classic textbook for Emergency Medical Technicians (sometimes called the "Orange Book")
Emergency First Aid for Your Child, Editors of Consumer Guide, pub. Consumer Guide
Emergency Medical Procedures for the Outdoors, Brenner and Church and Field – important items for backpack or survival kit; fast format for easy-to-follow first aid instructions; list of supplies needed, tips and illustrations
Emergency Medical Procedures—for the Home, Auto, and Workplace, Patricia B. Hill, Editor, pub. Prentice Hall Press – manage potentially dangerous or troublesome situations; unique flowchart format helps you act quickly, calmly and correctly
Emergency Preparedness and First Aid Guide, Menasha Ridge
Emergency Preparedness—The Right Way, author/publisher Howard Godfrey, P.O. Box 3214, Bowman CA95604 – experienced fire service, law enforcement, and military; teacher of preparedness and organizer of Preparedness Shows presents current information in a concise manner with supporting references and resources
Emergency War Surgery (2nd US Revision), Thomas E. Bowen, Editor, US Department of Defense – available from Government Printing Office (GPO) Bookstores; 2nd edition adds wound dynamics, organization and administration of medical resources, triage, evacuation, updated techniques
Essential Wilderness Navigator, David Seidman and Christine Erikson, pub. McGraw-Hill – find your way in the great outdoors
Everybody's Outdoor Survival Guide, Don Paul, pub. Pathfinder Publications – Green Beret's guide to outdoor survival; wilderness skills
Family First Aid Guide, The, Robert Fuentes, MD
Family First Aid Handbook—How to Handle Medical Emergencies, Thom R. Mitchell, pub. Nelson Thomas
Field Guide to Fishes, pub. National Audubon Society – durable plastic-bound guide; hundreds of high-quality color photographs and drawings

Outdoor Skills & First Aid Books (continued)

Field Guide to Insects and Spiders, pub. National Audubon Society – durable plastic-bound guide; hundreds of high-quality color photographs and drawings
Field Guide to North American Mammals, pub. National Audubon Society – hundreds of high-quality color photographs and drawings to allow identification
Field Guide to Seashore Creatures, pub. National Audubon Society – durable plastic-bound guide; high-quality color photographs and drawings
Field Guide to The Night Sky, pub. National Audubon Society – durable plastic-bound guide; high-quality color photographs and drawings
Field Guide to Trees (Western or Eastern), pub. National Audubon Society – durable plastic-bound guide; high-quality color photographs and drawings
Field Guide to Weather, pub. National Audubon Society – durable plastic-bound guide; high-quality color photographs and drawings
Field Hygiene and Sanitation—Army Field Manual 21-10 / Air Force Manual 161-10 – basic field sanitation techniques
First Aid and CPR Manual, David M. White
First Aid Fast, American Red Cross
First Aid Handbook, National Safety Council – first aid and emergency care
First Aid Manual for Chemical Accidents, Marc J. Lefevre and Shirley Conibe
Gourmet Camping, Osborne – author with more than 20 years' experience camping and cooking; preparing in advance so that most meals take ½ hour in the field
Green Beret's Compass Course, Don Paul – stay found anywhere
Handbook for Wilderness Survival, A, Bob Harris
How to Stay Alive in the Woods, Bradford Angier, pub. MacMillan Publishing Co. – discover new ways for surviving in the wilderness; divided into four sections: living off the land, keeping warm, finding your way out, avoiding trouble; sensible guide to food, shelter, and self-preservation that makes starvation in the wilderness next to impossible
Hypothermia, Frostbite, and Other Cold Injuries, James A. Wilkerson – prevention, recognition and pre-hospital treatment
Hypothermia—Killer of the Unprepared, Theodore G. Lathrop, MD – author is experienced medical doctor and member of a climbing group; case studies; warning signs; prevention advice
Johnson & Johnson First Aid Book, The, Stephen N. Rosenberg, MD, pub. Warner Books, Inc. – authoritative guide to emergency care; systematic directions for any situation requiring first aid; step-by-step words and illustrations
Kids Outdoors—Skills and Knowledge for Outdoor Adventures; Frank Logue, Mark Carroll, and Victoria Logue, pub. McGraw-Hill
Land Navigation Handbook—Sierra Club Guide to Map and Compass, W. S. Kals, pub. Sierra Club Books – map and compass skills combined with special concerns for the wilderness wanderer; for beginning pathfinder or veteran woodsman; 5-color fold-out topographic map and 70 drawings and photos
Management of Wilderness and Environmental Emergencies, Auerbach and Geeher – medical textbook; simple and advanced treatments
Manual Del Aventurero—Adventurer's Handbook, Rudiger Nehberg
Map Reading and Land Navigation (Field Manual) – US Army field manual; illustrated
Map Reading, Army Field Manual 21-26 – using military-style lensatic compasses correctly; military grid systems, such as UTM (Universal Transverse Mercator)
Medical Specialist, US Army Field Manual – training manual for the combat medic; 20+ detailed chapters on life-saving medical skills; body systems, triage assessment, field treatment, sanitation, drugs, injuries, etc.
Medicine for Mountaineering and Other Wilderness Activities, James Wilkerson
Medicine for Mountaineering, pub. The Mountaineers – intermediate-duration care book, with heavy emphasis on mountains and problems encountered in wilderness
Medicine for the Backcountry, Tilton and Hubbell – emergency care of injured backcountry travelers; help victims of trauma, environmental, and medical emergencies
Medicine for the Outdoors, Paul S. Auerbach, MD, pub. Little Brown and Co. – guide to emergency medical procedures and first aid; information about emergency procedures that anyone can handle effectively
Military Mountaineering, Army Training Circular 90-6
Modern Outdoor Survival, Dwight Schuh, pub. Menasha Ridge Press – enjoy safe outings; use modern gear and knowledge to prevent or cope with emergencies
Morrow Guide to Knots, The, Bigon and Regazzoni – lots of different knots, how and when to tie them
Mosby's Outdoor Emergency Medical Guide, David H. Manhoff – what to do in outdoor emergency when help may take some time to arrive

Outdoor Skills & First Aid Books (continued)

Mountain Medicine, Fred Darvill, Jr., MD
– medical emergencies while backpacking or survival situations; reference for group leaders; easy-to-understand language for laymen

Mountaineering First Aid—A Guide to Accident Response and First Aid Care (4ᵗʰ Ed.), Jan D. Carline, Martha J. Lentz and Steven C. MacDonald, pub. Mountaineers Books
– preparation before mountaineering; treating specific injuries; edition includes treating animal bites and stings; first aid for children

Mountaineering Medicine—A Wilderness Medical Guide, Darvill
– the doctor's book about what medical emergency care to use while camping, hunting or fishing

Mountainman Crafts and Skills, D. Montgomery
– illustrated guide to practical clothing, shelter, equipment, and wilderness living

National Outdoor Leadership Schools Wilderness Guide, John Sullivan and Peter Simer

Natural Health First-Aid Guide, Mark Mayell
– handbook of natural remedies for treating minor emergencies

New Wilderness Handbook, The, Paul Petzoldt, pub. W. W. Norton and Co.

NOLS Wilderness First Aid, National Outdoor Leadership School
– first-aid guide by professional outdoors personnel

North American Indian Survival Skills, Karen Liptak

North American Vertical Rope Techniques, pub. National Speleological Society

Official Boy Scout Fieldbook, The
– one of the essential books for the preparedness library—by the group that first promoted being prepared

Official Pocket Medical Survival Manual, Robert W. Pelton, self-pub., Freedom and Liberty Foundation
– compact, 280 pages profusely illustrated; practical, easy-to-use, standard and emergency medical technology, a quick reference manual

Official Pocket Medicinal Plant Survival Manual, Robert W. Pelton, self-pub., Freedom and Liberty Foundation
– compact, practical, easy-to-use, medicinal plants information, profusely illustrated, quick reference manual for what-ails-you & how to treat it

Onboard Medical Handbook, The– First Aid and Emergency Medicine Afloat, Paul G. Gill

Outback Skills & Survival Techniques, MicroTek Publishers
– dual-indexed first aid & outback skills booklet; lifesaving techniques & details; simple illustrations; what to do & how to survive emergencies

Outdoor Cookbook, Dan and Inez Morris, pub. Hawthorn Books, Inc.
– all anyone needs to know about cooking out-of-doors

Outdoor Emergency Care, Bowman, pub. National Ski Patrol
– emergency medical text; care in wilderness situations

Outdoor Survival Handbook, Paul Bryant and Raymond Mears, pub. St. Martin's Press
– resources and materials available in wild and how to use them for food, shelter, warmth, and navigation; organized by season; explanation of essential everyday skills needed to get the most out of outdoor adventures, including fires, water, medicinal herbs, and more

Outdoor Survival Skills, Larry Dean Olsen, pub. Pocket Books
– basic information on existing in the wild; camping skills, hunting, fishing, emergencies, and tracking; classic manual on outdoors survival

Outdoor Survival Training—Instructor Manual; Dolly Garza, pub. University of Alaska Sea Grant

Outdoors Survival Manual—Survival Skills for Backpackers, Hikers, Campers, pub. Mother Earth News

Outward Bound Map and Compass Handbook, Glenn Randall
– concise book on land navigation

Outward Bound Wilderness First-Aid Handbook, Jeff Isaac

Pocket Guide to Outdoor Survival, Stan Bradshaw, pub. Greycliff Publishing Co.
– everything you need to know in a compact, lightweight, and easily-referenced book

Pocket Medic—The Indispensable First Aid Guide
– used to train soldiers in first aid on the battlefield or other emergency situations, handy pocket reference now available to the public; life-saving measures: restoring pulse or breathing, stopping bleeding, preventing shock, first aid for head injuries, fractures, wounds and burns; treatment for common emergencies such as choking, drowning, electrical shock, stings and bites, overexposure to heat, cold and more

Practical Camp Cook Book, Fred Bouwman
– for serious outdoorsmen, recipes & information based on field cooking conditions; preparing wild game & fish, gathering food, camp fires

Practical Outdoor Survival—A Modern Approach, Len McDougall, pub. Lyons and Burford

Practical Wilderness Survival Handbook, A, Vol. 1, Alan Fry
– all-season guide to short trip preparation and survival techniques for hiking, skiing, backpacking, and canoeing

Primitive Outdoor Skills, Richard Jamison
– primitive skills and techniques in easy-to-follow format; stone tools, snow caves, steam-pit cooking, etc.

Primitive Wilderness Living and Survival Skills, John and Geri McPherson, pub. John McPherson
– friction fire, shelters, trapping, hide tanning, primitive tools, containers, food preparation, sinew-backed bow and arrow, and more

Outdoor Skills & First Aid Books (continued)

Primitive, The, Martin	
– outdoor survival book; scrounging materials to build ingenious contraptions/devices for trapping and catching food, providing water, building hospitable shelter, special weapons, and ideas for keeping children busy	

Primitive, The, Martin
– outdoor survival book; scrounging materials to build ingenious contraptions/devices for trapping and catching food, providing water, building hospitable shelter, special weapons, and ideas for keeping children busy

Reading the Outdoors at Night, Tom Brown
– identify sights, sounds, and smells of the wilderness after dark in detail with a little practice

Reading the Water, Hughes
– fly fishers' handbook for finding trout in all types of water; stream structure, trout food and trout patterns; read and fish riffles, pocket water, mountain creeks, meadow streams, pools, runs, flats, etc.

Ropes, Knots and Slings for Climbers, Walt Wheelock, pub. Desert Publications
– hide things using the US Army Special Forces Caching Techniques

Roughing It Easy, Part 1 and Part 2, Dian Thomas
– camping out and cooking with improvised materials; woodcraft information and recipes

S. A. S. Survival Manual, John Wiseman
– from first aid to improvised shelters to navigation by stars; complete survival course—on land, sea, in any weather, anywhere in the world; full-color illustrations of edible, medicinal and poisonous plants, poisonous snakes and reptiles, dangerous insects and other creatures

Ships Medicine Chest and First Aid at Sea, pub. USPHS
– published primarily for the merchant marine; prescription drugs (legal and technical), lists of drugs and material for different ships; death, burial at sea; disease section (including VD), section on getting medical advise over HF radio from the USPHS

Special Forces Medical Handbook, US Army training handbook
– medical techniques as they apply to unconventional operations; chapters on sterilizing under field conditions, field dentistry, and obstetrics

Sports Afield Outdoor Skills, Vol. 1, Frank S. Golad, Ed., pub. Hearst Books

Staying Found—The Complete Map and Compass Handbook, June Fleming, pub. Mountaineers Books

Survival in the 90s—A Guide for Outdoor Enthusiasts, Bob and Susan Newman, pub. Menasha Ridge Press
– avoid likely and unlikely pitfalls on vacation or at home; stay alive in dangerous situations; from a Marine wilderness survival instructor and outdoor enthusiast, but provides valuable advice for those who wander in circles close to home

Survival Poaching, Ragnar Benson
– live off the land under emergency conditions utilizing the poacher's art

Survival With Style, Bradford Angier
– no-nonsense outdoor survival and woodcraft from experienced woodsman and survivalist; keeping body and soul together in the wilderness

Survival-Evasion-Escape, pub. Paladin Press
– survive at sea or tropics, improvise shelters and obtain food and water; color plates of snakes & plants for identification of poisonous species

Survival—How to Prevail in Hostile Environments; Xavier Maniguet, pub. Facts on File

Survivalist's Medicine Chest, Ragnar Benson, pub. Paladin Press
– using specialized medicines in world without doctors; preparing for diarrhea, tetanus, typhoid, pneumonia, VD, plague and gun-shot wounds without modern drugs; handbook for doctoring humans with readily obtainable, cheaply-priced veterinary medicines (***Caution:*** there is element of risk for self-treatment or non-professional treatment—this book is not for everyone!)

Tom Brown's Field Guide to Nature Observation and Tracking, Tom Brown

Tom Brown's Field Guide to the Forgotten Wilderness, Tom Brown and Jackie McGuire
– open your eyes to nature's abundance; attract wild animals; reading subtle trails of animals; observe animals without being noticed

Tracking, Jack Kearney
– follow people's and animal's tracks; avoid being tracked

Tricks of the Trail—A 90s Wilderness Guide, Roy J. Santoro, pub. Naturegraph Publishers

US Army Survival Manual FM 21-76 (Reprint), pub. Headquarters, Dept. of the Army
– for backpacker & survivalist; 100+ color photos of edible & poisonous plants; field-expedient weapons, cold-weather survival, & sea survival

Vehicle Recovery Operations, Army Field Manual 21-22
– get unstuck, information on moving large heavy objects with things at hand

Vivir Y Sobrevivir En LA Naturaleza—To Live and Survive in the Natural World, Coineau and Knoepfler

Way of the Scout, Tom Brown, pub. Berkley Publishing Group
– lessons of the scout; physical skills of ancient art of survival can lead to spiritual rewards of personal awareness and inner peace

Wilderness Basics—The Complete Handbook for Hikers and Backpackers, Jerry Schad and David S. Moser, pub. Mountaineers Books
– originally prepared for their own use by the San Diego Chapter of the Sierra Club

Wilderness Cuisine, Carole Latimer
– delicious foods while camping; pack food and keep it fresh; plan mouth-watering menus for weekend or week-long trips

Wilderness First Aid, Tod Schimelpfenig

Wilderness First-Aid Guide, Wayne Merry

Outdoor Skills & First Aid Books (continued)

Wilderness Medical Kit, Selection and Use of Field Medical Supplies, Dr. Nicholas Williams – booklet describing medical tools, supplies and medications useful for medical support in austere wilderness or disaster setting
Wilderness Medical Society Practice Guidelines for Wilderness Emergency Care; by William W. Forgey, MD, pub. ICS Books
Wilderness Ranger Cookbook, Brunell and Swain – by Forest Service rangers—their recipes, made with care, seasoned with experience, and perfected over time; practical camp stove cookery
Wilderness Route Finder, Calvin Rutstrum – non-military book discusses utilization of military-style lensatic compass, information on general route-finding
Wilderness Search and Rescue—A Complete Handbook, Tim J. Setnicka
Wilderness Survival Handbook, Alan Fry, pub. St. Martin's Press – clothing, sheltering, eating, staying warm, and finding one's way; what you need to know before starting: choosing appropriate clothing and footwear, signaling for help, starting and managing fire, building emergency shelter, first aid, and obtaining water and food; 100 illustrations
Wilderness Survival, Bernard Shanks, pub. Universe Publications
Wilderness Wayfinding—How to Survive in the Wilderness As You Travel, Bob Newman, pub. Paladin Press
Wilderness, Bob Newman – survive in the wilderness
Wildwood Wisdom, Ellsworth Jaeger
Woodsmoke, Richard L. and Linda Jamison, pub. Menasha Ridge Press
You Can Stay Alive, Larry Wells and Roger Giles – wilderness living and emergency survival techniques

When you find errors, please address the correct data to:
Doc@DoctorPrepper.com

B. Disasters (Natural, People-Caused, & Personal) and Survival

This category includes books about earthquakes, floods, hurricanes, tornadoes; biological, chemical, or nuclear disaster; civil disorder, general disasters skills; war, job loss, fire, and financial loss.

Chart 27–3
Disasters & Survival Books

America's Judgments Documentation Packet, pub. Militia of Montana, PO Box 1486, Noxon MT 59853 ☎(406) 847-2735 🖳**mom@logoplex.com**   – paperwork and documentation utilized by John Trochmann used in the making of the video **America's Judgments—*What Lies Ahead;*** 191 pages of government documents and photographs detailing the takeover of America by one-world elitists
Apocalypse Tomorrow, Duncan Long   – scenarios present in-depth forecasting the future survival scene
Bad Time, Good News, Bill Yatchman   – preparedness and survival; precious metals, food storage, MREs, water storage, medical supplies, firearms, survival checklist, and more
Basic Essentials of Desert Survival, Dave Ganci
Blueprint for Survival!, Stephen Quayle, pub. Safe-Trek Publishing   – food, water, self-dense, retreats, clothing, transportation, and survival products; physical and mental preparation with a framework & timeline
Book of Outdoor Lore, Clyde Ormond   – survival skills, equipment needed; edible plants and animals; gather/hunt/prepare them; making and using primitive weapons
Book of Survival, Anthony Greenbank, pub. Harper and Row   – how to think, act and stay alive in an emergency situation
Breathe No Evil, Stephen Quayle and Duncan Long, pub. Safe-Trek Publishing   – tactical guide to biological and chemical terrorism; biological and chemical warfare and how to protect yourself
California Wildfire Landscaping (or **Wildfire Survival Guide**), Maureen Gilmer, pub. Taylor Publishing Co.   – protecting your home from fire dangers when there's no fire department
Can You Survive, Robert B. DePugh, pub. Desert Publications
Checklist for Survival, Tony and Jo-Anne Lesce   – how, when, and where to prepare for and utilize the black market; hide, defend, flee, group, loot, ambush, grow food, get safe water, get fuel, obtain transportation, and forage for survival
Chernobyl Syndrome—and How to Survive It, The, Dean Ing, pub. Baen Books
Common-Sense Survival for Outdoor Enthusiasts, Bob Newman   – mini-guide to surviving for up to 5 days; *friendly* text for spouse or child to read without scaring them; for short-term survival in the woods
Complete Disaster Survival Manual, Ted Wright, pub. Hampton Roads Publishing Co., Inc.   – prepare for earthquakes, floods, tornadoes, and other disasters; simple planning can mean the difference between life and death
Crash of '97-'98: A Special Report, The, Geri Guidetti, pub. The, PO Box 364, Monkton MD 21111 ✉**arkinst@concentric.net**   – *why* it will happen and how to get out of debt and get prepared *now!*
Crisis Preparedness Handbook, Jack A Spigarelli, pub. Resource Publications   – food, communications, tools, transportation, fuel, water, radiological defense, etc.; food storage calculations by calories; recommended amounts of each group of foods; storing, gardening and foraging included
Desert Survival, Nelson Dick
Design Of Structures To Resist Nuclear Weapons Effects, pub. American Society of Civil Engineers   – revised *ASCE Manuals and Reports on Engineering Practice No. 42*
Disaster Survival Guide, Cass Igram   – survivors nutritional pharmacy
Earthquake and Disaster Preparedness, Eleanor Malin, pub. American Products Company   ✉**apc@american-products.com**   – surviving the next great disaster by being prepared—before, during, and after—whether at home or away
Earthquake Survival Guide, Fryar Calhoun   – emergency planning for your family, home, workplace, or school
Earthquake Survival Manual, Lael Morgan   – what to do before, during, and after an earthquake
Earthquake Terror, Peg Kehret
Emergency Medical Care For Disasters   – quick reference guide for health workers and trained laymen when there's no doctor; determine treatment of diseases, disorders and injuries
Emergency Survival Guide, Michael Borofka   – survive anything

Disasters & Survival Books (continued)

Emergency Survival Packs, Blair D. Jaynes
– family guide to preparing a low-cost, 4-day evacuation kit; includes different lists for adults and children (three children's age groups) on what should be included in kits
Emergency War Surgery (1992 Edition), US Army
– revised and updated; 33 chapters of life-saving information; every aspect of wound care in the field
Emergency…Survival Guide, Rev. William E. Dewey, self-pub.
– scientific and psychic evidence for violent changes now taking place, prepare spiritually and physically; checklists for emergency planning, evacuation, and what's needed while awaiting help; extensive bibliography and list of supply sources; condensed; easy to read
Encyclopedia Of Survival, W. R. Onslow and Rainer Stahlberg
– secrets and little-known information; 4-part book: *Survival Aspects; Food in the Survival Environment; Fire, Fuel & Shelter;* and *Survival Arms & Armaments;* survive an economic collapse: barter to avoid currency problems; full-scale nuclear attack and what food to store
Family Emergency Plan, Vol. 1, Barry G. and Lynnette B. Crockett, self-pub.
– simple outlines and worksheets for a family emergency response plan
Family Emergency Plan, Vol. 2, Barry G. and Lynnette B. Crockett, self-pub.
– what to do before, during and after natural disasters, hazardous material accidents and civil disturbances
Family Emergency Plan, Vol. 3, Barry G. and Lynnette B. Crockett, self-pub.
– actions to take before, during and after hurricanes, tornadoes, lightning and severe thunderstorms, floods, winter storms, drought and extreme heat, nuclear and radiological emergencies, and national emergencies
Fifty Ways To Improve Your Shortwave Listening, Bill Lauterbach, pub. DWM Communications
– cure noise and interference problems; build inexpensive antennas with parts from hardware store, frequency lists, & program information
Fighting Chance, Robinson and North
– written prior to dismantling of the Soviet Union; avoid any type of nuclear disaster
Guide to Emergency Survival Communications—How to Build and Power Your System, T. P. Harrington, pub. Universal Electronics
– receive and send information in time of crisis; types of systems available in time of need, where they can be found—SWR, citizens band, federal services, weather services, overseas news services, amateur radio, and other sources of vital information and programming; where to find necessary equipment, choose proper equipment, and build your communication equipment; power systems and build your own
How to "Be Prepared", Roland Page, pub. Horizon Publishers, Inc.
– suggestions for emergency preparedness
How to Be Safe in an Unsafe World, Gilbert
– down-to-earth security book dealing with what you can do to protect yourself without a barricaded fortress
How to Live Through a Famine, Dean L. Rasmussen, pub. Horizon Publishers, Inc.
– survive in a famine, real or situational
How to Survive a Nuclear Accident, Duncan Long
– if you live near, or downwind of a nuclear power plant, what you can do now and what to do in the event of an actual nuclear accident
How to Survive the End of the World as We Know It: Tactics, Techniques, and Technologies for Uncertain Times, James Wesley, Rawles **SurvivalBlog.com**
– JWR's latest nonfiction book on surviving TEOTWAWKI; good advice from the king of survivalism; highly-ranked & regarded author
Hurricane Handbook, The—A Practical Guide for the Residents of the Hurricane Belt, Sharon Maddux Carpenter and Toni Garcia Carpenter, Tailored Tours Publications
– 1,000+ suggestions to help Hurricane Belt residents know how to prepare for hurricanes, weather the storm, rebuild afterwards, and get their lives back together; lists for completion to assure your household is in order before the storm
Hurricanes—How to Prepare and Recover, pub. The Miami Herald
Life After Doomsday, Bruce D. Clayton, PhD
– survive a nuclear nightmare; survival strategies & problems for survivors; procedure for developing individual survival plans; information about shelters and their defense, food storage, home medical techniques, and psychology of survival; prime nuclear target areas in the US; short- and long-term effects of nuclear weapons use, ensuing medical consequences, and how to measure fallout radiation
Live Off the Land in the City and Country, Ragnar Benson
– practical survival using your common sense; finding fresh game (even in the city) using three keys: logic, physical laws and improvising
Manual De Supervivencia—US Armed Forces Survival Manual, John Boswell
Modern Weapons Caching, Ragnar Benson
– store most anything for the long term
Never Say Die!—The Canadian Air Force Survival Manual
– survival from desert to frozen arctic tundra; combat *fear, pain* and *panic*; find water, edible plants; improvise shelters, tools and equipment
Next New Madrid Earthquake, The—A Survival Guide for the Midwest, William Atkinson, pub. Shawnee Books
No Need to Die—Real Techniques of Survival, Eddie McGee

Disasters & Survival Books (continued)

No Such Thing As Doomsday—Underground Shelters, How to Prepare for Earth Changes, Wars, and Other Threats, Philip L. Hoag, pub. Yellowstone River Publishing
– general preparedness, preparing for earth changes; war and other threats; building underground shelters; surviving in a shelter environment

Nuclear Emergency, Ken Larson, pub. Rhema Publishing
– protect your family from radiation; understand nuclear plant meltdown, nuclear terrorism, and nuclear weapons; critical to family safety

Nuclear War and You—Before, During, After—You Are the Target, Jerrold Richards

Nuclear War Survival Skills, Cresson H. Kearney, pub. Oregon Institute of Science & Medicine
– facts and fallacies about nuclear weapons are discussed by America's foremost expert; what to expect, how to survive, water storage, shelter plans, etc.; life-saving instructions; originally published by DOE; contains plans for the original home-made radiation meter

Official Pocket Edible Plant Survival Manual, Robert W. Pelton, self-pub. Freedom and Liberty Foundation
– compact, illustrated, practical, easy-to-use; quick reference manual; for the survivalist or urbanite

Official Pocket Survival Manual, Robert W. Pelton, self-pub. Freedom and Liberty Foundation
– practical, easy-to-use, current technology, illustrated, quick reference manual; knowledge & equipment needed to survive in an emergency

Oregon Earthquake Handbook, The—An Easy-To-Understand Information and Survival Guide, Vern Cope

Patriots: A Novel of Survival in the Coming Collapse, James Wesley, Rawles **SurvivalBlog.com**
– part novel/part survivalist handbook; small group deals with America's worst nightmare—the total collapse of society.

Plan Not Panic—The 72-Hour Survival/Emergency Evacuation Manual, Barbara Salsbury, pub. Salsbury Enterprises
– differs from typical emergency evacuation lists & how-to books; how "lag-time" is villain in disasters; 2 types of emergency preparedness

Prepare Today Survive Tomorrow, Harold
– individual and group preparation, rural and urban defense; practical approach to match your needs and abilities

Preparing for Emergencies, Dr. James McKeever and Mrs. Jeani McKeever, pub. Omega Publications
– 11-step action plan in priority sequence helps avoid costly errors

Project Readiness, A Guide to Family Emergency Preparedness, Louise E. Nelson, pub. Horizon Publishers, Inc.
– planning and executing preparedness; dealing with short-term, long-term, natural and man-caused disasters

Protect Your Home, Geiger
– home security systems; dogs, locks, decals, timers, safes and home alarm systems

Radiological Defense Manual, CPG 2-6.2, Defense Civil Preparedness Agency
– fallout patterns and protection

Richard DeCastro's Survival Book List
– capsule reviews of frugal living titles

S. A. S Survival Guide, Collins Gem
– survive and handle every kind of situation—anywhere in the world; tested in training and operations; fully-illustrated

S. A. S. Survival Handbook, John Wiseman
– for civilians, survive in various situations and climate zones

S. A. S. Urban Survival Handbook, John Wiseman
– protect yourself and your family from dangers of urban jungle

Search and Rescue—Survival Training, Air Force Regulation 64-4
– textbook for survival

Sense of Survival, J. Allan South
– personal survival; emergency kits, what foods to store, attack survival, basic first-aid, excellent how-to manual

Shelter, pub. 10-Speed Press
– historical, cultural and practical perspective of shelter designs from around the world; aspects of water, food and waste (human, animal, food) management; what to do with food and animal waste

Short-Term Survival Techniques, John Tomikel, pub. Allegheny Press

Starting Over—A Guide to Fighting Back from Natural Disasters, Robert L. Williams
– after a tornado destroyed their home authors built 4,000 sq. ft. home with a chainsaw and $15,000; story of self-reliance and determination

Survival Book, The, Nesbit
– general survival techniques

Survival Books, Bruce D. Clayton, PhD, pub. Media West
– review of 300+ books on survival topics; helps make wise choices in building a survival library

Survival Family, Mary and Tom Bergman, self-pub.
– how one family prepared for disasters and lived one year as if there were no other choices

Survival Guide for the New Millennium, Byron Kirkwood
– survive coming earth changes by being prepared; how-to book for the uninitiated

Survival Handbook, Peter Darman, pub. Stackpole Books

Disasters & Survival Books (continued)

Survival in Today's Turbulent Times, Duncan Long – take control of your life and improve your chance of survival in today's world; steps to take now to survive in future
Survival Is A Dying Art, Barry Davies – knowledge and wisdom common to our forefathers explained and illustrated
Survival Retreat, Ragnar Benson – plan for the defense of survival retreat, win battles by avoiding them
Survival Skills of the North American Indians, Peter Goodman
Survival Skills, Libby Roberts
Survival, US Army Field Manual 21-76 – revised, global information about emergencies and survival under toughest conditions
Survival, Your First 72 Hours … *and Beyond*, E. J. Wilfley, pub. Survival Publishing Co., – individual & 72-hour survival packs; tips on basic bulk food storage, survival foods & goods, what to do to prepare for an emergency
Survival—A Manual that Could Save Your Life, Chris & Gretchin Janowsky, pub. Paladin Press (available from the authors) – long-term survival in typical North America; by the operators of **World Survival Institute** (AK)
Survival—A Manual that Could Save Your Life, Chris and Gretchin Janowsky, pub. Paladin Press – long-term survival in typical North American environment; life-saving first-aid and wilderness medical care, water procurement, improvised survival tools and weapons; using the *L.I.F.E.* system—a secret formula in emergency
Survive Disaster with Natural Medicines, Cass Igram, DO, pub. Cedar Graphics – home pharmacy manual for disaster survival; prescribes natural, non-toxic remedies for treatment of disaster-related injuries and illnesses
Survive the Coming Nuclear War, Ronald Cruit
Surviving Doomsday, C. Bruce Sibley – the effects of nuclear, biological and chemical warfare; for the true survivalist
Surviving Major Chemical Accidents, Duncan Long – techniques for responding to chemical and biological threats
Survivor, The, Volumes 1-4, Kurt Saxon – old time techniques
Tappan on Survival, Mel Tappan, pub. Janus Press – collection of articles from various magazines
Tom Brown's Field Guide to City and Suburban Survival, Tom Brown
Tom Brown's Field Guide to Wilderness Survival, Tom Brown, Jr., pub. Berkley Books
Urban Combat, US Army Manual, pub. Desert Publications – current doctrine for combat in urban areas, select and defend urban locations; standard military weapons
Urban Survival Handbook, John Wiseman – perils and dangers of urban living and how to eliminate them, cope with them and prepare for them; disasters, hazards, health, home security, poisons, safety, self-defense and terrorism; protect yourself and your family in urban environment
US Special Forces Medical Handbook, Glen K. Craig – new, updated quick-reference guide; diagnostic and treatment information; disease diagnosis and treatment, drugs and dosages, emergency paramedical skills and preventive medicine; burn and blast injuries; nuclear, biological and chemical warfare; emergency war surgery as well as primitive and veterinary medicine, obstetrics, pediatrics and orthopedics; additional life-saving information
Wallace Guidebook for Emergency Care and Survival, The, H. Wallace, pub. Survivor Industries, Inc. – survival techniques, simple scratch to head traumas to childbirth; indoor/outdoor lifesaving tips; comprehensive and easy to understand
Wright's Complete Disaster Survival Manual, Ted Wright – prepare for earthquakes, floods, tornadoes, and other disasters
You Can Survive It All, Marlene Geiser-Wiley – 550-page *Physician's Handbook of International and Nutritional Healing Modalities*; survival guide for difficult and extreme times; home and physician's reference

When you find errors, please address the correct data to:
Doc@DoctorPrepper.com

PREPAREDNESS LIFESTYLE BOOKS

These books provide information about activities that sustain life on a daily basis. Often, these activities require skills normally not utilized in today's lifestyle. These skills, though seldom used today, can make life more enjoyable.

C. Homesteading, Building, Maintenance, and Repair

This category includes books about do-it-yourself skills, animal husbandry, auto repair, bees and honey production, blacksmithing, burying the dead, butchering, electrical wiring and systems, home and outbuilding construction, plumbing systems, small-scale farming, soap making, and woodworking.

Chart 27–4
Homesteading, Building, Maintenance, & Repair Books

$50 and Up Underground House Book, Mike Oehler, pub. Mole Publishing – design and build underground; highly personal book; truly low-cost housing via earth-sheltering techniques
ABC and XYZ of Bee Culture, A. I. Root, pub. The A. I. Root Co. – an encyclopedic approach to beekeeping
Adobe and Rammed Earth Buildings, Paul Graham McHenry, Jr., pub. University of Arizona Press
Adobe Build it Yourself, Paul Graham McHenry, Jr., University of Arizona Press
Alex Wade's Guide to Affordable Houses, Alex Wade, pub. Rodale Press
Almanac of Rural Living, Harvey C. Neese, pub. NRN Resources – reprints of selected government agricultural-related pamphlets
Alternative House Building, Mike McClintock, pub. Popular Science Books
Art of Blacksmithing, The, Alex W. Bealer – blacksmithing using modern metals
At Home in the Woods, Bradford Angier – real-life story about how two people moved to the woods without a lot of money in the bank
Auto Repair for Dummies, Deanna Sclar
Back to Basics, Reader's Digest staff, pub. Readers Digest – broad coverage of urban and ex-urban household: home and property improvements, gardening to canning, minor repairs to building shelters; many illustrations and photographs
Backyard Homestead Mini Farm and Garden Log Book, The, John Jeavons
Backyard Livestock, Steven Thomas, pub. Countryman Press – raising good, natural food for your family; broad coverage of various kinds of livestock for the beginner; basics for non-farmers
Basic Butchering of Livestock & Game, John J. Mettler, Jr.
Basic Construction Techniques for Small Buildings Simply Explained, Navy – small structures and homes, everything from land preparation to final painting
Basic Home Wiring, Sunset Magazine – basic home electrical repairs
Basic Plumbing Techniques, pub. Ortho Books – basic home plumbing repairs
Basic Self-Reliance, pub. The Church of Jesus Christ of Latter-day Saints – instructor's manual for teaching people in underdeveloped countries how to care for themselves; make a hand-powered washing machine, a water clarifier (not purifier), evaporative refrigerator, and more; recognize and treat worms in humans; compost piles, and other low- and no-technology solutions to basic health in a survival situation
Becoming Self-Reliant, Ken Larson, pub. Rhema Publishing – become less dependent on society and government; return to respectful knowledge of the land, learn new skills, and store consumable goods
BeeHive Product Bible, Royden Brown, pub. Avery Publishing Group, Inc. – guide to bee pollen, propolis and honey products
Beekeeping, A Practical Guide, Richard E. Bonney – for beginner or experienced beekeeper; acquire bees, install a colony, manage a hive, take a crop of honey, prevent and treat varroa and tracheal mites, and learn about Africanized bees
Build a Yurt: The Low-Cost Mongolian Round House, Len Charney, pub. Collier Books div. Macmillan Pub.
Building Professional's Greywater Guide, pub. Oasis Biocompatible Products
Building Underground, Herb Wade, pub. Rodale Press
Butchering, Processing, and Preservation of Meat, Frank G. Ashbrook, pub. Van Nostrand Reinhold Co. – for home & farm, augment the food supply; butchering, processing & preserving beef, pork, lamb, wild game, poultry & fish

Homesteading, Building, Maintenance, & Repair Books (continued)

Canadian Beekeeping, self-pub.
– periodical on beekeeping and bee culture

Car Talk, Tom and Ray Magliozzi
– talk radio's most famous car experts; talk show questions and answers

Caring for Your Own Dead, Lisa Carlson

Cheese Making at Home—The Complete Illustrated Guide, Don Radke, pub. Doubleday & Co.
– recipes for cheesemaking at home; for the beginner or expert

Cheese-Making Made Easy, Ricki & Robert Carrol, pub. Garden Way Publishing
– making cheese; equipment to ingredients; soft to hard cheese; storing and aging of cheese

Chicken Health Handbook, Gail Demerow
– nutrition, infectious diseases, immunity, anatomy, parasites, and incubation

Christian Homesteading Movement, Jonathan Periam, pub. Crown Publishers
– classic 1884 edition reprint; 1,200+ engravings show what our forefathers knew and did

Clean Your House and Everything in It, Eugenia Chapman and Jill Major

Clutter's Last Stand, Don Aslett

Complete Book of Edible Landscaping, The, Rosalind Creasy

Complete Book of Meat, Phyllis Reynolds, pub. Barrows and Co.

Complete Herbal Handbook for Dogs and Cats, Juliette de Bairacli Levy
– alternative to processed pet foods, antibiotics, and hormone treatments

Complete Homesteading Book, David Robinson, pub. Garden Way
– for the budding homesteader; illustrations and photographs

Country Blacksmithing, Charles McRaven
– metalworking with limited equipment; section on tempering steels

Country Women, Sherry Thomas and Jeanne Tetrault, pub. Anchor Press/Doubleday
– handbook for the new farmer; information about animals and building

Designing and Maintaining Your Edible Landscape Naturally, Robert Kourik

Dr. Pitcairn's Complete Guide To Natural Health For Dogs and Cats, Pitcairn
– revised and updated edition

Dwelling on Earth, David Easton
– professional application of earthbuilding techniques; instruction manual for do-it-yourself home construction

Earth Ponds, Tim Matson
– country pond-maker's guide to building, maintenance, and restoration

Earth Sheltered Habitat, Gideon S. Golany, pub. Van Nostrand/Reinhold

Earth Sheltered Housing, Max Riterman, pub. Van Nostrand/Reinhold

Earthbuilders' Encyclopedia, pub. Southwest Solaradobe School
– includes UBC codes for building adobes in AZ, NM, TX, and CA

Earthships, Vols. I, II, III, Michael Reynolds, pub. Solar Survival Press

Electricians Toolbox Manual, Rex Miller, pub. ARCOS/Simon and Schuster
– electrical wiring, the National Electrical Code, and related issues

Encyclopedia of Country Living—An Old Fashioned Recipe Book, Carla Emery, pub. Sasquatch Books
– complete homesteading book; 850+ pages of information for the homestead-oriented; information and skills resource for anyone

Everyone's Knife Bible, Don Paul

Farmer's Dog, The, John Holmes, pub. Popular Dogs Publishing

Farming for Self-Sufficiency—Independence on a 5-Acre Farm, John and Sally Seymour, pub. Schocken Books
– English "smallholders" movement

Five Acres and Independence, M.G. Kains, pub. Dover Books
– small farm management; cropping methods, plants, and farming techniques for small farms (5 acres or less) based on 1940's technology

Flight From the City—An Experiment in Creative Living on the Land, Ralph Bordosi, pub. Harper and Row

Foxfire Series, (I-IX) Eliot Wigginton, Ed., pub. Anchor Press/Doubleday
– elderly hill people talk about old-time ways; maybe not most practical way, but interesting reading; not useful for die-hard urbanite

Future Is Abundant—A Guide to Sustainable Agriculture, pub. Tilth Organization
– annotated bibliography with ideas for everyone, aimed at Pacific Northwest residents

Golden Age of Homespun, Jared van Wagenen, Jr., pub. Cornell University Press
– US rural population reached maximum between 1860-1880; more country people and more individual farms then than ever before or
  since

Good House—Building a Life on the Land, Richard Manning

Grow It!, Richard W. Langer, pub. Saturday Review Press
– beginner's complete small farm guide for growing vegetables and grains and raising livestock in tune with nature

Guide to Bees and Honey, Ted Hooper, pub. Rodale Press
– recent bee culture book

Homesteading, Building, Maintenance, & Repair Books (continued)

Guide to Self-Sufficiency, John Seymour, pub. Harrowsmith Magazine – collection of articles
Handyman's Book, Tools, Materials and Processes Employed in Woodworking, Paul N. Hasluck, pub. 10-Speed Press – 760-pg. / 2,545 illustrations and working drawings; hand-craft almost anything from wood using hand tools; furniture, outbuildings, homes, tool boxes, etc.; selection, use, maintenance and care of hand tools
Hard Times in Paradise, David and Micki Crepin – biography of an American family homesteading in northern CA with their goats
Have-More Plan, Ed and Carolyn Robinson, pub. Garden Way – homesteading resource with illustrations and photographs
Heritage Farming—The People's Farm and Stock Cyclopedia, pub. Fairstone Press – reprint of state-of-the-art farming practices of late 1800's
Hive and the Honey Bee, edited by Dadant and Sons, pub. Dadant and Sons, Inc. – raise honey bees; history, anatomy, life within the hive, nutrition, genetics, behavior, nectar production, and more
Home and Farm Manual—A Pictorial Encyclopedia of Farm, Garden, Household, Architectural, Legal, Medical and Social Information, The, Jonathan Periam, pub. Crown Publishers – classic 1884 Edition; how much they knew over 100 years ago; 1,200+ exquisite engravings
Homemade Money, Barbara Brabec, pub. Betterway Publications – for home-based businesses: assessing situation, marketing strategy, time management, pricing for profit; direct and wholesale marketing; worksheets and resources
Homesteader's Handbook, James E. Churchill, pub. Stackpole Books
Homesteader's Handbook, Martin Lawrence, pub. Mayflower Books
Homesteader's Handbook, Rich Israel and Reny Slay
Homesteader's Manual, Editors of Farmstead Magazine, pub. T.A.B. Books – illustrated book about homesteading in general
Homesteading in the City, Nancy Seligman
Homesteading—A Practical Guide to Living off the Land, Patricia Crawford, pub. Macmillian Publishing Co. – presentation of homestead mentality
Horsekeeping On A Small Acreage, Cherry Hill – design safe and functional facilities for horses
How to Be Your Own Butcher, Leon Stanley and Evan Lobel, pub. Putnam Publishing Group – professional butchers explain all about butchering; author of these books: *Meat*, *All About Meat*, and *The Lobel Brothers' Meat Cookbook*
How To Buy Land Cheap (4th Ed.), Edward Preston – bargain-basement land buying
How to Fix Damn Near Everything, Franklin Peterson
How to Survive in the City and Country, Ragner Benson – trapping, diesel generators from China, gardening, building a home, personal and home defense, etc.
Integral Urban House—Self-Reliant Living in the City, The The Farallones Institute, pub. Sierra Club Books – small inter-city house with small lot turned into complete, self-contained eco-system; food production, water, waste, sewage, heat, using gray water, recycling, and small livestock management (rabbits, chickens, etc.)
Keeping Bees, John Vivian, pub. Williamson Publishing Co. – in-depth book with photographs; good bood for the beginning beekeeper
Kinbarra's Farm Journal, c/o Hoegger Supply Co. – loose-leaf format, plans, charts, formulas, and more
Land for the Family– A Guide to Country Living, A.F. Gustafson, E.V. Hardenburg, E.Y. Smith, and Jeanette McCay, pub. Comstock
Leather Makin', Larry J. Wells – patterns, photos, and detailed drawings for the leather worker
Living on a Few Acres, US Dept. of Agriculture – collection of articles written by extension agents in 1978
Making Cheeses at Home, Susan Ogilvy, pub. Crown Publishers
Managing Your Personal Food Supply—How to Eat Better for Less by Taking an Active Role in Producing, Processing, and Preparing Your Food, Ray Wolf, editor, pub. Rodale Press
Manual of Practical Homesteading, The, John Vivian, Rodale Press
Meat Handbook, The, Albert Levie, pub. The Avi Publishing Co.
Modern Homestead Manual, Skip Thomsen and Cat Freshwater, pub. Panandus – positive and negative sides of homesteading; what you need to start; illustrations; topics other books ignore
Mother's Home Building and Shelter Guide, Editors of Mother Earth News
Old Fashioned Recipe Book, Carla Emery – life under less "civilized" conditions; making butter to butchering animals
One Acre and Security, Bradford Angier, pub. Random House

Homesteading, Building, Maintenance, & Repair Books (continued)

Orchard Mason Bee—Life and History, Biology, Propagation and Use of a Truly Benevolent and Beneficial Insect, The, Brian L. Griffin – orchard mason bees are native to US and Canada; highly efficient pollinators; positive addition to your garden and orchard
Owner-Built Homestead The—A How-to-Do-It Book, Barbara and Ken Kern – site selection, water development, soil management, farming, farm machinery, bulk processing and marketing
Place of Your Own Making, A, Stephen Taylor, pub. Henry Holt
Plans Book; A Tiny Underground House, Malcolm Wells, pub. Underground Art Gallery – designs for underground homes that look like something out of Architectural Record, beautiful, not a survivalist bunker
Pork, pub. Time-Life Books – how-to book for the prodigal pig; prepare, utilize, store, and cook; recipes
Practical Beekeeping, Tompkins – A to Z for those planning to keep bees
Practical Blacksmithing, M. T. Richardson – classic from the turn of the century
Practical Electrical Wiring, Richter and Schwan – for homeowner, updated with advent of new NEC requirements, clear for untrained and pro
Practical Skills—A Revival of Forgotten Crafts, Techniques, and Traditions, Gene Logsdon, pub. Rodale Press – illustrated; old ways of small-scale grain growing, aquaculture, and berry raising
Radios that Work for Free, K.E. Edwards, pub., Hope and Allen Publishing Co.
Raising Rabbits, Ann Kanable – for serious rabbit raisers
Raising Sheep The Modern Way, Paula Simmons – revised for small-scale sheep raisers
Raising The Home Duck Flock, Dave Holderread
Reader's Digest DIY Manual – a general reference to the ordinary DIY, many details
Self-Sufficient Country Living, D.S. Savage, pub. St. Martin's Press
Short Kutz, Melanie Graham – make clothing repairs
Soap Book, The, Sandy Maine, pub. Interweave Press – recipe suggestions for various soaps
Soap Recipes, Elaine C. White, pub. Valley Hills Press – filled, aromatherapy, Castile, lye, and herbal soaps; soaps made from goat fat, beeswax, and milk; instructions and explanations
Step-By-Step Knifemaking, David Boye – each stage of design and fabrication of a knife
Successful Small-Scale Farming (An Organic Approach), Karl Schwenke
Super Formulas, Arts and Crafts, Elaine C. White, pub. Valley Hills Press – make 360+ useful products that contain honey and beeswax
Ten Acres Enough—The Small Farm Dream Is Possible, Ralph and Lynn Miller, pub. Mill Press, Inc.
This Old House Guide to Building and Remodeling Materials, Bob Villa and Norm Abram, pub. Warner Books – materials to build or rebuild structures; tools
Timber Reduced Energy Efficient Homes (aka TREE homes), Ed Paschich and Paula Hendricks, pub. Sunstone Press – total environmental impact of materials selected and used for building adobe or wood frame home
Tom Brown's Field Guide to Living with the Earth, Tom Brown, Jr., pub. Berkley Books – personal experiences of a expert on the secrets of adaptation; how-to section on earth shelters; using materials; making tools, weapons, furniture, utensils, and clothing; using plants found in the fields
Underground Houses, Robert L. Roy – of the Eastern or concrete construction school of underground house building; designs using cordwood masonry (using log ends in mortar as building material) as well as blocks
Veterinary Guide For Animal Owners, A – specific preventive measures and cures for pets and livestock
Village Technology Handbook, pub. VITA – elementary tips on appropriate technology for developing nations
Working at Woodworking, Jim Topin
World's Only Perfect Food, Royden Brown, pub. Hohm Press – all about the honey bee; perfect "miracle" foods from the beehive
Yankee Magazine Book of Forgotten Arts, Richard M. Bacon, pub. Simon and Schuster – cooking on wood stove, build a smokehouse, use root cellars, keep a family cow, work with draft horse, create dyes from common plants, make soap, wooden toys, paint, painting colonial patterned floors, and more

D. Water

This category includes books about water purification, storage, treatment dangers, and water systems.

Chart 27–5
Water Resources Books

Clean Water (Earth at Risk), Karen J. Barss
Climate Change and US Water Resources, Paul E. Waggoner
Community Water Safety, American Red Cross
Cottage Water Systems, Max Burns – out-of-the-city guide to pumps, plumbing, water purification, and privvies
Create An Oasis With Greywater, pub. Oasis Biocompatible Products – don't throw away your greywater, use it
Don't Drink the Water, Lono Kahuna Kupua A'o, pub. Kali Press – hundreds of pollutants are found in our drinking water; nearly ½ of all municipal water systems violate Federal health standards
Drinking Water Book—A Complete Guide to Safe Drinking Water, Colin Igram – determine what's in your tap water and safeguard your health; different kinds of filters and bottled waters; cheapest and best ways to have tap water tested; rates products on the market; make intelligent decisions about drinking water
Drinking Water Hazards, John Cary Stewart – determine if there are toxic chemicals in your water and what to do if there are
Drinking Water—Refreshing Answers to All Your Questions, Louise Lindsey, James M. Symons and Maria Leticia Ramirez
Finding Water, Rick Brassington – construction and maintenance of private water supplies
Good Water Guide—The World's Best Bottled Water, Maureen Green – describes and evaluates 250 different brands from 42 countries; each critically reviewed and its source and bottling procedure described; mineral contents are presented in easy-to-read tables along with full-color label illustrations and photos of springs and production facilities
Greenpeace Book of Water, Klaus Lanz
H₂0—The Guide to Quality Bottled Water, Arthur vonWiesenberger – best quality bottled water from around the world; which minerals and trace elements make a great water; read a water analysis, what to look for and what to avoid when buying bottled water
Handbook of Drinking Water Quality, John De Zuane
Home Water Supply, Stu Campbell – find, filter, store, and conserve water; money-saving answers about locating water, digging a pond, or hooking up the plumbing
Is Our Water Safe to Drink?, J. Gordon, MD – drinking water hazards and health risks
Last Oasis—Facing Water Scarcity, Sandra Postel
Nalco Water Handbook, Frank N. Kemmer
Plain Talk About Drinking Water, James Symons – questions and answers about the water you drink
Properties of Water, The, Ann Hood
Water Treatment Processes—Simple Options, C. Visvanathan and Saravanamuthu Vigneswaran
Water, A Resource in Crisis, Eileen Lucas
Water, Francois Michel
Water, Water Everywhere, Cynthia Overbeck Bix and Mark J. Rauzon – cycle of evaporation, condensation, and precipitation providing fresh water to the earth; how this supply brought to people's homes
Water—Almost Enough for Everyone, Stephanie Ocko
Water—Fact Finders, Chris Ellis

When you find errors, please address the correct data to:
Doc@DoctorPrepper.com

E. Gardening and Food Production

This category includes books about backyard gardening, composting, fruits, herbs, irrigation, mulching, mushrooms, organic gardening, pest control, vegetables, greenhouses, small-scale hydroponics, sprouts, and sprouting.

Chart 27–6
Gardening & Food Production Books

25 Vegetables Anyone Can Grow, Robbins
– complete information for growing a selected group of vegetables

A Grower's Guide To Marketing Fruits, Vegetables, & Herbs In Illinois, pub. Illinois Extension
– guide covers 20+ specialty crops in 100+ pages; designed to link producers with area wholesales and shippers; includes listing 100 major produce distributors in IL, WI, and MO; pricing, packaging, and quality standards

A Guide To Starting, Operating, & Selling In Farmers Markets, Charles Marr & Karen Gast, Cooperative Extension Service, KSU
– provides overview of the organization and operation of farmers' market; how to use the market effectively, pricing, and merchandising strategies, advertising, and display techniques

AHA Directory of Herbal Education, pub. American Herb Association
– 40 sources of where individuals may obtain herbal training, certification, and degrees

AHA Directory of Mail-Order Medicinal Herb Products, pub. American Herb Association
– mail-order resources for procuring herbs & herbal products

Along the Garden Path, Bill and Sylvia Varney, pub. Fredericksburg Herb Farm
– excellent information on growing herbs; many non-culinary recipes

Astrological Gardening, Louise Riotte
– ancient wisdom of successful planting and harvesting by the stars

Backyard Berry Book, Stella Otto
– "hands-on" guide to growing berries, brambles, and vine fruit in home garden

Backyard Bonanza, editors of Organic Gardening Magazine, pub. Rodale
– introduction to intensive gardening

Backyard Orchardist, The, Stella Otto, pub. OttoGraphics
– growing fruit trees in a home garden; list of resources

Basic Book of Organic Gardening, edited by Robert Rodale, pub. Ballantine Books, Inc.
– facts, notes, ideas, suggestions to move toward better way of living

Basic Hydroponics for the Do-It-Yourselfer (1ˢᵗ Ed.), M. Edward Muckle
– build a wide variety of gardens from basic materials; trouble shooting guide; all the popular systems; keys to successful operation; hydroponics gardens for every location indoor, greenhouse or outdoor

Beginning Hydroponics—Soil-less Gardening, Richard E. Nicholls, pub. Running Press
– beginner's guide to growing vegetables, house plants, flowers, and herbs without soil

Berries—Cultivation, Decoration, and Recipes, Mary Forsell and Tony Cenicola

Big Book Of Gardening Skills
– organized by topic, with charts, tables, and illustrations

Biodynamic Farm, A, Hugh Lovel
– oldest organic agriculture movement in the western world; move our evolution light years ahead with this nutrition

Botanical Series, Stephen Foster, pub. American Botanical Council
– information on botany, nomenclature, historical and modern usage, commercial aspects, and references

    #301 The Purple Cone Flowers   *#302 Siberian Ginseng*   *#303 Asian Ginseng*   *#304 Gingko*   *#305 Milk Thistle*
    #306 Peppermint   *#307 Chamomile*   *#308 American Ginseng*   *#309 Goldenseal*   *#310 Feverfew*
    #311 Garlic   *#312 Valerian*   *#313 Ephedra*   *#314 Passionflower*

British Herbs and Vegetables, George M. Taylor
– color and B&W photos and drawings of popular British herbs and veggies

Budget Gardener, Maureen Gilmer, pub. Penguin Books
– ideas to create a pleasant environment more economically

Bug Book, The, Philbrick
– controlling backyard garden pests from ants to cutworms without toxic materials

Bugs, Slugs & Other Thugs, Rhonda Hart

Building Healthy Gardens, Catherine Foster
– improving and maintaining plant virility

Carrots Love Tomatoes—Secrets of Companion Planting for Successful Gardening, Louise Riotte, pub. Garden Way Publishing
– plant companion gardens successfully; maximizing the home garden

Charmed Kitchen, The, Judi Strauss, pub. Goosefoot Acres Press
– try herbs without being too aggressive

Gardening & Food Production Books (continued)

Cold Climate Gardening, Hill – extend growing season for everything from shrubs to strawberries; snowbelt gardeners & those living in valleys, hillsides or dry climates
Commercial Hydroponics, John Mason – 86 alternatives for hydroponics culture; ideas for expanding your garden
Complete Gardener's Almanac, Marjorie Willison – month by month guide to successful gardening
Cooking with Herb Scents, pub. Western Reserve Herb Society
Cooking with Lavender, Joyce Ellenbecker, pub. Foundation House Publications – instructions for using lavender in recipes such as Lavender-Orange Ice Cream or Peach-Lavender Pie
Definitive Guide to Hydroponic Food Production (5th Ed.), Howard M. Resh – classic book for advanced hobby or novice commercial hydroponics; basic understanding of commercial hydroponics production
Dirt Doctor's Guide to Organic Gardening, J. Howard Garrett, pub. University of Texas Press – natural gardening, landscape, food crops, or house plants

Disease Compendium Series, pub. American Phytopathological Society
– series with information on several field crops, fruits, greenhouse crops, turf and ornamentals; descriptions of diseases; photographs of symptoms and causal agents; some abiotic or physiological symptoms and causes described; for professional or advanced amateur:
    Alfalfa Diseases   Peanut Diseases   Bean Diseases   Beet Diseases and Insects
    Potato Diseases   Pea Diseases   Tomato Diseases   Sweet Potato Diseases

Down To Earth Vegetable Gardening, Dick Raymond – revised and updated edition of gardening classic
Drip Irrigation for Every Landscape and All Climates, Robert Kourik – every component and step to putting in drip irrigation is clearly illustrated and explained
Encyclopedia of Herbs and Their Uses, Deni Bown, pub. Dorling Kindersley Publishing – basic material for study and appreciation of herbs
Encyclopedia of Organic Gardening, by the staff of **Organic Gardening and Farming Magazine** – whole field of horticulture from organic point of view— cultivate, fertilize and harvest
Essential Kitchen Gardener, The, Frieda Arkin, pub. Henry Holt and Co. – A-Z how-to in dictionary format: planting, growing, treating diseases, organic and conventional methods of soil control and cultivating
Field Guide to Western Mushrooms, Alexander Smith, pub. University of Michigan Press – popular, easy-to-use book for mushrooms found west of the Rockies; color photos
Four Season Harvest, Eliot Coleman, pub. R. R. Donneley and Sons – harvest fresh, organic vegetables all year long; escape confines of the growing season; composting, planning and preparing outdoor garden; planting and cultivating; cold frames, tunnel greenhouses, root cellars, and growing winter greens indoors
Fresh Vegetables and Herbs from Your Garden, Percy Thrower, VMH, pub. Crescent Books – planning, planting, growing and harvesting herbs and vegetables
Fruits and Berries in the Home Garden, Lewis Hill – master gardener provides instructions for beginner and pro
Gardener's Bug Book, Barbara Pleasant – natural pest control for beginners or advanced gardeners
Gardening by Mail, Barbara J. Barton, pub. Houghton Mifflin Co. – directory of resources for gardeners; includes seed companies, nurseries, garden suppliers, plant societies, magazines, libraries, and books
Gardening Indoors, George Van Patten, pub. Van Patten Publishing – hydroponics on a small scale for average home-owner
Gardening with Herbs for Flavor and Fragrance, Fox – grow herbs, purchasing seeds, harvesting, and drying for future crops
Gardening—The Rockwool Book, George F. Van Patten – introductory book for the hobby grower; simple presentation with clear definition of the equipment required
Gardens Without Soil—House Plants, Vegetables, and Flowers, Jack Kramer, pub. Scribner
Garden-Ville Method—Lessons in Nature (2nd Ed.),The, Malcolm Beck, pub. Garden-Ville, Inc. – authority and practitioner in organic growing tells how to work with nature to produce a productive organic garden
Greenhouse Gardener's Companion, Shane Smith – growing food and flowers in your greenhouse or sunspace
Grow More Nutritious Vegetables Without Soil, James D. Taylor, pub. Parkside Press – new organic method of hydroponics
Growing Food in Solar Greenhouses, Delores Wolfe
Growing Great Garlic, pub. Filaree Productions – information on growing 200+ strains of garlic; types, planting, cultivation, harvesting, storage, marketing and processing
Growing Herbs from Seed, Cutting and Root, Thomas DeBaggio, pub. Interweave Press – by commercial grower/professional; basics, problems

Gardening & Food Production Books (continued)

Growing Herbs, Deni Bown, pub. Dorling Kindersley – introductory book with color photographs of 60 herbs; pull chart has cultivation details for each herb at a glance
Growing Vegetables West of Cascades, Steve Solomon – guide to natural gardening for the Northwest
Guide for the Hydroponic and Soil-less Culture Grower, J. Benton Jones, pub. Timber Press
Harvest Gardener, Susan McClure – growing for maximum yield, prime flavor, and garden-fresh storage
Herb Garden, Frances A. Bardswell, pub. Florence Amherst and Isabelle Forrest – index, tables, and color illustrations
Herb Garden, The, Sarah Garland, pub. Penguin Books
Herb Gardening (1st Ed.), Eleanour Sinclair Rohde, pub. Medici Society – drawings, color and B&W photos
Holistic Garden, The, Clinton R. Kraft, pub. Aristera Publications – grow food holistically and organically with edible plants that grow naturally; small plot grows vegetables using rotation system; requires no chemical fertilizers, no soil depletion; produces good quality food; collect and grow open-pollinated varieties of vegetables
Home Garden Book of Herbs and Spices, Milo Miloradovich, pub. Doubleday – grow, prepare and preserve all culinary herbs and spices—for gardener, homemaker, and gourmet
Home Hydroponics and How to Do It, Lem Jones with Paul and Cay Beardsley, Crown Publishers – step-by-step on setting up hydroponics greenhouse; detailed plans for constructing, equipping, planting and growing practical home system; poor soil, no soil, or contaminated soil situation
How to Grow More Vegetables Than You Ever Thought Possible on Less Land Than You Can Imagine, John Jeavons – ordinary lawn area of 800 square feet provides family of four with fresh food for a year; methods proven during 20 years of trial to be among the most productive and successful in use; book introduces the Biodynamic French Intensive method of gardening
How to Identify Mushrooms Using only Macroscopic Features, David Largent, pub. Mad River Press – for the beginning mushroom student; easy-to-use, textbook quality volume for those not knowing where to start; quality line drawings
Humanure Handbook, The—A Guide To Composting Human Manure, pub. Jenkins Publishing – managing a compost toilet and compost pile
Hydroponic Crop Production, Joe Romer – for the serious hydroponics grower; illustrated
Hydroponic Food Production (4th Ed.), Howard M. Resh, pub. Woodbridge Press – soil-less food growing methods
Hydroponic Gardening, Raymond Bridwell, pub. Woodbridge Press – introduce children to hydroponics
Hydroponic Growing Systems, P.A. Schippers, pub. National Agricultural Plastics Association
Hydroponic Nutrients—Easy Ways to Make Your Own (3rd Ed.), M. Edward Muckle – current information on plant nutrition and nutrient formulation; simple method of making your own plant food
Hydroponic Tomatoes for the Home Gardener, Howard M. Resh – for beginner, with focus on world's most popular crop; several different systems presented in text and illustrations
Hydroponic Workbook—A Guide to Soil-less Gardening, Joseph Gooze
Hydroponics at Home, Extension Bulletin E-1853, Dara J. Philipsen, J. Lee Taylor, and Irvin E. Widders, pub. Michigan St. University
Hydroponics for Everyone, Dr. Struan K. Sutherland, pub. Hyland House – illustrated intro to hydroponics; designed to make your first garden simple, painless and easy to operate
Hydroponics for the Home Gardener, Stewart Kenyon, pub. Van Nostrand Reinhold – step-by-step guide for growing vegetables and herbs, even house plants, without soil
Hydroponics Gardening, Bridwell – grow fruits and vegetables year 'round, in 10 to 15 minutes a day on a minimum of space
Hydroponics Gardening, Steven Carruthers, pub. Family Resources
Hydroponics Home Food Gardens, Howard M. Resh, pub. Family Resources
Hydroponics Horticulture Facts—VC-19-82 (Rev. 4/85), John M. Gerber, pub. University of Illinois at Urbana-Champaign, College of Agriculture, Cooperative Extension Service
Hydroponics Plus—The Bentley System, Maxwell Bentley, pub. O' Connor Printers
Hydroponics Worldwide—State of the Art in Soil-less Crop Production, Adam J. Savage, Ed., pub. Internat'l Ctr for Special Studies
Hydroponics, John M.Gerber, pub. University of Illinois at Urbana-Champaign, College of Agriculture, Cooperative Extension Service
Hydroponics—The Complete Guide to Gardening Without Soil, Dudley Harris, pub. New Holland Publishers – for beginners, hobbyists and commercial growers
Independent Home, The—Living Well with Power from the Sun, Wind, & Water, Michael Potts – how to create a serlf-reliant home that is comfortable, natural, and sustainable; many ideas and details
Indoor Grower's Guide to Gourmet Sprouts, pub. The Book Publishing Co.
Joy Of Gardening, Dick Raymond – anyone, anywhere can turn any patch of ground into a veggie garden

Gardening & Food Production Books (continued)

Knott's Handbook for Vegetable Growers—3rd Ed., O. A. Lorenz and D. N. Maynard, pub. John Wiley and Sons
– handbook and reference book; general guidelines for production and plant characteristics of all vegetable crops; diseases, insects, pesticides, fertilizers, harvest, handling and storage, seeding rates, cold and heat susceptibility, plant nutrition, and food value

Let It Rot!—The Gardener's Guide to Composting, Stu Campbell
– natural way to recycle waste materials such as household garbage, grass clippings, and ashes to create useful, soil-nourishing compost

Lettuce from Eden, Albert Whiting, pub. A. Whiting
– hydroponic growing systems for small or large greenhouses

Mail Order Gardener, The, Hal Morgan, pub. Harper and Row

Market What You Grow, c/o Randy Whatley, pub. The Chicot Press
– idea book and hands-on workbook for small growers

Master Guide to Planning Profitable Hydroponic Greenhouse Operations (Rev.), Adam J. Savage, pub. Int'l. Ctr. For Special Studies

Modern Encyclopedia of Herbs, Joseph M. Kadans, pub. Parker Publishing
– reference about hundreds of herbs: common names, cooking uses, botanical names, cosmetic uses, growing conditions, & medical uses

Mulch Book, The, Stu Campbell
– everything you need to know about mulching

Mushrooms Demystified, David Aurora
– mushrooms for everyman; one of the best books about finding mushrooms and knowing what you've found

My Years in My Herb Garden, Helen M. Fox, pub. MacMillan
– experienced herb grower tells how it's done

Natural Insect Repellents for Pets, People and Plants, Janette Frainger and Connie More, pub. The Herb Bar
– book of ancient and safe natural pest control methods to which insects can never become immune

New Organic Grower, Eliot Coleman, pub. Rodale Books
– master grower presents simplest and most sustainable ways to grow top-quality organic vegetables; marketing the harvest, small-scale equipment, farming, and gardening for long-term health of soil; farm-generated fertility, winter garden, pests, and information resources

New Seed Starters Handbook, Nancy Bubel
– get your garden off to a good start

Old Fashioned Fruit Garden—The Best Way to Grow, Preserve and Bake with Small Fruit, The, Jo Ann Gardner
– useful information and country wisdom; every step of fruit season; planting and harvesting, preserving and packing

Organic Field Crop Handbook, pub. Canadian Organic Growers, Inc.

Organic Resource Guide, pub. Canadian Organic Growers, Inc.

Patio Garden, The Hazel Evans, pub. Penguin Books

Pay Dirt, How to Raise and Sell Herbs and Produce for Serious Ca$h, Mimi Luebbermann
– specialty herbs, fresh produce and dried herbs; profiting from these and other products

Peralandra Garden Workbook (1st Ed), Machaelle Small Wright
 – gardening with nature intelligences

Permaculture Way—Practical To Create A Self-Sustaining World, The, Graham Bell
– permanent methods of sustainable agriculture

Q and A—Hundreds of Can-Do Answers to a Gardener's Toughest Question, Editors of Organic Gardening Magazine
– answers 600 questions; building better gardens; growing better crops; growing great fruit; beautifying homes; keeping gardens healthy

Rita's Sprouting and Recipes, Rita Bingham, self-pub.

Rodale's All New Encyclopedia of Organic Gardening, pub. Rodale Press
– 400+ entries of gardening information; collected from garden experts and writers nationwide

Rodale's Book Of Composting, pub. Rodale Press
– improve your soil, recycle kitchen and yard wastes, grow healthier plants, create earth-safe garden

Rodale's Color Handbook of Garden Insects, pub. Rodale Press
– color illustrations, systematically arranged information

Rodale's Successful Organic Gardening – Companion Planting, pub. Rodale Press

Rodale's Successful Organic Gardening – Controlling Pests and Disease, pub. Rodale Press

Rodale's Successful Organic Gardening – Fruits and Berries, pub. Rodale Press

Rodale's Successful Organic Gardening – Herbs, pub. Rodale Press

Rodale's Successful Organic Gardening – Improving Soil, pub. Rodale Press

Rodale's Successful Organic Gardening – Pruning, pub. Rodale Press

Rodale's Successful Organic Gardening – Vegetables, pub. Rodale Press

Roses Love Garlic—Secrets Of Companion Planting With Flowers, Louise Riotte

Salad Garden, The, Joy Larkcom, pub. Penguin Books

Saving Seeds—The Gardeners Guide to Growing and Storing Vegetable and Flower Seeds, Marc Rodgers and Polly Alexander
– save seeds from growing crop for next crop

Gardening & Food Production Books (continued)

Secret Life of Compost, Malcolm Beck, pub. Garden-Ville, Inc. – compost lawn, garden, feedlot, and farm; maintain and improve the soil; improve food production through proper use of compost
Secrets Of Plant Propagation, Lewis Hill – start plants from seeds and cuttings, dividing, layering, and grafting
Seed to Seed—Seed-Saving Techniques for the Vegetable Gardener, Suzanne Ashworth, pub. Seed Savers Publications – saving seeds for self-sufficiency; seed-saving for 160+ vegetable crops; sustain seed production on small scale; for beginning or experienced seed savers who maintain unique varieties to conserve our vegetable heritage
Seeds & Sprouts for Life, Bernard Jensen
Self-Sufficiency Gardening, Martin Waterman – financial, physical, and emotional security from your own backyard
Self-Sufficient Gardener, John Seymour, pub. Doubleday and Co. – growing and preserving all your own food
Soil-less Culture of Greenhouse Vegetables—Bulletin 218, Hunter Johnson, Florida Cooperative Extension Service, Institute of Food and Agricultural Sciences, University of Florida
Solar Electric House, The, Steven J. Strong – definitive book on solar electric systems for the home; covers all aspects of energy independence
Solar Gardening—Growing Vegetables Year-Round the American Intensive Way, Leandre and Gretchen Poisson – gardening system allows concentration and retention of sun's energy; grow more vegetables—organically, efficiently, and 12 mo./year
Solar Independent Home Book, The, pub. Fowler Solar Electric, Inc. – the bible for the 12V home installation; illustration detail installations and applications
Soybean Cookbook—Growing and Using Nature's Miracle Protein, Garden Way Publishing – 200+ recipes: soups, casseroles, desserts; growing, harvesting and storing soybeans
Sprout Handbook, Stuart Wheelwright, pub. Research Technical Services
Sprout It!—One Week from Seed to Salad! Steve Meyerowitz, pub. The Sprout House, Inc.
Sproutchart, Michael Linden, self-pub. Sprouting Publications – utilize healthful sprouts of seeds and grains
Sproutguide, Michael Linden, self-pub. Sprouting Publications – guide book for the home sprouter
Sprouting Book, The, Ann Wigmore, pub. Avery Publishing Group, Inc. – recipe book and practical guide to sprouting
Sprouting for All Seasons, Larimore, pub. Horizon Publishers – how and what to sprout; recipes
Sprouts—The Miracle Food, Steve Meyerowitz, pub. The Sprout House – storage, harvesting, cleaning, mixing, refrigeration
Square Foot Gardening, Mel Bartholomew, pub. Rodale Press – maximum food production with minimum space
Survival Acre, Linda Runyon – use your family's garden space for security and survival
Survival Gardening, John Freeman
Tips for the Lazy Gardener, Linda Tilgner
Twelve Months Harvest, Chevron Chemical Co. – utilize garden space for virtually year-round food supply
Vegetable Garden Know-How, Raymond – beginner or expert, comprehensive
Vegetable Gardening, Editors of Sunset Books, pub. Lane Publishing Co. – growing vegetables in home gardens
Whole Grains—Grow, Harvest and Cook Your Own, Sara Pitzer, pub. Garden Way Publishing – 50 recipes for growing, harvesting, and cooking 7 grains—barley, buckwheat, corn, millet, oats, rice, rye, and wheat or triticale
Wild Garden, The, Violet Stevenson, pub. Penguin Books
Worms Eat My Garbage, Mary Appelhof – set up and maintain a worm composting system

When you find errors, please address the correct data to:
Doc@DoctorPrepper.com

F. Harvesting and Gathering Wild Foods

This category includes books about edible wild herbs, plants, roots, mushrooms, foraging, hunting, plant and weed identification, and sea vegetables.

Chart 27–7
Harvesting & Gathering Wild Foods Books

Acorn Pancakes, Dandelion Salad, and 38 Other Wild Recipes, Jean Craighead, George and Paul Mirocha
Audubon Field Guide to North American Mushrooms – edible mushrooms; color photos
Basic Essentials of Edible Wild Plants and Useful Herbs, Jim Meuninck
British Herbs, Florence Ranson, pub. Harmondsworth (div. Penguin) – illustrated with photos and drawings
Bull's Eye, Ragnar Benson – crossbow history, today's technology; using the crossbow from booby-trapping to spear fishing; manufacturers, models, and prices
Common Edible and Useful Plants of the West, Muriel Sweet – finding and utilizing forage plants
Dandelion Celebration—A Guide To Unexpected Cuisine, Dr. Peter Gail, pub. Goosefoot Acres Press – gathering, preparing, and savoring the entire dandelion; using dandelions in meals; appetizers, "coffee" and desserts from one of the most potent vegetable nutrient sources that exists; 75+ recipes and fascinating anecdotes, medicinal potential, and nutrition
Delightful Delicious Daylily, Dr. Peter Gail, pub. Goosefoot Acres Press – one of the top 10 most appealing flowers for cooking; use daylilies as exciting and nutritious ingredient of many dishes
Drinks from the Wilds, Steven A. Krause and Robert W. Freckman
Eat the Weeds, Ben Charles Harris – nature's abundant supermarket of free, flavorful, and delicious food
Edible and Medicinal Plants of the Rocky Mountains and Territories, Terry Willard, MH – master herbalist describes edible and medicinal herbs of Canada and northern Rockies
Edible and Useful Wild Plants of the United States and Canada, Charles Francis Saunders
Edible Wild Plants of Eastern North America, Merritt Lyndon Fernald
Edible Wild Plants, Oliver Perry Medsger, pub. McMillan – 150+ North American species and their habitats, photos, drawings, index, and index of scientific names
Edible Wild Plants—A North American Field Guide, Thomas S. Elias and Peter A. Dykeman
Field Guide to Edible Wild Plants, Bradford Angier – quick identification of edible wild plants in the US and Canada; color illustrations
Field Guide to Medicinal Wild Plants, Bradford Angier – from expert on survival
Field Guide to Mushrooms, pub. National Audubon Society – durable plastic-bound guide; hundreds of high-quality color photographs and drawings
From the Shepherd's Purse, Max G. Barlow, pub. Spice West Publications – find, gather and prepare infusions, decoctions, powders, drawing salves, etc.; photographs and charts
Great Dandelion Cookbook, Dr. Peter Gail, pub. Goosefoot Acres Press – recipes from *National Dandelion Cook-off;* dandy burgers, dandelion flower drop cookies, and more
Guide To Wild Foods—In the Footsteps of Our Ancestors (4ᵗʰ Ed.), Christopher Nyerges, pub. Survival News Service 🖥**http://home.earthlink.net/~nyerges** ✉*nyergees@earthlinknet* – thoroughly tested and full of first-hand experience; packed full of information that makes identifying food plants fun; an encyclopedia of knowledge about edible wild foods, including what and what not to eat!
Herb Walk Manual, The, LeArta Moulton, pub. L M™ Publications – discover how to use nature's herbal healers on a plant identification field trip without the thorns!; 135+ medicinal, edible, and poisonous plants found throughout the world's temperate zones identified in full color with detailed identifying characteristics; teaches the differences between useful and dangerous plants with details of identifying characteristics; gain confidence in how to find wild plants and save money utilizing their natural medicinal properties; reference manual with glossary and *Herb Walk Medicinal Guide* included
Herb Walk Video, The, LeArta Moulton, pub. L M™ Publications – video (VHS), full-color plant identification trip without the thorns; more than 135 medicinal, edible and poisonous plants found throughout the world's temperate zones; teaches the differences between useful and dangerous plants with details of identifying characteristics; teaches confidence in what to do with wild plants; how to save money utilizing natural medicinal properties of plants; manual included
Identifying and Harvesting Edible and Medicinal Plants in Wild (& Not So Wild Places), Steve Brill and Evelyn Dean
Instant Guide to Edible Plants, An, Pamela Forey and Cecilia Fitzsimons – illustrated; for the forager

Harvesting & Gathering Wild Foods Books (continued)

Instant Guide to Medicinal Plants, Pamela Forey and Ruth Lindsay – companion to **Instant Guide to Edible Plants**; illustrations, medical glossary, map showing locations
Introduction to Mushroom Hunting, Charles – 95 common mushrooms and fungi
Mushroom Book, The, Krienger – 500+ pages of pictures and descriptions of different wild mushrooms, their habitat and how to use them
Nature's Free Pharmacy, Ken Larson, pub. Rhema Publishing – home remedies using Nature's healing herbs; benefit from a knowledge of herbal medicine for healing and minor medical problems
Recipes for Backyard Weeds, Dr. Peter Gail, pub. Goosefoot Acres Press – forage for free, edible, nutritious vegetables—"weeds" that are among the topmost green leafy vegetables available
Roots—A Vegetarian Bounty, pub. Woodbridge Press
Sea Vegetable Gelatin Cookbook, Judith Cooper Madlener – foraging, harvesting, and preparation of highly nutritious sea vegetables, nearly 200 recipes from appetizers to desserts
Stalking Healthful Herbs, Euell Gibbons – beverages, recipes, remedies, and teas; culmination of Gibbon's study and exploration of wild herbs
Stalking the Wild Asparagus—Field Guide Edition, Euell Gibbons, pub. David McKay – field guide to edible wild plants
Story of Fruits and Vegetables, pub. Devin-Adair Publishers Co., Inc.
Tom Brown's Guide to Wild Edible and Medicinal Plants, Tom Brown – how to use every part of the plant—leaves, roots, and flowers; where to find useful plants; best harvest times; preparing delicious food dishes, soups, teas, and breads from the abundance of the great outdoors; proven medicinals for ills and maladies
Totally Free Lunch, The, Dr. Peter Gail, pub. Goosefoot Acres Press – harvesting your backyard; culinary and medicinal history of 26 common backyard weeds
Warm Climate Gardening, Barbara Pleasant – tips, techniques, plans, and projects for humid or dry conditions
Wild and Free Cookbook, The, Tom Squier – recipes that will turn roadkill into gourmet meals—if it doesn't turn your stomach…
Wild Cards® Edible Wild Food Cards, Linda Runyon, pub. US Games Systems – unique deck of playing cards with glossy photos and plant descriptions; 52 common wild edible food plants and their uses; companion to *Wild Food Guide Book*
Wild Food Trail Guide, Alan Hall
Wild Foods Guide Book, Linda Runyon – common and uncommon wild edible food plants and their uses
Wild Roots—Forager's Guide to Edible and Medicinal Roots, Tubers, Corms, and Rhizomes of North America, Douglas B. Elliott

When you find errors, please address the correct data to:
Doc@DoctorPrepper.com

G. Preserving and Storing Foods

This category includes books about brining, canning, curing, dehydrating and drying foods, freezing, pickling, refrigerating, smoking, and freeze-drying, storage tips, root cellaring; storage plans, and using stored foods.

Chart 27–8
Preserving & Storing Foods Books

ABC's of Home Food Dehydration, Barbara Densley
– several methods of drying foods at home; dry fruits, vegetables, herbs, meats, fish, and more; helpful hints and recipes included

All About Pickling, Editorial staff of Ortho Books, pub. Ortho Books
– ancient method of food preservation now returns as do-it-yourself pickling for pleasure, pride and economy

Ball Blue Book, New Revised Edition, pub. Ball Corporation
– home canning and freezing

Ball Freezer Book, Vol. 1, No. 1, pub. Ball Corporation
– home freezing

Bee Prepared with Honey, Arthur W. Anderson, pub. Horizon Publishers, Inc.
– utilize honey in your food storage program

Bernardin Home Canning Guide, pub. Bernardin, Inc.

Better Homes and Garden Presents, Better Homes and Gardens
– America's all time favorite canning and preserving recipes

Busy Person's Guide to Preserving Food, Janet Bachand Chadwick, pub. Garden Way Publishing

Canning, Freezing, Curing and Smoking of Meat, Fish and Game, Wilbur F. Eastman

Clearly Delicious
– preserving, pickling and bottling; full-color photos

Complete Book of Freezer Cookery, Seranne
– use the home freezer wisely and effectively

Complete Book of Home Storage of Vegetables and Fruits, Evelyn V. Lovedan

Dehydration Made Simple, Mary Bell
– dehydrate just about any fresh fruit, vegetable or meat; easy-to-follow recipes and many color photos

Don Holm's Book of Food Drying—Pickling and Smoke Curing, Don Holm

Essentials of Home Production and Storage, pub. The Church of Jesus Christ of Latter-day Saints
– 28-page pamphlet; determine what foods to store and how to store them; bibliography of related books

Family Storage Plan, Bob R. Zabriskie, pub. Bookcraft Publishers, Inc.
– preparation, preservation and storage of basics

Famine and Survival in America, Howard Ruff, pub. Publishers Press
– prepare for the coming famine and avoid deadly storage errors

Food and Water—Threats, Shortages and Solutions, Bernard S. Cayne and Jenny E. Tesar

Food Drying At Home The Natural Way, Bee Byer, pub. J. P. Tarcher/St. Martin's Press
– dehydrating foods and using them in everyday recipes

Food Keeper, The, pub. Food Marketing Institute
– pamphlet available for long SASE; tips on storage of foods plus chart of how long various items will keep in the refrigerator, pantry, and/or freezer with emphasis on current-use items (milk products, meats, etc.); helpful in planning a food reserve

Fruit Drying with a Microwave, Isabel Webb, pub. Sterling Publishing Co., Inc.
– dozens of recipes and photos; quick, easy method of drying fruit in the microwave

Fun with Fruit Preservation, Dora D. Flack, pub. Horizon Publishers, Inc.
– all aspects of fruit preservation

Garden Way's Guide to Food Drying—How to Dehydrate, Store and Use Vegetables, Fruits and Herbs, pub. Garden Way Pub.
– low-cost alternative to canning & freezing; equipment to use; make a dehydrator; hundreds of recipes for using what you've dried

Gateway to Survival is Storage, Walter D. Batchelor, pub. Horizon Publishers, Inc.
– developing an adequate food storage program in all climates

Home Canning, Sunset Books and Sunset Magazine Editors, pub. Sunset Books

Home Food Dehydrating, Jay P. and Shirley Bills, pub. Horizon Publishers, Inc.
– techniques for dehydrating food storage items

Home Food Systems—Rodale's Catalog of Methods and Tools for Producing, Processing, and Preserving Naturally Good Foods, Roger B. Yepsen, Jr., Ed., pub. Rodale Press
– make your own food and beverages; step-by-step processes and recipes

Honey—God's Gift for Health and Beauty, Joe M. Parkhill
– cooking and canning with honey, food value versus sugar

How to Develop a Low-Cost Family Food-Storage System, Anita Evangelista

Preserving & Storing Foods Books (continued)

How To Dry Foods, Deanna DeLong, pub. HP Books – select, prepare and dry fruits, vegetables, meats and fish; easy-to-use techniques
How to Enjoy Eating Your Food Storage Now!, Jay E. Ostler, self-pub. – method of consuming and replenishing your food supply
How-To Book —Canning, Freezing, Drying, pub. The Mirro Corp.
Just Add Water, Barbara G. Salsbury, pub. Horizon Publishers, Inc. – dehydrated food storage and usage
Just In Case, Barbara Salsbury, pub. Bookcraft Publishers – preserve food by canning, drying, freezing, brining; store food in basements, apartments, root cellars; grow food in home gardens and containers; prepare your family for almost any eventuality
Keeping Food Fresh—How To Choose and Store Everything You Eat, Janet Bailey, pub. The Dial Press – ensure you are getting food at its peak for maximum nutrition and taste; food science, kitchen crises, and kitchen systems
Keeping the Harvest—Preserving Your Fruits, Vegetables and Herbs, Nancy Chioffi and Gretchen Mead – preserve fruits, vegetables, & herbs by canning, jams, jellies, freezing, pickling, drying, curing, & cold storage; easy-to-read instructions
Kerr Home Canning and Freezing Book, Kerr Glass Manufacturing Corp. – home canning and freezing
Living Well on Wheat—How to Cook, Eat, Survive on the Golden Grain (Book II) Geri Guidetti**,** pub. The Ark Institute – grow, harvest, store, prepare and survive on inexpensive, wholesome wheat grain
Making Food Storage Fun, Fast and Easy, LauraAnne J. Logar, self-pub.
Making the Best of Basics–*Family Preparedness Handbook,* 10th Ed., James Talmage Stevens, pub. Gold Leaf Press – comprehensive information for becoming prepared for the uncertain future; charts, tables, recipes for basic foods, and 2400+ resources throughout the US & Canada providing foods & foodstuffs
Marlene's Magic with Food Storage, Marlene Peterson, pub. Marlene's Magic – turn "dry" storage foods into delicious meals and gourmet delights; recipes easily prepared and stretch budgets; ideas for calculating your family storage, foods for babies, sprouting, cooking tips, and drying fruits and vegetables; home-made tofu in 10 easy steps
Methods of Long-term Underground Storage – booklet; how to prepare items for long-term storage underground; plastic coatings, desiccants, burial locations, etc.
Natural Foods Storage Bible, Kendricks Dienstbier, pub. Horizon Publishers, Inc.
New Putting Food By, Ruth Hertzberg and Beatrice Vaughan and Janet Greene, pub. The Stephen Greene Press – best methods to can, freeze, pickle, dry, cure, and preserve foods; includes new technology, new ingredients and twice as many recipes
Passport to Survival, Esther Dickey, pub. Bookcraft Publishers, Inc. – four basic foods for preparation, preservation and storage
Perfect Preserves—Provisions from the Kitchen Garden, Nora Carey
Preserving Today, Jeanne Lesem, pub. Alfred A. Knopf, Inc. – new and faster techniques for preserving foods at their peak of flavor; 168 recipes
Putting Food By (4th Ed.), Greene, Hertzberg and Vaughn, pub. Penguin Group – updated; best ways to can, freeze, pickle, dry, cure, and preserve foods for storage
Revised Keeping the Harvest—Home Storage of Fruits and Vegetables, Garden Way Publishing – canning, freezing, bottling, pickling, steam juicing, curing, drying, and more; build and use root cellars and storage containers indoors and out
Rita's Powdered Milk, Cheeses, and Yogurt, Rita Bingham, pub. Meals in Minutes – making yogurt and cheeses from powdered milk—cottage, hard, parmesan, cream and more
Rodale's Complete Book of Home Freezing, Marilyn Hodges, pub. Rodale Press – freezing all kinds of foods; maintain and organize your freezer; recipes
Root Cellaring—Natural Cold Storage of Fruits and Vegetables, Mike and Nancy Bubel
Sam Andy's Food Storage Guide and Cookbook, pub. SAI Publishing – nutritional breakdown of each food, its calorie count, protein content, and complete guide to selecting foods for storage; good recipe book using dehydrated products
Stocking Up III—The Classic Preserving Guide, Carol Hupping and the staff at Rodale Food Center, pub. A Fireside Book – new edition, completely revised and updated, 300+ new recipes; latest home storage techniques; freezing, canning, drying and root-cellar storing, preparing virtually every food for storage; hints and tips for quick and easy home preservation
Stocking Up—How To Prepare The Foods You Grow, Naturally, Carol Hupping Stoner and staff, Organic Gardening and Farming – growing and preserving your own food; especially for those gardening without electricity
Survival Food Storage, Mark and Zhana Thomason, pub. TSI Publishers – store a year's supply of food and water for entire family in one or two rooms
Whole Food Catalog, Nava Atlas, pub. Ballantine Books, Inc., div. of Random House Publishing – complete guide to natural foods and how to store and use them
Year's Supply, A, Barry G. and Lynnette B. Crockett, pub. Barry Crockett – obtain and carefully store a year's supply of food, clothing, fuel, and other basic necessities
Your Guide to Home Storage, Alan K. Briscoe, pub. Horizon Publishers, Inc.

H. Cooking, Preparation and Utilization of Foods

This category includes books about beverages (herbs and teas), breads, cookbooks, cooking storage foods, food additives, grains, historical recipes, making sausages, resource guides, seasonings, tofu, miso, stored foods, natural, nutrition, organic, resources, vegetarian, Vegan, and special diets.

Chart 27–9
Cooking, Preparation, & Utilization of Foods Books

A Better Whey to Fine Cooking, pub. Cache Valley Dairy Association
– pamphlet on using whey

All About Yogurt, pub. Devin-Adair Publishers Co., Inc.

Alternate Egg Cookbook, Frances Naldrett
– use pasteurized, dried, or frozen eggs

Amazing Grains, Joanne Saltzman
– vegetarian main dishes with whole grains; collection of low-fat, high-fiber, virtually cholesterol-free, and ecologically sound recipes for nutritious main dishes with whole grains and vegetables

Amazing Wheat Book, The, LeArta Moulton, pub. L M™ Publications
– wheat meat, breads, pastries and desserts from the author of **The *New* Gluten Book;** how to make your own seasonings, to utilize wheat meat more effectively; basic batter for muffins, cakes, cookies, waffles, etc., that are ready-to-bake in minutes; how to overcome that tired, heavy feeling by using fiber-rich foods; delicious, wholesome, fast recipes that are easy enough for children to make; enjoy better health and prevent disease with vitamin and mineral-rich whole wheat

American Wholefoods Cuisine, Nikki and David Goldbeck, pub. The New American Library, Inc.
– 1300+ meatless, wholesome recipes; short order to gourmet; contemporary approach to cooking based on vegetable proteins and unrefined foods; food handling, storage, supplies, putting up produce and cooking techniques

Aproveche Mejor Frutas Y Verduras (La Huerta Familiar/Harvest Book), Editors of Organic Gardening

Art of Cooking, The, Arnold Zabert, pub. HPBooks, Inc.
– preparing and presenting fine food; prepare an endless repertory of dishes and present food in thousands of different ways

Art of Making Sausages, Patés and Other Charcuterie, Grigson
– the art of Charcuterie (French for preparing pork meat), recipes dating back to Roman times; use the entire pig

Art of Making Sprouted Bread, Steve Meyerowitz, pub. The Sprout House, Inc.
– make bread with all kinds of sprouts

Back To Eden Cookbook, Jethro Kloss
– recipes and information

Bake Your Own Bread, Floss and Stan Dworkin, pub. New American Library
– 100+ tested recipes for easy, wholesome breads, rolls muffins, biscuits, and ethnic specialties—pizza, croissants, bagels, and tortillas

Bean Banquets, Patricia Gregory, pub. Woodbridge Press
– recipes from around the world based on beans and legumes

Bean Cuisine, Janey Horsley
– cooking beans; meatless, budget-wise recipes

Beans and Peas, Inez M. Krech

Beansprout Book, Gay Courter, pub. Simon and Schuster

Best of the Herman Sourdough Herald 1980-1990, Dawn Johanson

Better Than Store-Bought, Helen Witty and Elizabeth Schneider Colchie, pub. Harper and Row Pub., Inc.
– formulas and techniques familiar to homemakers before commercially-prepared foods; foods people can make at home

Biscuits, Spoonbread, and Sweet Potato Pie, Bill Neal

Blue Collar Food, Christopher Styler and William Hodge, pub. Hearst Books, affiliate of William Morrow and Co., Inc.
– easy-to-follow recipes anyone can make and eat—real food for real people by two professional cooks with 25+ years experience

Book of Bread, Judith and Evan Jones, pub. Harper and Row
– 240 recipes for traditional and unique bread-baking; uncomplicated techniques; top-selling authors

Book of Miso, (1ˢᵗ Ed.), William Shurtleff and Akiko Aoyagi, pub. Ballantine Books
– for 1,000+ years, one of Japan's favorite foods; use like rich meat stock in soups, stews, and desserts; 400 recipes with easy-to-follow instructions; analysis of miso's nutritional benefits; history of use in Chinese and Japanese culture

Book of Miso, The, pub. Soyfoods Center

Book of Sushi, Hinjiro and Tachibana, Yuzuru Omae

Book of Tofu, The, pub. Soyfoods Center

Book of Tofu, The—Protein Source of the Future—Now! (Vol. 1), William Shurtleff and Akiko Aoyagi, pub. Ballantine Books
– make tofu in the kitchen; nutritional benefits; weight control recipes; cholesterol-free, tasty when prepared properly

Book of Whole Grains, Marlene Anne Bumgarner, pub. St. Martin's Press
– grain-by-grain guide to cooking, growing, and grinding whole cereals, nut, peas, and beans; 250 recipes; fit whole grain cooking into busy lifestyle; wheat, oats, rye, triticale, buckwheat, barley, corn, rice, millet, sorghum, nuts and seeds, dried peas, and beans

Cooking, Preparation, & Utilization of Foods Books (continued)

Book of Whole Grains, pub. Chesbro Press
Bread in Half the Time, Linda West Eckhardt and Diana Collingwood Butts, pub. Crown Publishers, Inc. – using the microwave and food processor to make real yeast bread in 90 min.; 68 recipes for bread machines; for the busy person
Bread Machine Cookbook IV, Donna German, pub. Bristol Publishing – whole grains and natural sugars
Bread Winners, Mel London, pub. Rodale Press – 200+ bread recipes from 45 bakers—none of whom are professional cooks or bakers; for anyone wanting to bake bread and other baked goods with natural ingredients
Breadman's Healthy Bread Book, The, George Burnett, pub. William Morrow and Co., Inc. – 100 foolproof recipes for electric bread machines
Breads, Sharon Tyler Herbst, pub. HPBooks – making bread as a creative process; basics make it easy
Bum Steers—How to Make Your Own Delicious Mock Meats, pub. Devin-Adair Publishers Co., Inc.
Chinese Vegetarian Cook Book, Gary Lee, pub. Nitty Gritty Productions – understand how; easy recipes; basics on gluten, soy bean sprouts and vegetables
Complete Book of Food, Carol Ann Rinzler, pub. Ballantine Books – nutritional, medical, and culinary guide to foods; storing, preparing, shopping, cooking & eating nutritious foods; food's importance to health
Complete Fish and Game Cookery of North America, Frances MacIlquaham, pub. Winchester Press – prepare fish and game for the table and storage
Complete Handbook of Brewing, Dave Miller – brewing from scratch for home-brewing types at any level of sophistication
Complete I Hate to Cook Book, Peg Bracken
Complete Kitchen Guide, Lillian Langseth-Christensen and Carol Sturm Smith, pub. Grosset and Dunlap – utensils, foodstuffs, weights, measurements and equivalents; much more
Complete Sprouting Cookbook, pub. Troubador Press
Complete Start-Your-Meal Cookbook, Johna Blinn, pub. Playmore, Inc., div. Waldman Pub. Corp.
Complete Whole Grain Cookbook, Carol Gelles, pub. Donald L. Fine, Inc. – buy, prepare, and cook all high-fiber grains; 400+ recipes, soups to desserts; each recipe has caloric, sodium, cholesterol, fiber content; grains as source of dietary fiber; incorporate grains into everyday diet; buying, cooking, preparing, and storing grains
Cookbook for People Who Love Animals, pub. Gentle World, Inc.
Cookin' With Home Storage, Peggy Layton – making meals from scratch or using storage foods; 550+ recipes; learn from storage expert how easy it is to use storage foods regularly
Cooking and Canning With Honey—Food Value Versus Sugar, Joe M. Parkhill
Cooking with 5 Ingredients or Less, Susan Kosoff and Teresa Kennedy, pub. Wings Books (div. Random House) – 300+ recipes for *"whipping up"* something delicious at a moment's notice with minimum ingredients
Cooking with Stored Foods, Carlene Tejada and Carroll Latham, pub. HP Books – full-color book with recipes for utilizing stored foods
Cooking With The Right Side The Brain – creative vegetarian cooking; recipes
Cooking with Wholegrains—The *Basic* Wholegrain Cookbook, Mildred Ellen Orton, pub. Farrar, Straus and Giroux – cook breads, rolls, cakes, scones, crackers, muffins, and desserts, using only stone-ground whole grains
Cooking, Berndt Berglund, pub. Book Society of Canada, Ltd.
Cook's Book of Essential Information—A Kitchen Handbook, Barbara Hill, pub. Sumner House Press – de-mystification of cooking; dictionary of terms, strategic meal planning, substitutions, supplies and equipment, knowing how to cook food, how to store (just about) everything; nutritional aids and food additives
Cook's Book of Indispensable Ideas—A Kitchen Sourcebook, Barbara Hill, pub. Sumner House Press – basic information for cooks; terms, definitions, substitution tables, nutritional information and more
Cook's Book of Uncommon Recipes, Barbara Hill, pub. Sumner House Press – 200+ recipes; clear, easy-to-understand explanations for cooking problems
Cook's Encyclopedia, The—Ingredients and Processes, Tom Stobart, pub. Harper and Row – information not found in cook books; comprehensive and reliable information for procedures and processes for even the most exotic foods; what each ingredient is and what it is used for and how to deal with it
Cook's Tales, Lee Edwards Benning, pub. The Globe Pequot Press – origins of 75 famous dishes; what inspired each of them, who improved or refined it, and who gave the dish its name; stories behind favorite appetizers, desserts, and entrees from European and American kitchens
Cornucopia—A Source Book of Edible Plants, pub. Kampong Publications

Cooking, Preparation, & Utilization of Foods Books (continued)

Country Beans, Rita Bingham, pub. Natural Meals In Minutes
– low-fat, heart-healthy, meatless recipes using fresh fruits, vegetables, and a combination of beans, wheat, & other grains to provide complete protein, high fiber, and super nutrition; 30-min. bean meals with bean flours in cream soups, sauces, gravies; desserts that cook in only 3 minutes; sprouting instructions; home canning recipes for beans & bean soups; most recipes are gluten-free for the growing number of people with wheat allergies or on rotation diets *(Rita is a daughter of Esther Dickey, author of Passport to Survival, an early book on food storage)*

Country Food– A Seasonal Journal, Miriam Ungerer, pub. Random House
– 150 recipes accompany the fresh provender which comes with the changing seasons; tips on food selections and preparation

Cut Your Food Bill in Half, Barbara Salsbury and C. Loveless

Deaf Smith Country Cookbook, Marjorie Winn Ford, Susan Hillyard, and Mary Faulk Koock, pub. Macmillan Publishing
– natural foods for family kitchens, 200+ recipes substituting natural foods

Dehydrated Food Cooking, Stan Smith
– use food storage in a simple manner; how much water to use, how long to rehydrate and how long to cook; recipes for apples to yams

Diet for a Small Planet, Frances Moore Lappe
– explains the efficiency of grain consumption instead of animals; recipes and guidance in balancing needed amino acids when avoiding meat

Don't Tell 'Em It's Good for 'Em, Nancy Baggett and Ruth Glick and Gloria Kaufer Greene, pub. Times Books
– make your family's favorite meals more nutritious with NUTRI-STEP system; 250+ recipes and tips on utilizing your storage foods better

Dress 'em Out, Captain James A. Smith, pub. Stoeger Publishing Co.
– for hunters who want more know-how on processing their catch

Dry Peas and Lentils, Betty Lowe Janson, Horizon Publishers
– delicious, nutritious meals from legumes using peas and lentils; live healthier and at a fraction of the cost of meat dishes; color photos

Dutch Oven Secrets, Lynn Hopkins, pub. Horizon Publishers
– detailed instructions for Dutch oven recipes; cooking for large groups; using Dutch oven in home food-storage program

Easy Basics for Good Cooking, Editors of Sunset Books
– cooking fresh, nutritious meals quickly and easily

Easy Gourmet Cookbook II, The, Elsie Lee, pub. Prestige Books, Inc.
– gourmet cooking that's table-ready in minutes

Edible Flowers, Marilyn Lande, pub. Lan-Design Publications
– recipes using edible flowers

Edible Flowers—A Kitchen Companion, Kitty Morse, pub. 10-Speed Press
– utilizing edible flowers for salads and entrees

Egg-Free, Milk-Free, Wheat-Free Cookbook, Becky Hamrick and S. L. Wiesenfeld, MD, pub. Harper and Row
– for those with food allergies to eggs, milk, and wheat; recipe ideas for breakfast, main dishes, vegetable dishes, desserts, appetizers and salads

Enchanted Broccoli Forest and Other Timeless Delicacies, Mollie Katzen
– more meals from author of the "Moosewood Cookbook"

Essential Cook, The, Charles Delmar, pub. Hill House Publishing Co.
– foods and cooking, utilizing basic foods and ingredients

Fabulous Egg Cookbook, The, Jeffrey Feinman, pub. Ventura Associates, Inc.
– 100's of recipes with high-protein eggs

Fake Fish and Dairy-less Desserts, pub. Devin-Adair Publishers Co., Inc.

Flora's Dictionary, Kathleen Gips, pub. TM Publications
– revised edition with more folklore on meanings associated with plants

Game Cookery in America and Europe, Raymond R. Camp, pub. HP Books
– prepare game when purchased; recipes for waterfowl, field birds, wild turkey, large game animals, rabbit, and squirrel; recipes and ideas for accompaniments for game meals; does not deal with dressing game

Garden Way Bread Book, pub. Garden Way Publishing
– 140+ *all-natural* recipes for novice and experienced bakers; fit bread-making into a busy schedule; *"can't-fail"* instructions

Good Breakfast Book, pub. Ceres Press

Gourmet Grains, pub. Woodbridge Press

Gourmet UnCook Book, Elizabeth Baker, pub. Drelwood Communications
– further raw foods recipes for elegant dieting with living natural foods; second book in the **UnCook…**Series *(see additional titles)*

Grains Cookbook, Bert Greene
– variety of recipes from great cooks around the world to get the most from your stored grains

Great American Chicken Cookbook, Iona Nixon, pub. Ventura Associates, Inc.
– recipes for standard favorites and way-out gourmet dishes

Great Cooks' Guide to Soups, pub. Random House
– America's leading food authorities share home-tested recipes and expertise on cooking equipment and techniques

Cooking, Preparation, & Utilization of Foods Books (continued)

Great Food Book, Luscious Lower-Fat Cooking, Julee Rosso, pub. Crown/Turtle Bay Books
– owner of her own inn, author is member of *Who's Who in American Cooking;* food that's in step with today's dieting lifestyle

Great Grains, Linda Drachman and Peter Wynne, pub. Fireside
– 125 recipes for grains—wheat, rice, corn, oats, barley, millet, buckwheat and amaranth; diverse assortment gives taste and texture to meals

Having Fun With Peanuts, Betsy H. Owens, Director, Virginia-Carolina Peanut Promotions
– recipes for peanuts: beverages, snacks, desserts

Herbal Guide to Food—Eating Healthy the Herbal Way, Jeanne Rose, pub. North Atlantic Books
– for those who want to use herbs in the diet; 120 recipes from teas to granolas to breads

Homemade Frozen Yogurt, pub. Triad Communications, Inc.

Instant Delite Recipes, Merrilyn Lloyd, pub. Carr Printing Co.
– recipes using *Instant Clear Jel,* pre-cooked food starch improves cooking habits & taste; food industry's secret applied in home kitchens

Japanese Vegetarian Cooking, pub. The Crossing Press

Joy of Cooking, The, Irma S. Rombauer and Marion Rombauer Becker, pub. The Bobbs-Merrill Co., Inc.
– *the* definitive American cookbook; simplified preparation process

Judith Olney on Bread, Judith Olney, pub. Crown Publishers, Inc.
– basics of bread baking; flours, tools, techniques, and recipes

Keep It Simple—30-Minute Meals from Scratch, Marian Burros, pub. William Morrow and Co., Inc.
– alternative to fast food outlets and factory-prepared food; fraud in the marketplace; consumers become self-reliant suppliers of cheaper, safer, quicker-to-fix, better, more abundant and more tasty food

Kitchen Garden Cookbook, Steve Meyerowitz, pub. The Sprout House
– sprout breads, cookies, soups, salads, and other low-fat, dairy-free recipes

Kitchen Magic—Cooking with Common Grains, Deanna Sudweeks, pub. Hawkes Publishing, Inc.
– use food storage grains in everyday meals; achieve higher nutrition by using common grains; save $$$ in food cost and preparation

Kitchen Science, Howard Hillman, pub. Houghton Mifflin Co.
– know the how and why in the kitchen; by author of 25+ books

L. L. Bean Game and Fish Cookbook, Angus Cameron and Judith Jones, pub. L.L. Bean Co.
– guide for the urban hunter and fisher in preparing game and fish

Laurel's Kitchen Bread Book, Laurel Robertson and the authors of "Laurel's Kitchen"
– whole-grain breadmaking; achieve superb results in a hit-and-miss undertaking; get yields that are soul-satisfying every time

Let's Cook It Right, Adelle Davis, pub. Harcourt Brace Jovanovich, Inc.
– 100's of recipes from America's foremost nutrition authority; preparing foods to protect essential nutrients and enhance natural flavors

Lifestyle for Health Cookbook, Cheryl Townsley, pub. Pinon Press
– prepare delicious health food; 180 recipes with nutritional analysis, alternatives for sugar, white flour, fat, salt, & dairy products

Lowfat Jewish Vegetarian Cookbook, pub. Vegetarian Resource Group

Madison Herb Society Cookbook, self-pub.
– recipes and ideas for picnics and cookouts, herbal liqueurs, and treats made in bread machine

Magic Mixes, Deanna Bean, self-pub.
– utilize storage foods to prepare mixes for tasty, easy-to-make dishes; save money & time with instant meals, sauces, baking, & desserts

Magic of Wheat Cookery, Lorraine Dilworth Tyler
– grinding wheat for cooking, baking and storing

Make a Treat with Wheat, Hazel Richards, pub. Hawkes Publishing
– use wheat in cakes and other treats

Make Your Own Convenience Foods, Don and Joan German, pub. MacMillan Pub.

Make Your Own Groceries, Daphne M. Hartwig, pub. Bobbs-Merrill Co., Inc.

Making Homemade Soups and Stews, Garden Way Publishing
– make hearty stews and chowders, gumbos, chilies and soups—hot and cold, clear and creamy

Meals in 30 Minutes, Cheryl Townsley, pub. Pinon Press
– fast, easy, delicious meals in minutes; menus and tips for bulk preparation, freezer, and leftover planning and management

Meatless Meals Guide, pub. Joy of Health

Mix-a-Meal Cookbook—Mixes and Recipes, Deanna Bean & Lorna Shute, Mix-A-Meal Company, Orem UT 84097
– fun meals and treats made the easy way with homemade dry mixes—convenience of store-bought at a fraction of the cost

Moosewood Cookbook, Mollie Katzen
– classic country cookbook

More Kitchen Wisdom—A New Treasury of Food and Cooking Lore, Helpful Hints, and Practical Pointers, Frieda Arkin, pub. Holt, Rinehart and Winston
– helpful, time-saving, money-saving lore on food: purchase, storage, cooking and serving; make meat out of wheat

More-with-Less Cookbook, Doris Janzen Longacre
– suggestions by Mennonites on how to eat better & consume less of the world's limited food resources; simple recipes; information on substitutions for ingredients; breads, cereals, meat, soup, veggies, complementary protein, allowances for energy & protein, garden

Cooking, Preparation, & Utilization of Foods Books (continued)

MRExcellence Cookbook– Your Guide to Making Ordinary Military MREs Extraordinary!, Vicki Walters, pub. Western Reserve Foods – 100s of ways to improve MREs and make them more than palatable
National Organic Directory, pub. Community Alliance with Family Farmers
Native Indian Wild Game, Fish & Wild Foods Cookbook, David Hunt – 340 recipes from Native American Native cooks
Natural Meals in Minutes, Rita Bingham, pub. Natural Meals in Minutes – heart-healthy foods from natural foods; basic foods and sprouting
Natural Nine, Lorraine D. Tyler – cooking with the 9 natural grains: barley, buckwheat, corn, millet, oats, rice, rye, sorghum (milo), wheat and triticale; breads, cereals, desserts (cakes, cookies and pies) and main and side dishes
Natural Sweets and Treats, Ruth Laughlin, pub. Bookcraft, Inc. – from experienced lecturer on how to change one's style of eating
New Complete Joy of Homebrewing, Charlie Papazian
New Concepts in Dehydrated Food Cookery, Barbara Densley – 100's of new ideas and tested recipes; using dehydrated foods as easily as fresh foods; 325+ recipes
New **Cookin' With Home Storage, The,** Vicki Tate, self-pub. – food storage cookbook—700 recipes using storage items, dehydrated foods, etc.; dairy products and cheesemaking, sprouting, survival foods, home remedies, household cleaners; pioneer cooking & recipes
New Doubleday Cookbook, Jean Anderson and Elaine Hanna, pub. Doubleday and Co., Inc. – 4000 recipes that are lighter and more nutritious (with calorie, sodium and cholesterol counts); simplify by utilizing kitchen equipment better; information at a glance in 135 charts
New **Gluten Book, The,** LeArta Moulton, pub. L M™ Publications – learn how to make meat out of wheat!; complete recipes and instruction for meats, sweets, and other treats made from wheat gluten; nutritious, low-fat, no-cholesterol main dishes, salads, sandwich spreads, soups, sauces, and desserts for healthy eating
New Simply Delicious, Rose Elliot – fast and easy vegetarian recipes
New York Times New Natural Foods Cookbook, Jean Hewitt, pub. Times Books – 725+ recipes without artificial flavors, colors, softeners, emulsifiers, bleaches, preservatives, chemicals, or hydrogenated fats
Not Just Cheesecake, pub. Triad Communications, Inc.
Not Milk—Nut Milks!, pub. Woodbridge Press
Nourishment for Life Cookbook, Rachel Albert-Matesz and Don Matesz, pub. Nourishment for Life
NutriSearch—The Database of the Natural Foods Industry, pub. Nutrisearch
Nutrition Secrets of the Ancients, pub. Prima Publishing
Oats, Peas, Beans and Barley Cookbook, Edith Cottrell Young, pub. Woodbridge Press – nutritionist presents 450 recipes for low-cost, tasty and nutritious dishes featuring natural or unrefined foods
Old-Fashioned Dutch Oven Cookbook, Don Holm – basic dutch oven care and use, Dutch oven recipes; emphasizes wild: information on gutting, skinning, and boning, sourdough cooking, drying and/or smoking meat; eating habits of the Lewis and Clark expedition
On Food and Cooking—The Science and Lore of the Kitchen, Harold McGee, pub. Charles Scribner's Sons – gastronomic science & lore; table ingredients and their interactions within our bodies; historical, literary, scientific and practical treatment of foodstuffs; nature of digestion & hunger; basic ingredient components; cooking methods & utensils; what happens when food spoils, why eggs are so nutritious; nature of foods, what they are made of, where they come from, how they are transformed by cooking
Once-a- Month Cooking, Mimi Wilson
One-hundred Ways to Use Wheat, Laura Hawkes
Organic Cooking for (Not-so-Organic) Mothers, pub. Chesbro Press
Organic Gourmet—Recipes and Resources from a Seasonal Kitchen, The, pub. North Atlantic Books and Frog, Ltd.
Organic Resource Guide, The, pub. Canadian Organic Growers, Inc.
Quick and Easy Cooking, Alona S. Perkes, pub. Horizon Publishing – busy person's guide to simple, nutritious meals
Quick Wholesome Foods Video, Rita Bingham, self-pub.
Recipes for a Small Planet, Ellen Buchman Ewald
Rita's Beans, Rita Bingham, pub. Meals in Minutes – "user-friendly" beans; "hide" beans in recipes; variety of sauces and gravies from beans
Rita's Introduction to Natural Foods, Rita Bingham, pub. Meals in Minutes – basic foods and delicious recipes for every meal of the day
Romancing The Bean, Joanne Saltzman – vegetarian bean dishes
Roots, K. Mayes and S. Gottfried – experience new appreciation for root vegetables

Cooking, Preparation, & Utilization of Foods Books (continued)

Roots—The Underground Cookbook, Barbara Grunes and Ann Elise Hunt, pub. Chicago Review Press
– 100+ recipes for root crops: potatoes, onions, garlic, beets, jicama, turnips, parsnips, carrots & others; selection and storage; nutritional, culinary, and medicinal characteristics & historical use of 20+ common backyard weeds; sources of seeds & commercial food products

Sampler of Wayside Herbs, A, Barbara Pond, pub. Greenwich House
– rediscovering old uses for familiar wild plants

Sauce It! Making Sauces, Purees and Gravies from Fruits and Vegetables, Garden Way Publishing
– make a puree of tomatoes, apples, or any fresh vegetable or fruit; use them fresh in 170+ recipes; best ways to preserve for future use

Simpler Life Cookbook, Frank Ford, pub. Harvest Press, Inc.
– living harmoniously in today's world; manual of preparedness for fulfillment and wholeness in use of resources

Six Ingredients Or Less, Carlean Johnson
– quick and easy recipes using six ingredients or less

Smoke and Spice, Cheryl Alters Jamison and Bill Jamison, pub. The Harvard Common Press
– 300 *real* barbecue recipes, for people who cook with smokers and other wood-burning equipment

Snack to Your Heart's Content, pub. Triad Communications, Inc.

Soup Alive, Eleanor S. Rosenast
– make vegetarian soups brimming with vital enzymes, vitamins, and flavor

Sourdough Cookin', Dean Tucker

Soya Bluebook, pub. Soyatech, Inc. — also: **Soya Bluebook Update**, pub. Soyatech, Inc.

Soybean Cookbook, Dorothea Van Gundy Jones, pub. Arco Publishing Co., Inc.
– practically everything about soybeans; 350 recipes

Soybean Granule Recipes, Alan Briscoe
– textured vegetable protein (TVP), convenient and tasty meat substitute; provide main meal dishes and snacks by using beef, bacon, chicken, or unflavored TVP

Soyfoods Cookery, pub. The Book Publishing Co.

Spirulina, Jack Joseph Challem
– nature's most perfect source of protein, minerals, and vitamins; recipes

Sprouter's Cookbook, for Fast Kitchen Crops, Marjorie Page Blanchard, pub. Garden Way
– grow sprouts; recipes; get fresh veggies from long-term storage

Spud Book, The, James Houston Turner, St. Martin's Press
– 101 ways to cook potatoes by a spud-lover; helps utilize potatoes in food storage program

Starting Over—Learning To Cook With Natural Foods, Polly Pitchford

Substituting Ingredients, Becky Sue Epstein and Hilary Dole Klein, pub. The Globe Pequot Press
– reference book for cooks who must plan for restricted diets or who want to whip up exotic fare but can't find the ingredients

Tasty Imitations, Barbara G. Salsbury, pub. Horizon Publishers, Inc.
– practical guide to meat substitutes

Tofu Cookery, Louise Hagler
– high protein, low-calorie, cholesterol-free, healthy recipes

Tofu Cookery, pub. The Book Publishing Co.

Turkey Cookbook, Rick Rodgers
– 138 new ways to cook America's best bird to the best advantage

TVP Cook Book, Dorothy R. Bates, pub. The Book Publishing Co.
– techniques for using quick-cooking meat substitute; recipes

Ultimate Soup Book, Julia Older and Steve Sherman, pub. A Plume Book
– 250 soups for appetizers, entrees, and desserts from ordinary supermarket ingredients; scratch recipes for using basic storage items (even though the book was not specifically written for this purpose)

Uncheese Cookbook, Joanne Stepaniak
– dairy-free cheese substitutes and classic "uncheese" dishes

Uninhabited Ocean Islands, Fisher
– 550+ recipes for basic garden and storage foods; simple, healthful recipes, many dating from early pioneer and Indian times; Grandma's home remedies and household cleaners

Uprisings, The Whole Grain Bakers Book, pub. The Cooperative Whole Grain Educational Association
– recipes for whole-grain cooking

Use-It-Up Cookbook, Lois C. Willand, self-pub.
– practical cookbook

Vegetarian Cooking Made Simple—Really!!, Susan Lapp, pub. Morris Press

Vegetarian Dining Using Tofu and Tempeh, Cheryl Townsley, pub. Pinon Press
– recipes with low-fat, sugar-free, and dairy-free options

Vegetarian Gourmet Recipes, Paul Bragg
– live better, longer, and cheaper with around-the-world recipes for nutritional power

Vegetarian Journal, pub. Vegetarian Resource Group

Cooking, Preparation, & Utilization of Foods Books (continued)

Venison—From Field to Table, John Weiss, pub. Outdoor Life Books – hunter's guide to preparing and cooking venison
Violets in the Kitchen, Dr. Peter Gail, pub. Goosefoot Acres Press – tasty violet flowers and greens; nature's richest source of vitamin C; 37 recipes for appetizers, salads, soups, ice cream and other desserts
Wheat for Man, Why and How, Vernice G. Rosenvall, Mabel H. Miller, and Dora D. Flack, pub. Bookcraft – standard in field of home storage; stone-ground wheat and how to use it
Wheatless Cooking, Lynette Coffey – gluten-free recipes
Whey Lover's Cookbook, The Secrets of Cooking with Swiss Whey D'Lite, pub. Country Fresh Farms Int'l., Inc. – 175+ recipes for making main dishes, soups, cakes, cookies, puddings, etc.
Whole Chicken Cookbook, Jim Fobel, pub. Ballantine Books, a division of Random House – 200 recipes for every part of chicken
Working a Duck, Melicia Phillips and Sean O. McElroy, pub. Doubleday – preparing duck, wild or farm-raised; 75+ recipes
Young Chef's Nutrition Guide and Cookbook, Carolyn E. Moore, PhD, RD, and Mimi Kerr and Robert Shulman, MD, pub. Barron's Educational Series, Inc. – especially for kids; recipes for beginners, intermediates and advanced junior chefs; nutritional information parents wish they'd known; for kids (and adults!) who want to utilize basic foods for improving and maintaining good healthy eating habits

When you find errors, please address the correct data to:
Doc@DoctorPrepper.com

Doctor Prepper

I. Medicine and Health

This category includes books about alternative and complementary techniques, aromatherapy, beauty aids, chiropractic, dental, homeopathy, enzymes, exercise, family health and first aid, fasting, folk remedies, herbalism, hydrotherapy, low-fat foods, macrobiotics, Oriental therapy, pain control, reflexology, and relaxation.

Chart 27–10
Conventional Medicine & Alternative Health Books

10 Essential Herbs, pub. HOHM Press
A New Day in Healing!, Valerie Seeman Moreton, ND, pub. Kalos Publishing
– pierce symptoms to expose the cause; resolving all types of conditions; support healing the body, renewing the mind, and living in the spirit
A Search for Wellness, pub. Hampton Roads Publishing Co.
Acquiring Optimal Health, pub. Hampton Roads Publishing Co.
Advanced Treatise in Herbology, Dr. Edward Shook, pub. Trinity Press
Alternative Medicine Yellow Pages, pub. Future Medicine Publishing, Inc.
Alternative Medicine—the Definitive Guide, pub. Future Medicine Publishing, Inc.
American Medicinal Plants, Charles F. Mills, pub. Davis Press
Amish Folk Remedies For Plain and Fancy Ailments, William R. McGrath
An Introduction to Young Living Essential Oils and Aromatherapy, D. Gary Young, ND Aromacologist, pub. Essential Press
– subtle, volatile liquids distilled from plants; essential oils and their importance to well-being; how they work in the body; chemistry of essential oils; use and application; treating diseases and conditions
Anti-Aging Manual—The Encyclopedia of Natural Health, pub. Information Pioneers, PO Box 7, South Woodstock CT 06267
– complete and intense information about the natural, complementary, and alternative modalities of healing
Are You Confused?, pub. Health Plus Publishers
Are You Poisoning Your Pet?, pub. Nature's Publishing, Ltd.
Aromatherapy Book—Applications and Inhalations, The, pub. New Age Creations
Aromatherapy Guide, (1ˢᵗ Ed.), Susan Hollick, pub. Vencom Publishing
– directory of aromatherapy products, essential oil suppliers, distributors, and associations
Aromatherapy, pub. Herbal Bodyworks
Aromatherapy, pub. Prentice-Hall
Aromatherapy—Complete Guide to the Healing Art, Kathi Keville and Mindy Green, pub. The Crossing Press
– information on aromatherapy as a science; material for using essential oils for cooking and body care products
Aromatherapy—The Essential Beginning, D. Gary Young, ND Aromacologist, pub. Essential Press Publishing
Attention Deficit Disorder, Polly Grissom, self-pub. Grissom Publishing
– natural methods for treating A.D.D. and Lupus; simple solutions for diets and all-natural methods to lessen effects of two misunderstood and mis-diagnosed conditions; experienced with herself and her own children; recipes for meals and dishes to help manage symptoms
Ayurveda and Aromatherapy, pub. Lotus Light Publications
AyurVeda, Chandrashekhar Thakkur, pub. Ancient Wisdom Publications
Back to Eden Cookbook, pub. Back to Eden Books Publishing Co.
Back to Eden, Jethro Kloss, pub. Lifeline Books
– classic guide to herbal therapy; gaining health using herbs, roots, and barks; herbal medicine, natural foods, and home remedies
Bantam Medical Dictionary, pub. Bantam Books
– layman's medical dictionary
BCH Miracle Foods Cookbook
– anti-oxidant rich vegetables and fruits that help you lose weight, fight disease, and slow aging
Be Your Own Doctor, Anne Wigmore
Becoming Vegetarian, pub. The Book Publishing Co.
Beginning Treatise in Herbology, Dr. Edward Shook, pub. Trinity Press
Better Health with Food Reflexology, pub. Ingham Publishing, Inc.
Biological Transmutations, Louis Kervran, pub. Swan House Publishing
Blended Beauty, Philip B., 10-Speed Press
– botanical body care using products from the kitchen; creator of Philip B. Hair and Skin Care line reveals many of his secrets—Oregano Hair De-tangler, Chocolate-Pumpkin Conditioning Hair Milk, and Cucumber-Parsley Facial Toner
Book Of Kuzu, Shurtleff and Aoyag
– Kuzu is more revered than ginseng in Japan for its medicinal qualities
Book Of Oriental Diagnosis, Kushi
– advanced book on the art of Oriental diagnosis
Botanical Influences on Illness, Melvyn R. Werbach and Michael T. Murray, pub. Third Line Press

Conventional Medicine & Alternative Health Books (continued)

Cardiologist's Painless Prescription for a Healthy Heart and a Longer Life, Joe D. Goldstrich

Childhood Diseases, John R. Christopher, pub. Christopher Publications

Clinical Pearls in Nutrition and Preventive Medicine, Kirk Hamilton, pub. IT Services

---

Colon Health Handbook, The, pub. Emerald Publishing Co.

Complete and Up-to-Date Fat Book, pub. Avery Publishing Group

Complete Home Healer, Angela Smyth
– treatment for 300 common health problems

Complete Home Health Advisor, pub. Woodland Publishing

Complete Illustrated Holistic Herbal, David Hoffmann, pub. Element Books
– reference for beginning herbal medicine; 200+ herbs described with pictures; parts used, constituents, actions and preparations and dosages

Complete Medicinal Herbal, The, Penelope Ody, pub. Dorling Kindersley, Inc.
– practical guide to the healing properties of herbs; 250+ remedies for common ailments from respiratory problems and digestive concerns to allergic conditions and varicose veins; full-color photographs of 120+ medicinal herbs

Complete Natural Health Encyclopedia, The, pub. Global Health, Ltd.

Conquer Stress, pub. KRS Edstrom

Cooking For Healthy Healing, Linda Rector-Page, ND, PhD, pub. Healthy Healing Publications, Inc.
– diets and recipes for alternative healing, healthy, fast, easy and delicious; companion and sequel to *Healthy Healing*

Creating Your Own Cosmetics—Naturally, Nikolaus J. Smeh, pub. Alliance Publishing
make-your-own skin care book; resources for all ingredients; comprehensive table of cosmetic chemicals causing adverse reactions

Crude Black Molasses, Byril Scott
– bio-available iron & other benefits of blackstrap molasses

Defeat Pain, pub. KRS Edstrom/Get Motivated

Dental Specialist, US Army Training Manual
– manual for the chair-side dental specialist, heavily illustrated; covers all aspects of dentistry

Different Bodies Different Diets—The 25 Body Type System™ *Men's Edition;* and
Different Bodies Different Diets—The 25 Body Type System™ *Women's Edition,* Dr. Carolyn L. Mein, pub. VisionWare Press (for personal communication with Dr. Mein: PO Box 8112, Rancho Santa Fe CA 92067 ☎(888) 2MY-TYPE or ☎(619) 756-3704 🖳(619) 756-6933 🖳www.bodytype.com
– health and diet system based on 25 different body types, developed after 25+ years of research; each body type system has its own unique and easy-to-follow diet; basis of system is that every person has a dominant gland, organ, or system, thus requiring certain support foods; knowing your body type helps determine what nutrients and eating plan is right; books make it easy to identify your specific body type; which foods and food combinations are most nurturing for your body; understand how to get most from your ideal food plan; how to help others determine their body type

Digestive Wellness, pub. Keats Publishing, Inc.

Directory of the Dietary Supplements Industry, pub. ITCM

Discovering Homeopathy, Dana Ullman, pub. Homeopathic Educational Services

Dixie Datebook, pub. Total Health

Doctor's Book of Home Remedies for Children, Editors of Prevention Magazine
– from allergies and animal bites to TV addiction

Doctor's Book of Home Remedies Vol. II—Over 1,200 New Doctor-Tested Tips and Techniques, Sid Kirchheimer

Doctors Book of Home Remedies, editors of *Prevention Magazine,* pub. Rodale Press
– medical companion for effective and safe treatment of almost *any* health problem; 1000s of tips and technologies anyone can use to heal

Don't Drink Your Milk, Frank Oski
– frightening facts about homogenized & pasteurized milk

Dr. Heimlich's Home Guide to Emergency Medical Situations, Henry J. Heimlich, MD, with Lawrence Galton, pub. Simon & Schuster
– identify what may be wrong and give successful treatment

Dr. Whitaker's Guide to Natural Healing, pub. Prima Publishing

Drugs and Beyond, pub. Global Health, Ltd.

Ear Acupressure Chart, pub. Joy of Health

Edgar Cayce Home Medicine Guide, Edgar Cayce

Electrolytes—The Spark of Life, pub. Nature's Publishing, Ltd.

Encyclopedia of Alternative Health Care, Kristin G. Olsen, pub. Pocket Books
– introduction to new choices in healing; how each therapy works; risks and rewards; how to choose a treatment and practitioner

Encyclopedia of Aromatherapy, pub. Healing Arts Press

Encyclopedia of Natural Medicine, pub. Prima Publishing

Book Of Shiatsu, Goodman
– introduction to learning Oriental massage

Conventional Medicine & Alternative Health Books (continued)

Encyclopedia of Natural Remedies, pub. Woodland Publishing
Essential Ohsawa, Ohsawa – writings of the founder of Macrobiotics
Family First Aid and Medical Guide—Emergencies, Symptoms, Treatments—in the Home, on the Road, on Vacation, Dr. James Bevan, pub. Simon and Schuster – advice on equipping home medicine cabinet; life-saving techniques, emergency survival techniques; medical encyclopedia with illustrations
Family Medical Encyclopedia, Schifferes – translates medical terms into everyday form; symptoms, what to do next; danger signs of mental and physical illness
Feel Better Cookbook—Tasty Remedies For Common Ailments, Susan A. Skolnick, pub. Wings Books – guide to health when you are not feeling well
Flower Essences and Vibrational Healing, pub. Cassandra Press, Inc.
Folk Medicine, D.C. Jarvis, MD
Folk Remedies For Common Ailments, Anne McIntyre
Food Combining and Digestion, Steve Meyerowitz, pub. The Sprout House, Inc. – improve digestion; get more nutrition from what's eaten; herbs, exercises, techniques to increase flow of digestive juices; digestion times of common foods; theories of chemistry, frequency, quantity, rhythm, mastication; effects of stress on nervous system
Food Combining Made Easy, Herbert Shelton – avoid indigestion, stress and toxemia
Food Enzymes—The Missing Link to Radiant Health, pub. HOHM Press
Food Smart—Eat Your Way to Better Health, Cheryl Townsley, pub. Pinon Press – replace self-sabotaging eating habits, conquer stressful lifestyle, convert to health-conscious pantry; plan great meals; on a small budget, achieve long-term health; strategy for making permanent changes in eating habits and lifestyle; resources for getting what you need
Foods That Heal, pub. Avery Publishing Group
Foot Massage Chart, pub. Joy of Health
For Goodness' Sake, Terry Joyce Blonder, pub. Camden House Publishing, Inc. – creative low-fat cooking from former chef at the Pritikin Center in Philadelphia
Garden Flower Folklore, Laura C. Martin
Gem Elixirs and Vibrational Healing, Vol. 1, pub. Cassandra Press, Inc.
Ginger—Common Spice and Wonder Drug, pub. Herbal Free Press, Ltd.
Global Herb Manual, pub. Global Health, Ltd.
Grape Cure, The, pub. Ehret Literature Publishing Co., Inc.
Gray's Anatomy – even old editions, or reprints of the "classic" editions are worthwhile, text on human anatomy and physiology
Great Book of Hemp, pub. Inner Traditions Int'l. – environmental, commercial, and medicinal uses of the world's most extraordinary plant
Great Book of Hemp,The, pub. Inner Traditions, Int'l. – complete guide to the environmental, commercial, and medicinal uses of the world's most extraordinary plant
Guide to Essential Oils, pub. Herbal Bodyworks
Hand Massage Chart, pub. Joy of Health
Heal the Cause!, Valerie Seeman Moreton, ND, pub. Kalos Publishing – creating wellness in body, mind, and spirit to allow the body to contact its innate healing powers; for those committed to taking responsibility for their own health and happiness through a comprehensive approach to resolving all types of conditions
Healing Clay, The, Abehsera – amazing health benefits and applications of green clay
Healing Herbs—Ultimate Guide to the Curative Power of Nature's Medicines, Michael Castleman, pub. Rodale Press – a compendium about the 5,000-year history of herbal healing; user-friendly, objective herbal guide, reviewed by a medical doctor
Healing Ourselves, Muramoto and Abehsera – Kampo: use of Japanese medicinal herbs; medicinal tea formulations
Healing Power of Aromatherapy, Hasnain Walji, PhD, pub. Prima Publishing – for beginner; specific oils and essential oil remedies for variety of ailments
Healing Power of Essential Oils, pub. Lotus Light Publications
Healing Power of Garlic, Paul Bergner, pub. Prima Publishing – editor of *Medical Herbalism*; how to use garlic to optimize its health benefits
Healing Power of Ginseng and The Tonic Herbs, Paul Bergner, pub. Prima Publishing – editor of Medical Herbalism condenses the literature on ginseng
Healing Power of Grapefruit Seed, pub. Lotus Light Publications
Healing Power of Herbs, pub. Prima Publishing
Healing with Whole Foods—Oriental Traditions and Modern Nutrition, pub. North Atlantic Books and Frog, Ltd.
Health Foods Business, pub. PTN Publishing Group

Conventional Medicine & Alternative Health Books (continued)

Health from God's Garden, Maria Treben, pub. Wilhelm Ennsthalen Steyr
Health News Naturally, pub. Keats Publishing, Inc.
Health through God's Pharmacy, Maria Treben, pub. Wilhelm Ennsthalen Steyr
Healthy Healing—An Alternative Healing Reference, Linda Rector-Page, ND, PhD, pub. Healthy Healing Publications, Inc.   – author of many books, booklets, and articles about natural foods and healing
Healthy, Wealthy andWise—A Step-by-Step Plan for Success Through Healthful Living, pub. KRS Edstrom
Heinerman's Encyclopedia of Healing Herbs and Spices, pub. Prentice-Hall
Heinerman's Encyclopedia of Healing Juices, pub. Prentice-Hall
Hemp for Health, pub. Healing Arts Press
Herb Book, The, John Lust, pub. Bantam Books   – hundreds of herbs; line drawings, descriptions, growth ranges, parts used and uses; techniques of herbal medicine, appendices of cross-references to Latin botanical names; extensive index
Herb Companion, **The,** pub. Interweave Press, Inc.
Herbal Bible—The Family Guidebook To Herbal Home Remedies, Michael Weiner
Herbal Medicine, Rudolf Fritz Weiss, MD, pub. Beaconsfield Publishers, Ltd.   – translation of the 6th edition *of Lehrbuch der Phytotherapie;* established modern text in field of medical herbalism
Herbal Medicine, The Natural Way to Get Well and Stay Well, Dian D. Buchman, pub. Gramercy Publishing
Herbs and Aromatherapy for the Reproductive System, pub. New Age Creations
Herbs and Health, pub. American Botanical Council
Herbs For Health, pub. Interweave Press, Inc.   – catalog of books on alternative healing, videos, audio tapes and seminars
Herbs of Choice, and The Honest Herbal, Tyler, Varro
Herbs of Life—Health and Healing Using Western and Chinese Techniques, Lesley Tierra, pub. The Crossing Press   – encyclopedia of herbal information; many charts simplify understanding of herbal treatments
Herbs to the Rescue, Herbal First Aid Handbook, Kurt King, MH, pub. Higher Ground Publications   – utilize herbs as alternatives to medical first aid; complete information
Holistic Protocol for the Immune System, A, Scott J. Gregory, OMD, pub. Tree of Life Publications   – holistic treatment of immuno-suppression health problems
Home Chiropractic Handbook, Karl V. Holmquist, DO
Home Remedies Handbook—Over 1,000 Ways to Heal Yourself, Editors of Consumer Guide
Home Remedies, Ott Wolff   – herbal and homeopathic treatments for use at home
Home Remedies—Hydrotherapy, Massage, Charcoal, and Other Simple Treatments, A. and C. Thrash
Home Remedies—What Works, Gale Maleskey   – thousands of Americans reveal their favorite home-tested cures
Homeopathic First Aid, Marilyn Moore   – method of healing that uses safe, inexpensive, natural remedies for numerous afflictions and illnesses; clear, concise, easy-to-understand   treatments for most common ailments
Homeopathy—Frontier in Medical Science, Bellavite, pub. Homeopathic Educational Services
Honey and Health, Laurie Croft, PhD, pub. Thorsons Publishers, Ltd.   – nature's oldest healer; analytical and medical view of the aspects of honey as an alternative or natural medicine
How to be Your Own Doctor (Sometimes), Sehnert   – deciding whether you need a doctor
How to Get Well, pub. Health Plus Publishers
How to Keep Slim, Healthy and Young with Juice Fasting, pub. Health Plus Publishers
How-To Herb Book, Velma Keith and Monteen Gordon, pub. Mayfield Publications
Hypoglycemia—A Better Approach, pub. Health Plus Publishers
Illustrated Encyclopedia of Essential Oils, Julia Lawless, pub. Element Books, Inc.   – updated version; color photographs and accurate information
Indian Herbology of North America, Alma R. Hutchens   – Native Americans herbals; applications for today's society
Instant Vitamin-Mineral Locator, Hanna Kroeger
Jeanne Rose's Herbal Body Book., pub. New Age Creations
Joni Loughran's Natural Skin Care, pub. North Atlantic Books and Frog, Ltd.
Joy of Health—A Doctor's Guide to Nutrition and Alternative Medicine, Zoltan P. Rona, MD, MS, pub. Llewellyn Publications   – medical doctor discusses his differences with "established" medicine and provides information for alternative medicine
Jude's Herbal Home Remedies, Jude C. Williams, Master Herbalist, pub. Llewellyn Publications   – natural health, beauty and home-care secrets; herbal self-care for beginning or experienced herbalist

Conventional Medicine & Alternative Health Books (continued)

Juice Fasting and Detoxification, Steve Meyerowitz, pub. The Sprout House, Inc.
– guide to detoxification and self-healing; types of fasts: juices, water, and herb teas; how to begin and end them; pre-fast, post-fast diet; negotiating a healing crisis; colonics, enemas, liver flushes; how to fast while working; exercises, massage, and purifying water

---

Kava—Medicine Hunting in Paradise, pub. Healing Arts Press

Kitchen Pharmacy—A Book of Healing Remedies For Everyone, Rose Elliot and D. C. Paoli

---

Let's Eat Right to Keep Fit, Adelle Davis, pub. Harcourt Brace Jovanovich, Inc.
– nutrition determines how you look and feel; how you may be injuring your health by what you eat

---

Light, Radiation and You—How to Stay Healthy, pub. Devin-Adair Publishers Co., Inc.

Little Herb Encyclopedia, pub. Woodland Publishing

Live Longer, Live Healthier—The Power of Pycnogenol, pub. HOHM Press

---

Making the Transition to Macrobiotics, Heidenry
– guidance and advice for the change to a whole foods diet

Mastering Bach Flower Therapies—A Guide to Diagnosis and Treatment, pub. Inner Traditions Int'l.

Meals that Heal, pub. Healing Arts Press

Medical Botany, W. H. Lewis and M. P. F. Elvin-Lewis, pub. John Wiley and Sons
– careful examination of the pharmacologic basis for medicinal properties attributed to many plants; field guide to the plants in your area; determine whether to use plants as supplement to your pharmaceutical supplies, which plants to use and how to use them

---

Medicinal Plants of the Mountain West, Michael Moore, pub. Museum of New Mexico Press

---

Merck Manual of Diagnosis and Treatment, pub. Merck
– diagnostic medical book, heavy on drug treatments rather than surgical interventions, new edition every 4-5years

---

Modern Day Plagues, Louise Tenney, MH

Modern Herbal, A, M. Grieve, pub. Penguin Books

More Chicken Soup and Other Folk Remedies, Joan and Lydia Wilen

---

Mrs. Reppert's Twelve Month Herbal, Bertha Reppert, pub. Remembrance Press
– 365 days of herbs with recipes, folklore, herbal healing, and gardening tips

---

Mucus-less Diet Healing System, pub. Ehret Literature Publishing Co., Inc.

Muramoto, ed. Michel Abehsera

Natural Healing for Babies and Children, pub. The Crossing Press

---

Natural Healing From Head To Toe, Aihara
– traditional Macrobiotic remedies

Natural Healing with Herbs, pub. HOHM Press

Natural Health Handbook, pub. Natural Health Publishing

Natural Health Shopper, pub. Natural Health Publishing

Natural Immunity, Sensei Muramoto
– theory of preventing AIDS and other degenerative diseases

Natural Remedy Book for Women, Diane Stein, pub. the Crossing Press
– a self-help guide to holistic health care and natural healing for women

---

Natural Resource—A Wealth of Wellness, pub. Natural Resources

---

Naturally Healing Herbs, Carly Wall, pub. Sterling Publishing
– making tonics of many types: blood purifying, strengthening, energizing, alterative, and renewing; how to make and how much to take

---

Nature's Medicine Chest, LeArta Moulton, pub. L M™ Publications
– 240+ full-color photos of medicinal and edible plants on 4"x 6" cards; 226 additional cards with home remedies and herb usage information

---

New Age Herbalist, Richard Mabey, pub. Macmillan Publishing Co.

New Age Journal Sourcebook, pub. New Age Journal

New Healing Yourself—Natural Remedies For Adults and Children, Joy Gardner

---

No More Ritalin—Treating ADHD Without Drugs, Dr. Mary Ann Black, pub. Kensington Publishing Corp.

Nontoxic, Natural and Earthwise, Debra Lynn Dodd, pub. Tarcher Publications

---

Northwind Farm's Herb Resource Directory, pub. Northwind Farm Publications

---

Nutrition Desk Reference, The, pub. Keats Publishing, Inc.

Nutritional Herbology, Mark Pedersen, pub. Pedersen Publishing

---

Nutritional Influences on Illness (1st **Ed.**)**,** Melvyn R. Werbach, pub. Thorsons

---

Nutritional Influences on Mental Illness, Melvyn R. Werbach, pub. Thorsons

---

One Minute Healer—500 Quick and Simple Ways to Heal Yourself Naturally, Dana Ullman

---

Opium Poppy—Botany, Chemistry and Pharmacology, L.D. Kapoor, PhD, pub. Haworth Press, Inc.
– everything about one of the oldest medicinal plants in history; cultivation and harvest

---

Optimal Wellness, Ralph Golan, MD, pub. Ballantine
– where mainstream and alternative medicine meet; alternative treatment for major health problems; A-Z self-care for 100+ common ailments; challenges "crisis/disease" orientation of modern medicine; describes comprehensive health care that heals the whole person

Conventional Medicine & Alternative Health Books (continued)

Our Earth Our Cure, Michel Abehsera, Ed. – benefits of French green clay to America; based on the writings of famous healer Raymond Dextreit
Over 50—Looking 30, pub. Nature's Publishing, Ltd.
Oxygen Therapies, Ed McCabe – medicinal uses of hydrogen peroxide, related technologies
Palm Therapy—Program Your Mind Through Your Palms, pub. Ultimate Mind Publisher
Physicians' Desk Reference (PDR), pub. Medical Economics – illustrated reference work about prescription drugs; identify any drugs
Planetary Herbology, Michael Tierra, pub. Lotus Press
Pocket Doctor, Bezruchka, MD – prevent illness or accident; when and how to treat yourself and others; when to get medical help
Pocket Guide to Ayurvedic Healing, pub. The Crossing Press
Pregnancy, Children and the Vegan Diet, pub. Gentle World, Inc.
Prescription for Cooking and Dietary Wellness, Phyllis A. Balch, CNC and James F. Balch, MD, pub. PAB Publishing, Inc. – quick reference charts combine nutritional healing and dietary wellness for speed healing
Prescription for Cooking—Astounding Health Cures Through Natural Foods, James F. Balch and Phyllis A. Balch, pub. PAB Publishing
Prescription for Dietary Wellness, pub. PAB Publishing, Inc.
Prescription for Nutritional Healing, James F. Balch, MD and Phyllis A Balch, CNC, pub. Avery Publishing Group, Inc.
Rational Fasting, pub. Ehret Literature Publishing Co., Inc.
Real Vitamin and Mineral Book—Going Beyond the RDA for Optimum Health, Shari Lieberman & Nancy Bruning, pub. Avery Pub. Group – nutritional supplements and their effective dosages; strengthening your immune system; what each vitamin, mineral, and newer supplement actually does in the body
Reiki—Way of the Heart, pub. Lotus Light Publications
Relax Mind and Body, pub. KRS Edstrom
Return to the Joy of Health, Zoltan Rona, MD, MS, pub. Alive Books / Canada – major health controversies; boost immunity & energy, take care of heart & circulatory system, improve digestion naturally; information on the brain, nerves & mind; women & complementary medicine; skin, hair & nails; muscles, joints & ligaments; healing foods & healing diets; recipes for better health and diet
Rodale Herb Book—How to Use, Grow, and Buy Nature's Miracle Plants, The, ed. William H. Hylton, pub. Rodale Press
RX Prescription for Cooking and Dietary Wellness, Phyllis A. Balch, CNC. and James F. Balch, MD, pub. PAB Publishing, Inc. – charts with healing foods, herbs, vitamins and juices using documented remedies for the speed healing of specific disorders
Say Yes to Life!, Leslie Nichols, self-pub. – whole herb catalog; brief chapters/treatises on many of man's ills; how natural products can cure all ills
School of Natural Healing, John R. Christopher, pub. Christopher Publications
Science of Herbal Medicine, John Heinerman, pub. Bi-World Publications
Scientific Validation of Herbal Medicine, The, Daniel B. Mowrey, PhD, pub. Comorant Books
Self-Healing Cookbook, The, Turner – best-selling macrobiotic cookbook
Sharks Don't Get Cancer, pub. Avery Publishing Group
Shiitake—The Healing Mushroom, Kenneth Jones, pub. Healing Arts Press – using this mushroom for protection against cancer and chronic fatigue
Sierra Club Guide to Safe Drinking Water, Scott Alan Lewis – description of contaminants; how to purify your water, possible illnesses if you don't; find out if water is safe, evaluate purification systems; merits of bottled water; ratings of 200 municipal water systems; 16 tables of information and analysis
Simple Guide to Nutritional Supplements, Sam Ziff and Micahel F. Ziff, DDS, pub. Bio-Probe, Inc. – removes confusion and mystery from field of nutritional supplementation; each nutrient is classified in easy-to-read standardized section: nutrient's role, deficiency symptoms, natural sources, synergists, depleting factors, therapeutic uses, and toxicity; index keyed to symptoms
Simply Vegan, pub. Vegetarian Resource Group
Smokers Guide to Vitamins and Health, pub. Vanguard Books
Spirit Medicine, Wolf Moondance, pub. Sterling Publishing – healing the spirit can lead to miraculous physical recoveries; Native American spirituality
Sports and Exercise Injuries, S. Subotnick, pub. Homeopathic Educational Services
Sprouting for Health in the 90's, pub. The Handy Pantry – build your immune system and detox your body; how sprouts can help you avoid the damaging effects of toxins in your body
Staying Healthy with Nutrition, The Complete Guide to Diet and Nutritional Medicine, Elson M. Haas, pub. Celestial Arts
Stopping the Clock, pub. Keats Publishing, Inc.

Conventional Medicine & Alternative Health Books (continued)

Super Foods—Allergy Recipes, Marjorie Hurt Jones, RN, pub. Mast Enterprises, Inc.   – for those with grain allergies; enjoy "lesser" grains and grain-like foods; not-too-complicated recipes; resources for grains
Super Healing Foods, pub. Prentice-Hall
Suppliers Directory of the Dietary Supplements Industry, pub. ITCM
Survival Medicine—Nature's Way, Marilyn Moore   – be physically prepared for any survival situation; heal yourself when doctor not available; preventive and curative techniques using backyard herbs, common fruits and vegetables; headaches and heartburn to serious bleeding and severe sickness
Swiss Nature Doctor's Home Treatment Of Common Ailments, Ann Vogel
Today's Herbal Health, pub. Woodland Publishing
Total Health, pub. Total Health
Traditional Home and Herbal Remedies, Jan De Vries
Turn Your Supermarket Into A Health Food Store, Lisa Messinger, pub. Pharos Books   – the brand name guide to shopping for a better diet; use food dollars on convenient packaged foods to improve your health
UnCook Book, Elton Baker, MD and Elizabeth Baker, pub. Elizabeth Baker Books   – all-raw food diet; original book in the Elizabeth Baker series
UnDiet Book, Elton Baker, MD and Elizabeth Baker, pub. Elizabeth Baker Books   – 7-phase weight-loss program that's not a diet; way of life that meets nutritional, spiritual, and physical needs
UnMedical Book, Elton Baker, MD and Elizabeth Baker, pub. Elizabeth Baker Books   – conquer disease, lose weight, avoid suffering and save money; natural healing for people who are sick or terminally ill; wellness guide for all
UnMedical Miracle—Oxygen, Elton Baker, MD and Elizabeth Baker, pub. Elizabeth Baker Books   – get enough oxygen in oxygen-poor world; *ozonated* (oxygenated) air and water; ozone/oxygen therapy to optimize health
Vegan Nutrition Pure and Simple, pub. Gentle World, Inc.
Vitamin and Herb Guide, **The,** pub. Global Health, Ltd.
Water Magic, Mary Muryn, pub. Fireside Books   – combinations of herbs and water; using herbs, homeopathic remedies, and flower essences
Weiner's Herbal, Michael Weiner, pub. Scarborough Press
Wellness Option, **The,** pub. Natural Resources
Wheatgrass—Nature's Finest Medicine, Steve Meyerowitz, pub. The Sprout House   – history, therapy, use, nutritional studies, and medicinal properties; compared to barley grass; anti-cancer benefits; detoxification methods; grow, cultivate, and juice; most effective methods for using; report on juicers
Where There Is No Dentist, Murray Dickson, pub. The Hesperian Foundation   – written for third world areas where there is minimum of tools, supplies and dentists; for emergency or survival situation; detailed drawings on making tools and taking care of dental problems
Where There Is No Doctor, David Werner, pub. The Hesperian Foundation   – take care of medical needs when far from medical help, manual for untrained individuals in establishing a health care system; oriented towards Latin America, but most information not geographically specific; information on diagnosis and treatment of various conditions without elaborate equipment; expanded update of 1st edition
Whole Food Facts—The Complete Reference Guide, pub. Inner Traditions Int'l.
Whole Foods Annual Source Book, pub. Whole Foods Magazine
Whole Foods, pub. Whole Foods Magazine
Why I Left Orthodox Medicine, pub. Hampton Roads Publishing Co.
Wilderness Medicine, William W. Forgey, MD   – complete instruction; goes well beyond first-aid information
Wise Woman Herbal for the Childbearing Years, Susan Weed, pub. Ash Tree Publications
Yeast Connection Cookbook, Crook   – combat yeast-related health problems
You Are All Sanpaku, translated and edited by William Dufty   – Zen macrobiotics with exposition of the art
Your Face Never Lies, Kushi   – introduction to Oriental diagnostic techniques using the shape of your face, your posture, skin tone, etc.
Your Guide to All Natural Anti-Aging Skincare, pub. Nature's Publishing, Ltd.
Your Herbal Medicine Chest, David Hoffman, BS, MNIMH, pub. Keats Publishing, Inc.   – 21 therapeutically valuable herbs that help in dealing with everyday health problems
Zen Macrobiotics, Ohsawa   – book that started the *Zen* macrobiotic movement

J. Home Management, Budgeting, and Organizing

This category includes books about living on less, self-reliance, and self-sufficiency; financial planning, insurance, money management, real estate, savings, and tax havens; bartering, cleaning, making money, self-employment, and simplification.

Chart 27–11
Home Management, Budgeting, & Organizing Books

101 Things To Do 'Til the Revolution, Claire Wolfe
– ideas and resources for self-liberation, monkey-wrenching and preparedness; generalities to precise instructions, these helpful hints are thought-provoking and sometimes humorous; if you are serious about being more self-sufficient in preparation for a major societal change
72-Hour Family Emergency Preparedness Checklist, Barry G. and Lynnette B. Crockett, pub. Barry Crockett
– assemble a quality, inexpensive 72-hour kit for each family member
A Place Called Simplicity, Claire Cloninger
– simple living for those who are serious about simplifying their life
Age of Inflation, Hans Sennhok, pub. Western Islands Publishers
– scholarly work dealing with causes of inflation, the federal reserve system, and monetary stability in our modem society
Alpha Strategy, The, John A. Pugsley
– financial self-defense; putting your savings into your home, food, clothing, and other consumables; investing in *real* goods to protect wealth
Art and Science of Dumpster Diving, John Hoffman
Backwoods Home Anthology—3rd Year, editors of Backwoods Home Magazine
– compilation of most of the bi-monthly articles for the 3rd year of publication
Backwoods Home Anthology—4th Year, editors of Backwoods Home Magazine
– compilation of most of the bi-monthly articles for the 4th year of Publication
Backwoods Home Anthology—5th Year, editors of Backwoods Home Magazine
– compilation of most of the bi-monthly articles for the 5th year of publication
Backwoods Home Magazine—Best of First 2 Years, Dave Duffy, Ed., pub. Backwoods Home Magazine
– best feature articles of *Backwoods Home Magazine's* initial 2 years; country living, gardening, alternative energy, jobs, self-sufficiency, etc
Bad Times Primer, C. G. Cobb
– survival on a budget; food storage, survival training, energy production; learn about survival skills; resources for survival equipment
Becoming Self-Sufficient with Dollars and Sense, Bruford S. Reynolds
– become more self-sufficient; get out and stay out of debt; loan payments; keeping fit and more; get control of your life
Beginners Guide to Family Preparedness, Rosalie Mason, pub. Horizon Publishers, Inc.
– food storage, back to basics, and survival facts; information that can help any family be prepared for emergencies that may arise
Best of Cheapskate Monthly, Mary Hunt
Big Book of Secret Hiding Places, Jack Lugar
– concealment of "stuff"; what searchers seek; everything about something to hide or should be hidden; excellent theft-protection ideas
Bite of Independence Through Self-Sufficiency, A, Marlynn, Venecia, and Jenny Phipps and Jan Woolsey, pub. SSL, Inc.
– utilizing food storage on a daily basis; feed a family of 4 for as little as $10.00 per week; for the self-reliant or wannabe; enjoy being prepared and living from storage fare; simplify your lifestyle and improve your life by utilizing your food storage; save money on your food budget
Build Your Ark! How to Prepare for Self-Reliance in Uncertain Times...Book I: Food Self-Sufficiency, Geri Guidetti, pub. The Ark Institute
– one-stop solution to learning how to grow a self-sufficient garden organically; how to provide your family food security
Buying Produce, Jack Murdich, pub. William Morrow
– understand selection, buying, and utilizing produce
Can You Trust a Tomato in January?, Vince Staten, pub. Simon and Schuster
– what's in grocery-store food and how some food products came to be
Cheap Eating—How To Feed Your Family Well and Spend Less, Pat Edwards, pub. Upper Access Books
– pinch pennies, improve nutrition, cut costs, & shop effectively for best foods at lowest prices; save money & have what you want to eat
Cheap Tricks—100s of Ways You Can Save 1000s of Dollars!, Andy Dappen, pub. Brier Books
Cheaper and Better Homemade Alternatives to Store Bought Goods, Nancy Birnes, pub. Shadow Lawn Press, Inc.
Cheapskate Monthly Book, The, Mary Hunt, pub. St. Martin's Press
Choose to Reuse, Nikki and David Goldbeck
Common Sense Economics, John Pugsley, pub. California Common Sense Press
– what the small investor can do to stay abreast of widening inflation on all fronts in order to protect family wealth today and in future

Home Management, Budgeting, & Organizing Books (continued)

Complete Book of Self-Sufficiency, John Seymour, pub. Faber and Faber, Unlimited   – foremost British survivalist author discusses how to be self-sufficient
Consumer Survival Book, The, Marvin Bittinger
Crisis Investing, Douglas R. Casey, pub. Harper and Row   – opportunities and profits in the coming great depression; investor's manual covering the inevitability of depression, the causes of economic failure; what will happen to stocks, bonds, real estate, insurance, collectibles, gold, gold stocks, silver, and overseas investing
Cut Your Bills in Half, Rodale Press
Eat Healthy for $50 a Week, Rhonda Barfield   – how to feed your family nutritious, delicious meals for less
Eating Cheap, Ragnar Benson   – eat and survive on $5 or less per week, even if you live in the city; cheap recipes to save you a lot of money fast
Food Finds—America's Best Local Foods and the People Who Produce Them, Allison and Margaret Engel, pub. HarperCollins Publishers   – 400 of the best small businesses making all-American foods; reflects ethnic idiosyncrasies and traditions of America's regional fare
From Pantry to Table, Marlena Spieler, pub. Addison-Wesley Publishing Co., Inc.   – get organized, prepare a shopping list, and set up a basic, intermediate, or advanced pantry
Frugal Mind, The, Charlotte Gorman, pub. Nottinham Books   – 1479 money saving tips for surviving the 1990's
Garage Sale Magic! How to Turn Your 'Trash' into Cash Simply and Easily!, Michael Williams
Garage Sale Mania! How To Hold A Profitable Garage, Yard, Or Tag Sale, Chris Stevenson
Garage Sales For Profit and Fun!, William C. Stratas
Getting Started in the Underground Economy, Adam Cash   – learn the do's and don'ts; wide range of topics covered
Go Underground and Save, Rickman and Bennett
Good Life, The, Helen Nearing
Good Work—A Guide for the Perplexed, E. F. Schumacher
Great Living in Grubby Times, Don Paul   – by author of *The Green Beret's Guide to Outdoor Survival*
Guerrilla Capitalism, Adam Cash   – first how-to-do-it book on the underground economy; make money in the underground economy; practice true free enterprise; for those serious about the underground economy
Hard Money Book, Steven Becknor, pub. Capitalist Reporter Press   – placing dollars in more inflation-proof investments; set up, manage, and deal with alternatives in today's fluctuating markets
How To Barter, David W. London, pub. Comstock Trading Co.   – alternatives to money for getting what you want
How To Become Financially Successful By Owning Your Own Business—A Step-by-Step Guide to Independence and Profit, Albert J. Lowry, pub. Simon and Schuster Publishing   – buying decisions, finding bargains, evaluating opportunities, income statements, the paperwork involved, money management, and many tips on running a successful operation
How to Bury Your Goods, Eddie the Wire   – for hard-core individualists who don't trust banks—or anybody; burying valuables and defeating those who look for them; when and how to bury goods and properly protect them
How to Do Business Off the Books, Adam Cash   – know secrets of the underground economy and keep your underground income "off the books"
How to Get Off the Fast Track, M. M. Kirsch
How to Hide Almost Anything, Krotz   – ideas about hiding small items in your home, in false panels, cabinet fronts, etc.
How to Hide Anything, Michael Connor   – hide cash, self-protection weapons, etc., in your home; construct dozens of hiding places for jewelry & survival supplies; 100+ drawing
How To Live Cheap But Good, Martin Poriss
How to Live on Almost Nothing and Have Plenty, Janet Chadwick
How To Live On Nothing, Joan Ranson Shortney, pub. Doubleday and Co.   – make do with what you have at your disposal
How to Prepare for the Coming Crash, Robert L. Preston   – steps to take now so you can live comfortably in a bad situation, due to a depression, strike, power loss, disaster, or being unemployed
How to Profit from the Next Great Depression, Dr. John L. King   – highly-respected economic historian shows step-by-step why a depression is inevitable; protect yourself and profit in the years ahead
How To Prosper During The Coming Bad Years, Howard J. Ruff   – course in personal and financial survival; soon to be re-printed

Home Management, Budgeting, & Organizing Books (continued)

How To Run a Small Business (4th Ed.), J. K. Lasser, pub. McGraw-Hill Books – all important aspects of operations from basic buying/starting up decisions to financing, management, records control, taxes, & selling
How To Save Money On Just About Everything, William Roberts, pub. Stebor Publications – hundreds of ways to save on large or small purchases for individuals, families and small businesses
How to Start and Operate a Mail-Order Business, Julia L Simon, pub. McGraw Hill Books – possibilities of mail-order, methods of setting up and operating business, calculating costs, legal, tactical, and functional options
How to Succeed In Your Own Business, William R. Park and Sue Chapin Park, pub. John Wiley and Sons – finding, buying, and running a small business operation; techniques, economics, and principles of money management
How To Successfully Manage Real Estate in Your Spare Time, Albert J. Lowry, pub. Simon and Schuster – management strategy, securing accounts, operating methods, financial tracking, pitfalls of property management, and wise investing
How to Survive Hard Times, Fred E. Jayne – budget resources effectively by planning ahead with a garden and food reserves
Miserly Moms, Jonni McCoy – wonderful book with practical steps for living well on a limited budget
Saving Money Any Way You Can, Mike Yorkey – how to become a frugal family helpful book with lots of practical suggestions
Simple Living, Debi Simple, self-pub. Simple Pleasures Press, PO Box 941, Auburn WA 98071 – easy, practical money-saving tips, ideas and resources
How to Survive Without a Salary—Coping in Today's Inflationary Times, Charles Long, pub. Sterling Publishing Co. – reducing needs to ditch the 9-5 lifestyle; second-hand sources (including 'trash'), auctions, barter/swap, & frugal attitude and philosophy
How to Want What You Have—Discovering the Magic and Grandeur of Ordinary Existence, Timothy Miller, PhD, pub. Henry Holt – accepting, and recognizing attributes and problems already owned; how the pursuit for more causes many problems; frugal life style
How You Can Become Financially Independent By Investing in Real Estate, Albert J. Lowry, pub. Simon and Schuster – strategic planning and decision-making for tapping into real estate options, buying and selling, and manipulating markets
How You Can Use Inflation To Beat The IRS, B. R. Anderson, pub. Harper and Row Publishers – legal ways to keep your money to yourself and find tax-exempt wealth; protection for profits in gold, silver, precious stones, and other hard money investments; primer on bartering; planning manual
Inflation Swindle, Emest J. Oppenheimer, pub. Prentice-Hall Press – classical perspectives on inflation; who is responsible in today's society; background reader for better understanding of inflation crisis
Inflation-Proofing Your Investments, Harry Browne, pub. Warner Books – investment principles in times of inflation; equity & dollar investments; avoiding taxes; creating a portfolio for today's economy
Invisible Crash, James Dines, pub. Ballantine Books – protecting the position of your money in times of runaway inflation
Leftover Gourmet, Patricia Rosier and Jessica L. Weiss, pub. Wings Books – preserving ingredients and buying the right foods less often
Live Rich When You're Not, Rebecca Greer
Living Cheap, Larry Roth
Living Cheaply with Style, Earnest Callenbach, pub. Ronin – improve your quality of life while spending less; food, housing, clothing, children, health, etc.; analyze your needs
Living More With Less, Doris J. Longacre, pub. Herald Press
Living on a Shoestring, Mike Edelhart
Living On Flood Plains and Wetlands—A Homeowner's High-Water Handbook, Maureen Gilmer, pub. Taylor Publishing Co. – navigate the maze of flood insurance programs, emergency procedures, and unique problems of lowland living; simplifies complex issues of wetland regulation; National Flood Insurance Programs
Living the Good Life, Helen Nearing
Living Well on Practically Nothing, Edward H. Romney – advice on how to get by with minimum money
Loving and Leaving the Good Life, Helen Nearing
Mark Skousen's 30-Day Plan To Financial Independence, Jonathan D. Pond, pub. Laissez Faire Books – 1001 ways to cut your expenses
Mary Ellen's Best of Helpful Kitchen Hints, Mary Ellen Pinkham, pub. Warner Books, Inc. – save time, trouble and money in shopping, cooking, serving and cleaning; reduce your stress levels around the kitchen
Miserly Moms—Living On One income In A Two-Income Economy (1st Ed.), Jonni McCoy, pub. Full Quart Press
Money Makeover—The Cheapskate Monthly Book, Mary Hunt
Money Saving Strategies for the Owner/Builder, Robert L. Roy, pub. Sterling Publishing Co., Inc.
Mother Earth News Guide to Self-Reliant City Living, **The,** pub. Mother Earth News – gardening, energy, transportation, food, livestock, health, home business and community
Mother Earth News Handbook of Home Business Ideas and Plans, The Mother Earth News Staff, pub. Bantam Books, Inc. – first-person articles of various at-home business ventures

Home Management, Budgeting, & Organizing Books (continued)

Moving to A Small Town, Wanda Urbanska and Frank Leverig, pub. Simon & Schuster
– complete how-to for those contemplating a move to rural America; for the country-bound

Muddling Toward Frugality, Warren Johnson

National Green Pages, pub. Co-op America
– yellow pages for people and the planet

Never Throw Out a Banana Again, Darcie Sanders and Martha Bullen

Not **For Packrats Only,** Don Aslett
– evaluate "stuff" and what it's costing to hang onto it

Parenting For The First Time—Raising Your Child To Be The Best He Or She Can Be, Dale Olen, PhD

Penny Pincher's Almanac—Handbook for Modern Frugality, Dean King

Penny Pinching Hedonist—How to Live like Royalty with a Peasant's Pocketbook, Shel Horowitz

Penny Pinching, Lee and Barbara Simmons

Place Called Simplicity—The Quiet Beauty of Simple Living, Claire Cloninger, pub. Harvest Press, Inc.

Plain and Simple, Sue Bender
– living among the Amish

Poisons In Your Food, Ruth Winter, MS, pub. Crown Publishers, Inc.
– dangers you face and what to do; review of America's diet and every aspect of the food service industry by award-winning science writer and author of numerous consumer dictionaries about food additives, cosmetics, cancer-causing agents, etc.

Price Waterhouse Book of Personal Financial Planning, Stanley H. Breitbard and Donna Sammons Carpenter, pub. Henry Holt
– money management; personal finance planning, investment strategies, debt management, insurance, tax planning, company benefits, retirement nest eggs and estate planning

Ready or Not!—A Practical Guide to Preparedness, Robert Bowden, Spencer-Barrus Publishers, Inc.
– compilation of newsletters; emergency preparedness, money, taxes, insurance, travel, education, and much more

Rodale's Book of Hints, Tips and Everyday Wisdom, Carol Hupping, Cheryl Winters Tetreau, and Roger B. Yepsen, pub. Rodale Press
– 1100+ tips on health, food, fitness, car care, home energy, the workshop and more

Saving Money Any Way You Can, Mike Yorkey, self-pub.

Secret Guide to Computers, Russ Walter

Self-Reliant Living, Dr. James McKeever and Mrs. Jeani McKeever, Omega Publications
– provide for yourself now and when you retire; be independent of fragile distribution service systems; good for beginning homesteader; references and resource listings

Self-Reliant Workbook, Jeani McKeever, Omega Publications
– companion to *Self-Reliant Living*; loose-leaf binder contains information about being self-reliant; how accomplished by author

Sell What You Sow, Eric Gibson
– grower's guide to successful produce marketing

Shopper's Guide to Natural Foods, editors of the East West Journal, pub. Avery Publishing
– guide to buying and preparing foods for good health; determine natural food by reading labels; categories of natural foods available

Simple Living, Frank Levering and Wanda Urbanska

Simple Living—One Couple's Search for a Better Life, Frank levering and Wanda Urbanska, pub. Viking Penquin
– how two southern California fast-trackers gave it all up for the country life

Simplify Your Life, Elaine St. James

Simply Ready—A Complete Guide for Provident Living and Personal Preparedness (1st Ed.), Terri Johnson, pub. MTJ Publishers
– planning; suggestions for basic food storage, food preservation, gardening, outdoor cooking, survival, soapmaking, etc.

Skills for Simple Living, ed. Betty Tillotson, pub. Hartley & Marks
– compilation of best articles in *The Smallholder* (Canadian homesteading magazine); essentail for real homesteaders

Survival Bartering, Duncan Long
– survive when bartering becomes necessary; good insurance for future

Tightwad Gazette I and II, Amy Dacyczyn
– selected issues of newsletter on cutting expenses

Tightwad Gazette, Amy Dacyczyn, a.k.a. The Frugal Zealot, pub. Villard Books
– thrift as a viable alternative lifestyle; save your money, time, environment; tips, tricks, strategies, recipes, & crafts for the tightest budget

Too Busy To Clean, Patt Barrel
– 500+ simple ways to make housecleaning easier

Un-Jobbing—The Adult Liberation Handbook, Michael Fogler, pub. Free Choice Press
– freedom from earning a paycheck; reclaim lifestyle/alignment with personal values; tools to change one's life & do what you really want

Voluntary Simplicity, Duane Elgin

Wealthy Procrastinator, Henry Cimmer

Working for Yourself—How to Be Successfully Self-Employed, Geoff Hewitt, pub. Rodale Press
– experiences of 100+ self-employed people

Your Money or Your Life—Transforming Your Relationship with Money and Achieving Financial Independence, Joe Dominguez and Vicki Robin, pub. Penguin Books

K. Light, Heat, and Power

This category includes books about alternative power and fuels technology: alcohol stills, alternative fuels, alcohol fuel, solar power, water power, wind power, and wood stoves.

Chart 27–12
Light, Heat, & Power Books

Appropriate Technology Sourcebook, PO Box 5453, Stanford CA 94039 ☎(800) 648-8043
– environmentally sustainable living, products, information and systems; reviews more than 1000 titles on up-to-date practical information about today's technology; guide to practical books for village and small community technology

Automotive Engineering Publications, pub. Burgess Publishing Co.
– convert your car to run on alcohol fuel

Brown's 1st Alcohol Fuel Cookbook, Michael Halsey Brown, pub. T.A.B. Books

Brown's Alcohol Motor Fuel Cookbook, Michael Halsey Brown, pub. Desert Publications

Complete Battery Book, Richard A. Perez., TAB Books, Inc.
– storage batteries illustrated for the layman; explains all types of batteries: lead acid, ni-cad, Edison cells, primary cells, methods, and machines to charge; using batteries effectively; inverters; energy management; and new battery technologies; formulae and conversion factors

Consumer Guide to Home Energy Savings, Alex Wilson and John Morrill

Convert Your Car To Alcohol, Keat B. Drane, pub. Love Street Books

Forget The Gas Pumps, Jim Wortham, pub. Love Street Books
– make your own fuel

Fuel Alcohol, How to Make It, How to Use It, James R. Ross, pub. St. Martin's Press

Heaven's Flame—Guidebook for Building Solar Cookers, pub. Home Power Magazine

How To Make Your Own Alcohol Fuels (1st Ed.), Larry W. Carley, pub. TAB Books, Inc.

Independent Home—Living Well With Power from the Sun, Wind, & Water, *(A Real Goods Independent Living Book)*, Michael Potts
– lessons on using energy better; harvest every electron, teaspoon of water, and therm of heat; prepare for the final fossil fuel energy crisis; phantom loads, free energy sources, and small habit changes to help "on-the-gridders" reduce their energy bills by 30– 60%

Introduction to Solar Energy for Scientists and Engineers, An, Sol Wieder
– reprint of 1982 edition

Makin' It On The Farm, Micki Nellis, pub. American Agriculture News
– alcohol fuel, the road to independence

Making Alcohol Fuel, Lance Crombie, pub. Rutan Publishing
– recipe and procedures

Making Moonshine Fuel, Ozzie McCoy, pub. Love Street Books

Making Your Own Motor Fuel, With Home and Farm Alcohol Stills, Fred Stetson, pub. Garden Way Publishing

Moonshine Motorfuel—Practical Fuel-Alcohol Handbook, Tom Hamn, self-pub.
– make it and use it

Mother Earth News Alcohol Fuel Handbook, pub. Mother Earth News

New Electric Vehicles—A Clean and Quiet Revolution, pub. Home Power Magazine

New Solar Electric Home, Joel Davidson, pub. Warner Books
– materials for building or rebuilding structures; use construction tools

New Woodburners Handbook
– safe, healthy, and efficient woodburning; select right stove for your needs

Passive Annual Heat Storage, John Hait and The Rocky Mountain Research Center [available from Whole Earth Access]
– using polyethylene and insulation to maintain constant year-round temperature in underground house

Producing Your Own Power—How to Make Nature's Energy Sources Work For You, Carol Hupping Stoner, ed., pub. Rodale Press

Secrets of Warmth, Hal Weiss

Survival Scrapbook #3—Energy, Stefan A. Szczelkun
– energy from variety of sources—solar, wind, fires, water, heat, electricity generation, animal power, bio-fuels, and methane from wastes

Vehicle Modification For Alcohol Use, pub. National Technical Information Service

Woodstove Cookery—At Home On The Range, Jane Cooper
– buying, setting-up, cleaning, and enjoying a woodstove in your home

Your Affordable Solar Home, Dan Hibshmann, Sierra Club Books

When you find errors, please address the correct data to:
Doc@DoctorPrepper.com

L. General, Experiential, and Spiritual

This category includes books about attitudes, body energy, dangers, healthy living, philosophy, human potential, spiritual insights, and successful living subjects.

Chart 27–13
General, Experiential, & Spiritual Books

Adventures in Simple Living, Rich Heffern
– creation-centered spirituality

Ageless Body, Timeless Mind, Deepak Chopra, MD
– quantum alternative to growing old; mind/body medicine; dramatically shape the aging process by creating new perception of aging; harness the power of awareness; experience timelessness

Awakening Spirits, Tom Brown

Bulletproof Privacy, Boston T. Party
– how to live hidden, happy, and free!; learn how to travel discreetly, relocate and reappear, not leave a paper trail, use the mail privately, buy and sell without a trace, make encrypted phone calls, and become invisible to databanks

Celestine Prophecy, James Redfield, pub. Warner Books, Inc.
– an adventure story exploring the heightened perception of the way our lives move forward—seemingly chance events occur at just the right moment, bringing us *just the right individuals*—thus our lives are suddenly sent off in new and important directions

Creating Covenant Communities, Robert J. Spear
– relocate with other patriots; form a community for self-reliant living

Food and Water—Threats, Shortages and Solutions, Bernard S. Cayne and Jenny E. Tesar

Good-Bye April 15th!, Boston T. Party
– how to legally opt out of the IRS system; legal aspects of taxation and the agency of government that abuses the nation

Hologram of Liberty, Kenneth W. Royce (a.k.a. Boston T. Party)
– the Constitution's shocking alliance with Big Government; how the Constitution was purposely left weak; discussion of how 3 peaceful solutions could be utilized to prevent the imminent insurrection now fomenting

LifeBalance, Linda and Richard Eyre, pub. Ballantine books, div. Random House, Inc.
– achieve priority balance, attitude balance, and goal balance in all areas of life

Mutant Message Down Under, Marlo Morgan, pub. MM Co.
– American & her adventures with an Australian aboriginal tribe on walkabout; what she learned from them & how this information applies to life

Positive Living and Health, Editors of Prevention Magazine, pub. Rodale Press
– nutrition to neuroscience, brain/body healing and mental empowerment

Quest, The, Tom Brown, Jr., pub. Berkley Books

Search, The, Tom Brown

Small Is Beautiful, E. F. Schumacher, pub. Harper and Row
– what to do about our culture diverging from our spiritual needs; economics as major source of errors; causal factors

Spiritual Properties of Herbs, pub. Cassandra Press, Inc.

Subtle Energy, John Davidson, MA, pub. The C. W. Daniel Co., Ltd.
– subtle energies (higher levels of energy beginning just beyond our normal perceptive abilities); role energies play in natural economy & healing

Tenth Insight, James Redfield, pub. Warner Books, Inc.
– sequel to *Celestine Prophecy;* another insight into other dimensions

Tracker, The, Tom Brown, Jr., pub. Berkley Books

Vibrations, Owen Lehto, pub. Nutritional Research Center
– positive and negative vibrations and how they affect health

Vision, The, Tom Brown, Jr., pub. Berkley Books

Votescam: The Stealing of America, James H. Collier and Kenneth F. Collier, pub. Victoria House Press
– discussion of the need to return to simple counting of the ballots without computers and other means that can be rigged, indicts Attorney General Janet Reno; non-fiction detective story

We Had Everything but Money—Priceless Memories of the Great Depression, pub. Country Books
– told in their own words by strong people; what it was like when banks closed and hearts opened

World Hunger—Twelve Myths, Frances Morre Lappe

You and the Police, Boston T. Party
– if you've ever been intimidated by the police, or didn't know how or when to stand your ground, or defended bogus traffic stops and tickets, checkpoint interrogation, intrusive questioning, needless arrest, or nasty roadside searches, this book will help you avoid the unpleasantness of dealing with the authorities

You Are Your Child's First Teacher, Rohima Baldwin
– enhance your child's development

You Can Predict Your Future, Tom Brown

M. "Country Wisdom"

The Country Wisdom series of books and booklets published by **Storey Communications, Inc.** provide answers for most activities around the home or homestead. There are more than 100 volumes with expert advice on country living and more information is available at http://www.storey.com.

When you find errors, please address the correct data to:
Doc@DoctorPrepper.com

PREPAREDNESS PRESS

Preparedness Publishers, Presses, Booksellers, & Catalog-Order Resources

The following alphabetical listing identifies the available publisher information for the books recorded in **Charts 27–2** through **27–14.** Refer to those charts for specific book titles. Titles and publisher information have been separated to save space. Note: publishers are listed by country of origin. Call your local library, bookseller, or use the Internet to locate many of the books you find of interest.

Associated with the written entries of these presses, publishers, and vendors you will also find names of other books and publications that are not found in **Charts 27–2** through **27–14.** These preparedness books resources may be able to act as "libraries" and help you procure, through their own inventories or research, some of the older books mentioned in the previous charts or other books not listed here.

Chart 27–15
Publishers, Presses, Booksellers, & Catalog-Order Resources

Canada
Canadian Beekeeping, Box 128, Oronon ON LOB 1MO
Vencom Publishing, PO Box 59007, Mississauga ON L4T 4J1 ✉*hollick@informamp.net*
Alternate Press, The, *(attn: Wendy Priesnitz, Editor)* RT. 1, St. George ON N0E 1N0 ☎/🖨(519) 448-4001 – publisher of books on organic gardening, healthy eating, wellness, homeschooling, home business, energy-efficient housing, voluntary simplicity, socially responsible business, the environment, eco-travel; alternative energy sources, and more
Cloudburst Press, 3661 W. Broadway, Vancouver BC V6R 2B8 ☎(604) 739-1771 – Canadian publisher for homesteaders
Albert Whiting, self-pub., A. Whiting, Cargill ON
Alive Books, 7436 Fraser Park Dr., Birnaby BC V5J 5B9 ☎(604) 435-1919 or (800) 663-6597 🖨(604) 435-4888 or (800) 661-0303 *(toll-free call from anywhere in North America)* – publisher and distributor of natural health and nutrition books in Canada and US
Institute for Nutritional Research, #81075, World Trade Centre, Toronto ON M5J 2V3 ☎(416) 969-3163 – publications, audio, and videos regarding health and wellness practices and issues
Boiling Kettle, The, PO Box 479, Wolfville NS B0P 1X0 🖳*www.netroute.net/altpress* ✉*kettle@glinx.com* – *online* mail-order store grew out of a search for a more inspiring way of life
Global Health, Ltd., 409 Estate Dr., Sherwood Park AB T8B 1L9 ☎(403) 449-1346 🖨(403) 449-4371
Canadian Organic Growers, Inc., Box 116, Collingwood ON L9Y 3Z4 ☎(705) 444-0923 or (613) 258-4045
England
C. W. Daniel Co., Ltd., 1 Church Path, Saffron Walden, Essex CB10JP
United States
10-Speed Press, PO Box 7123, Berkeley CA 94707
9-HEART-9 Publishing, Dallas TX
A. I. Root Co., PO Box 407, Medina OH 44256
Acres, U.S.A., PO Box 8800, Metairie LA 70011 ☎(504) 889-2100 🖨(504) 889-2777 – voice for eco-agriculture; books and videos about specialty crops, organics, healthy living, natural health, and more
Adventures Unlimited, One Adventure Place, PO Box 74, Kempton IL 60946 ☎(815) 253-6390 🖨(815) 253-6300 – publishes catalog of books for alternative science, philosophy, religion, alternative health, extra-terrestrial, & conspiracy
Alfred A. Knopf, Inc., New York NY
Alliance Publishing, PO Box 399, Garrisonville VA 22463
Alternative Power, Renewable Energy Center, 701 S. Main, Westby WI 54667 ☎(608) 634-2984 – renewable energy center; mail order company; free *"Catalog and Design Guide"*
Amazing Reprints, Box 5931, Austin TX 78763 – mail-order homesteading and preparedness books
America West Distributors *(attn: Grant)*, PO Box 3300, Bozeman MT 59772 ☎(406) 585-0700 🖨(406) 585-0703 – books for the independent thinker and the self-reliant
American Academy of Dissident Sciences, 13002 San Vicente Blvd., Los Angeles CA 90049 ☎(310) 458-6338 – non-profit organization for the dissemination of alternative and politically-incorrect knowledge, blacklisted by the *Illuminati* in the last 100 years and expunged from the public—especially academic libraries and databases in the best *Orwellian* tradition of 1984

Publishers, Presses, Booksellers, & Catalog-Order Resources (continued)

American Agrarian, Rt. 1 Box 229, Caledonia MN 55921 – preparedness books and information
American Botanical Council (ABC), PO Box 201660, Austin TX 78720 ☎(512) 331-8868 🖷(512) 331-1924
American Herb Association, PO Box 1673, Nevada City CA 95959 ☎(916) 265-9552
American Homestead Mercantile Co., PO Box 1354, Bonsall CA
American Phytopathological Society, 3340 Pilot Knob Rd., St. Paul MN 55121 ☎(612) 454-7250
American Products Company, 6750 SW 111th Ave., Beaverton OR 97008 ☎(505) 672-7502   ☎(503) 672-7104 🖳 *www.american-products.com* ✉*apc@american-products.com*
American Red Cross, call your Local Red Cross for information
American Society of Civil Engineers (ACSE), 345 East 47th St., New York NY 10017
Anchor Press/Doubleday, Garden City NY *(pub. in Canada)*
Angie's Country Books, 69 Elm St., Shelburne Falls MA 01370 – preparedness books and information
ANR Publications, University of California, 6701 San Pablo Ave., Oakland CA 94608 ☎(510) 642-2431
Antique Hardware Store, The, 1 Matthews Ct., Hilton Head SC 29926 ☎(800) 422-9982 – mail-order preparedness products
Appropriate Technology Sourcebook, The, PO Box 5453, Stanford CA 94039 ☎(800) 648-8043 – environmentally sustainable living; products, information, and systems; reviews more than 1000 titles on up-to-date   practical information about today's technology; guide to practical books for village and small community technology
Arco Publishing Co., Inc., 219 Park Avenue *S.*, New York NY 10031
Aristera Publications, PO Box 3764, Redwood City CA 94064
Ark Institute, The, PO Box 364, Monkton MD 21111 ☎(410) 343-0990 🖳www.arkinst.com ✉*arkinst@concentric.net*
Armor Plated Books, 5 Grogans Park Dr. #110, The Woodlands TX 77380 – avoid IRS attacks! learn about: independent contractors; clean, defensible tax records, & tax audits; secret IRS files; sur-   viving arbitrary gov't.
Aspen Cabin Wilderness Bookstore, 5038 Sixth Ave., Kenosha WI 53140 ☎(800) 397-6584 – books on wilderness living, survival, gardening, homesteading, hunting, fishing, construction, and other lifestyle subjects
Atomic Books, 1018 North Charles Street, Baltimore MD 21201 ☎(410) 625-7955 🖷(410) 625-7945 – excellent walk-in shop or mail-order catalog order for "weird" books and off-beat titles; also top-selling titles and Publi-   cations
Avery Publishing Group, 120 Old Broadway, New Hyde Park NY 11040 ☎(800) 548-5757 or (516) 741-2155 🖷(516) 742-1892
Back to Eden, pub. Back to Eden Books Pub. Co., PO Box 1439, Loma Linda CA 92354 ☎(909) 796-9615 🖷(909) 796- 9746
BackHome Books, PO Box 70, Hendersonville NC 28793 ☎(704) 696-3838 or (800) 992-2546
Backwoods Home Books, 29545 Ellensburg Avenue, Gold Beach, OR 97444 – bookstore of preparedness, homesteading, survival, and country living books
Backwoods Home Magazine, 29545 Ellensburg Avenue, Gold Beach, OR 97444
Badger Books, 518 W. 4th Street, Neillsville WI 54456 ☎(715) 743-4533 – publications for those on a tight budget; *"Feasting for Less than 50 Cents"* and *"The Soup Kitchen"*
Ball Corporation, Consumer Affairs, Muncie IN 47302
Ballantine Books, Inc., div. Random House Publishing, 200 Park Avenue, New York NY 10166
Barron's Educational Series, Inc., 250 Wireless Blvd., Hauppauge NY 11788
Barry Crockett, self-pub., PO Box 1601, Orem UT 84059
Beaconsfield Publishers, Ltd., Beaconsfield
Beginning of Wisdom, The, 54 Plumb Hill Washington CT 06793 – preparedness books and information
Bernardin, Inc., Evansville IN
Better Life Publishing, *(attn: Lana J. Chandler, Owner/Editor),* 3002 Penna Ave., Charleston WV 25302 ☎(304) 343- 0206 – directory of 115 sources of free recipes; $3.00
Betterway Publications, PO Box 219, Cozet VA 22932
Bio-Probe, Inc., PO Box 608010, Orlando FL 32860 ☎(407) 290-9670 or (800) 282-9670
Blue Dolphin Publishing, Inc., PO Box 1920, Nevada City CA 95959 ☎(800) 643-0765

Publishers, Presses, Booksellers, & Catalog-Order Resources (continued)

Bluestocking Press, PO Box 1014, Placerville CA 95667 ☎(800) 959-8586 or (916) 621-1123 📠(916) 642-9222
– catalog/resource for materials to challenge students' thinking and encourage children to think and discuss pertinent issues

Bobbs-Merrill Co., Inc., 4300 W. 61st Street, Indianapolis IN

BOHICA Concepts, PO Box 546, Randle WA 98377 ☎(360) 497-7075
– distributor of politically incorrect Publications; something to offend everyone…

Book Publishing Co., The, PO Box 99, Summertown TN 38483 ☎(615) 964-3571 📠(615) 964-3518

Bookcraft Publishers, Inc., 1848 Printers Row, Salt Lake City UT 84119 ☎(801) 972-6180

Bookfinder, 209-C Piedmont, Blacksburg VA 24060 ☎(800) 846-4231
– out-of-print book service; find old preparedness books; send or call for information

Books Plus, 468-L Glen, Fruit Heights UT 84034
– preparedness books and information

Books, PO Box 327, Prairie Grove AR 72753
– preparedness books and information

Brier Books, PO Box 180, Mountlake Terrace, Seattle WA 98043 ☎(800) 356-9315

Cache Valley Dairy Association, Smithfield UT 84335

California Farm Fresh Directory, pub. Community Alliance with Family Farmers (**CAFF**)

Camden House Country Life Books, Box 1004 Ferry Rd, Charlotte VT 05445 ☎(800) 344-3350

Cassandra Press, Inc., PO Box 150868, San Rafael CA 94915 ☎(415) 382-8507

Ceadrebrae Retreat, RT. #2, Tiverton ON N06-2T0

Cedar Fort, Inc., 925 N. Main, Springville UT 84663 ☎(801) 489-4084 📠(801) 489-9432
– publisher / distributor of preparedness books

Cedar Graphics, 311 Parsons Lane, Hiawatha IA 52233 ☎(800) 243-5242

Ceres Press, PO Box 87, Woodstock NY 12498 ☎(914) 679-5573 ✉*dgoldbeck@aol.com*

Charles C. Thomas, Publisher, Ltd., 2600 S. 1st St., Springfield IL 62794 ☎(800) 258-8980 📠(217) 789-9130
– books about police and their jobs: criminals, violence, survival thinking, coping with crises, survival tactics, protecting themselves against the unlawful, terrorism, and other issues

Chelsea Green Publishing Co., *(attn: Stephen Morris, Publisher),* 205 Gates Building, White River Junction VT 05001 ☎(800) 639-4099 or (802) 295-6300 📠(802) 2956444
– publisher of books and videos for sustainable living: gardening, food, shelter, energy, and nature

Chesbro Press, PO Box 1326, Morgan Hill CA 95038 ☎(408) 779-5930

Chicago Review Press, Inc., 814 North Franklin, Chicago IL 60610

Chicot Press, Box 5198 Atlanta GA 30355 (800) 888-6088

Christian Family's Organizer *(attn: G. Harris),* ☎(507) 433-4912

Christian Light Education, PO Box 1212, Harrisonburg VA 22801 ☎(540) 434-0750 📠(540) 433-8896
– full Christian homeschool curriculum for grades 1-12; library books for homeschoolers

Christian Patriot Association, PO Box 596, Boring OR 97009 ☎(503) 668-4941
– bookstore offering hard-to-find books: Christianity, alternative health, conspiracies, IRS, survival, and more!

Christian Research, PO Box 385, Eureka Springs AR 72632 ☎/📠(501) 253-7185 ✉**clibrary @ipa.net**
– books, tapes, & videos about preparedness, food production, & survival subjects

Christopher Publications, PO Box 412, Springville UT 84663 ☎(800) 372-8255 or (801) 489-4254
– audio cassettes selected from the popular radio show *"A Healthier You"*; collection of Dr. John Christopher's herbal seminar videos, books, and lectures, other books and booklets about herbal treatments, and his **Natural Healing Newsletters**; books by other authors of note in the nutrition, herbal medicine, herb identification and reference, preparations, botany and horticulture, reflexology and iridology, and other herbal reference books and video instructional materials

Common Sense, PO Box 668, Lake Stevens WA 98258 ☎(206) 335-3765
– *Crisis in Our Courts,* lawyer Steve Bertsch; *One Nation Under God,* Lawrence D. Blanchard; *Economic Solutions* exposes unlawful money

Community Alliance with Family Farmers (CAFF), PO Box 464, Davis CA 95617 ☎(916) 756-8518 📠(916) 756-7857

Complete Guide to Exercise Videos, The, Collage Video Specialties, Inc. 5390 Main St. NE, Minneapolis MN 55421 ☎(800) 433-6769
– collection of over 250 exercise and fitness videos; ratings by participants

Cookbook Shoppe, *(attn: Vicki Tate)* 302 E. 200 North, Manti UT 84642 ☎(801) 835-8283
– books, tapes and videos on foods, food storage, and preparedness; books on food storage, food utilization, preparation, and preservation

Publishers, Presses, Booksellers, & Catalog-Order Resources (continued)

Cooperative Extension Service, Kansas State University, Manhattan KS 66506 ☎(913) 532-6170

Cooperative Grocer, PO Box 597, Athens OH 45701 ☎(800) 878-7333 or (614) 592-1912 🖷(614) 594-4504

Country Books, PO Box 990, Greendale WI 53129 ☎(800) 558-1013

Country Store Books, Box 6025 #57, Columbia MO 65205
– free catalog for LSASE; books about the country way of life, especially good on exotic animals and draft horses

Country Wisdom Bulletins, div. Storey Communications, Inc., Schoolhouse Rd., Pownal VT 05261 ☎(802) 823-5811 or (800) 827-8673 ☎(800) 865-3429

Countryman Press, PO Box 175, Woodstock VT ☎(800) 245-4151 05091
– preparedness books and information

CPA Book Publishers, pub. Christian Patriot Association, 33838 SE Kelso Rd. #6, Boring OR 97009
– Publications for Christian political education; catalog contains 1000's of Publications

Cross-Current Publishing, 333 North 425 East, Alpine UT 84004 ☎(801) 756-2786 🖷(801-492-3393 www.cross-current.com or www.crisispreparednesshandbook.com.
– publisher of *Crisis Preparedness Handbook: A Comprehensive Guide to Home Storage and Physical Survival*, 2nd ed., by Jack A. Spigarelli

Crossing Press, The, PO Box 1048, Freedom CA 95019 ☎(800) 777-1048 or (408) 722-0711 🖷(800) 549-0020 ✉*crossing@aol.com*
– books about herbal medicine, natural health, healthy lifestyle; women's interests; aging; new age and native American; cookbooks; contemporary issues; poetry and photography

Crown Publishers, Inc., 201 East 50th Street, New York NY 10022

Crown/Turtle Bay Books, div. Crown Publishers, Inc., 201 East 50th Street, New York NY 10022

Dadant and Sons, Inc., 51 *S.* Second Street, Hamilton IL 62341

Daniel Hill, PO Box 49, Dixmont ME 04932 ☎(207) 234-2315

Davidson's, PO Box 588, Marshall AR 72650
– homesteading/survival pamphlets

Deborah Marzek's Books, 3198 S. Peach St., Fresno CA 93725
– lifestyle books and information

Delta Press, PO Box 1625, El Dorado AR 71731 ☎/🖷(501) 862-9671 *order line:* (800) 852-4445
– books about ditch medicine, emergency medical situations, survival medicine, and medical care for disasters

Desert Publications, PO Box 1751, El Dorado AR 71731

Devin-Adair Publishers Co., Inc., 6 N. Water St., Greenwich CT 06830 ☎(203) 531-7755

Dial Press, The, div. Doubleday and Co., Inc., Garden City NY

Disability Bookshop Catalog, The, PO Box 129 Vancouver WA 98666 ☎(360) 694-2426
– books about traditional and alternative approaches to a variety of physical and mental disabilities

Don Boal Marketing, PO Box 236, **Curwensville** PA 16833 ☎(717) 236-1013
– distributor of preparedness books, videos, and audio publications; Patriot and Christian literature

Don Fallick's Books, Rt. 3 Box 72, Davenport WA 99122
– homesteader and author of quality how-to information about male-traditional homesteading skills; materials include: *A Rank Beginner's Guide to: Logging, Basic Building Materials; Easy Lifting with a Rope; Building A Safe; Wood-Fired Water Heater; Splitting Firewood; Getting Started in Blacksmithing;* series of guides to *Building a House-Heating Solar Greenhouse; A Pallet Fence; Colonial Shoulder Yoke*

Donald L. Fine, Inc., New York NY

Donna McKenna, self-pub., 106 Bedford Street, Statesboro GA 30458

Dorling Kindersley, Inc., 232 Madison Ave., New York NY 10016

Doubleday and Co., Inc., div. Bantam Doubleday Dell Publishing Group, Inc., 666 Fifth Ave., New York NY 10103

Drelwood Communications, Inc., PO Box 149, Indianola WA 98324 ☎(206) 297-2271
– publisher of the Elizabeth Baker series of books and videos about raw foods and oxygen in the restoration of health and disease treatment

DWM Communications, POB 87, Hanover MI 49241

Earthhaven Community, *(attn: Chuck Marsh),* 205 Jones Rd., Leicester NC 28748 ☎(704) 526-2634

Earthwood, 366 Murtaugh Hill Road, West Chazy NY 12992 ☎(518) 493-7744
– organization run by experienced alternative building field; author, publisher, and distributor of books related to the alternative housing techniques, skills, and interests since 1981; books, videos, and plans for the novice or expert

Publishers, Presses, Booksellers, & Catalog-Order Resources (continued)

Eating Well Magazine and Books, PO Box 1001, Charlotte VT 05445 ☎(802) 425-3961 🖳(802) 425-3307 ✉*ewelledit@aol.com*
Ehret Literature Publishing Co., Inc., 19 Babcock Pl, Yonkers NY 10701 ☎(800) 527-8123 or (914) 376-1000 🖳(914) 376-1001
Element Books, Inc., PO Box 830, Rockport MA 01966
Elizabeth Baker Books, PO Box 149, Indianola WA 98342 ☎(206) 297-7789
Emerald Publishing Co., PO Box 11830, Reno NV 89510 ☎(702) 324-2624
Emporium, The, c/o Pilgrim Goose Hatchery, PO Box 95, Williamsfield OH 44093 – homesteading and survival pamphlets and products
Essential Press Publishing, PO Box 9282, Salt Lake City UT 84109 ☎(800) 763-9983
Eureka Resource, Box 53565, San Jose CA 95153 – homesteading and survival pamphlets; survival products; gardening, energy; backpacking, wildlife, survival; health, nutrition, medicine; crafts, tools, building methods; legal self-help
Exceptional Living, 300 Plaza Middlesex, Middletown CT 06457 ☎(800) 700-8869 – books, videos, and audio tapes for the terminally ill
Fairstone Press, PO Box 777, Lake Orion MI 48631
Family Preparedness Network, Inc., PO Box 118, Salt Lake City UT 84110 *(out of business)*
Family Resources, PO Box 1027, Corvallis OR 97339 ☎(503) 757-0028
Farrar, Straus and Giroux, Inc., 19 Union Square W., New York NY 10003
Fear Not Foundation, PO Box 403, Syracuse NY 13215 – **"knowledge replaces fear"**; the *Preparedness Papers* are the most comprehensive source of information on how to survive and prevail in any disaster; little-known preparedness secrets of how to protect yourself and your family in any emergency or disaster
Fireside Books, div. Simon and Schuster, Rockefeller Center, 1230 Avenue of the Americas, New York NY 10020
Firing Pin Enterprizes, Box 80696 Rt. C, Phoenix AZ 85060 ☎(602) 275-1623 🖳(602) 275-5954 🖳**www.firingpin.com** – books, manuals, booklets, and a host of other items; many titles are exclusive to *FPE*; specific information on the fabrication and/or conversion of weapons to full automatic and the construction of sound suppressors (silencers)—with a warning it's illegal now!
Focus Books, 94 Holmes Mill Rd., Creamridge NJ 08514 – homesteading and survival pamphlets and products
Food Marketing Institute, 800 Connecticut Ave. NW, Washington DC 20006
Food Place, The, PO Box 482, Provo UT 84603 ☎(801) 374-1858 or *toll-free* ☎(888) 554-3727
Foundation House Publications, 5569 North County Rd. 29, Loveland CO 80538
Fredericksburg Herb Farm, PO Drawer 927, Fredericksburg TX 78624
Free American Newsmagazine, The, 🖳 www.freeamerican.com – hundreds of hard-to-find conservative and Patriotic books in stock
Free Choice Press, PO Box 1027, Lexington KY 40588
Free Enterprise Society, 738 Shaw Ave. #205, Clovis CA 93612 ☎(209) 294-0665 – educational library for freedom; membership society for Constitutional, lawful taxes, privacy, and money issues; conducts seminars to help people learn about their heritage in America & overcome fear of government
Freedom and Liberty Foundation, PO Box 12619, Knoxville TN 37912
Future Medicine Publishing, Inc., 10124 18th St. #E, Puyallup WA 98371 ☎(206) 952-1130 🖳(206) 952-1129
Gamaliel, Box 1160, Why AZ 85321
Garden Way, div. Storey Communications, PO Box 445, Schoolhouse Rd., Pownal VT 05261 ☎(800) 441-5700 🖳(800) 865-3429 – growing, storing, or using food; for home gardeners, natural gardening enthusiasts or cooks concerned with healthful eating and living; major publisher of titles in the field of self-reliance
Garden-Ville, Inc., 7561 E. Evans Rd., San Antonio TX 78266
Gary Davis Co., c/o Kitchen Garden Co., Bountiful UT
Gentle World, Inc., PO Box 110, Paia HI 96779 ☎(808) 572-1560 🖳(808) 572-3522
GESCO, 254 SW Rogue River Ave., Grants Pass OR 97526 – mail-order "how-to" and lifestyle books
Globe Pequot Press, The, 6 Business Park Rd., Old Saybrook CT 06475

Publishers, Presses, Booksellers, & Catalog-Order Resources (continued)

Good Advice Press, (*attn: Marc Eisenson or Nancy Castleman*), Box 78, Elizaville NY 12523 ☎(914) 758-1400 ▤(914) 758-1475 *Info@GoodAdvicePress.com*
– publications for non-consumers who are trying to get ahead; publisher of tools for creating the life you want

Good Earth Books, 7400 Redwood Ave., Evansville IN 47720 ☎(812) 963-3960
– books for independent living at affordable prices; 100's of new, used, and out-of-print books and magazines on practical skills, homesteading, small farming, rural life, frugal living, food preservation, organic gardening, folk/herbal medicine, alternative energy/shelter, survival, and other self-sufficiency subjects

Good Earth Publications, RR 2 Box 1875, Green Creek Dr., Columbus NC 28722 ☎(704) 863-2288
– homesteading and survival pamphlets and products

Goosefoot Acres Press, (*attn: Peter A. Gail, PhD*), PO Box 18016, Cleveland Heights OH 44118 ☎(216) 932-2145 ▤(216) 932-2187
✉*petergail@aol.com*
– educational programs, Amish products and services, Publications about edible wild plants

Gramercy Publishing, New York NY

Grass Farmer's Bookshelf, The, PO Box 9607, Jackson MS 39286 ☎(800) 748-9808
– homesteading and survival pamphlets and products

Great Books Educational Supplies, 9797 W. Colfax Ave., Lakewood CO 80215 ☎(800) 555-1610 ▤(303) 274-0288
– homeschool supplies and curriculum, testing materials, library reference works, and more!

Grissom Publishing, PO Box 300295, Escondido CA 92030 ☎(888) 224-3438

Grosset and Dunlap, New York NY

Growing Edge, The c/o New Moon Publishing, PO Box 1027, Corvallis OR 97339 ☎(800) 888-6785 or (541) 757-8477 ▤(541) 757-0028 🖥www.teleport.com/~tomalex/GE.html ✉*talexan@peak.org*
– books, magazines, videos on hydroponics food growing and other innovative gardening and indoor growing

GSG and Associates, PO Box 6448, San Pedro CA 90734 ☎(310) 548-7267 ▤(310) 548-5802
– publisher of books about New World Order: *Goals 2000 Intelligence*

Hampton Roads Publishing Co., 134 Burgess Ln., Charlottesville VA 22902 ☎(804) 296-2772 ▤(804) 296-5096
🖥www.hamptonroadspub.com ✉*hrpc@mail.hamptonroadspub.com*

Hands-On Health Care Catalog, *Acupressure Institute*, 1533 Shattuck Ave., Berkeley CA 94709 (800) 442-2232
– catalog of books, videos, and audio tapes on acupressure

Handy Pantry, The, 2129 E. Cedar #3, Tempe AZ 85281 ☎(602) 967-4338 or (800) 735-0630 ▤(602) 921-4232 🖥 www.handypantry.com

Harcourt Brace Jovanovich, Inc., 757 Third Ave., New York NY 10017

Harder Supply, Rt. 1 Box 97, Shumway IL 62461
– mail-order homesteading and preparedness products

Harper and Row Publishers, Inc., 10 East 53rd Street, New York NY 10022

Harper Perennial, div. Harper Collins Publishers, 10 E. 53rd Street, New York NY 10022

Harvard Common Press, The, 535 Albany Street, Boston MA 02118

Harvest Press, Inc., PO Box 3535, Ft. Worth TX 76105

Hawkes Publishing, Inc. (*out of business,*), see **Spencer-Barrus Publishers, Inc.**

Haworth Press, Inc., 10 Alice St., Binghamton NY 13904

Hawthorn Books, Inc., 260 Madison Ave., New York NY 10016

Healing Arts Press, PO Box 388, Rochester VT 05767 ☎(800) 246-8648 or (802) 767-3174 ▤(802) 767-3726 ✉*orders@gotoit.com*

Health Plus Publishers, PO Box 1027, Sherwood OR 97140 ☎(503) 625-0589

Healthwise, Inc., PO Box 1989, Boise ID 83701

Healthy Healing Publications, Inc., 2715 Porter Street #206, Soquel CA 95073

Hearst Books, div. William Morrow and Co., Inc., 1350 Avenue of the Americas, New York NY 10019

Heartwood Publications, 5808 S. Pacific Coast Hwy. #14, Redondo Beach CA 90277
– homesteading and survival pamphlets and products

Henry Holt and Co., 115 W. 18th Street, New York NY 10011

Herb Bar, The, 200 W. Mary, Austin TX 78704

Herbal Bodyworks, c/oJeanne Rose, 219 Carl St., San Francisco CA 94117 ☎(415) 564-6785 ▤(415) 564-6799

Herbal Free Press, Ltd., 4 High St. #11, Brattleboro VT 05301 ☎/▤(802) 254-6142

Heritage Farming—The People's Farm and Stock Cyclopedia, Fairstone Press, PO Box 777, Lake Orion MI 48631

Publishers, Presses, Booksellers, & Catalog-Order Resources (continued)

Higher Ground Publications, PO Box 1045, Hamilton MT 59840

Hill House Publishing Co., Chapel Hill NC

HOHM Press, PO Box 2501, Prescott AZ 86302 ☎(800) 381-2700 ▤(520) 717-1779

Home Power Magazine—Bookstore, PO Box 520, Ashland OR 97520 ☎(916) 475-3179 or (800) 707-6585
▤(916) 475-0941🖳www.homepower.com/hp ✉*hp@homepower.org*
– books about energy-saving, self-produced heat, light and power systems

Homegrown Booklets, 67 Awosting Rd., Pine Bush NY 12566☎(914) 744-2245
– homesteading and survival pamphlets and products

Homeopathic Educational Services, 2124 Kittredge St., Berkeley CA 94704 ☎(510) 649-0294 ▤(510) 649-1955

Homestead Books, *(attn: John and Darlene Campbell),* Box 964, Poteau OK 74953 ☎(918) 647-7106
– books about self-sufficient living balanced with stewardship of the land; subjects include: backyard fish production, raising rabbits & tanning skins, rabbit recipes, plans for alternate shelter, housing small animals, & authentic Indian recipes

Hope and Allen Publishing Co., PO Box 926, Grants Pass OR 97526

Horizon Publishers and Distributors, Inc., 50 South 500 West, Bountiful UT 84010 ☎(801) 295-9451
– original publisher of many preparedness titles; many are still available

Hotline Printing and Publishing, PO Box 161132, Altamonte Springs FL 32716 ☎(407) 628-1377 ▤(407) 628-9935

Houghton Mifflin Co., 2 Park Street, Boston MA 02108

HP Books, Box 5367, Tucson AZ 85703 ☎(602) 888-2150 or (602) 288-2150

Huckleberry Books, 2220 W. Indiana, Evansville IN 47712
– mail-order "how-to" and lifestyle books

Hydroponic Society of America, Box 6067, Concord CA 94524 ☎(415) 682-4193

Ideals Publishing Co., Milwaukee WI

Illinois Extension Service #C1300, University of Illinois, **OACE** 69-R3 Mumford Hall, 1301 West Gregory Dr., Urbana IL 61801

Information Pioneers, PO Box 7, South Woodstock CT 06267
– author and publisher of **Anti-Aging Manual—The Encylopedia of Natural Health,** the complete information volume about natural, complementary, and alternative modalities of healing

Ingham Publishing, Inc., PO Box 12642, St. Petersburg FL 33733 ☎(813) 343-4811 ▤(813) 381-2807

Inner Traditions Int'l., One Park St., Rochester VT 05767 ☎(802) 767-3174 ▤(802) 767-3726

International Tesla Society, PO Box 5636, Colorado Springs CO 80931 ☎(719) 475-0918
– extraordinary science! Tesla technology, alternative (free) energy research, anti-gravity, medical alternative and previously suppressed information; the *International Tesla Society* is the best kept secret in science

Interweave Press, Inc., 201 E 4th St., Loveland CO 80537 ☎(970) 669-7672 or (800) 272-2193 ▤(970) 667-8317
✉*h4h@iwp.ccmail,compuserve*

IT Services, 3301 Alta Arden #3, Sacramento CA 95825 ☎(916) 489-4400 *(in CA)* or (800) 422-9887 ▤(916) 489-1710

ITCM, 25 Hanford Dr., Fairfield CT 06430 ☎(800) 643-2283 ▤(203) 255-3786

J. N. Townsend Publishing, 12 Greenleaf Dr., Exeter NH 03833
– mail-order "how-to" and lifestyle books

J. R. J. Enterprises, PO Box 29114, Oakland CA 94604
– mail-order "how-to" and lifestyle books

Javelin Press, Boston T. Party, 504 W. 24th St. #73P, Austin TX 78705
– **Good-Bye April 15th**, **Hologram of Liberty**, **Bulletproof Privacy**, &**You and the Police;** other books, videos, Tees, & Freedom products

JCL Books, c/o Ken Lietz, 353 Rockhurst, Bollingbrook IL 60440 (630) 739-7608
– books of all kinds; search service available

Jenkins Publishing, PO Box 607, Grove City PA 16127 ☎(814) 786-8209

John Birch Society, PO Box 8040, Appleton, WI 54913 ☎(414) 749-3783 or ☎(800) 341-1522 *order line*
– monthly Publication *The New American*; complete library of freedom materials

John C. Campbell Folk School, Rt. 1 Box 14-A, Brasstown NC 28902 ☎(800) 562-2440

John Wiley and Sons Publishers, One Wiley Drive, Somerset NJ 08875

Joy of Health, PO Box 2123, Chapel Hill NC 27515 ☎(919) 929-8672 ▤(919) 932-5200 ✉*efb95@aol.com*

Kali Press, PO Box 2169, Pagosa Springs CO 81147 ☎(970) 264-5200

Kalos Publishing, PO Box 270817, San Diego CA 92198

Kampong Publications, 1870 Sunrise Dr., Vista CA 92084 ☎(619) 726-0990

Publishers, Presses, Booksellers, & Catalog-Order Resources (continued)

Karen Oiler's Books, Box 33, Ash Fork AZ 86320   – mail-order "how-to" and lifestyle books
Kayo Fraser's Books, PO Box 330016, Gold Creek Rd., Gold Creek MT 59733 ☎(406) 288-3363   – mail-order "how-to" and lifestyle books
Keats Publishing, Inc., 27 Pine St., New Canaan CT 06840 ☎(203) 966-8721 ▤(203) 972-3991 ▯www.keats.com   ✉*publish@keats.com*
Kelly's Books, PO Box 574737, Orlando FL 32857   – mail-order "how-to" and lifestyle books
Ken Larson, pub. Rhema Publishing, ✉*keninga@aol.com*   – books about preparedness issues; problems and solutions
Kensington Publishing Corp., 850 Third Ave., New York NY 10022 ☎(212) 407-1500 ▤(212) 935-0699
Kerr Glass Manufacturing Corp., Sand Springs OK 74063 ☎(800) 323-2426
KRS Edstrom/Get Motivated, PO Box 8584, Universal City CA 91618 ☎(213) 851-8623 or (213) 851-8622   ▯www.audiobooks.com
L M™ Publications, PO Box 482, Provo UT 84603 ☎(888) 55-HERBS or ☎/▤(801) 374-1858   – publisher of LeArta Moulton's books and video publications: The Herb Walk Video, The Herb Walk Manual, The Amazing Wheat Book, The New Gluten Book, and Nature's Medicine Walk
Laissez Faire Books, 938 Howard #202, San Francisco CA 94103 ☎(415) 541-9780 ▤(415) 541-0597   ▯www.laissezfaire.org   – large selection of books on Liberty; monthly features on the most exciting and powerful titles available; philosophy, religion, politics, education, history, economics, science, and technology
Lancaster & Simpson, Ltd., 6292 Red Maple Lane, Lino Lakes MN 55014 ☎(612) 490-1132   – send **LSASE** for free catalog; out-of-print books of old-time ways of farming and gardening; subjects include: livestock, poultry, crops, homesteading, self-sufficiency, beekeeping, gardening, farming, etc.; many books are truly back-to-basics—pre-hi-technology
Lancaster's, Box 13636, Roseville MN 55113   – mail-order "how-to" and lifestyle books
Lancer Books, Inc., 1560 Broadway, New York NY 10036
Lan-Design Publications, 12202 East 203rd St., Raymore MO 64083
Lane Publishing Co., Menlo Park CA 94025
Latter-day Family Resources, 242 E. Southfield Rd., Spanish Fork UT 84660 ☎(801) 798-2106
LauraAnne J. Logar, self-pub., 17140 Oak Leaf Dr., Morgan Hill CA 95037
Lehman's, One Lehman Circle, Kidron OH 44636 ☎(330) 857-5757 ▤(330) 857-5785 ▯www.lehmans.com ✉*info@lehmans.com*   – books for simple, self-sufficient living; source for hard-to-find books on utilizing livestock, small-scale farming, homesteading, repairs, and maintenance to equipment and supplies from a past era
Lenon's Books, Box 455, Rochester MI 48308   – mail-order "how-to" and lifestyle books
Leslie Nichols, PO Box 510, Gainesville MO 65655 ☎(417) 679-4145 ▯(417) 679-3514
Let's Live Magazine, 320 N Larchmont Blvd. Fl. 3, Los Angeles CA 90004 ☎(213) 469-3901 ▤(213) 469-9597 ✉*letslive@caprica.com*
Library Builders, 11288-A San Juan St., Loma Linda CA 92354 ☎(909) 825-7207   – informative books revealing the New World Order; Health and global diseases, Religion; the economy, and control; learn protect yourself
Life Sprouts, PO Box 150, Paradise UT 84328 ☎(800) 241-1516   – books about sprouting and live food production
Lifetime Memories, 150 Monte Vista, Buckley WA 98321   – mail-order "how-to" and lifestyle books
Little Creek Bookshop, *(attn: Patrick and Rose Railey),* Route 1 Box 189C, Delmar DE 19940 ☎(302) 846-9930   – large assortment of affordable used books covering homesteading/simple living, gardening, farming, hunting/fishing, building/home construction, livestock, camping/outdoor skills, and nature essays
Little, Brown and Co., Boston MA
Live Free Int'l., *(attn: Jim Stumm, Owner),* PO Box 1743, Harvey IL 60426 ☎(312) 821-LIVE   – more than 25 reports/titles of self-reliance information

Publishers, Presses, Booksellers, & Catalog-Order Resources (continued)

Living Arts, 2434 Main St., Santa Monica CA 90405 ☎(800) 2-LIVING
– sources for mind and body processes

Llewellyn Publications, PO Box 64383, St. Paul MN 55164

Lotus Light Publications, PO Box 325, Twin Lakes WI 53181 ☎(414) 889-8561 🖹(414) 889-8591 ✉*santoshk@msn.com*

Lyons and Burford, New York NY

Macmillan Publishing Co., Inc., 866 Third Ave., New York NY 10022

Madison Herb Society, PO Box 8733, Madison WI 53708

Magic Mixes, 588 E. Park Drive, Elk Ridge UT 84651 ☎(801) 423-1991 ✉*magicmixes@Juno.com*

Malachite School and Small Farm, 8055 County Rd., 570 Pass Creek Rd., Gardner CO 81040

Marlene's Magic, PO Box 802, American Fork UT 84003 ☎(801) 756-6423

Marugg Co., The, PO Box 1418, Tracy City TN 37387
– mail-order homesteading and preparedness products

Mast Enterprises, Inc., 2615 N. Fourth Street, Coeur d'Alene ID 83814

Meals in Minutes, 2479 North 750 East, Provo UT 84604 ☎(801) 374-1858

Medical Economics Data, div. of Medical Economics Co., Inc., Oradell NJ 07649

Mel's Books, 1960 Harriman, Klamath Falls OR 97601
– mail-order "how-to" and lifestyle books

Merck Family Fund, ☎(301) 270-2970 Fax: (301) 270-2973 ✉*merck@igc.apc.org*

Metropolotian Museum of Art, The, New York NY

Michael Linden, Box 62, Ashland OR 97520 ☎(800) 746-7413
– publisher of *Sproutguide* and *Sproutchart*; *Cell-Tech* distributor

Michigan State University, Cooperative Extension Service, East Lansing MI

MicroTek Publishers, 8910 Sunset Ave. #H, Fair Oaks CA 96678 ☎(916) 966-7718 ☎(916) 966-7768

Mike Yorkey, self-pub. ☎(405) 336-9856

Mirro Corp, The., PO Box 409, Manitowoc WI 54220

Mischka Farm Books, N8246-A, Easterly Rd., Whitewater WI 53190 ☎(414) 473-5595
– mail-order "how-to" and lifestyle books

MM Co., PO Box 100, Lees Summit MO 64063 ☎(816) 246-6365

Mole Publishing *(attn: Mike Oehler),* Rt. 4 Box 618, Bonners Ferry ID 83805 ☎(208) 267-7349
– publisher of books and videos about alternative housing ; low-cost underground shelters; fall-out shelters

Morrow and Co., Inc., 105 Madison Ave., New York NY 10016

Mother's Bookshelf, c/o Sussex Publishers, Inc., 49 E. 21st St., Fl. 11, New York NY 10010 ☎(212) 260-7323 🖹(212) 260-7566
– book section of *Mother Earth News*; books about self-reliance, environmental, natural foods, gardening, natural remedies, cooking, home improvement, and country lifestyle

MTJ Publishers, 8020 Chestnut Hill Dr. SE, Olympia WA 98513

Natural Health Publishing, 17 Station St., Brookline Village MA 02147 ☎(617) 232-1000 🖹(617) 232-1572

Natural Meals In Minutes, PO Box 504, Edmond OK 73083 ☎(888) 232-6706 🖳www.NaturalMeals.com ✉*FasterBeans@worldnet.att.net*

Nature's Publishing, Ltd., PO Box 380361, Murdock FL 33938 ☎(941) 426-1929 or (800) 950-1929 🖹(941) 426-6871

New Age Creations, 219 Carl St., San Francisco CA 94117 ☎(415) 564-6785 🖹(415) 564-6799

New Age Journal, 42 Pleasant St., Watertown MA 02172 ☎(617) 926-0200 🖹(617) 926-5021 🖳www.newage.com/home/newage ✉*mc@newage.com*

New Age Publishing & Retailing Association (NAPRA), PO Box 9, Eastsound WA 98245 ☎(206) 376-2702
– retailers of metaphysical & *New Age* books, tapes & products; publishes *NAPRA Trade News* with information on new product releases

New American Library, Inc., The, 1633 Broadway, New York NY 10019

New Atlantean Resources *(attn: Nathan Wright),* 625 Galisteo Street, Santa Fe NM 87501 ☎/🖹(505) 983-1856
🖳www.new-atlantean.com/global ✉*global@ndw-atlantean.com*
– holistic products to stimulate thought, empower choices, and honor the freedom to live in harmony with others and the natural world

New Pioneer Hardware, PO Box 389164, Cincinnati OH 45238
– mail-order homesteading and preparedness publications

Publishers, Presses, Booksellers, & Catalog-Order Resources (continued)

Nitro-Pak Preparedness Center, 151 N. Main St., Heber City UT 84302 ☎(800) 866-4876
☎(435) 654-0099 ▤(435) 654-3860 🖳www.nitro-pak.com
– author and publisher of **The Five Deadly Enemies to Food Storage and How to Avoid Them;** producer of videos about preparedness and security: **Earthquake Preparedness (#9801), Fires and Personal Emergencies (#9803), Emergency Heat, Light and Cooking (#9804),** and **Severe Floods and Storms (#9808)**

Nitty Gritty Productions, PO Box 5457, Concord CA

North Atlantic Books and Frog, Ltd., PO Box 12327, Berkeley CA 94712 ☎(510) 559-8277 or (800) 335-2665 ▤(510) 559-8279

Northwind Farm Publications, Rt. 2 Box 246, Shevlin MN 56676 ☎(218) 657-2478 ▤(218) 657-2447 ✉*doliver@polaristel.net*

Nourishment for Life, 2210 N. 41st #A, Seattle WA 98103 ☎(206) 545-4325

Nutrisearch, 9201 Hwy G, Mount Horeb WI 53572 ☎(608) 832-4442 ▤(608) 832-4805 🖳**www.nutrisearch.com** ✉*csower@clearware.com*

Nutritional Research Center, PO Box 308, Keller WA 99140

Oasis Biocompatible Products, 5 San Marcos Trout Club, Santa Barbara CA 93105 ☎(805) 967-3222 ▤(805) 967-3229

Old and Out-of-Print Farming Books *(attn: Marvin Jager)*, Half Moon Pond, Box 241, Washington NH 03280
– used and out-of-print farming and country books, magazines, and periodicals

Omega Publications *(attn: Jeani McKeever, Editor,)* PO Box 4130, Medford OR 97501 ☎(541) 826-4512
– publisher of end-times information and preparedness books, audio tapes, and videos

Organic Gardening and Farming Magazine, c/o Rodale Books, Inc., 33 East Minor St., Emmaus PA 18098

Ortho Books, div. Chevron Chemical Co., Ortho Division, 200 Bush Street, San Francisco CA 94104

OttoGraphics, 80082 Maple City Rd. #B, Maple City MI 49664

Outdoor Life Books, div. Times Mirror Magazines, Inc., 380 Madison Ave., New York NY 10017

PAB Publishing, Inc., 610 W Main St., Greenfield IN 46140 ☎(317) 467-4666 ▤(317) 462-2232

Paladin Press, PO Box 1307, Boulder CO 80306 ☎(303) 443-7250 or (800) 392-2400 ▤(303) 442-8741
🖳**www.paladin-press.com** ✉*pala@rmii.com*
– publisher and distributor of the action library; books, videos, and audio cassettes for the survivalist; catalog of more than 650 action titles for dealers or consumers; books and videos about sometimes controversial subjects: guns, assault weapons, financial freedom, new ID and personal freedom, survival, knives and knife fighting, and more

Patriot Report, PO Box 437, Uniontown AR 72955 ☎(918) 498-3909
– books, videos, and audiocassettes about future gun confiscation and the encroachment of a One World Government

Pederson's Books, Rt. 1 Box 55, Aitkin MN 56431
– mail-order "how-to" and lifestyle books

Penguin Books, 375 Hudson St., New York NY 10014

Perigree Books, div. The Putnam Publishing Group, 200 Madison Ave., New York NY 10016

Permaculture Books, PO Box 65, Califon NJ 07830 ☎(800) 832-6285

Permaculture Institute, PO Box 156, Santa Fe NM 87504 ☎(505) 983-0663

Pharos Books, div. Scripps Howard Co., 200 Park Ave., New York NY 10166

Pinon Press, PO Box 35007, Colorado Springs CO 80935

Planetree Health Catalog, The, Planetree Health Resource Center at California Pacific Medical Center, 2040 Webster St., San Francisco CA 94115 ☎(415) 923-3681
– catalog of books, videos and audio tapes on a variety of topics relating to health

Playmore, Inc., div, Waldman Publishing Corp., New York NY

Pocket Books, 1230 Avenue of the Americas, New York NY 10020

Practical Cookbooks, 145 Malcolm Ave. SE, Minneapolis MN 55414 ☎(612) 378-9697

Prentice-Hall Press, 15 Columbus Circle, New York NY 10023

Prentice-Hall, 113 Sylvan Ave., Englewood Cliffs NJ 07632 ☎(800) 727-2047 ▤(201) 592-2950 🖳www.phdirect.com

Prescription Books for Health d.b.a. **PAB Publishing, Inc.,** 610 W Main St., Greenfield IN 46140 ☎(317) 467-4666 ▤(317) 462-2232

Prestige Books, Inc., 18 East 41st Street, New York NY 10017

Prevention Magazine Health Books, pub. Rodale Press, Emmaus PA 18098

Prima Publishing, 3875 Atherton Rd, Rocklin CA 95765 ☎(916) 632-4400 ▤(916) 635-4405
🖳**www.primaPublishing.com** ✉*kimt@primapub.com*

PTN Publishing Group, 445 Broadhollow Rd., Melville NY 11747 ☎(516) 845-2700 ▤(516) 845-7109

Publishers, Presses, Booksellers, & Catalog-Order Resources (continued)

Quest for the Best, PO Box 1775, Solana Beach CA 92075 ☎(619) 944-2934 or (800) 326-8589 – unique, uncommon books and products; **SASE** for free literature and information—and a $5.00 credit-voucher towards first purchase
Random House, New York NY
Reading Room, The, 264 S. Wabash, Wabash IN 46992 – mail-order "how-to" and lifestyle books
Real Goods, 555 Leslie St., Ukiah CA 95482 ☎(800) 762-7325 – publications for alternate and energy-efficient information
Rehoboth Ranch, 399-3400 Dr., Crawford CO 81415 ☎(303) 9213782
Remembrance Press, 120 S. Market Street, Mechanicsburg PA 17055
Research Technical Services, 3747 Quincy Ave., Ogden UT
Resource Publications, Provo UT
Rinehart and Winston, 383 Madison Ave., New York NY 10017
Robert Gear, Box 113, Greenfield MA 01302 ☎(413) 772-6576 – new and out-of-print books on responsible agriculture, livestock, poultry, gardening, and rural life
Rocky Ridge Enterprises, *(attn: Stephen J. Norling, Editor),* N2173 10th Ave., Montello WI 53949 ☎(608) 297-2199 – self-reliant booklets for the self-reliant; titles include: ***"Carp for Fun and Food", "Food for Survival", "The No-Chemical Survival Garden", "Sensible, Affordable Survival Living",*** and more
Rocky Top Publications, Stamford NY
Rodale Press, Inc., 33 E. Minor St., Emmaus PA 18098 ☎(610) 967-5171 📠(610) 967-8181 – wide range of books and a plethora of Publications by the premier publisher on various subjects about food preparation, gardening, organics, farming, cultivating, collecting, preparing, or utilizing it
Rodale Research Center, *(attn: Adele Weinberg),* RD #1 Box 323, Kutztown PA 19530 ☎(215) 683-6009
Safe-Trek Publishing, 90 Safe-Trek Place, Bozeman MT 59715 ☎(800) 424-7870 – publisher of Stephen Quayle's books about survival and preparedness: *Blueprint for Survival!* and *Breathe No Evil*
SAI Publishing, *(attn: John Sauer, Editor),* PO Box 140581, Irving TX 75014 ☎(800) 331-0358 – publisher of the **Common-Sense Survival Guides** series: *"How To Be A Survivor", "How To Survive Earthquakes", "How To Survive Hurricanes and Tornadoes", "How To Survive Floods", "How To Survive Fires", "How To Survive Manmade Disasters", "The Survivor's Guide to Emergency Preparedness", " How To Be A Survivor", "Cope, Survive and Conquer", "Survivor's Sourcebook",* and *"The Savvy Survivor's Sprouting Guide"*
Salisbury Enterprises, 1453 Mary Ann Drive, Santa Clara CA 95050 ☎(408) 984-8611 or ☎/📠(800) 972-7749
Sam Weller Books, 254 S. Main, Salt Lake City UT 84101 ☎(800) 333-7269 or (801) 328-2586   Also located at: 8191 South 700 East, Sandy UT 84070 ☎(801) 566-0219 – extensive collection of food storage and preparedness titles; search available; collector's editions of and local preparedness writers
Sasquatch Books, 1008 Western Ave. #300, Seattle WA 98104 ☎(206) 467-4300 – specializing in regional guidebooks and books on gardening, cooking, and travel for the Pacific Northwest
Seed Savers Publications, RR 3 Box 239, Decorah IA 52101
Sierra Sun Publishing *(attn: Skipper Clark, Editor and Publisher),* PO Box 6209, 96 Canyon Highlands, Oroville CA 95966 ☎(916) 534-3924 – book about the problems with food storage supplies based on testing and analysis performed by an independent lab
Simon and Schuster, 1230 Avenue of the Americas, New York NY 10020
Simple Pleasures Press, self-pub. Debi Simple, PO Box 941, Auburn WA 98071
Small Farm Family Program Leader, Lincoln Univ. Ext., 900 Moreau Dr., Jefferson City MO 65101 ☎(314) 681-5545
Smith's, Box 83, New Germantown PA 17071 – mail-order homesteading and preparedness products
Soyatech, Inc., PO Box 84, Bar Harbor ME 04609 ☎(800) 424-7692 or (207) 288-4969 📠(207) 288-5264 💻*www.soyatech.com* ✉*data@soyatech.com*
Soyfoods Center, PO Box 234, Lafayette CA 94549 ☎(510) 283-2991 💻*www.soyfoodsinfo.com*
Sprout House, The *(attn: Rick Kohn, Manager),* 7023 McLennan Ave., Van Nuys CA 91406 ☎(800) SPROUTS – publisher of **Sproutman**® books; kitchen gardening, juice fasting and detoxification, sprouting, wheatgrass, and food combining & digestion
Sprouting Publications *(attn: Michael Linden, President),* Box 62, Ashland OR 97520 ☎(800) 746-7413 – publisher of *"SproutChart"*, the definitive guide to sprouting, and *"SproutGuide",* how-to chart for sprouting 39 seeds

Publishers, Presses, Booksellers, & Catalog-Order Resources (continued)

SSL, Inc., PO Box 2050, Higley AZ 85236
St. Martin's Press, 175 Fifth Ave., New York NY 10010
Stebor Publications, div. American Consumer Group, Inc., PO Box 475, Laguna Beach CA 92652
Stephen Greene Press, The, Fessenden Rd., Brattleboro VT 05301
Sterling Publishing Co., Inc., 387 Park Avenue *S.,* New York NY 10016
Stoeger Publishing Co., 55 Ruta Ct., *S.* Hackensack NJ 07606
Storey Communications *(attn: John Storey, Editor),* Schoolhouse Rd., Pownal VT 05261 ☎(800) 441-5700 or (802) 823-5810   – publisher of books for country living; large selection of how-to books for gardening, harvesting, storing, and preparing foods
Stroud Booksellers, HC 68, Box 94, Williamsburg WV 24991   – mail-order "how-to" and lifestyle books
Sumner House Press, 2527 W. Kennewick Ave. #190, Kennewick WA 99336
Sunset Books, div. Lane Publishing Co., Menlo Park CA 94025
Survival News Service, PO Box 41834, Los Angeles CA 90041☎(213) 255-9502 🖳**http://homeearthlinknet/~nyerges** ✉*nyerges@earthlinknet*   – publisher of Christopher Nyerges' books and booklets about how to live off wild-growing plants and the environment; expert has experienced life and times of existing from nature's bounty
Survival Publishing Co., *(attn: E. J. Wilfley),* Box 1213, Mulino OR 97042 ☎(503) 829-5444   – publisher of *Survival, Your First 72 Hours … and Beyond*
Survivalist Papers, pub. Live Free, Int'l., PO Box 1743, Harvey IL 60426 ☎(312) 821-LIVE   – papers prepared by volunteers and staff for those who want and will work to survive; terse, down-to-earth information
TAB Books, Inc., Blue Ridge Summit PA 17214
Tailored Tours Publications, Box 22861, Lake Buena Vista FL 32830 ☎(407) 354-3070
Taylor Publishing Co., Dallas TX
Thorsons Publishers, Ltd., Wellingsborough, Northamptonshire NN8 2RQ
Time-Life Books, c/o Reader Information, 541 North Fairbanks Ct., Chicago IL 60611
Times Books, Three Park Avenue, New York NY 10016
TM Publications, 152 *S.* Main St., Chagrin Falls OH 44022
Total Health, 6001 Topanga Canyon Blvd. #300, Woodland Hills CA 91367 ☎(818) 887-6484 🖷(818) 887-7960
TRAX, *(attn: Jay Benson),* 32 W. Martin Lane, Salt Lake City UT 84107 ☎(801) 262-3601   – books about alternative and natural medicine, health, politically incorrect, and historical subjects
Tree of Life Publications, PO Box 126, Joshua Tree CA 92252
Tree Top Fulfillment Bookstore, c/o Tree Top Publications, Inc., PO Box 5326, Evansville IN 47716 ☎(812) 477-8670 or *orders only* ☎(800) 618-7772   – books about the subjects of the Constitution, Social Security, the IRS, US fiscal policy, and other political, economic, and social issues
Triad Communications, Inc., PO Box 13355, Gainesville FL 32604 ☎(904) 373-5800 🖷(904) 373-1488
Troubador Press, 385 Fremont St., San Francisco CA 94105
TSI Publishers, PO Box 22099, San Francisco CA 94122
Tusker Press, PO Box 1338, Sebastopol CA 95473
Ultimate Mind Publisher, PO Box 7371, Van Nuys CA 91409 ☎/🖷(805) 944-4909
Ultimate Preparedness, 931 North S. R. 434 #1201- 194, Altamonte Springs FL 32714   – books for spiritual preparedness, without which all else fails; backpack Bibles, study Bibles, health books, and videos
Underground Art Gallery, 673 Satucket Rd., Brewster MA 02631
Universal Electronics, Inc., 4555 Groves Rd #12, Columbus OH ☎(614) 866-4605 🖷(614) 866-1201
University of Texas Press, PO Box 7819, Austin TX 78713
Upper Access Books, One Upper Access Rd., PO Box 457, Hinesburg VT 05461
US Games Systems, Stamford CT 06902
Valley Hills Press, 108 E Garrard Rd. #202-A, Starkville MS 39759 ☎/🖷(601) 323-7100
Van Nostrand Reinhold Co., 135 W. 50ᵗʰ Street, New York NY 10020
Van Patten Publishing, c/o Family Resources, PO Box 1027, Corvallis OR 97339 ☎(503) 757-0028
Vanguard Books, PO Box 4028, Crofton MD 21114 ☎(301) 805-1483 🖷(301) 805-1086

Publishers, Presses, Booksellers, & Catalog-Order Resources (continued)

Vegetarian Resource Group, PO Box 1463, Baltimore MD 21203 ☎(410) 366-8343 🖷(410) 366-8804 – books, cookbooks, pamphlets, etc.; non-profit organization dedicated to education of the public about vegetarianism and the interrelated issues of health, nutrition, ecology, ethics, and world hunger
Ventura Associates, Inc., 200 Madison Ave., New York NY 10016
Vicki Tate, 302 E. 200 North, Manti UT 84642 ☎(801) 835-8283 – author and self-pub. of New Cookin' with Home Storage; also, library of cook books for the self-reliant homemaker
Victoria House Press, 67 Wall St., New York NY 10005
Virginia-Carolina Peanut Promotions, 109 *S.* Main Street, Rocky Mount NC 27802
VisionWare Press, 4118 Raya Way, San Diego CA 92122 ☎(619) 756-3704 or ☎(800) 247-6553 www.bodytype.com – publisher of Dr. Carolyn Mein's books: **Different Bodies, Different Diets—Men's Version** and **Different Bodies, Different Diets—Women's Version**
VITA, 1600 Wilson Blvd. #500, Arlington VA 22209
Volunteers in Technical Assistance (VITA), 1600 Wilson Blvd. #500, Arlington VA 22209
Warner Books, Inc., 666 Fifth Ave., New York NY 10103
Western Reserve Foods, PO Box 19175, Cleveland OH 44119☎(216) 383-1777 or (888) 366-3482 ✉*wrfood@cyberspace.net*
Western Reserve Herb Society, 11030 East Blvd., Cleveland OH 44106
Whole Foods Magazine, 3000 Hadley Rd, South Plainfield, NJ 07080 ☎(908) 769-1160 🖷(908) 769-1171
William Morrow and Co., Inc., 1350 Avenue of the Americas, New York NY 10019
Williamson Publishing, PO Box 185, Charlotte VT 05445 ☎(800) 234-8791 – free catalog; animal care books
Willowpoint Publishing, Box 302, Decatur MI 49045 – mail-order "how-to" and lifestyle books
Winchester Press, div. New Century Publishers, Inc., 220 Old New Brunswick Rd., Piscataway NJ 08854
Wings Books, div. Random House Co., 40 Engelhard Ave., Avenel NJ 07001
Wolfe Publishing Co., 6471 Airpark Drive, Prescott AZ 86301 ☎(520) 445-7810 🖷(520) 778-5124 – books on family defense, self-protection, personal self-defense, guns, and gun laws
Woodbridge Press, Box 209, Santa Barbara CA 93102 ☎(800) 237-6053 or (805) 965-7039 🖷(805) 936-0540 – publisher of vegetarian cookbooks only
Woodland Publishing, PO Box 160, Pleasant Grove UT 84062 ☎(801) 785-8100 🖷(801) 785-8511
World Research Foundation Catalog, 15300 Ventura Blvd. #405, Sherman Oaks CA 91403 ☎(818) 907-5483
Writer's Digest Books, 1507 Dana Ave., Cincinnati OH 45207

Notice:

**Some Publishers, Presses, Booksellers, & Catalog-Order Resources in this directory may no longer be in business. Phone and fax numbers may have changed.
Websites and email addresses may also have changed.
That is the natural consequence of publishing any list.**

**Luckily, there is the wondrous Internet and access to it through several browsers!
There's Amazon.com, eBay, and CraigsList.com—and dozens of sites I've yet to search—and some not yet visited.
There are so many sites and so little time!**

**When you find errors, please send the correct data to:
Doc@DoctorPrepper.com, or go to Contact Me and send me the details.**

We appreciate your interest in this information and will make changes upon verification.

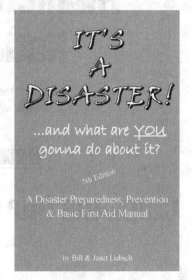

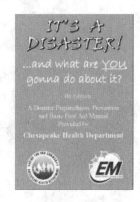

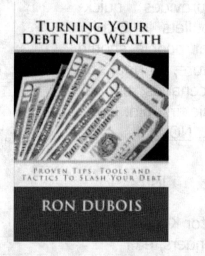

Section IX

Creating A Precious Metals Strategy

Chapter 28: Acquiring Gold & Silver

You are your personal Life Assurance Agent. Your commitments are the test of an effective agent. How are you going to insure yourself against the vulnerabilities in your life, career, retirement, education for your children, and protect all of you against future uncertainty?

Acquiring Gold & Silver

While getting your pantry ready for the unexpected, there is more to consider than just food, shelter, and clothing. We strongly recommend that you invest in yourself and your family by providing a financial cushion that contains a years' supply of reserves for housing and/or shelter for your family. In a financial emergency, when the entire *fiat* (paper money) system fails, there may be a need for a medium of exchange that is both *effective* and *outside* the fiat money utilized at the present time. This allows an effective and continuing medium of exchange with intrinsic value recognized by those with whom we deal. Any tangible asset that another will accept for goods or services will suffice, but reserves that are recognized worldwide have always been ***precious metals***.

Webster's dictionary defines the term precious metal very simply as a metal of the gold, silver, or platinum group. Some guidelines for understanding precious metals and their value in an investment portfolio are provided in this chapter. Our intent is to inspire all our readers to learn about the generalities of investing in precious metals.[1] Specific advice is

> Even if you do not fully grasp the necessity of holding precious metals, look at it as having *wealth insurance* on your financial assets.

[1]Information is given as generalizations of typical portfolios. Some of this information was provided by Patrick C. Gorman, President & Owner, Resource Consultants Incorporated, 6139 S. Rural Road Ste.103, Tempe AZ 85283 ☎(800) 494-4149 or 480-820-5877 🖷480-820-5905. Resource Consultants deals in all gold, silver, and platinum coins and bullion. Pat sells 90% silver in bags, gold and silver Eagle coins, silver dollars, and can recommend a strategy to fit individual need. His wife, Linda, has been in the business for 25+ years, and is experienced in every aspect of brokerage and precious metals management.

Mr. Gorman has been in the hard asset business for more than 27 years. For the past 19 years, he has also hosted his own live talk show, *"Hard Money Watch"* and has been rated in the area's top 5 radio shows for the last 6 years. Further, Pat Gorman and his company Resource Consultants is the most recommended prenot offered by this chapter, its author, publisher, or distributors—nor is any course of action recommended for the individual reader. In fact, we urge you to always seek expert advice and consult with a professional investment counselor prior to making any investments. Review the credentials of those investment consultants to assure they have the background and training to give competent advice about the acquisition and utilization of precious metals in your portfolio.

Precious metals are a real *and* enduring asset of true wealth and power. Gold's richness is attested to by the fact that it was used to decorate the temples of the Egyptian gods more than 3,000 years ago. Today when one sees new gold coins in brokers' showrooms, their luster and beauty capture the imagination with their richness and powerful warmth.

Knowledgeable investors have always valued the tangible and symbolic significance of precious metals. Both silver and gold were used as coins as early as the 6th century. Rulers struck gold coins or stamped bars with their personal heraldic emblems to create *coin of the realm* or legal tender for trade within their area of influence.

Precious metals have been used as money in the past and can be kept in reserve as money for the future. ***What is money?*** Money is defined here as stored-up work. It can take the form of anything anyone will accept in payment for goods and services rendered. Throughout history, people have accepted many things as money (*e.g.:* seashells, animal teeth, livestock, salt, sugar, furs, slaves, wives, gemstones, and precious metals), too many to mention individually. Some of these forms of money have proven to be much more enduring than others. In all of history, however, precious metals—usually in the form of gold and silver—have best served to determine the value of one's stored-up work. A note of caution, by their nature, precious metals markets can be very volatile, and can trap the unwary.

GOLD—THE ULTIMATE FORM OF MONEY

> The value of gold is the only constant that can keep a government from inflating a currency substitute into oblivion.
>
> Gold is a yardstick of value that keeps governments in line; governments staffed by power-crazy and greedy men whom—as history has proven—cannot be kept in control by any other means.
>
> Otto Scott,
> ***Otto Scott's Compass***

Do you recall the expression ***Good as gold***? For thousands of years, civilizations have looked upon gold as the ultimate form of money. No other substance embodies the unsurpassed luster and beauty of gold. Gold has unique characteristics in ease of workability for jewelry, excellent conductivity for electronic manufacturing, and is virtually indestructible.

Gold is a rare substance—during all recorded history, approximately 125,000 tons have been mined! Based on that figure, all the gold ever produced in history could fit in a cube with approximately 60-ft. sides—about the size of two hay barns on a typical farm. Gold production fulfills approximately 60% of the free-world demand for it.

Gold loans, forward selling, gold scrap, and gold from former USSR countries meet the free-world gold supply shortfall. Africa produces approximately one-third of the world's annual production of gold, the former Soviet Union countries about one-sixth, the US produces about 10%-11%, while Australia and Canada together produce another 15%. These supply-side facts certainly explain why increased demand for gold at the current price level creates a strong upward pressure on gold prices—there's just not enough of it to go around!

Additionally, worldwide gold demand has increased steadily, due to increased utilization by the jewelry industry, central bank purchases (to assure their ability to make international payments), gold investors, electronics manufacturing, dentistry, minting of official coins, government treasuries, and miscellaneous industry applications.[2] There is also

---

cious metals brokers in the country. They are recommended by more than 20 financial newsletter writers and investment analysts.

another indicator created by the Chinese peasants who are now able to have savings accrue privately. These people have been buying gold through the Chinese government, even though they are charged a price that is twice that of the free world price!

In the last several years, the Federal Reserve Bank (the US Central Bank) and the Federal government have tended to decry gold—because using gold as the reserve backing for the issuance of paper currency requires these entities to be accountable for adequate amounts of gold bullion in reserve. As you could agree, it seems the Federal government has chosen not to be accountable for their financial actions in the past several decades!

In 1933, President Roosevelt confiscated gold from American citizens. In 1934, after trusting citizens had turned their gold in, he raised the price 69%, to $35. None of the citizens participated in that profit, yet they reelected him three times! Is it any wonder we're in such a fiscal mess? It was not until 1974 that American citizens could own gold again. The scramble to get a piece of real money began in earnest, and continues today for those investors who seek long-term security. Indeed, when future monetary dislocation begins due to the loss of faith in and acceptance of the almighty dollar, gold coins may be the only form of money that will have enduring value.

Through continued government and banking market manipulation over the past years, most investors have ignored precious metals for the high-flying equity (stocks and bonds) markets. That market trend is now changing. More people are realizing the ultimate safety and monetary insurance that precious metals provide. In fact, since the market crash of 2008, demand for precious metals has increased three fold, by the regular investment public, searching safety for their diminishing dollar assets.

Based on industry reports, the precious metals vendors currently enjoy an inrush of new purchasers—it seems no one wants to sell their personal holdings. As available precious metals inventory is diminished, there will be increased selling pressure on institutions that hold precious metals in inventory. This will cause a volatile rise, creating wealth and protecting wealth that many people have built up over the years.

Remember, Gold is the ultimate insurance policy for wealth.

> ...the only valuable money Government has to spend is that money taxed or borrowed out of the people's earnings.
>
> When Government decides to spend more than it has thus received, that extra unearned money is created out of thin air, through the banks.
>
> When spent, this unearned money takes on value only by reducing the value of all money, savings, and insurance of the people.
>
> From:
> *The Ten Pillars of Economic Wisdom*

SILVER—EVERYMAN'S MONEY

Silver has also been a monetary[3] means of exchange for several thousands of years. Silver is much more abundant than gold, and therefore less costly and valuable. Yet, silver is considered by many to be the form of reserve money that most of us can afford. Silver is more accessible to the average person. Until 1965, the US government produced most of its coins with at least 90% silver content, but this practice was abandoned that year.

Perhaps one of the reasons the government changed this policy was to protect itself from being fiscally responsible to the public for reserves of silver to support the paper money. You probably don't recall when the bills were silver *certificates*—and could be redeemed––*by law*—for silver.

From the current indicators in the marketplace, fall of 2009, there seem to be several factors that make this a most propitious time to accumulate silver bullion coins before silver becomes a scarce commodity: inventories are lower than any time since 1950. Demand for silver is exceeding supply at this time, unequalled since 1978.

---

3 However, it is not now a "monetary" metal, and probably will never be again in our lifetime—except in India. Silver is strictly an industrial metal and most likely will fall dramatically with other commodities during the next depression. There is lots of silver and it's very unlikely that it will ever be scarce, though it may rise in price for a short period—i.e., in a time of hyperinflation—but during the next depression, it may just as well drop to the price of $0.25/oz.

PLATINUM—FOR THE SERIOUS INVESTOR

Platinum is the most precious metal[4], and is five (5) times scarcer than gold. Platinum is used primarily in automotive catalytic converters, and utilization has increased more than 50% over the last ten years. Now that the whole world is concerned about air pollution, its use in the auto industry will continue to grow. However, now the largest market for platinum is for jewelry—more than 35% of the total platinum utilized today. Increased purchases should occur as platinum bullion coins are being minted and circulated at a low premium.

THE 10 MOST ASKED QUESTIONS ABOUT PRECIOUS METALS

Many people have been conditioned to believe paper money is the ideal means of *storing* of their work's value. They simply don't understand the historic appeal and value of precious metals to those who are preparing for the uncertain financial future. Here are ten (10) of the most often asked questions about metals and coins we've encountered over the past 25 years.

Hopefully, the answers to these questions will provide both a working knowledge and some insight into the intrinsic value of precious metals, as well as why and how they provide long-term stability to their owner.

1. What Makes Precious Metals So Valuable?

Several factors determine the value of gold, silver, and platinum. First, all three precious metals have tremendous conductive properties, making many electronic devices more effective, durable, and less expensive.

Gold is one of the most malleable metals. An ounce of gold may be stretched into several miles of fine thread without breaking it. Its beautiful color enhances jewelry and fashion. However, the major aspect of gold that makes it so attractive is its diversity of investment interest. Here are some of the reasons why investors buy and hold gold in their portfolios as a financial asset:

➤ Hedge against both inflation and deflation

➤ Protection against currency market fluctuations

➤ Portfolio diversification

➤ Safe haven in times of economic and financial market instability

➤ Price based on supply and demand

➤ A store of value despite governmental despots—especially in developing countries

Silver is a key component of the precious metals complex. It has been used for several years in the photographic industry for clarity and to enhance film resolution. Even though we are now entering the age of digital photographic technology, it is projected that the photographic industry will continue to use 10s of millions of ounce each year going forward.

---

4 The above paragraph may also apply to platinum. It would probably appreciate faster than gold if inflation occurs in the economy as inflation occurs in the monetary system. However, if the economy has seen the largest proportion of inflation that's expected and also experiences a deflation of the economy—while the Federal Bank hyper-inflates the monetary system (*paper currencies*) in an attempt to keep the worldwide economy from crashing—then platinum and silver would most likely drop in value while gold rises. When the next depression occurs, platinum would drop while gold would retain a relatively high relationship to *all* commodities.

Increased use of silver in electrical contacts, fabrication of electronic components, and a myriad of other applications has far outpaced the total available *new* supply by a wide margin.

Also, silver has tremendous healing benefits as an alternative treatment modality. As of this writing, more than 600 silver-based antibacterial products are available, whether prescription or for over-the-counter sale. In the event of bacterial warfare, silver may be one of our best defenses to both protect and heal the body.

The four fundamentals to watch in the silver market are:
1. Total new supply
2. Fabrication demand
3. Investor demand[5]
4. Inventories

Often, silver is bought instead of gold because it seems less expensive. However, anyone who purchases silver for this reason simply does not understand the economics of precious metals. It may offer greater price volatility, thereby offering increased potential capital appreciation or losses.

Note that because of its volatility, silver may be better termed a *speculation*. Gold is purchased for its stability, and for this reason is very different from the other metals.

Silver is purchased for these and other reasons to diversify a portfolio within a sector:

➤ Sensitive to supply and demand trends
➤ Hedge against currency exchange rate fluctuations
➤ Inflation hedge
➤ Bought as substitute6 for gold investment

Platinum is a diversifier within a diversifier (precious metals sector.) The fundamental differences between platinum and gold make platinum an excellent complement to gold. Platinum prices are more responsive to changes in industrial demand, which tends to rise as economies expand.

Platinum comprises a smaller market, so prices tend to outpace gold prices in bull markets. Here are some of the reasons platinum is considered a means of diversification within the precious metals portfolio:

➤ Considered an industrial commodity
➤ Prices tend to rise sooner in the economic cycle than gold
➤ Used in wide variety of industrial products and applications
➤ Prices more volatile than those of gold
➤ No large above-ground inventories exist

Even without the monetary benefits that these precious metals provide, gold, silver, and platinum are substances without which the economic world could not prosper. Technology is a wonderful thing, yet gold, silver, and platinum have not, and cannot, be replaced—though demagogues have tried since the commencement of commerce.

---

[5] None of the metals can properly be termed "investments" because they don't pay any dividends or interest.
[6] Note: there is no *real* substitute for gold!

Gold, silver, and platinum are considered a long-term holding strategy. That does not, however, dictate that regardless of price, they should not be traded. (For example, many gold owners sold their stock of gold when it reached $875 in January 1980, and then were able to buy it at $290 during the first quarter of 1998.)

In fact, truly knowledgeable precious metals purchasers generally add to their holdings every year, and have not been net sellers of gold since the gold price was freed from governmental price control in 1974.

2. What Determines the Value of Precious Metals ?

Precious metals and coins trade on markets similar to those of equity stocks, options, and bonds. Gold, silver and platinum trade on the New York **NYMEX** market. Prices can literally change momentarily, just like International Business Machines (**IBM**) or Microsoft (**MSFT**). **CNBC** (cable television) reports real-time information daily during market hours.

All major and most local newspapers report the *precious metals futures* (contracts) and also the market *spot price* of the previous day. The market spot (cash) price reported is a precious metals *market indicator*—not the price of gold or silver bullion and coins.

The spot price reflects the price at which mining companies can sell their unrefined metals (in rough ingots) to the refining industry. After the gold is refined and made into planchets, it is then sold to the various mints. Private and government mints refine planchets into bullion bars and coins.

After minting, additional costs, such as shipping, distributing, marketing, and sales expense add to the final price to metals brokers, who then take their profit when selling to the consumer.

These processing factors are the reason the price of gold in the newspaper doesn't translate directly into the market cost of the American Gold Eagle. Actually, the price paid for coins varies with the size of the order, but should have a premium of approximately 6%-8% over the spot price.

3. How Much Gold and Silver Should Be in My Portfolio ?

Actually there is no set amount as far as a percentage basis in owning precious metals. Level of investment in precious metals depends on the individual's concern about current and future economic conditions.

Consider maintaining 15% to 17% of your portfolio in physical metals at all times, regardless of your feelings about precious metals.

The best investment portfolio is normally based on the asset *allocation method*. Asset allocation was conceived to protect the individual's investment portfolio against virtually any situation that might occur.

The premise for asset allocation of the typical portfolio dictated that assets should be divided among these equity investment categories: stocks; US Treasury, municipal, and corporate bonds; cash savings; and precious metals. Additionally, real estate and property should be included in the portfolio. This total investment protection package should endure any economic scenario inasmuch as possible in today's world.

Since you undoubtedly have fire insurance on your home, life insurance on your life, and car insurance for your car, doesn't it make sense to get some *insurance* for your finances? Even if no dire circumstances occur in your lifetime, you won't lose much in interest and dividends if you hold 15% of your net worth in gold.

However, if history does repeat itself *and* some of the dire predictions of levelheaded commentators do come true, that 15% in gold just may save your financial hide! Whether you believe in or trust precious metals, hold minimally 15%-17% of your total assets in precious metals—which you should have in your physical possession.[7]

This does not include stocks in metals mining companies—mining stocks are a totally different part of the investment portfolio! That percentage of your portfolio should remain a minor portion and is a relatively conservative position. When you sense rising indicators of economic dislocation, you may want to increase the amount of precious metals in your personal portfolio.

Remember, if others are managing your money, they should be able to help you get the growth, interest, income, and dividends you need with 83% to 85% of your portfolio. Shy away from those who want 100% of your liquid assets in their control. Some aggressive money managers will tell you to hold more precious metals. If you are able to do so, own 18%-20% in physically held metals that you control—never allow anyone else to hold or store your precious metals.

4. Do You Have A Suggested Portfolio of Precious Metals for Everyone ?

Everyone, regardless of current wealth, is different. Some people may believe that they can get by with only their food storage. Others believe their talents alone will get them through thick or thin situations.

Unfortunately, we will surely need everything that we currently have or can possibly acquire to be successful in rising to the challenges that seem to be just ahead.

As for precious metals and coins, a well-diversified portfolio will be the best choice. There is no assurance any portfolio will. Consider having the following the following selection in your portfolio:

➤ **Core Position for Wealth Insurance.**
  • **90% Silver coins.** Investigate the collection of pre-1965 dimes, quarters, and half-dollars. They are easily recognizable, manageable, and have high utility with those less informed during the transitional period following a financial collapse. They will come in handy for buying the basics during uncertainty.
  • **Gold coins.** Investigate the collection of 1-ounce, ½-ounce, ¼-ounce, and $^{1}/_{10}$-ounce fractional coins[8]. These coins should be tucked away in a safe place for instant access.

---

7 Always take physical possession of precious metals. As this overall paper market continues to crumble and brokerage firms disappear you may want to ask for your stock and bond and mutual fund certificates are delivered to you and hold them in your possession. if you are so courageous as to own other types of stocks, bonds, and treasuries, get those certificates also—even mutual fund shares!

8 There is a potential for confiscation of these and other gold coins as defined by the Supreme Court. There are certain types of coins, such as the British Sovereigns, Swiss Francs, and French Francs are much better for holding to avoid confiscation. Check with professional dealers to determine which coins are the highest risk—you could have your gold devalued by confiscation—the government could call in gold at about 14% of its purchase price today. Be aware that those who choose to buy these may be "flirting" with federal confiscation

It is not my intention to present reasons for not purchasing gold bullion bars or gold bullion coins, namely confiscation. There is perhaps equally important reasons—if not a compelling one—for holding "collector" gold coins (at least semi-numismatic coins), that being for their price appreciation. Collector Coins have a place in everyone portfolio. They might do and have done in the past perform better in a rising metals markets " In other words, gold coins that have at least some collector value will appreciate faster in a rising gold bullion market.

On the other side of the coin (*slight pun intended*), when gold bullion drops in value the collector coins have a tendency to stay higher in price. They don't make them anymore and if no one is selling them back to the market then the price should stay stable. So, in both rising and declining gold bullion markets, gold coins do a *better* job of maintaining the client's asset values and/or allow owners to experience value appreciation of their gold holdings.

> ➢ **Aggressive Position for Wealth Accumulation.** After the important core position is covered, investigate these coins, as appropriate, for your personal wealth accumulation:
> - **Silver dollars**
> - **US pre-1933 gold coins**—selected carefully at time of purchase
> - **Other collector coins**—based on your ability to accumulate them

Acquiring precious metals depends on the depth of the pocketbook. If you haven't diversified your portfolio, now is a good time to start. Identify qualified professionals and seek their advice.

Educate yourself, then proceed with caution. If you already own some precious metals, interview several professionals for a consensus to determine whether you have the best choices in your portfolio for today's risks.

5. I've Never Owned Precious Metals—What Items Do You Suggest ?

Initially, the answer to this question will deal only with the physical side of precious metals ownership—gold, silver, and platinum coins and bullion. We do not intend to make recommendations, but provide this information to encourage you to think about viable alternatives for your portfolio.

> **Remember:** the possibility of confiscation of certain coins could be a reality for US citizens in then future.

Gold would be your first choice for acquisition—perhaps 75-80% of the precious metals allocation should be in gold. You may start out by purchasing 1-ounce, ½-ounce, ¼-ounce, and $1/_{10}$-ounce gold bullion coins. Many different countries mint these coins: the US, Canada, Austria, China, South Africa—virtually every civilized nation.

Fractional gold coins, such as British Sovereigns and Swiss Francs, should be purchased in case paper currency becomes unstable and you need to barter for goods and services. Bullion bars of gold used to be looked at as a poor alternative to the coins. However recently the mints that make these bars have included an assay certificate and the bars are serial numbered. From this point forward we would not be worried about gold bullion bars.

Once you have a solid gold coin position, then begin acquiring some US pre-1933 coins as a way of increasing solid financial growth and value. Gold pieces of $5, $10, and $20 face values minted between 1849 and 1932 by the US Government are the only collector coins you might investigate owning.[9]

US collector coins can be an unforgettable experience—not only are they beautiful, but a piece of our history during previous fiscally stable periods. Collector coins can be very profitable if the right ones are purchased and preserved properly.[10]

In the precious metals sector of your portfolio, 10% might be held in silver. However, as inflation comes about and prices for food and other daily items increase exponentially, you might want to consider owning much more silver.

---

9 Foreign collector coins are not considered liquid—they never have been liquid and they never will be liquid. The seller of the foreign antiquities is the only person that makes any money on this acquisition. When it comes to buying collector coins it is definitely *Caveat Emptor*. Always check prices on these coins. This market is not regulated (and shouldn't be). Prices on the same coin and grade can vary sometimes as much as a $100 or more. Always check with at least three sources for competitive pricing before buying to assure value.

10 **An important note:** don't ignore all bullion coins because of the fear some of them they may be confiscated. Confiscation of gold in today's world is much more difficult—though not impossible. Get a copy of *The Value of Honest Money, a new book* by Patrick Gorman. It will provide interesting information about the issue of our current money system and help guide you through these tumuchulous times. Write, call, or fax for a free copy: Resource Consultants Incorporated, 6139 S. Rural Road, #103, Tempe AZ 85283 ☎ (800) 494-4149 or 480-820-5877 📠 480-820-5905.

Investigate owning silver coins, such as 90% pre-1965 dimes, quarters, and half-dollars as your first preference. In the 1970's and early 1980's, silver bullion bars were considered the investment of preference. Governments have also been minting 1-ounce silver coins, such as the US Silver Eagle and the 1-ounce Silver Canadian Maple Leaf. They are beautiful coins, but don't acquire them unless the premium over the spot price is minimal.

The key factor in acquiring silver is to purchase bullion or bullion coins as close to the spot price as possible. After silver bullion coins such as the 90% dimes, quarters, and halves, then consider US Silver Dollars. Silver dollars can be purchased in many different conditions. For use in barter situations, the silver dollars that are either lightly circulated or the lower graded uncirculated condition are considered best. Platinum is probably not a precious metal you could easily barter.

No more than 5% of your metals allocation should be in platinum[11]. Platinum is basically an industrial metal—it has no real *monetary* value. Generally, platinum is a good buy when less than 20% over the price of gold, and should not be acquired when the price exceeds that price point—it is then too late to consider it as a short-term strategy.

A good investment strategy is to buy platinum when the premium is less than 20% over gold, sell it when the price runs up, and put the profits into more gold. Platinum should be purchased in the form of coins minted by government mints. The US, Canada, Australia, and the Isle of Man all mint 1-ounce coins—which would be an acceptable way to buy it. Always buy the coins with the least amount of premium over the spot price. Avoid the esoteric (designer) platinum coins that sell for a very high premium.

Let's address some basic **Do** and **Don't** suggestions about getting precious metals, gold and silver coins, and collector coins for your diversified portfolio. Here are a few things to consider:

Five Things to Do

There are no perfect *general* solutions, and certainly no absolutes in these statements, but consider them seriously with your professional broker for *applicable* portfolio diversification:

1. Maintain at least 50% of your precious metals portfolio in quality coins. Determine which coins belong in your core position. Cover your core position or permanent holdings first. Needs are different for each person, based on amount to invest, age, and purpose of portfolio.
2. Buy pre-1933 gold coins. Some foreign coins are excellent for core positions.
3. Buy when prices dip. Recently, the gold and silver markets have been having larger than normal price swings. Take advantage of these swings to acquire more gold. Add to your core position when you can afford it. Be aware of the trends in the precious metals market to enhance your buying and selling opportunities.
4. Continue self-education about precious metals and the market indicators affecting them.
5. Select a reputable and reliable professional precious metals broker to help in the continuing evaluation of your diversification portfolio.

Five Things *Not* to Do

These suggestions are not cast in concrete. Don't be intimidated by what *others* may say—

---

[11]Local libraries should have *A GuideBook of United States Coins* by R. S. Yeoman. Read it before buying any coins that carry a collector premium. It's a great educational book about the history of US coins and provides accurate mintage information and how coins are graded. It is a must-read for those preferring to avoid the misery of learning the lessons of buying coins the hard way.

do what is applicable to your financial situation. Get professional advice and be aware of market conditions before committing your dollars.

1. Don't buy only foreign numismatic coins—watch the spread and consider their liquidity.
2. Don't buy only high-grade, rare/esoteric numismatic coins, *unless you understand the market strategy.*
3. Don't wait more than 2 weeks for delivery of coins or bullion. Once the payment has cleared the bank account of the broker, any delay is an interest-free loan to the seller.
4. Don't deal with any broker or dealer before checking credentials and business practices. Don't succumb to undue pressure from anyone with whom you deal—no deal is so good it can't wait or be checked out for legitimacy before investing.12
5. Don't keep large amounts of precious metals in your home or living area.

6. What Forms of Precious Metals Should I Avoid ?

This question is perhaps easier to answer. As mentioned in the previous section, some of the things to avoid are precious metals items that appeal only to the owner's emotions and ego. When it comes to protecting your portfolio of precious metals, avoid buying jewelry or trinkets fashioned with pure, filled, or plated gold, silver, or platinum. While these works of art are wonderful to wear, beautiful to regard, and give great pleasure to their owner when showing them off, they don't have much liquidity except in countries where jewelry is the primary form for holding gold.

Also, avoid high-grade, rare, esoteric, or high-priced coins where the bulk of the money spent on the coin is for its design or a high premium—not part of its intrinsic and long-term value. Examples are coins that are one-of-kind specimens advertised to increase 500% -1,000% when the market *heats up*. Indeed, some of these coins may well increase in a *hot* market.

However, the reality is that a rare ½-ounce gold coin that originally cost $2,000 will not buy more bread and milk in times of financial disintermediation than a gold coin that cost $500.

7. Where Do I Store My Precious Metals and How Do I Protect Them ?

This question has plagued many people for many years. There are those who don't own precious metals because of the fear of having them in their possession.

The **first rule** of storing precious metals is: don't let your broker or dealer hold them for you! The broker may not be accessible when you need your holdings!

If you don't want them in your possession for security reasons, then locate a private safety deposit box company. Check their business reputation by asking questions about confidentiality, hours of access, and what reporting is required of them to *any* government agency. Ascertain how long they have been in business.

Ascertain who would have access to your private box for any reason or on any basis.

Call the Better Business Bureau for references about the safety deposit box company and those dealing with them during the last three years.

---

[12] **Remember**: "deals" are like waves of the ocean—they just keep coming!

Some elect to use bank safe deposit boxes, but there are problems associated with that strategy should there be either a massive financial upheaval or federal confiscation order. There is another solution for this problem of safekeeping. In the local Telephone Company *Yellow Pages*® are listings of safe dealers. Quality safes are very expensive, very heavy, and require installation if they are not to be obvious in your home.

Call local safe dealers and ask them if they sell *used* commercial grade *TL15* or *TL30* safes. Frequently, this type of used or refurbished high-quality safe will cost only 30%-40% of a new safe. It's an excellent method of having your cake and eating it too. Given the value of precious metals, as well as other valuables, it is a small investment for security and safety.

8. What Are the *Rules of the Game* So I Don't Violate the Law ?

This question interests everyone desiring privacy. How can an investor or collector avoid giving his name and Social Security number when making precious metals transactions? Can one legally deal strictly in cash? The #1consideration required by both common sense and business practice is to avoid breaking the law. Anyone may buy precious metals with cash and keep the transaction private—as long as the purchase is less than $10,000. The Federal cash reporting laws are mandatory and requires that forms and filings *must* be made when transactions total $10,000 during any 12-month period. You can use personal checks, cashier's checks, bank wire transfers, or money orders for precious metals transactions in any amount.

When dealing with a firm via mail, personal checks are normally acceptable. The seller merely holds a personal check until it clears the bank account, then ships the order. Be aware that precious metals firms accepting credit cards must make up the cost of the processing fee and credit card discount in every transaction. There is no free lunch—buyers are paying for the service by paying higher prices.

Keep it simple—there is no need to get creative. Avoid the red flags by conforming to the rules. It is very difficult to hide money in our society. That is one of the reasons it takes time and patience to acquire and protect long-term investments. Don't wait until it's too late to begin the collection of precious metals.

9. Just How Liquid Are Precious Metals in A Crisis Situation ?

Precious metals and coins are one of the most liquid items available. There have been markets and market makers of gold and silver even before the time of Christ. There may be times when the mainstream market is not functioning (though it has never happened!) However, there will always be someone willing to trade precious metals coins for something you and your family may need.

That's where education becomes essential. Don't just buy gold and silver blindly—regardless of financial status. No one will take care of the ignorant—the ignorant will simply be taken! Educate yourself to your local area and get to know like-minded people. That doesn't mean to tell everyone about everything you have or own!

10. When Things Get Ugly, How Do I Use My Coins for the Things I Need ?

This is the part we don't like to discuss or portray. However, it is a reality of life that some rain must fall for the flowers to grow. Initially, there will be crooks of all kinds trying to take advantage of those with precious metals. Should the US national economy fail, it could become an everyone-for-himself society. Few people living today know what it was truly like during the Depression era—but projections are that a financial failure today will be much worse and a lot deeper—due to the nature of our urban lifestyle and lack of knowledge about taking care of ourselves.

In the future, we may well be required by circumstances to trade out or barter our time, talents, and our personal resources for the goods and services that we will need so desperately. In the past, this was the general manner of exchange—until gold and silver coins became the preferred method. The difference is that back then, most people had high ethics and a full measure of morality. Today, it seems many people have only one expectation or standard—**WIFM**—*what's in it for me*?

There are a number of books about barter, survival, and how to maximize future disastrous events in **Chapter 11. Books, Section J. Home Management, Budgeting, & Organizing,** page 12-41, for books relative to bartering, financial planning, self-reliance, and self-reliance.

Many people will become very frustrated and angry because of their jealousy of others who chose to be prepared. So be it. Make your choice now to be prepared for the uncertain future. The real threats to those who prepared are those who've chosen *not* to be prepared. It is our considered opinion that precious metals and coins are going to be the most liquid monetary form (except for food) for acquiring currency and the other necessities of life if we don't already have them beforehand.

There are a limited number of US citizens capable of living the austere life of the agrarian society of yesteryear. We've become accustomed to the *good life*—and all that living in the most prosperous times ever provides us. We may come to appreciate these wonderful times more if we choose not to get our preparedness act together!

See Chapter 6, *Getting Your Household in Order,* in **Making the Best of Basics** for more details.

Complete the charts and use them help you compile and keep detailed written records of all your financial investments, banking accounts, IRAs, retirement funds, debts, receivables, etc.

WHERE TO GO FROM HERE ?

In this chapter we've presented the ten questions (and answers) most frequently encountered on a daily basis in the precious metals market. Remember that stored work in the form of cash, gold, and silver can enhance your financial survival for the for years to come.

We suggest that for the sanctity of your mind and spirit, you make a special effort to accomplish minimally the following financial self-preservation measures.

✓	Personal Financial Preparedness Considerations
	Invest wisely now in a year's supply of food, clothing, and emergency equipment for your family's preparedness.
	Reserve at least 3-6 months' living expenses in cash or exchangeable monetary value.
	Reduce personal debt as quickly as possible—pay off smallest debt 1st, then larger debts.
	Collect on debts owed you by taking an aggressive stance to avoid or minimize loss.
	Hold majority of your liquid assets in physical precious metals—in your own possession!
	Sell for cash marginal personal property not directly related to your homeownership and business.
	Reduce your exposure to stocks, bonds, and mutual funds in retirement/pension funds, personal IRAs, insurance policies, and personal savings accounts.
	Consider short positions in stocks and bonds—get expert advice and qualified investment advisors to teach you these strategies!
	Keep bank deposits to a minimum and stay liquid in a privately owned, secure place.
	Consider converting existing IRA assets into the new Roth IRA, or even a Precious Metals IRA

Should you choose to acquire a reserve of money in your financial preparedness efforts, this information will serve to help you investigate the validity of precious metals. Implementing these important actions will help you avoid financial ruin and give you peace of mind today and provide future prosperity in the months and years to come.

The next few years will be interesting financial times to say the least! It will be important for all of us to be aware of the financial investments we've made and stay abreast of the changing markets.

Do not get too comfortable with your current investments in the equity markets. Protect yourself with a balanced portfolio based on what you have read in this chapter.

It seems ever to be the case that when food, foodstuffs, and the basic elements required to support life are in short supply, people become frightened, greedy, and try to take advantage of others to avoid loss of life or security—the same happens in the fiscal and equity markets!

Finally, we urge you to do the following to gain and maintain control over your financial future:

♦ Continue to educate yourself on the precious metals and coins markets.

♦ Study the potential fiscal, economic, and social problems—and their solutions.

♦ Get the help of wise counselors and trusted financial advisors to resolve your financial problems with the myriad of solutions available.

SOME CONCLUDING THOUGHTS...

In chaotic situations, remember who you are, hold to your personal standards and your integrity, treat others in the manner you want to be treated, keep a level head on your shoulders, and you will enjoy inner peace.

Remember: what goes around comes around. When the crisis is past, we will all be better for it. That which does not kill us makes us stronger.

People often are heard to say, *Knowledge is power.* I totally disagree! For example, information in a database is knowledge. However, it has value or power *only* when it is utilized to accomplish something of value outside itself.

❑ **Knowledge alone is *not* power—only the *application* of knowledge gives power to its owner.**

❑ **Applied knowledge *is* power! Use your knowledge about the uncertainty of the future to prepare for it in a timely manner.**

❑ **Make your decisions and act now for your future security.**

❑ **Now is the time to prepare for the future! After all, it's where you're going to live—prepared or not!**

AFTERWORD

This book was written for you the reader:

- To motivate and encourage you—yes, even urge you –to undertake a family preparedness plan;

- To provide you the information and tools to assist you in the planning process;

- To guide you in putting your family preparedness plan into practice; and

- To provide information about available resources for the products and services you require in completion of your task in becoming appropriately prepared.

There are many reasons for family preparedness. Some reasons are better than others. I have found that the most excellent reason is that parents love their family enough to make the sacrifice required. Even if you are a family of one you have extended family members, friends, neighbors, and/or co-workers. Each person has the responsibility of caring for himself or herself and loved ones.

Though I would want you to have your family prepared immediately, it won't happen at all without a great deal of personal and family effort.

No one knows your family's needs, nor can better care for your family than you—or perhaps stated more correctly—**no one else has that greater, sacred responsibility than you!**

You may not at this moment know what or how you're going to accomplish this worthy task, but if you have a television, radio, or know anyone who does—you surely know why!

In this book we don't deal with the causative factors–there are many organizations spending millions (verily, even multi-billions!) of dollars researching and reporting on the causes. The information in this **Family Preparedness Handbook** deals with solutions, focuses on giving you some planning tools, and encourages you to learn how to live a basic lifestyle.

We encourage you to begin your preparedness journey today! May you be greatly blessed for your efforts!

Should you have helpful comments or suggestions from your own experiences, contact me through my blogsite so they can be shared with others. We appreciate your input.

Doc@DoctorPrepper.com

A Modern Parable

By

James Talmage Stevens

Parable of the Fairway Ants

During the night, an ant colony moved onto the vast expanse of the verdant 9th fairway on a local golf course and dug themselves a great underground home. They brought a huge mound of loose dirt to the surface in the middle of the fairway. Now, it was just before daybreak when the move was completed, and the Queen had been safely ensconced in her chamber deep in the ground. The captain of the guard set sentinels in place at each entrance, giving instructions to them to be alert to all signs of conflict, since they were in a new and different environment.

It was barely daylight, the first rays of the sun barely visible in the East, when the sentinel ant on top of the mound saw a big comet shooting through the sky—coming on a parabolic path straight toward the mound. It only took a second for the sentinel ant to determine that the arcing body in the sky was directly on target to land somewhere on the anthill. He immediately shouted down the tunnel to his captain, *Sir, Emergency! Danger! There's a comet coming right at the anthill! This is going to be terrible! It's a natural disaster—and there's nothing we can do!! Get the ants to safety!*

The captain quickly relayed the information about the threat of the forthcoming natural disaster to the queen. Then, ushering her to safety, assured her the colony was safe, but informing her that there might be some individual ants lost. Before any of the ants could get to the deep shelters, the comet landed in the opening of the main entry to the anthill, burying itself several inches into the mound. Many topside worker ants were killed, including the sentinel ant.

Many worker ants scurrying about in the upper tunnels, trying to respond to the potential onslaught of the unexpected natural disaster, were also victims of the comet as it penetrated into the anthill.

The anthill shook slightly with the impact of the comet, the loud noise of its hitting the mound causing panic and terror in the upper tunnels and chambers. The captain went to the damaged area, noting how deeply into the anthill the comet had penetrated. He saw the whiteness of the foreign object, and in a flash he was able to identify the object—it was a golf ball!

He quickly examined the spent object that had forced itself deep into the anthill. Given his long experience on and around the golf course, he immediately determined it was not a natural disaster, but only the natural consequence of a bad drive!

The captain had seen golf balls occasionally around the former anthill in the rough off the fairway. Often the golfers came, angrily searching for their lost golf balls, tearing up the ant sanctuary with spears on their feet and beating the ground in frustration with their long sticks. Many ants had been killed by those barbaric weapons. In fact, this was one of the reasons the Queen chose to move the colony, hoping to find a more hospitable location.

The captain checked to make sure the Queen was not harmed, and reported to her that it was not a natural disaster, but a people-caused incident. He then spent a few moments digging through some dirt blocking a side tunnel so he could get to the top of the anthill to examine the damage for himself. He emerged into the morning light and he could see the ball, buried in the top of the anthill, and dead ant bodies all around.

As the captain was examining the damages, he sensed the ground vibrate. Turning toward the direction of the vibrations, he saw a small crowd of golfers approaching the mound. They were gesturing towards the anthill and the ball buried inside the mound entry, about a foot above the surface of the fairway. One of the golfers appeared very agitated about the situation.

The captain noticed that the group soon became quiet as the golfer moved to a position over the ball buried in the anthill. After some shifting of his feet and swinging a big stick in smooth curves toward the sunken ball, the golf person drew back over his head and swung at the ball with great force, digging up more loose dirt and a large number of innocent ants, just missing the captain, who barely had time to clamber away from the hole to a safer perch. Apparently the golf person had hit the ball on the top, driving it even deeper into the anthill.

The captain immediately charged down into the anthill, ran down the tunnel, found the Queen, and yelled, *Oh, Queen, it's worse than before! It's not a natural disaster, it's a people-caused problem, and they're taking it out on us!*

The captain quickly explained the details to the Queen, who urged him to send some experts on damage control to determine what should be done to protect the colony from the golf person swinging the stick—before they were all destroyed.

Meanwhile, the golfer, realizing he had topped the ball and just pushed it deeper into the softened soil, muttered some imprecations and turned to choose another stick. After selecting a club, the golfer proceeded to practice his swing, determined to get the ball out of the hole with this swing. By now, groups of ants were watching with intense interest, not sure what would happen next, mesmerized by the swinging of the stick by the golf person. It was then the ants realized the golf person was going to hit the ball again, so they scattered—well, like ants!

The captain, down below, saw the ball getting closer to the Queen's chamber, so he ran to protect her. The captain saw that the ball was dangerously close to crushing the lower chambers, indeed blocking off escape, and capable of killing the Queen.

Just then, the golf person swung with all the strength he had, and this time, once again hitting the top of the ball, drove the ball until it was just an ant antenna's length from collapsing the hill. The totally unnerved captain proclaimed to the Queen that he was out of options and didn't know what else to do.

The Queen ant, in all her majesty, looked at the Captain and said.

Captain, you first told me we were going to be victims of a natural disaster—a comet falling from the sky.

Then, you said it was a people-caused problem—a people hitting at us with a stick.

Now, the situation has become so bad that it's a personal problem. We'll be indeed fortunate if we live through this situation. I only see one recourse for all of us—if we're to survive what began as a natural disaster, then became a people-caused disaster, and now ultimately threatens to become a personal disaster—if we want to live through this disastrous event, we'd better get on the ball!

From the Desk of Rich & Annie Fleetwood
Founders - SurvivalRing

SurvivalRing started in early 1997 as a single page focused on building up a network of like minded individual websites via the technology of Web rings. In 1999, SurvivalRing became a household name as Y2k chaos loomed on the horizon.

Over the next few years, hundreds of megabytes, and then gigabytes, were uploaded and shared via many different sections of SurvivalRing. Traffic to our site jumped to over 100,000 unique visitors a month, and hundreds of gigabytes (1000 megabytes per gigabyte) were downloaded each year.

Our new site design is the culmination of years of study, new software, intense discussion, and many sleepless nights. Database driven info, multimedia delivery, unlimited expansion and upgrade capability, and a uniform presentation of all SurvivalRing content gives you faster and better access to all the ebooks, software, media and more.

Since 1997, SurvivalRing has been focused on providing documents, downloads, and information to all visitors in all areas of family preparedness, survival, self-reliance, and self-sufficiency. As founders, Annie & I both returned to college to increase skills, add new experiences, and actually live some of the things we talk about… frugality, self reliance, self sufficiency, and survival skills. We currently live on 10 acres in rural Wyoming, and are always developing more content and media to share on the SurvivalRing and other SR network websites.

What We Do...

Never heard of us? Visit our **About Us** page for details on what we do and why. Visit our many **awareness pages** for history and details of past

disasters and informational overviews. Drop by o **forums** and find lots of info on a myriad of topic: or over 1,200 new downloads in the forum downloads area. Our **chat room** is also available 24/7, and we have new content being uploaded every week. Questions? Comments? Use our **Contact page.** We also have **articles,** gigabytes o **downloads**, and I'll even personally respond to your emails if you're looking for specific info or are just getting started in preparedness.

Rich & Annie's lifestyle and experiences provide many key moments of having to learn self relianc and survival skills in a hurry. Weather disasters, home repairs, home schooling, car repairs, accidents, and more gave us reason to learn the hard way, and to avoid those situations in the future. Hurricanes & tornadoes wrecked some dreams and family, and were the real beginning of our quest for first learning, and then sharing solutions to regularly occuring threats.

All of the thousands of downloadable files, article: web pages, and content offered on the SurvivalRing network are available to a global audience. The target audience is the family unit. Information, skills, resources, and how to's are offered that any family, individual, or group can use to focus on making themselves better prepared for LIFE. New to the idea of self reliance? We have a starter page for you.

Do you live in the USA? Have you ever suffered from severe weather? Earthquakes? Flooding? Crimes or warfare? Other Accidents or Mass disasters? Start by learning what natural threats occur where you live. We can help you with all these things that you really need to be concerned with.

We've got those downloads I keep mentioning above. Here are links to a LOT of them…

- Download Set One
- All Hazards – Downloads
- Bunker – Downloads
- Field Manuals – Downloads
- Civil Defense Classics
- Download Set Two
- Download Set Three
- NBC Preparedness – Downloads

Many more publications are on the way in the coming months and years. From where, you might ask? We have bookshelves full of original US and other nation civil defense and survival documents going back decades. DECADES.

Here's a sampling of just ONE stack of documents we have.

http://www.survivalring.org/about/the-project/

And, we have eleven PUBLISHED CD Rom and DVD Rom disks of multimedia, featuring documents, videos, audios, and more. More on the way soon. Intrigued? Read below.

Yes, we have data. We have ebooks. We have videos. We have community via our Forums, chat, and email lists.

How do we offer it all?

SurvivalCD.com is our publication company for our disks. We will be publishing videos, DVDs. podcasts, and even books in the coming future. All will be available online, as well as tangible, in your hand, products.

First, take a look below at our recent disk publications. Learn more about them at the SurvivalCD.com website.

Below you will find links to detailed info about our packages, as well as direct links to purchase our CD & DVD publications with **PayPal**. In association with James, and the digital launch of hs book, we offer the "Basics" sale of all our products, giving you 30% ALL of our products.

The **"Basics"** sales page is protected with the password **basics.** Enter **basics** in the password box at the page above, and you'll get access to the very special prices we're offering. Look for this…

PROTECTED: MAKING THE BEST OF BASICS SPECIAL

This post is password protected. To view it please enter your password below:

Password:

Submit

This post is password protected. Enter the password to view comments.

PACKAGE	Retail Price	Discount Price	You Save	Info	Buy Now
MassPak	$40.00	$28.00	$12	(info)	PayPal
DigiPak	$30.00	$21.00	$9	(info)	PayPal
HazardPak	$35.00	$24.50	$10.50	(info)	PayPal
Appropriate Tech	$55.00	$38.50	$16.50	(info)	PayPal
ATtackPak	$75.00	$52.50	$22.50	(info)	PayPal
LifePak	$100.00	$70.00	$30	(info)	PayPal
Pandemic	$10.00	$7.00	$3	(info)	PayPal
SRCC 1 year	$89.00	$62.30	$26.70	(info)	PayPal
CivDef Classics	$30.00	$21.00	$9	(info)	PayPal

We've been building our websites and creating new files for over 12 years now. We have no intentions of stopping in the future. SurvivalRing has become our life's passion. Come see what we've done…just for you.

Thanks for reading this page. We look forward to serving you. Questions or Comments? **Click Here.**

Rich and Annie Fleetwood
Summer 2010